The Law of Consumer Protection and Fair Trading

'Suppose we turn goldsmiths?' said Schwartz to Hans, as they entered the large city. 'It is a good knave's trade; we can put a great deal of copper into the gold without anyone's finding out.'
The King of the Golden River JOHN RUSKIN

'If we had the Ten Commandments these days, there would have to be a Code of Practice attached to each of them.'
ANONYMOUS INDUSTRIALIST

'If the good Lord had wanted us to go metric, he'd only have had ten Apostles.'
SISTER INCARNATA, quoted by John Mortimer

Dedication

Emptori qui cavere debet, atque venditori cujus ignorantiam jus haud excusat.

The Law of
Consumer Protection
and Fair Trading

Fourth Edition

by

Brian W. Harvey MA, LLM (CANTAB)

Solicitor, Professor of Law at
the University of Birmingham

and

Deborah L. Parry BA (LAW) (Sheffield)

Senior Lecturer in Law at
the University of Hull

Butterworths
London, Dublin, Edinburgh
1992

United Kingdom	Butterworth & Co (Publishers) Ltd, Halsbury House, 35 Chancery Lane, LONDON WC2A 1EL and 4 Hill Street, EDINBURGH EH2 3JZ
Australia	Butterworths, SYDNEY, MELBOURNE, BRISBANE, ADELAIDE, PERTH, CANBERRA and HOBART
Canada	Butterworths Canada Ltd, TORONTO and VANCOUVER
Ireland	Butterworth (Ireland) Ltd, DUBLIN
Malaysia	Malayan Law Journal Sdn Bhd, KUALA LUMPUR
New Zealand	Butterworths of New Zealand Ltd, WELLINGTON and AUCKLAND
Puerto Rico	Butterworth of Puerto Rico, Inc, SAN JUAN
Singapore	Butterworths Asia, SINGAPORE
South Africa	Butterworths Publishers (Pty) Ltd, DURBAN
USA	Butterworth Legal Publishers, CARLSBAD, California and SALEM, New Hampshire

Reprinted 1994

A CIP Catalogue record for this book is available from the British Library

ISBN 0 406 54370 4

Typeset by Kerrypress Ltd, Luton, Beds
Printed and bound in Great Britain by
Redwood Books, Trowbridge, Wiltshire

∞ This text paper meets the requirements of ISO 9706/1994. Information and Documentation — paper for documents — requirements for permanence.

Preface

Recent years have seen a rapid increase in the volume of legislation to protect the consumer against not only fraud and dishonesty in commercial dealings but also against oppressive bargains and dangerous products. There is widespread public interest in 'consumerism' and an increasingly large number of professional and lay people are expected to be able to give advice on consumer problems and help to formulate consumer policy. Commercial litigation, at least as described in the leading textbooks on mercantile law, tends to be concerned primarily with disputes between business concerns, shipping companies and the like. There is a growing school of thought which holds that consumer protection law is at best only distantly related to commercial law, and it is legitimate as a separate exercise to focus on transactions between suppliers and the ultimate consumer. From that perspective it is fruitful to analyse the civil rights and duties and the criminal liabilities to which these transactions give rise.

What precisely should be covered by a comprehensive account of 'consumer protection law' is, as is the case with administrative law, for instance, the subject of legitimate debate. For present purposes we have looked at the body of law which exists to protect the private consumer from (a) unsafe products, (b) qualitatively deficient goods and services, (c) fraudulent, misleading or undesirable trading practices, (d) insufficient information, and (e) economic exploitation through lack of competition or excessive prices. To understand the working of the law it is also important to examine the voluntary or statutory provisions for giving the consumer redress when he has a legitimate complaint, whether it be against a nationalised industry or a producer of goods or services in the private sector. From this vast field we have necessarily had to be selective, particularly as to services. It could be argued, for instance, that the machinery regulating state welfare benefits is partly there to protect the consumer of these benefits, and certainly that public licensing systems relating to everything from taxi cabs to betting shops is an aspect of consumer protection. But the line has to be drawn somewhere, and the above topics are better dealt with in the specialist works that already exist. For this reason we have also ignored the protection given to purchasers of land under section 76 of the Law of Property Act 1925 (implied covenants for title) since this is a specialist topic appropriately left to textbooks on Conveyancing, and the same considerations apply to the complex body of law protecting various types of tenant from eviction or payment of excessive rent. In many of these more technical areas the 'consumer in the street' will often rely on professional advice, and if matters go wrong his first line of attack will be against his professional adviser – an aspect of consumer protection fully dealt with in this book.

In the preface to the first edition of this book it was mentioned that when this book was originally written there was very little published work intended for practising lawyers, law students and trainee or qualified trading standards officers, treating the whole field in some depth. Since then a number of books have been produced and we seem to have moved from famine to abundance in a very short time. In addition the comparative absence of published material on the relationship between law and economics in this field no longer applies, and the burgeoning interest in this interdisciplinary field in the UK is encouraging. The original justification of the treatment of the social, political and (particularly) economic context of the laws and institutions concerning consumer protection in an introductory way was stated as being that 'many law students will not have studied economics before, and, with a few distinguished exceptions, authors of academic law books in England have given their readers little encouragement to think about the relationship between law and economics. Whilst extreme statements which would deny the study of law any normative role or intrinsic intellectual interest at all are to be deplored, a moment's thought will show that both parliamentary and judicial law-making rests on certain usually unexpressed economic or socio-political premises. Evaluation of a particular law's merits or demerits should not rest entirely on whether it appears to work well. It is also necessary to estimate the effect that any consumer protection law will have on, for instance, the economics of the production of the particular goods or services in question, and on consumer behaviour generally. It would be possible, given sufficient space, to deal with this wider dimension in far greater detail than we have done, but we have both kept in mind and tried to deal with it in a way comprehensible to the person without any previous training in economics.'

As was the case with the last edition, the original author of the first two editions has been joined by Deborah L. Parry, Senior Lecturer in Law at the University of Hull. Consumer protection law is wide in scope and changes rapidly. Even the first chapter dealing with the context of the subject has been affected by the collapse of the former Soviet Union.

A number of people have read and commented upon parts of the text and it is not possible to mention everyone individually. But we would like to thank Holley Cullen (Hull) and George Applebey (Birmingham), together with correspondents from the British Standards Institution, the Citizens' Advice Bureaux, the National Federation of Consumer Groups and the press office of the Office of Fair Trading who have given us specific assistance, as has the Department of Trade and Industry.

Detailed changes of case law and statute have affected almost every page of the former edition. Much rewriting and reordering of the material has been necessary. We have divided this task between us but are jointly and severally responsible for the whole. We have endeavoured to state the law as at 31 March 1992. The prospective amendments to criminal penalties made by the Criminal Justice Act 1991, section 17, which are due to be implemented in October 1992, have been incorporated into the text where appropriate.

BRIAN W. HARVEY
DEBORAH L. PARRY

Contents

ix

Table of statutes and other legislation

References in this Table to *Statutes* are to Halsbury's Statutes of England (Fourth Edition) showing the volume and page at which the annotated text of the Act may be found.

Page references printed in **bold** type indicate where the Act is set out in part or in full.

List of cases

1 The historical, economic and philosophical background to consumer protection

The aim of this chapter is to introduce the economic and philosophical background to the widely accepted principle that the consumer of goods and services is entitled to protection under the law if the goods and services supplied to him for consideration are defective or falsely described. To be more precise, and as indicated in the Preface, the range of laws considered in this book are designed to protect the consumer in at least one of the following areas, namely against: a) unsafe products; b) qualitatively deficient goods and services; c) fraudulent trading practices; d) insufficient information to exercise a prudent buying decision; and e) economic exploitation through lack of competition or excessive prices.

The idea that the consumer is deserving of protection is not a new one in English law. A brief history of some aspects of consumer protection in England will perhaps assist in the appreciation of the impact of consumer protection in the twentieth century. It must be borne in mind, though, that the motivation for the early legislation was as much to protect the honest trader against dishonest competition as to protect the consumer.

1. HISTORICAL DEVELOPMENT

Early consumer protection machinery was closely linked to the then existing units of local government. The primary units of pre-nineteenth century local government were the county and the parish. The hierarchy of government would have been expressed as being the King in Parliament and, locally, the official dignitaries of the county – the Lord Lieutenant, the High Sheriff and the Justices of the Peace. The functions of the Justices of the Peace, as developed in the thirteenth and fourteenth centuries, were both judicial and administrative. In the sixteenth century their already increasing duties and jurisdiction were increased by giving them supervisory jurisdiction over the parish with regard to bridges and highways, and, a little later, the poor law, paving, lighting and cleansing of streets.

Outside this general scheme were the borough and the manor. A town which had secured its charter of incorporation and become a borough appointed its own justices and operated its own analogous system of local government through mayors, aldermen and burgesses. The manor was the residue of the feudal system of land tenure. Originally England had been parcelled out by William the Conqueror to his faithful followers, whose successors, after numerous subdivisions, were known as Lords of the Manor. Villeins within the Lord's demesne owed to him duties of service, and courts over which he presided regulated a large number of civil and criminal matters arising in the community. As the royal courts became established and offered a more efficient system of justice, manorial courts declined, but the manorial court known as the court leet had a persistent and important role in the main regulatory function of local government in the seventeenth century and beyond – the supervision of trading standards and the suppression of local nuisances. So, to summarise, the courts exercising functions which we would now associate with 'consumer protection' and 'public health' were primarily the petty sessional courts of the Justices of the Peace and the Manorial Courts Leet, whose jurisdiction was in practice concurrent.

The concept of consumer protection to the thinking person, throughout the eighteenth century at least, would mean a) protection from excessive prices levied on primary commodities, and b) protection from short measure. Protection from 'common nuisances' involving misuses of houses, streets and bridges is a separate area of activity which must be investigated by the historian of public health. (It is, of course, debatable how far the motivation for the regulation of trade came primarily from the honest traders seeking to preserve their own reputation and standards.)

Bread, beer, meat and fuel were singled out from earliest times as being commodities which the Crown, through the agency of the justices or other local courts, should regulate both as to quantity and quality. As to bread, a statute of 1709 recites that the existing law is so obscure that 'little or no observance hath in many places been made either in the due assize or reasonable price of bread, and covetous and evil disposed persons have for their own gain and lucre deceived and oppressed Her Majesty's subjects.' The justices of the peace or the mayors of boroughs were therefore empowered to fix the weight and price of bread and bakers had to mark their loaves with their size and quality. The price was to be fixed by reference to current market prices of grain, meal or flour. Setting the 'assize of bread' remained the function of the mayors or justices, together with the enforcement of criminal penalties for contravention, until the abolition of the assize in 1836 on the adoption of Adam Smith's principle that competition was the best regulator of these matters.

A somewhat similar system prevailed as regards the pricing, weighing and marking of coal from 1664. As regards ale, both the Justices of the Peace and the Courts Leet exercised jurisdiction over the price and measure of ale. This involved setting the price and ensuring that vessels made of 'wood, earth, glass, horn, leather, pewter, or some other good and wholesome metal', should be made and sized, and stamped or marked as a quart or pint (the half pint being nowhere mentioned, perhaps on the basis *de minimis non curat lex*). There is a reference in Shakespeare's *Taming of the Shrew* to Christopher Sly who is told that he would

rail upon the Hostess of the house
And say you would present her at the Leet
Because she brought stone jugs, and no sealed quarts.

The Court Leet's contribution to the assessment of the ale and beer was made largely through the investigations of its officer styled an aleconner. The aleconner is one of the direct ancestors of the modern weights and measures inspector, though his job was perhaps more interesting in one respect in that he was under a duty to undertake spot checks of the quality of ale by tasting. His duties, all officially described in a contemporary record, were 'to examine bread, weights, measures, ale and beer for sale, and to return such as offend against the assize or standard, or vend unwholesome liquor.' The aleconner was in fact one of many officials that a larger Court Leet might appoint; the others might include Constables, Market-lookers, the Searchers and Sealers of Leather, the Pecksealers, the Town-crier, the Town Scavengers, Dog-muzzlers, Clerks of the Wheat, Fish and Butchery markets.

Courts Leet were the manorial criminal courts, established by an actual or presumed grant. The steward who presided over them was normally a lawyer and could punish by fine (called 'amercement') or even by imprisonment if the fine was unpaid. An important and lucrative feature was that all fines imposed belonged to the lord or the steward. Whilst their quasi-criminal functions have been abolished, they still retain the right preserved by section 24 of the Administration of Justice Act 1977 to sit and transact such business as was customary before the passing of that Act, some of which is quaintly spelled out in the Fourth Schedule to the Act.

Here are a few examples, taken from the contemporary record of the Court Leet of the Savoy, indicating the type of offences concerned with weights and measures and 'unfair trading' dealt with:

Terence McMahon amerced £10 for exposing for sale thirty-one penny worth of bread wanting thirty-one ounces assize (1709);

Upon the return of the Aleconners, Mrs Fossick, cheesemonger, for selling with scales no true ballance, to the great prejudice of the fair trader, amerced £2 (1766);

Richardson amerced £20 for selling coal in sacks that want near 3 inches in length and near 2 inches in breadth of the standard or assize by law directed (1735);

Mary James, her weights being too light, amerced 5 shillings (1689);

Nicholas Baker, poulterer, amerced 3 shillings for vending and selling stinking and corrupt unwholesome pigeons (1694);

Upon the return of the fleshtasters, Mr Harrison, butcher, for exposing to sale fleshmeat not fit for Christians to eat, and refusing to remove the same, amerced 5 shillings (1761).

References in the above records to bread being too light or sacks of coal being too short of 'the standard or assize by law directed' remind us of the necessity of having constants by which weighing and measuring may accurately be assessed wherever the exercise is undertaken. For the need for accurate and widely understood weights and measures is as old as government. 'Without it there can be no civilisation and no society but the primordial. It is the first essential tool of material creation and the private and public economy are its dependants.'[1] The law and the administration designed to enforce it have for many years aimed at 1) standardisation of weights and measures, 2) control over the accuracy of the equipment used for weighing and measuring by traders, and 3) the protection of the consumer against short weight or short measure.

The search for a standard weight and measure has been a long one. The early inclination to measure weight by what a person could lift, quantities by grains of wheat and a measure by parts of the body, particularly the foot, led to many attempts at standardisation. Weight was essential for measuring gold and silver coins and bullion. By the reign of Henry VII the troy pound (of Mediterranean trade routes origin), ounce and pennyweight were established for silver, gold and some commodities. The main alternative system was avoirdupois, the pound consisting of 16 troy ounces or 7,680 grains. Wool had its own weight system. Sets of weights were kept at the King's Treasury. Length measurements were equally slowly standardised. Edward I enacted in 1305 that '3 grains of barley, dry and

---

1   O'Keefe *Law of Weights and Measures* (2nd Edn, by A. A. Painter), which contains an excellent and detailed history not only of the law (to which the authors are indebted) but of the emergence of weighing and measuring machinery.

round, make an inch, 12 inches make a foot, 3 feet make an Ulna' (Latin for 'elbow', later called a yard). Again the monarchs kept measuring rods in their Treasuries to set these standards, the yard-rod of Elizabeth I being the primary standard until 1824. Measurements of capacity were also crude and lacked uniformity. Measures such as gallons and pints were defined by the troy weight of the contents of the vessel containing threshed wheat, which varied with temperature and crop. In 1824 Imperial measurements were adopted, the Imperial Troy pound being 5,760 grains and the avoirdupois pound weighing 7,000 troy grains. The ounce was 1/16 of a pound, and the dram 1/16 of an ounce. A verified brass avoirdupois pound was constructed and deposited at the Treasury. Later in 1855 the Imperial standard Pound Avoirdupois of 7,000 grains was declared to be the only standard measure of weight. The Imperial gallon was standardised in 1824 by reference to ten pounds avoirdupois of distilled water weighed in air. The growth of science and technology has since required far more accurate measures. The metre is now defined as 'the length of the path travelled by light in a vacuum during a time interval of 1/299 792 458 of a second' (see Part I, Schedule 1 to the Weights and Measures Act 1985), and the yard is 0.9144 metres exactly. The four primary standards set out in section 2 of the Weights and Measures Act 1985 (yard, pound, metre and kilogramme) are in the custody of the National Physical Laboratory.

Of the two great measuring systems, the Imperial and the Metric, it is the latter with its more easily understood subdivision of weights and measures which is likely to gain almost universal acceptance. Introduced into France by the Revolutionary Government of 1799 it spread throughout continental Europe, Russia, Japan, China and most other non-English speaking countries. The United Kingdom legalised the use of metric terms in contracts in 1864 and by the Weights and Measures (Metric System) Act 1897 made metric weights and measures lawful in trade as an alternative to the Imperial system. Impetus towards metrication in the United Kingdom was added by the accession to the European Communities. The Weights and Measures &c Act 1976 gave power to the Secretary of State by order to prohibit unauthorised Imperial units of weights and measures pursuant to the metrication policy of and under obligations imposed by EEC Units of Measurement Directives. Section 1 of the Weights and Measures Act 1985 (which consolidated the material provisions of the Weights and Measures Acts 1963, 1976 and 1979) and Schedule 1 to the 1985 Act set out the only units of measurement by reference to which any measurement involving length or mass may be made in the UK. Schedule 1 sets out definitions of measurement of length, area, volume, capacity, mass or weight and electricity. It also defines a number of traditional Imperial units which may not be used for trade. The law is more closely examined in chapter 13.

The statutory powers to enforce uniformity in weights and measures also have a long history. There is a reference to uniformity of measures of wine, ale, corn and cloth in Magna Carta in 1215. The Assize of Bread and Ale of 1266 laid down a scheme to control the amount of bread or ale obtainable for a farthing or penny respectively, depending on the current price of wheat, barley or oats. Short weight or quantity was punishable by a fine or in more serious cases flogging or the pillory. The attempt to control the weight of bread obtainable for a specified price continued until the Bread Act 1836 which required bread to be unadulterated and sold by weight. There were similar attempts to control the sale of almost all primary commodities of everyday life (particularly grain, cloth, wine, cheese, fish, honey, coal, salt and butter) in many cases dating from the fourteenth or fifteenth centuries. The vital step of penalising those using unjust balances was taken in the middle of the fourteenth century, towns having common balances and weights in the custody of the Mayor and Constable, but enforcement was sporadic. Excommunication after the Archbishop of Canterbury's promulgated anathema in 1428 if unequal-armed balances were used seemed to prove the most efficacious device.

2. THE ECONOMIC CONTEXT OF CONSUMERISM[2]

Many assumptions are habitually made by those concerned with consumer protection as to the economic, philosophical and political nature of 'consumerism'. Statute law, comprising the State's view of the extent and nature of the protection which should be given to the consumer, proceeds on some of these assumptions but does not and cannot examine them. Nevertheless any informed view of the law, or an understanding of the writings on the philosophy of consumerism that follow, involve at least a nodding acquaintance with these assumptions, and an idea of how far they are open to challenge. A detailed analysis of any of these areas is outside the scope of this book; what follows is merely an attempt at looking at the 'context' of

---

2   See further David Morris (ed.) *Economics of Consumer Protection* (1980); Ogus and Veljanovski *Readings in the Economics of Law and Regulation* (1984); Burrows and Veljanovski *The Economic Approach to Law* (1981); Iain D. C. Ramsey *Rationales for Intervention in the Consumer Market Place* (OFT Occasional Paper, 1984). On the persistent failure of law teachers to recognise the importance of the nexus between law and economics in the UK, see Ogus 'Economics, Liberty and the Common Law' [1980] JSPTL 42.

the law. It is appropriate to look first at some economic theories of consumer behaviour in the economy as a whole, explained in a way professional economists would regard as grossly over-simplified, but perhaps at some gain in comprehensibility to the layman.

Demand

There is alleged to be an economist who taught his parrot the distillation of a lifetime's study of the 'dismal science'. It merely repeated 'supply and demand'. As far as consumer behaviour is concerned we are dealing primarily with aspects of 'demand' in microeconomic theory.

Who is 'the consumer', the subject matter of this book? The Molony Committee on Consumer Protection regarded a consumer as one who purchases (or hire-purchases) goods for private use or consumption (para. 2). The private consumer of services is equally 'a consumer', as the Molony Committee admitted, but this aspect of consumerism was rejected in the Report as a matter for investigation for reasons of practicability. (A transaction whereby goods are purchased from a retail shop does in any case involve both goods and services, the mark-up over the wholesale price being the payment for the services involved in the purchase.) More recently it has been realised that the definition of 'a consumer' should be broadened to include anyone who consumes goods or services at the end of the chain of production, thus catching the otherwise excluded plaintiff in *Donoghue v Stevenson*,[3] for example. In some countries 'consumerism' embraces pressure groups concerned primarily with the environment and its preservation. However it is not practicable to discuss here such laws which protect the public generally and which do not give to the individual (except in rare cases) the right to take legal action against infringement. Nor is it appropriate here to discuss the government or public authorities as consumers, though they do of course 'consume' goods and services as do firms not publicly owned.

In economic theory the picture of consumer behaviour is drawn on a much larger canvas. The dramatis personae of economic theory consists of three groups – 'households', 'firms' and 'central authorities'. The stage on which they act is called 'the market'. When economists speak about 'the consumer' they refer to the group of individuals comprising the household. Unrealistically 'households' are deemed as consistent decision-taking units as individuals are. Again, perhaps unrealistically, households are assumed to know what they want and to act rationally. (Broadly these generalisations

---

3   [1932] AC 562. The case is discussed further in ch 6.

can be substantiated; on an isolated basis there will be found many aberrants.) So households are assumed to desire their well-being, 'satisfaction' or 'utility' as this concept is called. They operate in a market which is, for present purposes, an area over which buyers and sellers negotiate the exchange of a well-defined commodity.[4] In a competitive market the diversity of buyers and sellers is large enough to prevent any one of them being able to influence price, and this we assume to be the norm. In recent times neither completely free-market economies nor entirely centrally controlled, or 'command', economies have existed. But the degree of central control has significantly varied from one political bloc to another and from one country to another. The British economy is a mixed economy, so the consumer finds that in the case of some commodities he is facing a price and quality control dictated by the State or a public corporation (coal, railways, the Post Office etc.), in other areas price may be less controlled but subject at least to some regulation (e.g. rents of private housing), and in other areas price is dictated purely by market considerations (television sets, motor cars etc.). Whether or not there is State regulation of price, quality and range of choice is, of course, a vital consideration in considering the shape and effectiveness of consumer protection in a given sphere.

Three hypotheses can be deduced about the nature of a household's demand. Firstly, a household's demand for a commodity is influenced by the price of that commodity and the prices of other goods. Assuming other factors such as income and preference (or taste) remain constant, normally if price rises a lesser quantity will be consumed, often because a substitution can be made. Thus a typical household might react to high potato prices by buying fewer potatoes and more, cheaper, rice, or to high coffee prices by buying tea, in both cases as a substitute. Similarly, and bound up with this thesis, a fall in the price of (expensive) coffee should result in less (comparatively cheap) tea being consumed. The two commodities are said to be 'substitutes'. But if two sorts of commodity tend to be consumed together, so that a fall in the price of one increases demand for the other, the two commodities are termed 'complements'. Thus we would expect a fall in the price of motor vehicles to be accompanied by increased demand both for motor vehicles and petrol.

Secondly, a rise in the 'income' of the household is associated normally with a rise in demand. We say 'normally' because there are many exceptions to this. A household living well above subsistence level is unlikely to alter the quantity of salt consumed whether

4   See Lipsey *An Introduction in Positive Economics* ch 6.

household income drops or rises (provided any drop is not too dramatic). And in some cases an inferior substitute might be abandoned in favour of a superior one, e.g. the demand of a household with increasing income for British sherry might cease altogether as Spanish sherry is substituted. Similarly, the total 'income' of the household marks the limit of its total spending in a given period. 'Income' here has to be defined very broadly to include savings, cash value of non-liquid assets and credit available. And as far as 'income' is concerned, the consumer's spending power is more likely in practice to be limited to the net 'take-home' sum received from all sources after tax and other deductions have been made – often called 'disposable income'.

Thirdly, the demand for a commodity depends upon the preferences, or taste, of the household. The question of varying taste is usually regarded as outside the realm of economic measurement, though taste or fashion are very real factors as far as production and marketing of goods are concerned and can be affected by advertising and publicity. Variations of taste are likely to lead to increase of demand for some commodities and decrease in demand for others.

Utility

The above three hypotheses help to explain, on a large scale, why consumers behave as they do. The concept of 'best value for money' is at the root of much of the legal and administrative machinery for consumer protection. It implies that the consumer will get the best return that he can for his expenditure just as a firm will seek to maximise the output from their inputs and, accordingly, its profit. How can this element of 'yield' that consumers are assumed to wish to maximise be measured? A fundamental concept, highly developed in the nineteenth century and still often referred to, is the concept of utility, particularly diminishing marginal utility.

Basic needs for housing, food, clothing and the like generate a large variety of specific wants. These wants can be satisfied by acquiring goods and services. The capacity of goods and services to satisfy wants is called 'utility'. Wants are subjective, and the concept of utility should not be confused with any objective assessment of 'usefulness'. Spectacles without which the wearer cannot see and eyeshadow without which the wearer will not be seen have equal utility for the person who wants each of them. But the intensity of demand, because of the level of satisfaction to be derived from the goods, is likely to affect the price of it unless supply of the goods can be increased to meet demand at the same price (i.e. supply is perfectly elastic). Therefore the relative price of commodities will be at least in part determined by the utility they have for consumers.

However, from the point of view of the individual consumer, a saturation point is likely to be reached if he consumes an ever increasing quantity of one good. To a thirsty man the first two pints of beer may be extremely satisfying, but after a certain number of pints in excess of this (depending on the capacity of the drinker) less and less satisfaction is derived. This principle applies to many commodities, even assuming there are no budgetary restraints because the beer is free or the consumer of the commodity has unlimited financial resources. So the principle of decreasing marginal utility is simply that although the utility derived from a good increases with the amount consumed, it does so less than proportionately. After a point utility starts to become reduced and continued consumption would confer a negative marginal utility (or a 'disutility').

Although this may seem somewhat abstract and unreal, the relevance of the theory to consumer behaviour may be seen by posing a series of choices. Which would you prefer – a visit to the opera or a hot bath? A person living in a comfortable house in Cornwall might prefer to go to the opera, since it is normally relatively inaccessible, whereas a man living in a condemned shack in East London, equally musical, might prefer a hot bath. The consumer is not comparing the *total* utility of opera performances in general and of hot baths in general (although many opinion polls proceed on the assumption that such a comparison is a useful exercise); he is comparing the *marginal* utility of each commodity. To the affluent Cornishman, another hot bath has low marginal utility, perhaps zero marginal utility if he has already bathed that day. But to the bathless slum dweller the marginal utility of a bath is high. Of course, choice of goods to satisfy various competing demands of the consumer is complicated by the fact that commodities vary in price per unit. So economists apply the principle of diminishing marginal utility to the behaviour of the household by saying that, to quote Lipsey, 'the household maximising its utility will so allocate its expenditure between commodities that the utility of the last penny spent on each is equal'.

It is fair to add that in the twentieth century economists have invented more sophisticated ways of mapping consumer behaviour and choice. Because utility cannot accurately be measured, they have concentrated instead on preferences. Thus, for example, if food and clothing were rationed, it might be possible to show that consumers would prefer six points for food and four points for clothing, rather than five points each, out of a maximum of ten points. The precise amount of utility is not measured when assessing the two combinations, but it is possible to plot by means of 'indifference curves' the areas in which the consumer is indifferent to choice and those where he develops a distinct preference. The details of this need not unduly concern the layman. The statement at the end of the last paragraph is the critical one in assessing consumer behaviour.

The courts have been asked to authorise the compensation of consumers disappointed by, for example, a spoilt holiday or lost photographs of a family wedding. In doing so the judges have recognised that consumers make purchases for the pleasure or utility they confer. This type of loss cannot be measured in the way normally employed in business law – by reference to the price paid or diminished profits. This concept of consumer surplus is fundamental to consumer law and can be seen explicitly recognised in, for example, *Jarvis v Swan Tours Ltd.*[5]

Consumer sovereignty and the generation of wants

To Adam Smith, 'the interest of the producer ought to be attended to only so far as it may be necessary for promoting that of the consumer' (*Wealth of Nations* 1776). Despite the scorn that has been poured onto the idea of 'consumer sovereignty' in the modern economy, for the reasons mentioned below, examples of how in a free market economy producers have to adjust to changing consumer preferences still abound. The mini-skirt manufacturer must adjust to the maxi (ie longer hemlines) or risk going out of business. In general terms the flow of consumer expenditure, directed by the preferences of numerous individuals, either increases or decreases pressures on producers. These pressures will be measured by the price mechanism which, at least in the short run, will increase as demand increases (and vice versa) until it settles at the point of balance of supply and demand. And as producers respond to increased demand, productive resources will be adapted (men laid off and retrained, plant renewed or adjusted etc.) in order to attract as much as they can of consumer spending.

The contrary thesis, developed by Galbraith in, for example, *The New Industrial State*, argues that the initiative now lies with the skilled 'technostructure' inside the corporation who can manipulate prices and demand. Others have pointed out that some products of large corporations still fail despite powerful promotion, and that, therefore, consumer sovereignty still fundamentally operates. The control which consumers exercise is, in truth, a matter of degree. The State, even in a mixed economy, can greatly affect consumer behaviour by its own spending, or, for example, increasing excise

5 [1973] QB 233, [1973] 1 All ER 71 – £125 damages for loss of entertainment and enjoyment of a holiday. See also Harris, Ogus and Phillips 'Contract Remedies and the Consumer Surplus' (1979) 95 LQR 581.

duties on alcohol and tobacco for reasons of revenue or public health or both, and, demand is inevitably affected. In a centrally directed economy, such as that formerly in operation in the old Soviet Union, producers may be directed to concentrate on production which, in the State's view, is desirable (e.g. public education, recreation for working people, social security instead of luxury goods, drink, tobacco and so on). This system certainly avoids some 'abuses' occurring in free economies, but the incentive to satisfy consumers largely disappears in favour of the need to satisfy an insensitive bureaucracy. The Moscow queues for the bare essentials of life and the lack of choice for customers tenacious enough to get to the front continue to be a sad and depressing feature of seventy years of a 'Communist' economy. And the proponents of the free market would add, in the words of Milton Friedman, that a free market economy 'gives people what they want instead of what a particular group thinks they ought to want'.

Another objection to the idea of consumer sovereignty is the thesis that their allegedly voluntary wants are 'created' by producers by advertising on TV or in newspapers, posters and the like, or by other methods such as door-to-door canvassing. This manipulates consumer preferences into areas which suit the producer. However, powerful though demand creation by advertising undoubtedly is, there are limitations to its effectiveness. Completely impractical clothing for the UK climate, or completely unpalatable food or drink would be rejected however subtle the advertising. And to the producer, the increased profit brought about by the increased demand must always exceed the often very considerable cost of advertising for the project to be worthwhile. Much will depend on whether the product itself is genuinely desirable and prolonged positive response will be primarily due to the making of the information available to the consumer, rather than 'puffing', which in an advanced free economy is likely to be controlled by a legal requirement that it should be lawful, decent and honest. To this extent, the consumer retains his sovereignty.

In this connection, and associated with the colossal growth in technology over the last century is a problem with which consumer protection is much concerned, namely the accuracy and extent of a consumer's knowledge about a product and his use of that knowledge when he decides to purchase goods. Watches, television sets, motor cars and many more consumer durables are difficult to judge objectively (disregarding the producers' advertising) by an ordinary individual without extensive initial testing which is normally impractical. Consumers may rely instead on a global brand name or trade mark of a large producer without considering less well publicised alternatives. This, too, exists as a powerful limitation to consumer sovereignty and underlines the importance of such organisations as the Consumers' Association which makes comparative information available on the quality and price of a range of competing products.

3. THE PHILOSOPHY AND POLITICS OF CONSUMERISM

In Britain it is conventional wisdom, adopted by the major political parties, that consumer protection is by and large 'a good thing'. Much of the law studied in this book emanates from Parliament and consists of measures over which there has been little political disagreement. Thus the Conservative Government introduced a Consumer Credit Bill to give effect to the main recommendation of the Crowther Committee on Consumer Credit and though this Bill fell with the Government in February 1974 the Bill was reintroduced with few substantive changes later in 1974 by the Labour Government.

However, if the student or practitioner of consumer protection is to have a broader appreciation of the subject than is likely to be afforded by a study of its detailed machinery, he should be able to answer such basic questions as – Why protect the consumer? Against what are you protecting him? And by protecting him, towards what goal are you aiming? The US Special Committee on Retail Instalment Sales, Consumer Credit, Small Loans and Usury, in its Report had framed questions precisely along these lines:

> It is fair to ask precisely what it is that the consumer is to be protected from. Must he be protected from his own lack of knowledge or discipline which leads him to take advantage of easy credit to buy things he does not need or cannot afford? Is he to be protected from the 'fringe' operator who may take advantage of the ignorance and gullibility of the consumer to cause him to overbuy or pay too much?[6]

Why protect the consumer?[7]

We have already seen that for many centuries it has been thought appropriate to protect the consumer against fraudulent or dangerous practices. This reflects a moral and religious ethic and is an

---

6 Page 9, cited Trebilcock 'Consumer Protection in the Affluent Society' 16 McGill LJ 263, an article fully exploring these problems to which the authors are much indebted.

7 For a comprehensive study of the possible answers to this question (based on (i) the improvement of economic efficiency be remedying market failures and (ii) 'equity'), see Iain D. C. Ramsay *Rationales for Intervention in the Consumer Market Place* (OFT, Occasional Paper, December 1984). This study contains many further references to Commonwealth and USA monographs on aspects of the economics of consumer protection.

appropriate function of the criminal law. As such the proposition is hardly controversial. More difficult to answer briefly is the question, – why 'protect' the consumer when there has been no fraud by the producer or seller? Examples of this sort of consumer protection are the implying of non-excludable terms as to quality in contracts for sale of goods or reopening of 'extortionate' credit bargains by the court under sections 137 to 140 of the Consumer Credit Act 1974.

The paternalism which this sort of legislation provision implies is normally justified in modern times by the idea of inequality of bargaining power. An important consumer protection measure in Australia was justified as follows:

> In consumer transactions unfair practices are widespread. The existing law is still founded on the principle known as caveat emptor – meaning 'let the buyer beware'. That principle may have been appropriate for transactions conducted in village markets. It has ceased to be appropriate as a general rule. Now the marketing of goods and services is conducted on an organised basis and by trained business executives. The untrained consumer is no match for the businessman who attempts to persuade the consumer to buy goods or services on terms and conditions suitable to the vendor. The consumer needs protection by the law and this Bill will provide such protection.[8]

Another aspect of consumer protection relevant to this question is the problem of claiming compensation against the large producer where the goods or services are defective. Litigation is disproportionately costly and troublesome to the small consumer. So policy has been to encourage producers to adopt codes of practice whereunder legitimate complaints are promptly dealt with on the one hand, and also encourage small claims and arbitration procedures to solve actual disputes expeditiously, cheaply and relatively informally.

The philosophy embodied in this type of consumer protection, which is to be found now in most of the developed jurisdictions in Europe and elsewhere in the non-Communist world, has been attacked at its roots by both thinkers of the left and of the right.

A revealing slogan from the left describes this type of consumer protection as 'band-aid on the malignancy of capitalism'.[9] If non-centrally controlled production is regarded as against the interests of the 'sub-stratum of society', a continuing function of capitalism disguised only in that it supplies material comforts to those who

8   Senator Murphy, then Australian Attorney-General, introducing the Trade Practices Bill of the Commonwealth of Australia in the Senate – quoted John Goldring 'Consumer Protection and the Trade Practices Act 1974 – 5' 6 Federal L Rev at 288.

9   Quoted Goldring, op. cit. p. 288.

would otherwise be in the van of the revolution, the sooner it is destroyed the better. As Marcuse said of the American Economy:

Let me give a brief definition of what I mean by an affluent society. A model, of course, is American society today, although even in the US it is more a tendency, not yet entirely translated into reality. In the first place, it is a capitalist society. It seems to be necessary to remind ourselves of this because there are some people, even on the left, who believe that American society is no longer a class society. I can assure you that it is a class society. It is a capitalist society with a high concentration of economic and political power; with an enlarged and enlarging sector of automation and co-ordination of production, distribution and communication; with private ownership in the means of production, which however depends increasingly on ever more active and wide intervention by the government. It is a society in which, as I mentioned, the material as well as cultural needs of the underlying population are satisfied on a scale larger than ever before – but they are satisfied in line with the requirements and interests of the apparatus and of the powers which control the apparatus. And it is a society growing on the condition of accelerating waste, planned obsolescence and destruction, while the substratum of the population continues to live in poverty and misery.[10]

If this is believed, the present system of consumer protection is clearly merely propping up a corrupt system to supply palliative or cosmetic remedies to the abused substratum of society, remedies which fail to do anything to stop the system in its tracks. Consumer protection is also attacked, usually covertly, for being 'middle class', the middle classes for this purpose being defined as those with the opportunity and education to look after themselves. The implication is that the poor are out of reach of this movement since they are too ignorant or under too many pressures to resist exploitation.[11] Describing the attitude of consumer associations to this charge Eirlys Roberts wrote:

Compassion for those poorer than themselves was not overt with the consumer associations. They were not social workers nor charity organisations. But it was there, and would show itself later in the perpetual attempt they would make to spread their membership beyond

10   H Marcuse 'Liberation from the Affluent Society' in *The Dialectics of Liberation*, ed. David Cooper (1968).
11   See David Caplovitz *The Poor Pay More* dealing with the expenditure of Negro and Puerto Rican families in New York State. See also 'Market Considerations and Consumer Protection Policy' xxiii Univ Toronto LJ 396 (Cayne and Trebilcock), and 'Why the Poor Pay More' National Consumer Council (1977). The argument can be taken further by saying that as natural resources are finite, unless production is centrally regulated the earth will be laid waste and man may not survive at all. See further Layton and Holmes 'Consumerism – A passing malaise or a continuing expression of social concern' 46 Austr Quarterly 6 – 25.

the middle classes, who showed some enthusiasm for joining them, to the working class, who showed very little.[12]

From the left to the right, the objection to at least some aspects of consumer protection is that it represents undue 'molly-coddling' of the consumer. In a laissez-faire economic system, the way in which production is affected by demand is not through regulation by law (except to stop fraud or dangerous goods and the like) but by the flow of consumer expenditure, activated by a series of voluntary choices, bringing pressure at various points. Part of the doctrine of consideration in law is that its adequacy cannot be questioned in legal proceedings. Neither law nor equity will, as a general rule, mend any man's bargain, even today. Linked with this is the belief in the therapeutic effect of the individual looking after his own interests rather than the 'nanny-state' trying, often at great expense and little result, to do this for him. The centrally planned economy, whose 'Nanny' is transmogrified into 'Big Brother' and under which the State decides what the consumer shall or shall not have, would represent the ultimate of objectionable control.

The following extracts from an essay by Lord Coleraine are by no means necessarily antipathetical to a degree of consumer protection legislated for ad hoc as at present, but they do well explain the Conservative objections to the centrally directed economy desired by Socialists, Marxists or Neo-Marxists as the fundamental solution:

. . . a spontaneous order in the economic field does not depend upon the supposed infallibility of a few individuals at the centre, supported and nourished by a mass of information coming in from the periphery with varying degrees of unpunctuality and inaccuracy. It is created and sustained by the self-regarding activities of an almost infinite number of individuals, each of whom is in communication with only a very small number of others. Each one of these, in his turn, is linked to others again. Thus, the needs and ideas of a single person can be communicated through an endless chain to those utterly remote from him, of whose very existence he may be unaware; and everyone in the chain is free to respond to information reaching him, in any way he pleases – or not respond at all. It is this process, infinitely complex in its operation but infallible in its effects, which causes packets of tea, for instance, to appear in the grocer's shop in convenient sizes, with blends and flavours suited to the varying tastes of the housewife, and matched to the length of her purse, an operation which is carried out so smoothly that its complexity is not even suspected.

There are many who, admitting the greater efficiency of a spontaneous order, hold that the price exacted for it in terms of social cost is too high,

12 *Consumers* (New Thinkers Library) at 18.

and that even gross inefficiency is to be preferred to the suffering which follows the ruthless application of the principles of a free economy. Indeed, any exposition of the theory of a free economy can be counted on to arouse, even in those philosophically opposed to state intervention, dark mutterings about laissez-faire, or references to children aroused at three o'clock in the morning to work in textile mills, or to little chimney sweeps with cancer of the skin. But there are still such things as Factory Acts, and it is surely better to control the thoughtlessness, the cruelty or the cupidity of man by legislation than to attempt the impossible task of planning an economy in which there is not even the possibility of abuse.

A spontaneous economic order, then, is more efficient than an imposed order, and it need not be much less humane. It is necessary to stress again, however, that personal liberty is the necessary precondition for it. A spontaneous order is inconceivable without personal freedom and, in particular, without freedom of choice. The socialist dream, on the other hand, depends for realisation upon the limitation of freedom for the individual, and the dilution of his sense of responsibility for his own acts.[13]

The Crowther Committee addressed itself to the same problem in the field of consumer credit, and answered the question in a rather similar way:

> Given the principles of economic policy which we have advocated, our general view is that the state should interfere as little as possible with the consumer's freedom to use his knowledge of the consumer credit market to the best of his ability and according to his judgment of what constitutes his best interests. While it is understandable and proper for the state to be concerned about the things on which people spend their money and even to use persuasion to influence the scale of values implied by their expenditure patterns, it remains a basic tenet of a free society that people themselves must be the judge of what contributes to their material welfare.

> Our examination of the social effects of consumer credit has not uncovered any strong social reasons for departing significantly from this view. Since the vast majority of consumers use credit wisely and derive considerable benefit from it, the right policy is not to restrict their freedom of access by administrative and legal measures but to help the minority who innocently get into trouble to manage their financial affairs more successfully – without, however, also making conditions easier for the fraudulent borrower. The basic principle of social policy must,

13 'For Conservatives Only' quoted in *How Conservatives Think* (1975). For a succinct political history of the Consumerist Ideology see Leonard Tivey 'The Politics of the Consumer', in R. Kimber and J. J. Richardson (eds.) *Pressure Groups in Britain – a reader* (1974). See also R. Cranston 'Creeping Economism: Some Thoughts on Law and Economics' (1977) British Journal of Law and Society 103 (a critique of the Chicago School's free market approach to economic theory as applied to the legal system, with particular reference to consumer protection).

therefore be to reduce the number of defaulting debtors. This is in everybody's interest.[14]

The decay of centrally planned economies

Since this debate between those favouring a 'command', centrally directed, economy and those favouring a free market was outlined in earlier editions of this book, colossal changes have occurred in world economic order. The centrally directed economies of the Soviet Union and Eastern and Central Europe have either collapsed or appear to be in the process of collapse. Now, democratically elected governments are striving to 'privatise' their state run industry, one end product of which should eventually be a far more responsive meeting of consumer demand.

This collapse has thrown into high relief the inadequacies (to put it mildly) of centrally directed economies. It is not just that such systems inevitably involve state-paid bureaucrats in their administration, with all the opportunities for corruption that inevitably occur. It is also only too apparent that such systems do not work. The former USSR's predicament has highlighted the problem. In 1991 it was estimated that the Soviet budget deficit was 36 billion roubles, financed by printing money and pushing inflation up to about 120 per cent a year. Foreign debt is estimated at $60 billion. In the shops of Moscow and Leningrad the queues are as long as ever and consumer goods of any kind, including food, are difficult to obtain outside the inevitable black market. The solutions so far discussed will involve much greater economic aid from the West combined with rapid economic reform – 'the 500 day plan'.

This 'plan', drafted with the help of USA economists, is nothing if not optimistic. Positive thinking is clearly needed, but the complexity of Western models, often taken completely for granted in the West itself, does not make for quick transplants. The free market needs carefully structured checks, balances and safety nets to make it work in a widely acceptable way. To take a few points, central to the understanding of the relationship between consumer and producer, free competition is essential to make markets work. But the supervisory mechanisms developed in the West to combat monopolies and restrictive practices have taken over a century to develop. And if competition works there will be business casualties. There must therefore be a safety net to supply income support to those thrown out of work. Much of the funding for this is a charge on central government taxation and taxation in a democracy has to be subject to limitations and principles of economic equity acceptable

14   Cmnd. 4596 (1971), paras. 3.9.1 and 3.9.2.

to the electorate. The Social Security system administered by the State similarly needs impartially administered and adjudicated rules. Businessmen themselves need a clearly understood legal system and an independent and knowledgeable judiciary – a product of years of tradition and training. The transition from a system where the all-powerful state (usually personified by supporters of the relevant party) was in effect unchallengeable is likely to take more than 500 days to achieve, particularly in a country such as Russia with no tradition of democracy even before the 1917 revolution.

A similar picture emerges from a number of Third World countries which chose to drink from the fountain of Marxist-Leninist internationalism. Tanzania, for instance, the epicentre of African Socialism since 1967, managed to obtain $115 million of aid from the World Bank for a shoe factory designed in the Stalinist 'gigantic' tradition. Planned to produce 4 million pairs of shoes per year, it never produced more than 7 per cent of its capacity. Marketing, design and responsiveness to the actual requirements of the consumer were as ignored as the factory's demands for the requisite supplies of power and raw materials from other state-controlled 'enterprises'. Foreign aid to this type of economy is now often tied to economic reform and a demonstration of commitment to human rights, but there is still much evidence of dishonest or incompetent economic and administrative action on reform (see *The Economist*, 24 August 1991, 48 – 49).

To revert to the problem of the First World, since the United Kingdom in common with the USA, Australia, Canada and other jurisdictions having similar systems of consumer protection are likely to have mixed rather than centrally directed economies for the foreseeable future, our conclusion must be that the need for consumer protection in such an economy is part of its nature. A completely unregulated laissez-faire system is unacceptable as is a centrally-directed one, and a pragmatic compromise is to compensate for the inequalities of bargaining power and technological expertise by giving the private consumer protection in specific areas by legislation.

Against what are you protecting the consumer?

Implicit in the suggested answers to this question by the US Special Committee (reproduced above, p. 13) is the concept of the prudent shopping decision. A decision is imprudent if the buyer buys goods which he does not need or cannot afford, or if he buys too much in quantity or pays too much as a result of slick salesmanship. The mischief of an apparently ever expanding economy involving ever increasing consumption the price of which is waste has now been the subject of a number of critical exposés – see for instance Vance Packard's *The Hidden Persuaders, The Status Seekers* and *The Waste Makers.* Galbraith uses what are philosophically similar arguments in advocating a decline in artificially contrived consumer demands, (artificially contrived, that is, by producers' advertising and salesmanship as well as the psychological need to 'keep up with the Joneses') and a switch of productive resources into the public sector in response to an induced demand for better schools, better hospitals etc. *instead* of more consumer durables. Galbraith supports the doctrine of diminishing marginal utility in relation to consumer wants in arguing that as more and more additional wants are satisfied the consumer *ought* to want less:

> In the contemporary United States, the supply of bread is plentiful and the supply of bread grains even redundant. . . And having extended their bread consumption to the point where its marginal utility is very low, people have gone on to spend their income on other things. Since these goods entered their consumption pattern after bread, there is a presumption that they are not very urgent either – that *their* consumption has been carried, as with wheat, to the point where marginal utility is small or even negligible. So it must be assumed that the importance of marginal increments of all production is low and declining. The effect of increasing affluence is to minimize the importance of economic goals. Production and productivity becomes less and less important.[15]

Logically this can be attacked by arguing that basing patterns of production on what a consumer *ought* to want is another way of saying that the economy ought to be centrally directed by the State, and even if the vast majority are incapable of taking independent prudent shopping (or non-shopping) decisions, to have freedom of choice, including the right to choose imprudently, entirely eliminated is also to eliminate personal freedom for the small minority who will always dissent from or challenge the norm.[16]

It can be seen that the question raises fundamental issues. If the law is to avoid venturing into the area of *regulation* of production so as to change society for better or worse according to taste, its role outside the criminal law must instead be primarily both to protect the consumer against misrepresentations of a contractual nature and to protect the prudent shopper on the basis of information. If all relevant information about a class of goods is available to the prudent shopper, together with information about the true cost of

15   Galbraith *The Affluent Society* quoted Trebilcock, op. cit. p. 268.
16   See e.g. Hayek *The Road to Serfdom.*

the goods if credit is available, then at least a prudent shopping decision can be made with the consumers' eyes full open.

This idea can be taken further by asking whether the body of consumer protection laws is reconcilable with the economic concept of the 'perfect market'. If so, the proponents of the need for these laws have a ready made answer to the common assumption that they somehow interfere with a process that would be better left to automatic self-regulation. It is, therefore, worth examining the concept of the perfect market more closely.

The conditions for the operation of the perfect market may be summarised broadly as follows:

a) there must be no monopoly;

b) there must be no cartels;

c) there must be freedom of entry into the market;

d) it must be assumed that there are an infinite number of buyers – i.e. no buyer-monopoly;

e) there must be product homogeneity – i.e. comparisons must be made between similar goods and public controls must affect similar goods equally;

f) it must be assumed that all consumers have perfect knowledge – i.e. have all the requisite information to make informed choices between competing goods.

How far the UK's consumer protection and competition laws serve to promote the concept of the perfect market has been the subject of more detailed analysis elsewhere.[17] Suffice it to say here that the UK has for many years accumulated progressively more comprehensive anti-monopoly and cartel legislation and this is mentioned later in this chapter. The first four conditions mentioned above are consistent with the general objectives of the anti-monopoly provisions of the Fair Trading Act 1973, the Competition Act 1980, the Restrictive Trade Practices Act 1976 and the Resale Prices Act 1976. The condition as to ensuring that consumers have perfect knowledge of the market before the perfect market concept can operate is fundamental. In a highly technological society, the consumer cannot in reality be in possession of the requisite technological knowledge to assess the wide variety of goods in common domestic use, nor is there in reality any pre-buying opportunity to subject goods to scientific analysis. This is why, it may be argued, modern consumer law statutes tend to give the

17 See B. W. Harvey 'Consumer Protection Laws and the Concept of the Perfect Market', John O'Keefe Memorial Lecture, Institute of Trading Standards, 1980. See also Siegan (ed.) *Regulation, Economics and the Law* (1979), particularly ch. 4 and I. D. C. Ramsey *Rationales for Intervention in the Consumer Market Place* (OFT Occasional Paper, December 1984).

consumer inalienable guarantees of fitness and merchantability as well as guarantees as to the safe operation of the goods. The need for product homogeneity imposes a necessary uniformity on standard term contracts for goods sold to consumers and special terms, including exemption clauses, are heavily controlled or banned altogether.

The need for perfect knowledge also highlights the importance of the reports on comparative testing by the Consumers' Association and on comparative prices by some local authorities' consumer advice centres. Similarly it is reasonable to imply a measure of responsibility on the producer in respect of the quality of goods where this cannot readily be ascertained by inspection, as is commonly the case in English law. (Criminal misrepresentations and laws against unsafe goods are uncontroversially within the ambit of consumer protection, and have been for many years.) The Molony Committee, in substantial accordance with this philosophy, grouped their proposals for consumer protection as follows:

    a) arrangements to give the consumer a positive assurance that the goods on offer are safe (if safety is relevant) and of sound quality (shortly 'standards');

    b) the provision of information annexed to the goods which will assist the consumer to judge for himself whether or not they will satisfy his particular requirement ('informative labelling');

    c) the assessment of the merits of the goods on offer by independent agencies ('seals of approval' and 'comparative testing');

    d) the availability of adequate means whereby the justifiably aggrieved shopper may obtain fair redress;

    e) the restraint of misdescription of the significant characteristics of the goods on offer;

    f) the restraint of objectionable sales promotion methods, whether in the form of advertisements or otherwise, which are calculated to divert the shopper from a proper judgment of his best interests (Cmnd. 1781 (1962) para. 48).

The above discussion also indicates the alternative goals which a policy of consumer protection does or should aim towards. The Galbraith thesis is basically anti-materialist and would, it has been suggested, lead eventually to the sort of state-directed objectives which characterised the planning of an economy such as that of the now dissolved USSR. The philosophy of the UK's consumer protection policy (and that of Canada and Australia for example) is consistent with the more modest objectives indicated in the Molony Report above. But wider, anti-inequality of bargaining power, objectives are of increasing importance and may take the form of anti-monopoly legislation, encouragement of competition, control of excessive or misleading advertising, full disclosure requirements, powers to reopen extortionate bargains, better access to the legal system for the unrepresented consumer, and consumer education programmes.

Should (and can) a cost-benefit analysis be made?

Those to whom consumer protection is almost sacred would perhaps take the view that the consumer is now so much better off as a result partly of outstanding proselytisers such as Ralph Nader in the USA (and the privately mounted campaigns for safer cars and smoke-free zones in airliners) and partly of the official and voluntary framework of consumer protection that to question whether there should be financial limits to the umbrella of protection is unworthy. How can you measure, in financial terms, improvement of the human condition? However, the issue did not escape the Molony Committee, who stated with great cogency:

16. We received a great weight of criticism of the existing system of consumer protection, accompanied by suggestions for its replacement. Although we observed a measure of justification, as well as unanimity, in the criticism, we found that some of the suggestions were extravagant in the extreme – extravagant in terms of money cost as well as conception. The consumer, unlike some classes with claims on public bounty, is everybody all the time. The consumer is the taxpayer, and we see small merit in creating an elaborate new system to assist him in one capacity when he would have to pay for it in the other. In so far as any increased cost fell on industry, recoupment from the consumer would be no less inevitable. Further, in considering bold suggestions for reshaping consumer protection arrangements it was necessary, in our opinion, not merely to balance the money cost, but also the degree of interference with production and distribution methods, against the benefits to the consumer claimed by the proponents of reform. These factors have weighted with us in favouring more stringent legal provisions in aid of the consumer rather than an extensive protective machinery, operating administratively at considerable cost.[18]

As regards the cost, in the UK part of this is met by those who subscribe to a particular group such as the Consumers' Association, but central government or local government revenue is now used extensively to service the Office of Fair Trading, the National Consumer Council, the Department of Trade and Industry itself, Citizens Advice Bureaux, Local Authorities' Trading Standards and Consumer Advice Centres, and so on. The money to service these departments and agencies must be raised by taxes or borrowing.

18   Cmnd. 1781, para. 16.

'Compliance' cost to industry in respect of legislative regulation of their product or service can also be considerable and is, of course, passed on to the consumer in higher prices. Over-regulation can kill the goose that lays the golden egg.[19] In 1979, the Commercial Legislation Monitoring Group (an ad hoc group representing 18 leading businesses) estimated that consumer protection legislation might be costing £150 million per annum, or 14p per £100 of household expenditure. Subsidiary legislation, and in particular labelling requirements, were singled out for particular criticism. The National Consumer Council challenged these figures (commissioned from the Economist Intelligence Unit) and estimated the cost at nearer ½p in every £10 of consumer expenditure, but the Monitoring Group's chairman was confident that the Group's higher figure was a reliable estimate.

In 1985 the Department of Trade published its own report based on the scrutiny of administrative and legislative requirements on businesses entitled 'Burdens on Businesses'. This identified a number of areas as being noticeably burdensome to small firms, particularly VAT and taxation procedures, employment protection and health and safety. Regulatory provisions falling under the head 'Consumer Law' were classified as relatively light (11 mentions from respondents out of 200). There were mixed views produced by those surveyed on the fairness of regulatory consumer provisions and it was considered that little could be done to reduce the burden. It was suggested, though, that there should be 'greater use of common sense in balancing firms and consumer interests'. Of a total of 200 firms surveyed, an estimate of £47,000 has been produced as the relevant overhead expense (see pp. 31, 44 of the report).

Following the production of the 'Burdens on Businesses' report, an Enterprise and Deregulation Unit was established within the Department of Trade and Industry to implement the Deregulation Initiative, launched in 1985. Two further papers entitled 'Lifting the Burden' and 'Building Businesses not Barriers' have subsequently been issued. The Deregulation Unit assesses compliance costs with new and existing legislation. Subordinate legislation which has become out of date or, by virtue of frequent amendments, unduly complicated is being identified for early attention. The Deregulation Unit's Brief also includes a careful review of licences which must be held by businesses. These include the following:

---

19 Consider, for instance, the effect of the introduction of most stringent fire regulations on the small hoteliers, many of whom were unable to find the capital needed for required improvements and went out of business. Greater safety is in fact being substituted for the choice of a less safe but cheaper hotel. And see Goldring 6 Fed L Rev at 290.

a) Licences required under the Consumer Credit Act 1974;
b) Registration under the Data Protection Act 1984;
c) Game licences under the Game Act 1831 and Finance Act 1908;
d) Registration for the sale of poisons under the Poisons Act 1972;
e) Licensing of cinemas under the Celluloid and Cinematograph Film Act 1922;
f) Licensing of theatres under the Theatres Act 1968.

As regards the business licence review, a paper was submitted to the Minister of Corporate Affairs in December 1990. Over 300 licences were identified, 30 of which have been targeted for abolition and 24 for administration change. The review is continuing.

The latest paper, *Cutting Red Tape for Business*, was published by the DTI in April 1991 and described the work carried out by government departments under the Initiative, and set out the programme of work so far. The achievements listed in *Cutting Red Tape for Business* include:

- an increase in the VAT registration threshold – giving 150,000 businesses the option of staying out of the VAT net for longer;
- a simplified system of annual returns for companies – by using a computer-generated shuttle document; only changes to the existing return will have to be notified;
- the introduction of a three line statement of profits for small companies instead of full accounts;
- the abolition of 5,000 business forms and the simplification of 10,000 others.

Despite the difficulty of the exercise, attempts have been made at least to construct models of how the cost component of such a cost-benefit analysis should proceed. The model constructed should serve to measure the social cost to the community of the corrective action being contemplated. So, for example, Layton and Holmes proceed as follows:[20]

Where legislation is concerned, more is not necessarily better. For the total cost of corrective action is made up of at least three elements. First there is the transactional cost that the customer incurs in terms of searching time,[1] inconvenience and risk; a cost which is presumably reduced as the intensity of regulation increases. But with the extension of

20 'Consumerism – A passing malaise or a continuing expression of social concern?' 46 Austr Quarterly 6 at 23 – 4. See also E. P. Belababa 'Unfair Trade Practices Legislation; symbolism and substance in consumer protection' 15 Osgoode Hall LJ 327.

1 By 'searching time' is meant the cost of ascertaining the quality of goods or services by the acquisition of information about them, including the resources spent in testing alternatives.

legislation, a second cost becomes significant, that of enforcing and implementing the newly enacted orders. In turn, this spawns a third expense – that associated with the additional costs incurred by the business community in complying with all the relevant legal provisions. It would seem that in assessing any programme of consumer protection, we must consider the total of all three of these action components and seek to establish that particular balance between exploitation and over-protection that yields the minimum social cost to the community (see Fig 4).

Fig. 4 Cost of protection

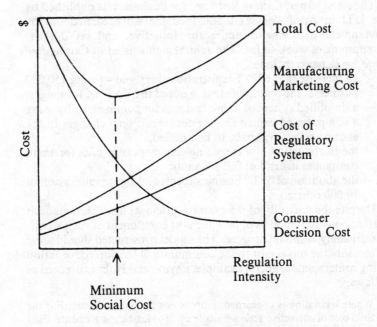

legislation, a second cost becomes significant, that of enforcing and implementing the newly enacted orders. In turn, this spawns a third expense – that associated with the additional costs incurred by the business community in complying with all the relevant legal provisions. It would seem that in assessing any programme of consumer protection, we must consider the total of all three of these action components and seek to establish that particular balance between exploitation and over-protection that yields the minimum social cost to the community (see Fig 4).

Another Australian study[2] proceeds on the basis that 'the law of consumer protection is in substance the use of legal machinery to allocate consumer losses between the purchaser or user of goods and

2   Merrilees and Cotman 'An Economic Analysis of Consumer Protection Law' (1976) Austr Quarterly (March) 79.

services and the vendor, manufacturer or others concerned with the production and distribution of goods and services'. This loss is both in Australia and the UK distributed in a somewhat random way. The loss falls on the purchaser if the seller or manufacturer effectively excludes contractual and tortious liability, or such liability does not necessarily arise in law – e.g. private sales of second hand motor cars, or where the State exacts criminal penalties without compensating the purchaser or user in respect of the deficient goods or services. Sometimes a user may obtain compensation in tort in respect of a manufacturer's negligence although a purchaser's right of action might be excluded by contract. In other cases the loss will fall on the seller, typically a retailer, where the purchaser pursues his non-excludable Sale of Goods Acts remedies against the seller but not the manufacturer, and the retailer finds his rights of indemnity barred by contract. As a further alternative, there may be an insurance fund on which consumers may claim in the absence of a remedy against the supplier, for example the compensation fund compulsorily covering the risk of defalcations by solicitors, or the ten year protection against certain building faults by builders on the register of the National House Building Council. Here the cost of the loss is spread evenly amongst contributors to the scheme. The Australian study discusses the economic impact of the various loss distribution models and one conclusion is that the consumer is better served by a regulatory system that encourages rigorous quality control at the production stage rather than one which relies for its sanctions on the consumer having the energy and funds to activate a breach of warranty claim in respect of defects which a less rigorous production system allows to occur.[3] Voluntary Codes of Practice such as those initiated with various suppliers of goods and services by the Office of Fair Trading in London can be helpful in both improving standards and streamlining complaints procedures. This idea has led representatives of both industry and consumer organisations to propose diminishing the extent of regulation for technical matters through the criminal law and adopting instead a system mid-way between the criminal and civil law, perhaps through universally applicable codes of practice[4] (Codes of Practice are discussed in chapter 11).

3 See also Jolowicz 'The Protection of the Consumer and Purchaser of Goods under English Law' (1969) 32 MLR 1, particularly at 7. The article is of fundamental importance, and proceeds in part on an analysis of the law as a system for the allocation of risks among the persons involved.
4 See in particular Gordon Borrie 'Laws and Codes for Consumers' [1980] Journal of Business Law 315 and David Tench *Towards a Middle System of Law* (Consumers' Association, 1981).

4. MONOPOLIES

The law of monopolies, mergers and restrictive practices is outside the scope of this book because of its complexity and its less direct importance to individual consumers, but a review of the economic and philosophical context of consumer protection would also be incomplete without at least some reference to monopolies.

In economic terms, consideration of monopolies involves the 'supply' side of the market place. In conditions of perfect competition the producer may assume that the price that he sells his goods at will be the market price. However, where a single producer either controls all the supply of a particular commodity or a combination of firms can control a very large proportion of total output, competition is imperfect and the monopolist may either fix his price (letting demand control his output) or restrict output (letting demand determine the price). As regards output, even a monopolist must take account of consumer demand and diminishing marginal utility. Therefore as the volume of production, and hence supply, increases the price of each unit of output will fall. In order to maximise profits he will therefore cease to increase supply beyond the point where the marginal cost of producing each unit of production exceeds the marginal revenue obtained by selling it. Accordingly the disadvantages to the consumer of monopolistic supply are:

   i) Output is generally restricted to maximise profits and keep up price. Furthermore, trade unions in the industry can develop a stranglehold to the disadvantage of the consumer.
   ii) Consumers have less choice than they would have where perfect competition exists, and perhaps no choice at all as regards a particular commodity (e.g. public utilities such as gas and electricity).
   iii) The existence of a monopoly discourages innovation. Dangerous competition which might result in more efficiency and lower prices is either bought up or stifled.

On the other hand, in some circumstances monopolies can be advantageous. Production can be better planned and trade stabilised. Distribution can be arranged economically, as would perhaps not be the case if, for instance, there were rival gas or electricity suppliers. It is also at least possible that since streamlined production and distribution save cost, the price of supply is lower than it otherwise would be.

In many countries anti-monopolies legislation exists. As long ago as 1890 the United States Government passed the Sherman Act and Theodore Roosevelt reinvigorated it in his 'trust-busting' operations at the beginning of this century. In the UK, besides the elderly provisions in the law of contract in respect of illegal arrangements in restraint of trade there are a number of statutes designed to secure the benefits of competitive trading conditions. The main ones are the Restrictive Trade Practices Act 1976, the Resale Prices Act 1976, the Fair Trading Act 1973 and the Competition Act 1980.[5]

In addition, the UK acceded to the Treaty of Rome on joining the European Economic Community on 1 January 1973, and this Treaty has as its major objective the elimination of customs barriers and free movement of 'persons, services and capital' (Art. 3). Accordingly the UK is now subject to the competition policy of the EEC. In particular Article 85 prohibits all agreements between undertakings, decisions by associations of undertakings and concerted practices which may affect trade between Member States and which have as their objective or effect the prevention, restriction or distortion of competition within the Common Market. The Article particularises five prohibited situations including those where the purchasing or selling prices are fixed or where markets or sources of supply are shared. The Article only catches agreements affecting trade 'between Member States', and the Commission has a circumscribed power to exempt certain agreements.[6]

---

5 For a more detailed account of competition policy see the second edition of this
   book. See also *Restrictive Trade Practices: Provisions of the Restrictive Trade
   Practices Act 1976* (OFT, Dec 1990) and *An Outline of United Kingdom
   Competition Policy* (OFT, April 1990).
6 The impact of Europe is discussed further in ch. 2.

2 UK consumer protection law in the European context

The European Community dimension

A fundamental principle of the European Economic Community and its founding Treaty, the Treaty of Rome, may be expressed as being that all the players in the competition of selling goods and services in the single marketplace should be required to play on a *level playing field*. Otherwise a moment's thought will show that competition becomes distorted (by, e.g., hidden subsidies or legislative indulgences which put external competitors at a disadvantage) and it is the consumer, finally, who either pays more for goods and services than if there were true competition, or is denied choice in some way. Ideally the laws of Member States in very wide areas including commercial law, safety law, environmental law and anything else affecting the costs of production and marketing ought to be the same. But as this is impracticable for political reasons, much of the energy of the EC institutions is put into formulating, and through the European Court of Justice, enforcing measures to harmonise these divergent laws. How far even this is truly practicable and enforceable is one of the key political questions of modern times.

In order to assist understanding of the impact of EC law on the UK domestic law, this chapter outlines the main institutions involved and then looks in particular at the impact of EC law on the consumer. It goes on to take advertising control as a case study.

EC institutions and aims

The European Economic Community is one of three Communities established between 1951 and 1957 by France, the German Federal Republic, Italy, Belgium, Holland and Luxembourg. With the approval of Parliament, the United Kingdom signed a Treaty of Accession in Brussels in 1972, to take effect from 1 January 1973. Denmark, the Republic of Ireland, Greece, Spain and Portugal have also become members of the EC (the European Communities). The European Economic Community is by far the most important of the three Communities (the others being the European Coal and Steel Community and the European Atomic Energy Community).

The main institutions of the EC are the Council of Ministers, the Commission, the European Parliament and the Court of Justice. The Court of Justice and the Court of First Instance (discussed in more detail below) have exclusive jurisdiction in the interpretation of Community law as between Member States *inter se*, and also between Member States and their nationals, or their nationals *inter se*, and the Court of Justice is the supreme tribunal on matters of interpretation of the Treaty of Rome (the Treaty giving rise to the European Economic Community) and the other treaties constituting the European Communities. The Council is the final decision-making body for major Community questions, and most of its decisions are taken as a result of a proposal from the Commission. Proposals are normally transmitted by the Council to the European Parliament for debate and an opinion.

With regard to the European Court of Justice, as was said in *The Times* on 23 June 1990: 'Few people know much about the European Court of Justice. Most confuse it with the European Court of Human Rights in Strasbourg or the International Court of Justice at the Hague. Yet the Luxembourg-based court is at the centre of British ideas on European political union'. The European Court was brought to the forefront of public notice in 1990 when it reaffirmed that Community law prevailed over national law, including Acts of Parliament – see *R v Minister of Agriculture, Fisheries and Food, ex p Factortame*[1] and in *Francovich v Italian Republic*.[2] The European Court of Justice held that in stated circumstances an individual could claim compensation from his or her government if that government had failed to implement a Community Directive by the time limit. As part of this principle, an interim injunction lay even against the Crown where, as in the *Factortame* case, the appellants were alleging that rights to fish under Community law were infringed by the quota provisions of the Merchant Shipping Act 1988. Here, the High Court had referred that question for preliminary adjudication under Article 177 of the EEC Treaty to the European Court, and the European Court held that the United Kingdom High Court had been right (despite having been reversed by the House of Lords) to suspend the operation of the 1988 Act as regards the appellants until the European Court had given a preliminary ruling to be implemented by the United Kingdom courts.

It will be seen from the above that the European Court's decisions

1 Case C-213/89 [1991] 1AC 603, [1991] 1 All ER 70, [1990] Eck 1 – 2433.
2 (1991) Times, 20 November (Case C-690) [1990] 1RLR 84, ECJ.

are designed to guide the courts of Member States on the interpretation of Community law (ie to decide whether those States have
obeyed treaty obligations), review the legality of acts of the
Commission and Council of Ministers (or their failure to act) and, as
in the above decision, to give preliminary rulings on points of EC law
for the national courts of Member States. It has no power to enforce
penalties, although perhaps because the United Kingdom has a good
record of compliance compared to, say, Italy and Belgium, the
United Kingdom Government has been proposing that it should
have the power to levy fines. Furthermore, EC citizens have no
power of *direct* access to the court on the matter of whether national
law complies with EC law. The matter has to be referred on by a
national court.

Because of the volume of business before the court, a new Court of
First Instance has been established since 1989 to determine facts in
complex cases and relieve the overburdened main court.

The main aims of the EEC are referred to as the 'four freedoms',
namely the freedom of movement of goods; the freedom of movement of persons; the freedom to provide services and the freedom of
movement of capital. The law of the EC has developed so as to
promote these objectives, together with that of the Common
Agricultural Policy. In addition the Single European Act 1986,
adopted by the heads of State or governments of the Member States,
was a treaty which envisages increasing the scope of Community
authority into such areas as social policy, technological development
and the environment. The treaty also envisages the adoption of
measures aimed at establishing the internal market (i.e. an area
without internal frontiers where there is free movement of goods,
persons, services and capital). The object is to complete the internal
market of the Community by the end of 1992. (The Treaty on
Political Union at Maastricht in 1991 extended EC jurisdiction yet
further, particularly in social matters.)

EC legislation

How are laws in the EC transmitted to the United Kingdom? The
answer to this question depends on the type of EC law which is being
considered. The European Communities Act 1972 both applied
existing Community law to the United Kingdom and made provision
for the law of the Community to grow by:

a) decisions of the European Court and

b) legislation in the form of regulations, decisions and directives.

A regulation is binding in its entirety and directly applicable in all
Member States to which it is addressed, but the form and method is

left to the national Government. A decision is binding in its entirety on those to whom it is addressed.

Directives are probably the most important source of EC law in the United Kingdom at present. Not being self-executing, a directive must be incorporated actively into the United Kingdom's domestic law (ie by statute or statutory instrument). An increasingly large volume of subsidiary legislation is now made under the European Communities Act 1972 pursuant to a directive. But a directive may also be implemented by primary legislation. An important example is Part I of the Consumer Protection Act 1987 which implements the Directive on Product Liability (85/374/EEC). As mentioned above, it is a matter of choice as to the method by which a directive is implemented in the United Kingdom's domestic law. If the matter is one of great importance, such as product liability, primary legislation may well be chosen. If the matter deals with detailed regulation of, for instance, labelling of food, the directive is more likely to be implemented by subsidiary legislation made either under the appropriate piece of primary legislation, eg the Food Acts or under the European Communities Act 1972. The European Court has developed the view that in some cases treaty provisions, decisions addressed to Member States, directives and certain agreements between Members and non-Members can be 'directly effective'. This means, in effect, that an individual can enforce a right conferred by, for instance, a directive against the State before the directive's implementation.[3]

The hierarchy of courts concerned with this type of legislation must be understood. If a question arises as to whether a directive has been correctly interpreted and implemented into the United Kingdom's domestic law by the appropriate deadline, this would be referred to the European Court of Justice, but in most other respects the fact that the directive has been implemented into the United Kingdom's domestic law, via its own primary or subsidiary legislation gives the United Kingdom court jurisdiction over any matter of application or enforcement of those laws. As has been explained, in addition to the European Court's jurisdiction directly to enforce Community law, it is open to any court or tribunal in the United Kingdom to refer for a preliminary ruling points arising in domestic cases which might conflict with Community law (Article 177 of the EEC Treaty).

The chronology of the legislative proposals affecting the consumer is that the Commission first prepares a preliminary draft of a directive or regulation, having consulted with governments, trade

---

3 See Smith and Bailey *Modern Legal System* (2nd Edn.) pp. 288 et seq.

associations, consumer representatives and other appropriate bodies or persons. The draft directive or regulation is then sent to the Council of Ministers, which consults the European Parliament and the Community's Economic and Social Committee (which has representatives of producers and consumers on its membership). On occasion a draft directive or regulation is withdrawn, but if it proceeds it becomes law in the way described above.

The single market

There has been a great deal of speculation about the significance of '1992' in terms of the development of the idea of the Common Market, but there is widespread ignorance of what the significance of this date really is and on the wider question of how EC law directly affects the producer and thus the consumer.

Firstly, what is the significance of 1992? It might make sense to spell out first what it is not. It is not about abolishing tariff barriers. Abolition of tariff barriers between Member States, in terms of quantitative restrictions on trade within the Common Market, happened many years ago and has affected the United Kingdom since it joined the Common Market in 1973. What it *is* about is the abolition of non-tariff barriers in the form of physical, technical and fiscal barriers which prevent the completion of the 'internal market'. The twelve separate Member States, with a population well exceeding 300,000,000 people, still remain very much twelve separate markets. By 'internal market' we mean an area without internal frontiers in which the free movement of - *goods, persons, services* and *capital* is ensured in accordance with the EEC Treaty. This is made clear by Article 13 of the Single European Act, in force since 1987. The idea is partly psychological. By the end of 1992 the objective involves the removal of the remaining non-tariff barriers to one complete market. The deadline gives a focus to this essential objective which was in danger of becoming atrophied.

Many of the matters which were considered to be in need of addressing in order to achieve the internal market by the deadline of midnight on 31 December 1992 are of direct or indirect relevance to those involved as producers - and, in turn, consumers as their customers who want a market with the optimum range of choice of goods and services at the most competitive price possible. So, for instance, physical barriers, involving delays at the frontiers when goods are transported, have to be removed as far as possible. Where these delays are caused by administrative problems reforms are needed. A major step forward was the introduction of the single administrative document.

Technical barriers are important too. For instance, if most of the twelve countries have different standards relating to goods which have to be complied with, the chances of achieving a single market are small. For a start, it can hardly be economic for manufacturers of mass-produced goods to make those goods to twelve differing standards. If there were one Community standard, manufacturing resources would inevitably be used much more efficiently. This problem has been one of the most deep seated in the development of the EC. Individual States may have a particular reason for imposing specific standards, and if these reasons are founded on the basic requirements of health, safety, consumer and environmental protection, they may well withstand a challenge from within the EC. However, following the decision of the European Court in the *Cassis de Dijon* case[4] where the German Government attempted to ban the sale in Germany of Cassis because it did not contain the minimum quantity of alcohol required by German authorities for drinks of that class, the court held that a minimum alcohol requirement was not a *necessary* provision for the protection of public health. German domestic law in this respect was therefore held to be unenforceable, and a similar decision has more recently been promulgated by the European Court as regards German legislative provisions restricting the use of the description 'bier' to beverages using particular ingredients.[5] The practical effect of the bier laws was to prevent the import into Germany of a large range of beers brewed in other Member States, which were perfectly acceptable under the laws of those other States. The ensuing result was to partition the Common Market and dilute competitive pressure. The only possible justification for the German law was that public health was being protected in this way, but the European Court dismissed this argument as unsubstantiated. Indeed, it is difficult to see how a minimum alcohol content requirement could be said to be in the interest of public *health*, though it might be consistent with consumer protection. A better way of avoiding misleading consumers on such matters is by labelling requirements.

The end result of this is that protectionism introduced, perhaps under the guise of consumer protection or protection of public health, by an individual Member State is likely to be struck down by the European Court unless it can be positively shown that health or other public policy principles are thereby prejudiced. The basis of the Court's jurisdiction here is Article 30 of the Treaty of Rome, with the exceptions mentioned above appearing in Article 36. Article 30

---

4 See under *Rewe-Zentral A G v Bundersmonopolverwaltung* [1979] ECR 649.
5 *EC Commission v Germany* Case 178/84 [1987] ECR 1227, [1988] 1 CMLR 780.

prohibits quantitative restrictions on importations and all measures with equivalent effect and the relevant texts are as follows:

30. Quantitative restrictions on imports and all measures having equivalent effect shall, without prejudice to the following provisions, be prohibited between Member States.

36. The provisions of Articles 30 to 34 shall not preclude prohibitions or restrictions on imports, exports or goods in transit justified on grounds of public morality, public policy or public security; the protection of health and life of humans, animals or plants; the protection of national treasures possessing artistic, historic or archaeological value or the protection of industrial and commercial property. Such prohibitions or restrictions shall not, however, constitute a means of arbitrary discrimination or a disguised restriction on trade between Member States.

It will be noted that the text of Article 36 does not refer directly to consumer protection, a concept which was not much in evidence when the Treaty was first designed and drafted. 'Public health' is the defence most usually argued and the court in effect weighs the conflicting policies of protecting the consumer and public health if there is a real threat to it by imported goods suffering from a health or safety risk not affecting similar domestic goods on the one hand and the prejudice to the producer in the stifling of external competition on the other. Recent cases suggest that the court leans in favour of the pro-competition argument on the grounds of 'proportionality'. Using 'a sledgehammer to crack a nut' is not justifiable. A consumer can be informed that a drink, for example, has a higher alcohol content that its rivals (and thus perhaps higher price) by mandatory labelling requirements. This is a neat application of the 'perfect knowledge' component of the concept of the 'perfect market' discussed in ch. 1.

A similar regime applies to prohibition of restrictions to the supply of services (Article 59) unless justified on the grounds of public policy, public security and public health (Articles 56 and 66). The concept of 'the interest of the consumer' can be seen to be capable of dual interpretations. On the face of it laws apparently protecting the consumer may infringe Article 30 as involving quantitative restrictions on imports or *'having equivalent effect'*. Consumers do not benefit from stifled competition. On the other hand there is a danger, unless Article 36 can be evoked, that the interest of the producer in a *free* market may swamp that of the consumer in a *safe* market.

The consumer interest

As has been remarked above, the EEC Treaty contains no direct and obvious provision designed to protect the consumer. Its purpose was to encourage and compel Member States to operate a truly free market, though there were nods in the direction of public policy and public health. When the need to promote consumer protection legislation became pressing the powers given by Article 100 were used, though this is very widely worded, providing for the issue of 'Directives for the approximation of such provisions laid down by law, regulation or administrative action in Member States as directly affect the establishment or functioning of the Common Market'. It was under this somewhat inapt provision that Directives on packaging or labelling of dangerous substances, solvents and cosmetics, control of the composition of articles coming into contact with food, product liability, contracts made away from business premises and consumer credit were in whole or part justified. Where a particular proposal of any sort is desirable but outside the ambit of Article 100, it may be possible to use the 'sweeping-up' power given to the Council to fill gaps in the powers to meet necessary objectives conferred by Article 235.

When the single market initiative presented a chance to amend the EEC Treaty the opportunity was taken to insert a much more satisfactory Article 100A, an article which had the added advantage of allowing the adoption of measures by a qualified majority vote rather than unanimity. The text empowers the Council, acting by a qualified majority on a proposal from the Commission in co-operation with the Economic and Social Committee, to adopt measures within the ambit of the (old) Article 100, and also states that the Commission, in its proposals concerning health, safety, environmental protection and *consumer protection*, will take as a base a high level of protection (Art. 100A(3)). Recent important Directives on such matters as toy safety (see ch. 9) and price indications on goods, other than food, have been made under Article 100A.[6]

Promotion of the consumer interest within the EEC

Consumer protection has increasingly in recent years been an important aspect of the Community's thinking and recommendations. Within the Commission there is an Environment and Consumer Protection Service responsible for representing the consumer interest in the Commission and formulating consumer policy. This

6 See generally Woodroffe (ed.) *Consumer Law in the EEC* (1984) A key article in this area is Stephen Weatherill '1992 and Consumer Law: Can Free Trade be Reconciled With Effective Protection?' (1988) 6 Trading Law 175; see also Wyatt and Dashwood *The Substantive Law of the EEC*, ch.6; Moyes (1984) 9 E L Rev 161; Weatherill (1988) 13 E L Rev 87; Shears (1992) 9 Trading Law 12.

Directorate-General is advised by a Consumers' Consultative Committee, established in 1973 and reconstituted in 1977. In addition, the Bureau Europeen des Unions de Consommateurs is a federation of the consumer associations within Member States and this also influences the Commission and undertakes studies for it. The Council and Commission also have to consult the 144-member Economic and Social Committee.[7]

In 1975 the Council adopted a consumer protection and information programme listing five fundamental rights of the consumer. These are: 1) the right to protection of health and safety, 2) the right to protection of economic interests, 3) the right to advice, help and redress, 4) the right to information and education, and 5) the right to consultation and representation. A further draft resolution concerning the second programme of the EEC for a consumer protection and information policy was submitted to the Council on 26 June 1979. It was expressed as being intended to enable new tasks to be undertaken in the years 1980 to 1985. The programme was approved by the Foreign Affairs Council in May 1981. The second programme was particularly concerned with the following matters arising out of the basic rights adopted by the first programme. These are 1) the protection of consumers against health and safety hazards, 2) protection of the economic interest of consumers, 3) improvement of the legal situation of the consumer, 4) improvement of consumer information and education, and 5) appropriate consultation and representation of consumers during preparation of decisions which concern them. On the tenth anniversary of the adoption of the Community consumer programme a document entitled 'A New Impetus for Consumer Protection Policy' was issued proposing a further timetabled programme for reform of this area.[8] The Commission identified the deep economic recession of the last decade as the main reason for slow progress but correctly added that the

---

7   In the UK the CECG (Consumers in the European Community Group) is an umbrella organisation which co-ordinates the research and representation of the UK consumer movement concerning EEC policies. It has regular discussions with the Ministry of Agriculture, Fisheries and Food, the DTI and the Department of Energy and has direct links with Brussels through members serving on the EEC committees mentioned above. See also Richard Lawson 'Progress on Consumer Protection' (1986) 5 Trading Law 118; Peter Shears 'European Consumer Law: Limping Towards "1992"' (1992) 9 Trading Law, 12; *Consumer Policy in the Single Market* (2nd Edn., 1990), Office for Official Publications of the European Communities, Luxembourg.

8   See Lawson (1986) 5 Trading Law 118 and (1987) 84 L S Gaz 39 for further detail. See also Peter Shears 'European Consumer Law: Limping Towards "1992"' (1992) 9 Trading Law 12.

consumer needs protection in times of recession quite as much as when economies boom.

The Maastricht Treaty also adds a New Title (XVIII) on Consumer Protection, which runs as follows:

Consumer protection

1. The Community shall contribute to the attainment of a high level of consumer protection through:
   a) measures adopted pursuant to Article 100A in the context of the completion of the internal market;
   b) specific action which supports and supplements the policy pursued by the Member States to protect the health, safety and economic interests of consumers and to provide adequate information for consumers.
2. The Council, acting in accordance with the procedure referred to in Article 189B and after consulting the Economic and Social Committee, shall adopt the specific action referred to in paragraph 1(b).
3. Action adopted pursuant to paragraph 2 shall not prevent any Member State from maintaining or introducing more stringent protective measures. Such measures must be compatible with this Treaty. The Commission shall be notified of them.

The reference to 'the attainment of a high level of consumer protection' is significant as indicating the increasing emphasis on this topic.

In connection with health and safety, Community directives on chocolate, some sugars, honey, fruit juices, and preserved milk and poultry health have (inter alia) been adopted by the UK and other similar proposals are under discussion. More generally, a directive aimed at harmonising consumer credit has also been promulgated, as have directives on 'doorstep contracts', advertising and product liability (all discussed elsewhere in this book). A directive on package travel was adopted in June 1990 for implementation by the end of 1992. It involves the licensing and bonding of all tour organisers, and confers various rights to accurate information on consumers. A draft directive is under discussion which would impose liability on producers of services for damage to the health and physical integrity of persons or the physical integrity of property (including animals) caused by their own fault while supplying the service, unless they can prove that they were in no way at fault – i.e. a reversal of the present burden of proof is involved – (December 1990), see further ch. 7. There are also draft directives under discussion which if adopted would extend yet further UK legislation on unfair contract terms and general product safety.

The OFT plays an important role in monitoring the application of the Community competition rules (particularly Articles 85 and 86 of the Treaty). It participates in meetings of the Community's Advisory Committee on Restrictive Practices and Monopolies.[9]

Outside the Community itself the Council of Europe was established in May 1949, having the membership of the UK and most of the other countries of Western Europe and some Central European states (e.g. Poland, Hungary, Czechoslavakia). Its membership clauses insist upon a state's adherence to the principles of freedom and human rights. Rather overshadowed in importance by the EEC, it has nevertheless had an important influence in a number of spheres – see, for instance, the Convention on Product Liability adopted by the Council of Ministers of the Council of Europe at Strasbourg in 1976 and discussed in ch. 6. A draft charter on consumer protection and assistance was adopted by the Consultative Assembly of the Council in 1973, and is similar to the EEC consumer protection and information programme discussed above.

In the context of advertising and the principle of freedom of expression, including commercial expression, the European Court will have regard to the Council of Europe's European Convention for the Protection of Human Rights and Fundamental Freedoms 1953. Article 10 of this Convention provides a right to freedom of expression which includes the right to receive and impart information and ideas without interference by public authorities, subject to some broad-based exceptions deemed necessary in a democratic society, e.g. the protection of public safety, health or morals. The application of Article 10 may strike down consumer-led advertising control legislation deemed to infringe the freedom of expression principle.

Advertising – a case study on EEC derived law

After many years of long and complex negotiations the EEC adopted a Council Directive on 10 September 1984 on misleading advertising. It was recognised that in the UK the combination of a substantial body of legislation including statutes dealing with trade descriptions, consumer credit, medicines and broadcasting and the self-regulatory system administered by the Advertising Standards Authority appear to deal well with most problems which arise. The only positive proposal of the Report of the Working Party of the Department of Trade in 1980 on this topic was that there should be an injunctive

9   See the DGFT's Annual Reports, 1985 and 1990. The OFT also participates in the competition work of the OECD. Some of the earlier directives have been castigated by Sir Gordon Borrie, then Director General of Fair Trading, as being irrelevant, retrograde and damaging to national interests. See Borrie *The Development of Consumer Law and Policy* (1984).

procedure whereby the Director General of Fair Trading would be able to obtain court orders preventing publication of advertisements likely to deceive or mislead. This was seen as a reinforcement of the existing self-regulatory system. The EEC Directive recognises the continuing role which self-regulatory bodies of this sort can play. In addition, the original 'unfair' advertising, a concept not recognised at present in UK law, was agreed to be left out for a further directive. Opposition to such a proposal is likely.

The Directive's main requirement is that Member States must establish procedures whereby those with a legitimate interest in prohibiting misleading advertising may either take legal action against it in the courts or bring the matter before an 'administrative authority' with competent jurisdiction and enforcement powers.

Government policy on implementation was that nothing should be done to hobble the ASA, which by its constitution and system of financing is regarded as more remote from industrial influence than, for example, a trade association enforcing a Code of Practice upon its members. As it operates on a non-statutory basis a great degree of flexibility is also maintained. The new powers which the Directive required to be introduced were therefore regarded as a 'long stop'.

Accordingly, subsidiary legislation made under the European Communities Act 1972[10] empowers the Director General of Fair Trading, in cases where he considers such measures to be necessary, and taking into account all the interests involved, in particular the public interest, to institute proceedings in the High Court for an injunction prohibiting misleading advertising. The definition of 'misleading advertising' is taken from Article 2 of the Directive and is stated to mean any advertising which in any way, including its presentation deceives or is likely to deceive the persons to whom it is addressed or whom it reaches and if by reason of its deceptive nature it is likely to affect their economic behaviour or which, for those reasons, injures or is likely to injure a competitor (reg. 2(2)).

In making injunctions the court is also required to take into account all the interests involved and, in particular, the public interest. It then has power to include in injunctions provisions prohibiting future advertisements about the same goods or services as those which give rise to the injunctions and which are misleading in substantially the same respects. The court also has power to require persons concerned with the dissemination of advertising material to furnish evidence as to the accuracy of factual claims and to consider factual claims as inaccurate if evidence is not furnished or

---

10   Control of Misleading Advertisements Regulations 1988, S.I. 1988/915.

is insufficient. The court may grant an injunction without proof of loss or damage to anyone (reg. 6(5)).

The DGFT as a precondition to court proceedings may require any complainant to satisfy him that established means of dealing with such complaints have been invoked (reg.4).

In the field of investment business advertising, the Securities and Investments Board are given similar powers to those given to the DGFT by rules made under the Financial Services Act 1986. Similar powers extend to advertising for which the Independent Television Commission and similar bodies have regulatory responsibility by virtue of the Broadcasting Act 1990 (commercial radio and television advertisements and cable advertisements). These bodies now have the additional duty of considering complaints about advertising alleged to be misleading in the sense of the Regulations and to take the necessary action, under their existing powers, to prevent the further dissemination of such advertising, taking into account all the interests involved and, in particular, the public interest, where they consider such action necessary. The bodies concerned are required to give complainants reasons for their decisions except where complaints are trivial or frivolous. In reaching their decisions the bodies will be entitled to regard factual claims as inaccurate if inadequate evidence is furnished by the advertiser as to the accuracy. This is in accordance with Article 6 of the Directive.

Modest activity has taken place pursuant to these Regulations, false nutritional or 'green' claims coming under particular scrutiny. Thus in *Director General of Fair Trading v Tobyward Ltd*[11] the DGFT had received complaints from Trading Standards Departments, the public and the ASA about a product of Tobyward Ltd called 'SpeedSlim' (which indicates the nature of the product). The court granted an interim injunction, later made permanent, restraining the publication of misleading advertisements for SpeedSlim and also any advertisement for any slimming product which is in similar terms or likely to convey a similar impression to the misleading claims.

Hoffman J in this case expanded upon the meaning of 'misleading' thus:

> 'Misleading', as I have said, is defined in the regulations as involving two elements: first, that the advertisement deceives or is likely to deceive the persons to whom it is addressed and, second, that it is likely to affect their economic behaviour. In my judgment in this context there is little difficulty about applying the concept of deception. An advertisement must be likely to deceive the persons to whom it is addressed if it makes false claims on behalf of the product. It is true that many people read

11   [1989] 2 All ER 266, Ch D.

advertisements with a certain degree of scepticism. For the purposes of applying the regulations, however, it must be assumed that there may be people who will believe what the advertisers tell them and in those circumstances the making of a false claim is likely to deceive . . . The other element, namely that the advertisement is likely to affect the economic behaviour of the persons to whom it is addressed, means in this context no more than that it must make it likely that they will buy the product.[12]

The above material shows how an EEC Directive was eventually implemented in the UK; it does not purport to give a full description of the law relating to advertising and its control. This is dealt with elsewhere in this book – e.g. see the discussion of the Trade Descriptions Act 1968 where relevant, in ch. 12 and, as to part of the civil law involved, the discussion of contract based remedies for misstatement in ch. 5.

12 Ibid at 270.

3 The institutional framework of consumer protection

1. CENTRAL AND LOCAL GOVERNMENT

a) Central government

Introduction. As a generalisation it can be said that the role of central government in consumer protection is to promote legislative policy (often involving preliminary research), oversee the implementation of legislation and oversee the work of various government agencies. Very often actual enforcement is left to local authorities.

An oft-repeated criticism of the organisation of central government consumer protection machinery is that responsibility is spread over too many Departments, some of which have possibly conflicting responsibilities to industries supplying to the consumer. The Co-operative Party, in particular, as early as 1955 advocated a Consumers' Welfare Ministry but this idea was rejected by the Molony Committee (para. 886 – 'we dismiss so grandiose a notion'). The Committee went on to recommend the establishment of a Consumer Council financed by government grant and this was established in 1963, concerned itself with consumer education and the promotion of consumer interests on a group (rather than individual) basis, but was abolished in 1971.

Central government was reorganised in 1970 and responsibility for consumer affairs passed to the new Department of Trade and Industry. A movement towards a separate Ministry for Consumer Affairs was made when Sir Geoffrey Howe QC was appointed as the first Minister for Trade and Consumer Affairs at the Department of Trade and Industry in 1972. Five junior ministers were appointed in other Departments concerned with consumer affairs (e.g. the Home Office and the Ministry of Agriculture, Fisheries and Food) and given responsibility for the consumer aspects of the Departments' work.

In 1974, after the February election had returned a Labour Government, three new Departments were established to replace the Department of Trade and Industry, namely the Department of

Industry, the Department of Trade and the Department of Prices and Consumer Protection (DPCP).

Further changes were made after the change of government in 1979. The new Conservative Government then abolished the DPCP and spread its functions amongst three divisions of the Department of Trade and Industry – the consumer affairs, competition policy, and metrology, quality assurance, safety and standards divisions. Transfer of functions from the Secretary of State for Prices and Consumer Protection to the Secretary of State for Trade was made by the Secretary of State for Trade Order 1979 by virtue of powers contained in the Ministers of the Crown Act 1975. Very few Departments exercise no functions which affect the consumer, but the main Departments so concerned are these:

Department of Trade and Industry

The Secretary of State of this Department is responsible, amongst other things, for policy and legislation on consumer affairs including trading standards, fair trading, weights and measures, consumer credit and consumer safety. The Department also has responsibilities under the Prices Act 1974, and for monopolies, mergers and restrictive practices. Agencies and similar bodies for whose work the Secretary of State is responsible include the Office of Fair Trading (see below), the Monopolies and Mergers Commission, the British Hallmarking Council, the Hearing Aid Council, the National Consumer Council and the Offices for regulation of water, gas, electricity and telecommunications (discussed in ch. 4). The Department also sponsors the British Standards Institute. The DTI's Consumer and Corporate Affairs Division is particularly relevant to many of the matters discussed in this book.

Office of Fair Trading

This is a government agency, established on 1 November 1973, the Director General of which is appointed by the Secretary of State for Trade. Its functions will be discussed in more detail in those parts of the book dealing with the Fair Trading Act 1973 (see ch. 11) and elsewhere as appropriate. It is the administrative headquarters from which the Director General of Fair Trading exercises his various statutory responsibilities in connection with consumer protection, consumer credit, and monopolies, mergers and restrictive or anti-competitive practices. The OFT in addition exercises important functions relating to consumer education by publishing various informative leaflets or booklets which are available locally through Consumer Advice Centres or Citizens' Advice Bureaux. It produces numerous helpful publications, many giving guidance to consumers affected by defective goods or services (including credit problems), and holds seminars and conferences. The Office also acts as a clearing house for information received at ground level from local authorities and Citizens' Advice Bureaux on areas causing difficulty. It is funded by the Department of Trade and Industry.

The Home Office

The main function of the Home Office as regards consumer protection is the supervision of the control of explosives, firearms, dangerous drugs, poisons and liquor licensing. Legislation on shops is within its responsibility and it advises on fire hazards in consumer products.

The Department of Health

This Department is, of course, primarily concerned with the administration of the National Health Service and welfare services concerned with the aged, handicapped or children. As regards consumer protection it works with the Ministry of Agriculture, Fisheries and Food in the area of food hygiene and safety, gives medical advice to government departments on chemical contamination of consumer products and is closely concerned with the control of drugs.

The Ministry of Agriculture, Fisheries and Food

A Board of Fisheries and Food was established in 1903 and in 1919 became a Ministry. In 1955 the Ministries of Food and Agriculture were amalgamated. As regards consumer protection the Ministry shares responsibility with the Department of Health, and with local authorities, in enforcing the Food Safety Act 1990 and the Medicines Act 1968 and the regulations made thereunder, and in particular has responsibility for standards of composition, labelling and advertising, and with regard to food additives and contaminants. Public health standards in slaughterhouses, cargoes and stores is another area of responsibility.

b) Local government

Enforcement

Responsibility for the enforcement of consumer protection legislation rests almost entirely with local authorities. As a general rule consumer protection functions are carried out by County Councils in England and Wales, the London Boroughs and the Regional or Islands Councils in Scotland, and in Northern Ireland, Area Trading

Standards Offices of the Department of Economic Development. Reorganisation by the Local Government Act 1972, operative from 1 April 1974, resulted in the number of authorities exercising these functions being reduced from 241 to some 88 in Great Britain. By the Local Government Act 1985 the former Metropolitan County Councils were abolished. They had been responsible for a population of over one million, the largest weights and measures authorities ever to have been created in the UK, and the economies of scale achieved are generally regarded as having produced exceptionally efficient and well-equipped enforcement departments. These units have now been fragmented by being split up between the Metropolitan District Councils. Although the 1985 Act requires the setting up of co-ordinating committees in the Metropolitan District, these are not thought to have been effective in maintaining standards. There is also power in the Act for the Secretary of State to establish by order a single authority in the Metropolitan areas but this power has not to date been exercised (see Sch. 8, para. 15).[1] The former Weights and Measures Departments are now generally called Trading Standards Departments or Consumer Protection Departments, and these Departments are responsible for the enforcement of most of the legislation discussed in chs. 9, 10, 12 and 13, particularly the Weights and Measures Act 1985, the Trade Descriptions Act 1968, the Food Safety Act 1990 and the Consumer Credit Act 1974. The Report of the Director General of Fair Trading, covering the year 1990, reveals that there were 238 convictions under the Weights and Measures Acts (of which 123 concerned short weight or measure), 1,258 convictions under the Trade Descriptions Act 1968 (leading to penalties of £828,680, mainly for false trade descriptions of goods), 26 convictions concerning false price claims, and 1,966 convictions under the Food Acts, mainly in respect of the supply of food not of the nature, substance or quality demanded. Much of the time of these Departments is of course spent in 'preventive' activities such as the statutory weighing and verification of weights and measuring apparatus (including, for example, the retesting and stamping of petrol measuring instruments following price changes) or the submitting of articles of food for chemical analysis. District Councils exercise certain functions concerning food hygiene and food safety and their joint responsibilities with County Councils are described more fully in ch. 13.[2]

The United Kingdom is probably unique amongst EEC Member

---

1 See the detailed critique in *O'Keefe's Law of Weights and Measures* (2nd Edn. by A.A. Painter), para. 130 et seq.
2 See the Food Safety Act 1990. See generally *Butterworths Law of Food and Drugs*, Div A.

States in relying on local authorities for the enforcement of basic trading standards legislation such as weights and measures. The reasons are historical, as outlined earlier in this book. The advantage is greater local accountability and, perhaps, sensitivity to the needs of a particular area than could be obtained if the legislation were enforced by divisional departments of central government. But a serious disadvantage is the tendency to uneven levels of enforcement of and varying interpretations of the legislation in different local authority jurisdictions. In recognition of this growing problem, agreement was reached in 1976 between the Association of County Councils and the Association of Metropolitan Authorities to set up a new co-ordinating body to be known as the Local Authorities Co-ordinating Body on Trading Standards (LACOTS). The main functions of this body are 1) to provide co-ordinated machinery for trading standards departments in Great Britain to liaise with central government and industry on relevant technical issues, 2) to co-ordinate operational practice of local authorities at the technical level and ensure uniform enforcement of legislation, including particularly legislation emanating from the EEC, and 3) to advise local authorities on interpretation and enforcement of specific legislation. Invaluable co-ordinating and educational services are also provided to trading standards officers by their professional association, the Institute of Trading Standards Administration.

In order to mitigate the evident dangers of inconsistent decision-making as between, and duplication of investigative effort by, two or more authorities, LACOTS has issued guidelines on what is called the 'Home Authority Principle'. Thus, where a company requires advice from a Trading Standards Department as to legal matters within the Department's remit, its 'home authority' is identified and initial guidance or advice is given. If this is complied with the home authority would not then institute proceedings against that company concerning the particular product or service. Unfortunately, this informal 'estoppel' does not prevent another authority from doing so, but the 'home authority' should be consulted first.[3]

Consumer advice centres

The activities discussed above pertain to the *enforcement* of consumer protection law. In addition the Local Government Act 1972 (sections 137, 142) and the Local Government (Scotland) Act 1973 enable local authorities to provide *advisory* services for the general public. Much of the impetus for the establishment of the advice

---

3   The guidelines in their up-dated form are reproduced in (1990) 7 Trading Law, p. 190.

centres which now exist came from the Consumers' Association which was concerned to make the type of information to be found in *Which?* available to a wider, perhaps, less middle-class, spectrum of the community. The CA advocated the setting up of advice centres to complement Citizens' Advice Bureaux and Weights and Measures Departments. Experiments were made in the London area from 1969 onwards, initially at the expense of the CA. The Advice Centre Servicing Unit of the CA was and is responsible for much of the information supplied to centres and the training of their staff.

About 120 Consumer Advice Centres and about 300 local price survey schemes existed in 1976 aided by grants from central government. These included mobile units to operate in rural areas. These Centres sought and, so far as they still operate, still seek both to assist consumers in getting satisfaction with complaints against retailers and other suppliers of faulty goods or services and to give pre-shopping advice primarily on the basis of price comparisons. The Centres were also a source of information via printed leaflets on matters affecting consumers generally.[4]

A change of policy occurred after the 1979 change of government. Shortly after taking office the Minister of State for Consumer Affairs announced that cash grants from central government for Centres and local price surveys were to end from April 1980, at a saving of £3.5 million annually. The reason given was that the Centres were thought not to be cost effective. Citizens' Advice Bureaux were the preferred vehicle for this type of advisory work, and financial support to them was doubled. Such Centres as have been continued are financed from local authority revenue.[5] The NCC in its Report *Ordinary Justice* (1989, pp. 52 – 53) found (in 1986) 29 remaining run by the Trading Standards Departments of 20 local authorities. Otherwise, Trading Standards Departments tend routinely to employ 'Consumer Advisers' who are not qualified Trading Standards Officers but may hold the Institute of Trading Standards'

4   A survey in the *Times* (24 November 1976) suggested that the Centres dealt primarily with complaints. In Wandsworth for example, about seven-tenths of complaints needed to be followed up and compensation of £1,777 was agreed with retailers in a year. Reactions of shoppers in London areas with Consumer Advice Centres ranged from ignorance of their existence to strong approval by those who made use of them. Because of their diminution since 1980, any impact tends to be local rather than national.

5   It is the opinion of some trading standards officers that public requests for advice, primarily on civil matters, are still significant and tend to be made to any trading standards officer available. A survey by the NCC, however, suggests that 47 per cent of such complaints are dealt with by solicitors, as opposed to 17 per cent by trading standards departments (see 'Simple Justice' p. 17). See also *Ordinary Justice*, NCC, (1989) ch.2. Citizens' Advice Bureaux and Law Centres also supply much advice in civil matters which could involve litigation at a later stage.

Diploma in Consumer Affairs (DCA) and specialise in advisory, rather than enforcement work.

2. BODIES SPONSORED DIRECTLY BY THE GOVERNMENT

The National Consumer Council

A White Paper entitled *A National Consumers' Agency* was put forward by the DPCP in 1974.[6] It was argued that the disappearance of the Consumer Council, a body recommended by the Molony Committee, established by subvention in March 1963 with the function of (inter alia) informing itself about consumers' problems and to consider action to further and safeguard consumers' interests, and abolished in 1971, left a gap. This gap could not, it was argued, be adequately filled by the Director General of Fair Trading. Accordingly it was proposed to establish a National Consumers' Agency whose main function should be to represent the consumer interest in dealings with the Government, local authorities, the Director General of Fair Trading, industry and any other sphere in which the consumer voice ought to be taken into account before policies are formulated or implemented.

This bore fruit in the setting up early in 1975 of the National Consumer Council (with Associated Councils for Scotland, Wales and Northern Ireland), with the assistance of a government grant (£300,000 initially, £2.178m in 1990). The Secretary of State for Trade and Industry has a general responsibility for its work, but it is non-statutory and independent of the Government. It has a part-time Chairman and Vice-Chairman. The Council does not deal directly with consumer complaints but seeks, by making representations, and by representing the consumer on public and other bodies, to influence policies affecting the consumer. Its work to date includes major reports on consumer representation in the nationalised industries and on energy tariffs for domestic fuels and the difficulties caused to those on low incomes. Both reports were made at the request of the Secretary of State. In 1977 a report was published on behalf of the NCC in a book entitled *Why The Poor Pay More* based on research into the consumer behaviour of the poorest sector in Britain. Since then the Council has published a critical review of official forms and leaflets (*Gobbledegook*, 1980), and *Plain language, plain law* (1990), a guide to the Credit Unions Act 1979 which it promoted, a report on Country of Origin Marking, and two on small

6   Cmnd. 5726.

claims, *Ordinary Justice* (1989) being of particular significance. In October 1981 its report entitled 'Service Please' recommended that all the consumer's existing rights should be re-enacted in one umbrella Act in an attempt to inform the consumer more clearly what these rights now are, which recommendation bore fruit in the Supply of Goods and Services Act 1982. Recent reports have scrutinised the quality of services supplied by local authorities, solicitors and the court system generally. The NCC interprets its remit sufficiently widely to cover many other matters of concern to the ordinary citizen, such as access to information, education, food quality, health and social services, housing and public utilities. The NCC, which is a company limited by guarantee, publishes an annual report listing in more detail its activities and reports. The trend of policy advocated by the Council generally is from one of consumer protection to consumer intervention.

The establishment of the Council was not supported by the major opposition party at the time but the Council survived the 1979 change of government and continues to do much vigorous work in identifying and representing the consumer interest, particularly where this is not being fully taken into account in decisions or proposals of central government, public authorities and privatised industries.[7]

The Consumer Protection Advisory Committee

This Committee was established under the Fair Trading Act 1973 (section 3) and its work will be more fully discussed in Chapter 11 dealing with that Act.

3. VOLUNTARY ORGANISATIONS

Citizens' Advice Bureaux (CABx)

The first Bureaux were started in 1939, just before the outbreak of war, by the National Council of Social Service as a voluntary enterprise. The object of the service is much wider than 'consumer protection' as normally understood. Any personal problems on which individuals welcome independent, confidential, practical, often legal-based, advice (such as landlord and tenant problems, divorce and family problems, problems with the police, problems with social security claims) are within the ambit of the service.

---

7 See *In the Absence of Competition* (1989), and *Out of Court* (1991) – low-cost trade arbitration schemes, including British Telecom.

Enquiries concerning consumer problems of the sort discussed in this book account for about 20 per cent of the total. (These enquiries include those as to fuel debts.)

Having fulfilled an identifiable need in wartime they have now expanded and are to be found in all parts of the country. In 1991 there were 712 bureaux with 1,346 outlets registered with NACAB (below). The National Association receives central government finance (£10.346m in 1990/91). In addition local bureaux are heavily dependent on local authority funding (£27.5m in 1990/91). Approximately 23,000 people work in the CAB Service, 90 per cent of whom are voluntary workers. Many bureaux have links with local solicitors, who may act as honorary legal advisers, and also have rota solicitor schemes whereunder solicitors alternate in giving free legal advice. On other occasions the CABx may assist people in filling in forms to enable them to get legal aid and advice from local solicitors in private practice.

Local CABx are independent autonomous bodies and are represented through area committees on the Council of the National Association of Citizens' Advice Bureaux. The Council supplies the policy of the movement and NACAB provides them with a comprehensive and up-to-date information service on new legislation and administrative developments.

Initiated by allegations of political bias on the one hand, and requests for more public money on the other, in 1984 a Report on the Service was produced by the Lovelock Committee (Cmnd. 9139 (1984)). This Report[8] contains much helpful information on the growth, work, aims and funding of the Service and prompted a constructive response from NACAB, 'Accepting the Challenge' (September, 1984).

In 1990/91 some 7 million enquiries were handled. Their work is fundamental to the operation of a complex law-based social system.

Consumers' Association

The primary aim of the Consumers' Association, a company limited by guarantee, is to provide information to the consumer about products and services by testing them thoroughly and giving the reader, through its magazine *Which?*, a frank appraisal. This results, in many cases, in the recommendation of a 'best buy'. The Association was formally brought into being in 1957 and the inspiration for this type of exercise came primarily from the USA

8　See M & H, pp. 295 – 299. See also J. Citron *Citizens' Advice Bureaux: For the Community by the Community* (1989); J. Richards, *Inform, Advise and Support: 50 Years of Citizens' Advice Bureaux.*

where since 1936 the Consumers' Union had been subjecting a wide range of goods to scientific testing and published the results to subscribers in the monthly Consumer Reports. This in turn was inspired by a book called *Your Money's Worth* by Chase and Schlink (1927) calling for the results of the tests made by the US Bureau of Standards to guide government purchasing policy to be made available to consumers generally.[9] Motivation was fivefold. Firstly, people should be encouraged to spend their money well amongst the variety of competing goods available. Secondly, it was regarded as desirable to do something towards reducing the inequality between the disadvantaged ordinary shopper and the technocratic manufacturer. Thirdly, there was the desire to improve Britain's economic performance by creating a more discriminating purchasing public for British goods which were not always of high quality. Fourthly, there was a resentment about the number of goods which were found to be unsatisfactory in some way and a desire to better the situation. Fifthly, there was a resentment of the power of advertising and the desire to find a means of choosing by rational rather than emotional means.[10] With the help of a charitable donation (£3,000) the first issue of *Which?* appeared in October 1957, issued to subscribers. At about the same time a rather similar magazine, *Shopper's Guide*, appeared under the sponsorship of the British Standards Institution, but ceased publication in 1963. There was considerable initial doubt as to whether the publication of comparative tests would, in Britain, lay the publishers open to be sued for the tort of malicious falsehood, also known as slander of title or slander of goods, the width of which had not been tested by much litigation. However, it had been authoritatively laid down in *Ratcliffe v Evans*[11] that the plaintiff must show (a) that the defendant made a false statement to someone else, (b) that it was made maliciously, and (c) that the plaintiff suffered damage (though in many circumstances it is no longer necessary to prove damage in these circumstances).[12] The requirement of *malice*, i.e. an improper motive or want of honest belief in the truth, in practice provides the necessary bar to actions founded on impartial tests of the kind sponsored by *Which?*.

The number of subscribers to *Which?* in 1992 was 800,000. 'Sister' magazines to which members may subscribe are *Holiday Which?*,

---

9 This plea was not finally granted until the (US) Freedom of Information Act 1966 made it a duty for government agencies and departments to give information to the public. Similar requests to the British government have been made, unavailingly; see Eirlys Roberts writing in *Which?*, 1975, p. 354.

10 The history of the movement is related by Eirlys Roberts in her book *Consumers* ch. V.

11 [1892] 2 QB 524.

12 Defamation Act 1952, s. 3.

Gardening from Which?, *Which? Wine Monthly* and *Which? Way to Health*. These are published by the Consumers' Association Ltd., which is the trading subsidiary of the Association for Consumer Research, a registered charity which exists to carry out research and comparative testing on behalf of consumers. In addition to its work 'on the ground' the Consumers' Association exerts a powerful influence in promoting public policy on consumer affairs, either by briefing members of Parliament, or representation on other bodies in the UK or in Europe. The Association is a member of the Bureau des Union de Consommateurs, the European Office of Consumers' Unions and the International Organisation of Consumers' Unions.

The Association is financed by members' subscriptions, donations, and fees from the letting of its advisory services. Ordinary members (those who successfully apply for ordinary membership after at least three years' subscription to *Which?*) may elect the governing Council. Members of the Council may not be directly engaged in the manufacture, distribution and sale of goods or commodities or in the rendering of services to the public.

Local consumer groups; the National Federation of Consumer Groups

Largely as a result of encouragement by the Consumers' Association there are about 20 local Consumer Groups in Great Britain, with 180 other corporate or individual subscribers to the National Federation. The first one was established in Oxford in 1961. They are independent, voluntary and non-profit-making. Their aim is to encourage interest in consumer affairs locally and to campaign for better local shops, services and facilities as well as to encourage helpful existing ones. Many publish their own magazine. The co-ordinating body is the National Federation of Consumer Groups, formed in 1963, which also has close links with the DTI, the Office of Fair Trading and many other consumer organisations. The Federation obtains a grant from the Consumers' Association, a grant from the DTI and receives subscriptions from federated groups and associated bodies. A National Executive Committee is elected by local Consumer Groups to govern the Federation.

The NFCG's Annual Report for 1990–91 highlights its report on the services offered by doctors, together with recommendations, its continued support for the completion of metrication in the UK and investigations into pricing by bar-code scanning.

British Standards Institution

The BSI originated in 1901 as the Engineering Standards Committee but was incorporated by royal charter under its present name in

1929. Its present charter dates from 1992. An independent, non-profit-making and non-political body, it is funded by sale of standards, subscriptions, testing and licence fees, and a grant from the DTI. Its objects may be summarised as 1) to co-ordinate the standardization of materials, products and processes so as to simplify production and distribution and eliminate the wastage involved in an unnecessary variety of patterns and sizes of articles serving the same purpose; 2) to set up standards of quality for goods and services and promote British Standards; 3) to register marks of all descriptions in the name of the Institution. Its Public Relations Department is responsible for educational work and for informing consumers about Standards and their impact.

A 'British Standard' is a published document laying down the specifications, testing or measurements with which an article must comply to ensure that it is efficient and suitable for the purpose. The Institution is responsible for over 11,000 of these Standards, each one of which is drawn up after consultation with representatives of manufacturers, distributors and users. Seventy-five per cent of BSI's projects are directly concerned with the production of European and international standards. Compliance with Standards by manufactures is usually voluntary, though in a few instances compliance is made compulsory by government regulation.

A manufacturer may claim that its goods are made in accordance with a certain British Standard by so stating and marking the goods with the BS number. But a more certain assurance of quality is where a manufacturer is licensed to apply a certification trade mark known as the 'kitemark' to his products. This involves testing for compliance by the BSI and regular spot checks by BSI inspectors thereafter. Failure to meet the Standard results in withdrawal of the licence. The 'registered firm' logo shows that a company's management and quality systems have been assessed as consistently meeting the requirements of BS 5750/ISO 9000/EN29000. (Allied organisations also exist in Britain which provide certification schemes, particularly for electrical goods under the auspices of the British Electrotechnical Approvals Board.)[13]

An important feature of the consumer protection side of the BSI is the work of its Consumer Policy Committee which comprises representatives of national consumer bodies and volunteer members of the public who work on standards where there is a consumer

---

13 Far more conformity has been required with safety requirements in domestic electrical equipment as a result of the Electrical Equipment (Safety) Regulations 1975, (implementing the EEC Directive on low voltage electrical equipment), now replaced by the Low Voltage Electrical Equipment (Safety) Regulations 1989, S.I. 1989/728.

interest. Safety experts advise members of the Consumer Policy Committee on matters of safety which may arise during the development of a Standard.

Other organisations to assist the consumer

There is a large number of organisations directly or peripherally concerned with assisting or protecting the consumer, and what follows is merely a brief selection of the more significant.

Advertising is in part controlled by legislation in the interests of consumer protection, but there is in addition a comprehensive code of practice promoted by the independent Advertising Standards Authority called the *British Code of Advertising Practice*. Under the code, advertisements must be legal, decent, honest and truthful, framed with a sense of responsibility to the consumer and conforming to the principles of fair competition. Detailed provisions apply to certain products, e.g. medicinal products, tobacco, consumer credit and mail order advertisements. Complaints about alleged breaches of the code may be made to the Authority by the public which are then investigated and the results may be published, warning offenders. There are certain other sanctions which may be applied through the trade. Although the code lacks the force of law, it can be justified by the claim that it is designed to achieve high professional standards and good taste which it may not be practicable to make the subject matter of legislation.

The Director General of Fair Trading presented a Review of the UK's self-regulating system of advertising control to the Secretary of State for Prices and Consumer Protection in 1978. The review concluded that the system was working well overall and that there was no evidence to suggest that comprehensive legal controls were needed. However, some improvements were recommended and in particular it was considered that the Director General should be given reserve powers. A further report of a working party of the Department of Trade on the Self-Regulatory System of Advertising Control was issued in 1980.

The adoption by the EC Council of Ministers on 10 September 1984 of a Directive on misleading advertising has already been commented upon.[14] In the context of the control which the Director General of Fair Trading has been given under the Control of Misleading Advertisements Regulations 1988 the government has stated:

In those areas of advertising where the ASA currently provides the main

14 See ch. 2.

control the Government see the new powers which the Directive requires to be introduced primarily as a 'long stop'. The Government hope that the effect will be to strengthen rather than diminish the authority of the self-regulation system.[15]

This attitude has been encouraged by the courts. Mr Justice Hoffmann, in *Director General of Fair Trading v Tobyward Ltd*,[16] where the first interlocutory injunction under the 1988 Regulations was granted, stated:

> . . . the regulations contemplate that there will only be intervention by the director when the voluntary system has failed. It is in my judgment desirable and in accordance with the public interest to which I must have regard that the courts should support the principle of self-regulation. I think that advertisers would be more inclined to accept the rulings of their self-regulatory bodies if it were generally known that in cases in which their procedures had been exhausted and the advertiser was still publishing an advertisement which appeared to the court to be prima facie misleading an injunction would ordinarily be granted (at p. 270).

There are numerous trade and professional associations whose functions include at least an element of consumer protection. To give some random examples, the National House Building Council, to which almost all house builders belong,[17] is an independent non-profit-making body whose aim is to improve the standard of house building and whose certificate is designed to ensure that the buyer does not suffer financially either from the financial failure of the builder or the seriously deficient building of the house. Its Council members are nominated by building societies, building employers' associations, consumer groups and the professions. It sets minimum standards of construction and has an inspection system of homes as they are built. A ten-year warranty is offered to protect buyers against losses, financed by means of a levy on builders.

The Association of British Travel Agents deals with complaints of disappointed travellers who have booked through members of the Association and provides replacement arrangements where a client is affected by the insolvency of his agent (see ch. 11).

As regards professional bodies, the Law Society protects solicitors' clients against the dishonesty or insolvency of their solicitors through a compensation fund to which all practising solicitors

15 Consultative Document, DTI, July 1985. See also Richard Lawson (1985) 4 Trading Law 38.
16 [1989] 2 All ER 266, Ch D. See further ch. 2.
17 Expulsion from the Register, or non-membership, usually results in the unavailability of mortgage finance. Further details of the new scheme in operation since 1989 can be found in (1989) 86 L S Gaz Pt 35, p. 17; and (1989) 86 L S Gaz Pt 36, p. 19.

contribute, and provides for compulsory insurance against negligence. It imposes strict disciplinary rules of conduct, breach of which may result in withdrawal of the right to practice, and has an independent system for investigating complaints against solicitors regarding their standard of work or scale of charges. There is also a quite separate Solicitors Complaints Bureau which dealt with 17,808 complaints in 1989. A legal services 'Ombudsman' reviews the way in which a legal professional body has handled complaints from clients not satisfied with the outcome of the investigation (see ch. 7).

Financial services have largely been omitted from this book because as regards investors they pertain to the raising of capital by offerors of financial services, and this is part of the apparatus of producers rather than consumers. But investors occupy a very similar position to consumers of services and investors have a considerable amount of protection against inadequate information about their investments or fraud. Once the capital is raised, providers of financial services sell them to consumers in the ordinary way – e.g. insurers through policies of various sorts, and where an industry is large and outside much consumer protection legislation[18] it may be justified to create special complaints mechanisms.

As examples of investor protection, complaints about companies authorised by the Securities and Investments Board, created by the Financial Services Act 1986, may if unresolved in a direct approach, be taken to the Board's Independent Investigator. That person can ultimately make an arbitral award binding on both parties. Arbitration, preceded by conciliation, is also offered to complainants dissatisfied with the services of the Securities Association and the Association of Futures Dealers and Brokers, and of the Financial Intermediaries, Managers and Brokers Regulatory Association (FIMBRA), and the Life Assurance and Unit Trust Regulatory Organisation (LAUTRO).

Since 1981 the financial sector has created a number of 'ombudsmen' in the private sector, typically financed by the subscriptions of those members of the particular sector joining the scheme. There are now ombudsmen for the insurance industry (336 companies are members representing 90 per cent of personal insurance business), banking (since 1986), building societies (who are required to have an adjudication scheme recognised by the Building Societies Commission under the Building Societies Act 1986); and, from 2 April 1991, a Pensions Ombudsman Scheme was established to deal with

---

18   For example, sections 2 to 4 of the Unfair Contract Terms Act 1977 do not apply to contracts of insurance – see Sch.1.

complaints against, and disputes with, trustees or managers of personal or occupational pensions schemes.

The actual powers of these ombudsmen vary from scheme to scheme, but at the minimum they carry a voice which is listened to in an often seemingly insensitive corporation and at best they require the company to pay compensation (eg in insurance cases). As a rule, a customer is not bound by the ombudsman's decisions and may resort to legal action if dissatisfied.

The effectiveness of these schemes (together with the Ombudsman for Corporate Estate Agents) was assessed in the Director General of Fair Trading's Report into Consumer Redress Mechanisms in November 1991. The report was critical of the bewildering variety of forms of redress in the financial sector, the varying standards of qualification required of ombudsmen, and the accessibility, simplicity and independence of some of the schemes.

These services are further discussed in ch. 7.

4 Nationalised or privatised industries and the consumer

1. INTRODUCTION

The nationalised industries considered in this chapter are (or were in their embodiment prior to privatisation) examples of public corporations. By 'public corporations' is meant, briefly, bodies having a separate legal personality conferred usually by statute but occasionally by charter,[1] having a specific range of functions often involving a statutory monopoly of the supply of goods or services and as regards management and finance, being independent of government except, in practice, on matters affecting national policy. This is not the place to endeavour to trace in detail the history of these corporations or assess their wider functions and significance.[2] Any survey now made must, in any case, take into account the government's privatisation policy which, at the time of writing, has deregulated (inter alia) the bus industry, telecommunications, British Gas, British Airways, water and electricity. In the case of telecommunications and gas supplies, both British Gas and British Telecom are dominant in their respective markets and the policy has been that, though privatised, they should be subject to a special regulatory regime some features of which are discussed below. Such machinery has not been necessary in, for example, the privatisation of the bus industry by the Transport Act 1985. This Act swept away a regime which was regarded as bureaucratic and which had effectively prevented competition by granting de facto monopolies. Under the new policy any operator can run services on unsubsidised routes provided safety requirements are met and notices given of intention to run such services. Subsidies for unprofitable routes must be awarded on the basis of competitive tender. Bus undertakings run by local authorities or Passenger Transport Executives have been

---

1 For example, the British Broadcasting Corporation.
2 For a thorough survey, see Tivey *Nationalisation in British Industry*.

transferred into free-standing, unsubsidised organisations and the National Bus Company (NBC) was broken up and more than 60 subsidiaries sold off. In these circumstances the consumer's interests must be enforced in the same way as against any other private operator, leaving the consumer to pursue his rights through the court and using, where appropriate, the Supply of Goods and Services Act 1982. In addition, British Rail remains nationalised and consumer complaints are routed through its Area Transport Users' Consultative Committees (TUCCs) – see the Transport Act 1962, section 56 as amended.

Leaving aside early and inexact nineteenth century precedents, an early twentieth century example is the Port of London Authority, established to run the London docks and waterfront by the Port of London Act 1908. But of the many public corporations which now exist, those in which the consumer has a particularly direct interest were mainly created as part of the nationalisation programme of the Labour Government in the years immediately following the Second World War. The vehicle of the public corporation was chosen to manage such industries as coal, gas, electricity, transport and, after many years as a government department, postal and telephone services so as, in theory at least, to combine the virtues of commercial and independent business management with public accountability and ultimate public control. 'Public enterprise' is the cachet which most aptly conveys the hermaphrodite status and objectives of this type of public corporation. The movement to establish public corporations of this type went into reverse in the 1980s with the government's privatisation policy, as mentioned above, though some important industries remain nationalised.

2. THE IMPLICATIONS OF MONOPOLY POWER

There is an immediate apparent contradiction in the state's economic objectives when one compares the elaborate machinery in the monopolies, mergers and restrictive practices legislation and the rules of the EEC to preserve an element of competition between producers in the consumer interest on the one hand, with the monopoly powers usually conferred by the nationalising statutes on the public corporations supplying essential goods and services on the other. Thus for example the Coal Industry Nationalisation Act 1946 (section 1 (1)(a)) states that the duties of the National Coal Board are 'working and getting the coal in Great Britain, to the exclusion (save in this Act provided) of any other person'. Other everyday examples of these monopoly powers are 1) the carriage of rail passengers by

British Rail and 2) in respect of the carrying of letters by the Post Office.[3]

The reasons for conferring these monopoly powers on public corporations of this sort included considerations arising from the colossal capital investment because of the nature of the service provided, the social responsibility of suppliers of energy to the community[4] and to the workers within the industry. Although there are formidable difficulties in contriving a fair system of competition in these fields of economic activity, the view currently taken by the government is that if the industry can be run profitably there is no intrinsic reason why ownership of it should not be vested in the public, through shareholdings, rather than in the state. The 'privatisation' policy adopted in recent years is discussed below. The legislation achieving the privatisation normally contains provisions at least narrowing down the areas in which the monopoly continues to exist.

Having pointed out the existence of legally enforceable monopoly powers it is necessary to qualify any impression that this necessarily puts the consumer into a straitjacket in the market place. For example, the consumer considering the installation of domestic central heating has the choice as regards fuel between oil, gas, electricity and solid fuel. In theory at least, even assuming that the particular industry is monopolistic, there is strong competition between the various industries to provide fuel at favourable rates. But in practice government may interfere either, as in the period from 1972 to 1975, by holding down prices below break-even level as a contribution to macro-economic anti-inflation policies, or, for example, by reducing the public indebtedness of the then nationalised gas industry by raising gas prices so that as a result, gas becomes less competitive with other sources of energy, or, more drastically, by

3   'Subject to the following provisions of this Part, the Post Office shall have throughout the United Kingdom the exclusive privilege of conveying letters from one place to another, and of performing all the incidental services of receiving, collecting and delivering, letters) (British Telecommunications Act 1981, s. 66(1)).

4   For example, the Gas Act 1948, s. 1 (1)(a) stated that it shall be the duty of every area board 'to develop and maintain an efficient, co-ordinated and economical system of gas supply for their area and to satisfy, so far as it is economical to do so, all reasonable demands for gas within their area' (see now the Gas Act 1986, s. 9). The Electricity Act 1947, s. 1(2) had a similar provision obliging boards 'to plan and carry out an efficient and economical distribution of those supplies to persons in their area who require them'. Professor Garner stated that 'there has yet been no litigant bold enough to ask for an order of mandamus against a public corporation, and it is perhaps doubtful whether he would achieve much by so doing': *Administrative Law* (4th Edn.) p. 315.

taking the same anti-monopoly actions as if the industry were a non-nationalised one.

3. PROTECTING THE CONSUMER'S INTERESTS

There are a number of legal and parliamentary controls upon public corporations and an analysis of these controls is more appropriate to works on administrative law. But, to give brief examples, a member of the public may sue a public corporation in the ordinary way, and in particular the corporation will be vicariously liable in tort for the negligence or other civil wrongs of its servants. This may be negatived by a specific statutory immunity, such as the Post Office's in relation to liability in respect of actions or omissions 'in relation to anything in the post', under section 29 of the Post Office Act 1969 (as amended).[5] Similar exclusions in respect of telecommunications were made by section 23 of the British Telecommunications Act 1981 which excludes British Telecom's tort liability in respect of failure to provide a service or apparatus and errors in telephone directories. As has already been pointed out it is probably not possible for a member of the public successfully to sue the corporation itself in respect of any alleged breach of statutory duty to provide, for instance, an efficient and economical supply of energy. Professor Garner has called this type of provision 'a duty of imperfect obligation'. Alternatively the appropriate minister might be required in Parliament to answer members' questions, often made on behalf of constituents, provided in fact there is a responsible minister, and sometimes where there is no such direct responsibility. Opportunities for debate may also occasionally occur, for example where a constituent statute is made or revised, or where a motion of supply includes a vote for financial assistance to the public corporation. Between 1956 and 1979 a House of Commons Select Committee examined the Reports and Accounts of the Nationalised Industries, and from time to time investigated and reported on a particular public corporation, or on general matters such as relations with the public, discussed below. But neither the Parliamentary Commissioner for Administration ('the Ombudsman') nor the Commissions for Local Administration cover the public corporations dealt with in this chapter.

It is widely, if by no means universally, conceded that it is also appropriate to represent the consumer in an advisory capacity in the

---

5   In *Harold Stephen & Co Ltd v Post Office* [1978] 1 All ER 939, the Court of Appeal refused to grant the plaintiff businessmen relief in respect of their mail detained by the 'blacking' action by Post Office workers.

policy-making of public corporations. This can either be justified on the grounds that it may help to prevent the irresponsible use of monopoly power or on the more general ground of the inequality of technological knowledge between consumer and producer. The main way in which Parliament has arranged for the consumer interest to be represented is by the creation of Consumer or Consultative Councils.[6] These exist, for example, for solid fuel (the Domestic Coal Consumers' Council), and postal services (Post Office Users' National Council – 'POUNC'). The effectiveness of these bodies is debatable though such independent surveys as have been made confirm that they can often deal effectively with consumer complaints and that their public profile is improving.[7]

4. PRIVATISATION OF FORMERLY NATIONALISED INDUSTRIES

The major examples of the privatisation of formerly nationalised industries affecting the everyday activities of the consumer are the gas industry, the electricity industry, the water supply industry and the telecommunications industry. Each will briefly be considered.

Gas

The Gas industry is now considered in its nationalised and then privatised form. The arrival of a central supply of natural gas from the North Sea accompanied by a system of trunk pipelines prompted the reorganisation of the gas industry on a unitary basis, under the British Gas Corporation, by the Gas Act 1972. The BGC had the duty of meeting all reasonable and economic demands for gas, avoiding undue preference. The BGC had a virtual monopoly of supply to the approximately 13 million domestic gas consumers. It competed with private firms on appliance sales, servicing and contracting but enjoyed about 60 per cent of domestic gas appliance

6   Emmanual Shinwell, Minister of Fuel and Power at the time of the Coal Industry Nationalisation Act 1946, justified a Coal Consumers' Council by stating, 'It was necessary to take account of public opinion, and though such a Council might prove abortive, it would be a body which would *appear* to be useful, and that was an important factor'. See also Rutherford 'The Consumer Voice in Nationalised Industries' (1980) 130 NLJ 620.

7   See Consumer Consultative Machinery in the Nationalised Industries (Consumer Council, 1968); HC Paper (1970–71) no 514; Consumers and the Nationalised Industries (NCC, 1976); 'The Citizen and Public Agencies' (Justice, 1976); White Paper on the Nationalised Industries (Cmnd. 7131 (1978)); Report on Non-Departmental Public Bodies (Cmnd. 7797 (1980)); Consumers' Interests and the Nationalised Industries (Do T, 1981).

sales. Management of the industry was through twelve Regions each of which was divided into Areas.

The Gas Act 1948 had created twelve gas consultative councils on an Area Basis. The 1972 Act preserved the regional structure by converting the Area Gas Consultative Councils into Regional Gas Consumers' Councils, and also set up a National Gas Consumers' Council (section 9). The National Council had a Chairman and not more than thirty members made up of the Chairmen of Regional councils and other members appointed, after consultation, by the Secretary of State. The BGC had to inform the National Council of its plans, tariff proposals and other matters involving consumers generally and the Council could make representations to the Minister (i.e. the Secretary of State for Energy). The Council's statutory duty was to consider 'any matter affecting the interests of consumers of gas generally or any class or description of consumers of gas' (section 10(1)).

The Regional Gas Consumers' Councils consisted of a paid chairman and between twenty and thirty members chosen from amongst local authority nominees and representatives of all classes of consumers in the area. Section 11 of the Gas Act 1972 required Regional Committees to appoint local, or district, committees to receive local representations and keep themselves aware of local requirements. Regional councils could make representations to the BGC or to the National Council, not to the Minister direct.

Under the government's privatisation policy provision was made for dissolution of the BGC and the vesting of its property, rights and liabilities in a company nominated for this purpose by the Secretary of State and limited by shares (Gas Act 1986, section 49). This 'successor company' (i.e. British Gas plc) was designed to be widely owned by gas consumers and investments in its shares are authorised as being appropriate for trustees (section 59). The Gas Act 1986 also removes the privilege (i.e. monopoly) with respect to the supply of gas through pipes conferred on the BGC by the Gas Act 1972. It is now open to any undertaking to supply gas to any premises provided the undertaking is authorised to do so under sections 7 and 8 of the Act as a 'public gas supplier'. Schedule 5 supplies a 'public gas supply code' with regard to the standard of service to be observed by public gas suppliers.

The Act also provides for the appointment of an officer to be known as the Director General of Gas Supply (section 1) whose office is known as OFGAS. Amongst his duties is the fixing of maximum prices at which gas supplied by public gas suppliers may be resold, and provision is made for the publication of such prices to secure adequate publicity. If any person resells any gas supplied by a public supplier at a price exceeding the maximum price, the amount of the excess is recoverable by the person to whom the gas was resold. The Act also contains the machinery for consumer representation. A new body corporate known as the Gas Consumers' Council is set up by section 2 to replace the old National Gas Consumers' Council. The Council consists of a chairman and such other members as the Secretary of State may from time to time appoint. Such members are required to represent and consider the interests of consumers of gas supplied through pipes in the different areas of Great Britain and understand the needs of small businesses. Schedule 2 further describes the status and duties of members of the Council which is funded by the Department of Trade and Industry. The Council has headquarters in London and regional offices in England, Scotland and Wales.

The Gas Consumers' Council (GCC) deals also with complaints about appliances sold by British Gas, or servicing and repairs, which do not come within the jurisdiction of OFGAS. During 1990 the GCC dealt with 80,000 enquiries and 21,700 complaints. The latter were mainly on accounts (32 per cent), services or repair (18 per cent) and general retailing activities (20 per cent). Details of complaints procedures should be found on the back of invoices.[8]

Telecommunications

The second example of the privatisation of a former public corporation is that of telecommunications. The history of the privatisation of telecommunications started with the British Telecommunications Act 1981. Under this Act provision was made for the establishment of a public corporation, called British Telecommunications, and also for the transfer to it of the relevant property, rights and liabilities of the Post Office in respect of telecommunications.

The 'privatisation' process was completed by the Telecommunications Act 1984. Amongst the important provisions of this Act are a) provision for the appointment of a Director General of Telecommunications to keep under review and to promote the provision of telecommunications in the UK, b) the removal of British Telecommunications' exclusive privilege to run telecommunications systems, and the requirement of all operators of such systems to be licensed by the Secretary of State or the Director, and c) the transfer of all British Telecommunications' property rights and liabilities to a successor company limited by shares (British Telecommunications plc) – the object of this provision, as in the case of gas, being to spread the

8   See *Consumer Redress Mechanisms* (OFT, 1991) para. 4.89.

ownership of the company as widely as possible. The government sold off a further tranche in 1991 leaving it with a holding of about 22 per cent.

Professor Sir Bryan Carsberg was appointed the first Director in 1984 and established his Office of Telecommunications (OFTEL). The general duties of the Director are laid down in section 3 and include the duty to exercise his powers so far as possible to secure that there are provided throughout the UK, save insofar as the provision thereof is impracticable or not reasonably practicable, such telecommunications services as satisfy all reasonable demands for them including, in particular, emergency services, public call box services, directory information services, maritime services and services in rural areas. The Director, together with the Secretary of State, is under a general duty to promote the interests of consumers, purchasers, and other users in the UK in respect of the prices charged for, and the quality and variety of, telecommunication services provided and telecommunication apparatus supplied. The Director, together with the Secretary of State, is also under a duty to maintain and promote effective competition between persons engaged in commercial activities connected with telecommunications in the UK.

OFTEL inherited the responsibilities formerly held by POUNC (mentioned earlier in this chapter) in respect of postal communications and telecommunications. But the Office was designed to have a broader brief; to ensure that British Telecom did not breach its operating licence, that it did not engage in unfair competition or abuse its size, and that its tariff was increased according to an agreed code setting it three percentage points behind the rate of inflation.

British Telecom, though privatised (in terms of *networking* rather than the supply of *equipment*), remains monopolistic (though described officially as a 'duopoly', the less dominant partner being Mercury (see below)). This status imposes a severe regulatory challenge. It is a tribute to its Director that OFTEL has been so relatively successful in publicising grievances and securing a measure of reform to British Telecom's operating practices. In 1991 it was reported that OFTEL received about 12,000 complaints per quarter of each year. The main areas of concern were tariffs and charges, quality of service and disputed telephone accounts.

With regard to competition, the only significant potential provider of a rival system of telecommunications to date is Mercury Communications Ltd which applied in 1985 to make interconnections with the British Telecom system. Most of its present business is commercial. The charges which BT makes for use of its network have been modest but are now under review. The provision of such a service by Mercury depends on purchasing a special telephone.

(There is, of course, competition in the supply of telecommunications *equipment*, and further competition is promised.)

The 1984 Act provided a Code of Practice (the Telecommunications Code, reproduced at the end of telephone directories) which the Director keeps under review, together with the terms of the contracts under which BT provides services. A new Code published on 5 November 1984 revised the previous Code and included provision for arbitration. The compensation scheme is referred to above. The arbitration scheme, and OFTEL's role in this area is assessed in the National Consumer Council's '*Out of Court*' report (1991).

Electricity

The Electricity Act 1947 nationalised electricity supply as from 1 April 1948. The Central Electricity Generating Board was responsible, in England and Wales, for the development and maintenance of an efficient bulk electricity supply to Area Boards. The Boards distributed electricity to consumers. The Energy Act 1983 removed the statutory prohibition (in force since 1909) on the supply of electricity by any person other than an Electricity Board and opened the way for the private generation of electricity and its sale to Boards as well as the right to use a Board's transmission and distribution system.

As regards the interests of consumers, 'consultative councils' were established under the Electricity Act 1947, section 7, to advise Area Boards and, in certain cases, to make representations to the Secretary of State.

The pattern of the privatisation of electricity followed a somewhat similar sequence to the other privatised industries considered in this chapter. In particular, the Electricity Act 1989 1) provided a new system governing the generation, transmission and supply of electricity and 2) removed electricity from state ownership and control into a number of regionally based successor companies which were then floated off to the public.

The regulatory mechanism involved the appointment of a Director General of Electricity Supply (operating through an office known as 'OFFER'). The duties of the officer include ensuring that all reasonable demands for electricity are met and protecting the interest of consumers in respect of prices, terms and quality of supply.

Section 2 of and Schedule 2 to the Electricity Act 1989 require the Director to appoint consumers' committees in relation to each of the authorised areas of public electricity suppliers or to two or more of such areas. The committees have a duty to make representations to, and consult with, their allocated public electricity supplier, keep matters affecting the interests of consumers in the area under review and advise the Director. There is an overarching National Consumers' Consultative Committee consisting of the Director and the chairmen of all the consumers' committees to review matters affecting consumers' interests (section 53).

If a consumer makes a complaint to the supplier which cannot be resolved it can be taken up with the regional office of OFFER. If this provides no resolution it may be considered by the local consumer committee. The committee cannot enforce decisions, but the Director General can – a decision by him has the same effect as a judgment of the county court or sheriff's court (Scotland).

In two important types of case the Director General might use his enforcement powers. These are where there is a proposed or actual disconnection when a public supplier is in contravention of its duty to give a supply; or when there is a breach of duty in meeting a reasonable request from a potential customer for a supply.[9]

Water

This industry was complicated by the existence of almost 200 'statutory water undertakers', some under the aegis of local authorities and most incorporated by a local Act of Parliament and formerly regulated by the Water Act 1945. The Water Act 1973 established ten water authorities to take over the functions of the former statutory undertakers. In turn, the Water Act 1989 transferred the functions of the ten water authorities to successor companies subsequently floated off to the public by the Crown. The relevant legislation was consolidated in 1991 and as far as regulation is concerned the relevant statute is now the Water Industry Act 1991.

Section 1 of the 1991 Act (consolidating the Water Act 1989, section 5, which, in turn, implemented the proposal in the government's 1986 White Paper *Privatisation of the Water Authorities in England and Wales,*) provides for the appointment of a Director General of Water Services, who operates through an office known as 'OFWAT'. The Director's primary duty is to secure that the functions of a water undertaker and sewerage undertaker are properly carried out in England and Wales. Important subsidiary duties include the protection of the interests of customers or potential customers in rural areas and to prevent undue preferences or discrimination in the fixing of charges.

As recommended by the White Paper, the consumer interest is more directly represented by the establishment of 'customer service committees' to whom every water company is allocated (section 28).

9 See *Consumer Redress Mechanisms* (OFT, 1991) para. 4.92.

Their duties are to keep under review the interests of the companies' customers or potential customers and to consult with and make representations to their companies. They are under a duty to investigate complaints by customers, unless frivolous or vexatious. The Director and the Secretary of State have reserve powers relating to certain classes of complaint.

Ten such committees (LSCs) have been set up by the Director General to protect consumers and investigate complaints. As with other public utilities, complaints about water or sewerage are first discussed with the relevant water company, but if resolution is not possible references are made to the Director General. LSCs advise the Director General on such matters as metering.

Privatisation policy – some problems

Privatisation of British Gas provides one of the more recently available case histories on the effects of the government's privatisation policy in the areas discussed in this book. The flotation of British Gas plc in 1986 resulted in the creation of about 5 million shareholders whose average holding was .00002 per cent of the total equity. It has been pointed out[10] that although this creates wider share ownership, the spread of the shareholders reduces rather than increases the ability of investors to influence the way British Gas behaves. The Japanese, by contrast, have arranged the privatisation of their Telecommunications System to favour the large investor rather than the small. And although John Moore, Financial Secretary to the Treasury, stated in 1983 that 'The primary objective of the government's privatisation programme is to reduce the power of the monopolist and to encourage competition' the machinery in the Gas Act 1986 for the promotion of competition appears to be weak. Since 1982 industrial consumers have had the facility of buying gas directly from oil companies but it is still necessary to use the British Gas network to transport the gas to the factory. Domestic consumers have no alternative but to use British Gas. Although the industry could have been split up into regional companies with a separate transmission company, this would, it is thought, have greatly reduced the value to the government of the flotation of British Gas. Incentives to more efficiency include, of course, the prospect of insolvency or being taken over. Effective monopolies such as British Gas are too large and too rich in assets for these considerations to be realistic threats.

10   See Professor John Kay writing in The Daily Telegraph, 10 December 1986. See also Kay, Mayer and Thompson (ed), *Privatisation and Regulation, the UK Experience* (Clarendon Press 1986).

The setting of prices by the industries' regulators is critical. The approved formula for pricing is known, shortly, as 'RPI-minus-X', which has the effect of making each industry limit its product price rises to x percentage points less than inflation. Thus, if inflation is at 6 per cent and x is set at 3, the industry may raise prices by the balance of 3 per cent. If the regulator considers that the monopoly profit is too high, x can be raised. BT's 'x' started at 3 per cent, rose to 4.5 per cent and is presently 6.25 per cent. Similarly British Gas's has risen from 2 per cent to 5 per cent. The regulator has to steer a difficult course between protecting the consumer and not discouraging investors.[11]

It is probably true to say, therefore, that it is the *management* of these industries which has been privatised. They are no longer directly accountable to the government and they have the ability to raise private capital. But except in the case of the fragmentation of the bus industry[12] the formerly nationalised industries remain monolithic, substantially free from the prospect of competition and, unlike under the old regime, government regulation. Such competition as there is must be between eg gas as an energy source and other sources such as electricity and oil.

The Citizen's Charter

In July 1991 the government published a White Paper entitled 'The Citizen's Charter – Raising the standard'. Its aim was to raise the standards of quality and efficiency where the citizen as 'customer' consumed services (or encountered administrative machinery) for which government departments were responsible, or which were connected with monopolistic suppliers. Education, health, employment opportunities, the inland revenue, police and social services are beyond the scope of this book. But British Rail, London Underground and the Post Office received attention and 'mini-charters' proposing better performance monitoring and targeting, compensation schemes for disappointed customers and possible future privatisation or increased competition are under discussion.

As regards the utilities which are the subject matter of this chapter, the Competition and Services (Utilities) Act 1992 was hurried through parliament prior to its dissolution and raises the powers of the regulators of the various offices – OFFER (Electricity), OFWAT (Water), OFGAS (Gas), OFTEL (Telephone) – up to the level of the strongest. It seems there is likely to be a move towards more customer-compensation schemes which, whilst to be welcomed by

11 See *The Regulation of BT's Prices*, Consultation Document of OFTEL, 1992.
12 Achieved by the Transport Act 1985 and mentioned above.

72   *Nationalised or privatised industries and the consumer*

consumers, may be to an extent self-defeating – for instance, where the loss-making British Rail finances the compensation payments made for its late trains by putting its fares up, instead of making efficiency gains.[13]

---

13   See *The Consumer Policy Review: Public Utilities* (Consumers' Association, 1992).

5 Supply of goods and contract-based remedies

When a consumer is supplied with goods which are subsequently discovered to be unsuitable for his intended purpose or of defective quality or not to comply with the supplier's description, may the consumer recover some or all of his money? Or more seriously still, where the goods cause damage to him or whoever uses the goods, may the injured person recover damages for the injuries?

For the answer to the first question it is necessary to examine the relevant parts of the law of contract as developed by the judges and as adjusted and amended by the legislature in the form of the sale and supply of goods legislation and the Misrepresentation Act 1967. The answer to the second question depends primarily on the development of the law of negligence in tort together with what might loosely be called the statute law of products liability. There is some danger in isolating parts of the complex body of contract and tort law and the sale and supply of goods legislation because one happens to be analysing the legal consequences of a transaction from the consumer's point of view. For instance, it must be borne in mind that whilst it can generally be assumed that where a consumer buys goods from a seller there has been a valid contract of sale of goods, occasionally this may not be the case since an apparently valid contract may be nullified or vitiated by some factor such as an operative mistake, or incapacity to contract, or illegality. Similarly, in cases where traders refuse to redeem 'money-off' vouchers and such like it is often of importance to analyse the actual or attempted purchase and sale transactions, bearing in mind that it is well established that goods on display in shops and marked at a price are not 'offered' to the customer. It is the customer who makes the offer for the article to the shopkeeper, who may or may not accept,[1] though display of goods at a false price may give rise to *criminal* liability under the Consumer Protection Act 1987, considered later in this book. A knowledge of the principles of contract and tort must

---

1 *Pharmaceutical Society of Great Britain v Boots Cash Chemists (Southern) Ltd* [1952] 2 QB 795, [1952] 2 All ER 456.

therefore be assumed since it is not appropriate in this book to attempt a global examination of them. Nor shall we attempt to deal with those provisions of the Sale of Goods Act 1979 which deal in detail with the transfer of property, risk of loss and proprietary remedies which are more appropriately left to works on commercial law.

CONTRACT-BASED REMEDIES

I) INTRODUCTION

Two associated principles permeated the nineteenth century development of contract – freedom of contract and, at ground level, *caveat emptor*, let the buyer beware. The idea of freedom of contract was part of the laissez-faire doctrine of liberal classical economics. Just as to the liberal, interference with religious freedom was anathema, so was interference with business. The duty of a government was to preserve law and order, promote foreign trade and defend the country from its enemies. Industry was left to look after its own interests, the inefficient going under in favour of the more cost-effective producer, except that the state could legitimately act against privileged monopolies which interfered with free competition. A perfect market responded automatically to the total pressure of self-interested but enlightened buyers and sellers. The system was manifestly sufficiently flexible to cater at a price for the needs of even the most individualistic consumer. Prices were the measure of the balance between supply and demand, cost and utility. 'Planning' and other collectivist intervention by government was unnecessary and harmful.[2] This philosophy was reflected by the judiciary. In an oft-quoted passage, Sir George Jessel, in 1875, said:

> . . . if there is one thing more than another which public policy requires, it is that men of full age and competent understanding shall have the utmost liberty in contracting, and that their contracts, when entered into freely and voluntarily, shall be held sacred and shall be enforced by Courts of Justice.[3]

The doctrine was harsh but, in terms of national wealth, highly successful. It still permeates many aspects of the law of contract; the parties will be held bound in the absence of some material vitiating

---

2 For a short but excellent account of the rise and decline of laissez-faire see Cairncross *Introduction to Economics* ch. 34.

3 *Printing and Numerical Registering Co v Sampson* (1875) LR 19 Eq 462, cited in Cheshire, Fifoot and Furmston's *Law of Contract* (12th Edn.) at p. 11, chs. 1 and 2 of which are an excellent introduction to the development of the law.

factor, however bad a bargain the buyer or seller has struck. But, without overtly replacing it, the twentieth century has seen increased intervention by both the judiciary and the legislature on behalf of the consumer[4] in recognition of the fact that in many transactions there is a significant inequality of bargaining power between the buyer and the seller, and it is accordingly unrealistic to ascribe to the buyer a freedom to contract and agree detailed terms when in practice he has little choice but to accept those terms. In other spheres, of which the contractual relationship between landlord and tenant or employer and employee are graphic examples, the state has intervened in favour of the tenant or employee respectively to give him a protected status irrespective of the terms of any contract.

II) EXPRESS TERMS

Undertakings and promises contained in a contract are known as terms of the contract, and may be express or implied by law or as a consequence of the presumed intention of the parties. As regards express terms, if the parties intended, or are deemed by the court to have intended, that a particular statement was to have a contractual and binding effect, the statement will be a term of the contract and its breach will result in the plaintiff being entitled to damages and, in some cases, rescission of the contract. Otherwise, the statement will be construed as a mere representation made before the contract was entered into and not forming part of the contractual promise. The plaintiff's remedies are then dependent on a) his being able to prove that the statement was a misrepresentation and b) the character of the misrepresentation, discussed below. There is often difficulty in deciding whether a statement is a term or a representation.[5] The attitude that the court tends to take is to regard statements as terms if the maker of the statement has greater expertise than the other party, or where the statement is of vital importance and is made with distinct promissory intention, or at a crucial stage of the pre-contract negotiations. But if the seller asks the buyer to verify the truth of a statement, such as where the seller of a boat said it was sound but advised the buyer to employ a surveyor to check it,[6] or in the ordinary case where the vendor or his agent states that his house is sound but leaves the purchaser free to have it surveyed, the statement will not normally be regarded as a term of the contract. Statements

---

4 The history of this development is well outlined in Borrie and Diamond *The Consumer, Society and the Law* (4th Edn.) ch. 1. See also Jolowicz (1969) 32 MLR 1.
5 See M & H pp. 2–10.
6 *Ecay v Godfrey* (1947) 80 Ll L Rep 286, KBD (Lord Goddard).

of unverifiable opinion are neither terms of the contract nor even material representations.

Three examples of how the Court of Appeal construed statements made in the course of selling a car in different ways may be noticed. Firstly, in *Oscar Chess Ltd v Williams*:[7]

> The seller, a private person, sold his car to the buyers, who were car dealers, stating that it was a 1948 Morris and the registration book confirmed this. In fact it was a similarly styled 1939 model and the registration book had presumably been altered by a previous owner. The 1939 model was worth £115 less than a 1948 model. It was held that the seller's statement was not a term of the contract, and being a mere innocent misrepresentation, no damages were recoverable.

By contrast, in *Dick Bentley Productions Ltd v Harold Smith Motors*:[8]

> The buyer, Dick Bentley, had been looking for a 'well vetted' Bentley car and the defendants through their respective companies sold him a Bentley which their manager told him had been owned by a German baron, had been fitted with a replacement engine and gearbox and since that time had done only 20,000 miles. The car turned out to be a considerable disappointment and the buyer brought an action for damages. The County Court judge awarded him £400 on the basis that the statement as to the mileage that the car had done was a term of the contract classified as a warranty, and the warranty had been broken, the car having actually done nearly 100,000 miles. This judgment was upheld by the Court of Appeal.

Thirdly, in *Beale v Taylor*:[9]

> A private motorist advertised his car for sale, describing it as a 'Herald convertible, white, 1961, twin carbs'. Unknown to either party the car was in fact the rear half of a 1961 Herald and the front half of an earlier model, and the seller was not regarded as careless in not knowing this. The private buyer was held entitled to recover damages for breach of the contractual term (possibly implied, as discussed below) that the car was a 1961 Herald.

Various attempts have been made to distinguish these cases. For instance Lord Denning suggested that in the *Oscar Chess* case the private seller was not penalised because he was not at fault, but in the *Dick Bentley* case the expert seller could have and should have verified the information. But this distinction is not possible to make in *Beale v Taylor*, where the fact that the seller appeared for himself

---

7   [1957] 1 All ER 325, [1957] 1 WLR 370, CA (by a majority).
8   [1965] 2 All ER 65, [1965] 1 WLR 623, CA; M & H p. 3.
9   [1967] 3 All ER 253, [1967] 1 WLR 1193, CA; M & H p. 68, and see *Cehave NV v Bremer Handelgesellschaft mbH, The Hansa Nord* [1976] QB 44, [1975] 3 All ER 739, CA.

in court may not have helped him, the *Oscar Chess* case not being cited. We are therefore left with the guidelines suggested above as supplying the best prediction of how a court will construe what was said in a particular transaction.

Once it has been determined that a particular statement is a term of the contract, it is classified as a *condition*, a *warranty* or a *'hybrid'* term[10] according to its importance. A condition is a vital term of the contract, breach of which entitles the plaintiff to rescind the contract if he so wishes and sue for damages in respect of past breaches. A warranty is described by the Sale of Goods Act 1979, section 61 as an agreement collateral to the main purpose of the contract. It is, in other words, a part of the contract not so vital that failure to perform it goes to the substance of the contract. The remedy for breach of warranty is damages only. A 'hybrid' term is one which, in a complex contract, can legitimately either be treated as a condition or warranty, the evaluation to be made primarily in the light of the parties' intention, express or implied, at the time of the contract, irrespective of the event resulting from the breach.[11]

In cases of hire-purchase it may be that the customer is persuaded by the dealer to enter into a hire-purchase agreement with a finance company, to whom the dealer then sells the car outright. The courts have classified this arrangement as a) a hire-purchase agreement between the customer and the finance company and b) a collateral contract embodying a warranty between the customer and the dealer. (The consideration is the entering by the customer into the hire-purchase agreement, thus enabling the dealer to sell the car to the finance company.) If the dealer wrongly warrants the goods sound, the customer may recover damages, from the dealer under contract (b). Thus in *Andrews v Hopkinson:*[12]

> The customer wished to take a second hand car on hire-purchase terms. The dealer recommended it by saying, 'It's a good little 'bus. I would stake my life on it. You will have no trouble with it.' The dealer then sold the car to a finance company which entered into a hire-purchase agreement for the car with the customer. The car was in fact in a dangerous condition owing to defective steering and the customer shortly afterwards collided with a lorry,

10 See generally M & H pp. 10–14; *Sale and Supply of Goods* Law Commission Working Paper No. 85 pp. 26–34; Law Com. No. 160 (Cm. 137) paras. 2.22–2.31 for useful discussions.

11 See *Bunge Corpn v Tradax SA* [1981] 2 All ER 513, [1981] 1 WLR 711, HL, where the court was unsympathetic to construing the effect of a commercial term (a stipulation as to time limits) in the light of the gravity of the events which occur. This is a problem unlikely to be met in ordinary consumer contracts; it seems unlikely that a condition implied under the Sale of Goods Act could be 'hybrid' or 'innominate'. Compare *Hong Kong Fir Shipping Co Ltd v Kawasaki Kisen Kaisha Ltd* [1962] 2 QB 26, [1962] 1 All ER 474, CA, favouring the view that evaluation should be in the light of the events occurring.

12 [1957] 1 QB 229, [1956] 3 All ER 422, Leeds Assizes.

wrecking the car and injuring himself. It was held that he was
entitled to recover damages for breach of the undertaking given to
him by the dealer.

III) IMPLIED TERMS

There are a number of situations where, apart from statute, a court
will be prepared to read into a contract an implied term or terms —
i.e. a condition or warranty not expressly stated but in accordance
with the presumed intention of the parties, or in accordance with
trade usage, or in compliance with the pattern of previous dealings
between the parties, or where the court otherwise deems it just to do
so.[13] Many of the cases on implied terms relate to contracts between
vendor and purchaser of land or landlord and tenant and the like,
rather than 'consumer' transactions.

Of fundamental importance when assessing the remedies of the
disappointed buyer of goods is the part of the Sale of Goods Act 1979
('the 1979 Act') implying various conditions into contracts of sale of
goods unless the parties agree to the contrary. The original Sale of
Goods Act 1893 ('the 1893 Act') was significantly amended by the
Supply of Goods (Implied Terms) Act 1973 ('the 1973 Act'), the main
object of which was severely to limit the seller's right to exclude these
implied terms, and this aspect of it is dealt with later.[14] The Act also
applied these conditions, suitably adjusted, to contracts of hire-
purchase, and these provisions have now been re-enacted, with
minor amendments, by the Consumer Credit Act 1974 (Schedule 4,
para. 35), and will not specifically be discussed further except to
point out that the debtor is better protected than the buyer in that his
rights are not diminished by the possibility that he has 'accepted' the
goods shortly after delivery. The 1973 Act also improves obligations
on the supplier of goods on redemption of trading stamps that are to
the same general effect as the implied conditions under a contract of
sale or hire-purchase (section 16, amending the Trading Stamps Act
1964). This legislation was consolidated by the Sale of Goods Act
1979.

It is not always the case that ownership or possession of goods is
obtained under a sale of goods contract governed by the 1979 Act. A
sale of goods contract is defined in section 2(1) of the 1979 Act as:

13   See *The Moorcock* (1889) 14 PD 64, CA; *Hollier v Rambler Motors (AMC) Ltd*
     [1972] 2 QB 71, [1972] 1 All ER 399, CA; *Reed v Dean* [1949] 1 KB 188 (a hired
     motor launch is impliedly warranted fit for the purpose of the hiring).
14   See below, p. 109.

a contract by which the seller transfers or agrees to transfer the property in goods to the buyer for a money consideration called the price.

If, therefore, ownership of goods is transferred for non-money consideration, for example other goods or a service (as in barter or exchange); if the possession but not ownership is transferred as, for example, in simple hire; or if goods plus services are supplied, as in work and materials contracts, then the Sale of Goods Act 1979 does not apply. Instead implied terms similar to those in the 1979 Act, regarding the nature of any goods supplied, are incorporated by the Supply of Goods and Services Act 1982 ('the 1982 Act').[15] These terms will be discussed in this chapter whilst the implied terms in the 1982 Act relating to any service element of a contract are discussed in chapter 7.

The contracts covered by the 1982 Act are those 'for the transfer of goods' and for 'hire of goods'. A 'contract for the transfer of goods means a contract under which one person transfers or agrees to transfer to another the property in goods, other than an excepted contract' (section 1(1)). Excepted contracts are those for the sale of goods, hire-purchase agreements, goods received on redemption of trading stamps, goods transferred by deed with no additional consideration and contracts by way of mortgage, pledge, charge or other security (section 1(2)). By section 6 a 'contract for the hire of goods' is defined as a 'contract under which one person bails or agrees to bail goods to another by way of hire, other than an excepted contract'. The excepted contracts are hire-purchase agreements and trading stamp agreements.

a) Title

To outline each implied condition in turn, referring in each case to the sections of the 1979 Act and the 1982 Act, we commence with section 12 of the 1979 Act which deals with implied undertakings as to title. It is, of course, vital in any commercial transaction that the buyer be assured that the goods which he is buying are the unencumbered property of the seller.

In practice it is not too uncommon to find cases where, for example, a buyer has innocently bought a car which is subject to an undischarged hire-purchase agreement or an antique which has been stolen. The normal rule here is *nemo dat quod non habet*, i.e. a seller cannot pass on a good title unless he himself has one. To this rule there are some significant exceptions. In the case of, for example, the

---

15 The 1982 Act is based in part on the Draft Supply of Goods (Implied Terms) Bill contained in the Law Commission Report No. 95 *Implied Terms in Contracts for the Supply of Goods.*

seller who is not the true owner of goods, he may nevertheless in specified circumstances pass a good title to the buyer if the seller is in possession of them with the owner's consent,[16] or in the unusual case where the sale is in 'market overt' — i.e. sales in a shop dealing in goods of that kind in the City of London or in a market in England held on days prescribed as market days by charter, custom or statute.[17] In cases of the sale of cars, a private purchaser in good faith of a car which is in fact 'owned' by the seller under a hire-purchase or conditional sale agreement obtains a good title as against the true owner if the private purchaser took without notice of the agreement.[18] In other cases, where goods are stolen and the thief convicted the court may order the restoration of the goods to the true owner under the Theft Act 1968, section 28(1)[19] and it is in these circumstances in particular that the buyer will look for redress to the seller, assuming that he is in a position to make compensation.[20]

In cases where there is no indication other than that the seller intended to pass a full title to the purchaser, section 12(1) of the 1979 Act states that there is:

> an implied condition on the part of the seller that in the case of sale he has a right to sell the goods, and in the case of an agreement to sell, he will have such a right at the time when the property is to pass.

Section 12(2) also implies warranties of freedom from encumbrances and of the right to quiet possession, which are likely only occasionally to be useful in view of the more fundamental implied conditions above.[1] Section 12(3) deals with the uncommon case where the seller

---

16   Sale of Goods Act 1979, s. 24, and Factors Act 1889, ss. 8 and 9. For discussion of sales by buyers in possession with consent, see ch. 10.

17   See *Bishopsgate Motor Finance Corpn v Transport Brakes Ltd* [1949] 1 KB 322, [1949] 1 All ER 37, CA (car sold in Maidstone market held sold in market overt). The sale must take place between sunrise and sunset — a factor fatal in *Reid v Metropolitan Police Comr* [1973] QB 551, [1973] 2 All ER 97, CA (stolen candelabra sold at Caledonian Market in Southwark before sunrise held not sold in market overt). The sale must also be within the physical limits of the market, not on adjoining land, see *Long v Jones* [1991] T LR 113, QBD.

18   Hire Purchase Act 1964, s. 27(2); if the hirer sells to a trade purchaser who sells to a bona fide private purchaser, the latter is still protected (s. 27(3)); the topic is further discussed in ch. 10.

19   The wrongful possessor of the goods is in any event liable to the true owner for the tort of wrongful interference with goods under the Torts (Interference with Goods) Act 1977.

20   Under the Theft Act 1968, s. 28(3) the court may order payment to the buyer of stolen goods out of money in the thief's possession when apprehended.

1   In *Microbeads AC v Vinhurst Road Markings Ltd* [1975] 1 All ER 529, [1975] 1 WLR 218, CA, the buyer having validly bought goods was prejudiced in his use of them by a patent acquired by a third party. This was held to be a breach of the warranty for quiet possession.

contracts to transfer only such title as he or a third party may have, in which case limited versions only of the two warranties mentioned above apply.

As to remedies where the condition as to the right to sell applies, there is an apparent difficulty where the goods have been accepted by the buyer and he wishes to reject the goods and have his money back. This is because section 11(4) of the 1979 Act states that where a contract of sale is not severable and the buyer has accepted the goods (as to which see section 35 and the discussion of 'acceptance' below – acceptance will normally be evidenced by conduct) 'the breach of any condition to be fulfilled by the seller can only be treated as a breach of warranty, and not as a ground for rejecting the goods and treating the contract as repudiated . . .'. The normal consequence of this is that the buyer who has accepted is limited to obtaining damages, which may amount to less than the purchase price. However, as regards the condition of title it was held in *Rowland v Divall*,[2] where a buyer of a stolen car had to return it to the true owner, that there was a total failure of consideration since what the buyer bargained for, ownership of the car, had never been transferred at all. He was therefore entitled to a full repayment, even though the car had been used for four months.[3]

The equivalent section in the 1982 Act dealing with title in contracts for the transfer of goods is section 2. In cases where there is an intention to pass full title there is an implied condition that the transferor has a right to transfer the property (section 2(1)) and implied warranties of freedom from encumbrances and quiet possession (section 2(2)). If it is intended that only limited title passes, then there are modified warranties of freedom from encumbrances and quiet possession (section 2(3)-(5)).

In contracts for the hire of goods there is clearly never any intention to pass title. Instead there is an implied condition that the bailor has a right to transfer possession and an implied warranty of quiet possession save for disturbance by the owner or other persons with a known or disclosed charge or encumbrance (section 7).[4]

---

2 [1923] 2 KB 500, CA.

3 In *Mason v Burningham* [1949] 2 KB 545, [1949] 2 All ER 134, CA, it was held that a buyer of a stolen typewriter was entitled not only to have her money back but to claim the cost of a repair she had paid for on the basis that there was a breach of the warranty of quiet possession.

4 For an early common law authority on this see *Lee v Atkinson and Brooks* (1609) Cro Jac 236.

b) Description

It is clear that where the seller sells goods by reference to a
description of them, the buyer should have a remedy if the goods fail
to comply with the description.[5] It could be argued that the
description should be regarded as an express term[6] but section 13(1)
and (2) of the 1979 Act categorises it as an implied condition:

> 13 (1) Where there is a contract for the sale of goods by description, there
> is an implied condition that the goods will correspond with the
> description.
> (2) If the sale is by sample as well as by description it is not sufficient
> that the bulk of the goods corresponds with the sample if the goods
> do not also correspond with the description.

Formerly section 14(2) of the 1893 Act stated that the implied
condition of merchantable quality only applied where the goods
were 'bought by description', and this was an encouragement to the
courts to interpret sales by description liberally. The terminology is
obviously appropriate to mail order sales and other cases where the
seller has not seen the goods before buying. But the courts have made
it clear that a sale by description can occur even where the buyer has
seen and examined the goods:

> . . . a thing is sold by description, though it is specific, so long as it is sold
> not merely as the specific thing but as a thing corresponding to a
> description, e.g. woollen under-garments, a hot water bottle, a second-
> hand reaping machine, to select a few obvious illustrations (per Lord
> Wright in *Grant v Australian Knitting Mills Ltd*).[7]

Dixon J in the High Court of Australia was equally explicit in the
same case:

> In the ordinary course of a sale over the counter by a shopkeeper to a
> customer, who calls for an article of a given description, inspects the
> specimens produced, and buys one, the transaction is a sale by
> description.[8]

However, it will not always be the case that sales of specific goods
with verbal or even written descriptions applied will be held to be *by*
description. In *Harlingdon & Leinster Enterprises Ltd v Christopher
Hull Fine Art Ltd*[9] the Court of Appeal decided that for section 13 to
operate the description had to be influential in the sale, thereby

---

5 See M & H pp. 67–71.
6 It is designated as an 'express warranty' in the USA's Uniform Commercial Code,
   art. 2–313(1)(b).
7 [1936] AC 85 at 100, PC (sale over the counter of some men's underwear held sale
   by description).
8 (1933) 50 CLR 387, at 418.
9 [1991] 1 QB 564, [1990] 1 All ER 737, CA. See also Lawrenson (1991) 54 MLR
   122.

becoming an essential term of the contract. There must be a common intention on the part of both parties for the description to become a term. In the words of Slade LJ:

> If the court is to hold that a contract is one 'for the sale of goods by description', it must be able to impute to the parties (quite apart from section 13(1) of the 1979 Act) a common intention that it shall be a term of the contract that the goods will correspond with the description (at p 751).

To help determine this issue the presence or absence of reliance on the description by the buyer was relevant. In this case a painting, stated to be by Gabriele Munter, was sold by an art dealer, who had no knowledge of the artist, to another dealer who had inspected the painting. The painting was found to be a forgery. In dismissing the buyer's claim of a breach of section 13, the court, by a majority, decided that, viewing the transaction objectively, there was no reliance by the buyer on the description applied by the seller.

The Molony Committee questioned whether sales in a self-service supermarket would qualify as being 'by description'[10] and the 1973 Act[11] accordingly added a new provision, now (slightly reworded) section 13(3) of the 1979 Act, which states:

> A sale of goods is not prevented from being a sale by description by reason only that, being exposed for sale or hire, they are selected by the buyer.

It may therefore be concluded that in shop sales in the normal way, goods with labelling of any sort to identify them would be sold by description, but goods such as green groceries not labelled would probably not be sold by description where selected without assistance by the shopper. Where *quality* is concerned the point will now usually be academic since the implied condition of merchantable quality, more usually involved, is no longer confined to sales by description. However, one case where the description condition may be of crucial importance is where the sale is a private one. Both the conditions relating to quality of goods considered below apply only to sales in 'the course of a business', but section 13 is not so confined. It may therefore supply a buyer with the necessary ground for action in a case such as *Beale v Taylor*[12] where it will be recalled that the seller who advertised what transpired as his hermaphrodite car in a motoring journal was a private motorist, not a dealer, and the buyer

10   Cmnd. 1781, para. 441.
11   Supply of Goods (Implied Terms) Act 1973, s. 2.
12   [1967] 3 All ER 253, [1967] 1 WLR 1193, CA; M & H p. 68; see above, p. 76. The cause of action was actually the alleged breach of the s. 13 condition, but it is not entirely clear from the report whether the court regarded the advertised description also as an express term.

recovered damages for breach of the condition, presumably assessed at the difference between the actual value of the car and the price paid. Where *quantity* is concerned the court may insist on exactitude if this is commercially reasonable:

> If the written contract specifies conditions of weight, measurement and the like, those conditions must be complied with. A ton does not mean about a ton, or a yard about a yard. Still less when you descend to minute measurements does ½inch mean about ½inch. If the seller wants a margin he must, and in my experience does, stipulate for it.[13]

The equivalent sections relating to description in the 1982 Act are section 3 for contracts for the transfer of goods and section 8[14] for contracts for the hire of goods.

c) Merchantable quality

The *caveat emptor* principle was firmly embedded into the 1893 Act, and it is now restated in section 14(1) of the 1979 Act:

> Except as provided by this section, and section 15[15] and subject to any other enactment, there is no implied condition or warranty about the quality or fitness for any particular purpose of goods supplied under a contract of sale.

There are similar provisions for contracts for the transfer of goods and the hire of goods in sections 4(1) and 9(l) of the 1982 Act respectively. However, the twin conditions of merchantability and fitness for purpose, particularly as broadened since the 1973 Act, have substantially eroded the *caveat emptor* principle. The condition of merchantable quality[16] in its amended form is comprised in section 14(2) of the 1979 Act, which states:

> Where the seller sells goods in the course of a business, there is an implied condition that the goods supplied under the contract are of merchantable quality, except that there is no such condition –

13 *Arcos Ltd v E A Ronaason & Son* [1933] AC 470 at 479, HL per Lord Atkin. See also the Sale of Goods Act 1979, s. 30 which confirms the buyer's right to reject for wrong quantities.
14 Restating the pre-Act position, see *Astley Industrial Trust Ltd v Grimley* [1963] 2 All ER 33, [1963] 1 WLR 584, CA.
15 1979 Act, s. 15 and 1982 Act, ss. 5 and 10 deal with sales by sample, and imply conditions i) that the bulk shall correspond in quality with the sample, ii) that there shall be a reasonable opportunity for the buyer/bailee to compare bulk and sample, and iii) as to merchantability except as regards defects apparent on examination.
16 See M & H pp. 73–81; Law Commission Working Paper No. 85 (October 1983) pp. 10–19; Law Com. No. 160 (May 1987, Cm. 137) pp. 6–11.

a) as regards defects specifically drawn to the buyer's attention before the contract is made; or
b) if the buyer examines the goods before the contract is made, as regards defects which that examination ought to reveal.

The equivalent provisions in the 1982 Act are sections 4(2) and (3) (transfer of goods) and 9(2) and (3) (hire contracts).

'In the course of a business'

It has already been noted that this excludes private sales. Business is defined to include 'a profession and the activities of any government department (including a Northern Ireland Department), or local or public authority'.[17] Whilst the purpose of this wide wording is 'to insure that the conditions implied by section 14 are imposed on every trade seller, no matter whether he is or is not habitually dealing in goods of the type sold',[18] the wording seems wide enough to catch, for instance, the sale of a doctor's professionally used car or a farmer's tractor, since in both cases any profit or loss would be reflected in his business accounts. There is considerable academic opinion, however, in favour of not including transactions ancillary to the normal course of a seller's business within the wording of the section.[19] Support for this approach can be derived from the Court of Appeal in *R & B Customs Brokers Co Ltd v United Dominions Trust Ltd*[20] where the same phrase was examined in the context of the Unfair Contract Terms Act 1977, section 12, to determine whether a company buying a car was doing so 'as consumer' or not. It was held that if a transaction was only incidental to the main business activity of the company, a degree of regularity was required before it was considered an intergral part of the business and thus 'in the course of a business'. To date this interpretation has not been applied to section 14 to determine whether a seller is selling in the course of a business, although it has been used in, and in fact derives from, the criminal sphere.[1]

---

17 1979 Act, s. 61(1); similarly 1982 Act, s. 18(1).
18 First Report of Exemption Clauses 1969 (Law Com. No. 24) para. 31. See M & H p. 72.
19 See e.g. Greig *Sale of Goods* (1974) p. 179; Miller and Lovell *Product Liability* (1977) p. 81. The Molony Committee uses the perhaps preferable expression, 'sells by way of trade': Cmnd. 1781, para. 443. But in *Buchanan-Jardine v Hamilink and Anor* 1981 SLT (Notes) 60 (Lord Ordinary, Scotland) it was held that the phrase is apt to describe the sales made by 'anybody who sells any part of his business equipment', there being no difference whether this was the sale of one item or, on termination of the business, the whole of the goods used for the purpose of the business. See [1981] JBL 380; M & H p. 73.
20 [1988] 1 All ER 847, [1988] 1 WLR 321, CA. See below p. 112.
1   *Davies v Sumner* [1984] 3 All ER 831, [1984] 1 WLR 1301, HL. See pp. 344-345.

'*Merchantable quality*'

There has been a large number of judicial attempts to define this phrase since its statutory birth in 1893. At the time considerations of the commercial saleability of the goods weighed as heavily in testing meaning as whether the consumer's expectations were fulfilled. As a result of recommendations by the Law Commission,[2] the 1973 Act inserted a definition into the 1893 Act and which now appears as section 14(6) of the 1979 Act, as follows:

> Goods of any kind are of merchantable quality within the meaning of subsection (2) above if they are as fit for the purpose or purposes for which goods of that kind are commonly bought as it is reasonable to expect having regard to any description applied to them, the price (if relevant) and all the other relevant circumstances.[3]

It has been suggested that the 1973 Act was an amending Act with a new definition included. As Mustill LJ indicates in *Rogers v Parish (Scarborough) Ltd:*[4]

> The language of section 14(6) is clear and free from technicality, and it should be sufficient in the great majority of cases to enable the fact-finding judge to arrive at a decision without exploring the intricacies of the prior law.

The core of this definition is the idea of fitness for reasonable use. The scope of this has been examined in relation to sales of new cars in particular. In the *Rogers* case Mustill LJ declared:

> Starting with the purpose for which 'goods of that kind' are commonly bought, one would include in respect of any passenger vehicle not merely the buyer's purpose of driving the car from one place to another but of doing so with the appropriate degree of comfort, ease of handling and reliability and, one may add, of pride in the vehicle's outward and interior appearance. What is the appropriate degree and what relative weight is to be attached to one characteristic of the car rather than another will depend on the market at which the car is aimed.[5]

The fact that a defect was repairable or that a vehicle could be started and driven from A to B did not necessarily mean it was merchanta-

---

2 (1969) Law Com. No. 24.
3 The equivalent definitions in contracts for the transfer of goods and hire are to be found in ss. 4(9) and 9(9) of the 1982 Act respectively.
4 [1987] 2 All ER 232 at 235, [1987] 2 WLR 353 at 358, CA.
5 [1987] 2 All ER 232 at 237, [1987] 2 WLR 353 at 359, CA. The case concerned a new Range Rover car costing £16,000 which had engine, gearbox and bodywork defects. After some 5,500 miles and six months of driving the plaintiffs rejected the vehicle. The court found that even though the vehicle was driveable it was not of merchantable quality and had been validly rejected by the plaintiffs.

ble. A number of factors were considered relevant in *Bernstein v Pamson Motors (Golders Green) Ltd*:[6] the intractability of the defect, the time which a repair took, the potential danger involved, the risk of knock-on effects and the price.

Pre-1973 cases may still be helpful regarding some matters. For example, in *Godley v Perry*[7] a six year old boy bought a cheap polystyrene catapult from a stationer. It fractured without abuse on his part shortly after purchase, blinding him in one eye. It was held that this was a breach both of the fitness for purpose condition (see below) and the condition of merchantable quality, and the boy recovered £2,500 damages. In *Wilson v Rickett, Cockerell & Co Ltd*[8] a consignment of 'Coalite' was bought by a consumer and this exploded when put in the grate owing to the extraneous presence of a charge of high explosive. It was held that the merchantable 'Coalite' could not be separated from the unmerchantable explosive. The entire goods were not of merchantable quality and the buyer could recover damages accordingly. But in *Heil v Hedges*[9] the presence of a harmful parasite worm in pork chops, which caused illness when the buyer ate the chops half-cooked, was held not to render the chops unmerchantable since the worm would have been killed had the chop been properly cooked. There seems little doubt that this type of case would be decided similarly even after the insertion of the definition of merchantability in the statute, since it is 'reasonable to expect' that pork will be properly cooked.

Second-hand goods involve more flexibility of treatment, since used goods may be expected to be less efficient or less long lasting than new goods and this is reflected in the price. But the courts will apply the condition of merchantability to second-hand goods where appropriate. Lord Denning suggested that merchantability 'means, that on the sale of a second-hand car, it is merchantable if it is in usable condition, even though not perfect. . . . A buyer should realise that, when he buys a second-hand car, defects may appear sooner or later; and in the absence of express warranty, he has no redress.'[10] This pre-dated the new definition of merchantable quality in section 14(6) and the wider test of merchantable quality as applied in *Rogers v Parish (Scarborough) Ltd*.[11] In *Shine v General Guarantee Corp Ltd (Reeds Motor Co (a firm), third party)*[12] the expectations of

---

6 [1987] 2 All ER 220, QBD. Here a new Nissan Laurel, costing about £8,000 seized up after 142 miles due to a blockage in the lubrication system.
7 [1960] 1 All ER 36, [1960] 1 WLR 9, QBD.
8 [1954] 1 QB 598, [1954] 1 All ER 868, CA.
9 [1951] 1 TLR 512, KBD.
10 *Bartlett v Sidney Marcus Ltd* [1965] 2 All ER 753 at 755, CA.
11 [1987] QB 933, [1987] 2 All ER 232, [1987] 2 WLR 353, CA.
12 [1988] 1 All ER 911, CA.

the purchaser of a second-hand enthusiast's car were examined in addition to the condition of the car to determine whether or not it was merchantable. In applying *Rogers*, the court found that the car, which had been submerged for over 24 hours, treated as an insurance write-off, and was without a rust-proof warranty, was unmerchantable. No reference was made to *Bartlett* in this case. Both *Bartlett* and *Rogers* were considered in *Business Application Specialists Ltd v Nationwide Credit Corpn Ltd (Marn Garage (Camberley) Ltd, third party)*[13] and the latter test preferred, although on its facts the defective second-hand car was found to be merchantable. Lord Justice Parker, whilst accepting that section 14(6) had changed the law, did agree with Lord Denning's suggestion that defects must be expected to arise sooner or later in second-hand cars.[14]

Whilst in the run-of-the-mill case of a consumer complaint it is usually clear that defective new goods (including any container that they are in) are not of merchantable quality, there may be cases where goods are perfectly fit for their functional purpose but too shoddy, dented or scratched in appearance to be merchantable at their full price[15] or merchantable at all.

The lack of certainty over the precise scope of this implied condition was highlighted by the Consumers' Association in an investigation of the buyer's rights where a new car was found to suffer from a large number of minor, remediable but inconvenient and irritating defects. The question was whether the buyer, after using the car for some twenty-two days during which the defects progressively developed, could reject it. A wide variety of legal opinion was sought in the answer to this all too common problem and the general consensus of opinion was that the buyer had no right of redress because the car would have been regarded as of 'merchantable quality' by the court (see 'Merchantable Quality: What does it mean?' Consumers' Association, November 1979). It was pointed out that, unless some trade usage in favour of the buyer under

---

13 [1988] BTLC 461, CA.
14 For discussion of the various new and second-hand car cases see Stephenson (1988) 6 Tr. Law 172; Barlow (1990) 7 Tr. Law 140; Whincup (1988) 138 NLJ 7; and Thomas (1989) 139 NLJ 1188.
15 See for instance *Jackson v Rotax Motor and Cycle Co* [1910] 2 KB 937, CA; M & H p. 75 (dented and scratched motor horns held unmerchantable); *Miller and Lovell* p. 85; Goode *Commercial Law* (1982) p. 262; Macleod *Consumer Sales Law* (1989) p. 364; Law Com. Working Paper No. 85 paras. 2.8–2.13; Law Com. No. 160 paras. 2.11–2.13. In *Bernstein v Pamsons Motors (Golders Green) Ltd* [1987] 2 All ER 220, QBD, it was suggested by Rougier J that in the case of a car, the price would be relevant: 'No buyer of a brand new Rolls-Royce Corniche would tolerate the slightest blemish on its exterior paintwork; the purchaser of a motor car very much at the humbler end of the range might be less fastidious' (at p. 228).

subsection (4) can be prayed in aid, there is no middle way. The defective goods are either sufficiently defective to be regarded as unmerchantable or not reasonably fit for the purpose of the buyer under section 14, in which case the buyer may reject and/or obtain damages, or they are not sufficiently defective to be so regarded and the buyer has no remedy whatsoever other than to rely on any enforceable manufacturer's guarantee that may exist. This argument is supported by reference to the House of Lords' decision in *B. S. Brown & Son Ltd v Craiks Ltd*[16] which seems to suggest that goods are merchantable if they are commercially usable even if not usable to the full extent of the buyer's expectations. The recent car cases, discussed above, would suggest that serious deviations from the expected standard may be classified as breaches of the condition but minor ones presumably will not. 'Whichever way one looks at it, I feel that in relation to defects of a kind commonly found in new vehicles and with which buyers commonly put up without rejecting motor cars the Court would be unable to say that such vehicles are not as reasonably fit for the purpose as is commonly required having regard to all the circumstances' (Michael Spencer, Barrister, in 'Merchantable Quality: What does it mean?' pp. 36–37).[17]

In the light of public concern about the Consumers' Association case (which was never litigated) the Rt Hon Donald Stewart introduced a private member's Bill in November 1978, the Supply of Goods (Amendment) Bill. This Bill was later withdrawn and instead it was announced that the Lord Chancellor had referred the matter to the Law Commission. The English and Scottish Law Commissions produced a Working Paper (No. 85) entitled 'Sale and Supply of Goods' in 1983.[18] This was then followed by the Report of the same name, published in May 1987.[19] The recommendation concerning merchantable quality is that the present statutory definition in section 14(6) of the 1979 Act (and its equivalent in sections 4(9) and 9(9) of the 1982 Act) should be redefined. The new definition should consist of two elements: a basic principle, formulated in language sufficiently general to apply to all kinds of goods and all kinds of transactions; and a list of aspects of quality, any of which could be

16 [1970] 1 All ER 823, [1970] 1 WLR 752, HL. See also *Millars of Falkirk Ltd v Turpie* 1976 SLT (Notes) 66, Court of Session; M & H p. 78.

17 This is supported by Rougier J in the *Bernstein* case: 'no system of mass-production can ever be perfect: mistakes and troubles of one sort or another, generally minor are bound to occur from time to time. . . the buyer of a new car must put up with a certain amount of teething troubles and have them rectified, albeit generally under some sort of manufacturer's warranty' (at pp. 228–229). See also 'Faulty Goods' (NCC,1981).

18 See also J Livermore 'Merchantable Quality' [1985] JBL 217 and 294.

19 Law Com. No. 160, Scot Law Com. No. 104, Cm. 137.

important in a particular case. The Report specifies that the basic principle should be 'that the quality of the goods sold or supplied under a contract should be such as would be acceptable to a reasonable person, bearing in mind the description of the goods, their price (if relevant), and all other circumstances (para. 8.1). The list of aspects of quality should include:

    a) the fitness of the goods for all their common purposes (para. 3.36);

    b) their appearance and finish (para. 3.38);

    c) their freedom from minor defects (para. 3.38);

    d) their safety (para. 3.46); and

    e) their durability (para. 3.57). (para. 8.1).

A draft Bill is included in the Report and in this 'merchantable quality' is replaced by the phrase 'acceptable quality'. Legislative change in this area was heralded in June 1991 by the Minister of Consumer Affairs[20] and this has been followed by a consultation paper[1] which adopts the Law Commission's proposals, though prefers 'satisfactory quality' instead of 'acceptable quality'.

Exceptions

The first case where the implied condition will not apply is where the defects are specifically drawn to the attention of the buyer before the contract is made. The only room for argument about what is otherwise a clear-cut and justifiable defence by the seller is whether the *extent* of a particular defect had been made clear, even though it had been mentioned 'specifically'. The wise seller will specify defects in writing and not minimise them, as can be seen, for example from the catalogue of any good antiquarian bookseller:

> VALERIUS FLACCUS, Argonautica. 72 leaves, 40 lines, Roman letter, folio, 18th century Italian vellum boards (joints cracked), a few very small worm holes, and small ink stain on title page covered with a slip of paper, large stain on verso of A4, Bologna, 1498 - £750.

Secondly, lazy buying seems to be encouraged by excepting the case where the buyer has examined the goods before the contract is made, as regards defects which that examination ought to reveal. There is a similarly circumscribed merchantability condition in sales by sample

---

20 Speech given to the Institute of Trading Standards Administration in Rotterdam, 4 July 1991, see (1991) 14 Consumer Law Today, Issue 8, pp. 1–2.

1 *Consumer Guarantees*, Department of Trade and Industry, February 1992.

under section 15. If the buyer apparently imprudently does not examine the goods at all, he preserves his full right to reject for unmerchantability. There is considerable academic debate on whether the quality of the examination is assessed objectively (as in *Thornett and Fehr v Beers & Son*)[2] or, more likely, subjectively, taking the word 'that' to mean the actual examination undertaken by the buyer.[3] It is consequently no less than prudent, for instance, that the Code of Practice for the motor industry states that 'dealers should provide all reasonable facilities to enable prospective customers or their nominees to carry out an examination of the car prior to sale, in order that any defects which ought to be revealed at the time of the sale are made known to both parties'.[4] There are of course many cases where examination is not possible at all, such as where there are harmful chemicals in the fabric of underpants[5] or arsenic in beer,[6] and the exception will accordingly have no relevance.

As a general comment on the merchantability condition, it is perhaps unfortunate that the 1973 Act patched up the provisions as drafted in the 1893 Act rather than rethinking them in the light of the current concern with consumer protection. The concept of merchantability seems more appropriate to mercantile transactions where the goods are to be resold rather than consumed, and the concept has proved very difficult to define satisfactorily.[7] In seeking to improve the situation the Law Commission comment:[8]

> Most of the criticisms of the present law (see paras. 2.5–2.16) have concerned new consumer durables rather than goods supplied under commercial contracts or second-hand goods. We do not, however, think that it is practical to provide different standards of quality for different types of transaction, different types of goods or even different classes of buyer and seller. Goods do not fall into neat categories and the result of such categorisation would be a regime of great complexity in which

2 [1919] 1 KB 486, KBD (barrels of vegetable glue examined externally only; no liability in respect of defect discoverable had the barrels been opened).
3 *Miller and Lovell* p. 97; *Benjamin on Sale* (1987, 3rd Edn.) para. 808; Atiyah *Sale of Goods* (8th Edn.) pp. 150–2; Goode *Commercial Law* p. 260; Macleod *Consumer Sales Law* p. 365.
4 Reproduced in O'Keefe *The Law Relating to Trade Descriptions* (Butterworths) Div. 5, para. 5[3908]. Note potential difficulties where a defect is discovered and notified prior to sale but sale proceeds as indicated by Dillon LJ in *R & B Customs Brokers Co Ltd v United Dominions Trust Ltd (Saunders Abbott (1980) Ltd, third party)* [1988] 1 All ER 847, CA, at p. 851.
5 *Grant v Australian Knitting Mills Ltd* [1936] AC 85, PC.
6 *Wren v Holt* [1903] 1 KB 610, CA. See also *Preist v Last* [1903] 2 KB 148, CA (burst hot water bottle).
7 See Law Com. Working Paper No. 85 paras. 2.6–2.7; Law Com. No. 160 para. 2.10.
8 Law Com. No. 160 paras. 3.13–3.66.

arguments as to which category applied would become of major and recurring importance. We think that in principle the term should be the same for all types of goods and all types of transaction, both consumer and non-consumer, and should have the necessary flexibility built into its wording. (para. 4.6).

This view was maintained in the final Report (paras. 3.8–3.10). To achieve a new standard of quality the Report recommends the introduction of a basic principle specifying a standard of acceptability coupled with a list of aspects of quality, as indicated above (paras. 3.13–3.66).

d) Fitness for the purpose

The reforms made by the 1973 Act to the 1893 Act, and the subsequent consolidation in 1979, have resulted in the renumbering in the 1979 Act of the original subsections of section 14 of the 1893 Act. The former condition of merchantable quality was contained in section 14(2), and remains in that subsection. The former condition of fitness for purpose was comprised in section 14(1) and is now to be found in section 14(3). This point must be borne in mind when studying the less recent cases if confusion is to be avoided. The new section 14(3) runs:

> Where the seller sells goods in the course of a business and the buyer, expressly or by implication, makes known to the seller. . . any particular purpose for which the goods are being bought, there is an implied condition that the goods supplied under the contract are reasonably fit for that purpose, whether or not that is a purpose for which such goods are commonly supplied, except where the circumstances show that the buyer does not rely, or that it is unreasonable for him to rely, on the skill or judgment of the seller.[9]

In the course of a business

The meaning of this phrase has been discussed above under 'merchantable quality'.

The purpose

In ordinary consumer transactions the courts will readily hold the buyer

---

9   The equivalent sections in the 1982 Act are s. 4(4)–(6) for transfer of goods and s. 9(4)–(6) for hire contracts.

impliedly to have made known his purpose. Obviously one buys food to eat it,[10] a catapult in order to shoot with it,[11] underclothing to wear[12] or a car to drive it. As to cars, the following case is illustrative of both the implicit nature of making known the purpose, and the fact that this condition too applies in appropriate circumstances to sales of second-hand goods. In *Crowther v Shannon Motor Co*,[13] a young man bought an eight year old Jaguar car from a dealer which had 82,000 miles on the odometer. The dealer commended it, saying that the engine was 'hardly run in'. 2,300 miles and three weeks later the engine seized up. The previous owner, when contacted, described the engine as 'clapped out'. The plaintiff-buyer claimed that the car was not fit for his purpose under what was then section 14(1) of the unamended 1893 Act. It was held that the buyer impliedly made known the purpose for which he wanted the car and had relied on the seller's skill or judgment. As a question of fact and degree the implied term had been broken. It is significant to note that the price paid was £390 and the damages awarded were £460, more than then could have been obtained had there been criminal proceedings and a compensation order by the magistrates' court, as discussed later in the book.

If the buyer requires goods for a particular purpose then this must be expressed. For instance, in *Baldry v Marshall*[14] the buyer claimed to reject an eight cylinder Bugatti car for breach of the implied condition of fitness when he had specified his purpose as being to acquire a fast, flexible and easily managed car which would be comfortable and suitable for ordinary touring purposes, which the Bugatti was not. Similarly if the buyer has some peculiarity, such as an abnormally sensitive skin, he will not be entitled to rely on this condition if he fails to reveal this and the goods are fit for the purpose

10 *Frost v The Aylesbury Dairy Co* [1905] 1 KB 608, CA (milk infected with typhoid germs probably without fault on seller's part, but held not fit for purpose); *Chaproniere v Mason* (1905) 21 TLR 633, CA (solicitor broke teeth on a stone in a bath bun; bun unfit for purpose of eating); *Wallis v Russell* [1902] 2 IR 585, CA – poisonous crabs unfit, though possibly a case of *expressly* making known the purpose, since the buyer asked for 'two nice fresh crabs for tea' – see Maurice Healy *The Old Munster Circuit* (1st Edn.) p. 209, for the bizarre background detail.
11 *Godley v Perry* [1960] 1 All ER 36, [1960] 1 WLR 9, QBD, see above.
12 *Grant v Australian Knitting Mills Ltd* [1936] AC 85, PC, see above.
13 [1975] 1 All ER 139, [1975] 1 WLR 30, CA; M & H, p. 83.
14 [1925] 1 KB 260, CA.

of a normal buyer.[15] The Act now specifically states that the goods supplied must be 'reasonably' fit for the purpose.

In general, consumer cases will involve a much higher degree of expertise in the seller than the buyer may be expected to have. The courts are correspondingly more inclined to imply the condition on the basis, no doubt, that it is not 'unreasonable' for the buyer to rely on the seller in these circumstances. In some commercial cases, where the goods are bought for resale, this may not be so. As Lord Wilberforce stated, the authorities show that the conditions respectively in section 14(2) and 14(3) are 'readily and untechnically applied to all sorts of informal situations – such as retail sales over the counter of articles whose purpose is well known – and are applied rather more strictly to large scale transactions carried through by written contracts'.[16] The private consumer can take comfort from the first part of this statement.

The history of the conditions of merchantability and fitness before the redrafting implemented by the 1973 Act involves some distortion of their natural meaning, since buyers could only use the merchantable quality condition where the sale was by description and the fitness condition did not apply to sales under patent or other trade names. Both these restrictions have now been removed. In many cases a buyer will be able to bring an action for breach of both conditions successfully, as in *Godley v Perry* above where the defective catapult was neither merchantable nor fit for the purpose. But if the buyer examines the goods, he may lose the right to sue in respect of the merchantability condition and have to rely on the fitness condition provided he could show that he did not rely solely on his own skill or judgment.[17] Similarly, whilst there is now no bar

---

15   See *Griffiths v Peter Conway Ltd* [1939] 1 All ER 685, CA; M & H p. 81 (coat caused buyer dermatitis, but only because her skin was particularly sensitive). See also *Manchester Liners Ltd v Rea Ltd* [1922] 2 AC 74, HL. The principle is that the buyer's statement must be sufficient to allow the seller to exercise his skill and judgment.

16   *Henry Kendall & Sons v William Lillico & Sons* [1969] 2 AC 31, HL at 123 (manufacturers had bought ground nut extract, without previous experience of it, from suppliers for making up poultry food which because of a too high concentration of a substance, poisonous to poultry but not cattle, killed a number of the ultimate buyers' birds. Despite a comparable level of expertise between manufacturer-buyer and supplier the groundnuts were held unfit for the purpose of use for cattle and poultry). See also the somewhat similar decision concerning foodstuffs unsuitable for mink in *Ashington Piggeries v Christopher Hill Ltd* [1972] AC 441, [1971] 1 All ER 847, HL.

17   See e.g. Dillon LJ in *R & B Customs Brokers Co Ltd v United Dominions Trust Ltd (Saunders Abbott (1980) Ltd, third party)* [1988] 1 All ER 847, CA, at p. 851.

to suing in respect of unfitness where goods are bought under brand names, if there is no preliminary advice given by the seller it may be difficult to show that the buyer relied in any way on the seller's, as opposed to the manufacturer's, skill or judgment.

It should also be noted that both implied conditions apply to goods 'supplied' under the contract. Whilst containers are normally sold with the goods contained therein, and there is liability where for instance a defective bottle breaks and injures the buyer,[18] this would still be the case where the bottle was returnable and remained the property of the seller, since he would still have 'supplied' the bottle under the contract.[19] In addition to the packaging and its contents, the Queen's Bench Division in *Wormell v RHM Agriculture (East) Ltd*[20] held that the instructions supplied with a chemical weedkiller were part of the 'goods'. If the instructions were missing, inaccurate or misleading so that the chemicals were not reasonably fit for their purpose, a breach of section 14(3) would be established, as it was in this case. On appeal the Court of Appeal took the view that the purchaser was prepared to take the risk that his crops might be damaged by the spray (as indicated in the instructions) and so, rather surprisingly, also took a risk that the spray might not work effectively (a fact not mentioned in the instructions). There was, thus, no breach of the implied terms.

e) *Liability without fault*

Where there has been a breach of either of these conditions, there is no effective defence by the seller of 'reasonable care'. Liability is strict. 'If there was a defect in fact, even though that defect was one which no reasonable skill or care could discover, the person supplying the article should nevertheless be responsible, the policy of the law being that in a case in which neither were to blame, he, and not the person to whom they were supplied, should be liable for the

---

18 *Morelli v Fitch and Gibbons* [1928] 2 KB 636; *Aswan Engineering Establishment Co v Lupdine Ltd (Thurgar Bolle Ltd, third party)* [1987] 1 All ER 135, [1987] 1 WLR 1, CA (on facts no breach of s. 14(3) when pails containing glue melted in the heat, either because of no reliance or, if reliance, pails suited normal purpose and no special purpose declared).

19 *Geddling v Marsh* [1920] 1 KB 668, KBD.

20 [1986] 1 All ER 769, [1986] 1 WLR 336, QBD, rvsd [1987] 3 All ER 75, [1987] 1 WLR 1091, CA.

defect.'[1] Of course, in most consumer sales the defendant will be the retailer who may well be blameless, a position which hardly accords with common sense in cases where the wrong clearly originates with the manufacturer. A survey undertaken on behalf of the Office of Fair Trading in 1988 showed that 40 per cent of those asked who would be responsible if an electric kettle had been bought which did not work either did not know or were incorrect.[2] As it stands at present the buyer's remedy is against the seller, and if that seller is a retailer he must rely on his similar rights under the 1979 Act against the wholesaler and so on until in this indirect (and economically very inefficient) way the manufacturer may[3] be made ultimately to bear the cost of the defect. This, in fact, remains the position for defective goods as opposed to dangerous goods since the implementation of the Consumer Protection Act 1987.[4] The Department of Trade and Industry consultation paper: *Consumer Guarantees*[5] does canvass the possibility of making manufacturers or importers liable, with the seller, under the Sale of Goods Act for the quality of goods. Further developments are awaited.

f) Is the consumer properly protected?

There are two fundamental criticisms that can be made of the present position. Firstly, as has already been mentioned in passing in the text, the 'merchantability' condition seems more appropriate to commercial transactions between dealers than to transactions between dealer and the ultimate consumer. The meaning of 'merchantable quality' can still give rise to expensive litigation despite the more helpful definition introduced by the 1973 Act which is now used in the 1979 Act and the 1982 Act. The exclusion of goods which have been examined can also give rise to difficulty in its present form. The other implied condition as to quality, namely 'fitness for purpose' is better understood but provides no protection where

1 *Randall v Newsom* (1876) 45 LJQB 364 at 365, per Blackburn J and *Frost v The Aylesbury Dairy Co Ltd* [1905] 1 KB 608, CA. See also statements to the same effect in *Henry Kendall & Sons v William Lillico & Sons* [1969] 2 AC 31, [1968] 2 All ER 444, HL and *Ashington Piggeries Ltd v Christopher Hill Ltd* [1972] AC 441, [1971] 1 All ER 847, HL. It is clear that the state of technical knowledge at the time (the 'state of the art' defence in negligence) is not a defence to an action under s. 14. This fact is often overlooked in the current debate on strict product liability in tort referred to in ch.6.
2 See *Bee Line* February 1989, p. 28. Also Jolowicz (1969) 32 MLR 1 at 5.
3 Note the problem of a retailer who cannot identify his source of supply as in *Lambert v Lewis* [1981] 1 All ER 1185, [1981] 2 WLR 713, HL; [1980] 1 All ER 978, [1980] 2 WLR 299, CA; M & H p. 35.
4 See further ch. 6.
5 February 1992.

goods are insufficiently defective to render them unmerchantable or not 'reasonably' fit for the purpose. A suggestion is made above under the discussion of 'merchantable quality' of a more apt implied condition proposed in Law Commission Report No. 160 and the preferred wording of the Department of Trade and Industry.

Secondly, it can be argued that the consumer is still not adequately protected from avoidable and common problems in consumer sales. Both implied conditions apply the test to the position *at the time of sale* and do not provide clear protection where a consumer durable breaks down within an unreasonably short time of purchase. Should there not be a condition that such goods remain durable for a reasonable time, or may the courts be relied upon to supply redress despite the present wording?[6] The Law Commission discusses this question in its 95th Report (*Implied Terms in Contracts for the Supply of Goods – July 1979), in its Working Paper No. 85 (Sale and Supply of Goods* – October 1983),[7] and in its 160th Report of the same name.[8] The Law Commission proposes that the durability of goods should be one of the matters listed as aspects of quality in deciding whether or not goods are of acceptable quality. The Report states: 'A requirement of durability should be such that the goods would be required to last for a reasonable time' (para. 3.51). The requirement should apply at the time of supply so that when goods are supplied they must have those qualities which will enable them to last in a reasonable condition for a reasonable period of time. The Law Commission, however, considered that no provision should be made for a term to be implied in contracts for the sale or supply of goods that the seller or supplier should keep spare parts and servicing facilities available.[9] It was felt that this may be better dealt with in self-regulating codes of practice for the industry in question. Thus, for instance, paragraph 5 of the Association of Manufacturers of Domestic Appliances' Code states that 'to enable the correct spares to be ordered and carried in store and van, the service organisation should ensure that it holds comprehensive spare-parts lists and service manuals covering those products on which service is undertaken'. Minimum periods for the keeping of spares are also laid down, the time (from five to fifteen years) depending on the applicance in question. No legislative action on improving the scope

---

6 *Lee v York Coach and Marine* [1977] RTR 35, CA; M & H, p. 94; cf *Crowther v Shannon Motor Co* [1975] 1 All ER 139, [1975] 1 WLR 30, CA; M & H p. 83.

7 See also M & H pp. 83–86; *Atiyah* pp. 169–170; *Goode* pp. 288–290; *Macleod* pp. 346–7; 'Faulty Goods', National Consumer Council, June 1981 paras. 3.1–3.52, 5.4; W. Richardson 'The Case for Quality' (1985) Vol 135 NLJ 6.

8 Cm. 137, May 1987, paras. 3.47–3.61.

9 Law Com. No. 95 paras. 115–129; Law Com. Working Paper No. 85 para. 2.17; M & H pp. 86–89; Law Com. No. 160 para. 3.66.

and definitions of the implied terms relating to goods has yet been taken and the problem is still under consideration.

Meanwhile the House of Lords in *Lambert v Lewis*[10] did supply some guidance as to the continuing nature of the implied condition for fitness appropriate to the sale of a towing hitch to a Land Rover owner (the facts of the case and the other issues involved are discussed in detail in ch. 6). As Lord Diplock stated,

> The implied warranty of fitness for a particular purpose relates to the goods at the time of delivery under the contract of sale in the state in which they were delivered. I do not doubt that it is a continuing warranty that the goods will continue to be fit for that purpose for a reasonable time after delivery so long as they remain in the same apparent state as that in which they were delivered, apart from normal wear and tear. What is a reasonable time will depend upon the nature of the goods.[11]

g) Remedies – rejection and damages

The remedies available for the breach of an implied term in a contract for the supply of goods depend in part on whether the term is classified as a condition or warranty. In addition, differences may occur depending upon which statute governs the contract. The Sale of Goods Act 1979 defines the word 'condition' indirectly in section 11(3) (see below) and the word 'warranty' specifically in section 61(1).[12] Neither of these terms is defined in the Supply of Goods (Implied Terms) Act 1973 (for hire-purchase contracts) or the Supply of Goods and Services Act 1982 (for transfer of goods and hire). The omission of any definition in the 1982 Act was based on the recommendations of the Law Commission in its 95th Report *Implied Terms in Contracts for the Supply of Goods* (para. 25), on the grounds of convenience and consistency with the 1973 Act. The whole area of remedies for breach of implied terms has been discussed extensively in the Law Commission Working Paper No. 85 *'Sale and Supply of Goods'*[13] and the final Report of the same name (Law Com. No. 160).

---

10   [1981] 1 All ER 1185, [1981] 2 WLR 713.

11   At pp. 1191, 720. Presumably one factor to be considered in deciding on the question of for how long goods should remain fit is the length of the manufacturers' guarantee usually given for that class of goods - but a longer period than this may in many circumstances be reasonable.

12   A warranty is 'an agreement with reference to goods which are the subject of a contract of sale but collateral to the main purpose of such contract, the breach of which gives rise to a claim for damages, but not to a right to reject the goods and treat the contract as repudiated'.

13   See also M & H pp. 90–105, 109–113; *Goode* chs. 10–13; *Atiyah* pts VI and VII; *Macleod* pt 7.

Rejection

The primary remedy for breach of either an express or implied condition is for the buyer to reject the goods and reclaim the price in full as well as additional damages for breach of contract in respect of losses not too remote in the light of the principles of contract law. Looking first at sale of goods contracts the right to repudiate the contract for breach of condition, rather than simply to reject performance as tendered and leave the seller the option of replacing the goods as some authorities suggest,[14] though nowhere explicitly stated, seems to be clearly inferred from the wording of section 11(3) of the 1979 Act (which refers to 'a condition, the breach of which may give rise to a right to treat the contract as repudiated . . . '), and by section 54 (which preserves the buyer's right to recover money paid where the consideration for the payment of it has failed).

Alternatively, the buyer may treat the breach of condition as a breach of warranty and retain the goods but claim damages for the breach by way of reduction of the purchase price, or by action if the price has been paid, or both (section 53). But where the buyer has 'accepted' the goods, as mentioned above under the discussion of the condition for title, he will have no option but to treat the breach of any condition (express or implied) as a breach of warranty (section 11(4)). The concept of acceptance[15] is explained primarily by section 35 of the 1979 Act (which re-enacts the law as amended here by the Misrepresentation Act 1967), and this now runs thus:

> The buyer is deemed to have accepted the goods when he intimates to the seller that he has accepted them, or (except where section 34 [of this Act] otherwise provides) when the goods have been delivered to him and he does any act in relation to them which is inconsistent with the ownership of the seller, or when after the lapse of a reasonable time he retains the goods without intimating to the seller that he has rejected them.

The concept is thus based on the buyer's conduct. An express acceptance is unequivocal, and is perhaps the exception rather than the rule in consumer cases. This may, however, occur if a consumer signs a delivery note or 'acceptance' note. It is debatable whether or not such a note constitutes express acceptance.[16] An act inconsistent with the seller's ownership would be, for example, reselling the goods, but this is subject to section 34 which states that the buyer is

14 See *Miller and Lovell* p. 111; *Goode* pp. 298–301, *Macleod* pp. 774–776. The right to repair or replace defective goods is considered 'uncertain' as to its existence or extent by the Law Com. Working Paper No. 85 para. 2.38.

15 See Law Com. Working Paper No. 85 paras. 2.48–2.60; Law Com. No. 160 paras. 2.40–2.49.

16 Law Com. Working Paper No. 85 para. 2.53; Law Com. No. 160 para. 2.45.

not deemed to have accepted the goods unless and until he had had a reasonable opportunity of examining them for the purpose of ascertaining whether they are in conformity with the contract. Most consumer cases will come under the third head of section 35 above which refers to the buyer's retaining the goods without intimating[17] that he has rejected them 'after the lapse of a reasonable time'. The word 'reasonable' provides a desirable flexibility which a court would apply by reference to such factors as whether the goods have been used and have deteriorated and whether the buyer has been unduly tardy in going back to the seller. Thus, for example, in *Leaf v International Galleries*[18] a buyer discovered that a picture that he had bought of Salisbury Cathedral, which was honestly represented by the seller to have been by Constable, was not a genuine Constable. Denning LJ stated:

> I think it right to assume in the buyer's favour that this term was a condition and that, if he had come in proper time he could have rejected the picture . . . In this case the buyer took the picture into his house and, apparently, hung it there, and five years passed before he intimated any rejection at all. That, I need hardly say, is much more than a reasonable time. It is far too late for him at the end of five years to reject this picture for breach of any condition. His remedy after that length of time is for damages only.

This offers valuable, if negative, advice. Would the discovery after five years that a vintage bottle of wine layed down was 'corked' prevent the buyer from rejecting it? He could hardly be said to be unreasonably tardy. The advice given in *Bernstein v Pamson Motors (Golders Green) Ltd*[19] suggests that section 35 does not refer to a reasonable time to discover the defects, it means a reasonable time to inspect the goods and try them out generally. Rougier J stated: 'The complexity of the intended function of the goods is clearly of prime consideration here. What is a reasonable time in relation to a bicycle would hardly suffice for a nuclear submarine'.[20] He held that 3 weeks and 142 miles driven in a new car was a reasonable time and that acceptance had occurred. Similarly, the common case of where the buyer first tries to get the seller to repair defective goods is not

---

17   Rejection must be unequivocally expressed, see *Lee v York Coach and Marine* [1977] RTR 35, CA; M & H p. 93 (two solicitor's letters requesting repairs and suggesting a right to reject not sufficient for rejection).
18   [1950] 2 KB 86, [1950] 1 All ER 693, CA.
19   [1987] 2 All ER 220, [1987] BTLC 37, QBD. See also M Whincup 'Purchaser's Acceptance of Defective Goods' (1986) 83 L S Gaz 3807; K Mullen 'Satisfaction Guaranteed or No Money Back?' (1988) 138 NLJ 280, 299.
20   At pp. 231, 50.

explicitly dealt with in the 1979 Act.[1] Is this tantamount to acceptance? There is conflicting judicial authority, but the more recent view seems to lean in favour of not regarding attempted repairs as necessarily evidence of acceptance.[2] The Law Commission considers: 'it is possible (though unlikely) that a buyer does an inconsistent act when he asks his seller to try to repair the goods, or agrees to the seller's offer to do so'.[3]

It is a common fallacy that the buyer can require the seller to repair defective goods. The statutory rights of the buyer are limited to rejection and/or damages. Any general right to require the seller to repair would need to be newly created by statute.

Where the buyer does have the right to reject the goods, section 36 makes clear that he is not bound to return them to the seller, but it is sufficient if he intimates to the seller that he refuses to accept them. In contracts other than sale of goods, for example hire-purchase, work and materials, hire and barter, the right to reject the goods is not governed by any statutory measure. Instead it is subject to the common law doctrine of affirmation[4] whereby once a person has been held to have affirmed the contract he may only sue for damages. In *Farnworth Finance Facilities Ltd v Attryde*,[5] a case concerning affirmation in a hire-purchase contract, Lord Denning MR indicated that: 'affirmation is a matter of election. A man only affirms a contract when he knows of the defects and by his conduct elects to go on with the contract despite them.'

Damages

Where damages are claimed for breach of condition or warranty in the circumstances discussed above, section 53(3) of the 1979 Act lays down a rule applicable in the many consumer cases when the claim is for loss due to defects in the goods under sections 13 and 14 of the 1979 Act, or in respect of broken express warranties:

1 Compare the US Uniform Commercial Code, art. 2608(1), where attempted curing of the defect does not prejudice non-acceptance.
2 Compare *Long v Lloyd* [1958] 2 All ER 402, [1958] 1 WLR 753, CA; M & H p. 95, (repair to lorry one factor in court's decision not to allow buyer to rescind purchase), and *Farnworth Finance Facilities Ltd v Attryde* [1970] 2 All ER 774, [1970] 1 WLR 1053, CA; M & H p. 100 (hire-purchase contract for motor frequently repaired during four months use still not affirmed). Neither case is *direct* authority on this point.
3 Law Com. No. 160 para. 2.47. See also M & H p. 98; *Goode* p. 310; Cranston *Consumers and The Law* (1984, 2nd Edn.) pp. 123–124.
4 See Law Com. Working Paper No. 85 paras. 2.61–2.63 (reproduced in M & H pp. 99–100) and Law Com. No. 160 paras. 2.50–2.52 for summaries of the doctrine.
5 [1970] 2 All ER 774 at 778, [1970] 1 WLR 1053 at 1059, CA; M & H p. 100.

In the case of breach of warranty of quality such loss is *prima facie* the difference between the value of the goods at the time of delivery to the buyer and the value they would have had if they had fulfilled the warranty.

In consumer cases the courts would normally take the difference between the contract price and the diminished value of the defective goods, either on a rough estimate or with the help of expert evidence.[6] The phrase 'at the time of delivery' should be noted, since it precludes increasing the claim in respect of inflationary rises in the cost of repairing or replacing the goods since the time of delivery.

Where there are consequential losses which may involve physical damage to the buyer or his property as a result of defective goods, or where the breach is of a condition other than a 'warranty of quality', the heads of loss for which the buyer may claim are those within section 53(2), modelled on the first part of the leading case in contract on remoteness of damage, *Hadley v Baxendale*.[7] The subsection states:

> The measure of damages for breach of warranty is the estimated loss directly and naturally resulting, in the ordinary course of events, from the breach of warranty.

To take a few examples of where consequential damage has been recovered, in *Bernstein v Pamsons Motors (Golders Green) Ltd*[8] the plaintiff was awarded the cost of returning home after the car broke down plus loss of a tank of petrol (£32.90), five days' loss of use of his car (£50) and £150 for a totally spoilt day out in the car. In addition the car had been fully repaired. No diminuition in value of the car was established so no damages were awarded under section 53(3). In *Godley v Perry*,[9] a case already referred to, a boy who lost his left eye because of a defective cheap catapult which broke with a dog-tooth fracture, recovered £2,500 in respect of pain and suffering, the loss of his eye and the discomfort of daily removal of his artificial eye. In *Wilson v Rickett, Cockerell & Co Ltd*,[10] also discussed above, the plaintiff's room and furniture were damaged by the explosive 'Coalite' and she recovered £117 for the damage done. Car owners whose vehicles have to be repaired owing to the fault of a third party

6   'It seems to me that one can very rarely arrive at an accurate figure of unsound value' per Devlin J in *Biggin & Co Ltd v Permanite Ltd* [1951] 2 KB 314 at 438, CA.
7   (1854) 9 Exch 341, Exchequer.
8   [1987] 2 All ER 220, QBD, see above.
9   [1960] 1 All ER 36, [1960] 1 WLR 9, QBD.
10   [1954] 1 QB 598, [1954] 1 All ER 868, CA.

are normally justified in hiring a temporary replacement.[11] All these losses arise 'directly and naturally' from the breach. If the parties are aware, at the time of making the contract, of 'special' losses which would arise on breach, as under the second part of *Hadley v Baxendale*,[12] these may also be recovered (section 54).

If the seller fails or refuses to deliver goods to the buyer then damages can be claimed under section 51. According to subsection (2):

> The measure of damages is the estimated loss directly and naturally resulting, in the ordinary course of events, from the seller's breach of contract.

If there is an available market in the goods concerned then subsection (3) awards damages on the basis of the difference between the contract price and the market price at the time of delivery or when delivery was refused.

As was the case with rejection, there are no statutory provisions relating to damages in the 1973 Act and the 1982 Act. Damages for breach of implied terms in work and materials, hire, barter and hire-purchase contracts will be assessed in a similar way to those under the 1979 Act.

Proposals for reform

The Law Commission has, in its Report No. 160 - *Sale and Supply of Goods*, considered remedies for breach of the statutory implied terms in detail. It proposes that in England and Wales in all contracts for the supply of goods, the implied terms of correspondence with description, the fitness of the goods and sales by sample should continue to be classified as conditions. In consumer transactions under the Sale of Goods Act 1979 the present law on remedies will be retained with an unrestricted right to reject the goods outright and claim a refund of money paid (para. 4.15). It is proposed to use the same definition of 'dealing as consumer' as that in the Unfair Contract Terms Act 1977[13] (para. 4.7).

In the case of non-consumer sales the Law Commission recommends that the statutory implied terms should remain as conditions but that where the breach is so slight that it would be unreasonable for the buyer to reject the goods, the breach should be treated not as a breach of a condition but as a breach of a warranty and thus

---

11 See Philip Naughton 'Damages for Loss of Use of Chattels and Inconvenience' (1977) 121 Sol Jo 700; 'Damage to Motor Cars – The Problem of Hiring a Substitute' I. Goldrein (1985) 135 NLJ 370.
12 (1854) 9 Exch 341, Exchequer.
13 See below, p. 111.

damages only being claimable (para. 4.21). Similar provisions are suggested for other contracts for the supply of goods (para. 4.32).

On the loss of the right to reject goods in sale of goods contracts, the proposals are that the buyer, be he consumer or non-consumer, should not lose his right to reject the goods by signing an acceptance note unless he has had a reasonable opportunity to examine the goods. In a non-consumer sale it would be open to the buyer to contract out of this provision provided the exclusion satisfied the requirements of the Unfair Contract Terms Act 1977 (paras. 5.22 and 5.24). There should be clarification that a request for, or agreement to, a cure should not of itself constitute acceptance. The 'inconsistent act' rule should be retained but with certain clarifications. A buyer will not be deemed to have accepted the goods merely because he has delivered the goods to a third party under a sub-sale, gift or other disposition (paras. 5.37–5.38). For all other supply of goods contracts the Law Commission recommends that the law should remain unaltered (paras. 5.46 and 5.49). Clause 2 of the Draft Sale and Supply of Goods Bill which is appended to the Report seeks to implement the various changes proposed.

IV) MISREPRESENTATION

Whether a seller's or supplier's statement about goods to be sold constitutes a promissory term of the contract or is merely a misrepresentation can be problematic, and the way the courts tend to find a solution has already been discussed. If the statement complained about is found to have no promissory effect but was a mere representation, the buyer still has useful remedies provided he can show that the statement was at least one of the factors that induced him to contract. If the buyer pays no regard to the statement or was aware that it was untrue, no complaint can be made.[14] The statement, to give rise to legal effects, must be more than an unverifiable opinion and must not be a mere advertiser's 'puff' - *simplex commendatio non obligat*, as every successful estate agent knows to his relief.

Where a misrepresentation has been made, remedies depend on its nature. A fraudulent misrepresentation is one made either knowingly, or without belief in its truth, or reckless as to whether it be true or false.[15] The buyer will often find this element of fraud by the seller difficult to prove and certainly dangerous to allege since heavy costs

---

14 See *Horsfall v Thomas* (1862) 1 H & C 90 (buyer bought dangerously defective gun, the seller having tried to conceal the defect, but no misrepresentation (by conduct) because buyer had not examined the gun).

15 *Derry v Peek* (1889) 14 App Cas 337, HL.

may be involved in the event of failure. However, if he is successful he is entitled to seek the discretionary remedy of rescission of the contract and an indemnity for his expenses, and is entitled as of right to damages for the tort of deceit. At common law if the misrepresentation was made innocently, without intention to deceive and not recklessly, the buyer had no right to sue for damages. Further he often found that because of 'sleeping on his rights' or the impossibility of restoring the goods in the same condition as when the contract is made, or the acquisition of rights to the goods by an innocent third party, he had lost as well his equitable right to rescind the contract.[16] The House of Lords in 1963[17] mitigated the rigour of this principle by holding that there are circumstances where careless advice can give rise to an action in tort based on the negligent misstatement, though there remains doubt as to whether this extends to advice given other than by professional advisers. The doctrine can be used where there is also a contractual relationship between the parties.[18] In the ordinary case of misrepresentation made by the seller or supplier to the buyer it will rarely now be necessary to go beyond the Misrepresentation Act 1967 which significantly increased the buyer's remedies in respect of innocent misrepresentations.

Section 2 of the Misrepresentation Act 1967 in subsection (1) states that where there is an operative misrepresentation which, had it been made fraudulently, would have made the person making it liable to damages,

> that person shall be so liable notwithstanding that the misrepresentation was not made fraudulently, unless he proves that he had reasonable ground to believe and did believe up to the time the contract was made that the facts represented were true.

Thus if a misrepresentation has been made honestly but negligently – in the sense that the maker of the statement must disprove his negligence by showing that he reasonably believed its truth –

---

16 See, for example, *Long v Lloyd* [1958] 2 All ER 402, [1958] 1 WLR 753, CA; M & H p. 95.

17 *Hedley Byrne & Co Ltd v Heller & Partners Ltd* [1964] AC 465, [1963] 2 All ER 575, HL.

18 See *Esso Petroleum Co Ltd v Mardon* [1976] QB 801, [1976] 2 All ER 5, CA; M & H p. 5; *Batty v Metropolitan Property Realisations Ltd* [1978] QB 554, [1978] 2 All ER 445, CA. The usual rule in professional cases was that a client must sue his negligent solicitor in contract not in tort, see *Clark v Kirby-Smith* [1964] Ch 506, [1964] 2 All ER 835, Ch D. However, in *Midland Bank Trust Co Ltd v Hett, Stubbs and Kemp* [1979] Ch 384, [1978] 3 All ER 571, Ch D, Oliver J held that an action against a firm of solicitors for not registering an option to buy land lay both in contract and tort. Cf *Bell v Peter Browne & Co (a firm)* [1990] 2 QB 495, [1990] 3 All ER 124, CA. See further ch. 7 at p. 168.

damages may be awarded.[19] The existing remedy of rescission is available as well as damages, or as the only remedy where there is no element of negligence. Subsection (2) gives the court a discretion to award damages in lieu of rescission, in addition to any damages awarded under subsection (1), though damages awarded under subsection (2) must be taken into account in awarding damages for negligent misrepresentation under subsection (1) (section 2(3)). The Act does not affect the pre-existing equitable limits to rescission mentioned above - excessive delay, impossibility of restoring the goods in the same condition as when supplied, or where an innocent third party has acquired rights to the property.

V) EXEMPTION CLAUSES

Introduction

There has long been something of a war of attrition between large scale sellers of goods, or suppliers of services, and their customers with regard to exemption clauses. We are here concerned with exemption clauses affecting the buyer's rights if the goods he buys are defective. Exemption clauses in contracts for services are dealt with in ch. 7. Both types involve clauses normally only found in 'standard form' contracts which the consumer must take or leave without alteration and where there is marked inequality of bargaining power between manufacturer-retailer on the one hand and consumers on the other.

In the field of the supply of goods statutory reforms in the form of the Unfair Contract Terms Act 1977, sections 6 and 7 have made the position between a business seller and a consumer comparatively straightforward. There is also limited protection where a business to business sale is involved. In the latter case in particular it may be important to analyse whether a particular exemption clause is binding at all because, for instance, the wording is not apt to cover the event complained of,[20] or where the exemption clause is not

---

19 Damages are to be assessed on a tortious basis, using the test applicable in the tort of deceit - that is any loss flowing from the misrepresentation, even if not reasonably foreseeable. Authority for this is *Royscot Trust Ltd v Rogerson* [1991] 2 QB 297, [1991] 3 All ER 294, [1991] 3 WLR 57, CA.

20 Exemption clauses are construed by the courts *contra proferentem*, i.e. ambiguities are construed against the person relying on the exemption clause. See e.g. *Wallis, Son and Wells v Pratt and Haynes* [1911] AC 394, HL ('no *warranty* express or implied' does not protect against breach of implied *condition*); and *Andrews Bros (Bournemouth) Ltd v Singer & Co Ltd* [1934] 1 KB 17, CA (exclusion of conditions and warranties *implied* do not include express conditions). See generally *Benjamin's Sale of Goods* (1987, 3rd Edn.) ch. 13.

incorporated into the contract at all[1] or is inconsistent with express undertakings that have been given at the time of making the contract.[2] Even where a clause appears part of the contract, by inclusion in a written document provided by one party to the other, if this contains onerous provisions these may not be enforceable in the absence of evidence to show that they have been fairly and reasonably brought to the attention of the other party. This can be seen in the case of *Interfoto Picture Library Ltd v Stiletto Visual Programmes Ltd.*[3] Here a provision in a delivery note, seeking to impose a penalty of £5 per day per item for each day any colour transparencies were retained beyond 14 days, which led to a bill for £3,783.50 being sent to the defendants, was held not to be part of the contract for the hire of the transparencies. The court took the view that nothing was done to draw the defendants' attention to this clause which was described by Bingham LJ as 'unreasonable and extortionate' (at p. 357). An award based on a quantum meruit was substituted.

If an exemption clause is incorporated into the contract it is generally not a defence to plead that the clause was not understood[4] or read, particularly if signed.[5] In this event, in order to do justice in cases where buyers or hire-purchasers of goods have been denied any remedy because of a comprehensive and binding exemption clause the courts steadily enlarged the idea of 'fundamental breach' of contract, a topic fully discussed in the standard textbooks on contract. The idea originates from the self-evident proposition that 'if a man offers to buy peas of another, and he sends him beans, he does not perform his contract';[6] no exclusion clause can avail the seller since beans are not merely defective peas and there is complete

---

1 Usually because it is introduced after the offer has been accepted - see *Chapelton v Barry UDC* [1940] 1 KB 532, [1940] 1 All ER 356, CA (deck chair hire document receipt), and *Olley v Marlborough Court Ltd* [1949] 1 KB 532, [1949] 1 All ER 127, CA (notice in hotel bedroom too late).

2 *Couchman v Hill* [1947] KB 554, [1947] 1 All ER 103, CA (statement that heifer was 'unserved' in auction catalogue overrode general disclaimer in conditions of sale); *J Evans & Son (Portsmouth) Ltd v Andrea Merzario Ltd* [1976] 2 All ER 930, [1976] 1 WLR 1078, CA (oral assurance that goods would be carried on deck overrode exemption clause giving carriers complete freedom of transportation and exemption from liability for loss).

3 [1989] QB 433, [1988] 1 All ER 348, CA. See also *Thornton v Shoe Lane Parking Ltd* [1971] 2 QB 163, [1971] 1 All ER 686, CA.

4 *Thompson v London Midland and Scottish Rly Co* [1930] 1 KB 41, CA (plaintiff illiterate).

5 *L'Estrange v F Graucob Ltd* [1934] 2 KB 394, CA (signed contract not read but contained effective comprehensive exemption clause). See the critical analysis of this principle in [1973] CLJ 104 (Spencer).

6 Per Lord Abinger CB in *Chanter v Hopkins* (1838) 4 M & W 399 at 404.

failure of consideration. The problem is often one of identity. Is an object suffering from a long line of defects still recognisable as that object? In the well known case of *Karsales (Harrow) Ltd v Wallis,*[7] the defendant having inspected a car which was then in good order, was eventually delivered, under a hire-purchase contract, with a 'shell' which had a broken cylinder head, burnt out valves and two broken pistons. This had been towed in late at night. The defendant had signed a contract containing an exemption clause excluding all express or implied conditions and warranties as to road worthiness or fitness for purpose. It was held that the plaintiffs were disentitled to rely on the exemption clause since there had been a fundamental breach of contract. 'In the true meaning of words a car that will not go is not a car at all'.[8] But the House of Lords has re-affirmed in *Photo Production Ltd v Securicor Transport Ltd*[9] that the 'doctrine' of fundamental breach is one of interpretation only and in this particular case refused to apply it where the parties were of equal bargaining power and well able to insure against the risk, the subject matter of the purported exemption clause. As a working rule for consumers it is safer to assume that a breach of the conditions of merchantability or fitness is not likely to be classified as fundamental provided the object contracted for is recognisably delivered. Nor, as will be seen next, is the private consumer of goods likely to need to rely on the doctrine to escape from the meshes of exemption clauses, owing to the relieving provisions of the Unfair Contract Terms Act 1977.[10] Indeed, Lord Denning, in *George Mitchell (Chesterhall) Ltd v Finney Lock Seeds Ltd,*[11] having provided a useful catalogue of the various techniques used to defeat exclusion clauses including fundamental breach concludes that: 'We should no longer have to go through all kinds of gymnastic contortions to get round them'.[12]

---

7 [1956] 2 All ER 866, [1956] 1 WLR 936, CA.
8 Per Birkett LJ at 869, 942. Parker LJ elaborated on this dictum by suggesting that not every defect temporarily rendering a car unusable would amount to a fundamental breach, 'but where, as here, a vehicle is delivered incapable of self-propulsion except after a complete overhaul. . . it is abundantly clear that there was a breach of a fundamental term' (at 871, 943). For an example, where cleaners who lost a customer's carpet were disentitled to rely on an exemption clause because of a fundamental breach, see *Levison v Patent Steam Carpet Cleaning Co Ltd* [1978] QB 69, [1977] 3 All ER 498, CA. As mentioned in the text, since the passing of the Unfair Contract Terms Act 1977 there can be few cases where the consumer would need to rely on arguing fundamental breach.
9 [1980] AC 827, [1980] 1 All ER 556, HL.
10 See discussion in *Benjamin's Sale of Goods* (1987, 3rd Edn.) para. 973.
11 [1983] QB 284, [1983] 1 All ER 108, CA; M & H p. 233.
12 At pp. 299, 115 respectively; M & H p. 235.

Freedom of contract

In accordance with the theory that there should be freedom to contract in any form between parties of full capacity, the 1979 Act gives the parties the right to negative or vary such provisions as those implying conditions as to the quality of goods. Section 55(1) states as follows:

> Where any right, duty or liability would arise under a contract of sale of goods by implication of law, it may (subject to the Unfair Contract Terms Act 1977) be negatived or varied by express agreement, or by the course of dealing between the parties, or by such usage as binds both parties to the contract.

The same is true in contracts for the transfer or hire of goods. Section 11(1) of the 1982 Act has very similar wording. The freedom to exclude the implied conditions and warranties on standard form sales agreements was for many years objected to by consumer organisations, and these objections were supported by the Molony Committee, paragraph 435 of whose Report states:

> The overriding argument in favour of prohibiting 'contracting-out' is that it enables well-organised commerce consistently to impose unfair terms on the consumer and to deny him what the law means him to have.
>
> This benefit is obtained without the consumer knowing how he is being treated. If a particular consumer is alive to the position he will find it difficult, and sometimes impossible, to avoid submitting to the terms of business universally adopted. Because the percipient customer is in a small minority the trades concerned can afford to refuse to modify their usual terms at his behest. He possesses no bargaining power of sufficient weight to compel. This is the essence of the case for intervention in support of the consuming public. We endorse the soundness of the case and accept the need to ban 'contracting-out'. To be effective the prohibition must extend to the efforts of any person to relieve the retailer of liability whether made before, at or after the moment of sale. The prohibition we have in mind is not a dictate supported by criminal law but a denial of legal effect to provisions relieving the retailer of statutory liabilities. The safeguard thus provided would be additional to any other rule of law (of which the Consumer Protection Act 1961, section 3 affords the most recent example) annexing obligation to a contract of sale.

The Law Commission also studied and reported on the position, and the Supply of Goods (Implied Terms) Act 1973 was based on the Commission's First Report on Exemption Clauses[13] to which passing reference has already been made. The 1973 Act amended section 55 of the 1893 Act by adding to it a number of subsections the primary purpose of which was to prohibit contracting out of the

---

13   (1969) Law Com. No. 24. See also M & H pp. 236–238.

implied conditions relating to description, merchantability and fitness in sales to consumers. The Act did not prevent exclusion or restriction of other obligations under the 1893 Act, such as to deliver the goods in reasonable time under section 29, and this remains the position.

The current position is stated by the Unfair Contract Terms Act 1977 ('the 1977 Act'), a private member's bill based on the draft bill contained in the Law Commission's Second Report on Exemption Clauses (1975).

The 1977 Act generally only applies to 'business liability' as defined in section 1(3) as amended.[14] This is liability for breach of obligations or duties arising a) from things done or to be done by a person in the course of a business or b) from the occupation of premises used for business purposes, subject to certain exceptions for recreational and educational uses. Purely 'private' transactions are, therefore, usually outside the scope of the Act. An exception under section 6 is discussed below.

Exclusions of statutory implied terms

Sections 6 and 7 of the 1977 Act contain similar provisions to deal with attempts to exclude or restrict statutory implied terms relating to title, description, fitness of the goods and sample. Section 6 governs contracts for the sale of goods, under the 1979 Act, and hire-purchase, under the 1973 Act. Section 7 governs other contracts where ownership or possession of goods is transferred, primarily work and materials, barter, and hire under the 1982 Act.

Title

The implied undertakings as to title provided by section 12 of the 1979 Act (sale of goods) and section 8 of the 1973 Act (hire-purchase) are protected by section 6(1) of the 1977 Act and those under section 2 of the 1982 Act (work and materials and barter) by section 7(3A).[15] In each case any attempt to exclude or restrict the liability by a contract term is rendered void. In other contracts (eg hire under section 7 of the 1982 Act) liability in respect of the right to transfer ownership or possession of the goods, or to have quiet possession is protected by subjecting any exemption clause to a reasonableness test (section 7(4) of the 1977 Act).[16]

---

14   By the Occupiers' Liability Act 1984, s 2.
15   As inserted by s. 17(2) of the 1982 Act.
16   As amended by s. 17(3) of the 1982 Act.

Description, quality and sample

As against a person dealing as consumer (see below) the implied undertakings as to conformity with description or sample, quality and fitness contained in sections 13, 14 and 15 of the 1979 Act (sale of goods) and sections 9, 10 and 11 of the 1973 Act (hire-purchase) are non-excludable by virtue of section 6(2) of the 1977 Act. Similarly, the equivalent terms for work and materials and barter (sections 3, 4 and 5 of the 1982 Act) and hire (sections 8, 9 and 10 of the 1982 Act) are non-excludable (section 7(2) of the 1977 Act).

In all cases where a person is not dealing as consumer the implied undertakings are excludable if the term satisfies a reasonableness test (section 6(3) of the 1977 Act for sale of goods and hire-purchase, section 7(3) for supply of goods contracts).

Before examining what is meant by 'deals as consumer' it is worth noting that, whilst section 7 of the 1977 Act only applies to business liability (see section 1(3) and above), section 6 applies to *all* contracts of sale and hire-purchase, not purely those containing 'business liability' (section 6(4)). Thus exemption clauses inserted in contracts for sale of goods between two private individuals will be affected by section 6.

'Dealing as consumer'

Section 12(1) indicates that a person 'deals as consumer' in relation to another party if a) he neither makes the contract in the course of a business nor holds himself out as doing so; and b) the other party does make the contract in the course of a business; and c) in the case of contracts of sale of goods, hire-purchase, or the miscellaneous contracts such as hire, barter and exchange obliquely referred to by section 7 of the 1977 Act, the goods in question are of a type 'ordinarily supplied for private use or consumption'. Sales by auction or competitive tender are excluded.[17] It is for those claiming that a party does not deal as a consumer to show that he does not (section 12(3)).

A problem to which the disparate treatment of consumer and non-consumer sales might give rise is that whilst a consumer can ignore a purported exemption clause caught by section 6 of the 1977 Act, a retailer who buys from a wholesaler or manufacturer may find that the clause binds him on the 'reasonableness' test. It is unlikely that a

---

17 Section 12(2). It is important to note that it is standard practice in salerooms to stipulate that lots must be taken with all faults and misdescriptions, any statements as to description being statements of opinion only. There is sometimes a right to return deliberate forgeries within a stipulated short period. The position is extensively discussed in Harvey & Meisel *Auctions Law and Practice*.

retailer (if without insurance) in similar circumstances to the one in *Godley v Perry*[18] would be in a position to bear heavy damages, and this would in turn gravely prejudice the consumer in the absence of an alternative right of action against an intermediate wholesaler, or the manufacturer – who could be abroad and difficult to sue.

With regard to consumer sales with which we are primarily concerned, it should be noted that sales by private sellers of second-hand goods are not 'in the course of a business'. Such a seller would only be free when selling to a consumer to exclude or restrict the implied condition of compliance with description under section 13 of the 1979 Act if the term was reasonable but the other implied conditions of merchantability and fitness are not applicable in this situation. The buyer must also not be one buying, or holding himself out to buy in course of a business, for example for resale. Problems may arise in deciding whether, for example, a professional man buying an asset partly for business and partly for private use (such as a doctor's car) would be buying the asset 'in the course of a business'. However, two decisions suggest that the courts apply the provision liberally in the consumer's interest. In *R & B Customs Brokers Co Ltd v United Dominions Trust Ltd*[19] a new car was bought from the defendants on credit. The plaintiffs, as purchasers, were a private company of shipping brokers, and the car was for the directors of the company. The car proved defective in that it leaked. The court held that the plaintiffs were 'dealing as a consumer' and thus the exclusion clause (which specifically did not apply to a buyer who dealt as consumer) was inoperative. Applying the criminal case of *Davies v Sumner*,[20] a case concerning the Trade Descriptions Act 1968, section 1, the court took the view that to fall outside the category of a consumer sale by virtue of the company's buying in the course of business, the buying of cars must form at the very least an integral part of the buyer's business and, if only incidental to the business, a sufficient degree of regularity is required. Only in those circumstances could the buyer be said to be on an equal footing with the seller.[1] In the words of Dillon LJ:

> . . . there are some transactions which are clearly integral parts of the business concerned, and these should be held to have been carried out in

18   [1960] 1 All ER 36, [1960] 1 WLR 9, QBD, considered above, p. 87.
19   [1988] 1 All ER 847, [1988] 1 WLR 321, CA.
20   [1984] 3 All ER 831, [1984] 1 WLR 1301, HL, see p. 344.
 1   A similar result was achieved in the earlier case of *Peter Symmons & Co Ltd v Cook* (1981) 131 NLJ 758, QBD; M & H p. 259. See further 'Business or Consumer? A Trap for the Unwary' D Parry (1988) 6 Trad Law p. 270 and discussion of the Consumer Transactions (Restrictions on Statements) Order 1976, S.I. 1976/1813, below at p. 118.

the course of those businesses; this would cover, apart from much else, the instance of a one-off adventure in the nature of trade where the transaction itself would constitute a trade or business. There are other transactions, however, such as the purchase of the car in the present case, which are at the highest only incidental to the carrying on of the relevant business; here a degree of regularity is required before it can be said that they are an integral part of the business carried on and so entered into in the course of that business.[2]

A further illustration of the fact that the *apparent* status of the buyer can be misleading, arises in *Rasbora Ltd v JCL Marine Ltd*.[3] Here a private individual contracted to buy a boat which was later sold to a company incorporated in Jersey by the buyer for the purpose of the transaction, thus avoiding VAT. The original contract was clearly a consumer sale and the court held that, despite the substitution of the corporation as the final buyer, this did not alter the character of the original transaction to a non-consumer sale.

Section 12 of the 1977 Act also stipulates that the goods must be of a type ordinarily supplied for private use or consumption. It will normally be clear into which category goods fall; a motor car or television set will qualify but a lorry or a large computer would be unlikely to. The word 'ordinarily' could conceivably give rise to problems over the years as buying patterns change.

Reasonableness

The concept of reasonableness is incorporated into exemption clauses in non-consumer transactions under sections 6(3) and 7(3) of the 1977 Act. Section 11 of that Act provides the explanations of the test. Section 11(5) makes it clear that:

> it is for those claiming that a contract term or notice satisfies the requirement of reasonableness to show that it does.

Thus the clause is deemed unreasonable unless proved otherwise. The basic test of reasonableness for a contract term is:

> that the term shall have been a fair and reasonable one to be included having regard to the circumstances which were or ought reasonably to have been, known to or in the contemplation of the parties when the contract was made. (section 11(1)).

Section 11(2) specifies that for sections 6 and 7, in assessing whether the clause is then reasonable, regard should be had to the matters specified in Schedule 2 to the 1977 Act. These 'guidelines' are (summarised):

2 At pp. 854, 330.
3 [1977] 1 Lloyd's Rep 645, QBD.

a) the relative strength of the bargaining positions of the parties, taking into account alternative means by which the customer's requirements could have been met;

b) whether the customer 'received an inducement to agree to the term', or whether he could have entered into a similar contract with other persons not containing such a term;

c) whether the customer knew or ought reasonably to have known of the existence and extent of the term (having regard, among other things) to any trade custom or previous course of dealing;

d) if liability is excluded if some condition is not complied with (e.g. giving notice of a claim within a time limit), whether it was reasonable to expect that compliance with that condition would be practicable;

e) whether the goods were manufactured, processed or adapted to the special order of the customer.

In addition where the restriction relates to a person's liability to pay a maximum sum of money, regard must be had to the resources available to him to meet the anticipated liability, and to how far it was open to him to insure against the risk (section 11(4)).

Two cases have examined the reasonableness of clauses under section 55(4) and (5) of the Sale of Goods Act 1893/1979 (the predecessors of s 6 of the 1977 Act). In *R. W. Green Ltd v Cade Bros Farms* the terms of a contract of sale limiting liability to repay the price between seed potato merchants and a farming business were upheld as being reasonable on the ground that the form of contract had been in use for many years with the approval of the negotiating bodies acting on behalf of both seed potato merchants and farmers.[4] The *Cade* case was distinguished in *George Mitchell (Chesterhall) Ltd v Finney Lock Seeds Ltd*[5] where the defendants sought to limit liability for supplying cabbage seeds which proved to be commercially useless. Here the clause had been inserted by the seed merchants without negotiation with the farmers and there had been negligence on the part of the seed merchants or their suppliers. Factors considered by the House of Lords included the relative bargaining strength of the parties, the opportunity to buy seeds without a limitation of liability, the ease and cheapness of insurance available to the defendants and the defendants' negligence. In particular the court, in deciding the clause was unreasonable, noted that in other cases of seed failure a negotiated settlement in excess of the limitations imposed would be agreed with an aggrieved farmer,

4   [1978] 1 Lloyd's Rep 602, QBD. A term imposing a short time limit for claims was, however, held unreasonable as to latent defects.

5   [1983] QB 284, [1983] 1 All ER 108, CA; M & H p. 233; [1983] 2 AC 803, [1983] 2 All ER 737, HL; M & H p. 263.

though this had not been achieved in this case. Lord Bridge examined the role of the appellate court in assessing the reasonableness of a clause and said:

> . . . the court must entertain a whole range of considerations, put them in the scales on one side or the other and decide at the end of the day on which side the balance comes down. There will sometimes be room for a legitimate difference of judicial opinion as to what the answer should be, where it will be impossible to say that one view is demonstrably wrong and the other demonstrably right. It must follow, in my view, that, when asked to review such a decision on appeal, the appellate court should treat the original decision with the utmost respect and refrain from interference with it unless satisfied that it proceeded on some erroneous principle or was plainly and obviously wrong.[6]

Liability arising in contract

The 1977 Act also attempts to deal with exemption clauses purporting to relieve the party in breach from the consequences of that breach. Section 3 applies where one party to a contract deals as a consumer or on the other's written standard terms of business. As against that party, the other cannot by reference to any contract term a) when himself in breach of contract, exclude or restrict any liability of his in respect of the breach; or b) claim to be entitled either to render a contractual performance substantially different from that which was reasonably expected of him; or c) in respect of the whole or any part of his contractual obligation, render no performance at all, except, in any of the cases mentioned above, in so far as the contract term satisfies the requirement of reasonableness. The requirement of reasonableness is partly the same as that discussed above. This is that the term shall have been a fair and reasonable one to be included having regard to the circumstances which were, or ought reasonably to have been, known to or in the contemplation of the parties when the contract was made (section 11(1)). There is, however, no specific requirement to refer to the guidelines in Schedule 2, although reference is being made in some cases.[7]

Section 3 gives rise to a number of difficulties of interpretation. It will be seen that the section applies in two circumstances, firstly where one of the contracting parties deals as a consumer (as defined by section 12 of the Act above) and secondly the section applies where one party contracts on the other's written standard terms of business. There is no statutory definition of 'written standard terms

6 [1983] 2 AC 803 at 816, [1983] 2 All ER 737 at 743; M & H p. 264.
7 See *Rees Hough Ltd v Redland Reinforced Plastics Ltd* (1984) 134 NLJ 706, QBD; *Keeton Sons & Co Ltd v Carl Prior Ltd* [1986] BTLC 30, CA, cited in Law Com. No. 156 (1986) para. 3.8.

of business'. The Law Commission's original comment (see Law Com. No. 69, para. 157) explains why: 'We think that the courts are well able to recognise standard terms used by persons in the course of their business, and that any attempt to lay down a precise definition of "standard form contract" would leave open the possibility that terms that were clearly contained in a standard form might fall outside the definition.' This issue would only be of importance where both parties were businessmen, since a person dealing as a consumer is already protected. It is thought that the phrase would cover standard form contracts prepared by professional and trade associations to be used by all those engaged in the relevant profession or trade and those prepared by individual contractors for use in all cases. It is common to find such standard form contracts in daily use in commerce, both as to conditions of sale and conditions of purchase. Occasionally it can be difficult to establish which of two conflicting sets of standard conditions have actually been incorporated in the contract – see *Butler Machine Tool Co Ltd v Ex-Cell-O Corpn (England) Ltd*.[8]

A second problem of interpretation concerns the nature of the exemption clauses covered by this section and which are subject to the requirement of reasonableness. Taking each in turn, with regard to clauses which, when one party is in breach of contract, exclude or restrict any liability of his in respect of the breach, this is essentially aimed at the restriction of the exercise of rights or remedies to which the other party might otherwise then be entitled. Examples are provisions in carriage contracts that the carrier shall not be liable for loss from a consignment unless he is advised of the loss in writing within seven days from the date of delivery, or a term in a building contract that the builder's liability for failure to complete within the contract period shall not exceed £X.

With regard to the other types of exemption clause mentioned in this section, an example of rendering a contractual performance substantially different from that which was reasonably expected of him would be the circumstances in issue in the case of *Anglo-Continental Holidays Ltd v Typaldos (London) Ltd*.[9] The defendant travel agents agreed to book for the plaintiffs cruises on a named ship following a fixed itinerary. There was a clause, printed on the back of their handbook, which read: 'Steamers, Sailing Dates, Rates, and

---

8 [1979] 1 All ER 965, [1979] 1 WLR 401, CA.
9 [1967] 2 Lloyd's Rep 61; M & H p. 253. See also *Askew v Intasun North Ltd* [1980] CLY 637. The county court held in this case that a clause in the defendants' brochure, entitling the defendants to change the place of holiday, did not exclude liability since it was inadequately worded. The facts of the case occurred before the Unfair Contract Terms Act 1977 came into force.

Itineraries are subject to change without prior notice'. On the basis of this clause the defendants offered the plaintiffs cruises on a different ship following a different itinerary, and in the event the Court of Appeal held, probably as a matter of construction, that the defendants could not rely on the clause to alter the substance of the arrangement. Minor variations in itineraries or in other contracts for goods or services, would probably be excluded from the scope of this section by the use of the words 'substantially' and 'reasonably'.

With regard to the purported exclusion of liability for rendering no performance at all in respect of the whole or any part of a person's contractual obligation, it is probably already the position at common law that a clause purporting to exclude all one's obligations is void at common law, since this would amount to a mere declaration of intent – see *Firestone Tyre and Rubber Co v Vokins & Co*.[10] This principle would not necessarily apply to the question of non-performance of part only of the contractual obligation. The Law Commission, in the explanatory notes to their draft Bill in similar language to the form that the 1977 Act eventually took, comment that 'this would apply to various terms excusing non-performance or entitling a party to cancel a contract'. (See also paras. 141–146, on which the above examples are founded.) It must be emphasised, finally, that such exemption clauses are not void but are deemed to be unreasonable until the person relying on the contract term or notice in question satisfies the court to the contrary on the basis of the statutory definition of the reasonableness test.

In the construction of section 3, there is every reason to think that courts would be more likely to regard such clauses as being reasonable where the contract is a commercial one between two traders of roughly equal bargaining power than where the party complaining was dealing as a consumer. In *Stag Line Ltd v Tyne Shiprepair Group Ltd, The Zinnia*[11] the clause in question sought to exclude liability for economic loss which arose after wrong materials were used in the repair of a ship. The court, in view of the bargaining positions of the two business parties, decided the clause was reasonable. The views of Lord Wilberforce in *Photo Production Ltd v Securicor Transport Ltd*,[12] where he favoured commercial undertakings of equal bargaining strength being allowed to apportion the risk as they wished, were supported.

Since the passing of the 1977 Act some abuses relating to void exclusion clauses have continued and attracted the attention of the Director General of Fair Trading. In particular, a seller might be

10　[1951] 1 Lloyd's Rep 32.
11　[1984] 2 Lloyd's Rep 211, Commercial Court, QBD.
12　[1980] AC 827, [1980] 1 All ER 556, HL.

tempted to purport to exclude a buyer's right to reject defective goods by a 'no refunds' notice, or any other notice purporting to take away the rights conferred by the sale of goods legislation ('goods returned for credit notes only', 'once sold goods may not be returned' were once common examples) and many consumers being ignorant of their rights would be disposed to accept this. As a result of a proposal by the Director General and a supporting Report of the Consumer Protection Advisory Committee in 1974, an order was made under the Fair Trading Act 1973, section 22[13] making it a criminal offence in the case of sale of goods or hire-purchase to display this type of notice, or display similar advertisements – or label goods and containers with similar notices.[14] It is also an offence to supply statements either about the retailer's obligations to the buyer or to supply statements made by third parties (e.g. in manufacturers guarantees) unless that statement is accompanied by a further statement that the consumer's statutory rights are not affected. The offence carries a maximum penalty of £5,000 on summary conviction[15] and a fine or imprisonment not exceeding two years, or both, on conviction on indictment (Fair Trading Act 1973, section 23, as amended). There is no such protection for contracts governed by the Supply of Goods and Services Act 1982, a factor which has resulted in continued monitoring by the Director General.[16]

The comparative absence of legislative protection given to buyers from private sellers can also be abused by a business seller purporting to be a private seller and contacting buyers through classified advertisements in newspapers. This practice was referred to the CPAC by the Director General, and the supporting CPAC Report[17]

---

13   Consumer Transactions (Restrictions on Statements) Order 1976, S.I. 1976/1813, as amended by S.I. 1978/27.

14   In *Hughes v Gillian and Owen Hall* [1981] RTR 430, QBD, M & H p. 281, sales of second-hand cars 'sold as seen and inspected' were held to infringe the terms of this order since prima facie such a phrase negates the implied condition of compliance with description under the Sale of Goods Act 1979, s. 13. In contrast in *Cavendish-Woodhouse Ltd v Manley* (1984) 82 LGR 376, QBD, the words 'bought as seen' were held not to amount to an offence as they reflected the fact that the customer had seen the goods he bought, the sale not being one by description. See further E. Jacobs 'The Pitfalls of Consumer Protection' (1985) 4 Tr L 297; R. G. Lawson 'Consumer Transactions (Restrictions on Statements) Order' (1986) 150 JPN 420; D. Parry 'Criminal Controls over Exemption Clauses and Guarantees' (1990) 2 Law for Business 307.

15   Increased from £2,000 in October 1992 by virtue of the Criminal Justice Act 1991, s. 17(2).

16   See O'Keefe *Law Relating to Trade Descriptions* paras. 1[5051]-[5052]; *Annual Report of the Director General of Fair Trading 1983* (HC Paper (1984) No. 495) at p. 14; M & H pp. 274–275.

17   Disguised Business Sales - HC Paper (1976) No. 355. See further the discussion of the Fair Trading Act 1973 in ch. 11.

resulted in the Business Advertisements (Disclosure) Order 1977[18] similarly making non-disclosure of business status a criminal offence.

Misrepresentations

The 1977 Act (section 8) also amended the statutory provisions dealing with clauses exempting a party to a contract from liability for misrepresentations by substituting a new section 3 into the Misrepresentation Act 1967 (and a new section 8 into the Misrepresentation Act (Northern Ireland) 1967). The former provision stated that any such exemption clause must be 'fair and reasonable', the criteria for which were not stated. This section was criticised, but had given rise to little litigation.

Section 3 now reads as follows:

If a contract contains a term which would exclude or restrict
a) any liability to which a party to a contract may be subject by reason of any misrepresentation made by him before the contract was made; or
b) any remedy available to another party to the contract by reason of such a misrepresentation,
that term shall be of no effect except in so far as it satisfies the requirement of reasonableness as stated in section 11(1) of the Unfair Contract Terms Act 1977; and it is for those claiming that the term satisfies that requirement to show that it does.

In the 1977 Act no guidelines for the interpretation of the substituted section 3 above are given except that the term must have been a fair and reasonable one to be included having regard to the circumstances which were, or ought reasonably to have been, known to or in the contemplation of the parties when the contract was made (section 11(1)). There now exists some judicial guidance as to the way these provisions (both pre and post the 1977 substitution) are to be construed. In *Overbrooke Estates Ltd v Glencombe Properties Ltd*[19] a clause limiting the authority of auctioneers and the firm's employees to make or give representations or warranties was held to fall outside the scope of the original version of section 3 since it was a limitation on the apparent authority of the auctioneers rather than an exemption clause. This case was followed in *Collins v Howell-Jones*.[20] In *Cremdean Properties Ltd v Nash*[1] and *Howard Marine and*

18 S.I. 1977/1918; M & H pp. 418–424. See also *Blakemore v Bellamy* [1983] RTR 303, QBD; M & H p. 421; Harvey (1983) 127 Sol. Jo. 163 and 179; Edmondson (1983) 147 JPN 309; Bragg (1983) 91 ITSA MR 182.
19 [1974] 3 All ER 511, [1974] 1 WLR 1335, Ch D.
20 (1980) 259 Estates Gazette 331, CA; see Murdoch (1981) 97 LQR 522.
1   (1977) 244 Estates Gazette 547, CA; M & H p. 261.

Dredging Co Ltd v A. Ogden & Sons (Excavations) Ltd[2] the court expressed the view that the clauses in question with respect to exemption from liability for misrepresentations were unreasonable.

Moving now to cases decided on section 3 as substituted by the 1977 Act, in a decision of great potential importance for conveyancers, *Walker v Boyle*,[3] Dillon J held that in the circumstances of this case a standard condition in the National Conditions of Sale (19th Edn.), which stated that 'without prejudice to any express right of either party or to any right of the purchaser in reliance on section 24 of the Law of Property Act 1969 to rescind the contract before completion, no error, misstatement or omission in any preliminary answer concerning the property . . . shall annul the sale' was ineffective to exempt from liability for a pre-contractual misstatement. The misstatement by the vendor was as to the absence of any boundary dispute, this being the subject matter of a specific preliminary enquiry by the purchaser. There was in fact a boundary dispute, the existence of which persuaded the purchaser not to proceed with the purchase after exchange of contracts. Dillon J said that the standard condition of sale in question did not meet the requirements of fairness and reasonableness required by section 11 of the 1977 Act. He ordered that the deposit paid by the purchaser should be returned with interest and the contract rescinded. Most conveyancing transactions were subject either to the National Conditions of Sale mentioned above or to the Law Society's Conditions of Sale. Since March 1990 these have been replaced by the Standard Conditions of Sale (1st Edn.). Condition 7.1 now entitles rescission of the contract only:

a) where the error or omission results from fraud or recklessness or
b) where he would otherwise be obliged, to his prejudice, to transfer or accept property differing substantially (in quantity, quality, tenure or otherwise) from what the error or omission had led him to expect.

It remains to be seen whether or not this satisfies the reasonableness test.

A further example of an exclusion clause failing to satisfy the reasonableness test of section 3 occurs in *South Western General Property Company Ltd v Marton*.[4] Here a clause which purported to exclude liability for a misrepresentation, that land sold at an auction could be used for building on providing a planning application was

2 [1978] QB 574, [1978] 2 All ER 1134, CA.
3 [1982] 1 All ER 634, [1982] 1 WLR 495, Ch D. See Aldridge (1981) 125 Sol Jo 731.
4 (1982) 263 Estates Gazette 1090, (1982) Times, 11 May, QBD.

made, was not shown to be reasonable in a contract with a private purchaser of the land.

The above decisions show the willingness of the courts to interpret the wide guidelines laid down by the Act in a sensible manner and in the interests of the consumer. The policy embodied in the Act of 'leaving it to the courts' has, however, not always attracted judicial support. Lord Hailsham described some of the 1977 Act's provisions as 'ban-yan tree justice' when debating it as a Bill. Certainly isolated attempts to legislate in this manner in the nineteenth century also do not seem to have met with approval.

Apropos of the Railway and Canal Traffic Act 1854, section 7, which made the enforceability of clauses exempting railway companies carrying goods dependent on the courts thinking it 'just and reasonable', Lord Bramwell said:

> It seems to me perfectly idle, and I cannot understand how it could have been supposed necessary, that it should be referred to a judge to say whether an agreement between carriers, of whose business he knows nothing, and fishmongers, of whose business he equally knows nothing, is reasonable or not.[5]

In the modern context of 'fair rents' and discretionary family and divorce laws, this policy is more likely nowadays to be regarded as a proper recognition of the futility of trying to legislate for widely differing circumstances except within broad principles, rather than an abrogation of its duty by the legislature. Modern legislation has forced sellers of goods to consumers to live without the exemption clauses which were almost automatically inserted in many standard form contracts before 1973, and this is a welcome development. The matter is not so straightforward as between two businessmen of equal economic power, since the allocation of deliberately assumed risks can be carefully costed and insured against. This is not an area where there is any obvious moral basis for interference by the legislature.

European developments

There is currently a revised EC Draft Directive on Unfair Terms in Consumer Contracts.[6] This, if adopted, will affect aspects of the Unfair Contract Terms Act 1977 discussed above. It applies to all

---

5 *Manchester Sheffield and Lincolnshire Rly Co v Brown* (1883) 8 App Cas 703 at 718 referred to in the Law Commission's Second Report on Exemption Clauses 1975, para. 66. The case involved a contract to carry fish at a reduced rate. It was held that a clause excluding liability for delay in delivery was 'reasonable'. See further Grunfeld, 17 MLR 119, *Borrie & Diamond* p. 62.

6 Com (92) 66 final, 5 March 1992.

consumer-business contracts, but not to business-business contracts, unlike sections 6(3) and 7(3) of the 1977 Act. Member States will be required to prohibit the use of unfair terms in contracts concluded with a consumer by any person acting in the course of his trade, business or profession. A contractual term is currently defined, in the Draft Directive, as 'unfair' if:

> of itself or in combination with another term or terms of the same contract, or of another contract upon which it is dependent contrary to the requirements of good faith:
>
>> it causes to the detriment of the consumer a significant imbalance in the parties' rights and obligations arising under the contract;
>> or
>> it causes the performance of the contract to be significantly different from what the consumer could legitimately expect.

The Annex declares certain types of terms to be unfair.

Article 6 requires Member States to ensure that the consumer is guaranteed, as purchaser under a contract for the sale of goods the right to receive goods which are in conformity with the contract and are fit for the purpose for which they were sold, and to complain that the goods contain hidden defects.

Consumers will have to be guaranteed the choice of the following options:

> (i) the reimbursement of the whole of the purchase price, or
> (ii) the replacement of the goods, or
> (iii) the repair of the goods at the seller's expense, or
> (iv) a reduction in the price if the consumer retains the goods;
>
> and the right to compensation for damage sustained by the consumer which arises out of that contract.

It can be seen from the above that new rights and remedies are created by the above provisions, for example under (iii), as currently there is no right of repair for defective goods. The Draft Directive requires adequate and effective means to be introduced to control unfair terms, including actions by persons or organisations, if regarded under national laws as having a legitimate interest in protecting consumers. Negotiations on the Draft are continuing and further developments are awaited. The implementation date was scheduled for 31 December 1992 but this is unlikely to be achieved.

6 Product liability and tort-based remedies

1. NEGLIGENCE-BASED LIABILITY

The majority of consumer complaints concerning defective goods are by purchasers whose expectations are disappointed and who are usually claiming for purely economic loss. The law is now almost as clear as can be expected in this area and in practice the vast majority of complaints which would, if litigated, be under the Sale of Goods Act 1979 are settled. This is either because the result of any litigation is predictable and the cost of remedying the defect is comparatively small, or because, even if the complaint is doubtful or clearly unjustified – retailers often complain that customers damage their goods *after* purchase and bring trumped-up complaints – sellers wish to preserve their goodwill and avoid troublesome disputes. From the consumer's point of view, liability based on contract is in practice strict. Once the plaintiff has established unfitness or unmerchantability the claim cannot be defeated by a defence that all reasonable care was taken to prevent the defect.[1] It is perhaps surprising that English law should put liability for consequential loss and injury on the shoulders of the retailer when it might involve damages of many thousands of pounds[2] on a sale of a cheap article in these circumstances,[3] but there are undoubted advantages to the consumer. In addition, where there is no damage to persons or property and the complaint is that the goods are shoddy or inefficient, the consumer's remedies lie in contract and not in tort.

These contract-based remedies have been given a statutory basis

---

1 *Frost v The Aylesbury Dairy Co Ltd* [1905] 1 KB 608, CA (typhoid in milk); *Wren v Holt* [1903] 1 KB 610, CA.
2 See *Godley v Perry* [1960] 1 All ER 36, [1960] 1 WLR 9, QBD, discussed above.
3 See Waddams 'Strict Liability, Warranties and the Sale of Goods' (1969) 19 Univ Toronto L Jo 157.

since 1893 and had a common law one for many years before.[4] They suffer, as was mentioned above, from a defect fatal if the consumer does not happen to be the purchaser, or if the purchaser for some reason cannot or does not wish to sue the seller. Being contract-based, privity of contract is essential. The purchaser must be the person suffering the loss, and it is he that must sue the seller under the 1979 Act unless the purchaser can show that he was acting as agent for the injured consumer – and here unless the purchaser was expressly authorised to contract for the principal, such a contract can only be ratified if the purchaser *at the time of making the contract* professed to contract on the principal's behalf.[5] The case of *Daniels and Daniels v R. White & Sons Ltd and Tarbard* [6] is often taken as an example.[7] Mr. Daniels purchased a bottle of lemonade from Mrs. Tarbard, a publican. It had been manufactured by R. White & Sons Ltd and contained a quantity of carbolic acid. Mr. and Mrs. Daniels both became ill as a result of drinking it. As between the buyer, Mr. Daniels, and the seller, Mrs. Tarbard, the conditions implied by the 1893 Act were capable of applying and it was found that whilst there was no implied condition of fitness (since the buyer had not relied on the seller's skill or judgment) the implied condition of merchantability applied and had been broken. Mr. Daniels was able to recover from Mrs. Tarbard damages for personal injuries without proving that she had been negligent. Mrs. Daniels could not sue Mrs. Tarbard, but could properly sue the manufacturers, Whites, for the tort of negligence. On the facts she failed to prove breach of the necessary duty of care, though in this respect the decision would probably not be followed today.[8] Mr. Daniels could also have sued the manufacturers successfully in tort had negligence been provable. Mrs. Tarbard would not necessarily have borne the loss. Either by joining in her supplier (who would in turn join in his supplier and so on down the line of suppliers to the manufacturer in theory) or by separate proceedings, she could recover on an indemnity basis for the

4   See e.g. *Gardiner v Gray* (1815) 4 Camp 144 for an early case holding that bags of silk must be 'saleable in the market under the denomination mentioned in the contract between them. The purchaser cannot be supposed to buy goods to lay them on a dunghill', per Lord Ellenborough.

5   *Keighley, Maxsted & Co v Durant* [1901] AC 240, HL. The injured person may be presumed to be the purchaser in such cases as where two or more people buy food together in a restaurant; see *Lockett v A. and M. Charles Ltd* [1938] 4 All ER 170, KBD; M & H p. 21.

6   [1938] 4 All ER 258, KBD; M & H p. 19.

7   See Law Com Working Paper No. 64 *Liability for Defective Products* (1975), paras. 8, 120; *Miller and Lovell* p. 23.

8   See *Hill v James Crowe (Cases) Ltd* [1978] 1 All ER 812, QBD; M & H p. 151. In addition, strict liability would now arise under the Consumer Protection Act 1987, s. 2, see below.

supplier's breach of the implied condition. Insolvency, inaccessibility or an effective exemption clause would break the chain at an intermediate stage.

Normally, tort-based remedies will be pursued in those circumstances where the consumer is debarred from using the Sale of Goods Act remedies. In cases where the consumer, having suffered damage to person or property, has a choice of either suing in contract or tort he would normally have chosen to sue in contract because of the absence of need to prove fault. With the introduction of the Consumer Protection Act 1987, for products put into circulation after 1 March 1988, strict liability is also available in tort.[9] Other factors are unlikely to be decisive either way. The limitation period during which an action must be brought if personal injuries are involved, three years from the time the plaintiff knew or ought to have known of the damage, is the same whether suing in contract or tort[10] and is six years in other cases.[11] An action under Part I of the Consumer Protection Act 1987 cannot be commenced after 10 years from the product being put into circulation.[12] Although the tests for remoteness and measure of damages have detailed differences in contract and tort respectively, in practice whether the damages recovered are in respect of the defective goods themselves or consequential loss the amount recovered will be similar.[13]

Torts generally

Although the tort of negligence has, until the introduction of the strict liability tort under the Consumer Protection Act 1987, overshadowed most of the other torts in importance, as in contract-based remedies the person advising a consumer contemplating legal action must do so with the whole of the law of tort in mind. This is

9 See below pp. 148–164.
10 Limitation Act 1980, s. 11.
11 Limitation Act 1980, ss. 2 and 5. This period might commence later in tort-based actions since the period commences at the moment the loss occurs, whereas in contract the period commences when the defective goods are delivered. The tort test gave rise to considerable problems in cases of latent damage - e.g. where the effects of negligence by a house builder, surveyor or solicitor do not become apparent for some time. Now under the Limitation Act 1980, s. 14A as inserted by the Latent Damage Act 1986, s. 1 in cases of latent damage not involving personal injuries, the period is the longer of six years or three years from the date of discovery or reasonable discoverability of significant damage. There is a cut-off point of 15 years from the last negligent act or omission (s. 14B).
12 Limitation Act 1980, s. 11(A) as inserted by the Consumer Protection Act 1987, s. 6(6) and Sch. 1, see p. 162.
13 For an example of one rather extreme case where this might not be so, see *Miller and Lovell* pp. 54–55.

not simply a question of bearing in mind such matters as the defences available generally in the law of tort. It may also be wise, for instance, to consider whether there might be liability for the tort of deceit,[14] or for supplying irresponsible persons with dangerous articles such as airguns or petrol to children[15] as well as or as an alternative to actions based on the breach of a duty of care.

Consideration should also be given to the possibility of action for the tort of breach of statutory duty,[16] particularly where the consumer has been injured by a defective article covered by regulations made under the Consumer Protection Act 1987, section 11. Section 41(1) of the 1987 Act gives a specific civil right of action in these circumstances. (A general duty is imposed upon manufacturers etc. to ensure that articles used at work are, so far as reasonably practicable, designed and constructed so as to be safe when properly used, but no civil right of action lies for breach - see the Health and Safety at Work etc. Act 1974, sections 6 (as amended) and 47, which is not strictly a consumer protection enactment since it pertains to the production process.)

The Donoghue v Stevenson duty

This well known decision of the House of Lords was something of a watershed in the law of tort since the wide dicta of the judges encouraged vigorous development of the use of the tort of negligence in a variety of situations. We are concerned here with the 'narrow' principle in the case defining the nature of the duty that the manufacturer owes to the ultimate consumer of his products.

In *Donoghue v Stevenson*[17] the appellant and a friend went to a cafe where the friend bought some ice cream and ginger beer in a bottle made of dark opaque glass. After the appellant had consumed some of the ginger beer the friend poured out the remainder of the bottle revealing a decomposed snail. The appellant suffered shock and gastroenteritis as a result of the impure ginger beer. It will have been noted that the appellant was not the purchaser and could not therefore sue the cafe proprietor in contract. It was held that the manufacturer owed a duty of care to the ultimate consumer. Lord Atkin explained the nature of this duty in the following words:

---

14   *Langridge v Levy* (1837) 2 M & W 519, affd. sub nom *Levy v Langridge* (1838) 4 M & W 337 (false statement about dangerous gun which exploded).

15   See *Bebee v Sales* (1916) 32 TLR 413 (airgun); *Yachuk v Oliver Blais Co Ltd* [1949] AC 386, [1949] 2 All ER 150, PC (petrol); *Miller and Lovell* pp. 300 et seq.

16   The constituent elements of this tort are breach of the relevant statutory duty by the defendant resulting in damage to the plaintiff. See further p. 235, below.

17   [1932] AC 562, HL.

A manufacturer of products, which he sells in such a form as to show that he intends them to reach the ultimate consumer in the form in which they left him with no reasonable possibility of intermediate examination, and with the knowledge that the absence of reasonable care in the preparation or putting up of the products will result in an injury to the consumer's life or property, owes a duty to the consumer to take reasonable care.[18]

Bearing in mind that 'negligence means more than heedless or careless conduct. . .; it properly connotes the complex concept of duty, breach, and damage thereby suffered by the person to whom the duty was owing,'[19] the following matters need some further elucidation when considering a consumer's possible cause of action against a manufacturer in negligence.

'The consumer'

Possible plaintiffs in an action against the manufacturer go beyond the purchaser to include, to adapt another of Lord Atkin's well known dicta in *Donoghue v Stevenson*, anyone who is so closely and directly affected by the manufacturer's act that he ought to have them in contemplation as being so affected when directing his mind to the acts or omissions called in question. As in *Donoghue v Stevenson* itself, friends of the purchaser are obviously included, as are members of the purchaser's family, persons to whom the purchaser has given or lent the product, employees who handle it,[20] and even bystanders who are injured by it.[1] The age of the consumer is immaterial. A child born disabled now has a right of action in negligence in respect of pre-natal injuries under the Congenital Disabilities (Civil Liability) Act 1976, e.g. where the foetus is affected by drugs having a teratogenic effect. It is immaterial that the product was given away free.

The parties liable

The primary duty is the manufacturer's, but liability has been extended to cover almost anyone responsible for the marketing of goods who can be shown to be at fault including sub-contractors,

---

18   Ibid at 599.
19   Per Lord Wright in *Lochgelly Iron and Coal Co Ltd v M'Mullan* [1934] AC 1, HL, at 25.
20   *Vacwell Engineering Co Ltd v BDH Chemicals Ltd* [1971] 1 QB 88, [1969] 3 All ER 1681, QBD; M & H p. 154.
 1   *Stennett v Hancock and Peters* [1939] 2 All ER 578 (plaintiff injured in leg by piece flying off inefficiently repaired lorry).

assemblers, packagers and bottlers, wholesalers, distributors, repairers, letters on hire and occasionally even retailers.[2]

Proving negligence

The burden of proving negligence is on the plaintiff. He must prove that the defendant owed him a duty of care, that this was broken and as a result he has suffered injury to person or property (and not purely economic loss).[3] In an increasingly complex technological age this can be a difficult task and may involve an expensive investigation of the producer's system of work and testing, safety record with other goods and so forth. However, in products liability cases where the 'snail in the ginger beer bottle' type of situation exists, the courts will readily infer negligence on the manufacturer's behalf which will only be displaced by strong rebutting evidence.[4] The manufacturer may be able to shift the blame by showing that the fault was caused by an independent contractor who was carefully chosen and whose work was checked,[5] or, perhaps because of the length of time the product has been used before the defect materialised. It is also a defence to show that an intermediate examination sufficient to reveal the defect was to be reasonably expected. Goods sold in opaque bottles or definitively pre-packaged cannot come within this defence.

The standard of safety

Almost any goods can be dangerous if abused. Tobacco is thought to be carcinogenic and certainly can cause other health problems; alcohol taken to excess can be dangerous; a car driven too fast can be dangerous; materials used in commonly produced goods,

2 See *Fisher v Harrods Ltd* [1966] 1 Lloyd's Rep 500, QBD; M & H p. 164 (retailer responsible for loss resulting in selling unsafe and improperly tested or labelled jewellery cleaning fluid, which splashed into plaintiff's eye). See also *Devilez v Boots Pure Drug Co Ltd* (1962) 106 Sol Jo 552 (inadequately bottled corn solvent).
3 See below p. 132.
4 See remarks of the Privy Council in *Grant v Australian Knitting Mill Ltd* [1936] AC 85. See also *Ward v Tesco Stores Ltd* [1976] 1 All ER 219, [1976] 1 WLR 810, CA (customer slipped on supermarket floor owing to spilt yogurt; held, that it was for the supermarket to *disprove* that this was due to lack of care on their part which, here, they could not do); and *Hill v James Crowe (Cases) Ltd* [1978] 1 All ER 812, QBD; M & H p. 151 (lorry driver injured when defective wooden packing case on which he stood collapsed – perhaps an example of foreseeable misuse. Negligent manufacture was assumed.)
5 *Taylor v Rover Co Ltd* [1966] 2 All ER 181, [1966] 1 WLR 1491, Birmingham Assizes (chisel splintered through excessive hardening by independent contractor); *Evans v Triplex Safety Glass Co Ltd* [1936] 1 All ER 283, KBD; M & H p. 152 (manufacturer of windscreen not responsible for shattered windscreen possibly caused by defective assembly by car manufacturer).

particularly man-made fibres, can be inflammable and dangerous. So how would a court react when faced with a claim, for example, by the representatives of a deceased smoker who has died from cancer after smoking a large number of the defendant's cigarettes?[6] In America, over 300 law-suits have been brought[7] but as yet none successfully. In one major test case, *Cipollone v Liggett Group Inc*,[8] the claim was successful at first instance but was reversed on appeal. The Supreme Court has now decided to re-open arguments in the case. The cigarette company is claiming inter alia that the health warnings given on the cigarette packs protects them from liability for the death from cancer of the plaintiff's wife who had smoked 30 cigarettes a day for 40 years. Another case *Claire Dewey v Brown & Williamson Tobacco Co*[9] has ruled that the Federal Cigarette Labeling and Advertising Act of 1965, which requires health warnings on cigarette packets, does not pre-empt a claim by a widow for the death of her husband. The plaintiff also faces problems of proving the causal link if several brands have been smoked and possibly the defence of *volenti non fit injuria*, or the partial defence of contributory negligence because of misuse in smoking to excess. Litigation was commenced in Australia by a terminally ill woman, only to be abandoned when she became too ill to testify. A test case may arise in the United Kingdom from victims of Buerger's Disease, a smoking-related illness which leads to the amputation of a limb.[10]

The manufacturer is entitled to expect reasonable and proper use of the product by the consumer. Damage caused by a product which is safe when used by normal people, but which causes injury when used by an abnormally sensitive or allergic person, will not be compensated since no general duty of care has been broken.[11] But whether the defendant is sufficiently abnormal to be outside the class of consumers to whom the duty is owed is a matter of degree. A product is dangerous 'if it might affect normal users adversely, or

---

6   See M Humphries 'Cigarette Litigation: English Prospects' (1989) 86 LS Gaz No 19, p. 14; N Gerrard and C Leech 'Cigarette smokers – more sinned against than sinning', (1990) 140 NLJ 1141.
7   See M Humphries 'Cigarette Litigation: The American Experience' (1989) 86 LS Gaz No 17, p. 14.
8   828 F 2d 335 (1988); 12 S Ct 335 (1991); USLW 3497 (1992), 21 January 1992; also (1992) 15 Consumer Law Today, Issue 2, p. 8.
9   577 A 2d 1239 (1990), Supreme Court New Jersey; see (1991) 14 Consumer Law Today, Issue 7, p. 5.
10 The Times, 20, 23 July and 17 September 1986, 5 August 1991.
11 This seems to follow from the non-breach of the implied condition of fitness where e.g. dermatitis is caused to an allergic person, who gives no warning of it, by the use of hair dye as in *Ingham v Emes* [1955] 2 QB 366, [1955] 2 All ER 740, CA.

even if it might adversely affect other users who had a higher degree of sensitivity than the normal, so long as they were not altogether exceptional'.[12]

If the product is known to be capable of causing danger if improperly used, and it is reasonable to anticipate that improper use might occur, then there is a probability that the manufacturer will be liable to damages for negligence unless a proper warning was given. The case of *Vacwell Engineering v BDH Chemicals Ltd*[13] is revealing on this and a number of other related points. The defendants began manufacturing and marketing for industrial use a chemical named boron tribromide. It was put up in glass ampoules with a warning label marked 'harmful vapour'. After discussion with the plaintiffs and visits to their plant the plaintiffs bought a supply of the chemical. In order to manufacture transistors the ampoules were put in a sink of water and detergent to wash off the labels. A visiting Russian physicist was engaged in doing this when there was a violent explosion which killed him and extensively damaged the plaintiff's property. The overwhelming probability was that an ampoule had been dropped into the sink, and then broken, and as a result the chemical came into contact with water. This caused a violent reaction which in turn broke the glass in the other ampoules in the sink, and the explosion occurred.

The plaintiffs successfully claimed damages for negligence and (inter alia) breach of the implied term of fitness for purpose under the 1893 Act. As regards the negligence action, the defendants were held to be in breach of their duty of care in not ascertaining that the chemical exploded when mixed with water (a fact which had been noted in French scientific journals in 1878 and again in 1899, though omitted from some more modern textbooks). Having ascertained the hazard the defendants should have at least put a warning such as, 'Warning – Harmful Vapour. Reacts violently with water and explodes'. Finally, the explosion and damage being foreseeable, the defendants were liable therefor, the magnitude and extent of the actual damage being irrelevant.[14] The Court of Appeal later upheld an agreed settlement of the appeal on the basis that the damages recoverable on the above basis should be reduced by 20 per cent in

12 Per Denning LJ in *Board v Thomas Hedley & Co Ltd* [1951] 2 All ER 431, CA, at 432.
13 [1971] 1 QB 88, [1969] 3 All ER 1681, QBD; M & H p. 154.
14 Applying dicta in *Smith v Leech Brain & Co Ltd* [1962] 2 QB 405, [1961] 3 All ER 1159, QBD (foreseeable burn to plaintiff's husband followed by unforeseeable cancer; damages awarded in respect of husband's death to widow).

respect, presumably, of contributory negligence.[15] To this the caveat must be added that a manufacturer's warning which really amounts to an exemption clause, in that it imposes 'restrictive or onerous conditions' within the Unfair Contract Terms Act 1977, section 13 will be rendered nugatory (or subject to the reasonableness test) imposed by section 2 of that Act.[16]

Damages

As will have been inferred from the *Vacwell* case considered above, a small degree of carelessness can result in an apparently disproportionate amount of damage. A crucial consideration is how much of the damage is recoverable from the defendant when claiming in tort. As in the *Vacwell* case the test adopted is whether the damage is of a type or kind which ought reasonably to have been foreseen, though the extent of the damage need not have been foreseen. If an explosion should have been foreseen, the fact that its magnitude exceeded all expectation is immaterial.[17] Where property damage is sustained the measure of damages is normally the cost of replacement.[18] For physical injuries the courts and insurance companies operate a rough tariff according to the nature and extent of the injury.[19] It still seems to be generally accepted in English tort law that pure economic loss cannot be compensated. There must be some preceding physical loss, even if minimal. This was established in *Spartan Steel and Alloys Ltd v Martin & Co (Contractors) Ltd.*[20] Although the House of Lords, in *Junior Books Ltd v Veitchi Co Ltd*,[1] permitted a claim for pure economic loss where the relationship

---

15   [1971] 1 QB 88 at 112. See also *Hurley v Dyke* [1979] RTR 265, HL, for the extent of a vendor's duty of care when an unroadworthy car which subsequently crashes and causes personal injuries is sold at auction 'as seen and with all its faults and without warranty' – a warning held adequate on the particular facts by the House of Lords.

16   See Macleod (1981) 97 LQR 550.

17   See in general, *The Wagon Mound* [1961] AC 388, [1966] 1 All ER 404, PC; *Hughes v Lord Advocate* [1963] AC 837, [1963] 1 All ER 705, HL.

18   See e.g. *Harbutt's Plasticine Ltd v Wayne Tank and Pump Co Ltd* [1970] 1 QB 447, [1970] 1 All ER 225, CA (factory burnt down due to overheated plastic piping which was unsuitable for purposes. Damages of £146,000 awarded).

19   See e.g. Kemp and Kemp *The Quantum of Damages*.

20   [1973] QB 27, [1972] 3 All ER 557, CA.

1   [1983] 1 AC 520, [1982] 3 All ER 201, HL; M & H p. 168. Here the appellants (sub-contractors) laid a concrete floor in the respondents' factory. The floor was defective and the appellants were found liable for the cost of replacing it, although the floor was not dangerous to health or property and there was no contractual relationship between the appellants and the respondents.

between the parties was sufficiently close, in the majority of cases
there will not be sufficient proximity between the parties and the
necessary element of reliance will be missing, thus preventing
successful claims for pure economic loss. This can be seen in
Muirhead v Industrial Tank Specialities Ltd [2] where damages for pure
economic loss were denied, although damages for physical loss to
property and losses consequential on this were allowed. Here the
plaintiff lobster farmer lost his stock of lobsters when the pumps,
manufactured by the third defendant and used to oxygenate the
water, failed. The court decided that the relationship between the
plaintiff and defendant did not demonstrate the required degree of
proximity and reliance to permit recovery for pure economic loss.
The House of Lords in *Murphy v Brentwood District Council* [3]
confined recovery for pure economic loss to cases where there is a
special relationship of proximity, akin to contract, with an element
of reliance present. Lord Bridge indicates:

> . . . if a manufacturer produces and sells a chattel which is merely
> defective in quality, even to the extent that it is valueless for the purpose
> for which it is intended, the manufacturer's liability at common law arises
> only under and by reference to the terms of any contract to which he is a
> party in relation to the chattel; the common law does not impose on him
> any liability in tort to persons to whom he owes no duty in contract but
> who, having acquired the chattel, suffer economic loss because the chattel
> is defective in quality. If a dangerous defect in a chattel is discovered
> before it causes any personal injury or damage to property, because the
> danger is now known and the chattel cannot safely be used unless the
> defect is repaired, the defect becomes merely a defect in quality. The
> chattel is either capable of repair at economic cost or it is worthless and
> must be scrapped. In either case the loss sustained by the owner or hirer
> of the chattel is purely economic. It is recoverable against any party who
> owes the loser a relevant contractual duty. But it is not recoverable in tort
> in the absence of a special relationship of proximity imposing on the
> tortfeasor a duty of care to safeguard the plaintiff from economic loss.
> There is no such special relationship between the manufacturer of a
> chattel and a remote owner or hirer. (at pp. 475, 926).

2   [1986] QB 507, [1985] 3 All ER 705, CA. See also *Candlewood Navigation Corpn
   Ltd v Mitsui OSK Lines Ltd* [1986] AC 1, [1985] 2 All ER 935, PC; *Leigh & Sillivan
   Ltd v Aliakmon Shipping Co Ltd, The Aliakmon* [1986] AC 785, [1986] 2 All ER
   145, [1986] 2 WLR 902, HL; *D & F Estates Ltd v Church Commissioners for
   England* [1989] AC 177, [1988] 2 All ER 992, HL; and *Simaan General
   Contracting Co v Pilkington Glass Ltd (No 2)* [1988] QB 758, [1988] 1 All ER 791,
   CA.
3   [1991] 1 AC 398, [1990] 2 All ER 908, HL. See also pp 190–191.

Exemption clauses and manufacturer's guarantees

The type of exemption clause which was often contained in a document in the name of the manufacturer and purported to be a guarantee, but which in fact gave the buyer less rights than he had under the 1893 Act, is as a result of the 1973 Act and subsequent legislation a thing of the past.[4] The manufacturer's objective was both to negative the consumer's rights against the retailer and to negative his own in respect of any liability in negligence. It is this aspect of the matter which must now be considered. The enforceability of these guarantees is somewhat conjectural since this depends upon there being a contract between manufacturer and consumer. If construed as a unilateral contract, that is one where an offer is made to a range of possible offerees and is accepted by a particular offeree doing the contemplated act, the contract would probably be completed by purchase of the article. This would both operate as acceptance and furnish consideration by the purchaser, provided he could be taken to know of the existence of the guarantee at the time of purchase. If the contract is construed as a bilateral one, involving a communicated acceptance by the buyer, 'registration' of the guarantee by filling it in and posting it would probably constitute both acceptance and furnish consideration by the buyer.[5] If a contract can be established between the parties a manufacturer could rely on a clause in the 'guarantee' exempting him from negligence. Alternatively the guarantee might operate as a non-contractual notice and, in exceptional cases, thereby exclude liability.

Exemption clauses in manufacturers' guarantees are now regulated by the Unfair Contract Terms Act 1977, section 5. This section applies only to cases where possession or ownership of the goods does not pass pursuant to the contract. So in contracts between seller and buyer, as opposed to manufacturer and buyer, exemption clauses relating to negligence will be avoided or regulated under section 2 (considered in detail in ch. 7), rather than section 5.

Section 5 provides that in the case of goods of a type ordinarily supplied for private use or consumption, where loss or damage a) arises from the goods proving defective while in consumer use, and b) results from the negligence of a person concerned in the

---

4   Such 'guarantees' are not necessarily objectionable. They may, and modern ones often do, give the consumer valuable rights over and above those implied by the Sale of Goods Act 1979.

5   *Chappell & Co Ltd v Nestle Co Ltd* [1960] AC 87, [1959] 2 All ER 701, HL (useless chocolate wrappers accompanying money sent to Nestle's for a copy of 'smash hit' record held to be part of the consideration).

manufacture or distribution of the goods, any exemption clause in the guarantee excluding or restricting liability for the loss or damage is void. For these purposes 'guarantee' and 'in consumer use' are defined. A guarantee is anything in writing if it contains or purports to contain some promise or assurance (however worded or presented) that defects will be made good by complete or partial replacement, or by repair, monetary compensation or otherwise. Goods are regarded as in consumer use when a person is using them, or has them in his possession for use, otherwise than exclusively for the purpose of a business.[6]

It will be appreciated that section 5 operates only where a) it can be proved that loss or damage of any sort has occurred owing to the negligence of the manufacturer or distributor, and b) there has been what would, apart from section 5, have been a successful attempt to negative or restrict such liability by a contractually binding exemption clause or an effective non-contractual notice.

The Department of Trade and Industry has, in a consultation paper *Consumer Guarantees*,[7] mooted changes in the law relating to guarantees. In particular there is the suggestion that manufacturers who choose to offer guarantees should be legally liable for their performance. As this would be achieved by statute, the measure of damages introduced could be made either tortious or contractual. In cases where the manufacturer is outside the United Kingdom, the importer would have the responsibility for the guarantee. The paper also canvasses making the retailer jointly and severally liable with the manufacturer for such guarantees.

Two case studies on design defects

Introduction. In the field of product liability, design defects in products are regarded with particular horror by manufacturers. Manufacturing defects, which no doubt give rise to the largest number of claims based on defective products, can at least be prevented in future by tightening quality control processes. But design defects can affect a huge number of individual products which may be awaiting sale or already sold and, once the defect is identified, can involve the manufacturer in frightening financial liability in

---

6 See Macleod 'Instructions as to the Use of Consumer Goods' (1981) 97 LQR 550.
7 February 1992. See also *Consumer Guarantees: A Discussion Paper*, OFT, August 1984; *Consumer Guarantees: A report by the Director General of Fair Trading*, OFT, June 1986; and *Competing in Quality*, NCC, April 1989. For further discussion of proposals see below p. 148.

modifying the product, often after an expensive recall.[8] The reluctance of some manufacturers to recall suspect products in time is illustrated by the Thalidomide saga to which reference is made in Ch. 8 and by the first of the two cases considered below, *Walton v British Leyland (UK) Ltd* (1978).

The second case selected for a more detailed analysis is *Lambert v Lewis* (1981). This case does not involve the sometimes complex question of whether a product *is* defective on an application of the current rules relating to the rules of negligence (an illustration of the standard of care laid down by which having already been provided in *Vacwell Engineering Co Ltd v BDH Chemicals Ltd*).[9] Both cases, however, provide graphic examples of the difficulty of apportioning blame (in terms of damages) 1) where a product is defectively designed and 2) this fact comes to light some time after its being marketed and 3) the product could perhaps have been prevented from causing damage had a third party taken proper action.

Walton v British Leyland (UK) Ltd, Dutton Forshaw (North East) Ltd and Blue House Lane Garage Ltd (12 July 1978, unreported), QBD[10]

Mr. and Mrs. Walton, the plaintiffs, were travelling as passengers in an Austin Allegro car which was being driven along a motorway by Mr. Walton's brother, Albert. As the vehicle was travelling at about 60 mph the rear nearside wheel came off. As a result the vehicle collided with the central crash barrier. Mr. Walton escaped with minor injuries but his wife was thrown from the car and suffered injuries so catastrophic that she was left a quadriplegic.

The car had been bought by Albert in 1974. It was described by Willis J as a 'thoroughly bad car'. It had been in and out of Duttons, the second defendants, for repair throughout 1975; the clutch having been replaced four times. The first symptom of the ultimate disaster was in early 1975 when Albert noticed a noise in the rear offside wheel and Duttons then replaced the bearing and fitted the larger

8   Whilst there is no general duty to recall defective products in the UK, failure to do so when the defect has been identified can greatly increase the liability to pay damages. In the case of motor vehicles the Department of Transport is entitled to information on safety defects and to put its views to the manufacturer on remedial action under the Code of Practice on Action concerning Vehicle Safety Defects between the Department of Transport and the Society of Motor Manufacturers and Traders Ltd. See Anthea Worsdall *Consumer Law for the Motor Trade* (3rd Edn.) pp 243–246.

9   [1971] 1 QB 88, [1969] 3 All ER 1681, QBD; M & H p. 154; above, p. 131.

10 This case does not appear to have been officially reported but a transcript appears in Product Liability International, August 1980, 156, and the decision received some publicity in newspapers. For detailed extracts see M & H pp. 159–163.

washer, recommended by the manufacturers, to that particular wheel only. The car was later taken to Blue House Lane Garage Ltd, the third defendants (who, unlike Duttons, were not franchised dealers for Leyland's) and they gave it a 6,000 mile service and later a 12,000 mile service. At the latter service the brakes and bearings were adjusted and the wheels changed. The accident occurred some 1,400 miles later without warning.

The case revealed a great deal of detailed evidence, no doubt produced under the rules relating to discovery of documentary evidence in civil proceedings, as to the history of 'wheel adrift' problems in Allegro cars in the early 1970s. To summarise, by February 1975 some 104 cases of 'wheel adrift' problems had been reported to Leyland's from the UK and abroad. The problem was regarded as serious. As the learned judge remarked, 'lives were plainly at risk, but so were sales, and a solution, or at least a palliative, had to be found urgently'.

At first the blame was put on servicing mechanics unfamiliar with the type of end float bearings used on this model (along with others, such as Marinas). If overtightened it was considered that this would lead to overheating, bearing collapse and, in the worst cases, wheels coming off. In fact after September 1974 the cars were manufactured with large washers in the rear hub assembly 'to improve bearing security' and all dealers were both warned of the dangers of incorrect adjustment and urged to fit larger washers when servicing earlier models. The judge described this 'palliative' as 'a limited education programme directed to mechanics working in distributors' garages'. The effect of fitting a larger washer was admitted to be not to prevent bearing failure but to prevent the wheel coming off should bearing failure occur. A revealing memorandum from a chief engineer at Leyland's in late 1974 stated: 'The design was introduced to satisfy performance demands at lower cost, and it is true to state that provided design requirements are adhered to no problem would be experienced. Unfortunately the design is not "idiot-proof" and will therefore continuously involve risk. The risk becomes greater as vehicles become older and ever more carelessly maintained. Had we incorporated the large washer from the commencement the risk would have been tolerable . . . Engineering have considered the possibility of recall action but do not favour it owing to the fact that it would damage the product' (i.e. adversely affect sales). In fact a recall campaign would have cost, in 1974, £300,000, and an education campaign to franchised outlets was chosen instead.

Expert evidence at the trial was to the effect that the outer bearing had collapsed and that the inner cone had been welded by excessive heat onto the stub axle. The probable, but not certain, cause of the accident was overtightening of the retaining nut, exacerbated by lack of grease.

The case against Duttons was that they should have fitted the larger washer to both hubs, instead of just one, when the car was brought in to them. But the learned judge was not convinced that the instructions they had had from Leyland's gave any indication of the real gravity of the problem and thought them ambiguous as to the need in all circumstances to change *both* hub washers following a complaint about only one. He went on to hold Duttons blameless.

The case against Blue House, and its allegedly negligent mechanic, was that the accident was caused by the overtightening of the vulnerable wheel bearing. Again the judge held this garage, who were not Leyland dealers and had no knowledge of the desirability of fitting larger washers, not negligent even if overtightening were the cause of the breakdown (which he did not regard as by any means established).

As to Leyland's responsibility, this was held to be 'total'. Having become aware of the 'wheel adrift' problem on this model, what was Leyland's position?

> The duty of care owed by Leyland to the public was to make a clean breast of the problem and recall all cars which they could, in order that the safety washers could be fitted. I accept, of course that manufacturers have to steer a course between alarming the public unecessarily and so damaging the reputation of their products, and observing their duty of care towards those whom they are in a position to protect from dangers of which they and they alone are aware. The duty seems to me to be the higher when they can palliate the worst effects of a failure which, if Leyland's view is right, they could never decisively guard against. They seriously considered recall and made an estimate of the cost at a figure which seems to me to be in no way out of proportion to the risks involved. It was decided not to follow this course for commercial reasons. I think this involved a failure to observe their duty of care for the safety of the many who were bound to remain at risk, irrespective of the recommendations made to Leyland dealers and to them alone.[11]

By way of footnote to this decision it might firstly be noticed that no Sale of Goods Act claim could be made by the plaintiffs since they were not the buyers. Subject to the possible problem of durability, there is little doubt that a breach of section 14 of that Act would otherwise have occurred. Secondly, the design problem was not clearly identified in the decision. The bearing in question was made by a respectable third party manufacturer, Timken, and was fitted to cars of various types world wide. It was clear that Leylands were not negligent in using this component. Thirdly, it was clear that the critical breach of the duty of care was not to instigate a recall, apparently for commercial reasons, after a large number of similar

11   Per Willis J.

faults had been reported. Fourthly, it was clear that the limited warning system adopted by Leyland's was not adequate to shift responsibility to third parties for improper servicing. It was not regarded as any excuse that unfranchised repairers were involved. This is presumably because no car owner is obliged to use franchised dealers for repair work.[12] If, therefore, a design is not 'idiot proof' manufacturers must anticipate that unfranchised garages, or even do-it-yourself owners, will fall into the trap that the design lays for them if it is not completely unreasonable for them to do so.

Lambert v Lewis[13]

The facts of this case concerned a tragic motor accident in 1972. The plaintiffs, a mother and daughter, were travelling in a Reliant car driven by the father in which the son was also a passenger. As their car approached an oncoming Land Rover, driven by a farmer's employee, a trailer being towed by the Land Rover became unhitched and slewed across the road into the path of the plaintiffs' car. In the ensuing accident the father, who was driving the car perfectly properly, was killed together with his son, and the mother and daughter injured. The mother sued on her behalf and on behalf of her deceased husband and son under the provisions of the Fatal Accidents Acts 1846 to 1959 and the Law Reform (Miscellaneous Provisions) Act 1934. The daughter sued in her own right through her mother as next friend.

In an accident of this sort the plaintiffs will be advised that it is highly likely that negligence will be involved on at least one person's behalf, since trailers should not become detached from towing vehicles. Assuming for the moment that the fundamental fault was in the design or manufacture of the hitch, though careless maintenance or driving might have exacerbated the problem, and bearing in mind the Sale of Goods Act 1979, section 14, the possible defendants can be illustrated diagrammatically as follows:

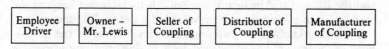

| Employee Driver | Owner – Mr. Lewis | Seller of Coupling | Distributor of Coupling | Manufacturer of Coupling |

Unfortunately, there was one vital link missing from this chain. The sellers and suppliers of the coupling, Lexmead, could not identify the stockist or distributor who sold them the Dixon-Bate trailer coupling, thus preventing any possible indemnity to them under the Sale of Goods Act. In the event the plaintiffs sued as joint defendants the employee-driver, the owner, the seller of the coupling and the manufacturer. By a process of third and fourth party notices the driver and owner claimed indemnity from the seller of the coupling should they be held liable to pay damages, and the seller sued claimed an indemnity or contribution from the manufacturers in the event that the seller was held liable to pay damages. It can thus be seen that the manufacturer was under attack on two fronts. There was the direct claim by the injured plaintiffs based on the consequences of failure to take care in the manufacture of the coupling. There was also the potential claim by the driver and owner of the Land Rover for indemnity from the seller who in turn looked for indemnity from them, the manufacturers, under the principles of the Law Reform (Married Women and Tortfeasors) Act 1935 – the law of *contract* not being available in this particular instance owing to the failure to identify the distributor, the missing link in the chain. However, whether there was any claim at all by the seller against the manufacturer depended, of course, on the seller first being made liable either to compensate the plaintiffs for negligence or to indemnify the driver or owner in respect of any negligence attributed to them.

At first instance[14] Stocker J formulated three issues for decision. The first was: why did the trailer become detached from the Land Rover? The judge found this was because of the defective coupling. It was a dual purpose towing hitch which could be used either attached to a cup-type trailer attachment, as here, or to a ring-type trailer attachment. It consisted of a towing pin ending at the top in a ball, and also locked at the bottom by a brass spindle and spiral pin with handle. What had happened was that the towing pin, securely locked at the top, rose out of the jaws of the towing assembly to which it should have been locked at the bottom. On subsequent examination the brass spindle and handle were found to be missing, and the hitch dirty. In fact it was only dirt which was keeping the towing pin in position and it only needed a jolt to dislodge it.

The second issue was – who was primarily liable for the detachment of the trailer? The judge held the manufacturer responsible. He held the coupling unsafe for the use for which it was designed and that the designers ought to have realised that the adaptation of a dual purpose coupling of this sort from ring-type to cup-type attachments resulted in a fundamental change in its function. It became subject to vertical stresses to which it would not have been subject if coupled to

14   [1979] RTR 61.

a ring attachment. That made the handle, and through it the spindle on which the integrity of the lock depended, vulnerable. He therefore found the manufacturers liable in negligence for the plaintiffs' loss and damage, and the finding was not challenged by the manufacturers.

The judge also considered the farmer-owner's liability, it having been established that the driver was not negligent. The owner had coupled the Land Rover to the trailer and moved it up and down to make sure it was secure. But 'he continued to use this coupling over a period of months in a state in which it was plainly damaged without taking steps to have it repaired or even to ascertain whether or not it was safe to continue to use it in such a condition'.[15] He was thus held to be negligent also, in that he had been insensitive to public safety and to the condition of the vehicle. The judge also went on to consider whether the seller of the coupling ('the suppliers') had been negligent, but held that this was not so since they had purchased the component from reputable manufacturers and the design defect could not have been identified by intermediate examination.

The judge therefore awarded the plaintiffs a total of £45,000 attributable as to 75 per cent to the manufacturers and 25 per cent to the farmer-owner.

The third issue was whether the owner could claim indemnity from any other party along the line. The owner claimed against the suppliers on the basis that the implied conditions of fitness for purpose and merchantable quality under the Sale of Goods Act 1979, section 14 had been broken, and that the damage caused by the accident resulted from these breaches. The judge held that the sale of the badly designed coupling did break both conditions, but the owner could claim nominal damages only. This was because the damages for which the owner was held liable (25 per cent of £45,000) were caused by his own independent negligence in continuing to use the defective coupling, and the damage suffered was therefore too remote from the seller's breach.

It was this latter point on which the substance of the appellate litigation in this case depended. The Court of Appeal[16] held that the seller of goods was responsible for all damage which flowed naturally and directly from a breach of warranty or condition in a contract of sale,[17] and this damage included the accident here because the suppliers should have foreseen that some such negligence might occur. The Court of Appeal therefore held the suppliers liable to indemnify the owner in respect of his liability for damages. The

15 At p. 87.
16 [1980] 1 All ER 978, [1980] 2 WLR 299.
17 See 1979 Act, s. 53(2) and *Hadley v Baxendale* (1854) 9 Exch 341.

suppliers, however, were unable to establish that the manufacturers were in turn responsible to indemnify them because of their dangerous design (thus being 100 per cent liable) because a) no special relationship existed for a claim for negligent misrepresentation, and b) the loss to the suppliers caused by the manufacturers' negligence was purely financial loss, and 'pure economic loss' unaccompanied by physical damage is not recoverable.[18]

The House of Lords in effect restored the substance of the position following Stocker J's judgment by reversing the Court of Appeal and finding the suppliers not liable to indemnify the owner. Lord Diplock formulated the issue thus:[19]

> In what circumstances can a party ('A') to a contract who has been found liable for a breach of a duty of care owed by him to a stranger ('X') to the contract, recover from the other party ('B') to the contract as damages for breach of warranty the amount of damages for negligence which 'A' himself has been ordered to pay to 'X'?

The answer to this was held to be in the ratio decidendi of *Mowbray v Merryweather*,[20] as restated by Winn LJ in *Hadley v Droitwich Construction Co Ltd*:[1]

> . . . in a case where A has been held liable to X, a stranger, for negligent failure to take a certain precaution, he may recover over from someone with whom he has a contract only if by that contract the other contracting party has warranted that he *need not* – there is no necessity – take the very precautions for the failure to take which he has been held liable in law to [X].

Did any or all the implied conditions under the Sale of Goods Act amount to such a warranty? The House of Lords held that they did not. They might have had continuing force for 'a reasonable time' which here might be some three to six months before the accident at which time the farmer should have become aware that the handle of the locking mechanism was missing. But if the accident had happened before then, the owner could not have been held to be negligent in the first place. After the owner should have noticed the defect in the coupling,

> the only implied warranty which could justify his failure to take the precaution either to get it mended or at least to find out whether it was

18 See *SCM (United Kingdom) Ltd v W J Whittall & Son Ltd* [1971] 1 QB 337, [1970] 3 All ER 245, CA, and *Spartan Steel and Alloys Ltd v Martin & Co (Contractors) Ltd* [1973] QB 27, [1972] 3 All ER 557, CA, which were followed on this difficult and controversial point. See ante at p. 132.

19 [1981] 1 All ER 1185 at 1190, [1981] 2 WLR 713 at 718.

20 [1895] 2 QB 640, CA.

 1 [1967] 3 All ER 911 at 914, [1968] 1 WLR 37 at 43, CA.

safe to continue to use it in that condition, would be a warranty that the coupling would continue to be safely used to tow a trailer on the public highway notwithstanding that it was in an obviously damaged state. My Lords, any implication of a warranty in these terms needs only to be stated, to be rejected.

It therefore followed that there was no need to consider the suppliers' claim for indemnity against the manufacturers, since there was no liability imposed on the suppliers to indemnify the owners.

It has been suggested by some commentators[2] that the issue in *Lambert v Lewis* would have been more simply resolved if manufacturers' strict liability for defective products had then been part of English law, as it now is under the Consumer Protection Act 1987. This, it is submitted, is not necessarily true. To start with, the same preliminary work must be done by the plaintiff's advisors to establish the cause of the accident. In *Lambert v Lewis* expert evidence had to be adduced that submission to a steady upward thrust of 1.05 tons would be enough to bring the towing pin out of the jaws if the pin had not been worn, and where it was worn (as here) a pressure of 0.87 tons would have been sufficient. The evidence of engineers would also be needed to establish that this degree of upward thrust, given the dual design of the coupling, rendered its design defective. Exactly the same investigation is needed successfully to sue the producer under the strict liability regime, since such liability depends on identifying a defect in the product. At that point a plaintiff would no doubt limit his own action to suing the producer unless he had doubts about the producer's ability to pay. It is, however, the case that the existing law of negligence remains and applies in particular to the liability of 'producers' inter se and their rights of recourse against third parties.[3] Nor are rights under the Sale of Goods Act 1979 affected. Therefore a plaintiff in a similar situation to that arising in *Lambert v Lewis* will be primarily interested in redress from the manufacturer, though it is usual practice to rely on 'belt and braces' and sue anyone else who might be liable as well. It is quite likely that the owner, who will still be liable for any independent negligence, will be joined in as co-defendant. Even if not, the producer might well seek contribution from the owner in respect of his independent negligence, in which case he will be joined in as a third party.[4] It might be argued that the existence of strict liability

2   See e.g. *Which?* October 1980, p. 596.
3   Consumer Protection Act 1987, s. 2(6).
4   See Civil Liability (Contribution) Act 1978, s. 1(1) of which states that 'any person liable in respect of any damage suffered by another person may recover contribution from any other person liable in respect of the same damage (whether jointly with him or otherwise)' and the Consumer Protection Act 1987, s. 2(5).

makes litigation less probable, but it should be understood that insurers are likely to remain hidden parties behind the producer and probably the vehicle owner. Where large amounts of money are at stake – the actual amount depending on the chance consequence of the financial status of the party or parties killed, and if injured rather than killed the extent of those injuries – the insurers may insist on their right to have their insured's liability properly established.

It is also of interest to focus on the position of the 'consumer' in *Lambert v Lewis*. Here he was the defendant rather than the plaintiff, the vehicle owner who had bought a coupling hitch which was badly designed and caused a catastrophic accident. The damage resulting was primarily his own liability to pay damages for negligence as a result. The owner's attempt to transfer on this liability to the seller of the towing hitch was finally defeated in the House of Lords on the somewhat recondite grounds of causation described above. Perhaps the lesson is that whilst there is always scope for rationalisation of the law, it cannot be 'made simple' if justice is to be done as between the various parties involved in this type of accident.

The evolvement of strict liability for defective products

The object of this part of the chapter is to trace the proposals for reform made over the last 20 years or so, the developments which have taken place, culminating in the Consumer Protection Act 1987, which will be considered in detail later in the chapter, and to see what the future might hold. In North America in particular, but also in some parts of Europe, the idea of strict liability for defective products has to a greater or lesser extent taken root and is now growing in the United Kingdom.

A regime of strict liability for defective products is one in which the claimant will succeed if he can prove that 1) the product was defective, 2) that there was a causal link between that defect and his injuries, 3) there are no defences available to the defendant.

Theories of strict product liability first gained acceptance in the USA, initially as an extension of implied sales warranties to others in the distributive chain[5] and then as part of the developed law of tort.[6] There has been considerable alarm in some quarters as to developments in the USA, and even reluctance by some non-USA manufacturers to export their products to North America. In the USA an

---

5 See *Henningsen v Bloomfield Motors Inc* 161 A 2d 69 (NJ, 1960), M & H p. 27.
6 See in particular *Greenman v Yuba Power Products Inc* 377 P 2d 897 (Cal, 1962); M & H p. 177, (Traynor CJ). See also the formula for strict tort liability stated in the American Law Institute's *Restatement of Tort*, 2d, s. 402A, and generally M & H pp. 172–192 and Miller and Lovell *Product Liability*.

'Inter-Agency Taskforce' was set up in 1975 as a result of allegations that insurance cover was difficult to obtain, but the subsequent report found no problem of widespread unavailability. It should also be borne in mind that although there have been a number of spectacular decisions emanating from the USA in this area of law, there are a number of important divergencies in the way the law is formulated and in the underlying legal system there from the new system operating in the UK. These differences include a) the USA system of contingency fees for lawyers, which encourages 'try on' litigation; in the UK lawyers are more cautious about risking clients' money and in legal aid cases the case has to be regarded as a reasonable one by the certifying committee; b) in the USA verdicts and damages (including the possibility of punitive damages) are left to juries; in civil cases in the UK this position only obtains in Northern Ireland; c) in most American states liability extends beyond the producer to other commercial suppliers; under the Consumer Protection Act 1987 strict liability only attaches to the producer, 'own brander' or Community importer (with limited responsibility on suppliers), liability of others continuing to depend on the law of negligence.

In Europe theories of strict liability were developed in France and the Netherlands in the 1960s and by the German Supreme Court in 1968. The debate on reforming English tort law centred on proposals from Europe and from the English and Scottish Law Commissions. In addition, the Royal Commission on Civil Liability and Compensation for Personal Injuries (Chairman, Lord Pearson) specifically considered compensation in respect of death or personal injury suffered 'through the manufacture, supply or use of goods or services'. The Commission in its Report (1978, Cmnd. 7054) concluded that there was no justification at that time for introducing a 'no-fault' scheme for injuries caused by defective products, but considered that a scheme involving strict liability (i.e. liability without proof of actual negligence), along the lines recommended by the Council of Europe Convention and the EC Directive discussed next, should be introduced.

Dealing with the main proposals chronologically, a proposal for a Council Directive[7] (the 'EC Directive') was presented by the Commission to the Council of the EC on 9 September 1976. A revised draft Directive was submitted to Council on 1 October 1979[8] in the light of criticisms from many quarters of the first Draft and of the opinions of the European Parliament (27 April 1979), its Legal

7   OJ No. C 241, 14 October 1976, p. 9.
8   OJ No. C 271, 26 October 1976, p. 3; M & H p. 197.

Affairs Committee and the Economic and Social Committee. This was followed by lengthy discussions on areas of disagreement including a) whether or not there should be a 'development risks' defence, b) the extension of liability to property damage and c) the imposition of maximum limits of liability.[9] The Directive was finally adopted on 25 July 1985 and was notified to Member States on 30 July 1985.[10] The main feature of the Directive, under Art. 1, is to make the producer strictly liable for damage caused by defects in a product. The Directive was introduced into English law in the Consumer Protection Act 1987, which is discussed fully below.

The economic assumption behind the Directive was, according to its accompanying memorandum of September 1976, that 'the compensation paid forms part of the general production costs of the product. This increase in cost is reflected in the pricing. The damage is thus, from an economic point of view, spread over all the products which are free from defects.' The Council has been accused of acting ultra vires, in that such matters as product liability fall outside the ambit of Art. 2 of the EEC Treaty which sets out as an object 'a harmonious development of economic activities'. However, the preamble to the Directive reflects the EC view that 'the approximation of the laws of the Member States concerning the liability of the producer for damage caused by the defectiveness of his products is necessary, because the existing divergencies may distort competition and affect the movement of goods within the common market and entail a differing degree of protection of the consumer against damage caused by a defective product to his health or property'.

Strict liability also forms the basis of the European Convention on Products Liability in regard to Personal Injury and Death (the 'Strasbourg Convention') adopted by the Committee of Ministers of the Council of Europe at Strasbourg in September 1976 and open for signature on 27 January 1977. Although some Member States have signed the United Kingdom does not propose to sign in the light of the EC Directive.[11] The Convention would oblige contracting States to make their national law conform with the provisions of the Convention. Article 3 obliges the producer to pay compensation for death or personal injuries caused by defects in products. A 'producer' is a manufacturer of the product or a component part, or a producer of natural products, or a business importer, or a person

9   See M & H pp. 196–204.
10   85/374/EEC, OJ No. L 210, 7 August 1985, p. 29.
11   *Implementation of EC Directive on Product Liability – An Explanatory and Consultative Note*, DTI, November 1985, Annex II.

branding the product with a distinguishing feature. Whilst there is no limitation on total damages, these will be reduced or disallowed if the injured person was at fault. There are also defences based on the producer not having circulated the product, or the defect coming into being after circulation, or the producer not acting as such in a business capacity. There are limitation periods of three years from awareness of injury and ten years from circulation of the product, with a prohibition of exemption clauses.

The Law Commission and the Scottish Law Commission produced a Report entitled *Liability for Defective Products* which included detailed comment on the EC Directive and the Strasbourg Convention (1977, Cmnd. 6831). The Commissions regarded the law in 1977 as inadequate and proposed remedies by way of amendment to the law of tort rather than by altering the rules of contract. It was recommended that as a general rule producers should bear the risk of and be strictly liable for injuries caused by defects in their products irrespective of fault. The plaintiff would therefore need to prove i) that an injury had occurred, ii) that the injury was attributable to a defective product, and iii) that the defendant had produced the product or was otherwise within the definition of 'producer'. 'Producers' included persons putting a brand mark on the product, a person supplying a defective product if there was no indication of the identity of the producer, and the first distributor of an imported product. Pharmaceutical products should be subject to the same rules as regards strict liability, though whether a central compensation fund would be appropriate for these or other products was regarded as a matter for the Royal Commission on Civil Liability. The Law Commission recommended that strict liability should also rest on the producer of components whether or not another producer incorporates it into his own product. The Scottish Law Commission disagreed, and recommended that strict liability for components should cease if the component were incorporated into another product which is itself put into circulation. The Scottish Law Commission also disagreed with the Law Commission's view that strict liability should rest on the producer of natural products as on other producers and recommended the exclusion of primary agricultural and fishery products from the regime of strict liability.

There was agreement that defences of 'assumption of risk' and 'contributory negligence' should be available, but exemption clauses should be void. The assessment of compensation for death and personal injuries should be in accordance with general tort law, and without financial limit.

Strict liability would be limited to death or personal injury. It would not apply to claims for damage to property or pure economic loss.[12]

Common threads in these proposals are a) the principle that there should be strict liability for defective products in respect of at least death or personal injury to both consumers and other 'bystanders' sustaining injury; b) that the producer of the finished article and in some cases producers of components and importers should be held liable, and that all commercially marketed products, other than products causing a nuclear accident, and possibly some natural products, should be included; and as regards the UK c) a preference for liability without financial limit based on existing tort law.

The chart on pp. 149–150 illustrates diagrammatically the points of difference and similarity in the proposals or reports of the various bodies discussed.

With regard to the future, a revolutionary proposal for reform is contained in *Consumer Guarantees*.[13] Here the question is raised of whether or not manufacturers should be jointly and severally liable with retailers for the *quality* of goods under sale of goods provisions. This, if adopted, would change entirely the manufacturer-retailer-consumer relationship. By establishing a form of vertical privity between manufacturers and consumers, this would enable many who, for some reason are prevented from suing in contract and are affected by the rules relating to pure economic loss in tort, to receive compensation under a form of strict contractual liability. Claims could then be directed against those responsible for producing defective goods rather than those who happen to sell them. As a consequence, much of the law of tort, both fault-based and strict, would become redundant where goods are involved, as contractual actions would be available. Further developments in this area are awaited with interest.

2. CONSUMER PROTECTION ACT 1987

Part I of the Consumer Protection Act 1987 ('the 1987 Act') seeks to implement the EC Directive on Product Liability[14] (section 1(1)).

12 See Law Com. No. 82 paras. 117–121; M & H p. 202.
13 Department of Trade and Industry, February 1992.
14 85/374/EEC. For further reading on the 1987 Act see Fairest *Guide to the Consumer Protection Act 1987*; Hewitt *Manufacturers' Liability for Defective Goods*, ch. 10; Lowe and Woodroffe *Consumer Law and Practice*, ch. 5; Macleod *Consumer Sales Law*, ch. 17; Merkin *A Guide to the Consumer Protection Act 1987*; Miller *Product Liability and Consumer Safety Encyclopaedia*, Div III and tort textbooks. See also A Clark, 'The Consumer Protection Act 1987', (1990) 50 MLR 614.

Subject Matter	EEC	Strasbourg	Law Com.	Pearson
(1) Terms of strict Liability	Producer liable for damage caused by a defect in his product (Art. 1).	Producer liable in respect of 'injuries caused by a defect in his product' (Art. 3).	Producer strictly liable for 'injuries resulting from defects in products that are put into circulation in the course of a business' (para. 38).	Producer should be strictly liable in tort for death or personal injury caused by defective products (para. 1236).
(2) Definition of 'Producer'	Producer of finished product or any raw material or component, persons putting marks on product and importer into EEC (Art. 3). Member States may, by derogation, include primary agricultural products and game as 'products' (Art. 15(1)(a)).	Manufacturer of finished product and of natural product and of component parts (Art. 2); importers and branders of 'own brand' (Art. 3).	Producer of all kinds of movable products (but not their agents or distributors), and subject to certain exceptions. Also component manufacturers (? if incorporated into another product), markers and importers (para. 50–103). ? Natural products (para. 83).	Producers of finished products, component producers, branders of 'own brand' products and importers but not other distributors (paras. 1235–1250).
(3) Definition of 'defect'	Product defective if 'it does not provide the safety which a person is entitled to expect', taking into account all the circumstances, including 'its presentation the use to which it could reasonably be expected that the product would be put and the time at which it was put into circulation' (Art. 6).	Product has a defect when it 'does not provide the safety which a person is entitled to expect, having regard to all the circumstances including the presentation of the product' (Art. 2).	Product defective if it does not comply with standard of reasonable safety that a person is entitled to expect; this is to be determined objectively in the light of circumstances, instructions or warnings and reasonable user (para. 48).	As per Strasbourg Art. 2 – 'presentation' to include warnings and instructions (para. 1237).
(4) Damage covered	Death, personal injuries, damage or destruction of property other than defective product if amounting to at least 500 ECU (£275) and 'private' non-business property (Art. 9).	Death or personal injuries (Art. 3).	Death or personal injuries but not property or pure economic loss (e.g. repairs to defective product to make it safe) (paras. 117–121).	Death or personal injury (para. 1236) (other types of injury beyond terms of reference).

Subject Matter	EEC	Strasbourg	Law Com.	Pearson
(5) Financial limits to liability in respect of one product or per capita	Optional limit of not less than 70m ECU (£41m) for death and personal injury (see Art. 16).	Option for States to enact global limit of 10m IMF. Special Drawing Rights for all damage caused by identical product and 70,000 SDR per capita as minima (see Annex).	No financial limits in respect of personal injury or death (para. 116).	No financial limits (para. 1264).
(6) Time limits for claims	Three years from awareness of injury; ten years from circulation of product (Arts. 10 and 11).	Similar to EEC (Arts. 6 and 7).	Ten years (English Law Com); no cut-off (Scottish Law Com) (para. 153; 160).	Similar to EEC and Strasbourg (para. 1269).
(7) Development risks	Defence under Art. 7 from which Member States may derogate (Art. 15(1)(b)).	Not available.	Not available if goods 'defective' as defined (para. 105).	Not available (para. 1259).
(8) Defences	Did not put product into circulation or not defective when put into circulation or not manufactured or distributed in the course of producer's business, or due to compliance with mandatory regulations (Art. 7), or contributory negligence by the victim (Art. 8(2)).	Contributory negligence (Art. 4). Also as EEC (Art. 5) (except re compliance with regulations).	(a) Voluntary assumption of risk. (b) Contributory negligence (paras. 106–110).	(a) Did not put product into circulation. (b) Ditto in course of a business. (c) Not defective when circulated. (d) Contributory negligence. N.B. No defence as to development risks or attempts to withdraw or official certification (paras. 1250–1260).
(9) Prohibition of contracting out	Yes (Art. 12).	Yes (Art. 8).	Yes (para. 112).	Yes (para. 1261).

The effect of this is to impose strict tortious liability on producers of goods which prove to be defective and which cause damage to persons or, in some circumstances, property, subject to certain defences.

The Bill had its first reading in the House of Lords on 19 November 1986 and received Royal Assent on 15 May 1987. The Committee stage, Report stage and Third Reading in the House of Commons were all curtailed to enable the Bill to be completed before the recess of Parliament for the election in June 1987. There was, therefore, very little chance to debate amendments in the Commons.

Part I of the 1987 Act came into force on 1 March 1988 and, by section 50(7), liability for defects under the Act only arises as regards those products supplied to others by their producers after that date. As the provisions of the 1987 Act are in addition to existing contractual and tortious rights (section 2(6)), this means that for new products supplied after 1 March 1988 there is potential liability under both the 1987 Act and the pre-existing law, whilst in the case of products supplied before 1 March 1988 only the pre-existing law is applicable. For many years it will, therefore, be important to know when a producer supplied a product before advice as to liability can be provided.

Before looking in detail at the liability created under the Act it is necessary to define two of the terms used.

Product. This is defined in section 1(2) as 'any goods or electricity'; goods being defined in section 45(1) as including substances (natural or artificial, in solid, liquid or gaseous form), growing crops, things comprised in land by virtue of being attached to it, ships, aircraft and vehicles.[15] In addition 'product' includes component parts and raw materials incorporated into finished products. Although buildings are included within the definition of goods, section 46(4) excludes from Part I 'supplying goods comprised in land where the supply is effected by the creation or disposal of an interest in land'. This means that if a building causes damage, for example by collapsing due to a design defect or defective construction, no claim can be made under the 1987 Act against the builder. However a claim may be made if any of the component parts of the building e.g. the brick, tiles, cement etc are defective and cause damage to persons or other property. This is as a result of section 46(3) which establishes that where goods are provided by their incorporation into buildings this

---

15 Note that this is a different definition from that under the Sale of Goods Act 1979, s. 61(1).

is a supply of goods. A detailed enquiry into issues of causation will therefore be needed where defects in a house cause claimable damage.

Producer. By section 1(2) a 'producer' of a product means:
   a) the person who manufactured it;
   b) in the case of a substance which has not been manufactured but has been won or abstracted, the person who won or abstracted it;
   c) in the case of a product which has not been manufactured, won or abstracted but essential characteristics of which are attributable to an industrial or other process having been carried out (for example in relation to agricultural produce), the person who carried out that process.

This definition covers: under a), the manufacturer; under b), producers of products like minerals and natural gas; and, under c), those who, for example, refine petroleum or process food, activities which cannot be described as 'manufacturing' in the usual sense. With regard to the processing of food there is much debate over such activities as canning and freezing – do these processes have the effect of giving the product 'essential characteristics', or are they simply a method of preserving the food, without affecting its characteristics? If the former is the case, then the person responsible for the canning or freezing will be a 'producer' and liability will fall on that person for defects in the food, whether these are caused by the processing itself or are inherent in the food. If the latter applies then the processor will not acquire the status of a 'producer' and will not, therefore, be liable for the defective food, even if his or her handling of it caused the defect to arise. It is necessary to consider defective foodstuffs in conjunction with section 2(4), discussed below.

Who is liable?

Section 2(1) places the liability for damage caused by defective products on three classes of person identified in subsection (2). These are a) producers of products (as defined in section 1(2), see above); b) certain own branders; and c) importers of products into the Community. In the case of an own brander liability arises if he has put his name on or uses a trade mark or distinguishing mark in relation to the product where he 'has held himself out to be the producer of the product' (section 2(2)(b)). Thus if, for example, a supermarket chain sells its own branded goods, representing itself as the producer and without revealing the actual manufacturer's name, this will result in the supermarket being liable as producer.[16] If the actual manufacturer's name is indicated then the supermarket will simply be a 'supplier' (see below). One slightly more problematic case is where supermarket X has products labelled as 'made for X', without revealing by whom they have been produced. Here it could be argued that the supermarket has not 'held [it]self out as the producer' and is therefore only a 'supplier'.

Where a defective product has been imported by someone into the Community from outside the Community in order, in the course of any business of his, to supply it to another, then that importer is liable for the product. If a non-Community product is imported into Great Britain via another Member State (e.g. Germany) then the liability will fall upon the person who imported the product into Germany. The action will depend upon the rules of private international law to determine who has jurisdiction and what laws are applicable. It is, therefore, important to all Community citizens how each Member State implements the Directive, in particular as regards the optional derogations.[17]

To deal with situations where the producer or importer may not readily be identifiable, section 2(3) places some responsibility on the supplier of goods. A supplier here is one who supplies[18] the defective goods to the person who suffers the damage, to the producer (in the case of component parts and raw materials) or any other person. The retailer of goods will clearly come under this definition. The supplier's liability only arises if: a) the person suffering damage asks the supplier to identify one or more persons falling under section 2(2) (i.e. producer, own brander or importer); b) that request is made within a reasonable period after the damage occurred and at a time when it is not reasonably practicable for the person making the request to identify all those persons; and c) the supplier fails, within a reasonable period of time after receiving the request to comply with the request or identify the person who supplied the product to him. It can be seen that the supplier's liability will not arise very often. It will need a product which does not bear marks identifying a

16 This considerably extends its liability. The strict liability for the quality of goods implied under the Sale of Goods Act 1979 only applies to those privy to the contract of sale (see ch. 5) and ordinary tortious actions require proof of negligence. Under the 1987 Act there is no privity requirement, anyone injured may sue, and without the need to prove negligence.

17 I.e. whether or not 'products' includes primary agricultural produce and game, the development risk defence and a ceiling for total liability for a producer of identical products with the same defect. See Annex III *Implementation of the EC Directive on Product Liability,* DTI, November 1985.

18 Defined widely in s. 46, including such things as sale, hire, hire-purchase, trading stamp redemption, work and materials contracts, prizes and gifts.

producer, own brander or importer and the supplier can completely discharge the liability either by identifying the person or persons requested or by identifying the person from whom the product was obtained. In the latter case the person suffering the damage would then have to repeat the process up the distribution chain until the person properly liable for the product is identified or no response is received to a request for information. It is easy to foresee practical difficulties arising over what is a reasonable period of time, both in terms of delays by the consumer as he or she slowly works back up the distribution chain and by the supplier on whom liability will rest if there is undue delay in providing the necessary information. Suppliers of goods from reputable manufacturers who clearly mark their goods have nothing to fear from section 2(3). It is only those who supply goods of undisclosed origin that may be affected by it.

The discussion of section 2 has so far omitted to mention one rather important exception to both subsections (2) and (3) contained in subsection (4). This is the controversial exclusion of persons who supply game or agricultural produce to others when at the time of supply it had not 'undergone an industrial process'. The Directive permitted Member States to include such products if wished (Art. 15(1)(a)) but the British Government chose not to.[19] The Act defines 'agricultural produce' as 'any produce of the soil, of stockfarming or of fisheries' (section 1(2)) but provides no definitions of 'game' or 'industrial process' and so litigation is likely over each, in particular the latter. It remains to be seen whether the shelling and freezing of peas or the filleting and freezing of fish are industrial processes. The situation is further complicated by the problem of identifying a 'producer', as mentioned above, for even if the food has 'undergone an industrial process', unless that process has changed the 'essential characteristics' of the item, the person processing it will not be classified as a 'producer' and no liability will be placed upon that person. It is interesting to note that the Act has not here followed the wording of the Directive, where under Art. 2 reference is made to products which 'have undergone initial processing'. This is, perhaps, a clearer concept than 'industrial processing'.[20]

The operation of subsection (4) will lead to many anomalies. If, for example, a person becomes ill as a result of eating potatoes which have absorbed a harmful chemical from the soil and the potatoes have been made into frozen chips or formed the topping on a ready-

19   For further discussion see Merkin *A Guide to the Consumer Protection Act 1987* paras. 2.2.3 and 3.3.3; Miller *Product Liability and Consumer Safety Encyclopaedia* para. III[254].

20   For a discussion of the arguments see *The Implementation of the EC Directive on Product Liability*, DTI, November 1985, paras. 28–34.

made shepherd's pie, then there may be a remedy against the producer under the 1987 Act. There will be no need to prove fault as the liability is strict, nor is there any need for the affected person to be privy to a contract. If instead the person bought unprocessed potatoes then the best action will be in contract under the Sale of Goods Act 1979, section 14, against the retailer. Again the liability is strict. If, however, the person was unfortunate enough to be served the potatoes, bought unprocessed by someone else, then the only chance of a remedy is to sue the producer under the pre-existing tort of negligence where proof of fault is required. It seems strange that, at a time when for health reasons people are encouraged to eat unprocessed foods, the law provides greater protection for those who consume processed foods which contain an inherent defect compared to identical foods which have not been processed. If the food has become defective due to the processing it has undergone then, providing the processor is a 'producer', clearly there is an action under the 1987 Act against the processor involved.

Under section 2 it is possible for more than one person to be responsible for the liability imposed. In these cases subsection (5) stipulates that such liability is joint and several. This will give an injured consumer a better chance of obtaining full compensation, for if there are several possible defendants it will mitigate the effects of insolvency of one of them. However, since all potential defendants in the chain will, if they are prudent, insure against the risks, the costs of this insurance will inevitably be passed on to consumers generally. There are, of course, rights of recourse, contribution and relief between co-defendants such as assemblers and component part manufacturers.[1]

When is there a 'defect'?

In order to have a claim under the Act it must be shown that the product in question is defective. Under section 3(1) of the 1987 Act there is a defect in a product 'if the safety of the product is not such as persons generally are entitled to expect'. The meaning of 'safety' is further explained in that subsection. It includes safety in the context of risk of damage to property as well as risk of death and personal injury;[2] also it refers to safety with respect to component parts comprised in the product. It is important that the definition is not confined to products which are dangerous to health as many will prove only to be a risk to property but may cause considerable damage and inconvenience.

---

1 See Civil Liability (Contribution) Act 1978, mentioned above p. 143.
2 See below for a discussion of what types of damage are recoverable.

The test of the expected level of safety is clearly an objective one and guidance is given in section 3(2) as to what sort of factors should be taken into account. First, under a) 'the manner in which, and purposes for which, the product has been marketed, its get-up, the use of any mark in relation to the product and any instructions for, or warnings with respect to, doing or refraining from doing anything with or in relation to the product'. This covers a number of matters. It is obviously important to examine the purposes for which a product is marketed, how and where it is advertised, whom it is aimed at (children or adults, expert users or amateurs), packaging (including safety catches, child-proof features, etc.), labels, instructions, warnings and the like.

The second consideration is 'b) what might reasonably be expected to be done with or in relation to the product'. In addition to examining the normal uses to which a product may be put, this requires manufacturers to take into account foreseeable misuses of their products and perhaps guard against some of them by warnings, etc. A product causing harm whilst being misused in an unreasonable or unforeseeable way would not, however, be considered as defective. An example may help to illustrate the effects of a) and b).

Typewriter correction fluid is marketed to do the job its name suggests and it would presumably meet the safety requirements when being so used. It is, however, capable of causing accidental harm if swallowed or inhaled and so it has long been the practice of manufacturers to indicate such risks on the labels. The accuracy and clarity of such warnings in preventing accidental harm are further factors to be examined in determining the safety of the product as a whole. An additional problem arises with this type of product in that it may be deliberately misused by inhaling it, sometimes with fatal results. Providing no encouragement for such misuse is given in the advertising of the product and clear warnings are given on the labels, the product is likely to satisfy the safety requirement even if it did cause harm when being misused. It is interesting to note that Tipp-Ex was reported to be considering removing its solvent-based thinner (used with the correction fluid) from the market following reported deaths from inhalation in England and Belgium.[3]

The third consideration specified in section 3(2) is 'c) the time when the product was supplied by its producer to another'. It is further stipulated that a product is not defective simply because a safer product is later produced. These are obviously important provisions for manufacturers; otherwise there would be a reluctance to improve the safety levels of products, lest earlier versions were

3   The Times, 17 October 1991.

then branded as defective. It also recognises that standards do improve over the years and that when judging the safety of a product it should be looked at, at least to some extent, in the light of expectations and standards current at its time of supply.

When considering the level of safety that people are entitled to expect from medicinal products particular problems arise. It is recognised that many drugs have side effects, some of which may be harmful in themselves. In deciding the safety issue a balance has to be drawn between the risks of harm from the illness compared to those from drugs. In the case of very serious illness a drug may satisfy the safety requirement despite its side effects whereas if used for minor illnesses it may not.[4] This cost-benefit analysis approach may well be relevant for other products also.[5]

'Damage'

Liability under Part I of the 1987 Act is for any 'damage' as defined in section 5. This covers death and personal injury and also loss or damage to any property including land (subsection (1)). 'Personal injury' is defined in section 45(1) as 'including any disease and any other impairment of a person's physical or mental condition'. It would seem, therefore, that claims for nervous shock are permissible. It is also important to note that there is no mention of being able to claim for pure economic loss, an important issue in many pre-Act negligence cases. The 1987 Act does not alter the law on this area in any way.

There are several restrictions on claims for property damage. First, under section 5(2), there is no liability for the loss of or damage to the defective product itself. Thus if the defective product self-destructs the only remedy available would be for the purchaser to sue in contract, there being no claim for such events under the law of negligence either. In addition there is no liability for any loss or damage to the whole or part of any product supplied with the defective product 'comprised in it'. This means that if a car is supplied with a defective tyre, which causes the car to crash, there is no liability for the loss of or damage to the car, nor, of course, for the tyre. In contrast if the tyre were supplied separately as a replacement then there would be liability for the damage to the car under the Act, though still not for the tyre itself.

The second restriction on property claims is under section 5(3). If the property, at the time it is damaged, is not:

---

4   *Implementation of EC Directive on Product Liability*, DTI, paras. 53–54.
5   See, for example, Miller *Product Liability and Consumer Safety Encyclopaedia* Div. III [121]; C Newdick (1987) 103 LQR 288 at 300.

    a) of a description of property ordinarily intended for private use, occupation or consumption; and

    b) intended by the person suffering the loss or damage mainly for his own private use, occupation or consumption

then there is no liability under the Act. It is necessary to look both at the nature of the property itself and the particular use to which it was being put at the time it suffered the damage in question.[6] Several significant product liability cases decided under the law of negligence would therefore be outside the scope of the 1987 Act, for example *Aswan Engineering Establishment Co v Lupdine Ltd*[7] and *Muirhead v Industrial Tank Specialities Ltd.*[8] The third restriction on property claims is that under section 5(4). The damage suffered to the property must exceed £275. The reason for this minimum limit is to prevent numerous small claims being pursued. It will, however, produce anomalies: a defective television set which explodes only destroying a £276 video will enable a claim to be made under Part I for the video, whereas if the video was worth £274 it will not.

    Section 5(5)-(7) assist in determining who has suffered property damage and when it occurred, an important consideration when limitation periods are involved (see below). Damage to property is deemed to occur at the earliest time someone who has an interest in the property has knowledge of the material facts about the loss or damage.

Defences

The 1987 Act provides a number of defences in section 4. In all of them it is up to the person proceeded against to establish the defence. First, under section 4(1)(a), it is a defence to show that the defect is *attributable* to compliance with any statutory requirement or Community obligation. This does not mean that by complying with statutory requirements (such as safety regulations under section 11[9]) there is an automatic defence. The defence only arises if, in complying with the regulations, this causes the defect. It is going to be unusual for a producer to be able to show that the consequence of complying with a statutory requirement or Community obligation is to make a product defective, especially as most such provisions are designed to make products more not less safe.

    The second defence, under section 4(1)(b), is that the person

---

6 It is unfortunate that yet another 'consumer use' definition is provided. The wording of the subsection does not correspond with that used in the Unfair Contract Terms Act 1977, s. 5 nor that in s. 12 of that Act, see pp. 135 and 111.

7 [1987] 1 All ER 135, [1987] 1 WLR 1, CA.

8 [1986] QB 507, [1985] 3 All ER 705, CA. See ante p. 133.

9 See ch. 9, p. 233.

proceeded against did not at any time supply the product to another. This will cover cases of mistaken identity, where a wrong distributor or manufacturer is sued, and products which cause harm before they leave the producer, for example to the producer's employees. It would also apply if the goods were stolen from the producer and then distributed. The Department of Trade and Industry Consultation Document[10] suggests drugs used in trials before marketing would be covered here. They are not 'supplied' in terms of the definition in section 46.

Under section 4(1)(c) the third defence has two limbs. The only supply by the person proceeded against must be otherwise than in the course of a business of that person and either s 2(2) does not apply to that person (i.e. not a producer, own brander or Community importer, discussed above) or, if it does apply, that the activity was not done to make a profit. Put simply it is a defence that the person supplied the goods privately, for example selling one's own goods second-hand or giving gifts to friends. Also, even if the person is a producer, etc. of the goods as long as they were not distributed to make a profit for that person there is a defence. This provides a vital defence for, for example, ladies who make cakes and jams for Womens' Institute stalls.

A fourth defence is that the defect did not exist in the product at the relevant time (section 4(1)(d)). The relevant time is explained under section 4(2). For electricity it is when it was generated, before transmission or distribution. Electricity companies will be able to use this defence to avoid liability under the Act for damage caused by voltage surges or falls caused by distribution faults. For defendants falling under section 2(2) (see above) the relevant time for all other products is when the person supplied the product to another. This means that a producer, own brander or Community importer will not be liable for defects caused by others further down the distribution chain, such as unauthorised removal of labels, warnings, etc. by suppliers, alterations to or adaption of the products which cause them to become defective, subsequent deterioration of food-stuffs, etc. This is akin to a plea of *novus actus interveniens*.

For defendants who do not fall under section 2(2) such as retailers, the relevant time for seeing if a defect exists is when the product was last supplied by someone coming within section 2(2). A retailer will have no liability under the Act if, when the goods were last supplied by the producer, own brander or Community importer, they were not defective. If they were defective at that time the retailer will incur the liability of a supplier as discussed above. This will mean that

---

10 *Implementation of EC Directive on Product Liability*, para. 56.

where a product becomes defective by, for example, a retailer removing a warning label, the producer will have a defence under section 4(1)(d) as there was no defect when it left the producer. The retailer will also have the same defence for the same reason, the defect being absent at the relevant time (when the product left the producer). In such a case the victim of the defective product will be without a remedy under the Act. It would still be open to the injured person to take a negligence action against the retailer.[11]

Perhaps the most important and certainly the most controversial[12] defence is that under section 4(1)(e). This states:

> that the state of scientific and technical knowledge at the relevant time was not such that a producer of products of the same description as the product in question might be expected to have discovered the defect if it had existed in his products while they were under his control.

The Directive made the adoption of this defence optional for Member States (Art. 15) and despite strenuous attempts by the consumer lobby to have it rejected, the Government included it in the Act. The defence is sometimes referred to as the 'development risks' defence; on other occasions as the 'state of the art' defence. Both of these expressions can have several different meanings and this can lead to confusion. Here 'development risks' will be used to cover the defence under section 4(1)(e) as it more accurately reflects the nature of the defence.

The test is objective, based on a reasonable producer, so the resources and experience of the particular producer will not be relevant. The words 'expected to have discovered the defect' may refer either to the issue of whether any producer ought to have been looking for the particular defect (such as the presence of the AIDS HIV virus in blood before much was known about it) or alternatively the problem of devising suitable tests to discover if a contemplated or known defect is present (e.g. tests for screening blood products for HIV virus). It is suggested that just because a producer follows all the tests and procedures fellow producers use, this may not in itself be sufficient to establish the defence if further testing would be

11 See, for example, *Holmes v Ashford* [1950] 2 All ER 76, CA; *Kubach v Hollands* [1937] 3 All ER 907, QBD.
12 See M & H pp. 199–202; C Newdick 'The Development Risk Defence of the Consumer Protection Act 1987' (1988) 47 CLJ 455; 482 HL Official Report (5th series) col. 1003 et seq (2nd Reading, 8 December 1986); 483 HL Official Report (5th series) col. 819 et seq (Committee, 20 January 1987). The suggestion of such a defence was rejected by both the Law Commission, Law Com. No. 82, Cmnd. 6831, para. 105 and the Pearson Commission. Cmnd. 7054, para. 1259.

expected, given the state of scientific and technical knowledge at the time.

The 'relevant time' is that defined under section 4(2) (see above) and here it is the time when the product was *supplied* by the producer, not when it was manufactured. This means a producer has to keep abreast of developments until the product leaves the producer's control. As has been seen earlier, just because safer products are subsequently produced this does not necessarily mean that a product was defective when put into circulation. In such cases there is no need for the producer to resort to the development risks defence; instead it can be argued that the claimant has failed to establish a defective product under section 3 or, if this is unsuccessful, section 4(1)(d) above can be raised. The main area of likely argument over the applicability of the development risks defence is that of new drugs with unexpected side effects. If all that is required by the courts to satisfy the defence is that producers perform the standard tests drug companies generally undertake then much of the anticipated benefit of the introduction of strict product liability will be lost. All that would be achieved would be effectively a reversal of the burden of proof with the producer having to show the absence of negligence rather than the victim having to establish its presence. If, on the other hand, the defence is applied stringently as the Department of Trade and Industry assert will be the case[13] then it will be difficult for a producer to establish that a particular defect could not have been discovered.

The final defence under section 4(1)(f) concerns component parts. It is a defence if the defect is in a finished product in which the component part is incorporated and the defect is wholly attributable either to the design of the finished product or to compliance by the component producer with instructions provided by the producer of the finished product. To qualify for the defence the component producer must have no responsibility for the design of the finished product or be simply following specifications which prove to be unsuitable. The producer of the finished product will in such cases be liable for the defects.

Linked with the defences provided under section 4 is the availability of a plea of contributory negligence on the part of the person injured. Section 6(4) applies the Law Reform (Contributory Negligence) Act 1945 and the Fatal Accidents Act 1976, section 5, (relating to contributory negligence) to claims under Part I. The claims of a person suffering damage as a result of a defective product can

---

13 *Implementation of the EC Directive on Product Liability*, para. 22.

therefore be reduced (or even completely removed) if that person was in some way to blame for the harm suffered.[14]

Limitation periods

Section 6(6) and Schedule 1 operate to amend the Limitation Act 1980 and to introduce time limits for actions under Part I of the 1987 Act. There is an overall cut-off point for any proceedings to be brought which is ten years after the 'relevant time' (Limitation Act 1980, section 11A(3) as inserted by Schedule 1, para. 1 of the 1987 Act). The 'relevant time' is that defined in section 4 of the 1987 Act. For producers, own branders and importers it is the time when they supplied the product to another. For others, for example retailers, it is the time when the product was last supplied by a producer, own brander or importer (see above). A right of action is 'extinguished' after the ten years, irrespective of whether or not it accrued and whether or not time had begun to run under section 11A(4) (see below). This fixed cut-off point assists producers to know the likely time period during which they can expect claims to be made and may assist in obtaining insurance against potential liability. It will mean that victims of products which may take many years to demonstrate their harmful effects, such as drugs and chemicals, may have lost their right of action long before they even realise that any harm has been suffered. In such cases there would, however, still be the possibility of an action in the tort of negligence.[15] It is clear that producers, importers and own branders will have to keep very careful and detailed records of when they supplied products if they are to take full advantage of the ten year limitation on claims.

The second limitation on actions is contained in the Limitation Act 1980, section 11A(4) (as inserted by the 1987 Act, Schedule 1). Claims for personal injuries or property damage cannot be brought more than three years after the later of:

a) the date on which the cause of action accrued; and
b) the date of knowledge of the injured party or, in the case of loss or damage to property, the date of knowledge of the plaintiff or (if earlier) of any person in whom his cause of action was previously vested.

The cause of action accrues when the damage or loss is suffered. In many cases this will be immediately appreciated by the victim and so

---

14   The risk of harm from a product may be so obvious (e.g. sharp knives) or the acts of the person harmed so unreasonable (e.g. solvent abusers) that the product is not found to be defective anyway. See above p. 156.
15   See Limitation Act 1980, s. 14 and, for example, *Wright v Dunlop Rubber Co Ltd* (1972) 13 KIR 255, CA (long-term carcinogenic properties of chemicals).

time will begin to run from then. If, however, the victim is not immediately aware of the damage then the alternative starting date may apply. The 'date of knowledge' is defined in the Limitation Act 1980, section 14(1A) (inserted by the 1987 Act, Schedule 1, para. 3). This requires knowledge about the damage caused by the defect, the causal link between the damage and the alleged defect and the identity of the defendant. Special provisions are included in both the amendments to the Limitation Act 1980 and in section 6 of the 1987 Act to cover the position where the victim has died.

Exclusion of liability

Section 7 of the 1987 Act prevents the exclusion or limitation of the liability of a person under Part I of the Act, whether by any contract term, notice or any other provision. It would, however, be open to a producer to prevent any liability arising by providing detailed warnings and instructions so as to ensure that the product in question is not found to be defective (see above).

Conclusion

The implementation of the EC Directive on Product Liability in Part I of the Consumer Protection Act 1987 undoubtedly simplifies the plaintiff's task in establishing liability, since fault no longer has to be proved and often there will be several potential defendants to sue. By no means all the difficulties have disappeared however. In particular the allegation that a product is defective may be strongly contested with lengthy debate over the level of safety that persons generally are entitled to expect. Also it will still be necessary to prove that the damage incurred was attributable to the defect, and problems over causation have in England and in other jurisdictions given rise to great difficulty in complex cases. Whilst it is reasonable to provide for a reduction in damages if the plaintiff has contributed to the accident, this also inevitably brings in the proof of fault and complicates the trial process. Above all in cases of new products with unexpected defects the availability of the development risks defence will raise the whole issue of fault and may result in the new strict liability tort action being much less of a revolutionary development than expected. In keeping with the provisions of Art. 15 of the EC Directive (which enables modification of the development risks defence under the Directive) section 8 of the 1987 Act provides a power to modify Part I of the Act by Order in Council. It may be that some time in the future the defence will be removed. It is interesting to note that the EC Commission is unhappy about some aspects of implementation of the Directive in United Kingdom law, including the development risks defence. The Commission has not yet decided whether or not to institute formal proceedings against the United Kingdom Government.[16]

The balance sheet reflected by the Consumer Protection Act 1987 nevertheless shows a clear gain by consumers and others injured by defective products. The cost of the new provisions is likely to be an increase in the price of all products, safe or unsafe, approximately equivalent to the cost of insurance of the risks. It is to be hoped that any such increase will be small. The benefit to many injured consumers will, however, be great. Although retailers may not in future be burdened with quite so many claims regarding damage done by products, it is interesting to note that the retailer's strict contractual liability will remain more onerous than the producer's strict tortious liability since only the latter will be able in some cases to plead the development risks defence and/or contributory negligence.

16   See (1991) 14 Consumer Law Today, Issue 12, p. 1.

7 The supply of services

Chapters 5 and 6 have been concerned with consumer transactions involving goods. Where the contract between consumer and supplier is one of services, the hallmark of which is that the consideration consists of value other than the primary (as opposed to incidental) supply of goods,[1] and the services are defective, the consumer's legal rights again depend on a) any express or implied terms applicable to the contract of services, and b) any right of action he or she might have in tort, particularly the tort of negligence.

1. IMPLIED TERMS

Prior to 1982, the implied terms in services contracts depended largely on the common law. Following the recommendations of the National Consumer Council in its report *Service Please – Services and the law: a consumer view* (October 1981) to codify certain of the common law implied terms, a Private Member's Bill was introduced in January 1982. This received Royal Assent on 13 July 1982 as the Supply of Goods and Services Act 1982 ('the 1982 Act'). Part I of the Act is concerned with the implied terms in contracts for the supply of goods,[2] whilst Part II, which came into force on 4 July 1983,[3] involves the supply of services.

In July 1982 the Law Commission was asked by the Lord Chancellor to consider if any reforms were needed to the implied terms in contracts for the supply of a service, the exclusion of liability and the consequences of breach and to make recommendations. The Report (Law Com. No. 156) was published in April 1986 and concluded that no immediate amendment of the 1982 Act was called for and that it would be premature to consider changes to the law concerning exclusion clauses.

---

1 Contracts for work and materials are mentioned above, ch. 5.
2 See ch. 5.
3 Section 20(3) and the Supply of Goods and Services Act 1982 (Commencement) Order 1982, S.I. 1982/1770.

Contract for the supply of a service

Section 12 of the 1982 Act defines a contract for the supply of a service as 'a contract under which a person ("the supplier") agrees to carry out a service'. Subsection (2) makes it clear that contracts of service or apprenticeships are not included in the definition. It does not matter that the contract may also involve the transfer or hire of goods, for example work and materials contracts, and any consideration will suffice, it need not be money (subsection (3)). Power is given to the Secretary of State for Trade and Industry to exempt, by statutory instrument, specified services from all or any of the implied terms (subsections (4) and (5)).[4] It can be seen, therefore, that a very wide range of contracts for services are included within the definition, from hairdressers and shoe repairers to solicitors, architects and doctors providing private medical treatment, and from high-street consumer deals to industrial services such as cleaning and security.[5]

Reasonable care and skill

Where advice is given which falls below the standard of expertise reasonably to be expected, or in the common case where services are defectively performed, what remedy has the disappointed consumer in contract? It must be shown that there is an express or implied term that the service would be rendered with reasonable care and skill and that the supplier is in breach of this term. If the contract is one where the supplier is acting in the course of a business[6] then section 13 of the 1982 Act implies such a term. This reflects the common law position and there are many decisions prior to the Act to give guidance. The standard of care in contracts is the same as that in tort:

> the standard of the ordinary skilled man exercising and professing to have that special skill . . . It is well-established law that it is sufficient if he exercises the ordinary skill of an ordinary competent man exercising that particular art.[7]

---

4   See discussion re s. 13 below for orders made to date. This power to exclude can be used to ensure that the legislation does not extend the existing law, merely codify it.

5   See Law Com. No. 156, paras. 2.7–2.17; and generally M & H pp. 114–127; G Woodroffe *Goods and Services - The New Law* (1982); R. G. Lawson *The Supply of Goods and Services Act 1982* (1982).

6   Defined in s. 18(1) as including 'a profession and the activities of any government department or local or public authority'.

7   McNair J, *Bolam v Friern Hospital Management Committee* [1957] 2 All ER 118, at 121, [1957] 1 WLR 582, at 586, QBD; as approved in *Whitehouse v Jordan* [1981] 1 All ER 267, [1981] 1 WLR 246, HL.

The test is an objective one – the supplier of the service must come up to the standard of an ordinary supplier of that type; if special skills are claimed then the supplier is judged against someone possessing that special skill.[8]

Any attempt to exclude the implied term is permissible (section 16(1)), but may be subject to the Unfair Contract Terms Act 1977, section 2.[9] In addition, certain types of services have been excluded from the operation of section 13 by statutory instrument. These are:

1) the services of an advocate in court or before any tribunal, inquiry or arbitrator and in carrying out preliminary work directly affecting the conduct of the hearing;[10]
2) the services of directors of companies in their capacity as such;[11]
3) the services of directors of building societies;[12]
4) the services of members of the management committees of industrial and provident societies;[12] and
5) the services of an arbitrator (including an umpire).[13]

In many cases it is not material whether a professional or skilled contractor is sued in contract for breach of the implied term above or whether action is taken for breach of a duty of care using the tort of negligence. It may be of significance, however, where limitation periods are involved since time starts to run from when the term is broken in contract and from when the damage is sustained in tort.[14] On many occasions the courts have considered whether or not to restrict claims against professional people privately engaged by a client to those in contract when there is the possibility of both

---

8 See Law Com. No. 156 paras. 2.19–2.27.
9 See below p. 175.
10 The Supply of Services (Exclusion of Implied Terms) Order 1982, S.I. 1982/1771, art. 2(1), see below pp. 184–185.
11 Ibid, art. 2(2). For the common law liability of directors see *Re City Equitable Fire Insurance Co Ltd* [1925] Ch 407, [1924] All ER Rep 485.
12 The Supply of Services (Exclusion of Implied Terms) Order 1983, S.I. 1983/902. For the common law position see *Sheffield and South Yorkshire Permanent Building Society v Aizlewood* (1889) 44 Ch D 412.
13 The Supply of Services (Exclusion of Implied Terms) Order 1985, S.I. 1985/1. The common law position is governed by *Sutcliffe v Thackrah* [1974] AC 727, [1974] 1 All ER 859, HL, and *Arenson v Casson Beckman Rutley & Co* [1977] AC 405, [1975] 3 All ER 901, HL. See also 'The Judicial Immunity of Arbitrators' F. Miller (1991) 141 NLJ 633.
14 In the case of latent damage, in the tort of negligence a plaintiff may obtain the benefit of the Limitation Act 1980, s. 14A which allows three years from the date of 'the knowledge required to bring an action' or six years from accrual. This is not permitted where the action is based in contract for breach of a negligence based term, see *Iron Trade Mutual Insurance Co Ltd v J K Buckenham Ltd* [1990] 1 All ER 808, QBD.

contractual and tortious liability arising. The restrictive approach was favoured for many years, the argument being that 'where the complaint made is of failure by him to do the very thing which he contracted to do, there is no room for saying that any duty other than the contractual duty has been broken'.[15] In *Clark v Kirby-Smith*[16] it was held, following 'a line of cases going back for nearly 150 years' that clients' causes of action against their solicitors were in contract not tort; similarly, the relationship which created the duty of exercising reasonable skill and care by architects to their clients arose out of the contract.[17] The point was reiterated and the duty again defined in *Greaves & Co Contractors Ltd v Baynham, Meikle & Partners*[18] by the Court of Appeal when explaining that whilst a term that parts of a building would be fit for the purpose that the parties had in mind could be implied in this particular case, the general duty 'is cast by law on every professional man holding himself out as an expert in any particular field', namely the contractual duty as described by McNair J in *Bolam v Friern Hospital Management Committee*.[19]

In contrast in *Midland Bank Trust Co Ltd v Hett, Stubbs and Kemp*[20] Oliver J refused to follow the restrictive approach and held a firm of solicitors liable in tort (as well as contract) for neglecting to register an option to purchase land. This decision was applied regarding insurance contracts in *Forsikringsaktieselskapet Vesta v Butcher*[1] and medical treatment in *Thake v Maurice*.[2] Subsequent cases involving solicitors have also accepted the joint contractual and tortious liability including *Foster v Outred & Co*[3] and *Bell v Peter*

---

15 Counsel *arguendo* in *Bagot v Stevens Scanlan & Co Ltd* [1966] 1 QB 197, QBD.
16 [1964] Ch 506, [1964] 2 All ER 835, Ch D, see also *Heywood v Wellers* [1976] QB 446, [1976] 1 All ER 300, CA (solicitors liable for client's distress and inconvenience amounting to breach of contract when not properly conducting litigation).
17 *Bagot v Stevens Scanlan & Co Ltd* [1966] 1 QB 197, [1964] 3 All ER 577, QBD.
18 [1975] 3 All ER 99 at 106, CA, per Geoffrey Lane LJ.
19 [1957] 2 All ER 118 at 121, QBD. See above, p. 166.
20 [1979] Ch 384, [1978] 3 All ER 571, Ch D; Cheshire Fifoot & Furmston's *Law of Contract* (12th Edn.) pp. 280–281; Jones *Textbook on Tort* (3rd Edn) pp. 6–7. See also *Ross v Caunters* [1980] Ch 297, [1979] 3 All ER 580, Ch D, solicitor held liable in negligence for financial loss to third party caused when that person's spouse executed will under which testator left her property, thus disqualifying her from any benefit. See also *Batty v Metropolitan Property Realisations Ltd* [1978] QB 554, [1978] 2 All ER 445, CA, discussed below, p. 171.
 1 [1986] 2 All ER 488 at 507, QBD, [1988] 2 All ER 43 at 47, CA.
 2 [1986] QB 644, [1986] 1 All ER 497, CA (doctor liable in negligence for failing to warn of risks of reversal of a vasectomy, performed as a private operation).
 3 [1982] 2 All ER 753, [1982] 1 WLR 86, CA.

Browne & Co.[4] In the latter case doubt was expressed over the advisability of concurrent liability when Mustill LJ declared:

> I think it a pity that English law has elected to recognise concurrent rights of action in contract and tort. Other legal systems seem to manage quite well by limiting attention to the contractual obligations which are, after all, the foundation of the relationship between the professional man and his client: as for example, in the case of French law, via the doctrine of non cumul. That precisely the same breach of precisely the same organisation should be capable of generating causes of action which arise at different times is in my judgment an anomaly which our law could well do without. Nevertheless the law is clear and we must apply it.[5]

This concern over concurrent liability had already been expressed by the Privy Council in *Tai Hing Cotton Mill Ltd v Liu Chong King Bank Ltd*[6] where Lord Scarman indicated that:

> Their Lordships do not believe that there is anything to the advantage of the law's development in searching for a liability in tort where the parties are in a contractual relationship. This is particularly so in a commercial relationship.

The debate concerning the existence of concurrent liability is likely to continue, with legislation as the only satisfactory method of resolving the issue.

Time for performance

Where the contract for the supply of a service is one where the supplier is acting in the course of a business then, if no time for carrying out the service has been fixed by the contract, nor any method for determining it stipulated, there is an implied term under section 14(1) of the 1982 Act that the service will be carried out within a reasonable time.[7] It is a question of fact what is a reasonable time (section 14(2)). A pre-Act example of this can be seen in *Charnock v Liverpool Corpn*.[8] Here a car which should have been repaired in five weeks took eight weeks. Damages were awarded for breach of the implied term of completing the work within a reasonable time.

---

4   [1990] 2 QB 495, [1990] 3 All ER 124, CA. Here the decision in *Midland Bank Trust Co Ltd v Hett, Stubbs and Kemp* [1979] Ch 384, [1978] 3 All ER 571, Ch D, was not followed on the question of time limits. Damage accrued in both contract and tort at the time when a solicitor negligently failed to protect his client's equitable interest in a property, there being no continuing contractual relationship between the solicitor and client, unlike in the *Midland Bank* case. For further comment on limitation aspects and negligent solicitors see H. Brayne and G. Martin (1991) 88 LS Gaz, No. 11, p. 25.
5   At pp. 511, 134.
6   [1986] AC 80 at 107, [1985] 2 All ER 947 at 957, PC; see (1986) 83 LS Gaz 3348.
7   See M & H pp. 118–121; Law Com. No. 156, paras. 2.28–2.29.
8   [1968] 3 All ER 473, [1968] 1 WLR 1498, CA; M & H p. 119.

Consideration

Section 15 of the 1982 Act implies a term, in any contract for the supply of a service, where the consideration has not been provided for by the contract or by a course of dealings, that the customer will pay the supplier a reasonable charge.[9] It is a question of fact as to what is a reasonable charge (section 15(2)). The section applies irrespective of whether or not the supplier is in the course of a business. Reference is made to 'consideration' and 'charge' as there is no requirement for payment to be in the form of money in such contracts.[10] Services may be provided for goods and/or other services, as well as money. Section 15 does not, however, deal with the situation where an exorbitant charge has been agreed under the contract.[11]

Stricter and additional obligations

The terms implied under Part II of the 1982 Act are not exhaustive.[12] Section 16(3) preserves any rule of law imposing a stricter duty than that under sections 13 and 14 and any additional implied terms which are not inconsistent with Part II. Also by section 16(4) it is 'subject to any other enactment which defines or restricts the rights, duties or liabilities arising in connection with a service of any description'. An area where liability has been extended beyond that provided by the 1982 Act is that involving the fitness of buildings.

Fitness of buildings

At common law 'it is quite clear . . . that when a purchaser buys a house from a builder who contracts to build it, there is a threefold implication: that the builder will do his work in a good and workmanlike manner; that he will supply good and proper materials; and that it will be reasonably fit for human habitation'.[13]

This common law duty was reinforced and expanded by the provisions of the Defective Premises Act 1972.[14] Under section 1, a person taking on work for or in connection with the provision of a dwelling (by erection, conversion or enlargement) owes a duty to the

---

9 See M & H pp. 121–123; Law Com. No. 156 paras. 2.30–2.33.
10 Section 12(3).
11 See below p. 187 for the position re solicitor's charges.
12 See M & H pp. 123–127; Law Com. No. 156 paras. 2.3–2.6 and 2.34–2.36.
13 Per Denning MR in *Hancock v B. W. Brazier (Anerley) Ltd* [1966] 2 All ER 901 at 903, CA.
14 The Act substantially implemented proposals of the Law Commission's *Report on Civil Liability of Vendors Etc. for Defective Premises* (Law Com. No. 40).

person ordering the work and to subsequent owners of a legal or equitable interest in the dwelling to see that the work is done in a workmanlike or professional manner, with proper materials so that the dwelling will be fit for habitation when completed. Any cause of action in respect of a breach of this duty is deemed to accrue when the dwelling was completed (section 1(5)). The duty cannot validly be excluded or restricted by agreement (section 6(3)). Section 3 also abolished the common law rule that vendors, lessors and other contractors were generally not liable in negligence if they carried out the work before the ownership of an interest in the land of a person subsequently injured by that negligence.

As to the question of 'fitness for habitation', in *Batty v Metropolitan Property Realisations Ltd*[15] developers acquired a site on a hill on which builders erected houses. The site appeared to be suitable, but there was evidence from surrounding land that land slips might occur. The plaintiffs took a long lease of a house on a plateau from the developers, who expressly warranted that the house had been built in an efficient and workmanlike manner and of proper materials and so as to be fit for habitation. Three years later the garden of the house was affected by a severe land slip, and the evidence showed that the house would also be affected by further slippages within the next ten years, rendering it valueless. It was held that the developers were liable under their warranty of fitness for habitation, which extended beyond the mere manner of building or materials used. The developers were liable in contract and in tort.

In the case of buildings for commercial purposes the courts have, on occasions, implied a term that the building should be fit for the purpose for which it was required.[16] This imposes on the builder 'a higher duty than is ordinarily implied in a contract for the design of a building by an architect. The latter, like the engineer, solicitor, doctor and other professionally qualified persons, has only to use reasonable care and skill'.[17]

15 [1978] QB 554, [1978] 2 All ER 445, CA. The builders were also liable in negligence for not having conducted sufficient tests on the site having regard to the defects in the surrounding area. Following *Murphy v Brentwood District Council* [1991] 1 AC 398, [1990] 2 All ER 908, [1990] 3 WLR 414, HL, this aspect of the decision has been overruled as it involved pure economic loss, see below p. 190.

16 *Greaves & Co (Contractors) Ltd v Baynham, Meikle & Partners* [1975] 3 All ER 99, [1975] 1 WLR 1095, CA; M & H p. 123; *Basildon District Council v J E Lesser (Properties) Ltd* [1985] QB 839, [1985] 1 All ER 20, QBD.

17 Judge John Newey QC, *Basildon District Council v J E Lesser (Properties) Ltd* [1985] 1 All ER 20 at 26, QBD.

Damages

The principles on which the courts assess damages in cases of breach of contract for the supply of goods have been discussed in ch. 5. Similar principles apply to breach of contract to provide services, the damages recoverable being in respect of consequences 'arising naturally, i.e. according to the usual course of things' from the breach, or 'such as may reasonably be supposed to have been in the contemplation of both parties, at the time they made the contract, as the probable result of the breach of it' under the rule in *Hadley v Baxendale* referred to above. On the face of it, because of the principles of privity of contract, where for instance the husband pays for a 'package' holiday for himself and his family which proves sufficiently irreconcilable with the tour operator's promises to amount to a breach of contract, the husband's claim would be limited to claiming in respect of his own losses and disappointment. But the Court of Appeal held in *Jackson v Horizon Holidays Ltd*[18] that in these circumstances the husband could recover not only in respect of his own discomfort and disappointment, but also that of his wife and children.

The Law Commission, in its Report *Implied Terms in Contracts for the Supply of Services*,[19] examined the existing remedies and canvassed the creation of new remedies. It concluded that any proposals for change would be premature and inappropriate.

2. NEGLIGENCE

The basis of this tort has already been discussed in connection with defective goods. As regards services, there are many cases where the provision of defective services may involve liability both for breach of a term of the contract between the consumer and provider and also in tort and some where, since there is no contract between the parties, liability is in tort alone, probably the tort of negligence. Examples of the latter are where there is breach of the limited duty of care by persons taking it upon themselves to give advice or information to someone who they should have known would rely on it and without any effective disclaimer, under the principle formulated in *Hedley*

---

18 [1975] 3 All ER 92, [1975] 1 WLR 1468, CA; M & H p. 22. But see also the criticism of the *Jackson* case in *Woodar Investment Development Ltd v Wimpey Construction (UK) Ltd* [1980] 1 All ER 571, HL; M & H p. 24. See H. Tomlinson and J. Wardell 'Damages in Holiday Cases', (1988) 85 LS Gaz No. 3, p. 28 for a number of examples of amounts of damages awarded.

19 Law Com. No. 156, April 1986, Part IV.

Byrne & Co Ltd v Heller & Partners Ltd[20] or in cases of medical negligence where a National Health patient may have no contract with the doctor or alternatively may contract privately with a doctor or surgeon for an operation on his child (the plaintiff being the child).

Examples of situations where providers of services are liable to consumers, and indeed any 'neighbour' injured by the negligence under the *Donoghue v Stevenson* principle, are legion. A repairer of goods owes a duty of care to their users, breach of which, in *Haseldine v Daw & Sons Ltd*,[1] was expressed as involving i) a want of care on his part in the performance of the work he was employed to do, and ii) circumstances which show that the employer (i.e. the customer) will be left in ignorance of the danger which the lack of care has created. The latter stipulation seems appropriate only to the type of situation under review in this case – i.e. where the plaintiff was injured in a lift that fell down a shaft because of a defective repair by the landlord's agents. It is part of the general principle that 'a repairer of a chattel stands in no different position from that of a manufacturer, and does owe a duty to a person who, in the ordinary course, may be expected to make use of the thing repaired'.[2]

Another fertile source of difficulty arises where the customer's property is left with the provider of the service and is misappropriated. It is an advantage of suing in negligence that under the principle of vicarious liability an employer is liable in respect of the torts committed by his employees in the course of employment. There may, therefore, be a good case for suing the owner of a restaurant or other place where the customer's goods are left and from where the theft of them is known to have been effected by an employee. The nature of the duty of care where the goods the subject matter of the bailment are lost or damaged was explained by Denning MR in *Morris v C W Martin & Sons Ltd*,[3] (where the customer's mink coat had been left with a furrier for cleaning and he sent it, with her consent, to the defendants where it was stolen by one of their employees). If the bailment is a gratuitous one, for example where a coat is left in a host's hall and stolen by a servant, the host is not liable because he is under no duty to prevent it being stolen, but only to 'keep it as his own'.[4] Somewhat similarly, if an actor's clothes are stolen from his theatre dressing room owing to a negligent porter

---

20 [1964] AC 465, [1963] 2 All ER 575, HL.
 1 [1941] 2 KB 343, [1941] 3 All ER 156, CA.
 2 Ibid per Goddard LJ.
 3 [1966] 1 QB 716, [1965] 2 All ER 725, CA.
 4 See *Coggs v Bernard* (1703) 2 Ld Raym 909 at 914 per Holt CJ — 'so far is the law from being unreasonable as to charge a man for doing such a friendly act for his friend'.

allowing a thief to enter, the employing theatre is not liable for the loss because the relationship of master and servant gives rise to no duty to protect the actor's belongings from theft (nor is the theatre proprietor a bailee of the clothes).[5] But where the bailment is for reward, as it will be when a consumer enters into a contract for the cleaning of clothes, it is the bailee's duty to take reasonable care to keep the bailed goods safe, and this duty cannot be delegated to a servant. The bailee's only defence is to show that the loss was without any fault on his or his servants' part. And in this particular case it has been held that a sub-bailee owes to the owner all the duties of a bailee for reward and could be sued successfully for the misappropriation by the servant to whom the master gave the duty of taking reasonable care (but not, apparently, if it had been by some other unconnected servant). In the case of thefts of the customers' goods from restaurants it is not always certain that there has been sufficient delivery of possession to the restaurant proprietor to constitute a bailment, as opposed to a mere licence whereunder the owner is permitted to leave possessions on the premises. But if there is a bailment, the bailor may be held responsible for loss either because of the breach of the obligation to take reasonable care imposed by the law of bailment or for negligence.[6] Vehicles left in car parks can also give rise to problems of whether there has been a bailment or a mere licence. In *Ashby v Tolhurst*[7] it was held that a car parked in the defendant's car park in return for a shilling fee and a 'Car Park Ticket' was not bailed to the defendant and that he was not liable for its theft; an exemption clause in any event absolved the defendant from liability for loss or damage to cars. Likewise in *Fred Chappell Ltd v National Car Parks*[8] the payment of £2, retention of the keys by the owner and no actual transfer of custody when parking in an open car park, without a barrier, did not result in the creation of a bailment. This was despite the inappropriate wording of the parking ticket which referred to 'misdelivery' and 'right to refuse to release

5   See e.g. *Deyong v Shenburn* [1946] KB 227, [1946] 1 All ER 226, CA; *Edwards v West Herts Group Hospital Management Committee* [1957] 1 All ER 541, [1957] 1 WLR 415, CA.

6   See *Ultzen v Nicols* [1894] 1 QB 92 (restaurant proprietor liable for loss of diner's coat hung on a hook behind him by a waiter). See also *Samuel v Westminster Wine Co Ltd* [1959] CLY 173.

7   [1937] 2 KB 242, [1937] 2 All ER 837, CA; M & H p. 132, followed in *Tinsley v Dudley* [1951] 2 KB 18, [1951] 1 All ER 252, CA. But see now the Unfair Contract Terms Act 1977, s. 2(2), below.

8   (1987) Times, 22 May QBD. Here, obiter, the judge decided that a term purporting to reverse the burden of proof in respect of any alleged breach of bailment would be reasonable under the Unfair Contract Terms Act 1977, s. 2(2) (below) considering the small charge, the nature of facilities offered and the difficulties in protecting the vehicles.

any vehicle'. Handing over keys or putting a car in an hotel's covered garage will normally[9] give rise to a bailment and the bailee must then disprove negligence.

Avoidance of liability for negligence

Finally on the topic of negligence, it is appropriate to draw attention to the important reform effected by the Unfair Contract Terms Act 1977, section 2.[10] This section was based on the recommendations of the Law Commission in their Second Report on Exemption Clauses (1975).

Section 2 provides that 1) a person cannot by reference to any contract term or notice exclude or restrict his liability for death or personal injury resulting from negligence, and 2) in the case of other loss or damage, a person cannot so exclude or restrict his liability for negligence except in so far as the contract term or notice satisfies the requirement of reasonableness. This means by virtue of section 11(1), that the term must be regarded by the court as a fair and reasonable one to be included having regard to the circumstances which were, or ought reasonably to have been, known to or in the contemplation of the parties when the contract was made. In the case of a non-contractual notice, section 11(3) indicates that 'it should be fair and reasonable to allow reliance on it, having regard to all the circumstances obtaining when the liability arose or (but for the notice) would have arisen'. Section 2 also makes it clear that the defence of *volenti non fit injuria* (based on the voluntary assumption of risk), is not necessarily available to the supplier simply because the injured person has agreed to or is aware of a contract term or notice excluding or restricting liability for negligence.

The wide scope of this provision should be noted. Within the scope of the Act any exemption clause in respect of negligence which results in death or personal injuries is void. Exemption clauses in respect of other loss or damage caused by negligence, such as 'goods accepted at owner's risk', must satisfy the reasonableness test provided that the person causing the loss is under the general law liable in negligence for it. This may not necessarily be the case where e.g. the bailment is entirely gratuitous and for the benefit of the bailee alone – in which case it could well not be relevant to consider section 2 since there was never any pre-existing liability for negligence out of which to contract. Whilst such exemption clauses might normally have been found in contracts for services of one sort and another, the

---

9 See *B G Transport Service v Marston Motor Co* [1970] 1 Lloyd's Rep 371, QBD. See generally N. E. Palmer *Bailment*, ch. 5.

10 See M & H pp. 239 and 245–253 and Law Com. No. 156, paras. 3.3–3.12.

section also applies to such clauses in contracts for sale or other disposition of goods under which ownership or possession passes. Provided the clause relates to business liability as defined by section 1(3) – i.e. obligations or duties arising from things done or to be done in the course of a business, or from the occupation of business premises – and provided the contract is not one of insurance (which industry has entered into a voluntary code of insurance practice) or otherwise within the isolated exceptions listed in Schedule 1 (contracts relating to land, intellectual property, companies and securities) – such exemption clauses are regulated by section 2. It matters not whether they are in respect of 'consumer transactions' or otherwise.

In respect of liability for 'negligence', negligence is defined (in section 1(1)) for the purposes of the Act as meaning the breach –

   a) of any obligation, arising from the express or implied terms of a contract, to take reasonable care or exercise reasonable skill in the performance of the contract;
   b) of any common law duty to take reasonable care or exercise reasonable skill (but not any stricter duty);
   c) of the common duty of care (owed by occupiers of premises to their visitors) imposed by the Occupiers' Liability Act 1957 and equivalent legislation in Northern Ireland.

There has been some reported judicial guidance as to how the concept of reasonableness must be implied into the many contracts into which consumers enter for services to be supplied on standard terms. In *Waldron-Kelly v British Railways Board*[11] the effect of the reasonableness test laid down by the 1977 Act on a standard form contract for carriage of goods by British Rail was discussed. The plaintiff had contracted with British Rail for his suitcase to be sent from Stockport to Haverford West by rail at owner's risk for a charge of £6.03. The standard form contract contained comprehensive exemption clauses in respect of loss, misdelivery, damage or delay unless the plaintiff could prove wilful misconduct by British Rail. If the goods failed to arrive at all, financial liability of British Rail was limited to a sum by reference to the weight of the goods (£27) as opposed to their value (£320.32). The suitcase never materialised and the plaintiff sued for the loss of the value of his goods and for compensation for distress and inconvenience. The judge held that in the case of non-delivery of goods, it was for the bailee to show that the loss was not his fault,[12] and this British Rail

---

11   [1981] CLY 303, Stockport County Court; M & H p. 250.
12   See *J Spurling Ltd v Bradshaw* [1956] 2 All ER 121, [1956] 1 WLR 461, CA; *Levison v Patent Steam Carpet Cleaning Co Ltd* [1978] QB 69, [1977] 3 All ER 498, CA.

had failed to do. British Rail's exemption clause did not apply because it failed to satisfy the test of reasonableness set out in sections 2, 3 and 11 of the 1977 Act. In consumer cases the 1977 Act had supplanted the doctrine of fundamental breach, and the court should not look outside the terms of the 1977 Act. Accordingly the plaintiff was awarded the value of the suitcase and its contents (£320.32) but nothing for general damages. In contrast in *Wight v British Railways Board*[13] the court accepted the limitation by reference to weight clause as reasonable. The reasons given included the fact that British Rail had no means of knowing the true value of the goods whereas the owner did and could insure them and competitors used similar, and often less generous, limitation clauses.

Exclusion clauses in film processors' contracts have been examined in *Woodman v Photo Trade Processing Ltd*[14] and *Warren v Truprint Ltd*.[15] In the *Woodman* case a clause limiting liability to the cost of a replacement film was held to be unreasonable. Reference was made to the fact that the clause offered no insurance facility, no advice was given to insure and the customer's attention was not specifically drawn to the clause. The court noted that the Code of Practice for the Photographic Industry[16] recommended a two-tier system of a normal service with total exclusion of liability and a special service at a higher charge with full acceptance of liability. No such special service was offered here. In the *Warren* case an alternative service *was* offered with the clause indicating 'We will undertake further liability at a supplementary charge. Written details on request.' Even this did not satisfy the reasonableness test as the alternatives were not plainly and clearly explained: the company could have set out the 'further liability' and the cost to the consumer.

An example of a non-consumer dispute concerning section 2(2) arose in *Phillips Products Ltd v Hyland*.[17] Here the negligent driver of a hired excavator damaged the hirer's factory. The clause, which purported to place responsibility for the driver's actions on the hirer, failed to satisfy the reasonableness test. The hirers did not regularly hire plant and drivers, had no control over the driver and had little opportunity to arrange insurance. The court supported the view of Lord Bridge in *George Mitchell (Chesterhall) Ltd v Finney Lock Seeds*

---

13 [1983] CLY 424, Bloomsbury and Marylebone County Court.
14 (1981), unreported, Exeter County Court; see M & H p. 245; *Which?* 1981 p. 426 (lost wedding photographs).
15 [1986] BTLC 344, Luton County Court (lost photographs of silver wedding and an award presentation).
16 See ch. 11, p. 334.
17 [1987] 2 All ER 620, [1987] 1 WLR 659n, CA. See also (1985) 82 L S Gaz 2393.

Ltd[18] that in such cases appellate courts should be reluctant to overturn decisions at first instance and emphasised that the issue of reasonableness was specific to the particular contract involved. The subjective nature of the test was confirmed in *Stevenson v Nationwide Building Society*.[19] Here an exclusion clause in a mortgage application form, which accepted no liability for the value or condition of a property, was held to be reasonable using section 11(3). The building society was offering a valuation without liability or, if the purchaser wished, he could have a full survey at additional cost with acceptance of liability. The purchaser chose not to have the full survey and could not then sue for the negligent valuation.

The House of Lords has examined the operation of section 2(2) in two cases, heard together, concerning disclaimers of liability made by surveyors: *Smith v Eric S Bush (a firm), and Harris v Wyre Forest District Council*.[20] In the first case the plaintiff received a copy of the survey report prepared, by the defendants, for her building society prior to obtaining a mortgage. She relied on the report, having no further survey done. In assessing the reasonableness of provisions seeking to exclude liability for the negligence of surveyors, Lord Griffiths declared that certain factors should always be taken into account: 1) the bargaining powers of the parties, 2) in the case of advice, the practicality of consulting alternative sources, 3) the difficulty of the task undertaken and 4) the practical consequences of the decision on the question of reasonableness. This involves the sum of money potentially at stake and the availability of insurance. He indicated:

> We are dealing in this case with a loss which will be limited to the value of a modest house and against which it can be expected that the surveyor will be insured. Bearing the loss will be unlikely to cause significant hardship if it has to be borne by the surveyor but it is, on the other hand, quite possible that it will be a financial catastrophe for the purchaser who may be left with a valueless house and no money to buy another. . . . The result of denying a surveyor, in the circumstances of this case, the right to exclude liability will result in distributing the risk of his negligence among all house purchasers through an increase in his fees to cover insurance, rather than allowing the whole of the risk to fall on the one unfortunate purchaser. (at pp. 858, 531).

Different considerations may operate regarding industrial properties, blocks of flats and very expensive houses, where purchasers may

---

18   [1983] 2 AC 803 at 816, [1983] 2 All ER 737 at 743, HL; M & H p. 264. See ch. 5 at p. 115.
19   (1984) 272 Estates Gazette 663, QBD.
20   [1990] 1 AC 831, [1989] 2 All ER 514, HL. See below p. 192.

be expected to have their own surveys done, thus enabling surveyors acting for the providers of finance to exclude or limit their liability.

In the second case the appellants applied to a local authority for a mortgage. The local authority had the premises valued and, on the basis of this, offered to advance 90 per cent of the asking price for the house, conditional on some minor repair work. The appellants assumed the house was worth at least the amount of the valuation and purchased the house without their own survey. An unsuccessful attempt was made by the respondents to argue that liability never arose under *Hedley Byrne & Co Ltd v Heller & Partners Ltd*[1] because of the disclaimer of liability and that therefore section 2(2) of the 1977 Act did not apply. In the words of Lord Templeman 'This construction would not give effect to the manifest intention of the 1977 Act but would emasculate the Act.' He referred to sections 11(3) and 13(1) and said that 'these provisions support the view that the 1977 Act requires all exclusion notices which would in common law provide a defence to an action for negligence must satisfy the requirement of reasonableness.' The clause did not satisfy the reasonableness test and in the words of Lord Templeman:

> It is open to Parliament to provide that members of all professions or members of one profession providing services in the normal course of the exercise of their profession for reward shall be entitled to exclude or limit their liability for failure to exercise reasonable skill and care. In the absence of any such provision valuers are not, in my opinion, entitled to rely on a general exclusion of the common law duty of care owed to purchasers of houses by valuers to exercise reasonable skill and care in valuing houses for mortgage purposes. (at pp. 853, 527).

Section 3 of the 1977 Act, discussed in ch. 5 in the context of the supply of goods, can be relevant also to contracts for services.

3. EUROPEAN DEVELOPMENTS – DRAFT DIRECTIVE ON SERVICES

In November 1990 the European Commission agreed a proposed Draft Directive on the liability of suppliers of services.[2] If adopted this will require changes to the Supply of Goods and Services Act 1982. The proposals will make suppliers of services liable for damage to people and movable or immovable property caused by fault on the part of the supplier. The burden of proving the absence of fault rests on the supplier (art. 1). Services are any transactions carried out on

1 [1964] AC 465, [1963] 2 All ER 575, HL.
2 OJ No C 12, 18.1.91, p. 8. For criticisms see (1991) 88 LS Gaz No 45, p. 7.

a commercial or public basis (except to maintain public safety, e.g. the police) which do not have as a direct and exclusive object the manufacture of movable property (art. 2). Thus work and materials contracts will be included. Damage encompasses a) 'death or any direct damage to the health or physical integrity of persons', b) damage to the physical integrity of property, including animals, providing the property is of a type intended for private use and is intended for or used principally for private use, and 'financial material damage resulting directly from the damage referred to at a) and b)' (art. 4). Economic loss is excluded so suppliers of legal, financial and insurance services are unlikely to be affected. Liability will be non-excludable (art. 6). Injured parties will have five years from the supply of the service to initiate proceedings, extended to 20 years regarding the design or construction of immovable property (art. 9), with respectively 3 and 10 years limitation periods (art. 10). The reversal of the burden of proof and non-excludability of the liability are perhaps the two most significant departures from the current provisions of the 1982 Act. It is intended that the Directive, if adopted, is operational from 31 December 1992, but this looks unrealistic.

4. SPECIAL CONSIDERATIONS AFFECTING SPECIFIC SERVICES

As a tailpiece to this chapter, it is worth mentioning that a consumer with a complaint against a provider of a service must be prepared to consider remedies lying outside the law of contract and tort as so far discussed in this chapter. It must also be borne in mind that the provider of services may have specific rights against the customer's goods.

Innkeepers

The ancient strict liability of the 'common innkeeper' for the safe-keeping of his guest's property, the historical reason for which is the former tendency of some innkeepers to work in close association with highwaymen and footpads, is now modified by the Hotel Proprietors Act 1956. Establishments formerly styled common inns are now 'hotels', and are within the ambit of the statute if they hold themselves out as offering food, drink (alcoholic or otherwise) and, if required, sleeping accommodation to any traveller appearing to be able and willing to pay a reasonable sum for the services provided and in a fit state to be received (section 1(3)). ('Private hotels' may be outside this definition.) Failure to accept a traveller when there is sufficient room renders the hotelier liable for damages. If the traveller has engaged sleeping accommodation the hotelier is an 'insurer' of any luggage other than that left in a car or the car itself. The only defences are act of God, act of the Queen's enemies, or the guest's own negligence.[3] The hotel proprietor may limit liability by the prominent exhibition of a notice in accordance with the Act which states that liability is limited to £50 for one article or £100 in total per guest unless either the hotel or its servants are guilty of neglect or wilful default, or the property has been deposited expressly for safe custody with the hotel proprietor. (Private hotels and boarding houses are within the ordinary law of negligence only.) The other side of the coin is that the innkeeper enjoys the right to detain, under a lien, the guest's goods brought to the hotel until the cost of food and lodging is met. If the goods are detained for six weeks the goods may be sold if the sale is advertised as specified by the Act at least a month beforehand (Innkeepers Act 1878).

Repairers

Again, a consumer whose goods are sold without agreement by a repairer may not have a valid complaint if the sale was within the terms of the Torts (Interference with Goods) Act 1977. Repairers, in common with many other providers of services, may detain the goods until their charges are met (solicitors, bankers, factors and wharfingers also have rights of lien). But if the customer never returns at all – a common complaint of tailors and shoe repairers, for instance – the repairer needs to sell the goods to defray any charges. It is possible, and is perhaps advisable, to reserve the right to do this on the terms stated in the contract. If goods are sold without such a contractual right the repairer will commit the tort of wrongful interference with goods[4] and must reimburse the owner on the basis of the value of the article when sued, less the value of any improvement. In an inflationary period this can be an open-ended commitment. The 1977 Act enables repairers or other persons providing treatment to sell the goods and account for the net proceeds to the owner after deducting charges and costs. The bailee has the right to sell the goods by the best method of sale reasonably available in the circumstances. To exercise this right the following factors must be present. Firstly, the bailor must be in breach of an obligation to take delivery of the goods, or the bailee must have taken reasonable steps to trace the bailor in order to impose such

3 See *Shacklock v Ethorpe Ltd* [1939] 3 All ER 372 (hotel liable even though guest, whose jewellery was stolen from a locked dressing case, did not lock the door).
4 Under the Torts (Interference with Goods) Act 1977.

obligation on the bailor by the notice mentioned below, but without success. If such an obligation does not already exist by virtue of the terms of any contract, the bailee may impose such an obligation on the bailor by serving him with a notice stating (inter alia) that the goods are ready for delivery and specifying any amount due to the bailee. The requirements of such a notice are specified in more detail in Part I of Schedule 1 of the Act. Secondly, the bailee must serve a notice (concurrently with the notice mentioned above, if appropriate) that the bailee intends to sell the goods on or after a specified date. The date must be sufficient to afford the bailor a reasonable opportunity of taking delivery of the goods, and if an amount is owing to the bailee, the period must be not less than three months. The notice must also specify the name and address of the bailee and specify the amount due to the bailee by the bailor. The notice must be in writing and sent by registered letter or by the recorded delivery service (Schedule 1, Part II). A sale duly made gives a good title to the purchaser as against the bailor.

The bailee is then liable to account to the bailor for the proceeds of sale less a) the costs of sale, and b) sums payable in respect of the goods by bailor to bailee before notice of sale was given (see generally section 12).

Where the complaint against a provider of services does not arise out of a clear cut breach of contract or a tort, and the objective is to obtain redress by other means, the point has already been made at various junctures in this book that it may be worthwhile considering a complaint to any professional association to which the provider of services belongs. This is particularly so if a) membership of such an association obliges the member to adopt a Code of Practice which has been infringed or b) a Code of Practice has been agreed with the Office of Fair Trading (considered in more detail in ch. 11) and there are facilities for arbitration of disputes, or c) there is statutory or other machinery for handling of complaints against a particular profession.

Bankers

In the case of banker and customer the relationship may be governed both by common law and specific statutes dealing with obligations as well as rights to the customer,[5] although the bank's fundamental duty is the contractual one of obeying its customer's mandate (and thus not to pay out on a cheque bearing a forged signature) and the customer's fundamental duty is to exercise reasonable care not to facilitate fraud by the manner in which cheques are drawn, breach of

5 Bills of Exchange Act 1882; Cheques Act 1957; Cheques Act 1992.

which will result in the customer's being responsible for losses sustained by the bank.[6] The details of this complex relationship are properly within the sphere of commercial law.

With effect from 16 March 1992 a new Code of Banking Practice is operational.[7] It provides a minimum standard for all banks with many banks likely to provide their own versions, giving additional rights to customers. The Code covers such matters as putting a £50 limit on liability for losses from cash dispensers and the use of cards for electronic funds transfers (Switch cards and the like) unless the bank can establish 'gross negligence' on the part of the account holder; greater confidentiality of information on accounts, mailing lists etc; prevention of levying current account charges when bank charges alone have made an account overdrawn; and the publication of tariffs covering basic account services.

In addition to legal action, an aggrieved banking customer can refer a complaint to the Banking Ombudsman if the bank concerned is a member of the scheme. This option commenced in January 1986 and only applies to personal banking services. Compensation of up to £100,000 is possible. The Ombudsman's decisions are binding on the banks but not the customers. The 1990–91 Report of the Ombudsman, Mr Lawrence Shurman, shows 6,327 complaints were received, 746 of which needed full investigation, with 30 per cent decided in favour of the complainant.[8]

Medical profession

With regard to complaints against members of a profession, the position of medical practitioners is particularly important. In the case of complaints against doctors for inadequate treatment under the National Health Service reference should be made to the complaints machinery under the National Health Service Act 1977.[9] The Secretary of State for Social Services must establish bodies, originally called family practitioner committees, now known as family health services authorities.[10] A person entitled to complain (normally the dissatisfied National Health Service patient) may complain to the general manager of the relevant authority or the

6 *London Joint Stock Bank Ltd v MacMillan and Arthur* [1918] AC 777.
7 See 'Legal aspects of the new Code' R Lawson (1992) 142 NLJ 346; *Bee Line* No. 91/4, p. 1.
8 See also *Consumer Redress Mechanisms*, OFT, 1991, paras. 4.75–4.76 and Appendix 2, Table 4 which reviews complaints dealt with 1986–90.
9 Section 129 and Sch. 14, paras. 1(1) and 2.
10 National Health Service Act 1977, s. 10 as substituted by the Health and Social Security Act 1984, s. 5 and see also the National Health Service and Community Care Act 1990, s. 2.

principal officer of the district health authority in writing, stating the substance of the complaint, within thirteen weeks of the event giving rise to the complaint. Complaints made against doctors in respect of an alleged failure to comply with the terms of service are investigated by the medical service committee of the family health services authority, consisting of a chairman and six other persons, three of whom are lay members. In the event of a hearing (i.e. when the complaint is not regarded as frivolous or vexatious) the complainant may be assisted in presenting the case by some other person but not a barrister or solicitor. The hearing is in private and the service committee then makes a report to the family health services authority. If the complaint is upheld there is no power to award compensation as such, but the authority may order recovery of the patient's expenses by deduction from the doctor's remuneration. The authority has other powers, such as to order reduction of the doctor's list of patients, or impose a fine, or it may make representations to the tribunal established under section 46 of the 1977 Act for removal of the doctor's name from the medical list. Either party may appeal to the Secretary of State for Social Services. Somewhat similar provisions apply to complaints against dentists, chemists and opticians in respect of National Health Service work. In the case of serious professional misconduct by doctors, disciplinary action may be taken by the General Medical Council to whom complaints can also be made. It must be emphasised that this complaints machinery is in addition to the patient's common law rights as previously discussed.

Legal profession

Complaints against lawyers pose slightly different problems.[11] It was held by the House of Lords in *Rondel v Worsley*[12] that a barrister was not liable for negligence in the conduct of litigation or in advising in connection with it. The immunity, which is justified on grounds of public policy, also extends to solicitors in respect of advocacy work. In *Saif Ali v Sydney Mitchell & Co*[13] it was held that this immunity extended to a barrister advising in connection with pre-trial work only as regards matters which are so intimately concerned with the conduct of the case that they may fairly be described as preliminary decisions affecting its conduct. Here, the barrister's advice and the

---

11 See generally *Ordinary Justice*, NCC, ch. 7.
12 [1969] 1 AC 191, [1967] 3 All ER 993, HL.
13 [1980] AC 198, [1978] 3 All ER 1033, HL. The Royal Commission on Legal Services reporting in 1979 (Cmnd. 7648), recommended compulsory insurance by barristers against liability for negligence. For a summary of its recommendations generally, see (1979) 129 NLJ 964, 988.

pleadings that he had drafted prevented the plaintiff's case from coming to court at all (because the limitation period had expired). The work thus fell outside the area of immunity for negligence. Accordingly, a barrister is liable in respect of negligent work or advice unconnected with impending litigation and it is of course well established that solicitors are so liable (for breach of contract, as discussed above). The immunity of advocates is also recognised in connection with the Supply of Goods and Services Act 1982. A contract for the services of 'an advocate in court or before any tribunal, inquiry or arbitrator and in carrying out preliminary work directly affecting the conduct of the hearing'[14] does not include the implied term of reasonable care and skill under section 13.[15] In addition, a consumer may wish to use other avenues of complaint, either because negligence is not necessarily involved or because there is professional immunity from liability for negligence. In the case of barristers, complaints concerning professional misconduct may be made in writing to the Bar Council. The complaint is referred to and investigated by the Professional Conduct Committee which has both barristers and lay members. The Committee can dismiss the complaint, refer the matter to the relevant Inn, deal with the matter informally or by a summary procedure. If there is sufficient evidence for a prosecution for professional misconduct or breach of professional standards the complaint is taken to a disciplinary tribunal, appointed by the Council of the Inns of Court and chaired by a judge. If the complaint is upheld, a barrister may be reprimanded, suspended or, in serious cases, disbarred by his or her Inn of Court (and thus disentitled to practise). Any fees received may be ordered to be returned but there is no power to award compensation where negligence has resulted in financial loss to a client.[16]

Complaints against solicitors are much more common than against barristers, which is to be expected since all clients' work must go through solicitors and they undertake responsibility for a far wider spectrum of work. Complaints about professional misconduct (for example, undue delay in the transaction of business or misappropriation of funds) or unsatisfactory service should be made in the first instance to the solicitors' firm involved. Since May 1991, each firm must establish an internal complaints handling process.[17] If the complaint is unresolved it may then be directed to the solicitors' governing body, The Law Society. In respect of defalcations, a

---

14 Supply of Services (Exclusion of Implied Terms) Order 1982, S.I. 1982/1771, art. 2(1).
15 See above p. 166.
16 See (1986) 83 L S Gaz 3229.
17 Solicitors Practice Rules 1990, Rule 15.

Compensation Fund is maintained by the Society out of which it may compensate clients who have been unable to recover money owed to them by their solicitor. As regards professional conduct generally, the Society has power to make rules for the regulation of discipline.[18]

The Report of the Royal Commission on Legal Services (1979, Cmnd. 7648) recommended that The Law Society should investigate not only allegations of professional misconduct but also allegations of bad professional work, irrespective of whether or not the client may be entitled to pursue a claim in the courts.[19] This was introduced in the Solicitors Act 1974, section 44A[20] and has been replaced by the Solicitors Act 1974, section 37A and Schedule 1A.[1] The Law Society Council may, if the services provided by solicitors are 'not of the quality which it is reasonable to expect of them' (section 37A), impose sanctions on the solicitors. The sanctions include remission of the solicitor's costs, rectification by the solicitor of any error or omission, payment of compensation of up to £1,000 and taking specified actions in the interest of the client.[2]

All complaints to The Law Society about solicitors are directed to the Solicitors Complaints Bureau (SCB) which was set up in 1986 following a review of The Law Society's role by management consultants Coopers and Lybrand.[3] Following reorganisation of the SCB in 1991 a complaint goes first to the Diagnostic Unit to decide the best method of handling it. Where possible the matter is referred to a conciliator. If this is not possible or if no agreement is reached then an Assistant Director will review the case. Complaints requiring formal investigation will either be considered by an Assistant Director or a Sub-Committee of the Adjudication and Appeals Committee. The Adjudication and Appeals Committee consists of a solicitor chairman, 14 solicitor members and 11 lay members. These members also sit as several Sub-Committees. There is an appeal process against decisions: matters concerning conduct or regulation go to the Conduct Appeals Sub-Committee, those concerning inadequate professional services (IPS) or awards of compensation go

---

18   Solicitors Act 1974, s. 31 and see Solicitors Practice Rules 1990.
19   Para. 25.24.
20   As inserted by the Administration of Justice Act 1985, s. 1, operative from 1 January 1987, S.I. 1986/2260.
 1   As inserted by the Courts and Legal Services Act 1990, s. 93 and Sch. 15 as of 1 April 1991.
 2   Solicitors Act 1974, Sch. 1A as inserted by the Courts and Legal Services Act 1990, s. 93(3) and Sch. 15.
 3   See (1986) 83 LS Gaz 3229 and generally SCB Annual Report 1990 and SCB Leaflet 'How and When' which provides information on how and when to complain about the service or behaviour of a solicitor.

to a Compensation (IPS) Appeals Sub-Committee. Alternatively the Assistant Director may decide to close the file as disclosing no grounds for further action. If dissatisfied with this, the complainant may appeal to the Termination Sub-Committee.

Cases of serious misconduct are referred by the Adjudication and Appeals Committee to the Solicitors Disciplinary Tribunal. This Tribunal is constituted by the Master of the Rolls from experienced solicitors and lay members. The Tribunal is a judicial body independent of The Law Society, and if the Tribunal finds the complaint proved it may strike the solicitor off the Roll (thus removing the right to practise) or suspend or fine the solicitor up to £5,000.[4] Either party may appeal to a divisional court of the Queen's Bench Division.[5] Similarly a solicitor or barrister may be excluded from undertaking work under the legal aid and advice scheme for misconduct,[6] and the solicitor or barrister has a final right of appeal to the High Court against such exclusion.[7]

Complaints involving alleged professional negligence may enable a client to seek damages through the courts. All solicitors are required to be insured against 'claims in respect of any description of civil liability'.[8] Instead of taking negligence claims to court, since June 1986 the Solicitors Arbitration Scheme has been available. The independent scheme is run by the Chartered Institute of Arbitrators and is decided on the basis of written submissions only. It is necessary to get the consent of both parties to go to arbitration and the decision is binding on both parties.[9]

Complaints about solicitors' bills are governed by different procedures. The client has two methods of safeguarding against excessive charges. Firstly there is the right to have the bill taxed by the court. The bill will be taxed on a 'solicitor and own client' basis so that all costs are allowed except so far as they are unreasonable in amount or have been unreasonably incurred. In contentious bills many items are fixed in accordance with scales laid down by the Rules of the Supreme Court. Thus unless the taxing master certifies certain items as being unreasonable the client must pay the costs as a contractual debt. Alternatively, and without prejudice to the right to have the bill taxed, the client may require the Society to certify that the sum is fair and reasonable, a procedure more apt for bills in

4 Solicitors Act 1974, s. 47 as amended by the Courts and Legal Services Act 1990, s. 92.
5 Ibid, s. 49.
6 See Administration of Justice Act 1985, ss. 40–44 as amended by Legal Aid Act 1988, s. 33.
7 Administration of Justice Act 1985, ss. 42(2) and 43(5).
8 Solicitors Act 1974, s. 37 and Solicitors' Indemnity Rules 1990.
9 See (1986) 83 LS Gaz 1876; (1986) 136 NLJ 649.

respect of non-contentious business where the solicitor's remuneration is such sum as may be fair and reasonable having regard to all the circumstances of the case. The Solicitors Remuneration Order 1972[10] lays down a number of guidelines which must be considered in non-contentious business. These include the complexity of the matter, the skill involved, the time spent on business and (very often the most important) the amount or value of the property involved and the importance of the matter to the client. A solicitor cannot bring proceedings to recover costs on a bill for non-contentious business unless the client has been informed of the right to obtain a certificate from the Society or to have the bill taxed by the court. The client must require the solicitor to obtain a certificate within one month of being informed of the right to do so.

Legal Services Ombudsman

The Solicitors Act 1974, section 45 made provision for the establishment of a 'Lay Observer' to examine written complaints from the public as to The Law Society's treatment of complaints about solicitors or their employees. The White Paper *Legal Services: A Framework for the Future* proposed[11] the abolition of the office of Lay Observer and the creation of a new statutory office of Legal Services Ombudsman to cover solicitors, barristers and licensed conveyancers. This has been brought about by the Courts and Legal Services Act 1990, section 21, the first English ombudsman, Michael Barnes, taking up office in January 1991. Appointment is made by the Lord Chancellor for a renewable three year period.

The functions of the ombudsman are specified in section 22 and involve investigation of any allegation relating 'to the manner in which a complaint made to a professional body' regarding authorised advocates and litigators, registered foreign lawyers, recognised bodies or duly certified notary publics, members of the professional body and any employee of such a person, has been dealt with by the professional body (subsection (1)). He thus has power to investigate both the matter which gave rise to the original complaint and also how that matter has been dealt with by the professional body. Any ombudsman enquiry cannot proceed whilst the matter is still under investigation by the professional body, pending any appeal against a determination by that body or until expiry of the appeal period (subsection (5)). He may, however, investigate if the complaint concerns failures by the body to investigate or delays in completion

10   S.I. 1972/1139.
11   Cm. 740, 1989, para. 10.13.

of an investigation. Certain matters are excluded from the ambit of the ombudsman to prevent 'retrials': issues which are being or have been determined by a court, the Solicitors Disciplinary Tribunal, the Disciplinary Tribunal of the Council of the Inns of Court or other specified tribunal (subsection (7)).

On completion of an investigation the ombudsman produces a written report of his conclusions under section 23. He may recommend reconsideration by the professional body, that the body considers exercising its powers with regard to the person with respect to whom the complaint was made or anyone connected with him, that specified compensation be paid by the person complained against or the body to the complainant for 'loss suffered by him, or inconvenience or distress caused to him', and reimbursement by the person or body of the cost or part of the cost of making the allegation (subsection (2)). The recipients of any such recommendations must indicate to the ombudsman, within three months, what action they propose to take to comply with the recommendation (subsection (7)). Failure to comply with a recommendation must be publicised, with reasons given, in a manner specified by the ombudsman (subsection (8)). It can therefore be seen that the ombudsman has no powers of compulsion but can ensure that full publicity is given to any cases where his recommendations are not followed. In addition to investigating complaints the ombudsman also has an advisory function concerning investigation procedures of the professional bodies (section 24).

Surveyors

It is well established that a surveyor who, for a fee, surveys a client's building and does so negligently is liable for the consequent loss to the client along the same lines as apply to other professional people (discussed above). If the surveyor negligently fails to identify defects in a property problems concerning quantification of damages may arise if the cost of repairing those undisclosed defects exceeds the diminution in value of the property (i.e. value with known defects compared with the price actually paid for the property). The current position is that the purchaser can only recover the diminution in value. This was decided by the Court of Appeal in *Watts v Morrow*.[12] In addition damages for distress and inconvenience were only recoverable when caused by the physical consequences of the breach; claims for general disappointment, anxiety etc. would not be allowed.

---

12   [1991] 4 All ER 937, CA.

The purchase of a house is likely to be the most expensive transaction the ordinary consumer undertakes. In the comparatively uncommon case where the purchase is not financed by a mortgage from a building society or bank the house buyer is entirely free to choose whether to have a preliminary survey or not before entering into a binding contract. In an effort to encourage surveys the Royal Institution of Chartered Surveyors introduced in 1981 a 'House Buyer's Report and Valuation' scheme. This provides house buyers with a truncated standard survey report following a limited inspection by the surveyor, plus some indication of the value of the house. The fee for the service is usually considerably less than that for a full structural survey. The RICS scheme seeks to limit the potential liability to negligence of surveyors offering this service, since there may be some defects which only a more detailed survey would have revealed. It is uncertain whether this type of exemption clause would be upheld as reasonable within the Unfair Contract Terms Act 1977, section 2(2) discussed above in this chapter.

The position of surveyors vis-à-vis third parties affected by their surveys has changed considerably in recent years. The first situation to consider is when a surveyor is acting for a local authority under statutory powers to ensure that local byelaws are complied with during the construction of houses. In 1990 the House of Lords in *Murphy v Brentwood District Council*[13] overruled its earlier decision of *Anns v Merton London Borough Council*[14] and denied the owner of a house affected by defective foundations a claim for compensation against the local authority whose negligent consulting engineers had approved the plans for the house. The house had been purchased in 1970 having been constructed on a concrete raft foundation to prevent settlement damage. The raft foundation proved to be defective and the house settled, causing cracks which were visible by 1981. Repairs to the foundations would have cost £45,000 but the plaintiff did not undertake these. Instead he sold the house for £35,000 below the market value if in sound condition in 1986. In the absence of actual damage to the owner's property (other than the house itself) or personal injury no claim for what is effectively pure economic loss could be made. The *Anns* case had allowed a claim on the basis that there was an imminent danger to the health or safety of the occupiers and that the cost of averting such danger was claimable against the local authority. In the light of subsequent cases, which

13   [1991] 1 AC 398, [1990] 2 All ER 908, [1990] 3 WLR 414, HL.
14   [1978] AC 728, [1977] 2 All ER 492, HL.

had considerably restricted the scope of the *Anns* decision,[15] it was not surprising that the House of Lords in *Murphy* declared the damage suffered as pure economic loss and denied the existence of a duty of care to prevent such damage.

The other situation in which a house buyer is vitally concerned with a survey of the house, undertaken for another, is where the house purchase is financed by a mortgage. By the Building Societies Act 1986, section 13, a building society is under a duty to make arrangements for the valuation of properties offered as securities for advances. Their practice is to appoint a surveyor in the locality who makes a survey and valuation to the building society. The building society makes its decision on whether or not to lend on this basis. The borrower, as a term of the loan, must normally repay to the society the cost of such valuation. In *Yianni v Edwin Evans & Sons*[16] a firm of surveyors and valuers who made a survey and valuation of a London house for the Halifax Building Society in connection with a loan application by the plaintiffs, Mr. and Mrs. Yianni, negligently reported to the building society that the property was suitable security for a loan of £12,000. In fact the property was subject to serious defects and the report of the surveyors was described by the judge as 'grossly incompetent and negligent'. The plaintiffs were sent a statutory notice by the building society saying that the making of the advance would not imply any warranty by the society that the purchase price was reasonable. The plaintiffs had not purchased a house before, nor did they requisition an independent survey. The surveyor's report to the building society was not shown to them. Nevertheless, it was held that the surveyors in this case knew the purpose of the report and that the plaintiffs would know, if the building society made an advance, that the surveyors must have

15   See e.g. *Governors of the Peabody Donation Fund v Sir Lindsay Parkinson & Co Ltd* [1985] AC 210, [1984] 3 All ER 529, HL; *Investors in Industry Commercial Properties Ltd v South Bedfordshire District Council* [1986] QB 1034, [1986] 1 All ER 787, CA; and *D & F Estates Ltd v Church Comrs for England* [1989] AC 177, [1988] 2 All ER 992, HL.

16   [1982] QB 438, [1981] 3 All ER 592, CA; M & H p. 147. According to *Secretary of State for the Environment v Essex, Goodman & Suggitt* [1986] 2 All ER 69, [1986] 1 WLR 1432, QBD, in the case of a surveyor the cause of action accrues when the person relying on the survey acts on the report, thus distinguishing *Pirelli General Cable Works Ltd v Oscar Faber & Partners* [1983] 2 AC 1, [1983] 1 All ER 65, HL, where actual occurrence of damage was the significant date for engineers, builders and architects. Cases governed by the Limitation Act 1980, s. 4A (as inserted by the Latent Damage Act 1986, s. 1) may benefit from the new provisions whereby the limitation period runs from the later of 6 years from accrual of the cause of action or 3 years from the earliest date on which the plaintiff had the 'knowledge required for bringing an action for damages in respect of the relevant damage and the right to bring such an action' (s. 14A (4)-(10)). Note, however, the 15-year long stop provision of s. 14B.

recommended that their house was suitable for a mortgage of £12,000, being 80 per cent of its price. The defendants therefore owed a duty of care to the plaintiffs since they should have foreseen that carelessness on their part might be likely to cause damage to the plaintiffs. The damages obtainable would be related to the £8,000 worth of remedial work which was required.

The House of Lords confirmed the existence of a duty of care owed by valuers to purchasers when valuing for local authority or building society mortgages in *Smith v Eric S Bush (a firm), and Harris v Wyre Forest District Council*.[17] In the words of Lord Templeman:

> . . . in my opinion the valuer assumes responsibility to both mortgagee and purchaser by agreeing to carry out a valuation for mortgage purposes knowing that the valuation fee has been paid by the purchaser and knowing that the valuation will probably be relied on by the purchaser in order to decide whether or not to enter into a contract to purchase the house. The valuer can escape the responsibility to exercise reasonable care and skill by an express exclusion clause, provided the exclusion clause does not fall foul of the Unfair Contract Terms Act 1977.[18]

Lord Griffiths indicated that it matters not whether the valuer is employed by the mortgagee, acting on his own account or is employed by a firm of independent surveyors, the duty as a professional person remains the same. The duty would, however, be limited to the purchaser of the house, there would be no duty to subsequent purchasers. It is interesting to note that here liability is imposed for economic loss suffered by the purchaser. Lord Griffiths explains that the necessary proximity between the valuer and purchaser 'arises from the surveyor's knowledge that the overwhelming probability is that the purchaser will rely on his valuation, the evidence was that surveyors knew that approximately 90 per cent of purchasers did so, and the fact that the surveyor only obtains the work because the purchaser is willing to pay his fee.' (at pp. 865, 536).

Estate agents

For many years concern has been felt regarding the inadequacies of controls over the activities of estate agents.[19] There is no prohibition on anyone setting up as an estate agent, whatever his or her qualifications or lack of them, and in the course of that business

---

17 [1990] 1 AC 831, [1989] 2 All ER 514, HL. See above p. 178.
18 At pp. 847, 524. For discussion of the exclusion of liability see above p. 178.
19 See, for example, *The Regulation of Estate Agency: A Consultative Document*, Dept of Prices and Consumer Protection, 1975; *Estate Agents Act 1979: A Review by the Director General of Fair Trading*, OFT, December 1988; *Review of Estate Agency*, DTI, June 1989; *Estate Agency: A consultation document by the Director General of Fair Trading*, OFT, September 1989; *Estate Agency: A report by the Director General of Fair Trading*, OFT, March 1990.

receiving deposits from potential purchasers. Of course, it would be an offence under the Trade Descriptions Act 1968 for such a person wrongly to be described as, for instance, an Associate of the Royal Institution of Chartered Surveyors, but there is nothing to prevent an unqualified person freely engaging in most of the activities of a professionally qualified auctioneer and estate agent. The Estate Agents Act 1979, which contains the main statutory controls over the activities of estate agents, falls far short of ensuring that estate agents must have followed a standard course of education and training (as is the case with medical practitioners, barristers, solicitors etc.). There is, however, provision in section 22(1)[20] for making regulations prescribing minimum standards of competence for those engaged in estate agency work.

The 1979 Act indicates that the profession of estate agency is open to any person until such time as that person is declared by the Director General of Fair Trading to be unfit to practice under section 3. Lessons having been learned from the huge expense of the licensing system under the Consumer Credit Act 1974, this Act in effect imposes a system of negative licensing – i.e. a person can practise until forbidden to do so or restricted in so doing.[1] Initially the grounds in section 3 which could be used to declare a person unfit to carry out estate agency work centred on convictions for offences such as fraud, dishonesty or violence, certain offences under the 1979 Act itself, discriminatory practices (as detailed in Schedule 1) and failures to comply with obligations imposed under sections 15, 18, 20 and 21 of the 1979 Act (see below). In response to the Director General's report *Estate Agency* (March 1990), regulations have been made under section 3 to extend these grounds. Convictions for a number of specified offences, for example unlawful harrassment of debtors, licensing, canvassing and advertising offences under the Consumer Credit Act 1974 and pricing offences under the Consumer Protection Act 1987, now enable prohibition proceedings to be taken.[2] Furthermore certain practices have been declared undesirable and thus grounds for prohibition or restriction.[3] These include

---

20 This section is not yet in force. The Director General did not believe implementation of these provisions would assist consumers as most are affected by unethical practices rather than incompetence; see *Estate Agency*, OFT, March 1990, para. 2.3.

1 For details of people prohibited from practising or restricted in their activities see Annual Reports of Director General of Fair Trading. Up to the end of 1991 150 estate agents had been banned, 9 restricted and 9 warned.

2 Section 3(1)(a)(iii) and the Estate Agents (Specified Offences) (No. 2) Order 1991, S.I. 1991/1091.

3 Section 3(1)(d) and the Estate Agents (Undesirable Practices) (No. 2) Order 1991, S.I. 1991/1032. See OFT booklet *The Estate Agency Guide – What you need to know if you are engaged in estate agency work*.

failure to disclose a personal interest in the property, promptly and in writing, discriminating against prospective purchasers who do not desire other services from the estate agent and failing to give clients prompt, written notification of offers received from prospective purchasers. Failure to comply, without reasonable excuse, with a prohibition or restriction order is an offence under section 3(8). Provision is also made, under section 4, for warnings to be issued in cases of failure to comply with obligations under the Act or for engaging in undesirable practices; future misbehaviour could then lead to a banning order being made.

The Act also imposes certain duties on practising estate agents. These are contained in sections 12 to 21 and include the following duties or obligations:

a) The duty to give certain information about charges and the point of time when these charges become payable (it having been for many years controversial as to whether estate agents earn their fee on 'introducing a person ready and willing to buy' or on actual exchange of binding contracts), additional services offered and explanations of certain terms used (section 18 and regulations made thereunder[4]).

b) A duty to declare any conflict of interest, actual or potential, or any personal interest of the estate agent with respect to the transaction (section 21).

c) No estate agent may seek from a purchaser a pre-contract deposit in excess of a prescribed limit (section 19).[5]

d) Where a deposit is taken from a purchaser, either as a pre-contractual deposit or as a deposit on exchange of contracts, there are duties relating to the keeping of such money in separate 'client accounts' in a manner comparable to that applicable to solicitors (sections 12–17).[6]

These duties are designed to encourage fairness and openness in dealings with vendors and purchasers and to avoid a number of well-publicised incidents where estate agents have decamped with purchasers' deposits, there being no compulsory compensation scheme applicable in this type of case. Failure to comply with

---

4   Estate Agents (Provision of Information) Regulations 1991, S.I. 1991/859.

5   This section is not yet in force.

6   See Estate Agents (Accounts) Regulations 1981, S.I. 1981/1520. For comment on the practical aspects see C. Sweeting 'Little Ado About Something' (1985) 93 ITSA MR 216.

Provisions relating to insurance cover for client's money under ss. 16 and 17 are not yet in force. In *Estate Agents Act 1979: A review by the Director General of Fair Trading*, OFT, 1988, it was felt that implementation of these provisions would be too costly for both government (local and national) and estate agents' customers in view of the few problems which arise (see paras. 16.1–16.3).

provisions concerning the keeping of clients' accounts is an offence (section 14(8)) and failure to provide information under section 18 makes any contract unenforceable without a court order (section 18(5)).

The enforcement of the Act is under the overall supervision of the Director General of Fair Trading. Local weights and measures authorities in Great Britain and the Department of Economic Development in Northern Ireland are also enforcement authorities. They are given powers, under section 11,[7] of entry and inspection. They may use these powers to require production of books or documents and to seize and detain any books or documents which may be required as evidence in proceedings, provided that the authorised officer has reasonable cause to suspect that an offence has been committed under the Act. Most of the Act came into force on 3 May 1982 although, as already noted, some sections are still awaiting commencement regulations.

Two additional developments affect estate agents. First the Property Misdescriptions Act 1991 will create criminal liability for misdescriptions of property. This is discussed further in ch. 12. Second, the Director General, in his report *Estate Agency*, advocated a voluntary code of practice for estate agents to supplement the legal framework, with a redress procedure incorporated. In 1990 the Ombudsman for Corporate Estate Agents (OCEA) was set up by the 15 largest corporate residential agencies, now there are 28 members. The scheme has adopted a code of practice with an ombudsman who can award up to £100,000.[8]

Insurance

A review of insurance law is outside the scope of this book but the conduct of insurance business and of claims made by consumers of the services of insurers has for some years been the subject of various criticisms.[9] In particular, the following two matters give rise to difficulties:

a) Duty of disclosure. Since the insurance contract is one 'of the utmost good faith' it has long been established 'in connection with insurance of all sorts, marine, fire, life, guarantee and every kind of policy that, as the underwriter knows nothing and the man who comes to him to insure knows everything, it is the duty of the assured

---

7   See also the Estate Agents (Entry and Inspection) Regulations 1981, S.I. 1981/1519.
8   See (1990) 87 LS Gaz, No. 33, p. 7 and *Consumer Redress Mechanisms*, OFT, November 1991, paras. 4.81–4.83.
9   See M & H pp. 134–146; *Which?* March 1991, p. 133.

. . . to make a full disclosure to the underwriters without being asked of all the material circumstances'.[10] The failure to disclose material facts by the insured entitles the insurance company to refuse to honour claims. A rather dramatic application of this principle occurred in *Woolcott v Sun Alliance & London Insurance Ltd.*[11] There the insured had been sentenced to 12 years' imprisonment for robbery and had other criminal convictions. In 1972 he had applied for a loan of £12,000 through his building society towards the purchase of a house. Under the terms of the mortgage the building society insured in the joint names of themselves and the insured. The insured never completed a proposal form but filled in an application form for a loan in which he was asked to state the amount for which he wished his house to be covered. No mention was made of his previous convictions. Having purchased the house, some two years later the house was totally destroyed by fire. The insurance company indemnified the building society to the extent of the advance but refused to meet a claim for the balance by the insured on the grounds that he had failed to disclose his previous robbery conviction. The High Court upheld the insurers on the principle that the insured was under a duty to disclose such facts as a reasonable and prudent insurer might have treated as material. A previous conviction for such a serious offence as robbery was clearly a fact which came within this category. The insurance company was therefore within its rights in refusing to honour the insured's part of the claim. The insured here was not assisted by the Rehabilitation of Offenders Act 1974 which makes provision for convictions to be regarded as 'spent' after a certain period has elapsed, the maximum period being ten years. This does not apply to serious sentences including imprisonment for a term exceeding 30 months.

The Law Commission in its report on Non-Disclosure and Breach of Warranty[12] stated that 'the present law as to non-disclosure is defective. The mischiefs in the present law cannot be cured by voluntary measures of self-regulation by the insurance industry such as Statements of Insurance Practice. In the absence of effective administrative control of underwriting, reform of the law is therefore required.' (para. 10.5). The Law Commission went on to propose that the duty of disclosure should be modified along the lines suggested in the Fifth Report of the Law Reform Committee. Under

10   *Rozanes v Bowen* (1928) 32 Ll L Rep 98 at 102. See Law Com. No. 104, Pt. 3, Cmnd. 8064 and 'Of reciprocity and remedies – duty of disclosure in insurance contracts' H Y Yeo, (1991) 11 Legal Studies 131.
11   [1978] 1 All ER 1253, [1978] 1 WLR 493; M & H p. 134.
12   Law Com. No. 104, October 1980.

these proposals a fact should be disclosed to the insurer by an applicant if:

a) it is material in the sense that it would influence a prudent insurer in deciding whether to offer cover against the proposed risk and, if so, at what premium and on what terms; and

b) it is either known to the applicant or it is one which he can be assumed to know; for this purpose he should be assumed to know a material fact if it would have been ascertainable by reasonable enquiry and if a reasonable man applying for the insurance in question would have ascertained it; and

c) it is one which a reasonable man in the position of the applicant would disclose to his insurers, having regard to the nature and extent of the insurance cover which is sought and the circumstances in which it is sought.[13] (N.B. it should be particularly noted that the duty to disclose material facts, both under the existing law and under the proposed reforms, continues to apply in the case of annual renewals of policies. Most insurance policies in England, other than policies of life insurance, are contracts for a term of one year and are renewable annually.)

b) Warranties. A second feature of insurance contracts which has given rise to concern relates to 'warranties'. Warranties are those statements actually made by the insured in the course of filling in the proposal form which are incorporated into the insurance contract. If any answer to a question asked is untrue the insurers may refuse to pay out on a claim on the ground of 'breach of warranty'.

Again the Law Commission regarded the present law in regard to warranties as defective and recommended statutory reform. In particular, it is proposed that a term of a contract of insurance should only be capable of constituting a warranty if it is material to the risk. This proposal is designed to negate the harsh result of the House of Lords' decision in *Dawsons Ltd v Bonnin*[14] where it was held that a wrong answer in the proposal form relating to the address at which a motor vehicle was to be garaged, though admittedly immaterial, nevertheless entitled the insurers to avoid liability under the policy.

It is further to be noted that the Unfair Contract Terms Act 1977, section 1(2) and Schedule 1 state that sections 2 to 4 of that Act (relating to the avoidance of liability for negligence, breach of

---

13 Law Com. No. 104, paras. 4–47 et seq, para. 10–5, and see also draft Bill attached to that Report. See NCC response *Insurance law – non-disclosure and breach of warranty* (1981); M & H p. 136.

14 [1922] 2 AC 413; M & H p. 142.

contract and indemnity clauses) do not apply to any contract of insurance.

It is clear that in the light of the Law Commission's Report above referred to, there is now considerable impetus towards reform on a number of aspects of insurance law in the consumer interest. To date no legislation has been forthcoming; instead the insurance industry has modified its Statements of Insurance Practice to require disclosure of facts one could reasonably be expected to disclose.[15]

Meanwhile a welcome development relating to the treatment of claims by insurance companies was the launching, in 1981, of an 'Insurance Ombudsman Bureau' to deal with complaints as to the handling of claims by consumers.[16] This Bureau was devised initially by the Guardian Royal Exchange, the General Accident and the Royal Insurance companies. In 1990 it merged with the Unit Trust Ombudsman scheme and now has over 330 members. The Bureau provides a conciliation service for United Kingdom personal policy holders of the member companies and individual unit trust holders.

In 1991 the Insurance Ombudsman received 4,334 new cases; of completed investigations he rejected two-thirds of them and upheld the policy holder's complaint in 910 of them. In addition he received 13,899 written enquiries and 26,048 telephone enquiries. Awards of up to £100,000 may be made by the Ombudsman. His decision is binding on the member companies but a complainant may still take court action if the complaint is rejected or the complainant is dissatisfied. Another method of deciding insurance disputes involves the Personal Insurance Arbitration Service (PIAS) to which a number of insurance companies belong. Here disputes are, with the consent of the member insurance company, resolved by arbitrators from the Chartered Institute of Arbitrators. The decision is binding on both parties and the service is free.

---

15   See *Which?* June 1986; Forte (1986) 49 MLR 754.
16   See M & H pp. 324–6 and *Consumer Redress Mechanisms*, OFT, November 1991, paras. 4.73–4.74 and Appendix 2, Table 2.

8 The enforcement of consumer rights – civil and criminal proceedings

1. CIVIL PROCEEDINGS

Introduction

The object of this chapter is first to describe and assess the formal machinery for recovery of compensation by a consumer where his claim lies, as it is likely to, in contract or in tort. Legal aid and advice is also explained. The second part of the chapter describes the criminal process which may be involved where a crime is committed against the consumer and in particular describes how compensation may now be obtained in criminal cases without the necessity of separate civil proceedings.

Courts exercising the relevant civil jurisdiction

If a consumer wishes to pursue a complaint about the defective quality of goods or services provided or about personal injury or loss caused by defective goods or services his cause of action will lie in contract or tort. The accompanying diagram on p. 201 indicates the relevant courts and avenues of appeal available in a typical consumer complaint case. The action will originate in either the Queen's Bench Division of the High Court or in the county court.

The relationship and division of business between the High Court and the county court has frequently been debated, as has the possibility of integration of the two courts, with their differences in practice and procedure so perplexing to the layman.[1] Unfortunately what might have been a desirable development from the litigant's point of view has been frustrated by such considerations as rights of audience and restrictions thereon imposed upon solicitors and their supposed adverse effects on the status of High Court judges. The latest thinking reflects the deliberations of the Civil Justice Review

---

1 See for example the Gorell Committee on County Court Procedure 1908–09, H C 71; Beeching Commission on Assizes and Quarter Sessions, Cmnd. 4153, 1969, p. 73.

Body.[2] The former mechanical criteria were almost entirely dependent on whether or not the debt, demand or damage did not exceed £5000, in which case the county court took jurisdiction. Now by virtue of the High Court and County Courts Jurisdiction Order 1991 (made under the Courts and Legal Services Act 1990) from 1 July 1991 county courts have unlimited jurisdiction for general list cases. Criteria for trial allocation depend upon substance, importance and complexity. Generally cases involving amounts below £25,000 are tried in a county court while those above £50,000 are tried in the High Court. Cases falling in the middle, where the amounts involved are between £25,000 and £50,000 are tried in either court according to the above criteria and judicial availability. (All personal injury cases under £50,000 start in the county court.) The idea is to identify cases which really need the expertise of the High Court.

It is not proposed to deal with the procedure involved in High Court civil actions, which differs in some important matters of detail from the simpler procedure of the county court. A case of sufficient importance for the High Court will usually, though not necessarily, be taken by solicitors and barristers (solicitors normally having no right of audience at the hearing) on behalf of the parties. Legal aid will often be available to help meet the cost of professional representation.

The county court

Civil judicial statistics show that over 90 per cent of all civil proceedings have, over recent years, been commenced in the county court. These include the vast majority of claims by or against buyers of goods and services. The total not only applies to claims brought under the court's general jurisdiction in contract and tort mentioned above but also under its special jurisdiction given by some 150 statutes dealing with specific areas – hire-purchase and landlord and tenant being two very prevalent examples.

County courts were created by the County Courts Act 1846 to try, on a local basis, cases involving smaller sums of money. They are not in any way based on geographical counties. The county court operates in about 300 towns and cities, and these are grouped into over 60 districts to each of which is allocated at least one circuit judge. On the passing of the Courts Act 1971 existing county court judges became circuit judges. New appointments are made by the Crown on the recommendation of the Lord Chancellor from amongst barristers or solicitors who have enjoyed general rights of audience in the Crown Court or in county courts for 10 years. A

2   See Cm. 394, 1988, Ch. 3.

Courts exercising civil jurisdiction (England and Wales)

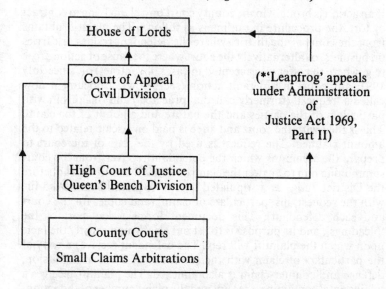

*Appeals may, exceptionally, go from the Queen's Bench Division direct to the House of Lords if the trial judge, the parties and the House of Lords agree and a point of law of general public importance is involved relating to statutory interpretation or if the judge was bound by a previous decision of the Court of Appeal or House of Lords.

District Judge of at least three years' standing is also eligible. Each district must also have a District Judge, formerly known as a Registrar, assisted by Deputy District Judges (usually local solicitors in practice). The Courts and Legal Services Act 1990 took away the administrative functions of the former Registrars and District Judges, who are required (in effect) to be barristers or solicitors of at least seven years' standing, are responsible for the procedural steps in county court litigation and, of particular importance to consumer claims, the trying or arbitration of 'small claims' (discussed later). In this connection it should be noted that after 1 July 1991 any proceedings in which the sum claimed or amount involved does not exceed £1,000 stands referred for arbitration to the District Judge upon receipt by the court of a defence to the claim.[3] The District Judge may then refer the proceedings to the circuit judge or an outside arbitrator.

3 County Court (Amendment No. 2) Rules 1991, S.I. 1991/1126.

Procedure

If an action is brought in the county court on a claim lying in contract or tort, the procedure in outline is as follows. The plaintiff obtains from the court of the district where the defendant resides or carries on business, or alternatively the court where the cause of action arose (e.g. where the offer was accepted in cases of contract) or, since July 1991, any court in a default action (see below), a document now called a 'request' (formerly called a 'praecipe') and fills this in with particulars of the parties and the nature and amount of the claim. This is filed with the court and a fee is paid on a scale related to the amount claimed. The request is used by the staff of the court to prepare the summons which the defendant receives from the court summoning him to answer the claim or admit it and to appear before the District Judge at a stipulated date. The plaintiff must also file with the request, his 'particulars of claim' (and copies for the court and each defendant). This document forms a key part of the 'pleadings', and its purpose is to set out clearly and shortly the facts upon which the plaintiff will rely. The defendant receives a copy of the particulars of claim with the summons. A form of admission, defence and counter-claim is also annexed. The plaintiff receives a 'plaint note' containing a receipt and the plaint number of the action.

The defendant may admit the claim, in which case he must within fourteen days pay the whole or part of the sum into court, plus costs on a fixed scale as indicated in the summons. If less than the full amount claimed is paid in the plaintiff has an option whether to accept this lesser sum, and if he does not the action proceeds. If the defendant proposes to pay by instalments the plaintiff similarly has an option whether or not to accept this offer, and if he does not accept the action proceeds.

If the defendant disputes the claim he must file a defence (and counter-claim in respect of a set-off if appropriate) within fourteen days. If he does nothing, he may still appear on the return day and dispute the claim, but rules provide that he be then responsible for any extra costs incurred and he may even be debarred from defending altogether. On the filing of a defence in an action for a liquidated sum (e.g. an alleged debt) the action is automatically transferred to the defendant's home court.

Assuming that the claim is defended, the next step in an ordinary action is the 'pre-trial review' where the parties meet privately and informally before the District Judge. The District Judge must consider the course of the proceedings and give all such directions as appear to him necessary or desirable for securing the just, expeditious and economical disposal of the action. The District Judge at this stage endeavours to ensure that all admissions and agreements that ought reasonably to be made are made. If the defendant does not appear the plaintiff may at this stage obtain judgment after proving his case by giving evidence on oath (and by affidavit if necessary). Documentary evidence in the form of letters, bills, receipts and so on may be produced in support of the plaintiff's case. In other cases where the defendant does appear, the case is often settled by agreement at this stage. If, however, a trial is required, a day is fixed and notice is given to all parties. (In more complicated proceedings interlocutory orders concerning such matters as third party proceedings, further and better particulars of claim, and discovery and inspection of documents are made at the pre-trial review, or there may be a series of pre-trial reviews if a prevaricating defendant persuades the District Judge that he needs more time.)

The trial is held either before the District Judge (usually in the case of claims not exceeding £5,000 or cases where the defendant is not expected to appear) or in other cases before the county court judge. (Juries are in practice obsolete in the county court.) The hearing is relatively formal with the lawyers involved wearing robes. The plaintiff opens the case and calls his witnesses, who may be cross-examined. The defendant then similarly calls his witnesses, and then makes a speech. The plaintiff may reply to this, and then judgment is given.

The above applies to the conduct of ordinary actions. There is a special procedure, particularly appropriate for collecting debts, known as a default action. The key feature of a default action is that if the defendant fails to respond appropriately, judgment may be requested in default without the need for a trial. A special form of request is used for this action. This form of action must be used (subject to certain exceptions) where the claim is for a set, arithmetically produced, sum of 'liquidated damages' rather than in cases where the claim is for general unliquidated damages. Claims for undischarged debts in respect of goods and services or the cost of repairing a vehicle damaged in an accident alleged to have been caused by the defendant are liquidated or treated as liquidated. Any other claim (e.g. for personal injuries or damages for defects in goods) must be made by an ordinary action. Litigants in persons will be helped by the county court staff to decide on the correct form of summons on the basis of the particulars of claim.

Arbitration

In commercial dealings in particular, the solution of disputes by referring them to arbitration as an alternative to proceedings in the ordinary courts has long been commonplace in the UK and abroad. Many commercial contracts, including insurance contracts, contain provisions whereunder parties must refer a dispute to arbitration before court proceedings are started, and in *Scott v Avery*[4] it was established that court proceedings could be stayed if this step had not first been taken. In these circumstances the agreement to refer to arbitration is contractual, but there are in addition a number of statutes which lay down arbitration procedures. Procedure is governed by the Arbitration Acts 1950–1979 and the 1979 Act[5] in particular has radically altered the former power of appealing to the High Court on the basis that an arbitrator should state a case for the court's opinion. This power was abused and brought English arbitration awards into disrepute on the grounds that the arbitrator's opinion was rarely final in any case of importance and proceedings were accordingly long drawn out and expensive. The 1979 Act now provides that parties may enter into an agreement excluding the jurisdiction of the High Court, but in arbitrations between UK residents, only after the arbitration has commenced. This effectively blocks any right of appeal, and unless the arbitrator has misconducted himself his award will be final. In other cases there is a right of appeal on a question of law, but only with consent of both parties or with leave of the court. The court will not grant leave unless it considers that the determination of the question of law could affect substantially the rights of the parties, and conditions, such as provision of security for the amount claimed, may be laid down. The High Court also has jurisdiction, save where excluded by agreement, to determine any question of law arising in the course of a reference with the arbitrator's consent or the consent of all the parties. This now very limited power of the court to intervene should be borne in mind by the consumer who decides to make use of arbitration procedures, whether under the provisions of a contract or Code of Practice, or by invoking the 'small claims' jurisdiction of the county court considered below, to which similar considerations apply.

A systematic attempt to deal with consumer small claims on a voluntary arbitration basis was made in 1971 in Manchester by the formation of an Arbitration Scheme for Small Claims, and a Small Claims 'Court' was established in Westminster in 1973. Much good work was done by these arbitration panels and their organisers

---

4   (1856) 5 HL Cas 811. Note, however, the Consumer Arbitration Agreements Act 1988, discussed in ch. 11.

5   See (1980) 43 MLR 45. See further *Pioneer Shipping Ltd v BTP Tioxide Ltd, The Nema* [1982] AC 724, [1981] 2 All ER 1030 on the circumstances governing the discretion as to whether to give leave to appeal against an award to the High Court on a question of law. See also [1980] JBL 348; [1981] JBL 362 and *Antaios Cia Naviera SA v Salen Rederierna AB, The Antaios* [1985] AC 191, [1984] 3 All ER 229, HL.

claimed that since there were no pleadings and no pre-trial review they were speedier and simpler than county court proceedings. Arbitrators, usually solicitors, were appointed from a rota of those willing to do the work for a nominal fee. However, the preliminary difficulty of securing the consent of *both* parties, since the schemes were voluntary, the lack of any easily operated enforcement procedure and, most critically of all, the lack of any public or charitable funding to continue the schemes led to their demise by 1980. Interestingly, there is in the early 1990s a movement to introduce alternative dispute resolution (ADR), where, essentially, a skilled conciliator guides the parties towards an agreed settlement of the dispute outside the court system altogether, but has no power to act further if agreement cannot be reached.[6]

At the same time a parallel development was taking place in the county court itself, no doubt in response to the criticism of over-formal, slow and expensive court procedures mentioned below. The Administration of Justice Acts 1973 and 1977, amending the County Courts Act 1959,[7] gave power for County Court Rules to prescribe cases in which proceedings may be referred to arbitration, either automatically or by order of the court, and enacted that the order of the arbitrator shall be as binding and effectual as if given by the judge. Order 19 of the County Court Rules, as amended by the County Court (Amendment No. 2) Rules 1991,[8] governs the position as from 1 July 1991. The scheme has the following main features:

a) Any proceedings involving an amount of £1,000 or less stand referred automatically to the District Judge as soon as a defence to the claim is received. (In 1989, 68% of money claims in the county court were for less than £500, the then limit.) The District Judge may, on a party's application, appoint the circuit judge or an outside arbitrator instead of himself.

b) If one of the parties so applies, the District Judge may subsequently rescind the arbitration referral, but only in certain circumstances. These are that he must be satisfied that a difficult question of law or a question of fact of exceptional complexity is involved, or a charge of fraud is in issue, or the parties agree to trial by the court, or that it would be unreasonable for the matter to proceed to arbitration having

---

6 See, for a vigorous promotion of ADR, *Judgement Day – The Case for Alternative Dispute Resolution* Adam Smith Institute, London (1992); also K.J. Mackie (ed.) *A Handbook of Dispute Resolution* (1991) Routledge.

7 See now s. 64 of the County Courts Act 1984 as amended.

8 See rr. 5 and 8.

regard to its subject matter and the interests of third parties likely to be affected.[9]

c) A simpler procedure is laid down for resolving the dispute. A date for preliminary consideration is, except in very simple cases, first appointed by the arbitrator, and at that stage the arbitrator will fix a hearing date and indicate what further steps should be taken before and at the hearing, though by the agreement of the parties the arbitrator may decide the case purely on the basis of statements and documents.

d) By consent of the parties, and before making an award, the arbitrator may take the evidence of expert witnesses.

e) At the hearing the proceedings 'shall be informal and the strict rules of evidence shall not apply'. Since representation by lawyers will normally be absent, the arbitrator is required to give each party a fair and equal opportunity to present his case. The parties' position is strengthened since 1992 when, by Order made under section 11 of the Courts and Legal Services Act 1990, they have a statutory right to lay representation. Under section 11(4) of that Act if a representative is behaving in an unruly manner 'the court may refuse to hear him'.

f) Generally no legal costs are allowed in respect of arbitrated claims of £1,000 or below.[10] The exceptions are the costs stated on the summons, any costs of enforcing the award and costs certified by the arbitrator as having been incurred by the unreasonable conduct of the other party. Travelling expenses and other incidentals may also be allowed (and these can in practice be significant, particularly where claims for witnesses' fees and for loss of wages are involved).

g) The arbitrator may proceed at a hearing despite the other party's absence, but there is a discretion to set aside such an award.

h) An award may be enforced as a judgment of the court. Accordingly all the machinery of the county court for enforcement of judgments, particularly warrants of execution against the debtor's property and attachment of earnings orders, are available.

i) The procedure may, of course, be used *against* consumers as well as by them, a point sometimes overlooked.

As mentioned above, this procedure involves an arbitration not a

---

9   For an example of where this occurred in facts arising out of a motor accident where the plaintiff was insured for third party risks only and the defendant comprehensively, see *Pepper v Healey* [1982] RTR 411, CA. See also generally M & H p. 312 et seq.

10   Ord. 19, r. 1(11).

trial and the possibility of appeal is very limited. For all practical purposes the arbitrator's decision is final on the facts. The circuit judge has power to set aside an award,[11] but this power can only be exercised if there is an error in law on the face of the record or misconduct by the arbitrator. It is in deference to this that the forms used in connection with an arbitration carry a warning that 'where a defended claim is arbitrated the right of appeal against the arbitrator's award is very limited'.

It will also be noted that because no legal costs are normally awarded in respect of the hearing legal representation is discouraged, but not forbidden. However, consumers and other litigants are of course entitled to avail themselves, if eligible, of the 'green form' scheme of legal advice from a solicitor in preparing a claim or defence.[12]

Litigants in person

Particularly with the advent of the small claims arbitration procedure in the county court, there has been a move to reduce the cost of litigation by litigants dispensing with solicitors, and acting and appearing for themselves. At the same time county courts have tried to change their rather forbidding image and become more accessible and helpful to such litigants. In particular the Lord Chancellor's Office has produced four leaflets, namely 1) 'What is small claim?'; 2) 'How do I make a small claim in the county court?'; 3) 'No reply to my summons – what should I do?'; 4) 'The defendant admits my claim – what must I do?'. These present most helpful guidance on steps to be taken and have been awarded the Crystal Mark for clarity approved by the Plain English Campaign. Every litigant in person unused to court procedures should study these leaflets, available free from the courts and some Citizens' Advice Bureaux and Advice Centres, which perform a valuable service in the administration of justice at ground level.

With regard to costs in actions when the claim involved exceeds the financial limit below which solicitors costs, other than those shown on the summons, are not allowed, the successful litigant in person was formerly not entitled to remuneration in respect of time and labour involved. Mainly as a result of pressure from the Consumers' Association the Litigants in Person (Costs and Expenses) Act 1975 abrogated this rule as from 1 April 1976. The lay

11 See County Courts Act 1984, s. 64(4), and Ord. 37, r. 7.
12 The small claims procedure is likely to undergo further reforms in the near future. See *Civil Justice Review* (1988) ch. 8; G. Applebey, 'Justice Within Reach?' (1987) 6 CJQ 214; *Ordinary Justice*, NCC, 1989.

litigant may now recover up to two-thirds of the sum which would have been allowed by his solicitor in accordance with an hourly rate. Guidance to litigants in person in drafting 'bills' is issued by the Lord Chancellor's Office and is available at the courts and in Citizens' Advice Bureaux.

The trend towards official encouragement, or at least absence of positive discouragement, to litigants in person continues with the projected setting up of an office in the Royal Courts of Justice in London whose staff will be available with advice on procedures for the common forms of action. There have long been personal application facilities for obtaining grants of probate and letters of administration, and divorce procedure in undefended cases has also been simplified to enable parties to act for themselves.

Class actions

In the UK the remedies available to a consumer must generally be obtained by personal initiative, often accompanied by the expenditure of time and money. This factor no doubt accounts for the comparative paucity of reported cases in the UK on sale of goods problems where one party is a consumer as opposed to where both parties are in business. In the UK there is no real equivalent to the 'class action' for ordinary civil claims as understood in the USA. In England and Wales plaintiffs must normally take action personally. Admittedly Order 15, rule 12 of the Rules of the Supreme Court makes provision for representative actions where numerous persons have the same interest in any proceedings, and judgments and orders are binding on all the persons as representing whom the plaintiff sues. However, the phrase 'same interest' was narrowly interpreted in *Markt & Co Ltd v Knight SS Co Ltd*[13] on the basis that where an identical term in separate contracts made with a number of shippers was broken there were nevertheless distinct contracts giving rise to quantifiably different claims for damages.

However, in three cases the court appears to have taken a more liberal view of the scope of representative actions. In *Prudential Assurance Co Ltd v Newman Industries Ltd*[14] the plaintiff company was a shareholder in Newman Industries Ltd. In connection with a takeover bid the plaintiffs brought an action claiming damages for conspiracy against the defendants, the chairman and the vice-chairman alleging (inter alia) that a circular issued was misleading. The plaintiff proposed to bring a representative action on behalf of the shareholders of Newman seeking a declaration that all such

13   [1910] 2 KB 1021. See generally M & H ch. 8.
14   [1981] Ch 229, [1979] 3 All ER 507.

shareholders who had suffered damage as a result of Newman's conduct should be entitled to damages for conspiracy. Vinelott J held that the court had jurisdiction to entertain a representative action by a plaintiff suing on behalf of a class where the cause of action of the plaintiff and each member of the class was alleged to be a separate cause of action in tort. However there were certain conditions which must be present. These included a condition that the court must be satisfied that no member of the class would, by virtue of the representative action, be able to claim a right which he could not have claimed in a separate action and, therefore, a plaintiff in his representative capacity would normally be able to obtain only declaratory relief (as opposed to damages). Further conditions were that the members of the class shared an interest which was common to all of them; and that the court was satisfied that it was for the benefit of the class that the plaintiff be permitted to sue in a representative capacity. In this particular case permission was given for the plaintiffs to sue in a representative capacity. In *EMI Records Ltd v Riley*[15] Dillon J came to a somewhat similar conclusion in allowing a member of the British Phonographic Industry Ltd (BPI) to sue on its own behalf and on behalf of all other members of BPI a market trader who was alleged to be manufacturing, selling and distributing 'pirate records'. Furthermore, in the particular circumstances of this case, the judge held that it was appropriate that damages should be recoverable by the plaintiff in its representative capacity since this would avoid the procedural complication that for the purpose of the enquiry into damages which the court had to make, either all the members of BPI would have to be joined as co-plaintiffs or they would have to issue separate writs. *Prudential Assurance Co Ltd v Newman Industries Ltd* (above) was distinguished in this respect. Where there is a multiplicity of plaintiffs, Order 15 rule 4 allows joinder of these plaintiffs where 'some common question of law or fact would arise in all the actions' and all rights to relief claimed arise out of the same transactions or series of transactions. This is a 'group action' rather than a representative action. A detailed 'Guide for Use in Group Actions' has been issued by the Supreme Court Procedure Committee covering the procedural technicalities and explains how economies in time and documentation may be made. In particular it is possible to have one master statement of claim setting out all the general allegations with the addition of a schedule from each plaintiff specifying which of the general allegations are relied on and setting out the specific facts

15   [1981] 2 All ER 838, [1981] 1 WLR 923.

relevant to that plaintiff.[16] As to legal aid, the Board is of the view that funding should be concentrated in one co-ordinating solicitor or a small group of firms, who would have conduct of the case. The solicitor first instructed by the client would deal with the client on a day-to-day basis.[17]

Before considering the third case, *Davies v Eli Lilly & Co*[18], the problem of dealing with a large number of plaintiffs individually, particularly as to quantum, needs discussion in the light of the history of Thalidomide.

Even though representative or group actions are now becoming better recognised, they cannot be regarded in practice as a panacea for all the ills of the consumer, even in what might be thought of as a fairly obvious case, such as the circumstances arising out of the use of the drug Thalidomide. There, sixty-two actions for damages for negligence were initially brought against the manufacturers of the drug, Distillers Ltd, who had always denied negligence. Negotiations for settlement proceeded on the basis that 40 per cent of what a court would have awarded for a successful negligence claim would be paid to the affected children, and this was approved by the court (as is required where a minor settles a civil action). However, the notional amount that a court would have awarded could not be agreed[19] and two test cases were brought. As a result a total of £1 million was paid by Distillers, apportioned according to disability. Other parents were dissatisfied with this amount and the Court of Appeal upheld the right of dissident parents to have their children's interests considered separately.[20] Public opinion had also gathered in force, and following public discussion and adverse criticism of Distillers a greatly increased sum, involving an estimated total of £20 million, was paid partly in lump sum compensation and partly with a trust fund into which the government also paid £5 million to offset the effects of taxation of the income of the fund. The point of this saga, for present purposes, is that even where there is a mass tragedy on

16   For litigation arising out of claims for personal injuries based on the use of the tranquillisers Ativan and Valium – 'a group pharmaceutical action' involving well over 900 plaintiffs – see *B v John Wyeth & Brothers Ltd* [1992] 1 All ER 443, [1992] 1 WLR 168, CA.

17   See Legal Aid Board Report, Cm. 688, 1989.

18   (1987) 131 Sol Jo 807; affd [1987] 3 All ER 94, [1987] 1 WLR 1136, CA – (concerning the sharing of costs).

19   A difficulty compounded by the uncertainty of whether a plaintiff could recover in respect of ante-natal injuries – see now Congenital Disabilities (Civil Liability) Act 1976.

20   See *Re Taylor's Application* [1972] 2 QB 369, [1972] 2 All ER 873. The Thalidomide affair is briefly outlined in ch. 26 of the Pearson Royal Commission's Report on Civil Liability and Compensation for Personal Injury (1978), Cmnd. 7054.

this scale it is essential that the interests of each affected plaintiff should be separately considered. Furthermore, the judge may feel that he should be properly satisfied as to proof of injury in each case, particularly where alleged drug reactions may in fact be symptoms wholly or partially attributable to some other cause. Economies can be made in England where, particularly if legal aid is involved, the same firm of solicitors and the same counsel can be held to represent all claimants.

The drug Opren

Owing to widespread concern about the alleged side-effects of the anti-arthritis drug Opren, the Opren Action Group was formed in 1982. The Law Society, in view of the very considerable number of potential claimants, agreed to liaise with all those solicitors contemplating the issue of proceedings for their clients. By 1986 a very large number of actions for personal injuries allegedly caused by this drug were instituted both against the manufacturers of Opren, the Eli Lilly group, and against the Committee on Safety of Medicines and the Department of Health and Social Security who were involved in licensing Opren for use in this country. Negligence was alleged on the footing that the Lilly defendants were negligent in the testing and marketing of the drug, and that the government defendants were negligent in its licensing. Since the great majority of Opren cases were legally aided so that the expense of conducting this huge volume of litigation on the plaintiffs side predominantly fell to the public purse, Hirst J in *Davies v Eli Lilly & Co*[1] laid down the procedure which he wished to be followed. He explained that a very substantial proportion of the actions were being conducted by six firms who in close co-operation advised and acted for members of the Opren Action Group. They represented 679 individual plaintiffs or potential plaintiffs. There were known to be a significant number of actual or potential plaintiffs outside this organization. The learned judge drew attention to the following cost saving measures:

1) Making use of short two-page specimen pleadings or schedules, cross-referenced to the very long and complicated master statement of claim and the two master defences of the respective groups of the defendants.
2) Organising one single discovery process to cover as many actions as possible.
3) In the light of the very complex technical and scientific questions arising, for the purpose of the trial on liability it was

---

1   (1987) 131 Sol Jo 807. See O. Hansen (1986) NLJ 883. Rvsd on issues of disclosure [1987] 1 All ER 801, [1987] 1 WLR 428, CA.

feasible and necessary to select an appropriate group of 'lead plaintiffs' who were suitably representative of the various categories into which Opren plaintiffs could be divided, having regard to the plaintiffs' medical history, to represent the various different aspects relevant to the issues of liability.

4) Meanwhile all other Opren actions should be stayed pending the conclusion of the main trial on liability.

5) A timetable should be agreed for issuing the writ (if not yet issued) for delivery of the details of the claim, for notification to the defendants of the wish to join in the 'Opren scheme' outlined by the judge above, and notification by all concerned of the proposed lead actions. The judge concluded:

It will be appreciated that this is a most unusual procedure devised to fit the special needs of this litigation. The intention is to be fair to all interested parties, including the present plaintiffs, serious claimants, and all the defendants, and to strike a fair balance between their interests.

The only other significant exception to the general rule that plaintiffs must normally take action personally is in respect of relator actions under which the Attorney-General appears for a section of the public in such cases as public nuisance or some other non-criminal complaint where an ordinary member of the public lacks the locus standi to sue. In *Gouriet v Union of Post Office Workers*[2] the House of Lords made it clear that a refusal by the Attorney-General to bring relator proceedings (to restrain the union from breaking the law as it had threatened to do) could not be reviewed by the courts. It also held that public civil rights could only be asserted by the Attorney-General as an officer of the Crown representing the public and individuals could not sue unless their private rights were affected or they could show damage over and above the rest of the public.[3]

Conclusions

Despite some recent streamlining, the county courts in many areas have not entirely shed their reputation for excessive proceduralism and delay. There is still no formal procedure allowing 'skeleton legal arguments' to be filed – the key points have to be extracted from the often too voluminous pleadings and other filed documentation. But mainly thanks to the far-reaching suggestions for reform of the Civil Justice Review, change is occurring and the idea that courts are there

2   [1978] AC 435, [1977] 3 All ER 70.
3   In consumer cases the powers of the Director General of Fair Trading to intervene against individuals or traders collectively under the Fair Trading Act 1973, Parts II and III constitute the most potent weapon for preventive action, but injured individuals do not obtain direct redress as a result.

for the benefit of litigants as consumers of the services of lawyers and judges is no longer heretical. From the courts' point of view, the requirement that they should take on an increased volume of work has not always been accompanied by the necessary resources in trained administrators. But until, for example, small claims in particular are able to be heard on Saturdays and one or two late evenings, so that litigants do not need to take so much time off work, many consumers will continue to find the legal process 'user unfriendly', however co-operative the staff of the courts actually try to be.

Sir Jack Jacob is not alone in questioning whether the present small claims arrangements provide 'a procedure which is simple, inexpensive and fair'.[4] An underlying difficulty, however, is that the applicable substantive law is not necessarily 'simple' just because the amount of money in issue is 'small'. District Judges are mitigating the problems by being prepared to take a more 'interventionist' or 'inquisitorial' role and those concerned with further reform might usefully compare the modus operandi of such tribunals as Social Security Appeal Tribunals.[5]

Legal aid and advice

Since 1949 litigants who satisfy certain financial tests have been able to sue or be sued and have their legal costs met in whole or in part from public funds. The present scheme for legal aid and advice is contained in the Legal Aid Act 1988 which deals with both legal aid and advice in civil cases and with legal aid in criminal cases. Consumers of legal services are, of course, likely to wish to use all types of legal aid and advice, but it is more appropriate here to outline the assistance available with civil claims. The administration of the scheme was undertaken by The Law Society under the guidance of the Lord Chancellor. From 1 April 1989 administration passed to the Legal Aid Board, under the Legal Aid Act 1988. Applications for representation certificates are made to an Area Director, and there is a right of appeal to an area committee against a refusal.

Legal aid may be given in the form of representation by a solicitor and, where necessary, a barrister, chosen by the applicant from those undertaking legal aid work. Legal aid is available for civil litigation

---

4 Address to conference at Institute of Judicial Administration, University of Birmingham on 'Reforming Small Claims', reported in Applebey (1987) 6 CJQ 214. See also the NCC's *Ordinary Justice* (1989).
5 An outstanding exposition and critique of the operation of both county courts and this type of statutory tribunal will be found in Smith & Bailey *The Modern English Legal System* (2nd Edn.), particularly chs. 2, 11, 12, 14 and 15.

in certain family-orientated proceedings in the magistrates' courts and in the county court, High Court, Court of Appeal and House of Lords (except in cases of defamation). Tribunals are not within the scheme, (except the Employment Appeal Tribunal, and the Lands Tribunal), nor are arbitrations. Application is made on a form obtainable from solicitors, Citizens' Advice Bureaux or legal aid offices. The form declares the applicant's financial position and contains a statement of the reason for the application which, to be successful, must persuade the Area Director that he has reasonable grounds for taking, defending or being a party to the proceedings.[6]

The financial limits imposed are stringent and are gauged by reference to the concepts of 'disposable income' and 'disposable capital'. Disposable income means gross income less certain necessary deductions including tax, rent, rates and maintenance of dependants. 'Disposable capital' is the applicant's total capital excluding, primarily, the value of the home. The limits may be altered by regulations, but were as from 1 April 1992 £6,800 per annum for disposable income and normally £6,750 for disposable capital. Below these limits the applicant may obtain free legal aid or may be required to make an assessed contribution. The Department of Social Security, who are sent details of the applicant's statements of means, may interview the applicant and investigate the position before legal aid is offered. If the offer is accepted within 28 days a legal aid certificate is granted.

The 1988 Act also makes provisions for legal advice to be given under the scheme. The applicant must approach a participating solicitor and fill in a green form to enable that solicitor to assess disposable capital or income. If his disposable income does not exceed £145 per week, or he is in receipt of income support or family credit, and his disposable capital does not exceed £1,000 he may receive advice or assistance orally or in writing, including assistance with settling a claim, bringing or defending proceedings or preparation of tribunal cases (but not representation at tribunals). With limited exceptions[7] this facility does not extend to the actual institution or conduct of proceedings or, since 1989, to conveyancing or the making of wills. A solicitor can on his own authority provide up to two hours' worth (exclusive of VAT) advice and assistance

---

6   Legal Aid Act 1988, s. 15(2).

7   Assistance may extend to representation by a solicitor where so requested by the magistrates' or county court, or on the solicitor's own proposal if accepted by the court whilst the solicitor is in the court precincts. 'Duty solicitor' schemes exist whereunder ABWOR (assistance by way of representation) is available without a means test etc., covering advice and assistance at police stations and magistrates' courts. Assistance with a will may be given to a client over 70 or to one who is disabled.

(three hours in undefended divorce proceedings). Over this approval must be obtained from the Legal Aid Office. The hourly rate of remuneration from 1 April 1991 was £42, or £44.50 in London. The applicant may be required to make a contribution, calculated according to income only, unless he or she is on income support or family credit or has a disposable income of less than £75 per week. £145 per week is the top limit. These limits are subject to frequent review.

In addition the Legal Aid Act 1979, now Part 3 of the Legal Aid Act 1988, added to the scheme 'assistance by way of representation' (sometimes called ABWOR) which allows representation in domestic and certain child care proceedings in magistrates' courts and tribunals specified by regulations (presently only the Mental Health Review Tribunal). The capital limit here is £3000, unless the client is on income support.

Where legal aid for an action has been granted, the assisted person is only liable to pay the costs of his solicitor and barrister up to the amount of his contribution. He may also be required to pay his successful opponent's costs up to such amount (if any) as is reasonable. A successful unassisted litigant has since 1964 been able, at the court's discretion, to have part or all of his costs paid out of the Legal Aid Fund where his opponent was assisted

However, because the court must be satisfied that severe financial hardship would be caused unless the order for costs is made, this concession is often worthless. It can easily be seen that an assisted litigant has a great (and often unjust) tactical advantage over an unassisted opponent. There appears to have been a slight relaxation of the application of this draconian test since the Court of Appeal's decision in *Hanning v Maitland (No 2)*.[8]

Payments to successful unassisted parties in 1989–90 were £524,381. If the assisted party wins, costs paid by the unsuccessful party are paid into the Legal Aid Board, and the Board has a first charge as regards any balance on any property recovered or preserved.

Conclusions

The Legal Aid and Advice Scheme has played a major part in making the administration of justice available to some of those who would otherwise not be able to afford the cost of professional representation

8 [1970] 1 QB 580.

or advice.[9] Being means-tested and geared to the recovery of some of the expense by way of contributions from assisted persons and payment of costs by unsuccessful unassisted opponents, it has also been administered comparatively economically. But the scheme is subject to some serious criticisms. In brief these are:

i) Legal aid is not at present available in most tribunals, but it is fair to add that there is little agreement amongst chairmen of tribunals on whether legal representation is necessarily desirable;

ii) There is a disparity in bargaining power as between an assisted litigant and his unassisted opponent. The former may tend to resist a settlement and prolong the proceedings in the knowledge that they are at public expense and that, if the plaintiff loses, costs will not be likely to be granted out of the Legal Aid Fund to the unassisted opponent. This is discussed in more detail above. Completely unmeritorious claims may be pursued in the knowledge that the other party will find it cheaper to settle than contest;

iii) The financial limits are arbitrary and cause substantial injustice to many litigants. In particular, a) the middle socio-economic groups are likely to be disqualified on both income and capital grounds and yet often cannot without hardship afford to litigate, particularly in the High Court or above, unless they are assured of success and of the opponent's ability to pay damages and costs; b) the capital limit causes injustice to all groups, particularly the lower socio-economic groups, where the applicant has been provident enough (and unwise enough?) to make savings. These have often involved considerable self-sacrifice in the past and the disqualification of such people is a highly objectionable feature of the scheme.

As Sir Gordon Borrie, has stated:

We are still far from the ideal of Magna Carta: 'To none will we sell, deny or delay right or justice . . .' For people in the upper working or middle classes, litigation is an uncertain and costly venture and the risk of ruinous financial loss is the greater because of the general rule that the loser pays the winner's costs.[10]

---

9   The alleged inaccessibility of solicitors' offices to the lower socio-economic groups, geographically and in terms of opening hours, has been the subject of published comment – see e.g. Ken Foster 'The Location of Solicitors' (1973) 36 MLR 153. The Royal Commission on Legal Services (Cmnd. 7648) allude to the problem in paras. 4.28 et seq. Law Centres, of which there were fifty-eight in 1986, are deliberately situated in densely populated urban areas. For the Royal Commission's assessment of them, see ibid, ch. 8. See also M & H p. 301.

10   Borrie 'Law Reform: A Damp Squib' University of Birmingham, 1970.

One possible solution presently under investigation is a development of the contingency fee system, perhaps a public Contingency Legal Aid Fund as has been suggested by *Justice*. The President of The Law Society said in his inaugural Address in 1977 that the Society would fully support the setting up of any such scheme.[11]

An authoritative survey of the legal aid scheme was conducted by the Cabinet Office Efficiency Unit in 1986 which published 'the Scrutiny Report'.[12] This Report, regarded as the most fundamental review of the legal aid scheme since its inception in 1949, mainly dealt with matters which would streamline the administration of civil and criminal legal aid and advice. The motivation of the exercise was to make savings in the estimated cost of legal aid, which in 1986/87 was £400 million, of which nearly £100 million was attributed to advice, over £260 million to assistance and legal proceedings and a further £35 million was spent on administration. There are separate additional administration costs in respect of the work of the courts and the DSS. These were estimated at £10 million in 1985/86. The administration of legal aid deals with nearly one million applications a year, and deals with one million green form bills and 800,000 legal aid bills. The existing procedures were called 'costly, complicated and overlapping'. There were also criticisms of inconsistency in the grant of applications and the levels of payment.

Amongst the main recommendations was the establishment of a nationally based Legal Services Board responsible for all aspects of legal aid and advice. The Board should be responsible to the Lord Chancellor. The extreme option of setting up a salaried service to provide *all* legal aid service and advice was rejected. The Report recommended the restructuring of the legal aid and advice system using the existing system as a basis.

Perhaps the most controversial recommendation was that the green form scheme should be abolished and in future legal advice should be obtained first from an advice agency in all except criminal cases. The Review commented that there was evidence of a substantial overlap between the advice provided by solicitors and that provided by other agencies. Furthermore there was no co-ordination of the work of advice agencies so that the availability of suitable advice depended very much on where the client lived or where he

11 See Law Society Gazette, 6 October 1977, and Lawyers and the Legal System, *Justice* 1977. See also ch. 16 of the Royal Commission on Legal Services (Cmnd. 7648), 'Alternatives and Supplements to Legal Aid'. The Report recommends the abolition of eligibility levels for both capital and income (paras. 12.31; 12.32) and states that 'we are satisfied that the costs of any substantial piece of litigation will be formidable and beyond the pockets of nearly all private individuals' (para. 12.31).

12 See (1986) Law Society's Gazette 2050.

could reach easily. A good example of this was representation at Tribunals. This is explicitly excluded from the green form scheme. Its availability depended on whether applicants lived in an area where another advice agency provided it. The Scrutiny Report's aim was expressed, however, as being 'to ensure co-ordinated provision of legal advice and Tribunal representation, using lay advisers and lawyers as appropriate'.

The Law Society's response, published in October 1986, was unsympathetic to many of the suggestions made. In particular, the Society considered that the Scrutiny Team's proposals for legal advice would lead to a worse service for the public and yet fail to meet the government's need for cost-effectiveness. Criticism was also received from other concerned bodies and a White Paper,[13] while proposing that responsibility for the scheme should be transferred from The Law Society to the new Legal Aid Board, rejected the abolition of the green form scheme in favour of improving it to provide better service at lower cost. There remains considerable concern about areas of unmet need for legal services in a country with a legal substructure which annually gets more complex. It is unclear how long the service provided by networks of solicitors' offices throughout the country can be taken for granted. Many of them depend on fair rates of legal aid remuneration. The working of the legal aid system is kept under annual review by the Legal Aid Board which reports to the Lord Chancellor, who also has an Advisory Committee. The Lord Chancellor commenced a review of the controversial financial eligibility conditions for the award of legal aid in 1989.

Reform in this vital area inevitably comes up against government restraints on public expenditure. The volume of litigation is increasing and likely to continue to do so as the citizen influenced perhaps by what is seen to be happening in the USA, becomes more aware of his or her 'rights'. Demand for legal services is not easily 'capped'. Government budgets are therefore easily overrun. On the other hand there is abundant evidence from practitioners of costs thrown away by wasted attendances at abortive hearings, and that many court proceedings are over-elaborate and unduly dependent on the adversarial process. It is in this area that reform priorities should lie.

A consultation paper[14] was issued in June 1991 and a proposal is made (as an alternative to the known options of private legal expenses insurance and state-run contingency legal aid) which, if adopted, could save a great deal of public funding. Briefly the

---

13   Cm. 118, 1987.
14   *Review of financial conditions for legal aid and eligibility for civil legal aid* (Lord Chancellor's Department).

proposal would involve scrapping the existing means-tested scheme for civil legal aid and replacing it with a system whereby litigants must first finance their own litigation up to a certain level, according to their means, before they can qualify for legal aid. Litigants would therefore begin their cases privately and could then apply for legal aid if, and only if, the actual costs exceeded a level commensurate with their means. That level could be anything from £50 to £11,000. But those who are presently entitled to free legal aid would continue to be so. The scheme, it is thought, under the 'safety net' principle would help those presently ineligible who are discouraged from litigation by the possibility of high costs arising. A private litigant would have to undertake to spend his or her own funds up to a level between £50 and £11,000 plus. It is thought that where legal aid was not granted from the start and litigants had to undertake a proportion of the risk themselves, this would encourage litigants to take more realistic decisions about proceeding in the first place and settling when the case is underway.

The proposal comes against a background where between 1985 and 1990 the number of legal aid certificates issued rose by 22 per cent, gross spending by 120 per cent from £17 million to £153 million and the average legal aid bill from £950 to £1,526. A survey of 17,000 legal aid cases showed that in 86 per cent of them legal aid was less than £2,500 and in 56 per cent less than £1,000.

The proposal is not without its difficulties, not least in respect of the uncertain and possibly large liability in respect of the opponent's costs.

2. CRIMINAL PROCEEDINGS

Introduction

The consumer will not usually be a direct party to criminal proceedings in the common case of a trader committing a trade descriptions, weights and measures, or food and drugs offence. The prosecution here will be undertaken by a solicitor or an officer of the responsible authority and in the former two cases usually by a trading standards or weights and measures inspector.[15] It is not therefore proposed to deal with the details of criminal procedure and evidence. A large number of offences by traders involving the consumer are treated as summary offences triable in the magistrates'

---

15 By s. 223 of the Local Government Act 1972 a local authority may authorise any member or officer to prosecute, defend or appear on its behalf in a magistrates' court whether or not he is a solicitor.

court. Thus section 84 of the Weights and Measures Act 1985 provides penalties under the Act 'on summary conviction'. Where the offence is tried on indictment the case will have started at the magistrates' court whose magistrates sit as examining justices and remit the case for trial by the Crown Court before judge and jury.

Classification of offences

Before the coming into force of Part III of the Criminal Law Act 1977 the determination of the mode of trial, whether summary or on indictment, was beset by complexities. In some cases summary offences could be tried on indictment and in others indictable offences could be tried summarily. 'Hybrid' offences could be taken either summarily or on indictment according to elections made by the prosecutor or accused.

As a result of the implementation of many of the recommendations of the James Committee on the Distribution of Criminal Business Between the Crown Court and Magistrates' Courts (1975, Cmnd. 6323), Part III of the Criminal Law Act 1977 ('the 1977 Act') creates three categories of offence, namely:

  a) offences triable only on indictment;
  b) offences triable only summarily;
  c) offences triable either way.

At common law all offences are indictable and it follows, therefore, that where there is no express statutory provision an offence is triable only on indictment. In addition an offence can be made triable only on indictment by statute – a classification in practice restricted to offences of an especially serious character. It also follows that an offence triable only summarily must be so designated by statute – see in particular Criminal Law Act 1977, Schedule 1. Most of the offences dealt with in this book are within the third category above, that is triable either way. This is because this third category includes not only the offences formerly listed in Schedule 3 to the 1977 Act and now in Schedule 1 to the Magistrates' Courts Act 1980 ('the 1980 Act') but also those offences which the statute creating them expressly makes triable either summarily or on indictment (1977 Act, section 16(4)). An example is section 14 of the Trade Descriptions Act 1968 (considered in ch. 12).

Procedure with 'either way' offences

Where a person aged at least seventeen is charged with an offence triable either way, the procedure to be adopted is laid down by sections 17 to 28 of the 1980 Act. The main steps involved where the prosecutor is not the Attorney-General, the Solicitor-General or the Director of Public Prosecutions are as follows:

1) The court must cause the charge to be written down, if this has not already been done, and read to the accused (section 19(2)).

2) The court must afford first the prosecutor and then the accused an opportunity to make representations as to which mode of trial would be more suitable (section 19(2)).

3) The court then considers which mode of trial is the more suitable in the light of these representations and in the light of the following matters: whether the circumstances make the offence one of serious character; whether the punishment which a magistrates' court has power to inflict would be adequate (see below); any other circumstance which appears to the court to make it more suitable for trial one way rather than the other (section 19(3)).

4) If the court regards summary trial as appropriate it must then be explained to the accused in ordinary language that he can either consent to such trial or, if he wishes, be tried by jury. It must also be explained to him that if he is convicted and, in the light of his character and antecedents, the court is of the opinion that greater punishment should be given than the magistrates' court has a general power to inflict, the court may commit him for sentence to the Crown Court under section 38 of the 1980 Act. If the accused elects for jury trial by the Crown Court the court must proceed as examining justices, but the accused's decision if he is later convicted may both involve him in heavier costs and, in the case of 'either way' offences such as those under the Trade Descriptions Act 1968, make him liable to the higher penalties (unlimited fine or imprisonment for a term not exceeding two years or both in this case) applicable to a conviction on indictment.

5) If, on the other hand, the court decides that the offence is more suitable for trial on indictment, the court so informs the accused and proceeds as examining justices (section 20(3)). Neither the prosecutor nor the accused can object to this course of action.

6) The court may change from summary trial to committal proceedings at any time before the conclusion of the evidence for the prosecution, and may change from committal proceedings to summary trial at any time during the inquiry into the information as examining justices, with the consent of the accused in the latter case (section 25).

7) Section 23 of the 1980 Act states that where the accused is represented by counsel or a solicitor who in his absence signifies the accused's consent to the proceedings for the determination of the mode of trial, and the court is satisfied that there is good reason for proceeding in the accused's

absence, the court may proceed in his absence. Any necessary consents to summary trial may be given by the accused's counsel or solicitor.

As referred to above, the power of a magistrates' court to sentence is limited. In particular, a magistrates' court has no power to impose imprisonment for more than six months in respect of any one offence (section 31(1)) or in aggregate except in the case of either way offences when the total of consecutive sentences must not exceed twelve months (section 133). But where an adult is tried for an either way offence and convicted by a magistrates' court and the court considers that because of the defendant's character and antecedents greater punishment should be inflicted than the justices have power to impose, they may commit the defendant to the Crown Court for sentence (section 38).

Penalty

Section 32 of the 1980 Act makes specific provision for penalties on summary conviction for offences triable either way. In the case of such offences which are not listed in Schedule 1 to that Act, that is, inter alia, offences under the Trade Descriptions Act 1968, the maximum fine is the 'prescribed sum' unless a particular statute specifically imposes a larger fine. With few exceptions, the maximum punishment for an 'either way' offence tried summarily is six months imprisonment and/or a fine of £2,000 (£5,000 from 1 October 1992) (Criminal Justice Act 1991, section 17).

Territorial jurisdiction

As a general rule a British subject cannot be tried under English law for what would have been offences e.g. under the Trade Descriptions Act 1968 if they had not been committed abroad. There are, however, exceptional cases where a domestic criminal court can take jurisdiction in such circumstances. These include:

a) offences under statutes which, exceptionally, confer such jurisdiction – e.g. Offences against the Person Act 1861, section 9 (murder by a British subject abroad);

b) offences committed by anyone on board British ships whether or not on the high seas and even if a foreign court has concurrent jurisdiction;

c) offences committed on foreign ships within British territorial waters – see Territorial Waters Jurisdiction Act 1878; or on foreign ships not in territorial waters by British subjects not 'belonging' to the ship – see generally Merchant Shipping Act

1894, section 686, considered by the House of Lords in *R v Kelly*;[16]

d) offences committed on installations or designated parts of the continental shelf adjacent to the United Kingdom – see Oil and Gas (Enterprises) Act 1982, s 22;

e) offences committed on British controlled aircraft whilst in flight – see Civil Aviation Act 1982, section 92 and *Air-India v Wiggins*.[17]

In addition, specific statutes may make it an offence to assist or induce the commission abroad of what would be an offence in the United Kingdom – see, for example, Trade Descriptions Act 1968, section 21 (accessories to offences committed abroad).

With regard to jurisdiction over offences committed within England and Wales, a magistrates' court for a county has jurisdiction to try all summary offences committed within the county (Magistrates' Courts Act 1980, section 2(1)). A magistrates' court also has jurisdiction over a person charged jointly with another person who is in custody or is to be proceeded against within the county (ibid, sections 1(2)(b) and 2(2)). Similarly, a magistrates' court by which any person is tried for any offence has jurisdiction to try him for any other summary offence, wherever committed (ibid, section 2(6)).

With regard to indictable offences, a magistrates' court has jurisdiction as examining justices over a person whether the offence was committed in the county or not, and the same applies with regard to its power to try summarily an offence triable either way (ibid, section 2(3) and 2(4)).

Time limits and procedure

In summary proceedings section 127 of the Magistrates' Courts Act 1980 imposes a general time limit on trying an information within six months from the time when the offence was committed. This does not apply to indictable offences including offences triable either way (see further Trade Descriptions Act 1968, section 19, discussed later).

Taking a weights and measures offence by way of example, the genesis of the case may well be a complaint by a member of the public to a trading standards officer who will take down particulars on a form designed for the purpose. If an offence appears to have been committed and the time limit, in this case twelve months from the time of the commission of the offence or three months from when the prosecutor has sufficient evidence to prosecute (whichever first

16 [1982] AC 665, [1981] 2 All ER 1098.
17 [1980] 2 All ER 593, [1980] 1 WLR 815, HL.

occurs)[18] has not expired, the complainant may be asked to give a written and signed statement which may be given in evidence in court.[19] An inspector will then interview the trader and, if appropriate, make tests. The relevant Code of Practice under the Police and Criminal Evidence Act 1984 applies in these circumstances and if there are reasonable grounds for suspecting that a person has committed an offence he or she should be cautioned thus: 'You do not have to say anything unless you wish to do so but what you say may be given in evidence.' A record is then made of questions asked and statements made (normally tape recorded).

A policy decision is then made as to whether or not to prosecute. This may turn on whether the trader has been warned or prosecuted on previous occasions. If prosecution is decided upon it is commenced by an information being laid before a justice of the peace (in the jurisdiction where the offence was commited[20]) to the effect that a stipulated person has committed or is suspected of committing an offence. In this case it will be in writing and signed by an officer authorised by the local weights and measures authority. Otherwise, only a chief police officer (now via the Crown Prosecution Service (see Prosecution of Offences Act 1985)) may lay an information in respect of a weights and measures offence – it is not open to a member of the public to do so. (This is in contrast with the Trade Descriptions Act 1968, under which a lay person may lay an information.[1]) A summons, specifying the defendant, the alleged offence and the date and place of the hearing, and signed by a justice, is then served on the defendant. Had the offence been serious, or the address insufficient for service of the summons, a warrant for the defendant's arrest would have been issued instead.

At the hearing, summary trial having been decided upon, if there is a plea of guilty (the clerk to the justices having first read out the offence with which he is charged and asked him to plead) the prosecutor outlines the circumstances in which the offence was committed and informs the bench of any previous convictions. The defendant may then plead in mitigation of sentence, after which the magistrates pronounce the appropriate sentence. Penalties on summary conviction for offences triable either way are limited to a maximum of six months' imprisonment or the presently prescribed sum of £5,000 (section 32 as amended), though in serious cases the

18   Weights and Measures Act 1985, s. 83.
19   Under Criminal Justice Act 1967, s. 9; Magistrates' Court Act 1980, s. 102. The witness must attend personally if there is an objection to written evidence.
20   Magistrates' Courts Act 1980, s. 1.
1   This is because the Act contains no limitation on the common law right of any person, whether aggrieved or not, to prosecute privately.

magistrates' court may commit the defendant to the Crown Court for sentence under section 38 of the Magistrates' Courts Act 1980. If the actual offence is giving short weight contrary to section 28 of the 1985 Act, the court must refer to the Act to ascertain the correct penalty. Under section 84 this is a fine of up to £5,000.

If the accused pleads not guilty the prosecutor is required to prove his case beyond reasonable doubt. The prosecutor will outline his case and call his witnesses who will give evidence on oath. They are examined (avoiding leading questions) by the prosecutor and may be cross-examined by the accused or his advocate. The questioning of witnesses in accordance with the complex rules of evidence is a skilled art, but where the accused is unrepresented he may in practice be assisted a little by the justices' clerk. The accused then calls any witnesses of his own, who go through the same process of examination-in-chief, cross-examination and, if necessary re-examination, and finally may address the court summarising in what ways the prosecutor's case is not proved. Only if the bench then convicts may evidence of previous convictions be given.

Appeals

The defendant may appeal against either sentence or conviction to the Crown Court and against sentence only if he pleaded guilty. On an appeal against conviction the case is completely reheard, though sentencing powers are limited to those available to magistrates' courts (from which it follows that the Crown Court can increase the severity of sentence within these limits). Alternatively, appeals may lie on a point of law by way of case stated to the Divisional Court of the Queen's Bench Division of the High Court. It will be observed that most of the decisions on trade descriptions discussed in ch. 12 arose in this way. The appeal may be by defendant or prosecutor. The Crown Court in its appellate jurisdiction may also state a case for the opinion of the Divisional Court. If a point of law of general public importance is involved and the Divisional Court gives its certificate to this effect and either it or the House of Lords gives leave to appeal, there may be further appeal to the House of Lords. If the trial was on indictment, appeal against conviction and/or sentence goes from the Crown Court to the Court of Appeal (Criminal Division) and from thence by either party to the House of Lords provided a) a certificate is given by the Court of Appeal that a point of law of general importance is involved and b) leave to appeal by either the Court of Appeal or the House of Lords is given (Criminal Appeal Act 1968, section 33).

Compensation orders

A development of great importance to the consumer is the power of
magistrates' courts and the Crown Court to make compensation
orders in favour of victims of offences. Such a power was introduced
in 1972 and is now to be found in the Powers of Criminal Courts Act
1973 (sections 35 to 38 as amended by sections 104 and 105 of the
Criminal Justice Act 1988). Although there was power to award
compensation for loss of property under section 4 of the Forfeiture
Act 1870 in the case of indictable offences, the power was held to be
inapplicable in a case arising under the Trade Descriptions Act 1968
because, inter alia, there was no loss of property in the particular
case.[2] The aggrieved consumer's only remedy was therefore to bring
a civil action in which, under section 11 of the Civil Evidence Act
1968, the criminal conviction may be pleaded to prove that the
defendant committed the offence. There was criticism of this too
cumbersome procedure in the House of Commons during debate on
the Criminal Justice Bill in 1971, particularly as the Trade Descriptions Act was intended to protect the consumer and this could be
better achieved if a magistrates' court could award compensation.
The Bill was eventually amended to embody what now appears in the
Powers of Criminal Courts Act 1973.

Section 35 of the 1973 Act (as partly replaced by the Magistrates'
Courts Act 1980, section 40) states that the court after convicting for
any offence may, instead of or in addition to its sentencing power,
and on application or otherwise, make a compensation order
requiring the defendant to pay compensation for any personal
injury, loss or damage resulting from the offence or any other offence
taken into consideration by the court in determining sentence. The
question of whether to make an order and, if so, of what amount,
must be judged with regard to the means of the defendant. If there is
a choice, the court should give preference to a compensation order.
At present a magistrates' court may not make an order for more than
£5,000[3] in respect of each offence of which the offender is convicted.
Compensation orders in respect of offences taken into consideration
may not exceed any balance of each £5,000 in respect of offences
which have led to the conviction after deducting compensation
orders actually made (see Magistrates' Courts Act 1980, section 40).
This provision can result in injustice. If the prosecutor charges a
number of offences separately a compensation order can be made in
respect of each 'victim' adversely affected by the offence. But if a

2   *Lieske v Blakemore* (1971) 135 JP Jo 826, Croydon Quarter Sessions.
3   The amount was raised from £2,000 by s. 17(3) of and Sch. 4 to the Criminal
    Justice Act 1991 from October 1992.

number of offences are taken into consideration, the amount of compensation available is arbitrarily lowered. This can be serious in the case, for instance, of a large tour operator whose holidays brochure contains material misdescriptions affecting a number of different consumers.[4] If subsequent civil proceedings are brought, damages are assessed without regard to the compensation, but credit is given in the amount actually awarded for the amount of any compensation order. The compensation order is enforced in the same way as a fine.[5]

A number of decisions[6] have indicated that compensation orders should only be made in clear and simple cases where the defendant has the means to satisfy the order. Magistrates' courts in particular are ill-equipped to measure disputed problems of causation and loss, and such matters are as a general rule left to the civil courts to assess.

As regards the consumer, the power to make compensation orders is particularly valuable in trade descriptions cases where the prosecuting officer of the trading standards authority should in appropriate cases ask for a compensation order on the consumer's behalf, thus saving the trouble and expense of bringing subsequent civil proceedings. The raising of the maximum in magistrates' courts to £5,000 gives the power added importance.[7] Since the Criminal Justice Act 1988 the court must give reasons if it fails to make an order.

The Annual Reports of the Director General of Fair Trading always present an invaluable compilation of statistical data on the volume of both consumer complaints and of convictions under specific legislation, broken down under sectors of trade. Amounts awarded under compensation orders are now given and for 1990 £80,349 was granted in respect of compensation for false descriptions

---

4 It is conceivable that if offences so taken into consideration were subsequently prosecuted a plea of autrefois convict would be unsuccessful. See generally H. Street 'Compensation Orders and the Trade Descriptions Act' [1974] Crim LR 345.
5 Magistrates' Courts Act 1980, s. 76.
6 *R v Kneeshaw* [1975] QB 57 at 60; *R v Daly* [1974] 1 All ER 290, [1974] 1 WLR 133; *R v Vivian* [1979] 1 All ER 48, [1979] 1 WLR 291 – but see the author's criticism of this decision in (1979) Local Government Chronicle 75. See also J. Vennard 'Magistrates' Assessments of Compensation for Injury' [1979] Crim LR 510. See also *R v Boardman* (1987) 9 Cr App Rep(s) 74, (following *R v Vivian* (above)) and *R v Horsham Justices, ex p. Richards* [1985] 2 All ER 1114, [1985] 1 WLR 986. (Where the question of whether there had been loss, and if so what loss, is raised, evidence should be produced in support of representations made by the parties).
7 See generally Home Office Report No. 102, 1988, by T. Newburn, *The Use and Enforcement of Compensation Orders in Magistrates' Courts.*

of goods alone. Of this sum, £64,341 related to offences concerning second-hand cars.[8]

9 A survey of the protective legislation

1. INTRODUCTION

This chapter surveys the umbrella of protection given to the consumer by a considerable number of statutes creating various criminal offences. Some also give certain civil rights in England and Wales to the consumer, and where appropriate these are mentioned too. It will be seen from the tables in chs. 12 and 13 that certain of these, namely the Weights and Measures Act 1985, the Trade Descriptions Act 1968, the Food Act 1984 and the Food Safety Act 1990 give rise to the largest number of consumer complaints and cases reported to the Office of Fair Trading. These, together with the Fair Trading Act 1973, will be dealt with in greater detail in subsequent chapters.

The following table gives an idea of the ambit of the main statutes affecting the consumer. The size and complexity of the legislation merely outlined in this chapter, much of it enforceable by local authorities, is better appreciated when it is realised that a number of these statutes have spanned subsidiary legislation which is both highly technical and extremely voluminous. There are, for example, over 150 regulations made under the food and drugs legislation alone and a substantial percentage of this is pursuant to EEC Directives.

The main criminal statutes affecting consumers

Subject matter	Legislation
Inaccurate quantities	Weights and Measures Act 1985.
Statement of and control of prices	Consumer Protection Act 1987; Mock Auctions Act 1961; Prices Acts 1974, 1975.
Food quality and hygiene	Food Act 1984; Food Safety Act 1990.

229

False descriptions	Trade Descriptions Act 1968; Trading Representations (Disabled Persons) Act 1958; Food Safety Act 1990.
Unsolicited goods and services	Unsolicited Goods and Services Acts 1971 and 1975.
Consumer credit	Consumer Credit Act 1974 (contains some criminal provisions).
Consumer safety; licensing labelling of dangerous products	Consumer Protection Act 1987; Animal Health Act 1981; Petroleum (Consolidation) Act 1928; Explosives Acts 1875 and 1923; Poisons Act 1972; Medicines Act 1968; Farm and Garden Chemicals Act 1967.
Road safety	Road Traffic Act 1988 (selling defective motor cycle crash helmets (section 17) and offences relating to the condition of vehicles).
Insurance policy holders' protection	Insurance Companies Act 1982; Policyholders Protection Act 1975; Financial Services Act 1986.
Pressurised selling	Consumer Credit Act 1974; Timeshare Act 1992; Consumer Protection (Cancellation of Contracts Concluded away from Business Premises) Regulations 1987.
Trading stamps	Trading Stamps Act 1964.
Hallmarking of precious metals	Hallmarking Act 1973.
Handling stolen goods/ obtaining money by deception	Theft Act 1968 (sections 22, 15).

2. LOCAL AND CENTRAL GOVERNMENT ENFORCEMENT AND ADMINISTRATION

It is broadly true that the Departments of State are responsible for legislative policy and administration of consumer protection statute law creating criminal penalties, and local government trading standards and environmental health departments are charged with the enforcement of the legislation. This not only involves the prosecution of offenders but also the prevention of offences by warnings to and education of traders affected by the legislation. There is in addition some central government responsibility for enforcement of particular statutes. For instance, the Director General of Fair Trading has various enforcement powers under Part III of the Fair Trading Act 1973 in respect of (inter alia) those who are trading unfairly.

The department primarily involved with consumer protection is the Department of Trade and Industry which administers the Weights and Measures Act 1985, the Consumer Protection Act 1987, the Prices Acts 1974 and 1975, the Consumer Credit Act 1974, the Fair Trading Act 1973, the Hallmarking Act 1973, the Trade Descriptions Act 1968, the Unsolicited Goods and Services Acts 1971 and 1975 and all aspects of competition policy including the European Community competition rules. The Ministry of Agriculture, Fisheries and Food is concerned with food supplies and food hygiene. It is primarily responsible for administering matters relating to the composition, labelling, marking and advertising of food and also for slaughterhouses and meat inspection. It shares administrative responsibility for the Food Safety Act 1990 with the Department of Health. The Home Office has a general responsibility for the administration of criminal justice and supervises the control of explosives, firearms and dangerous drugs.[1]

3. SUMMARY OF SPECIFIC CRIMINAL LEGISLATION

I) CONSUMER SAFETY AND LICENSING

a) Introduction

A number of statutes seek to use the criminal law to ensure that consumers are protected from unsafe goods. Before examining the relevant provisions it may be helpful to outline the developments which have taken place since the 1960s.

---

1 The institutional framework of consumer protection is further discussed in ch. 3.

In 1961 the Consumer Protection Act 1961 was passed. It was inspired by the need for preventive legislation in respect of dangerous goods identified by the Molony Committee.[2] The 1961 Act was subsequently amended by the Consumer Protection Act 1971 and then in 1976 the government published a Green Paper entitled '*Consumer Safety – A Consultative Document*'.[3] This considered such issues as the possibility of recalls, seizure and destruction of unsafe goods, problems encountered over making regulations, compliance with recognised standards and enforcement procedures.

The then government was unable to introduce the necessary legislation because of pressures on parliamentary time but it was able to support a private member's Bill which became the Consumer Safety Act 1978.[4] The 1978 Act was designed to strengthen and consolidate consumer safety legislation other than in the field of food and drugs. It came into force on 1 November 1978 except for those provisions repealing the Consumer Protection Acts 1961–1971, the Regulations under which also continued in force. It was intended that the Regulations made under the 1961 Act would eventually be re-made as safety regulations under the 1978 Act. The delays in this process were recognised[5] and the enforcement powers under the 1961 Act were improved by being made the same as those under the 1978 Act.[6]

The effectiveness of the 1978 Act, coupled with the Acts of 1961–1971, was reviewed in the White Paper *The Safety of Goods* published in July 1984.[7] Several of the recommendations of the White Paper were then incorporated in a private member's Bill which became the Consumer Safety (Amendment) Act 1986.

Finally in the autumn of 1986 the government introduced the Consumer Protection Bill in the House of Lords. As well as dealing with product liability[8] and the pricing of goods and services,[9] it sought to consolidate existing laws on consumer safety and to introduce a general safety duty as proposed in the White Paper *The Safety of Goods*.[10] The Bill received Royal Assent on 15 May 1987 and Part II (dealing with safety matters) came into force on 1 October 1987. The 1961–71 Acts, the 1978 Act and the 1986 Act were

2   Cmnd. 1011 (Interim Report).
3   Cmnd. 6398; M & H pp. 455–456, 458–459.
4   M & H pp. 456–458; G. Stephenson *The Criminal Law and Consumer Protection* (Barry Rose, 1983) ch. VI.
5   *The Safety of Goods* Cmnd. 9302, para. 54.
6   Consumer Safety (Amendment) Act 1986, s. 16 and Sch. 1.
7   Cmnd. 9302 (1984); M & H pp. 460–461.
8   See further ch. 6.
9   See further ch. 12.
10 Cmnd. 9302, paras. 33–48; M & H pp. 460–461.

all repealed although Regulations made under them were continued, with some modifications.[11]

It is proposed to examine the Consumer Protection Act 1987 ('the 1987 Act') first, followed by other statutes affecting safety.

b) Consumer Protection Act 1987[12]

Discussion of the 1987 Act will begin with those areas which consolidate and improve on earlier legislation and then move to the newly introduced general safety duty.

Section 11 enables the Secretary of State to make 'safety regulations' to secure that goods are 'safe', that unsafe goods are not made available either generally or to particular classes of person and that appropriate information is, and inappropriate information is not, provided (subsection (1)). This is similar to section 1(1) of the 1978 Act, though the specific reference to availability of goods is new. 'Safe' is defined in section 19(1) and (2). It means 'such that there is no risk or no risk apart from one reduced to a minimum' that death or personal injury will be caused by the goods, their keeping, use or consumption, assembly, any emission or leakage from the goods or reliance on the accuracy of any measurement, calculation or other reading made by or by means of the goods. Safety is, therefore, not only concerned with the use of the goods but also their storage. Goods excluded from consideration for safety regulations include food, controlled drugs and licensed medicinal products (section 11(7)). Section 11(2) lists the types of provisions which the safety regulations may contain e.g. with respect to composition, design, construction, finish or packing, approval schemes, testing, inspections, disposals, instructions and prohibitions on supplying etc. the goods.[13] Further provisions concerning prosecution aspects such as time limits are detailed in subsection (3).

The requirement of consultations by the Secretary of State prior to laying a draft safety regulation before Parliament and procedures for parliamentary approval are specified in section 11(5) and (6). In *R v Secretary of State for Health, ex p United States Tobacco International Inc*[14] an application for judicial review was granted against the decision by the Minister to make the Oral Snuff (Safety)

---

11 Section 50(4) and (5) and Consumer Protection Act 1987 (Commencement No. 1) Order 1987, S.I. 1987/1680.
12 See also Fairest *Guide to the Consumer Protection Act 1987*, Merkin *A Guide to the Consumer Protection Act 1987;* D Parry 'Criminal Liability for the Safety of Goods' (1989) 1 Law for Business 219.
13 Similar to 1(2) of the 1978 Act.
14 [1992] 1 QB 353, [1992] 1 All ER 212, QBD.

Regulations 1989.[15] The applicant company was the sole manufacturer and packager of oral snuff in the United Kingdom. Because of the company's special position, the fact that it had been encouraged, by the government, to set up business in Scotland and the catastrophic effect on its business of any ban, the Secretary of State, when proposing new Regulations, should have given the company a full opportunity to know and respond to the proposals. The court decided that there had been unfairness in the way these Regulations had been made and they would therefore be quashed. Taylor LJ indicated that draconian measures require procedural propriety to be observed and fair treatment for those concerned.

Unlike the 1978 Act, the 1987 Act does not contain special provisions for making Prohibition Orders[16] to deal quickly with dangerous goods as they come on to the market. Instead, section 11(5) enables the consultation process to be by-passed if a safety regulation is not to last more than 12 months and the Secretary of State specifies that it appears to him that 'the need to protect the public requires that the regulations should be made without delay'. Such an 'emergency' safety regulation could be replaced, on its expiry, by a permanent safety regulation introduced after full consultation.

Breach of safety regulations is not an offence in itself (section 11(4)). However it is an offence to supply[17] etc. where the regulations prohibit such a supply (section 12(1)). There are also offences connected with the testing of goods, provision of prohibited information and failure to supply correct information (section 12(2)-(4)). There is a penalty of 6 months' imprisonment (compared to the previous 3 months) and/or a fine of up to level 5 on the standard scale for these offences. It is a defence to show that all reasonable steps have been taken and all due diligence exercised (section 39(1)). Seven days' notice to the prosecutor is required for an allegation of act or default of another or reliance on information given by another (section 39(2)). In addition, a defence based on reliance on information supplied by another will not be accepted unless the defendant shows it was reasonable in all the circumstances to rely on the

15   S.I. 1989/2347, see post p. 418.
16   These were designed to prevent anyone from supplying etc. particular goods which were considered unsafe. They involved a 28-day consultation procedure or, in emergency, could be made at once. The Order lasted for one year and could be renewed or replaced with a Safety Regulation. Examples covered children's nightwear, toy tear-gas capsules, toy water snakes, gas catalytic heaters, expanding novelties and scented erasers.
17   A wide definition of supply is provided in s. 46, including selling, hiring, hire-purchase, trading stamps and giving as prizes and gifts. The supply must be in the course of a business (s. 46(5)).

information, having regard to the steps he took or might reasonably have taken to verify the information and whether he had any reason to disbelieve the information (section 39(4)).[18]

In *Rotherham Metropolitan Borough Council v Raysun (UK) Ltd*[19] the court confirmed the need for positive and sufficient steps to be taken to satisfy the reasonable precautions and due diligence defence under section 12 of the 1986 Act, now replaced by section 39(1) of the 1987 Act. Here agents of the respondents in Hong Kong did partially supervise the producer of crayons and one packet out of 10,000 dozen packets was tested in the UK. More recently, in *P & M Supplies (Essex) Ltd v Devon County Council*,[20] where a company had operated a sampling and testing system for toys (378 (0.49 per cent) of 76,960 toys imported sampled, 18 sent to public analyst), the court emphasised that it was up to the defendant to establish that there had been sufficient sampling to satisfy the defence requirements. The need for assistance to be given to magistrates by the defendant, preferably in the form of independent statistical evidence as to what should be done by a reasonable trader in the circumstances, was highlighted.

A by-pass provision is included in section 40 to enable the prosecution of the person, in the course of any business of his, whose act or default caused another to commit an offence, e.g. manufacturers or importers.

In addition to criminal proceedings being taken for certain breaches of obligations under safety regulations, section 41(1) provides (unless excluded in regulations) for a civil action for breach of statutory duty for anyone who has been 'affected by a contravention of the obligation'.[1] The constituents of this tort are that the plaintiff must prove that a) a statutory duty existed, b) this was broken by the defendant, c) damage was suffered. The liability

---

18 This re-enacts the provisions of s. 12 of the 1986 Act which were introduced following the recommendations in para. 20 of *The Safety of Goods* Cmnd. 9302 (1984).

19 (1988) 153 JP 37, QBD.

20 (1991) 156 JP 328, QBD.

1 In many other criminal statutes no such express stipulation is made and a litigant may have to establish the right to sue for breach of statutory duty in the courts. This is unnecessarily unhelpful and has been rightly criticised; see e.g. Borrie and Diamond *The Consumer, Society and the Law* (4th Edn.) p. 148, and compare *Buckley v La Reserve* [1959] Crim LR 451 (Westminster County Court) (no right to sue in tort where food unfit for human consumption (snail) supplied contrary to Food and Drugs Act 1955, s. 8). See commentary [1959] Crim LR 452–3. There is a presumption against the availability of an action for breach of statutory duty when the statute is silent. However, proof of a criminal conviction in a subsequent civil case affords prima facie evidence of the facts on which it was based (Civil Evidence Act 1968).

cannot be limited or excluded by contract terms or notices (section 41(4)) but contributory negligence by the plaintiff is a partial defence.

Section 13 of the 1987 Act re-enacts the provisions, first introduced in section 3 of the 1978 Act, relating to prohibition notices and notices to warn. A prohibition notice is directed at a named trader to prevent that trader from supplying dangerous goods. It may be used against, for example, the sole manufacturer, importer or retailer of a particular item or against a retailer who creates risks by selling certain goods to a particular class of person, for example children, or by the way he sells them, for example without assembling them properly or carrying out the necessary safety checks. The procedures for making prohibition notices are laid down in Schedule 2, Pt I and involve at least a 21-day consultation process. An example of a prohibition notice under section 3 of the 1978 Act illustrates its use. In March 1983 the then Minister for Consumer Affairs, Dr. Gerard Vaughan, issued a warning about gas catalytic heaters, some of which contained asbestos. The main suppliers were asked to stop supplying them and all voluntarily did so except for Impact Heaters (UK). On 26 September 1983 a prohibition notice was issued against Impact Heaters (UK) prohibiting sales. This was then followed by a Prohibition Order, the Gas Catalytic Heaters (Safety) Order 1983,[2] which in turn was replaced by the Gas Catalytic Heaters (Safety) Regulations 1984,[3] thus permanently banning the dangerous heaters. Each step which was taken helped to deal with the immediate problem and enabled time for the necessary consultations before the next stage. Similar steps could be used under the 1987 Act, with the emergency procedure for Safety Regulations being used in place of the Prohibition Order (see above).

The provisions for notices to warn require a person to publish at his own expense warnings about specified goods considered by the Secretary of State to be unsafe. The procedures for issuing such notices are contained in Schedule 2, Pt II and involve a 28-day consultation process. To date no notices to warn have been issued although the Department of Trade and Industry does regularly issue warning notices about the safety of goods.

Contraventions of prohibition notices or notices to warn are offences under section 13(4) with the same penalties, defences and by-pass provisions as for breaches of Safety Regulations. There is no action for breach of statutory duty for harm resulting from either prohibition notices or notices to warn (section 41(2)). This can be

2   S.I. 1983/1696; see also DTI Press Notice, 21 November 1983.
3   S.I. 1984/1802, see below p. 422.

contrasted with the previous position under section 6 of the 1978 Act where there was such an action in the case of prohibition notices.

Section 14 of the 1987 Act re-enacts, with minor alterations, the provisions of section 3 of the 1986 Act relating to 'suspension notices'. It enables the stopping of the supply of goods believed to be dangerous whilst they are tested or a prosecution brought.[4] If an enforcement authority has reasonable grounds to suspect that any safety provision[5] has been contravened in relation to any goods, it may serve a suspension notice on a person. The notice prohibits that person from supplying etc. those goods without the consent of the authority, for a specified period of up to six months (section 14(1)). Breach of a suspension notice is (subject to the defence provisions of section 39) an offence with up to six months' imprisonment and/or a fine of up to level 5 on the standard scale (section 14(6)). To enable the enforcement authority to keep track of suspended goods the notice may require their whereabouts to be notified to the authority throughout the suspension period (section 14(3)). An appeal procedure is laid down in section 15 and compensation may be payable if the goods in fact conform to safety requirements (section 14(7) and (8)).[6]

The case of *R v Birmingham City Council, ex p Ferrero Ltd,*[7] examined the provisions of section 14 and considered the methods of appeal available to a producer who wished to challenge a suspension order. The judgment of the Queen's Bench Division,[8] which had granted judicial review of the decision by Birmingham City Council to suspend the supply of 'Kinder Surprise Eggs', was overturned by the Court of Appeal. Producers aggrieved by the issue of a suspension order against their products have to use the appeal process laid down in section 15 to seek removal of the order by establishing that the goods in question are safe. The case concerned small toys depicting the Pink Panther, contained in the chocolate eggs. A child had died from swallowing part of one of the toys and, as a result, supply of the eggs was suspended for six months under section 14. In rejecting the use of judicial review in such circumstances Taylor LJ stated:

> The real issue was whether the goods contravened a safety provision and the section 15 appeal was geared exactly to deciding that issue. If the

4   See Cmnd. 9302, paras. 23–25.
5   Defined in s. 45(1) as the general safety requirement in s. 10 (see below) or any provision of safety regulations, a prohibition notice or suspension notice.
6   See Cardwell and Kay 'The Consumer Protection Act 1987: Liability of the Enforcement Authorities' (1988) 6 Trad Law 212.
7   (1991) 155 JP 721, CA.
8   (1990) 154 JP 661, QBD.

goods did contravene the safety provision and were dangerous to children then, surely, procedural impropriety or unfairness in the decision-making process should not persuade a court to quash the order. The determining factors are the paramount need to safeguard consumers and the emergency nature of the s 14 powers.[9]

As under section 6 of the 1986 Act, section 16 of the 1987 Act allows enforcement authorities to apply for an order forfeiting goods which contravene safety provisions. The court, if satisfied of the contravention, may order the destruction of the goods or their release to a specified person for possible repair or as scrap (section 16(6) and (7)). An appeal process is provided under section 16(5) with power to delay the destruction of the goods pending the appeal.

The enforcement provisions, under Pt IV of the 1987 Act (sections 27–35),[10] reflect the recommendations in the White Paper *The Safety of Goods*,[11] which were subsequently introduced in the 1986 Act. Enforcement officers can inspect and seize goods for testing, inspect documents etc. at the point of first supply i.e. before they have been supplied to consumers in the United Kingdom (section 29). It is thus possible to check goods for compliance with relevant safety provisions both at the retail stage and at the manufacture/import stage. There is an appeal procedure against any seizure of goods, together with the possibility of compensation if there has been no breach of safety provisions (sections 33 and 34). The Commissioners of Customs and Excise may, under section 37, disclose to trading standards officers, information on goods imported into the United Kingdom (subject to confidentiality restrictions contained in section 38). In addition, customs officers are given powers to seize and detain goods for up to two working days to enable trading standards officers to inspect the goods (section 31).[12]

The provisions of the 1987 Act discussed so far have been those covering areas already dealt with under previous legislation. The 1987 Act does, however, also create a new general safety duty. The idea of such a duty was mooted in the White Paper *The Safety of Goods*[13] because of the problem with existing safety legislation that 'only a limited number of categories and aspects of consumer goods'

9   (1991) 99 ITSA Trading Standards Review Pt 8, p. 16, at p. 18.
10 See further K Cardwell 'The Consumer Protection Act 1987: Enforcement of Provisions Governing the Safety of Consumer Goods' (1987) 50 MLR 622.
11 See Cmnd. 9302 paras. 21–22.
12 See Cmnd. 9302 paras. 27–32.
13 Cmnd. 9302 paras. 3348; M & H pp. 460–461; see also *Implementation of EC Directive on Product Liability* Department of Trade and Industry November 1985, pp. 8–10.

are covered (para. 33). The White Paper proposed 'to place a general obligation on the suppliers of consumer goods to achieve an acceptable standard of safety where it is reasonable to expect them to anticipate and reduce the risks arising from those goods' (para. 34). This has been implemented in section 10 of the 1987 Act. The section makes it a criminal offence for a person to supply,[14] offer or agree to supply or expose or possess any consumer goods 'which fail to comply with the general safety requirement'. 'Consumer goods' are defined, in subsection (7), as goods ordinarily intended for private use and consumption, but excluding such things as water, food, feeding stuff, controlled drugs, licensed medicinal products, aircraft (other than hang-gliders) and motor vehicles. These areas are, according to the White Paper, excluded from existing safety legislation or are 'already adequately covered by other statutes' (para. 44). Also excluded is tobacco as the application of a general duty 'could raise particular problems' (para. 44).

Consumer goods will fail to comply with the general safety requirement if they are not reasonably safe having regard to all the circumstances including the manner in which and purposes for which they are marketed, their get-up, use of marks, instructions and warnings,[15] any published standards of safety for such goods and the existence of reasonable means (considering cost, likelihood and extent of any improvement) for making the goods safer (section 10(2)). This is quite wide in its scope and is not limited to situations where published standards and regulations exist. The main difficulty with such a safety requirement, is that, in imposing strict criminal liability, there is a need for certainty – to know what is and is not permitted by law – and yet the definition of what fails to satisfy the requirement is very general and flexible. It is likely that, in cases where there is no clear and straightforward breach of a published standard or regulation, defendants will argue strenuously that their goods are not in breach of the safety duty. The similarity of the general safety duty to the meaning of a defect under Part I of the 1987 Act may also mean that civil claims under Part I are challenged more frequently. Compliance with statutory requirements or Community obligations will not be regarded as a failure to comply with the safety requirement, nor will failure to do more than is required by safety

---

14 Section 46(5) makes it clear that any such supply etc. must be in the course of a business.
15 See similar wording re the meaning of a defect in Pt. I of the 1987 Act (s. 3) in ch. 6 at p. 155.

regulations or certain other specified standards[16] or legislation (subsection (3)).

A conviction under section 10(l) may lead to imprisonment for up to six months and/or a fine of level 5 on the standard scale (section 10(6)). In addition to the standard defence of reasonable steps and due diligence under section 39, section 10(4) provides further defences. These are a) reasonable belief that the goods would not be used or consumed in the United Kingdom, or b) that the supply etc. was in the course of a retail[17] business and at the time of supply etc. the supplier neither knew nor had reasonable grounds to believe that the goods failed to comply with the general safety requirement, or c) that the terms of supply etc. indicated that the goods to be acquired[18] were second-hand. The exclusion of second-hand goods and goods for export was suggested in the White Paper (para. 41) but has attracted much criticism from consumer organisations.

Contrary to the recommendations of the White Paper (para. 48), there is no action for breach of statutory duty available for breach of the general safety requirement (section 41(2)).

Active use is being made, by trading standards departments, of the provisions of section 10 with a considerable number of successful prosecutions being taken.[19] Appeal cases have not yet been reported.

Appendix I contains a summary of current Regulations made under section 11 of the 1987 Act, the Consumer Protection Act 1961 and the Consumer Safety Act 1978. Also listed are Regulations made under the European Communities Act 1972.

c) Future Developments – Europe

The European Community has been active in the area of consumer safety and the effects of several Directives can be seen in the Regulations detailed in Appendix I. In particular, as part of the progression towards free movement of goods and services between Member States, there has been harmonisation of many safety provisions.[20] This is usually achieved by a general standard being imposed, which can be satisfied by compliance with national

---

16　The Secretary of State has, under s. 11, made the Approval of Safety Standards Regulations 1987, S.I. 1987/1911, see p. 416, to enable approval to be given to standards. The current list of approved standards is Notice No. 8, see Miller *Product Liability and Consumer Safety Encyclopaedia* Para. VI [3001].

17　As defined in s. 10(5).

18　Section 10(4)(c)(ii) refers to 'the acquisition of an interest' in the goods so cases of hire would be excluded from the special defence.

19　These are regularly reported in Consumer Law Today.

20　See further *Consumer Policy in the Single Market* (2nd Edn., 1991) Office for Official Publications of the European Communities.

standards or with European standards devised by the private standards organisations CEN (European Committee for Standardization) and Cenelec (European Committee for Electrotechnical Standardization). Currently under consideration is a proposed Directive on general product safety.[1] This will establish a general safety requirement for all products available within the Community, enforcement provisions for the control of and, where necessary, the banning of unsafe goods, information exchange procedures to ensure that the existence of dangerous products is known throughout the Community and create a new body, the Committee on Product Safety Emergencies, to assist the Commission to deal with products which pose a 'grave and immediate risk'. Although much of the proposed Directive reflects the position in the United Kingdom currently found in the Consumer Protection Act 1987, Part II, clearly a number of changes will be necessary should the Directive be accepted, for example relating to its coverage of *all* goods, both new and second-hand. Further developments are awaited.

d) Petroleum (Consolidation) Act 1928

Petroleum spirit may not be kept without a licence issued by a local authority, and it is an offence to do so, or to contravene a condition of a licence. There are exceptions in favour of the storage of small quantities for private use, and storage without a licence in well ventilated places of up to two gallons in one metal vessel is permitted for certain engines such as lawn mowers by the Petroleum Spirit (Motor Vehicles etc.) Regulations 1929 (as amended).[2] Since 1982 storage in plastic containers, not exceeding 5 litres capacity, which comply with the Petroleum Spirit (Plastic Containers) Regulations 1982[3] has also been permissible.

e) Explosive Acts 1875 to 1976 (as amended)

This legislation mainly concerns the manufacture in licensed factories of gunpowder, nitro-glycerine, dynamite and other explosives. It

1　Original version: OJ C 193, 31 July 1989, p. 1; amended version OJ C 156, 27 June 1990, p. 8. The Council of Ministers has approved the proposal which will now go to the European Parliament, see (1992) 15 Consumer Law Today No. 2, p. 1. See also J. Bradgate 'Product Safety: The EEC Follows UK Lead' (1990) 7 Trading Law 2.
2　S. R. & O. 1929/952 as amended by S.I. 1979/427 and S.I. 1982/630.
3　S.I. 1982/630.

is an offence to keep explosives in an unauthorised place, except small quantities for private use. Licences are granted by the Health and Safety Executive and local authorities. It is an offence to hawk explosives in public places (1875 Act, section 30) to sell them to children under 16 (1875 Act, section 31 as amended by Explosives (Age of Purchase &c.) Act 1976 and the Consumer Protection Act 1987), or to sell explosives except in properly labelled and constructed packages (1875 Act, section 32). The Act also makes it an offence to throw a firework in a public place (1875 Act, section 80 as amended) and the manufacture of fireworks is controlled by the Fireworks Act 1951.

f) Pharmacy and Poisons Act 1933; Poisons Act 1972; Medicines Acts etc.

This legislation forms part of a series of Acts which, amongst other matters, control, under the criminal law, the sale of poisons and medicines. For example, retail chemist shops must be under the personal control of a registered pharmacist and the name and certificate of registration of the person having control of the business must be conspicuously exhibited on the premises (Medicines Act 1968). The Poisons Act 1972 prohibits the sale of specified poisons in Part I of the Poisons List other than by authorised sellers; and poisons may not be sold by automatic machine. Certain other persons as listed by local authorities may sell poisons in Part II of the Poisons List. Enforcement is by the Pharmaceutical Society and by local authorities.

Regulations made under the Medicines Act 1968 provide, inter alia, that all pre-packed medicines shall have written on a label or container so as to be clearly legible the appropriate designation of the substance or its active constituents. In addition certain medicines may only be sold by authorised sellers, but there is an elaborately described class of proprietary medicines outside this prohibition.

The Medicines Act 1968 makes it an offence to sell any medicinal product which is not of the nature or quality demanded by the purchaser to his prejudice (section 64) and it is also an offence to adulterate medicinal products (section 63). Some classes of medicine may be sold only on prescriptions by doctors, dentists or vets (section 58). Part VI of the Act contains an elaborate code prohibiting false or misleading advertisements relating to medicinal products. Also relating to advertisements, the Cancer Act 1939 makes it an offence to take part in the publication of an advertisement offering to treat a person for cancer, prescribing remedies or giving advice in connection with such treament. There are exceptions in respect of advertisements not aimed at the general public.[4]

The Farm and Garden Chemicals Act 1967 gives power to make Regulations as to the labelling and marking of substances including insecticides and weedkillers commonly used in farming and gardening. It is an offence to sell or consign for sale an unlabelled product required by the regulations to be labelled (see the Farm and Garden Chemicals Regulations 1971).[5]

II) ROAD SAFETY

Road Traffic Act 1988

The Road Traffic Act 1988 contains numerous provisions as to the construction, use and safe loading of vehicles which benefit consumers directly or indirectly, but this topic must be left to works of a specialist nature.

With regard to sales of vehicles or accessories, section 75 (as amended)[6] contains a general prohibition of the supply of motor vehicles or trailers which are unroadworthy by reason of defective brakes, steering gear or tyres and generally as to construction, weight, or equipment or where its condition would involve a danger of injury to any person if used on the road. Nor may vehicles be altered so as to render them unroadworthy or so that they would involve a danger of injury to any person. Subject to the defence that the vehicle was supplied or believed to be for use abroad, any person who sells, offers to sell or supply or exposes for sale or alters a vehicle in contravention of these provisions is guilty of an offence punishable on summary conviction with a fine up to level 5 on the standard scale.[7] It is also an offence to fit or sell defective or unsuitable vehicle parts (section 76).

By section 17 it is an offence to sell or offer for sale for use in Great Britain a motor cycle crash helmet other than one conforming to regulations designed to afford protection to motor cyclists in the event of accident. Section 18(4) makes it an offence to sell or offer for sale unauthorised head-worn appliances for use on motor cycles, for

4 See also the Medicines (Labelling and Advertising to the Public) Regulations 1978, S.I. 1978/41, which, inter alia, prohibit advertisements for medical products available on prescription only and also advertisements relating to medical products for the treatment of specified diseases; these include V.D., tuberculosis, cancer, diabetes, cataracts and glaucoma. Advertisements of spermicidal contraceptives are stringently controlled.
5 S.I. 1971/729.
6 As amended by the Road Traffic Act 1991, s. 16.
7 Road Traffic Offenders Act 1988, s. 9 and Sch. 2.

example visors, eye protectors[8] and earphones. The penalty for either offence is a fine up to level 3 on the standard scale on summary conviction, and local authorities are empowered to institute proceedings.[9]

III) PRICES

a) Mock Auctions Act 1961; Auctions (Bidding Agreements) Acts

It is an offence, punishable by maximum sentences of a fine of level 5 and/or imprisonment of three months on summary conviction (unlimited fine/two years on conviction on indictment), to promote or conduct or assist in the conduct of a mock auction. A sale of goods by way of competitive bidding is a mock auction if during the course of sale i) a lot is sold to a person bidding for it at a price lower than the amount of his highest bid for that lot, or part of the price is repaid or credited to him or stated to be so (unless the goods are found to be defective), or ii) the right to bid is or is stated to be restricted to persons who have bought or agreed to buy one or more articles, or iii) any articles are given away or offered as gifts (section 1). 'Competitive bidding' is defined as including 'any mode of sale whereby prospective purchasers may be enabled to compete for the purchase of articles whether by way of increasing bids or by the offer of articles to be bid for at successively decreasing prices or otherwise' (section 3(1)). In *Lomas v Rydeheard*[10] it was held by the Divisional Court (on appeal from the Crown Court) that where the defendant offered articles for sale to customers assembled in his salerooms, calling out a series of progressively decreasing prices, but not asking for bids until his final price when he offered the item to an individual in the crowd who bought it without bargaining, this was still 'competitive bidding' since it could be inferred that prices would have been reduced further if people had been unwilling to buy. The Act applies to lots comprising plate, linen, china, glass, books, pictures, prints, furniture, jewellery, articles of household or personal use or ornament or any musical or scientific instruments or apparatus (section 3).

8 Motor Cycles (Eye Protectors) Regulations 1985, S.I. 1985/1593 as amended by S.I. 1987/675 and S.I. 1988/1031.
9 Road Traffic Offenders Act 1988, s. 9 and Sch. 2 and s. 4 respectively. It is also an offence for an accused defendant wilfully to apply to a helmet or headworn appliance a warranty not given in relation to that helmet (Road Traffic Act 1988, Sch. 1, para. 6) or to give to a purchaser a false warranty in writing (ibid). See also s. 80 – applying false approval marks to vehicles (indicating conformity with EEC or international standards) is an offence under the Trade Descriptions Act 1968.
10 (1975) 119 Sol Jo 233, QBD.

In *Clements v Rydeheard,*[11] the defendant held sales at which he offered, at a fixed price, a number of boxes with undisclosed contents and selected the purchasers from those who put up their hands. Purchasers of later lots were similarly selected but only from those who had purchased boxes. The Divisional Court held that this was a sale by competitive bidding.

Competitive bidding includes any mode of sale whereby persons can compete for the purchase of articles in any way, whether or not by reference to price. In *Allen v Simmons,*[12] the audience was asked by the respondent who would pay him 30p for a set of glasses. Hands were raised. There was only one set of glasses. The successful 'bidder' was sold the glasses for 1p and a similar performance took place relating to an offer for sale of an undisclosed item for 50p.

In the view of Melford Stevenson J it was difficult to form a precise view of the meaning of the word 'otherwise' in section 3(1), but the subsection did contemplate bidding in what was or appeared to be competition with other bidders. The mere fact that the effect of the bid depended on the whim of the person conducting the so-called auction did not matter. Following *Clements v Rydeheard* above, the court in effect construed section 3(1) set out above as stopping at the words 'may be enabled to compete for the purchase of articles', and the offence had accordingly been committed. As has been pointed out[13] there seems to be no point, and indeed no justification in law, in construing section 3(1) in this curtailed way. Either decision could be justified by simply relying on the words 'or otherwise'.

The Court of Appeal in *R v Pollard*[14] agreed with the decisions in *Clements v Rydeheard* and *Allen v Simmons* above. It refused to apply the *ejusdem generis* rule to the words 'or otherwise' and require the competitive bidding to be on a financial scale. The fastest hand up was a competitive bid. May LJ drew attention to the words 'includes any mode of sale' which widened the ambit of the subsection.

The Act is designed to prevent fraudulent practices at auctions covering the lots as specified above. It was introduced as a Private Member's Bill and as will be inferred from the above litigation, doubts have arisen as to its precise ambit. Its existence has certainly not prevented the fairly common practice of 'one day sales' with all the problems of enforcing civil remedies for defective goods that they bring. The OFT in 1979 wrote to all chief trading standards officers suggesting local codes of practice to protect consumers. The assumption is that all those who hire out public halls in a particular

11 [1978] 3 All ER 658, QBD.
12 [1978] 3 All ER 662, [1978] 1 WLR 879, QBD.
13 [1978] Crim LR 362 at 363.
14 (1984) 148 JP 679, CA.

area can guard against abuses by incorporating appropriate conditions in the letting contract.[15] A number of such codes have been adopted and hirers of halls have been asked to notify Trading Standards Departments in advance of all proposed sales.

Other legislation exists to prohibit dealers' bidding rings. By the Auctions (Bidding Agreements) Act 1927, if a dealer induces another person to abstain from bidding, both commit an offence carrying a maximum fine of level 5 and/or six months' imprisonment, and persons convicted may be ordered by the court not to participate in auctions for up to three years (Auctions (Bidding Agreements) Act 1969).[16]

b) Prices Acts 1974 and 1975

These Acts authorise the payment of food subsidies, and provide for the regulation of prices of food and other commodities essential in low-income household budgets by the Secretary of State. By section 2 of the 1974 Act (as amended by section 2 of the 1975 Act) the Secretary of State may make Orders regulating prices and Orders have been made relating to (inter alia) bread, butter, cheese, flour, and tea.[17] By section 4 (as amended) Orders may be made regulating the way prices are marked and indicated, including unit pricing (price per pound weight or other unit). Some Orders relate to specific locations: pre-packed milk in vending machines[18] and food and drinks offered for retail sale for consumption on the premises.[19] As to the display of prices in restaurants (a matter on which the law seems in some areas to be more honoured in the breach than in the observance) the Order[19] requires (inter alia) prices to be easily legible to an intending purchaser (normally near the entrance to the eating area) and prices must include VAT in all cases and also cover charges

15　For a helpful account of the objectives of the Act, see (1981) 131 NLJ 49 (A. T. H. Smith). Trading Standards Departments' experience with many mock auctions is that the proceedings often involve the commission of other offences, e.g. under the Trade Descriptions Act 1968, as well as under the 1961 Act.

　　North Yorkshire County Council have devised an interesting method of controlling such sales under their own private Act of Parliament, see S Pudney 'North Yorkshire County Council Act 1991' (1991) 99 Trading Standards Review, Pt 12, p.8.

16　It can often be difficult to distinguish between bidders acting as partners as opposed to forming an illegal bidding ring. For a review of the law see A. T. H. Smith 'Auction Rings' [1981] Crim LR 86. See also *R v Jordan* [1981] CLY 131, Swansea Crown Court. See for further detailed discussion of this legislation, Harvey & Meisel *Auctions Law and Practice*.

17　There are no Orders currently in force.

18　Price Marking (Pre-packed Milk in Vending Machines) Order 1976, S.I. 1976/796.

19　See Price Marking (Food and Drink on Premises) Order 1979, S.I. 1979/361.

etc. unless the contrary is clearly indicated in the same way as the price of the food is required to be displayed. The Order does not apply to bona fide clubs, staff canteens and the like. Also controlled are price displays at hotels for sleeping accommodation (maximum and minimum charges).[20]

Of considerable significance is the Price Marking Order 1991[1] which seeks to implement the EEC Directives on indicating prices of foodstuffs and non-food products.[2] The object of the Directives is that consumers should know the price of items they wish to buy prior to purchase and to enable comparisons to be made. The 1991 Order seeks to achieve this by removing the previous piecemeal provisions for price indications and creating new requirements for the majority of products sold by retail. The scope of the Order is indicated in article 2, with certain items, for example works of art and antiques, being excluded. Also excluded are private sales, sales of goods for trade or commercial activities and goods supplied in the course of a service (article 1(2)). Article 3 stipulates that a selling price for all goods for sale by retail (except motor fuel – see below) must be given in writing. The price may, in the case of goods sold from bulk, be by reference to units of measurement, single items or specified quantities. For other goods it must be the price of a single item or a specified quantity. Unit pricing of many items is required by article 4 with a complex system of exemptions, restrictions on permissible units of measurement (articles 6 and 7, dealing with imperial and metric units) and special provisions for meat, cheese and milk sold pre-packed in pre-established quantities (article 5).

Traders are not required to price each item individually as article 8 permits shelf-markings, notices and price lists displayed in close proximity to the goods. This does nothing to assist consumers to keep a check on shelf prices compared with the prices they are charged where bar-codes are used to record prices at the till. VAT-inclusive prices must be given unless sales are mainly to business customers and traders are allowed to use general notices for 14 days to adjust prices following changes in VAT or other tax rates (article 9). Where differential pricing operates depending upon the method of payment used, the Order only requires one method to be shown when indicating the selling or unit price (article 11). This is, however,

20 See Tourism (Sleeping Accommodation Price Display) Order 1977, S.I. 1977/1877 (made under the Development of Tourism Act 1969, s. 18).
 1 S.I. 1991/1382 as amended by S.I. 1991/1690.
 2 Council Directive 79/581/EEC (OJ No L 158, 26.6.79, p. 19) as amended by Council Directive 88/315/EEC (OJ No L 142, 9.6.88, p. 23) and Council Directive 88/314/EEC (OJ No L 142, 9.6.88, p. 19).

subject to the requirements of the Price Indications (Method of Payment) Regulations 1991.[3]

Indications of the price of motor fuel are governed by articles 12–16 and Schedule 2 and apply to all fuels, including diesel. Prices at pumps, on road-side displays and at points of payment are all regulated, together with detailed requirements for fuel sold by the litre. Finally special provisions are included for the sale of jewellery and precious metals (article 17) and to cover general reductions during sales (article 18).

Section 5 of the 1974 Act relates to the information to be displayed by 'price range notices'.[4] The Schedule to the 1974 Act relates to the enforcement of these provisions and puts this duty on local weights and measures authorities who are solely responsible for prosecutions. Persons contravening Orders made under sections 2, 4 and 5 are liable to an unlimited fine on conviction on indictment and a fine not exceeding £5,000 on summary conviction.[5]

IV) TRADE REPRESENTATIONS

Trading Representations (Disabled Persons) Acts 1958 and 1972

The 1958 Act makes it an offence to represent when selling, exchanging or soliciting orders for goods by house-to-house visits, by post or by telephone, that blind or otherwise disabled persons are employed in the production of, or benefit from the sale of the goods. There are exceptions in favour of local authorities, institutions and associations registered under various Acts or by the Government and persons carrying on a business who are substantially disabled. In England and Wales a local authority may institute proceedings. Offenders are punishable by a fine not exceeding £5,000[6] on summary conviction, or an unlimited fine and/or up to two years' imprisonment on conviction on indictment (section 1 of the 1958 Act as amended by section 1 of the 1972 Act).

V) TRADING STAMPS

Trading Stamps Act 1964

This Act originated as a Private Member's Bill. It is designed to regulate the promotion of trading stamps and the conditions under

3 S.I. 1991/199, see further ch. 12 p. 382.
4 Retailers may be ordered to display information as to the range of prices within which specified goods are commonly sold by retail in the UK at a particular date or period. No such Orders apply currently.
5 Increased from £2,000 in October 1992 by virtue of the Criminal Justice Act 1991, s. 17(2).
6 Increased from £2,000 in October 1992 by virtue of the Criminal Justice Act 1991, s. 17(2).

which retailers may use them. 'Trading stamps' are widely defined to include coupons, vouchers and tokens whether adhesive or not.

The Act makes it an offence for any person other than a company (i.e. a registered limited company) or an industrial and provident society to carry on business as a promoter of trading stamps (section 1). It is also an offence to issue any trading stamp on any sale or credit transaction unless it bears on its face in clear and legible characters a value expressed in or by reference to current coins of the realm.[7]

Trading stamps and stamp books must also bear the promoter's name and catalogues must indicate the number of stamps needed to obtain anything described in the catalogue. It is an offence to contravene these provisions (sections 2, 5). It is also an offence to advertise the cash value of trading stamps by associating the worth of any trading stamps with what the holder pays or may pay (for goods) to obtain them, or in misleading or deceptive terms. The offences carry varying fines.

Shops are required to post notices showing the cash value of trading stamps and giving sufficient particulars to enable customers to ascertain the number of trading stamps to which they are entitled on a purchase, and a copy of any current catalogue must be kept where customers may conveniently consult it. If these provisions are contravened without reasonable excuse, the occupier or person having control of the shop is liable on summary conviction to a fine up to level 1 on the standard scale. A person pulling down such a notice is also liable to a similar penalty.[8]

The Act also incorporates two useful civil rights in favour of the consumer. By section 3 the holder of trading stamps having an aggregate cash value of not less than 25p may insist on their being redeemed for cash. Where the stamps are redeemed for goods, section 4 implies warranties by the trader that he has the right to give the goods in exchange, for quiet possession and freedom from encumbrances and that the goods shall be of merchantable quality.

VI) UNSOLICITED GOODS AND SERVICES

Unsolicited Goods and Services Acts 1971 and 1975

The 1971 Act was designed to meet problems caused by 'inertia-selling'. Goods were sent to the potential customer without his prior knowledge or request and then various techniques, from the sending of an invoice to demands for payment and threats, were used to

---

7 Trading Stamps Act 1964, s. 2(1), as substituted by the Consumer Credit Act 1974, Sch. 4, para. 24.
8 Trading Stamps Act 1964, s. 7 as amended by the Criminal Damage Act 1971.

extract the notional price of the goods from the customer. The Act makes no specific provision for enforcement by public authorities.

The Act gives the recipient of unsolicited goods a conditional right to use, deal or dispose of them as if they were an unconditional gift to him so that the sender's title to the goods is extinguished, and creates certain offences. The conditions are that the goods were sent to the recipient with a view to his acquiring them, that the recipient had no reasonable cause to believe that they were sent to him for the purposes of a trade or business, and has neither agreed to acquire or return them and *either* a) six months has expired since receiving the goods and the seller has not attempted to take possession of them, *or* b) not later than thirty days before the six months has expired, thirty days' written notice is given to the sender stating the recipient's name and address and that the goods are unsolicited, during which time the sender has not attempted to take possession. In other words, the recipient may either do nothing for six months or send a thirty-day notice, at the end of which periods the recipient may keep the goods (section 1).

Section 2 makes it an offence (maximum fine of level 4 on the standard scale on summary conviction) to demand payment or assert a present or prospective right to payment in the course of business and in respect of goods known to be unsolicited goods.[9] Similarly, threatening legal proceedings or the placing of the name of a person on a debtors' or defaulters' list or invoking or threatening any other collection procedure is an offence (maximum fine level 5 on the standard scale on summary conviction).

Section 3 makes it an offence (maximum fine level 5 on the standard scale on summary conviction) to demand payment for unsolicited entries in respect of a directory relating to that person or his trade or business. There is no right to charge for such entries unless there has been signed by the directory entrant an order or note in the form specified in the Act.

Section 4 makes it an offence to send published material or advertisements which the sender knows or ought reasonably to know are unsolicited, and which describe or illustrate human sexual techniques. A prosecution under this section needs the consent of the Director of Public Prosecutions. The maximum penalty is level 5 on the standard scale.

The Act also (in common with many other criminal laws affecting the consumer) makes provision for offences by corporations. A director, manager or other officer of a company who consents to,

9   See P. I. Thomas 'The Unsolicited Goods and Services Act 1971 – Ten Years On' (1981) 89 ITSA MR 242 and, for an unusual case on the area, *Eiman v London Borough of Waltham Forest* (1982) 90 ITSA MR 204; M & H p. 474.

connives at or has been neglectful with regard to the commission of the offence, as well as the company, is liable to be proceeded against and punished (section 5).

VII) HALLMARKING

Hallmarking Act 1973

Hallmarking is one of the oldest, most important and most taken for granted forms of consumer protection. The fundamental need for protection arises because gold, silver and platinum are too soft to be of much practical use and normally need to be alloyed with other metals. But this lowers the intrinsic value of the article, and it is therefore essential to establish by chemical analysis what proportion the precious metal content bears to the whole. Accurate analyses are therefore carried out by Assay Offices on small samples removed from the article before polishing prior to the article being certified as containing metal conforming to one of the legal standards of fineness and purity. There are now four Assay Offices (Birmingham, London, Sheffield and Edinburgh) which are incorporated by Royal Charter or statute and are independent of trade organisations.

With regard to gold, a Gold Carat is 1/24, so an article of 22 carats consists of 22 parts gold and 2 parts alloy. Legal standards have varied since 1300 when hallmarking was introduced. In 1575 22 carats was the legal standard, and in 1798, 1854 and 1932 the current 9 carat, 14 carat and 18 carat standards were established. Standards of silver are 'Sterling' (925 parts silver in 1,000) and 'Britannia' (958.4 parts silver in 1,000) and the standard of platinum, which was first covered by legislation from 1 January 1975, is 950 parts in 1,000. The standard mark for gold is a crown and the standard of fineness in figures (916 for 22 carats, 750 for 18 carats, 585 for 14 carats and 375 for 9 carats). The standard mark, since ancient times, for Sterling silver is a lion and for Britannia silver the figure of Britannia. For platinum the standard mark is an orb surmounted by a cross (Hallmarking Act 1973, Schedule 2). Foreign hallmarks may be approved by order of the Secretary of State pursuant to an international convention or treaty (section 2(1)). These powers are being used to implement the International Convention on the Control and Marking of Articles of Precious Metals.

The following illustration of a hallmark shows first the sponsor's (or maker's) mark, then the mark for sterling silver, then the mark of the London Assay Office and finally the date letter for 1975:[10]

---

10 See generally 'British Hallmarks on Gold, Silver and Platinum', published by the Assay Offices of Great Britain and reproduced in O'Keefe *The Law Relating to Trade Descriptions*.

The main offence under the Act is, subject to certain exemptions in favour of articles such as coins, articles manufactured before 1900, articles of a minimum fineness and of a very light weight (gold, less than 1 gram, silver less than 7.78 grams, platinum less than 0.5 gram),[11] for any person in the course of a trade or business to apply to an unhallmarked article a description indicating that it is wholly or partly made of gold, silver or platinum, or to supply or offer to supply an unhallmarked article to which such a description is applied. Certain descriptions are exempted from this. These are 'plated' or 'rolled' gold, 'plated' silver and 'plated' platinum, provided the words 'plated' or 'rolled' are as large as any other lettering in the description. In addition the description must not be false or applied to an article of which the description is inappropriate. A description is also permissible if confined to the colour of an article (section 1 and Schedule 1).[12] Subject to an exception, it is also an offence to make any addition, alteration or repair to a hallmarked article, or to alter or deface any mark (except by battering an article to make it fit only for remanufacture) without the written consent of an assay office. The exception applies to making an addition to one article which is not a new ware if its character remains unaltered and the addition is of the same precious metal and fineness as the article and the weight of the addition does not exceed the standards laid down in the section (section 5).

Section 6 lays down offences in connection with the counterfeiting of dies and marks and section 9 states that it is the duty of every local weights and measures authority to enforce the Act within their area. Penalties for offences are on summary conviction a maximum fine of £5,000[13] or on indictment an unlimited fine and/or imprisonment for up to two years, or in the case of counterfeiting, ten years.

11   Exempted articles as listed in the Hallmarking Act 1973, Sch. I, Pt II (as amended) may be hallmarked voluntarily.
12   These provisions apply equally to imported articles. It is the importer's responsibility to send the articles for hallmarking.
13   Increased from £2,000 in October 1992 by virtue of the Criminal Justice Act 1991, s. 17(2).

VIII) INSURANCE POLICYHOLDERS' PROTECTION

Policyholders Protection Act 1975; Insurance Companies Act 1982; Financial Services Act 1986

The Policyholders Protection Act 1975 imposes a scheme funded by a levy on authorised insurance companies to ensure that if an authorised insurance company is unable to meet its liabilities policyholders nevertheless receive at least 90 per cent of the benefits that they would otherwise have received. It is an offence for such a company to give false information in a statement required to be made to the Board or to the Secretary of State or to make default in giving such information or statements.

The Insurance Companies Act 1982, Part I, restricts the carrying on of insurance business to authorised insurers. It is an offence to carry on business without authorisation or to furnish false information in order to obtain authorisation (section 14). Part II of the Act lays down detailed regulations for companies to deposit accounts and statements of their business with the Secretary of State, to apply assets relating to long term business alone thereto, and a number of other matters designed to prevent or give warning of insolvency. It is an offence not to comply with the various requirements (section 71). Part III (section 72) empowers the Secretary of State to make regulations controlling insurance advertisements. Section 133 of the Financial Services Act 1986 makes it an offence for any person to make false, deceptive, dishonest or reckless promises or forecasts to induce another person to enter into a contract of insurance. Prosecutions must have the consent of the Secretary of State, the Industrial Assurance Commissioner or the Director of Public Prosecutions (section 201(2) of the 1986 Act).

It is convenient to mention here an important non-criminal consumer protection scheme, insurance-based, in respect of holidays abroad. In recent years there have been some well publicised failures of package tour operators. There are now two lines of defence where foreign air travel is involved. The Civil Aviation Authority licenses travel organisers and requires them to provide a bond. This amounts to 15 per cent of licensable turnover, or 10 per cent if the licence holder is a member of the Association of British Travel Agents (which has its own mutual support arrangements). The fund so provided is used to repatriate stranded passengers and repay deposits if an air travel organiser fails financially. As a second line of defence, and in order to meet more serious cases such as the failure of Court Line in 1974, the Air Travel Reserve Fund Act 1975 set up a Reserve Fund to which all holders of air travel organisers' licences had to contribute 2 per cent of their turnover. In October 1977 the obligation to make contributions was suspended,[14] and in February 1986 the Fund was dissolved.[15] The funds were transferred to the Trustees of the Air Travel Trust with a view to improving the protection available.

IX) THEFT AND DECEPTION

The Theft Act 1968 is an important part of the general criminal law. Consumers are not, as such, more directly concerned with the Act than members of the public in any other capacity, but in the course of buying goods several sections could be material.

The problem of buying goods which turn out to have been stolen has already been discussed.[16] The Act states that a person handles stolen goods if knowing or believing them to be stolen goods he dishonestly receives the goods, or dishonestly undertakes or assists in their retention, removal, disposal or realisation by or for the benefit of another person. A person buying goods which he knows to be stolen 'receives the goods'. The penalty for 'handling' is a maximum of 14 years' imprisonment on conviction on indictment (section 22).

Cheating of various kinds is covered by section 15. This states that a person who by any deception dishonestly obtains property (defined in section 4 as including money) belonging to another with the intention of permanently depriving the other of it shall on conviction on indictment be liable to a maximum of ten years' imprisonment. 'Deception' is any deception, whether deliberate or reckless by words or conduct as to fact or as to law, including a deception as to the present intentions of the person using the deception or any other person. This section accordingly covers a large number of situations where money or property is obtained by deception, ranging from the alteration of a car's mileage to obtain a higher selling price, falsely claiming expensive repairs are necessary[17] or have been done, to the doorstep seller of goods and services taking money in advance with no intention of fulfilling the obligation. The Theft Act 1978 makes additional provision for dishonestly obtaining services by deception, evasion of liability by deception and making off without payment where payment on the spot is required or expected. The 1968 Act also

14   Civil Aviation (Air Travel Organisers' Licensing) (Reserve Fund) Regulations 1975, S.I. 1975/1196 (amended by S.I. 1977/1331).
15   Air Travel Reserve Fund (Winding Up of Fund and Dissolution of Agency) Order 1986, S.I. 1986/155. See also Law Com. No. 156 p. 38 and (1986) 9 Consumer Law Today No. 5 at p. 8.
16   See above, p. 79 and also below, p. 301.
17   See *R v King* [1987] QB 547, [1987] 1 All ER 547, CA.

makes clear that where property has been stolen or obtained by fraud or other wrongful means, the title to that or any other property shall not be affected by reason only of the conviction of the offenders (section 31). Questions of title to goods which have been stolen are therefore left to the civil law. The general principle involved is that the property in goods remains in the person from whom they were stolen.[18] Formerly the true owner had to sue for their return within six years but this rule was abrogated by the Limitation Amendment Act 1980, section 2 (now the Limitation Act 1980, section 4).

18 See above, p. 80.

10 Consumer credit

INTRODUCTION

Something has already been said of the economic background to consumer credit in ch. 1 and we commence this chapter with a description of the genesis of the present legislation governing this field, the Consumer Credit Act 1974 ('the Act').[1]

1. CONSUMER CREDIT – THE BACKGROUND

The Crowther Committee was appointed in September 1968 by the Secretary of State for Trade and Industry to carry out a wide ranging review of consumer credit. The Committee's terms of reference were:
  i) to enquire into the present law and practice governing the provision of credit to individuals for financing purchases of goods and services for personal consumption;
 ii) to consider the advantages and disadvantages of existing and possible alternative arrangements for providing such credit, having regard to the interests of consumers, traders and suppliers of credit including depositors;
iii) to consider in particular whether any amendment of the Moneylenders Acts is desirable; and
iv) to make recommendations.

The Committee's two volume report appeared in March 1971 (Cmnd. 4596). The Report made serious and far-reaching criticisms of the then existing law and in particular criticised the regulation of

---

1 See also M & H ch. 5; Bennion *Consumer Credit Control*; R. M. Goode *Consumer Credit Legislation*; Guest and Lloyd *Encyclopaedia of Consumer Credit Law*; O'Keefe *The Law Relating to Trade Descriptions*; (the latter four works being loose leaf encyclopaedias). Textbooks on the subject include Bennion *Consumer Credit Act Manual* (3rd Edn.); Goode *Consumer Credit Law*; Hill-Smith *Consumer Credit: Law and Practice*; Lawson *Consumer Credit*; Macleod *Consumer Sales Law* and Stephenson *Consumer Credit*.

transactions on the basis of legal abstractions rather than on the basis of commercial reality:

> The greatest weakness of the present law of credit, and that from which most of the other defects stem, is the failure to look behind the form of a transaction and deal with the substance. . . . Typical are the distinctions made by the law between a hire-purchase agreement and a conditional sale agreement; between a hire-purchase or conditional sale agreement and a purchase-money chattel mortgage; and between the discounting of debts with recourse (i.e. upon the terms that the assignor guarantees payment by the debtor) and the lending of money on the security of debts. None of these distinctions has any validity in the real world; yet the law continues to adhere to them in deference to theoretical concepts developed two centuries ago. (Para. 4.2.2.)

The Report also contains a full historical, economic and social critique of consumer credit and proposed a new legal framework. This involved repeal of the Moneylenders Acts, Bills of Sale Acts, Pawnbrokers Acts and Hire-Purchase Acts. The proposed legislation was to cover sums advanced of up to £2,000 (dropping the hire-purchase legislation's test of 'hire-purchase *price*' – i.e. the total payable by the hirer to complete the transaction) and, on the basis that there should be 'truth in lending', enable debtors to 'shop around' for credit on the most favourable terms (para. 3.8.2. et seq) by requiring that the effective cost of borrowing in terms of an annual percentage rate should be disclosed (para. 6.5.16). The Report also recommended introduction of a comprehensive licensing system administered by a single agency.

The Report was followed by a White Paper *The Report of the Law on Consumer Credit* (1973, Cmnd. 5427) which, after much consultation, affirmed the Government's intention to implement the Report with a few modifications. The shape of the future Consumer Credit Bill was foreshadowed, and the regulations to be made under it. Mathematical formulae for finding the true cost of borrowing at an annual percentage are included in Appendices. The government did not accept the need for a Lending and Security Act as recommended by the Report and recommended raising of the financial limits for statutory protection of credit from £2,000 to £5,000.

The Act was passed on 31 July 1974 and is designed to provide the framework for the implementation of the above proposals, the details being left to regulations. As a result, the supply to individuals of credit not exceeding £15,000 (raised from £5,000 in 1985) is comprehensively regulated throughout the United Kingdom by this Act.

In addition the EC Directive on Consumer Credit was agreed on

22 December 1986.[2] It is based to a great extent on the Consumer Credit Act 1974, although is not as extensive. It seeks to ensure that annual percentage rates of charge (APRs) are indicated in certain advertisements, to control the form and content of credit agreements, to provide information about credit charges, to make provisions concerning repossessions and early settlements, to provide connected-lender liability and to control credit grantors by means of a licensing or similar system. The Directive left the details of implementation to the Member States, requiring provisions to be operative by 1 January 1990. The Directive does not apply to certain agreements, in particular those of less than 200ECU (approximately £145) or more than 20,000ECU (approximately £14,500). Only a few minor modifications to Regulations were necessary in order to implement the Directive in the United Kingdom. An amendment to the Directive was passed on 22 February 1990,[3] with the ultimate aim of introducing a common Community method of calculating the annual percentage rate of charge. The new provisions specify the matters to be included and excluded from the calculations of APRs, require additional information to be given in writing to consumers and extend the exemption for loans guaranteed by a mortgage secured on immoveable property. Implementation of the amendments is required by 31 December 1992.

The British Government has also been examining the impact of consumer credit legislation on businesses and has considered ways of removing some controls from certain sectors of the business community. The White Paper '*Releasing Enterprise*' (1988, Cm. 512) recommends the removal of all business lending and hiring from the scope of the Act, simplification of several aspects of the Act and its Regulations and it outlines proposals for removing the necessity to possess a licence for many sectors of the credit industry. Developments on these matters are awaited.

2. FEATURES OF THE CONSUMER CREDIT ACT 1974

The draftsman of the Act, Mr. F. A. R. Bennion (who is well known for his criticisms of the usually unhelpful and obscure presentation of statute law) set new standards of comprehensibility in this particular measure. It does of course deal with a difficult area, perhaps too complex to be dealt with satisfactorily in one Act, however well

2   87/102/EEC, OJ No. L 42/48, 12 February 1987.
3   90/88/EEC, OJ No. L 61/14, 22 February 1990.

drafted, but those who have to study it in detail will find the following novel and helpful features:

a) Examples illustrating the application of the most important terms in the Act are set out in Schedule 2. Some of these are referred to later. In case of conflict, the provisions of the Act prevail over the examples (section 188).

b) The 35 offences created by the Act, and the penalties that they attract, are set out in tabular form in Schedule 1 (as amended). The onus of proof in various court proceedings is summarised in section 171.

c) In addition to a comprehensive definition section (section 189) Schedule 2 lists the new terminology used in the Act and refers the reader to the section and example where a definition and explanation are respectively to be found.

d) Schedule 3 deals with the commencement provisions in a comprehensible way. A note makes it clear that 'except as otherwise mentioned in this Schedule, the provisions of this Act come into force on its passing, that is on 31st July 1974'. Provisions awaiting commencement orders were listed and section 192 required the relevant provision in Schedule 3 to be amended when an order was made. Those with a fully up-dated text therefore do not need to delve into volumes of statutory instruments to find commencement dates. The Act became fully in force on 19 May 1985.

The Act is laid out in 12 Parts. Part I deals with the duties of the Director General of Fair Trading ('the Director') and in particular mentions his duty to 'keep under review and from time to time advise' the Secretary of State for Trade and Industry about social and commercial developments in the United Kingdom and elsewhere relating to the provision of credit and the working of the Act. Part I also deals with the powers of the Secretary of State and gives the Council on Tribunals a supervisory function over the adjudicating functions of the Director. Part II deals with the basic concepts relating to the provision of credit in its various forms, with particular reference to credit agreements, hire agreements and linked transactions. Part III deals with the licensing system administered by the Director, since all businesses which carry on a consumer credit (or hire) business where the agreements are regulated require a licence (section 21). Part IV relates to the advertising of such businesses. Parts V to X regulate the various types of individual credit and hire agreements. Part XI deals with enforcement of the Act and, in particular, lays down the powers of the Director, the powers relating to entry, inspection and the making of test purchases by local weights and measures authorities, and related provisions. Part XII ('Supplemental') deals with definitions and other residual matters.

Although the Act is fully in force, it is necessary when advising on particular credit transactions to check the commencement dates of relevant sections as many only apply to agreements *made* on or after the commencement date. Commencement dates are not generally included in the text, save where special problems arise, for example with section 75.

3. THE LAW OUTSIDE THE ACT

It must be borne in mind that the Act is not a comprehensive code relating to all aspects of contracts for consumer credit. The ordinary law of contract governs the formation of such contracts and such vitiating factors as misrepresentation or illegality. Furthermore the Act normally only applies where the credit does not exceed £15,000 or where the debtor is not a body corporate.

Where mortgages of personal property (i.e. property other than land) occur these are still governed by the Bills of Sale Acts 1878–82 as slightly amended by section 192 of the Act and Schedule 4. A bill of sale is a document by which the property in goods is transferred by one person to another, either absolutely or by way of security. Absolute bills, under which a person disposes of goods but remains in possession of them, are required to be registered under the 1878 Act in order to warn the public that the possessor is not the true owner. Bills of sale by way of security are governed by the 1878 and 1882 Acts. The latter Act is designed to safeguard the grantor of the bill against oppressive terms. If the provisions of the 1882 Act, which lay down a form for such bills, are not complied with the security may be void. The Crowther Report indicated that whilst 'absolute bills of sale are of little importance at the present time . . . on the other hand some 9,000 security bills of sale are registered (at the Filing Department of the Royal Courts of Justice) every year' (para. 4.1.35).

The hire-purchase conditions and warranties in the Supply of Goods (Implied Terms) Act 1973 remain, as slightly amended by Schedule 4 to the 1974 Act and the Unfair Contract Terms Act 1977. There are accordingly implied appropriately adjusted conditions of title, correspondence with description, merchantable quality, except as to defects specifically drawn to the consumer's attention before the agreement is made, and as to defects which any examination made ought to have revealed. There is also an implied condition of fitness for purpose where that purpose has been expressly or impliedly made known either to the creditor or credit-broker and the circumstances do not show that the consumer either did not rely, or that it was unreasonable for him to rely, on the other party's skill or judgment. These implied undertakings relating to quality and fitness also apply where a hire-purchase agreement is made by a person who in the course of a business is acting as agent for the creditor, thus embracing the common tripartite dealer-finance company-consumer relationship which usually occurs under a hire-purchase agreement.

Although the Hire-Purchase Act 1965 was completely repealed it continued to apply in part to contracts entered into before 19 May 1985, the appointed day for bringing in the appropriate substitutionary provisions of the Act. The Hire-Purchase Act 1964 was repealed except as to s 37 and Part III dealing with the title to motor vehicles dealt with below. Part III of this Act is conveniently reproduced, as amended by the new terminology introduced thereby, in Schedule 4, para. 22 of the 1974 Act.

4. DEFINITIONS AND SCOPE OF THE ACT

The meaning of credit

Although credit is purportedly defined in section 9, this section does not actually provide a full definition but merely states (inter alia) that 'credit' includes a cash loan, and any other form of financial accommodation. A clue to the concept of 'credit' in the Act lies, if anywhere, in the expression 'financial accommodation'. It is the presence or absence of this factor which dictates whether a simple case such as the payment of newspaper or milk bills monthly brings those transactions within the Act as 'credit' or whether there is some other element in the transaction which must be present before the Act applies. There is evidence of some misunderstanding on this fundamental point. As Goode points out[4] there must be a contractual deferment of the time when the debt would ordinarily be paid. For instance, in the common cases of newspapers or milk bills being paid monthly, there is no contractual deferment of the time at which the debt would have been paid under the contract to supply these commodities. Only when an extra contractual provision expressly defers the time for payment of the debt does 'credit', for the purposes of the Act, become a factor. In some cases it is necessary to make a sophisticated analysis under the ordinary law relating to the supply of goods and services as to when the debt would ordinarily become payable, but in everyday cases the principle is clear enough. The main subject matter of the Act is in fact agreements whereunder the debt in question is not only postponed but repayable by set instalments.

4 Goode *Consumer Credit Law* paras. 8.10–8.12.

Regulated agreements

Comprehension of the structure of the Act can only be achieved by understanding the meaning of the terms used to describe various types of agreement. An approximate picture can be obtained by studying the tabular illustration in Appendix III, p. 438.

A concept central to the working of the Act is that of the 'regulated agreement'. Only regulated agreements are governed by the requirements of the Act (including the licensing provisions, but this is not so with regard to advertising and the reopening of extortionate credit bargains which are governed by provisions of far wider scope; see sections 43 and 137 respectively). Section 189 defines a regulated agreement as 'a consumer credit agreement, or consumer hire agreement, other than an exempt agreement'. The agreement must also have been made not before 1 April 1977.[5] Each of the above expressions must therefore be examined separately.

Consumer credit agreements

A consumer credit agreement is a personal credit agreement by which the creditor provides the debtor with credit not exceeding £15,000 (section 8(2)[6]). A 'personal credit agreement' is also defined as an agreement between an individual ('the debtor') and any other person ('the creditor') by which the creditor provides the debtor with credit of any amount (section 8(1)). 'Individual' is defined as including a partnership or other unincorporated body of persons (not consisting entirely of bodies corporate) (section 189) and 'credit' includes a cash loan, and any other form of financial accommodation (section 9(1)). Consequently, the Act applies not only to the common form of instalment credit relating to goods, such as hire-purchase and credit sale agreements. A hire-purchase agreement is defined at some length in section 189, but in essence it is an agreement under which goods are bailed by the bailor in return for periodical payments by the bailee and the property in the goods will pass to the bailee a) on fulfilment of the terms of the agreement, and b) on the bailee exercising thereafter an option to purchase them. A conditional sale agreement is an agreement for the sale of goods or land under which the price is payable by instalments and the property is to remain in the seller until the specified conditions are fulfilled. A credit sale agreement is similar except that the property

5   Consumer Credit Act 1974 (Commencement No. 2) Order 1977, S.I. 1977/325, art. 2(1).
6   As amended by the Consumer Credit (Increase of Monetary Limits) Order 1983, S.I. 1983/1878.

passes to the buyer without any preconditions (section 189). The Act applies also to any other agreement to which credit is extended, such as budget and option accounts, credit cards, loans and overdrafts. It matters not that the debtor is a partnership and the transaction concerns goods required for their business. There is no concept of a 'consumer' as opposed to 'business' transaction such as is to be found in the Unfair Contract Terms Act 1977, section 6. The Act regulates all non-exempt credit agreements where the debtor is not a body corporate.

Consumer hire agreements

A consumer hire agreement is by section 15[7] declared to be an agreement made by a person with a hirer for the bailment of goods to the hirer, which
   a) is not a hire-purchase agreement, and
   b) is capable of subsisting for more than three months, and
   c) does not require the hirer to make payments exceeding £15,000.
Unless it is an exempt agreement a consumer hire agreement is a regulated agreement[8] (see below).

Exempt agreements

By section 16(1) (as amended) outside the scope of the Act are consumer credit agreements where the creditor is a local authority or some other body specified by Order being
   a) an insurance company,
   b) a friendly society,
   c) an organisation of employers or of workers,
   d) a charity,
   e) a land improvement company,
   f) a body corporate specifically referred to in any public general Act,
   ff) a body corporate specifically referred to in orders made under certain sections of the Housing Act 1985, the Housing (Scotland) Act 1987, the Housing (Northern Ireland) Order 1981 or the Housing (Northern Ireland) Order 1983,
   g) a building society, or

---

7 As amended by the Consumer Credit (Increase of Monetary Limits) Order 1983, S.I. 1983/1878.
8 See further Palmer and Yates 'The Application of Consumer Credit Act 1974 to Consumer Hire Agreements' (1979) 38 CLJ 180. See also OFT booklet 'Hire Agreements' (6th Edn., November 1990) for details of the provisions of the Act relating to hire contracts.

    h) an authorised institution or wholly-owned subsidiary of such
        an institution,

provided the agreement also falls within section 16(2) which, broadly,
relates to agreements concerned with the financing of land or
dwellings on any land. Thus, whilst mortgages granted by building
societies, banks and local authorities are exempt, those made by non-
approved credit organisations, together with many second mortgages will not be exempt, and, indeed, will be regulated, if the loan
does not exceed £15,000.

Section 16(5) gives the Secretary of State power to make orders
exempting agreements in various circumstances, e.g. where the
number of payments do not exceed a number specified or the total
charge for credit does not exceed a stipulated percentage. An Order
has been made exempting fixed-sum debtor-creditor-supplier agreements (see below for definition) where there are not more than four
instalment repayments payable in not more than 12 months and
which are not hire-purchase, conditional sale or pledge agreements,
or agreements financing the purchase of land, thus exempting many
ordinary credit accounts. Also exempted are running-account
debtor-creditor-supplier agreements where one repayment by the
debtor is due for each regular period. Thus, for example, weekly or
monthly trade credits are exempt, as are such credit card agreements
as Diners Club and American Express where the entire debt must be
discharged monthly (distinguish Visa and Access). Debtor-creditor
agreements at a comparatively modest rate of interest are similarly
exempted. The rate must not exceed the higher of 13 per cent per
annum and 1 per cent above the highest of the London and Scottish
clearing banks' base rates being the rate prevailing 28 days before the
agreement is made (see generally Consumer Credit (Exempt Agreements) Order 1989).[9] In addition certain credit transactions concerning the import into or export out of the United Kingdom of goods
and services are exempt if the debtor is provided with the credit in the
course of a business carried on by him.

    Consumer *hire* agreements are not exempt unless an Order is made
exempting consumer hire agreements a) relating to the supply of
electricity, gas or water by meter or b) where the owner of the thing
hired is a specified public telecommunications operator[10] (to cover
telephones). The 1989 Order mentioned above exempts hiring
agreements within category a).

---

9   S.I. 1989/869 as amended by S.I. 1989/1841, S.I. 1989/2337, S.I. 1991/1393 and
      S.I. 1991/1949. For further guidance see OFT booklet 'Regulated and Exempt
      Agreements' (CCP 10).

10   Section 16(6) as amended by the Telecommunications Act 1984, s. 109 and Sch.
      4, para. 60(1).

Whilst exempt agreements are outside the regulation provisions of the Act, such agreements are still subject to control by the courts if they fall within the description of extortionate credit bargains laid down by section 138.

Computing the £15,000 limit

The principle behind the regulation provisions of the Act is to fix control by reference to the credit loaned to the borrower. This represents a change of policy from the position under the hire-purchase legislation where the hire-purchase price included the interest element in the loan. To cover cases where interest rates fluctuate, interest or finance charges are excluded from the calculation of the loan. For instance, in hire-purchase cases the measure of the fixed sum credit supplied is 'an amount equal to the total price of the goods less the aggregate of the deposit (if any) and the total charge for credit' (section 9(3)).

Example (see Schedule 2, example 10)[11]

FACTS. C (in England) agrees to bail goods to D (an individual) in return for periodical payments. The agreement provides for the property in the goods to pass to D on payment of a total of £17,500 and the exercise by D of an option to purchase. The sum of £17,500 includes a down-payment of £1,000. It also includes an amount which, according to regulations made under section 20(1), constitutes a total charge for credit of £1,500.

ANALYSIS. This is a hire-purchase agreement with a deposit of £1,000 and a total price of £17,500 (see definitions of 'hire-purchase agreement', 'deposit' and 'total price' in section 189(1)). By section 9(3), it is taken to provide credit amounting to £17,500 – (£1,500 + £1,000), which equals £15,000. Under section 8(2), the agreement is therefore a consumer credit agreement, and under sections 9(3) and 11(1) it is a restricted-use credit agreement for fixed-sum credit. A similar result would follow if the agreement by C had been a hiring agreement in Scotland.

Running account, or revolving credit, is credit which fluctuates, as, for example in the case of a bank overdraft, or credit card or an option account. Running account credit is regulated by the Act if the credit limit as defined by section 10(2) does not exceed £15,000. Section 10(2) defines the credit limit as the maximum debit balance

11   Modified to take into account the increased financial limit of £15,000.

which is allowed to stand on the account during any agreed period, disregarding permitted temporary loans exceeding the maximum.

The credit limit is taken not to exceed £15,000, even if the agreement indicates a limit in excess of £15,000 if: i) the debtor cannot draw *at any one time* more than £15,000; or ii) the rate of the total charge for credit increases or some other condition favouring the creditor comes into operation at a figure below £15,000; or iii) at the time the agreement is made it is probable that the amount of credit will not rise above £15,000 (section 10(3)(b)). These rules are designed to prevent artificially high credit limits being used to avoid an agreement being classified as a 'regulated agreement'.

Fixed sum credit is any other facility whereunder a debtor is enabled to receive credit, whether in one amount or by instalments (section 10(1)(b)). Examples would be a fixed sum bank loan, hire-purchase, credit sale or conditional sale agreements, check or voucher trading.

'Restricted-use' and 'unrestricted-use' credit

Section 11 defines restricted-use credit as, essentially, a regulated consumer credit agreement whereunder the credit supplied is to finance a *particular* transaction. This may be a transaction between the debtor and the creditor, for example hire-purchase, conditional sale, or a shop providing its own credit card scheme or budget account (section 11(1)(a)). Second the credit may be to finance a transaction between the debtor and a supplier (someone other than the creditor), for example a loan from a finance company paid directly to a garage to purchase a car from that garage, credit card agreements such as Access and Visa and check and voucher trading agreements (section 11(1)(b)). Finally if the finance is to refinance any existing indebtedness of the debtor either to the creditor or to a third party this is also a restricted-use agreement, for example the consolidation of several separate credit agreements into one agreement (section 11(1)(c)). Unrestricted-use credit, under section 11(2), is credit supplied under any other regulated agreement, not falling under subsection (1). The hallmark of this is that the credit is at the disposal of the debtor, as where he has overdraft facilities or a personal loan, even though certain uses would contravene the agreement (section 11(3)).

Debtor-creditor-supplier agreements and debtor-creditor agreements

These mind-boggling terms are the shorthand way in which the draftsman has subdivided the structure of regulated credit agreements. The distinction is simply between those where the creditor is also the supplier of the goods, or has a pre-existing business connection with the supplier (a debtor-creditor-supplier agreement under section 12), and those where the creditor is not also the supplier and has no pre-existing business connection with the supplier (a debtor-creditor agreement under section 13). Perhaps the first expression might have been better written as a 'debtor and creditor-supplier agreement'. Examples of debtor-creditor-supplier agreements are 1) any arrangement where the supplier of goods also provides the buyer with credit within the financial limits or, 2) the arrangement under a hire-purchase transaction where a finance house agrees to buy goods from the dealer and let them on hire-purchase terms to the customer, or 3) credit card transactions, since there is a pre-existing connection between supplier and creditor. Examples of debtor-creditor agreements are agreements to re-finance existing debts of the debtor and personal bank loans or overdrafts not tied to any particular transaction. The expression is in fact defined so as to catch all regulated agreements which are not debtor-creditor-supplier agreements.

The distinction is important to understand not only because these terms are used throughout the Act but because, for instance, whilst debtor-creditor-supplier agreements may be canvassed off trade premises by specifically licensed lenders, it is an offence so to canvass debtor-creditor agreements (section 49). The object here is to prohibit 'doorstep' cash loan facilities and merely to regulate such activities as doorstep sale of goods transactions on credit terms.

Credit token agreements

Section 14(2) states that a credit token agreement is a regulated agreement for the provision of credit in connection with the use of a 'credit-token'. 'Credit-token' is defined by section 14(1) as a card, check, voucher, coupon, stamp, form, booklet, or other document or thing given to an individual by a person carrying on a consumer credit business who undertakes that on production of it (whether or not some other action is also required) the debtor is entitled to receive cash, goods or services from the creditor or a third party.[12] Examples are credit cards issued by individual stores, credit cards such as Access and Visa, checks and vouchers, and cash cards used to obtain cash from banks' computerised cash machines. Cheque cards guaranteeing cheques up to a stated amount are issued under a 'consumer credit agreement' but are not credit tokens since the bank is merely paying the cheques drawn on it pursuant to the guarantee, not paying for goods or services. Example 21 in Schedule 2 of the Act elaborates this point.

12 See generally M & H pp. 216–19; *Which?* December 1989 p. 607.

Amongst the specific provisions in the Act relating to credit tokens is section 51(1) making it an offence to supply unsolicited credit tokens. In *Elliot v Director General of Fair Trading*[13] shoe retailers circulated past customers with a cardboard replica credit card which stated, inter alia, that credit was 'immediately available if you have a bank account'. On a charge brought under section 51 the defence argued that the card was merely a promotion of sales and the real credit card would be issued only after an application form had been filled in. The Divisional Court, upholding the magistrates' conviction of the defendant retailers, held that the cardboard replica fell within the wording of the definition of a credit token in section 14(1) (see above) – the defendant had *undertaken* that on the production of a card he would supply credit (whether or not some other action was also required). Section 84 limits the debtor's liability arising out of accidental loss of a credit token to £50[14] though there is no such limit if the misuse is by a person acquiring possession with the debtor's consent. Liability for subsequent misuse ceases altogether after giving notice of loss to the creditor. Agreements for the issue of credit tokens are subject to Part V of the Act, relating to entry into, withdrawal from and formalities governing regulated agreements, and section 85 requires the creditor to give the debtor a copy of any executed agreement on issuing a new credit-token (other than the first).

Small agreements

A small agreement is a regulated consumer credit agreement or consumer hire agreement for credit or hire payments not exceeding £50, being an agreement which is either unsecured or secured by a guarantee or indemnity only (section 17[15]). Hire-purchase and conditional sale agreements are specifically excluded, but a credit-sale agreement where credit not exceeding £50 is repayable by instalments and the property in the goods passes to the buyer immediately would be a 'small agreement'. Whilst being generally subject to the Act as regards default, termination and control by the courts, there is relaxation of the requirements relating to form and content, withdrawal and cancellation under Part V of the Act if the agreement is a small debtor-creditor-supplier agreement for restricted-use credit.

---

13   [1980] 1 WLR 977, [1980] ICR 629, QBD; M & H p. 217. See also Fairest (1980) 130 NLJ 1194; reply, Lister (1981) 131 NLJ 73; West (1981) 145 JPN 113.

14   Increased from £30 to £50 by the Consumer Credit (Increase of Monetary Amounts) Order 1983, S.I. 1983/1571, as of 20 May 1985.

15   As amended by the Consumer Credit (Increase of Monetary Limits) Order 1983, S.I. 1983/1878.

Non-commercial agreements

A 'non-commercial agreement' is not subject to various provisions of the Act – e.g. the formal requirements of Part V of the Act relating to entry into agreements (section 74), connected lender liability (section 75) or the giving of certain information to the debtor or hirer under sections 77–79 or sections 107–110. A 'non-commercial agreement' is defined as a consumer credit agreement or consumer hire agreement not made by the creditor or owner in the course of a business carried on by him (section 189(1)) and occasional transactions belonging to a business of that type are ignored (section 189(2)). If A, a private person, lends B £20 as a friendly act or a solicitor makes a temporary and isolated loan to a client in respect of a conveyancing transaction, these would be non-commercial agreements.[16]

Multiple agreements

If a single agreement falls into more than one category each part is to be treated as a separate agreement and that separate agreement is then regulated by the appropriate part of the Act (section 18).

Linked agreements

These are defined in section 19. The object of the complex definition and provisions relating to linked agreements is to provide that a subsidiary agreement linked to a regulated agreement stands or falls with that regulated agreement. The section provides three criteria which, if any one of them fits the preliminary transaction (except if it is a provision of security such as a guarantee), results in that preliminary transaction being classified as a linked transaction. It is then automatically cancelled or terminated if the principal credit agreement is cancelled or terminated.

The three criteria are, summarised:

a) the transaction is entered into in compliance with a term of the principal agreement – e.g. a contract that the supplier of goods on credit shall also maintain them at the debtor's expense, or for insurance of the goods; or

b) the principal agreement is a debtor-creditor-supplier agreement and the transaction is financed by the principal agreement – e.g. under a tripartite credit-sale agreement between

---

16 For an example under the former legislation (the Money-lenders Act 1900) see *Wills v Wood* (1984) 128 Sol Jo 222, [1984] LS Gaz R 1211, CA; M & H p. 221; where a solicitor's client lending money to other clients, making seven loans over four years, was held not to be in the business of being a moneylender.

customer, dealer and finance house (by pre-existing arrangement) the purchase of the goods by the customer from the
dealer will be linked to the loan to the customer from the
finance house; or

c) a creditor (or other person similarly placed) initiates the
preliminary transaction by suggesting it to the debtor so as to
induce the creditor to enter into the principal agreement or for
a purpose related to it – e.g. a contract of life insurance is
entered into by D at the suggestion of C and C then enters into
a regulated agreement with D.

There is provision in section 19 for coupling an agreement made by
a debtor's 'relative' (as defined by sections 184 and 189) with the
debtor's principal agreement.

Total charge for credit

As was mentioned above, the Crowther Committee recommended
that debtors should have means of determining the true cost of credit
provided or to be provided – the 'truth in lending' principle. Rates of
interest can often be deceptively stated, either by a reference to an
amount of money rather than a true percentage rate per annum or,
for example, by not allowing for the effect of repaying a capital sum
on which an interest rate is based by instalments, the interest being
charged on the full amount borrowed. Section 20 empowers the
Secretary of State to make regulations to achieve this principle. This
has proved an immensely complex exercise, for not only must the
total charge be calculated by including such matters as the cost of
insurance of the goods if the debtor is obliged to insure, but statutory
assumptions must be made relating to the effect of the time element
in which the credit is advanced, when it is to be repaid, and whether
repayments are index-linked. These matters are dealt with in detail in
the Consumer Credit (Total Charge for Credit) Regulations 1980 (as
amended)[17] and fifteen volumes (or Parts) of Consumer Credit
Tables. Although the details of the Regulations cannot be dealt with
here, it is important to understand the basis of the cost of credit as
shown by many advertisements and all quotations for credit (see the
Consumer Credit (Advertisements) Regulations 1989[18] and the
Consumer Credit (Quotations) Regulations 1989[19]). The central idea
is first to calculate the total charge for credit taking into account all
relevant additional charges as indicated above, and then to express
this as an annual percentage rate of charge ('APR'). The APR then

17 S.I. 1980/51 as amended by S.I. 1985/1192 and S.I. 1989/596.
18 S.I. 1989/1125.
19 S.I. 1989/1126.

becomes a reliable yardstick to measure the cost of credit when comparing alternative sources. As an example, a creditor lends £156 to a debtor to be repaid with total interest of £23.40 by 52 weekly instalments of £3.45 each, commencing one week after the loan. The total charge for credit here is simply the £23.40. The Consumer Credit Tables then have to be referred to and they require the charge per £ lent to be calculated by using the formula C/P where C = total charge for credit, P = the amount of the credit supplied. Thus, here this amounts to 23.40/156.00 = 0.15. Part 1 of the Tables, covering equal weekly instalments, then indicates that if the charge per £ lent is .1500 and there are 52 weekly instalments, the APR is 32.4 per cent. This example is based on material to be found in the OFT's booklet on Credit Charges, and in connection with the Regulations referred to above controlling advertisements for credit or hire facilities, the OFT's booklet on the Advertisements and Quotations Regulations 1989 should also be consulted (see below).

The Consumer Credit Directive[20] uses a similar method for calculating the APR as it is currently operative, but some minor amendment of the Regulations may be necessary.

Licensing

The Act introduced a potentially powerful regulatory weapon by requiring all proprietors of consumer credit or hire businesses to be licensed by the Director General of Fair Trading (section 21). Section 21 exempts from this requirement a) local authorities and b) bodies corporate empowered by a public general Act to carry on a business, and section 189 makes it clear that only businesses concerned with *regulated* agreements are within the licensing provisions. Ancillary credit businesses as defined by section 145 (credit brokers, debt adjusters, debt counsellors, debt collectors and credit reference agencies) also require licences (section 147). The scope of the licensing requirement is therefore very wide – far wider, for instance, than the old system requiring moneylenders to be licensed. Now almost all businesses dealing with consumer credit or hire agreements as defined must be licensed. It was estimated that some 90,000 businesses would be affected. In fact, from 1976 to December 1990, 306,139 applications for new licences had been made and 291,092 licences granted.[1]

The original timetable for licensing in stages comprised the period from February 1976 over the following twelve months. This was later

---

20   90/88/EEC, OJ No. L 61/14, 22 February 1990.
1   Appendix I (D), Table 1, *Annual Report of the Director General of Fair Trading 1990* (1991 HCP 502).

extended to 1978 because of a flood of last-minute applications many of which were defective.[2] In 1989 a further category of traders was brought within the licensing system: those only making regulated agreements not exceeding £30.[3] It is of the essence of the scheme that the Director satisfies himself that the applicant is a fit person to hold the licence. There can, therefore, be no unauthorised short cuts in this process.

The detailed provisions regarding licensing[4] are to be found in Part III of the Act and these provisions are supplemented by Regulations.

Types of licence

Under section 22 these are of two types, namely standard licences issued by the Director to individuals, partnerships, incorporated or unincorporated bodies, and group licences. A group licence has been granted, for example, to The Law Society in respect of ancillary credit businesses carried on by solicitors.

Period of licence

Originally the standard period of licence was three years. This was extended, in 1979, to 10 years and then to 15 years in 1986. As of 1 June 1991, the licence period is five years.[5]

Authorisation of specific activities

A licence to carry on a business covers all lawful activities done in the course of that business, though the licence may limit the activities it covers. In particular a licence covers the canvassing off trade premises of debtor-creditor-supplier or regulated consumer hire agreements only if it so provides (section 23).

Administration

The applicant having applied for a licence on the specified form (section 6) and paid a fee, the Director must satisfy himself that the

---

2   See (1976) 95 Law Notes 226.
3   Consumer Credit Act (Commencement No. 10) Order 1989, S.I. 1989/1128.
4   See generally M & H pp. 207–216; G. Borrie 'Licensing Practice Under the Consumer Credit Act' [1982] JBL 91; *Bee Line* No. 90/1 pp. 7–9 and OFT booklet 'Responsibility of a Licensee' (CCP3).
5   Consumer Credit (Period of Standard Licence) Regulations 1975, S.I. 1975/2124 as amended by S.I. 1991/817. The reason for the extension was to enable the licensing system to be computerised prior to requests for renewals being received (see *Bee Line* No. 42 p. 8). Once achieved, a reduced licence period was introduced.

applicant is a fit person trading under a name which is not misleading or undesirable (section 25). Relevant factors listed in section 25 to be considered are whether the applicant or, in the case of a body corporate, anyone controlling it, has committed offences involving fraud or dishonesty, or unfair business practices. Before determining not to issue a licence he must allow the applicant to make representations after having explained the reasons why he is minded to refuse the application. (The Director has shown himself willing to use this machinery in the case of e.g. second-hand car sales businesses, dependent on credit facilities being available for custo- mers, but who persistently flout civil law or the Trade Descriptions Act 1968 and photocopier leasing firms with unfair selling practi- ces.[6]) There are provisions for renewal, variation, suspension and revocation of licences again accompanied by a duty to consider representations. Persons prejudiced by a refusal or compulsory variation have a right of appeal to the Secretary of State as specified more particularly in section 41.[7]

The sanctions for engaging in activities for which a licence is required whilst unlicensed are both criminal and civil. Section 39(1) makes it an offence to do so, the offence carrying a fine of up to £5,000 if the case is tried summarily, and up to 2 years' imprisonment[8] and/or a fine if tried on indictment (see sections 39, 167 and Schedule 1 (as amended)[9]). Similarly it is an offence for a licensee under a standard licence to carry on a business under a name not specified in the licence (section 39(2)) or not within 21 working days to notify the Director of changes in particulars entered in the register which the Director maintains of all licences and applications under section 35 (the register being open to public inspection at a fee – section 35(3)).

By section 147 the criminal sanctions which apply to unlicensed consumer credit businesses also apply to unlicensed ancillary credit businesses. Three criminal cases have examined the need for licences for credit brokerage, which under section 145(2) is, inter alia, the 'effecting of introductions' of people desiring credit to persons

6   For further details see *Annual Report of the Director General of Fair Trading 1988* (1989 HCP 440) at p. 30 and Appendix 1(E), Tables 4 and 5 at p. 53 and OFT Press Release 15/91 re car sales and OFT Press Release 2/92 and *Bee Line* 91/4 p. 12 re photocopier leasing.
7   See D. B. Williams 'Licensing Appeals under the Consumer Credit Act 1974' (1987) 84 LS Gaz 250 and *North Wales Motor Auctions Ltd v Secretary of State for Trade* [1981] CCLR 1, QBD.
8   See e.g. *R v Curr* (1980) 2 Cr App Rep (S) 153, CA (12 months' prison, £2,400 fine).
9   By the Magistrates' Courts Act 1980, s. 32 as amended (increased from £2,000 by the Criminal Justice Act 1991, s. 17(2) from October 1992).

carrying on a consumer credit business or other credit-brokers. In *Brookes v Retail Credit Cards Ltd*[10] it was held that, on its own, the provision of display boxes and application forms, belonging to the respondent company, in an unlicensed retail shop did not amount to 'introducing' persons seeking credit to a consumer credit business under section 145(2). The respondent company was thus not guilty of aiding, abetting, counselling or procuring an offence by the shop. In *Hicks v Walker*[11] the court held that a car dealer who, having been refused a credit licence, introduced customers to a licensed credit-broker with a view to introductions to a licensed credit business did effect introductions of credit brokerage facilities to a credit-broker and thus committed an offence under section 39. The number of transactions which can be involved before a credit-broking 'business' is established, thus requiring a licence to be obtained, was examined in *R v Marshall.*[12] As mentioned above in connection with non-commercial agreements,[13] section 189(2) recognises that 'occasional' entry into particular transactions does not amount to carrying on that type of business. The court decided that it was a question of fact for the jury to decide whether the activity was occasional or regular and, due to a misdirection on this point, the appeal against conviction for unlicensed trading was allowed.

The civil consequence of not obtaining a licence is that any regulated agreement not being a non-commercial agreement is unenforceable against the debtor or hirer (section 40). Section 40(2) gives power to the Director to remedy the position by making an order treating regulated agreements made during the unlicensed period as if they had been licensed. The Director must act judicially and consider representations by the trader as well as how far debtors have been prejudiced. There is, again, an appeal against refusal by the trader to the Secretary of State (section 41).[14] There are similar civil sanctions against agreements for the services of persons running ancillary credit businesses (no fees or commission can be claimed without an order from the Director) and regulated agreements made on introductions by unlicensed credit-brokers (sections 148, 149). It should be noted that the effect of the Act on the agreements mentioned above is to make them unenforceable against the debtor or hirer, not void. The debtor or hirer can exercise rights under the agreement against the creditor or owner.

In October 1988, coinciding with the publication of the White

10   (1985) 150 JP 131, [1986] BTLC 56, QBD.
11   (1984) 148 JPN 636, QBD; M & H p. 213.
12   (1989) 90 Cr App Rep 73, CA.
13   See above p. 269.
14   See D. Foulkes (1983) 113 NLJ 135.

Paper *Releasing Enterprise* (Cm. 512), the Department of Trade and Industry announced a review of consumer credit licensing.[15] Some proposals, for example the extension of licensing requirements to those only making agreements under £30 and the shortening of the period of licences, have been implemented. The major suggestion, that, in general, ancillary credit businesses should not longer be required to apply for a licence, has yet to be implemented. Ancillary licences would still be necessary if certain 'trigger' factors apply, for example previous adverse licensing decisions or convictions for specified offences and the Director General would be able to require licence applications in cases where he doubted the fitness of a trader. Reaction from consumer organisations and the Director General to the proposal of negative licensing for ancillary credit businesses has been unfavourable.[16]

5. SEEKING BUSINESS

Part IV of the Act and sections 151–154 are aimed at protecting the consumer from two mischiefs, namely uncontrolled advertising of credit or rental facilities and canvassing off trade premises of certain regulated agreements. As in many other Parts of the Act, a number of details are contained in Orders made by the Secretary of State.

The ambit of Part IV is delineated by section 43. An advertiser is within the scope of Part IV if an advertisement for the purposes of his business indicates that he is willing a) to provide credit, or b) to enter into agreements of bailment or hire. But this does not apply if the advertiser does not carry on a consumer credit or consumer hire business, or does not supply credit to individuals secured on land, or where the agreement is unregulated because the law applicable to the agreement is that of a foreign land. Nor does the advertisement come within the controls if it indicates that the credit must exceed £15,000 and that no security is required or that the security is to consist of property other than land, or that credit is available only to a body corporate (section 43(3)[17]). The categories exempted have been extended by Order.[18] The meaning of 'indicating' in section 43(1) has

15 (1988) 11 Consumer Law Today, No. 12, pp. 1–3.
16 See, for example, *Consumer Credit Licensing*, NCC Policy Paper, December 1988; *Review of Consumer Credit Licensing: Comments by the Director General of Fair Trading on the Proposals of the Department of Trade and Industry*, OFT, December 1988.
17 As amended by the Consumer Credit (Increase of Monetary Limits) Order 1983, S.I. 1983/1878 and the Contracts (Applicable Law) Act 1990, s. 5 and Sch. 4, para. 2.
18 See Consumer Credit (Exempt Advertisements) Order 1985, S.I. 1985/621.

been discussed in *Jenkins v Lombard North Central plc*,[19] where the court held that price stickers with the credit company's name and logo on them did not 'indicate' a willingness to provide credit. To be an advertisement covered by the Regulations it must state that the company is willing to provide credit. Suggestions that it is willing, based on the reputation of the company, are not sufficient.

The effect of this provision is to make Part IV apply to all consumer credit businesses, consumer hire businesses and any sort of agreement to provide credit to individuals secured on land *unless* the agreement falls within subsection (3) because, for example, the advertisement makes it clear that credit is available to a body corporate only.

The following are the main provisions regulating advertisements within the ambit of Part IV.

a) An advertiser advertising credit under restricted-use credit agreements relating to goods or services who does not also hold himself as prepared to sell the goods or services for cash commits an offence (section 45).

b) If an advertisement is in a material respect false or misleading the advertiser commits an offence. This includes falsely stating or implying an intention on the advertiser's part which he has not got (section 46).[20]

c) Advertisements contravening the above may also render others knowingly involved in the illegal advertisement criminally liable – e.g. the publisher or deviser of it (section 47).

The form and content of advertisements is governed by the Consumer Credit (Advertisements) Regulations 1989[1] made under powers contained in section 44. The section lays down that the framework of any provision made under it must be designed so that an advertisement conveys a fair and reasonably comprehensive indication of the nature of the credit or hire facilities offered by the advertiser and of their true cost to persons using them. The Regulations apply to all forms of advertising, including by radio, TV and film. Advertisements are divided according to the amount of information given, into 'simple', 'intermediate', and 'full'. Simple credit advertisements may only give the name of the person providing credit, a postal address, telephone number, logo, occupation – e.g. 'moneylender' and any other information other than that the person is willing to provide credit or the cash or other price of goods, services, land or other things. Intermediate credit adver-

19   [1984] 1 All ER 828, [1984] 1 WLR 307, QBD.
20   See e.g. *Home Insulation Ltd v Wadsley* [1988] BTLC 279, QBD and *Metsoja v H Norman Pitt & Co Ltd* (1989) 153 JP 485, QBD.
1   S.I. 1989/1125.

tisements must consist of the advertiser's name and postal address or telephone number (except in certain circumstances), warning notices for loans secured on land[2] and foreign currency mortgages, any other security requirements, insurance and deposit requirements, credit broker's fee, information about terms of business, cash price for debtor-creditor-supplier agreements, the APR where a cash price is given, if no APR is given, a statement that the total amount payable is no greater than the cash price and if the APR is not fixed, a statement that it is variable. Certain additional information is permitted, e.g. logo, restrictions on credit availability and advance payments requirements. Full credit advertisements must include the same compulsory information as intermediate advertisements, together with additional compulsory matters such as the frequency, number and amount of advance payments and of repayments, the total amount payable and details of other payments or charges. Certain other additional matters may also be included eg logos, occupation and rates of interest charged. The requirements for simple, intermediate and full hire advertisements are similar. The Regulations are lucidly explained, with examples, in the OFT's explanatory guide: 'Advertisements and Quotations Regulations 1989'.[3] Quotations must contain similar information to full credit advertisements. In both cases the form of the advertisement/quotation must be given clearly, together as a whole, and the APR be given the required prominence.

Section 167 and Schedule 1 (as amended) lay down penalties for the above offences. Section 168 provides general defences to criminal proceedings brought under the Act. It states that it is a defence to prove that the act or omission was due to a mistake, or to reliance on information supplied to the defendant, or to an act or omission by another person or to an accident *and* that the defendant took all reasonable precautions and exercised all due diligence to avoid the act or omission in question. There are provisions requiring notice of the defence that it was a third party's fault and identification of the third party. There is a similar defence in the Trade Descriptions Act 1968, section 24(1) (and also the Fair Trading Act 1973, section 25(1)). There has been considerable litigation on the defence under the Trade Descriptions Act 1968 – see e.g. *Tesco Supermarkets Ltd v Nattrass*,[4] as to the meaning of an 'act or omission by another person'.

---

2   The inclusion of such requirements for secured loans in the absence of similar warnings for unsecured loans was unsuccessfully challenged in *First National Bank plc v Secretary of State for Trade and Industry* (1990) 154 JP 571, CA.
3   See also P. Circus 'The new advertising regulations' (1990) 87 LS Gaz No 15 p. 20.
4   [1972] AC 153, [1971] 2 All ER 127, HL, see ch. 12.

Sections 48–51 deal with canvassing offences. Canvassing regulated agreements off trade premises is defined as where an individual ('the canvasser') solicits the entry of another individual ('the consumer') into the agreement by making oral representations to the consumer, or any other individual, at a place which is not the place of business of either of the parties or that of the creditor, owner or supplier, being a visit which is a) carried out for the purpose of making such oral representations and b) not carried out in response to a request made on a previous occasion (section 48). Note that the representations may be made e.g. to a member of the consumer's family, that the visit in question must be made *for the purpose of* making oral representations and a previous request legitimates the canvassing. Physical presence of the canvasser is required – a telephone call is not enough.

The offences are:

a) canvassing debtor-creditor agreements off trade premises (without a request);

b) canvassing debtor-creditor agreements off trade premises in response to a request unless the request was in writing and signed by or on behalf of the person making it (section 49);[5]

c) sending circulars to minors containing invitations to borrow money or obtain goods or services on credit or to apply for information about these matters. It is a defence that the minor was not known or suspected to be a minor (section 50(2));

d) giving persons credit-tokens who have not asked for them, the request being in a signed document, unless it is a small debtor-creditor-supplier agreement (section 51).

In connection with a) and b) it should be noted that only debtor-creditor agreements are within the ambit of the offence. A typical transaction would be a personal loan. Debtor-creditor-supplier agreements may be canvassed by specifically licensed suppliers, but in these circumstances the consumer may have rights of cancellation (see section 67). A request must be in writing and signed to take a debtor-creditor agreement out of the offence provisions. Under section 49(3) the Director can authorise[6] the soliciting of agreements to overdraw current accounts of existing customers.

In connection with credit-tokens, unsolicited credit-tokens such as credit cards are not permitted,[7] but excepted from this are tokens

---

5   See, for example, *R v Chadda* [1984] CCLR 1, (1983) 91 ITSA MR 43, Newcastle Crown Court.

6   See Determination of Director General, 1 June 1977, *Annual Report of Director General of Fair Trading 1977* (1978 HCP 228) p. 66.

7   See, for example, *Elliot v Director General of Fair Trading* [1980] 1 WLR 977, [1980] ICR 629, QBD; M & H p. 217.

issued under an existing agreement or renewals or replacements of tokens (section 51(3)). A request for a credit-token must be in a signed document unless it is a small debtor-creditor-supplier agreement. The definition of a credit-token in section 14 has been mentioned above.

Credit marketing has been reviewed by the Department of Trade and Industry. In December 1990 a consultative document[8] was published seeking views on a number of possible reforms and this has been followed, in December 1991, with a further consultative document.[9] Regarding circulars to minors, it is proposed to remove the defence in section 50(2). If a credit circular makes it clear that credit is not offered to those under 18, a new defence of taking appropriate precautions to minimise the risk of circulating under 18 year olds would be introduced (para. 2.2). In addition regulations regarding licensing would also cover the need to take precautions to prevent sending credit circulars to minors (para. 5.2). Recipients of unsolicited credit circulars should have the opportunity of putting a stop to further circulars, unsolicited increases in credit limits for running-account credit and inertia selling techniques, e.g. for credit insurance, would similarly be regulated (paras. 5.5–5.10). Proposed improvements to the Consumer Credit (Advertisements) Regulations 1989[10] include making all advertisements where information is given about the price of credit full advertisements, the inclusion of prescribed statements about secured and unsecured loans in all intermediate and full advertisements and fuller information where examples are given and where variable rates of interest may be charged (paras. 3.1–3.18). Some of the proposals would require legislative change, the others could be introduced by amending regulations.

6. FORMING AND CANCELLING AGREEMENTS

These matters are governed by Part V of the Act and regulations made thereunder.

Disclosure

Section 55 contains a preliminary requirement for disclosure of

---

8 *Proposals for New Legislation on Credit Marketing, A Consultative Document* DTI, December 1990.
9 *Revised Proposals for Legislation on Credit Marketing, A Consultative Document* DTI, December 1991.
10 S.I. 1989/1125.

information to the debtor or hirer as specified by regulation. Failure to do this results in the agreement being 'not properly executed', which means that the agreement is enforceable against the debtor or hirer on an order of the court only (section 65). There are no current plans for regulations to be made under this section.

Negotiator as agent of financier

Section 56 deals with 'antecedent negotiations', i.e. negotiations with the debtor or hirer a) by the creditor or owner in relation to the making of any regulated agreement, b) a credit-broker in relation to goods to be sold under a debtor-creditor-supplier agreement under section 12(a), and c) a supplier in relation to a transaction to be financed by a debtor-creditor-supplier agreement under section 12(b) or (c). Typically a dealer will negotiate with a 'customer' with a view to the formation of a hire-purchase agreement whereunder a finance company buys the goods from the dealer and then as creditor lets them on hire (with an option to purchase) to the debtor. Section 56(2) states that in the case of any debtor-creditor-supplier agreement negotiations with the debtor shall be deemed to be conducted by the negotiator in the capacity of agent of the creditor as well as in his actual capacity. Antecedent negotiations include any representations made by the negotiator to the debtor or hirer (section 56(4)), and agreements are void in so far as they purport to exclude liability for the acts or omissions of the negotiator (section 56(3)). The effect of this is therefore to give non-excludable rights to the debtor or hirer against the negotiator in respect of breaches of express conditions and warranties or of actionable misrepresentations. These rights under section 56 do not, however, apply to implied terms; nor do they apply to contracts of hire where no credit is provided. In *Moorgate Mercantile Leasing v Isobel Gell and Ugolini Dispensers (UK)*,[11] an attempt to make a hire company liable for the misrepresentations of the supplier of an ice shake dispenser failed as the contract was not a consumer credit agreement and the supplier was not a negotiator under section 56.

In some situations there is an overlap between sections 56 and 75[12] and one case decided under section 75 should, in fact, have been decided using section 56.[13]

---

11   [1986] CLY 371, Grays Thurrock County Court. See also Dobson [1983] JBL 312.
12   See post p. 285; also Fairest and Rudkin (1978) 128 NLJ 243, Hill-Smith (1983) 133 NLJ 1012 and 1063.
13   See *Porter v General Guarantee Corpn Ltd* [1982] RTR 384, QBD, post p. 286.

Making the agreement

The provisions relating to formalities are somewhat similar to those laid down by the former hire-purchase legislation. The formalities apply to all regulated agreements including hire-purchase and conditional sale agreements, but not to small[14] debtor-creditor-supplier agreements for restricted-use credit or non-commercial agreements (section 74).

By section 60 the Secretary of State must make regulations as to the form and content of documents embodying regulated agreements. The current regulations are the Consumer Credit (Agreements) Regulations 1983.[15] These are designed to ensure that the debtor or hirer is made aware of a) the rights and duties conferred or imposed upon him by the agreement, b) the amount and rate of the total charge for credit, c) the protection and remedies available to him under the Act, and d) any other matters which it is desirable for him to know about.[16]

The Department of Trade and Industry is proposing further improvements in the protection offered to debtors.[17] If adopted, credit agreements would have to include prescribed statements in the signature box relating to security, foreign currency mortgages and advice about the commitment about to be undertaken. In addition agreements will not be able to contain inertia selling provisions, whereby a debtor has positively to reject e.g. credit insurance (paras. 4.1–4.9).

A properly formed document must be signed by the debtor or hirer and by or on behalf of the creditor or owner (section 61). The debtor or hirer is entitled to at least one copy, delivered there and then if the document is 'an executed agreement' because the creditor or owner has also signed it. If the agreement has not yet been signed by the creditor or owner, the debtor or hirer is entitled to both a copy when he signs and a further copy within seven days of its being made (section 63). If the unexecuted agreement is, instead, sent to the debtor or hirer, a copy must accompany it. If when the debtor

---

14 For the purposes of Part V, if the agreement is one to which the Consumer Protection (Cancellation of Contracts Concluded away from Business Premises) Regulations 1987, S.I. 1987/2117, applies, a small agreement is one not exceeding £35, see post at p. 284.

15 See S.I. 1983/1553 as amended by S.I. 1984/1600, S.I. 1985/666 and S.I. 1988/2047.

16 For guidance see OFT booklets 'Cancellable agreements' (5th Edn., November 1990) and 'Non-Cancellable agreements' (5th Edn., November 1990).

17 *Revised Proposals for Legislation on Credit Marketing, A Consultative Document*, DTI, December 1991.

or hirer signs it has not been signed by the other party, a further copy must be given within seven days of its being made (sections 62, 63).

There are special provisions for cancellable agreements and regulated agreements secured on land. In the case of the former, section 64 imposes a duty[18] to include on every copy of such an agreement (see below) a notice of how and when it is cancellable.[19] In addition, if a second copy of the agreement is required under section 63, in the case of a cancellable agreement this must be sent by post (section 63(3)). The same provisions do not apply to second mortgages because of the conveyancing difficulties that would arise. Instead, the unexecuted mortgage agreement must contain a notice in a prescribed form[20] indicating the right to withdraw from the agreement (section 58, and see section 61(2)).

An improperly executed regulated agreement may be enforced, for example, by the retaking of goods or land, on an order of the court only (section 65).[1] In the case of a cancellable agreement, if the requirement to give a cancellation notice under section 64(1) has not been complied with then, by section 127(4), the court cannot make an enforcement order.

Withdrawal

The Act, under section 57, includes and extends the common law right to withdraw from an agreement before it has been accepted. The provisions apply to any regulated agreement, save those exempted under section 74. A written or oral notice of withdrawal, however expressed, may, as at common law, be given to the creditor or owner. In addition, by section 57(3), notice may be given to a credit-broker or supplier who acted as a 'negotiator' or any person, who in the course of a business, acted on behalf of the debtor in negotiating the agreement. The effect of withdrawal is the same as cancellation, bringing to an end both the prospective regulated agreement and any linked transaction, subject to certain exceptions (see below).

---

18 Subject to the Director General being empowered to make a determination exempting this requirement, see Consumer Credit (Notice of Cancellation Rights) (Exemptions) Regulations 1983, S.I. 1983/1558.

19 See Consumer Credit (Cancellation Notices and Copies of Documents) Regulations 1983, S.I. 1983/1557 as amended by S.I. 1984/1108, S.I. 1985/666, S.I. 1988/2047 and S.I. 1989/591.

20 S.I. 1983/1557 as amended and S.I. 1983/1553 as amended.

 1 The agreement is not, however, void, see *R v Modupe* [1991] Crim LR 530, CA.

Cancelling agreements

The law in the Consumer Credit Act 1974 is based on similar but not identical provisions in the Hire-Purchase Act 1965 designed to curtail over-enthusiasm by 'doorstep' salesmen. The provisions apply to all regulated agreements (save those exempted by section 74) subject to the following points:

1) They only apply where oral representations are made in the presence of the debtor by or on behalf of the negotiator (section 67);

2) They do not apply where the agreement is signed at the business premises of the creditor, a party linked to the transaction or the negotiator (section 67);

3) They do not apply to agreements secured on land, restricted use credit agreements to finance the purchase of land or agreements for bridging loans in connection with the purchase of land (section 67).

Special 'cooling-off' arrangements apply to agreements involving land mortgages, primarily because of the extra dimension which the proprietary rights acquired involve and the difficulties of 'cancelling' mortgages. If the various requirements in sections 58 and 61 are not observed, such an agreement is 'improperly executed' and unenforceable except by court order.

If the agreement is a 'cancellable' one, the debtor enjoys a cooling-off period. This is to the end of the fifth day following the day on which he receives the statutory copy of the agreement under section 63(2) or a notice under section 64(1), or where regulations dispense with the need for a copy, fourteen days following the day on which he signed the unexecuted agreement. Under section 63(2) the second copy must be given to the debtor within seven days of the making of the agreement. Accordingly, where an agreement is made on 1 July, the second copy received on 7 July, the agreement is cancellable until 12 July expires.

If within the cooling-off period the debtor serves a written cancellation notice on the creditor or his agent, 'however expressed', indicating his intention to withdraw from the agreement, the notice operates to cancel the agreement and any linked transaction (or promise to enter into a linked transaction) (section 69). Only three types of linked transactions continue despite cancellation: contracts of insurance, guarantees of goods and current and deposit accounts opened in pursuance of the agreement.[2] If the post is used to serve

---

2 See Consumer Credit (Linked Transactions) (Exemptions) Regulations 1983, S.I. 1983/1560. See also Bone & Rutherford [1985] JBL 209.

the notice of cancellation, it takes effect on posting, even if never received by the creditor or his agent (section 69(7)).

The effect of cancellation is to entitle the debtor to repayment of any sums paid and he has a lien on any goods in his possession pending repayment. Despite cancellation, there are provisions favourable to the debtor concerning the repayment by instalments of any credit and interest (see section 71). This is to discourage the making of advances of money during the cooling-off period, a factor which might otherwise discourage the debtor from exercising his cancellation rights. Goods acquired under a restricted-use debtor-creditor-supplier agreement must be restored to the person from whom the debtor obtained them (section 72). The debtor is not obliged to do so other than at his own premises and in pursuance of a written request by the creditor, but while the goods are in his possession he is under a duty to retain possession of them and to take reasonable care of them (ibid). Any breach of his duty is actionable as the tort of breach of statutory duty (ibid) and damages can thus be awarded. It is worth noting that the obligation to restore the goods does not apply in certain cases, for example if they are perishable goods or consumables which are consumed prior to cancellation (section 72(9)).[3]

There are proposals to extend further cancellation rights by amending the Act.[4] This would involve giving cancellation rights for debtor-creditor-supplier agreements and hire agreements signed on trade premises following face-to-face negotiations. Debtors, however, could contract out of such rights where goods are involved and the supplier either agrees to deliver the goods or to do work on them within the cancellation period. Suppliers would not be able to make waiver of cancellation rights a condition of any sale, but debtors could forfeit their rights to cancel if the goods are not returned or if they are returned in a significantly worse condition than when supplied. In addition it is intended to simplify the way of determining the length of the cancellation period and to bring it into line with the EC Directive on Doorstep Selling.[5]

As a result of this Directive, the Consumer Protection (Cancellation of Contracts Concluded away from Business Premises) Regulations 1987[6] were brought into force on 1 July 1988. The effect of

3 See Dobson (1978) Vol 128 NLJ 56 for possible abuses by consumers. On cancellation generally see OFT booklet 'Cancellable Agreements' (5th Edn., November 1990).

4 *Revised Proposals for Legislation on Credit Marketing, A Consultative Document*, DTI, December 1991, paras. 2.5–2.7.

5 Directive to protect the consumer in respect of contracts negotiated away from business premises, 85/577/EEC, OJ No L 372 p. 31, 20 December 1985.

6 S.I. 1987/2117 as amended by S.I. 1988/958.

these Regulations is to give protection, in civil law, to many non-credit consumers who make contracts away from business premises in a similar way to that given to those buying on credit. Certain contracts are excluded, for example food and drink supplied by regular roundsmen and where payments will not exceed £35. A seven day cancellation provision is included, with the contract being unenforceable if the customer is not informed of the right to cancel.

Problems encountered by consumers over the selling of timeshares has led to the Timeshare Act 1992[7] which is modelled on the cancellation provisions of the Consumer Credit Act 1974. Both cash and credit purchasers are covered, with a minimum 14 day cooling-off period for contracts made under United Kingdom law or where one of the parties is located in the United Kingdom. Failure to inform consumers of the cancellation rights is a criminal offence where a business is selling timeshare, although this does not apply to timeshare credit agreements (to maintain consistency with the provisions of the 1974 Act). The civil consequences of cancellation are similar to those under section 71, above, and the criminal provisions include a due diligence defence and the ability to prosecute employees.

7. DURING THE AGREEMENT

There are a number of matters which, if they arise during the currency of the agreement, are regulated by Part VI of the Act. The main provisions are now summarised.

Liability of creditor for breaches by supplier[8]

The object of section 75 is to make it clear that where there is a debtor-creditor-supplier agreement and the supplier is not also the creditor (such as where the debtor buys goods by using his Access or Visa card), the creditor is jointly and severally liable with the seller to the debtor for damages in respect of any misrepresentation or breach of contract – an apparent exception to the basic principle of privity of contract. In *United Dominions Trust v Taylor*[9] a debtor under an agreement within the ambit of section 75 to whom an unsatisfactory car had been sold in reliance on the supplier's misrepresentation, purported to rescind both the 'sale' contract and the loan agreement (although the finance company had made no misrepresentation

---

7 See T Bourne 'Cooling off on timeshares' (1992) 142 NLJ 418.
8 See M & H pp. 224–230 and OFT leaflet 'Equal Liability' (CCP 21).
9 1980 SLT 28, Sheriffs Court, Scotland; M & H p. 228.

itself). The debtor was held entitled to do this on the basis of the statement in section 75 that a debtor with a claim in respect of misrepresentation or breach of contract against the supplier 'shall have a like claim' against the creditor. The approach of section 75 'leaves no room for the idea of privity of contract which is fundamental to the common law of contract'.[10] It is, perhaps, unfortunate that the 'like claim' was interpreted as one of rescission instead of one for damages. Under the purchase contract, following rescission, the debtor would be entitled to payment of money sufficient to enable termination of the credit agreement. It would seem preferable to consider the creditor jointly liable to 'pay' this and thereby discharge the credit agreement, rather than suggesting that the credit agreement is rescinded following the rescission of the purchase agreement. A 'like claim' of rescission of the credit agreement would clearly not operate in cases where a credit card is used to fund the purchase of goods. Here, although the purchase contract for the goods might be rescinded by reason of a misrepresentation, the credit card agreement continues. By interpreting the 'like claim' as one for damages, confusion is less likely to arise in future cases, whilst still enabling the same result to be achieved.

Although the creditor has a right of indemnity from the supplier, if the supplier is insolvent the additional right will provide valuable, as for example, with the collapse of Lowndes Queensway in 1990 and International Leisure Group/Air Europe in 1991. This provision does not apply to non-commercial agreements or to agreements with a cash price of £100 or less or more than £30,000.[11] By virtue of the Consumer Credit Act 1974 (Commencement No. 3) Order 1977 this 'connected lender' liability applies to tripartite debtor-creditor-supplier agreements (under section 12(b) or (c)) made after 30 June 1977. Section 75 should not, however, apply to two party debtor-creditor-supplier agreements such as hire-purchase as section 12(a) is not mentioned in that section. Such agreements do not need the special protection granted by section 75 as with them the creditor is also the supplier of the goods or services. The debtor, therefore, has contractual rights against the creditor for defective goods etc. and by section 56(2) any representations by a negotiator are deemed to be made by him as agent for the creditor. However, in *Porter v General*

10   See also (1980) 130 NLJ 924; (1980) 96 LQR 343; (1981) 97 LQR 532; [1980] JBL 277; [1981] JBL 179; M & H pp. 224–230. For the possible interrelationship between s. 56 (in antecedent negotiations the negotiator is deemed to be the agent of the creditor) and s. 75, see (1978) 128 NLJ 243; also (1983) 133 NLJ 1012 and 1063; [1979] JBL 331. For a discussion on whether or not s. 75 applies to Electronic Funds Transfers see Dobson [1984] JBL 350–352.

11   Section 75(3) as amended by the Consumer Credit (Increase of Monetary Limits) Order 1983, S.I. 1983/1878.

Guarantee Corpn Ltd,[12] the court applied section 75 to a hire-purchase agreement to make the finance company responsible for the misrepresentations of the car dealer who had negotiated the deal. It is submitted that section 56 would provide a more appropriate basis for the decision (see above).

In connection with starting dates and the question of retrospection there has been considerable controversy as to whether section 75 protects a credit card holder whose card was first issued before 1 April 1977, since only consumer credit and consumer hire agreements made after that date are *regulated* agreements, this being the commencement date laid down by the Consumer Credit Act 1974 (Commencement No. 2) Order 1977.[13] The issuing banks take the view that since the credit card agreement was made before that date, section 75 does not apply to the subsequent use of the card. Goode takes the view that this position is unfounded. 'In the case of a unilateral contract established by a running-account credit agreement, there is a separate acceptance of the creditor's continuing offer each time the facility is utilised, so that on each occasion when the debtor uses the card a distinct contract is generated, governed by the terms of the running-account agreement.'[14] Following pressure from the Office of Fair Trading the banks have agreed to accept joint and several liability in respect of cards issued under agreements made before 1 April 1977. This liability is limited, however, to the amount of the sum advanced for the transaction in question.[15]

Further problems have arisen following the collapse of some major companies in that credit card companies have sought to limit their liability under section 75 to those contracts made by traders with whom they have a merchant acquirer agreement. For example, Barclaycard sought to deny responsibility for their Visa card-holders dealing with Lowndes Queensway because the company had been recruited into the Visa system by another bank. The Office of Fair Trading disagrees with this policy and takes the view that, where cards are issued to customers by one member of a network and the trader is recruited to the network by another, connected lender liability provisions apply fully. Currently liability is accepted by some banks on a voluntary basis.[16]

---

12 [1982] RTR 384, QBD. See also Thornley [1983] CLJ 201.
13 S.I. 1977/325.
14 See Goode *Consumer Credit Law* paras. 677, 1076. See also Dobson (1978) 128 NLJ 448.
15 See OFT leaflet 'Equal Liability' p. 3 and *Bee Line* No 91/2 p. 26.
16 See 'Equal Liability and Credit Cards', *Bee Line* No 91/2 pp. 25–26; *Which?* April 1991, p. 184 and June 1991, p. 304.

Duty to give notice before taking certain action

If the regulated agreement allows the creditor to demand earlier payment, recover possession of goods or land or treat any of the rights of the debtor as terminated, restricted or deferred, section 76 states that the creditor must give to the debtor at least seven days' notice of his intention to exercise such rights. The form such a notice must take is contained in the Consumer Credit (Enforcement, Default and Terminations Notices) Regulations 1983.[17]

Rights to information

Sections 77 and 78 confer upon the debtor the right to obtain information from the creditor as to such matters as the amount already paid and the amount owing. In addition section 97 supplements the debtor's right to complete payments ahead of time at a discount (see sections 94 and 95) by requiring the creditor to inform him of the amount needed to settle his account.

The debtor is also under a liability to tell the creditor where the goods are when the agreement requires the debtor to keep the goods in his possession or control (section 80).

Appropriation of payments

Where a debtor under two or more agreements with the same creditor makes one payment insufficient to discharge the total due on each, and does not specifically appropriate any particular sum to a particular agreement, the payment is to be appropriated towards the satisfaction of the sums due under the several agreements respectively in the proportions which those sums bear to one another (section 81). For example if £60 is due under one regulated agreement and £40 under another, the debtor's payment of £60 is appropriated as to £36 to the first agreement and £24 to the second.

Variation of agreements

There is, of course, no power to vary agreements unilaterally, but if the agreement itself permits this the effect, when exercised, is to revoke the inconsistent parts of the earlier agreement. Section 82 provides (inter alia) that this shall not be effective before notice of the variation is given to the debtor in the prescribed manner. The Consumer Credit (Notice of Variation of Agreements) Regulations

---

17 S.I. 1983/1561 as amended by S.I. 1984/1109.

1977[18] require seven days' written notice to be given personally to the debtor or hirer.

8. TERMINATION OF THE AGREEMENT

Hiring agreements

If the agreement is a regulated consumer hire agreement,[19] section 101 confers the right for the hirer to terminate it after at least eighteen months has expired, even if the hiring was for a fixed term of longer duration. The hirer must give notice equivalent to the shortest period between two payments, or of three months, whichever is less. In the case of some commercial agreements such a statutory licence to terminate prematurely would not be justified by public policy, so section 101 incorporates some exceptions. These relate to agreements involving 1) hiring rentals of more than £900 per annum (an amount which has been raised by Order[20] under section 181(1)), 2) goods hired for the purpose of the hirer's business, and including the business of hiring them to other persons in the course of business and persons carrying on consumer hire businesses in favour of whom 3) the Director directs (on their application) that section 101 shall not apply.

Where the agreement is terminated under the above, all liabilities accrued under the agreement up to termination must be discharged (section 101(2)).

Early settlement – consumer credit agreements

At any time during the lifetime of a regulated consumer credit agreement the debtor may give notice to the creditor that he wishes to complete his payments ahead of time (section 94). On payment of the required amount his indebtedness is then discharged. As the creditor is receiving his payment early, section 95 provides for regulations to be made to calculate the rebate of charges for credit which the debtor is allowed. The current Regulations are the Consumer Credit (Rebate on Early Settlement) Regulations 1983.[1] A number of formulae are provided to calculate the *minimum* rebate

18   S.I. 1977/328 as amended by S.I.s 1979/661 and 667.
19   See OFT booklet 'Hire agreements' (6th Edn., November 1990).
20   Increased from £300 to £900 by the Consumer Credit (Increase of Monetary Amounts) Order 1983, S.I. 1983/1571.
 1   S.I. 1983/1562 as amended by S.I. 1989/596. For discussion of rebates allowable on judgment debts, see *Forward Trust Ltd v Robinson* [1987] B TLC 12, Birmingham County Court; and *Forward Trust Ltd v Whymark* [1990] 2 QB 670, [1989] 3 All ER 915, CA.

permitted.[2] To enable the debtor to make an informed decision whether or not to settle early section 97 imposes a duty on the creditor to provide the required information within 12 days of receipt of a written request.[3]

Termination by debtor – consumer credit agreements

As under the old law (see Hire-Purchase Act 1965, section 27) the debtor under a regulated hire-purchase or conditional sale agreement may terminate it. The debtor can do so at any time before his final payment is due by giving to the creditor or owner notice (section 99). (The creditor may also terminate where there has been no default on giving the debtor at least seven days' notice (section 98).) The right to terminate does not apply to conditional sale agreements relating to land which has become vested in the debtor, but it does apply to conditional sale agreements for goods unless the property in the goods is transferred from the debtor to a third party. On such termination, the property in the goods reverts to the original owner if it is not already in him (section 99(3)–(5)).

The position following termination by the debtor is as follows (section 100):

1) He must discharge all accrued liabilities (section 99(2)).
2) Unless the agreement provides for a smaller payment or makes no provision, the debtor must pay to the creditor the amount (if any) by which one-half of the total price exceeds the aggregate of a) the sums paid and b) the sums due in respect of the total price at date of termination (section 100). This '50 per cent rule' is a long-standing one in hire-purchase law (see Hire-Purchase Act 1965, section 28). Where an installation charge is specified as part of the total price the debtor must pay this in full plus half the remainder of the total purchase price.
3) The court has a discretion to order payment of a lesser fraction of the total price if it considers such a sum would adequately compensate the creditor for the depreciation that inevitably occurs.
4) The debtor must pay compensation for any failure to take reasonable care of the goods or land.

---

2   See *Home Insulation Ltd v Wadsley* [1988] CCLR 25, QBD, for a case where the credit company literature indicated a higher rebate allowable, in error. Company obliged to allow the higher sum.
3   See Consumer Credit (Settlement Information) Regulations 1983, S.I. 1983/1564 and Consumer Credit (Prescribed Periods for Giving Information) Regulations 1983, S.I. 1983/1569. See generally OFT booklet 'Matters arising during the lifetime of an agreement' (6th Edn., October 1990). Note also *Home Insulation Ltd v Wadsley* above.

5) If the debtor wrongfully retains the goods the court must order their redelivery to the creditor, without giving the debtor an option to pay the value of the goods, unless it is satisfied that this would be unjust.

Termination of regulated agreements by the creditor on debtor's default

Where the debtor is in breach of his agreement, the creditor will probably wish to terminate the agreement and recover the goods. In the past there was abuse of the contractual position leading to situations where, for instance, a debtor had almost completed his instalments when, as a result of a minor delay in payment, the creditor 'snatched back' the hired goods. There has been legislation for many years protecting the debtor in these circumstances and this is repeated in an extended form in the 1974 Act.

A precondition of termination is the service on the debtor of a default notice. Section 87 states that this is necessary before the creditor can become entitled, by reason of any breach of the regulated agreement, a) to terminate the agreement, or b) to demand earlier payment of any sum, or c) to recover possession of any goods or land, or d) to treat any of the debtor's rights as terminated, restricted or deferred, or e) to enforce any security. The form of the notice is as prescribed by regulation (section 88 and the Consumer Credit (Enforcement, Default and Termination Notices) Regulations 1983[4]) and must specify the breach, what action is required to remedy the breach if capable of being remedied, or the notice may require compensation. In effect, seven days' notice to remedy is required, and the notice may state that the creditor will take one of the courses of action specified in section 87, e.g. demand repossession of the goods, unless the breach is duly remedied or compensation paid. If the debtor takes the action specified within the time limit the breach is treated as not having occurred (section 89). (See also section 76 – duty to give notice in other cases.)

Repossession of goods

In order to protect debtors from the risk of the 'snatch-back' of goods by creditors from debtors in circumstances where a considerable proportion of the total price of the goods has been paid, the concept of 'protected goods' is used. These provisions, in section 90, apply to regulated hire-purchase and conditional sale agreements only. The section provides that where the property in the goods

4 S.I. 1983/1561 as amended by S.I. 1984/1109.

remains in the creditor and the debtor has paid to the creditor one-third or more of the total price of the goods, the creditor is not entitled to recover possession of the goods without a court order. It is now also a precondition that the debtor is in breach of the agreement. Any installation charge included in the total purchase price must, in effect, first be paid and the one-third fraction applied to the balance (section 90(2)).

The consequences of contravening section 90 are serious. The regulated agreement, if not already terminated, terminates and the debtor is both released from all further liability and is entitled to recover from the creditor all sums paid by him under the agreement (section 91).

In the following cases there is no infringement of this provision:

i) Where the debtor consents to repossession (section 173(3)). Thus, in *Mercantile Credit Co Ltd v Cross*[5] a finance company obtained repossession of the debtor's motor cycle combination after he had paid more than one-third of the price, having first written him a letter terminating the agreement because of arrears. The hirer voluntarily returned the motor cycle to the shop from which he had obtained it. It was held by the Court of Appeal that this was not enforcing 'any right to recover possession . . . other than by action' contrary to the then legislation (Hire-Purchase Act 1938), and though the hirer's consent to repossession must be voluntary, in this case he was deemed to be aware of his statutory rights.

ii) The section envisages recovery 'from the debtor' and does not therefore cover repossession from a person other than the debtor as defined by section 189(1) (a definition which includes a person to whom the debtor's rights and duties have passed by assignment or operation of law). Thus if the goods are in the wrongful possession of a third party, or have been abandoned (see *Bentinck Ltd v Cromwell Engineering Co*[6] – debtor abandoned damaged vehicle at garage) the restrictions on repossession do not apply.

iii) The restrictions do not apply if the debtor terminates the agreement (section 90(5)).

Even if the goods are not 'protected goods' the creditor is not entitled to enter any premises to take repossession of goods under a regulated hire, hire-purchase or conditional sale agreement, or to recover possession of land under a conditional sale agreement relating to land, except under an order of the court (section 92), or unless the debtor consents (section 173(3)). Contravention of section

---

5 [1965] 2 QB 205, [1965] 1 All ER 577, CA.
6 [1971] 1 QB 324, [1971] 1 All ER 33, CA.

92 is actionable as a breach of statutory duty (section 92(3)). In addition, section 93 prevents the debtor from being charged an increased rate of interest when in breach of the agreement.[7]

Death of the debtor or hirer

In the event of the death of the debtor or hirer before the completion of a regulated agreement, other than an agreement of unspecified duration, if the agreement is fully secured the creditor is not entitled to do any act for which a default notice is required, for example terminate the agreement, demand earlier repayment or recover possession of the goods (section 86). If the agreement is partly secured or unsecured the creditor may only do any of those acts on the order of the court. The creditor may, however, restrict or refuse any further credit.

9. POWERS OF THE COURT

As before, most of the litigation concerning hire-purchase and similar regulated agreements will be within the jurisdiction of the county court (see definition in section 189). In Part IX of the Act wide discretionary powers are conferred on the court to control regulated agreements and securities, to grant relief to debtors and protection to the goods of creditors, and to reopen extortionate bargains, whether regulated or not.

i) Time orders (section 129) and enforcement orders (section 127)

Time orders made by the court are designed either to adjust the rate and time of payments of instalments if the sum is owed under regulated agreements (the most common type in practice) or to specify the period by which a breach of the agreement must be remedied, other than a breach relating to a non-payment of money.

The court can make such an order if it thinks it just to do so 1) on an application for an 'enforcement order' (an order to enforce an improperly-executed agreement under e.g. section 65(1), see section 127), 2) on an application by a debtor after being served with a default notice, a creditor's notice of calling-in under section 76, or a notice of termination in non-default cases under section 98, or 3) on a creditor's action to enforce any security or recover possession of any goods or land the subject-matter of a regulated agreement.

The time order must be made 'having regard to the means of the

---

7 See generally OFT booklet 'Matters arising during the lifetime of an agreement' (6th Edn., October 1990).

debtor' (section 129(2)(a)), unless the debtor makes an acceptable offer (section 130(1)) and the section applies also to hirers and sureties. Similar powers ('postponed orders') applied under the old law, but the power to make time orders is wider, not being confined to hire-purchase and conditional sale agreements except where the order relates to sums not yet due (section 130(2)). One situation where the use of such orders is appropriate is where mortgagees seek repossession of houses. In *First National Bank plc v Syed*[8] the Court of Appeal gave guidance on the factors to be considered in deciding whether or not to make a time order. The creditor's position must be considered as well as the debtor's. Here, in view of the history of default, sporadic repayments and the unlikelihood of improvement in the debtors' finances, a time order was refused and enforcement of a possession order permitted.

Enforcement orders under section 127 may be sought in cases of: a) improperly executed agreements (section 65), b) improperly executed security instruments (section 105), c) failure to serve a copy of a notice on a surety (section 111) or d) taking of a negotiable instrument in contravention of section 123 (section 124). The court must refuse to make an enforcement order under section 65 if the debtor has not signed a copy of the agreement (section 127(3)) or, in the case of a cancellable agreement, if the copies rules under sections 62 and 63 were not complied with and were not rectified before commencement of proceedings or if the provisions relating to cancellation notices under section 64(1) were not complied with (section 127(4)). In other cases the court has a discretion whether or not to enforce an agreement. It may, in granting an enforcement order, reduce or discharge any sum payable by the debtor, hirer, or surety to compensate for any prejudice suffered as a result of the contravention in question (section 127(2)).

ii) Protection orders (section 131)

In order to protect the goods of the creditor 'pending the determination of proceedings under this Act', the court on the application of a creditor under a regulated agreement may make an order protecting the goods against damage or depreciation, including orders restricting or prohibiting their use or as to their custody. Such an order can be made in respect of any goods under a regulated agreement whether or not they are 'protected'. (If the goods are perishable, the court may be requested to order a sale under its general jurisdiction – see e.g. County Court Rules 1981, Order 13, rule 7.[9])

8   [1991] 2 All ER 250, CA.
9   S.I. 1981/1687.

iii) Financial relief for hirer (section 132)

If, under a consumer hire agreement, the owner has repossessed the goods other than by action, the court may make an order for repayment for the whole or any part of the sum paid by the hirer and that the obligation to pay any sum owed by the hirer shall cease. The court makes such order as it thinks just having regard to the extent of the enjoyment of the goods by the hirer. The object of the section is to give some protection to the hirer, who is without the benefit of the 'protected goods' concept applicable to hire-purchase and conditional sale agreements only (see above, p. 291).

iv) Special powers relating to hire-purchase and conditional sale agreements (section 133)

The court has power to make a variety of orders as regards the above agreements in addition to time and protection orders. Section 133 provides that on an application for an enforcement order or time order or in an action by the creditor for recovery of possession of goods the court may if it appears just make a 'return' order or a 'transfer' order. A 'return order' is an order for the return of the goods to the creditor. Such an order may be suspended under the general power to make conditional or suspended orders in section 135.

A transfer order is the modern equivalent of a 'Solomon's judgment' – the order will be for transfer of the title to some of the goods to the debtor and the return of some to the creditor (though obviously the goods must be capable of division in this way unlike Solomon's child). A similar 'split-order' was within the powers of the court under the former hire-purchase legislation. The section lays down a condition which must be fulfilled before a transfer order can be made. This is that the 'paid-up sum' exceeds the part of the total price referable to the transferred goods by an amount equal to at least one-third of the unpaid balance of the total price (section 133(3)). Thus the debtor must have paid the value of the transferred goods plus at least one-third of the total price of all the goods before a transfer order can be made. The 'paid-up sum' is normally the sum paid by the debtor to the creditor to date, but adjustments are made for sums owed by the creditor to the debtor, or vice versa, in respect of the goods (section 133(2)). Subject to this, 'the transferred goods shall be such of the goods to which the agreement relates as the court thinks just' (section 133(3)).

After a return order or transfer order has been made, if the debtor pays the balance of the purchase price and fulfils 'any other necessary conditions', then provided the goods are not in the possession of the creditor the debtor may claim the goods back. If the debtor fails to comply with a transfer order the court, on the creditor's application, may revoke the order and instead order the debtor to pay the balance of the total price as is referable to the goods. Conditional and suspended orders may also be made (section 135).

v) Variation of agreements (section 136)

The court has a general power to make an order to amend any agreement or security. It is generally thought that this power would be used only in connection with the making of the orders discussed above.

vi) Extortionate credit bargains (sections 137, 138, 139)

The court has power to re-open a credit agreement so as to do justice between the parties if it finds a credit bargain extortionate.[10] This applies to all credit agreements, whether or not regulated, provided they are made with an 'individual', and not a body corporate. It does not apply to hire agreements. The credit 'bargains' may be examined generally. The power resembles provisions formerly in the Moneylenders Acts, and a similar equitable power has been exercised in land mortgage cases (see *Cityland and Property (Holdings) Ltd v Dabrah*).[11]

Some guidance is given by section 138 on when bargains are extortionate. A bargain is extortionate if the payments to be made by the debtor are grossly exorbitant or otherwise grossly contravene ordinary principles of fair dealing. There is a helpful list of factors to be taken into account in deciding whether a bargain is extortionate. These include interest rates prevailing at the time (there is now no presumption against interest rates exceeding 48 per cent), the age, experience, business capacity and state of health of the debtor and the degree of risk accepted by the creditor (see sections 138(2), (3) and (4)). The burden of disproving that the bargain is extortionate is on the creditor once the debtor has made such an allegation under section 139 (section 171(7)). The court should require the debtor to support his allegation with prima facie evidence. Under section 139 the court in re-opening extortionate bargains has wide powers including those to rewrite the agreement, set aside the debtor's obligations or order repayments to be made. The draftsman of the Act, when writing on this topic, expressed the view that although it

---

10   See M & H pp. 219–222; Wilkinson (1979) 8 Anglo-Am 240; Hill-Smith (1982) 126 SJ 530; Wilkinson (1986) 136 NLJ 796; Bently & Howells [1989] Conv 164 and 234; OFT leaflet 'Extortionate Credit' (CCP 21); *Unjust Credit Transactions*, Report by Director General, OFT, September 1991.

11   [1968] Ch 166, [1967] 2 All ER 639.

was likely that a body of case law on the exercise of this power would rapidly accumulate, 'it is likely that the courts will be sparing with relief. The bargain must after all be grossly exorbitant or unfair.'[12] This view has been borne out by the decisions of the High Court, with very few cases being re-opened.

In *A Ketley Ltd v Scott*[13] the defendants contracted to buy a flat but were unable to complete (because of lack of funds) on the due date. Mr. Scott, therefore, obtained a loan from the plaintiffs of £20,500 to enable him and his wife to complete. The interest was expressed as being 12 per cent over three months, this being equal to 48 per cent per annum. He did not declare to the plaintiffs that he had given a legal charge on the property to his bank to cover an overdraft and was liable under certain further guarantees to third parties. The loan not having been repaid the plaintiffs sued for payment due and possession and obtained judgment, but an inquiry was ordered into the question of whether the interest was 'extortionate'. The court held that material considerations were that the plaintiffs had lent 82 per cent of the value of the property without time for inquiry, the risk being highly speculative. Furthermore Mr. Scott had failed to disclose his overdraft at the bank and other financial commitments and these were deceitful acts. Having regard to the degree of risk the interest charged was not disproportionately high and it was therefore not just to re-open the credit bargain. This was followed, in 1984, by *Wills v Wood*[14] where a retired hotelier loaned money on security of mortgages to other clients of his solicitor. In deciding that an agreement with the defendant did not 'grossly contravene the principles of fair dealing' the court indicated that although the defendant may have been unwise in borrowing the money, the plaintiff had not dealt in any unfair or improper way. As Sir John Donaldson indicated 'the word is "extortionate" not "unwise"'. The same conclusion was reached in *Coldunell Ltd v Gallon*.[15]

The provisions of section 138 received detailed study in *Davies v Directloans Ltd*[16] where Edward Nugee QC (sitting as Deputy Judge of the High Court) indicated that it was unnecessary and not

12 F. A. R. Bennion (1979) 121 Sol Jo 485.
13 [1981] ICR 241, QBD; M & H p. 220. See (1980) 130 NLJ 749. Jurisdiction is now given to the county court in the case of applications by a debtor or surety for all regulated agreements and also all other agreements for fixed-sum or running-account credit (s 139(5) as amended by the High Court and County Courts Jurisdiction Order 1991, S.I. 1991/724, art. 2(1)(h),(8) and Sch, Pt I).
14 (1984) 128 Sol Jo 222, [1984] LS Gaz 1211; M & H p. 221. See also (1984) 134 NLJ 355.
15 [1986] QB 1184, [1986] 1 All ER 429, CA.
16 [1986] 2 All ER 783, [1986] 1 WLR 823, Ch D. See also (1986) 136 NLJ 796.

permissible to look outside the Act at earlier authorities to ascertain its meaning. He indicated that:

> Under the 1974 Act the test is not whether the creditor has acted in a morally reprehensible manner, but whether one or other of the conditions of section 138(1) is fulfilled, and, although it may be thought that if either condition is fulfilled there is likely to be something morally reprehensible about the creditor's conduct, the starting and ending point in determining whether the credit bargain is extortionate must be the words of section 138(1). (at pp. 789, 831.)

In deciding that the mortgage agreement in question was not extortionate the court noted that the borrowers had received independent advice from a solicitor, were not under greater than normal financial pressure, the degree of risk to the lender justified a significantly higher rate of interest than a building society would charge and the true rate of interest was not grossly exorbitant when compared with prevailing interest rates.

In four cases the credit agreement has been re-opened and the amount of interest charged altered. In *Barcabe Ltd v Edwards*[17] the court was influenced by the fact that a flat interest rate of 100 per cent, APR 319 per cent, was extortionate in comparison with other companies charging 18–20 per cent. The court reduced the interest rate charged to 40 per cent. The second case was *Devogate v Jarvis*[18] where an APR was reduced from 39 per cent to 30 per cent for a well-secured loan of £10,000. A flat rate of 42 per cent was halved to 21 per cent for an £18,000 mortgage in *Prestonwell Ltd v Capon*.[19] The comparative rates for loans elsewhere, the debtors' lack of business capacity, financial pressure and lack of access to legal advice all contributed to the decision. Finally, in *Shahabinia v Giyahchi*[20] the creditor appealed to the Court of Appeal over the interest rate of 15 per cent imposed by the Queen's Bench Division when it re-opened three agreements. A rate of 30 per cent was substituted so as to do justice between the parties, 15 per cent having been even less than bank rate for some of the relevant time.

In 1990 Mr Edward Leigh, Parliamentary Under Secretary of State for Industry and Consumer Affairs, requested that the Director General review the effectiveness of the extortionate credit provisions. Consultations took place during 1991 and his report was published in September 1991.[1] The Director General proposes

---

17 [1983] CCLR 11, Birmingham County Court.
18 (16 November 1987, unreported), Lexis transcript, Sevenoaks County Court.
19 (1988), unreported, Corby County Court.
20 (5 July 1989, unreported), Lexis transcript, CA.
 1 *Unjust Credit Transactions*, OFT, September 1991.

reform of the provisions of sections 137–140 by replacing the idea of an 'extortionate credit bargain' with that of an 'unjust credit transaction'. To determine whether or not a transaction is 'unjust' account could be taken of 'excessive' payments, the current factors under section 138(2), (3) and (4) and 'the lender's care and responsibility in making the loan, including steps taken to find out and check the borrower's credit-worthiness and ability to meet the full terms of the agreement' (para. 1.9, sub-para. 4). In addition it is recommended that, instead of 'otherwise grossly contravenes the ordinary principles of fair dealing' in section 138(1), the transaction be examined to see if it involves business activity which is deceitful or oppressive or otherwise unfair or improper, using the same terms as those for licensing decisions under section 25(2)(d). In addition to application by the debtor, the court should have power to re-open a credit transaction itself.[2] It is further proposed that the Director General and Trading Standards Departments should, in the public interest, be able to initiate proceedings for a declaration that particular credit transactions, or parts of them, are unjust. Government support was given to these proposals, with some modifications.[3] Payments should be 'grossly excessive' to qualify and it is proposed to detail the factors to be considered in deciding whether or not there is an unjust credit transaction in regulations to allow for greater flexibility.

Further reforms concerning extortionate credit bargains are advocated by the Law Commission in its report *Transfer of Land – Land Mortgages*.[4] Here it is proposed that all control over the form, content and enforcement of land mortgages be removed from the 1974 Act. In particular this would remove land mortgages from the provisions of sections 137–140 and replace these controls with similar, but more extensive, ones addressed specifically to the land mortgage contract.

10. CREDIT STATUS ENQUIRIES

There has been a great deal of concern by consumer organisations about the means used to assess a consumer's credit rating and the

2 See also *Releasing Enterprise*, Cm. 512, para. 6.8.8.
3 See (1992) 15 Consumer Law Today, Issue 4, p. 6 and *Bee Line* 91/4, p. 9.
4 Law Com. No. 204, see especially Pts VIII and IX.

accuracy of information obtained by potential creditors from credit reference agencies operating on a commercial basis, the term 'credit reference agency' being defined as a person carrying on a business comprising the furnishing of persons with information relevant to the financial standing of individuals, being information collected by the agency for that purpose (section 145(8)). Banks' status inquiries and solicitors' inquiries about e.g. the status of a potential tenant of their client landlord, do not bring them within the definition of a credit reference agency. The Act contains a number of provisions to remedy the main mischiefs that can arise.

Section 157 puts any creditor, owner or negotiator under a duty to disclose to the debtor or hirer at his request the name and address of any credit reference agency to which the creditor applied for information about his financial standing. The duty ceases after 28 days from the end of the antecedent negotiations. Section 158 then goes on to put credit reference agencies under a duty to give the consumer a copy of the file relating to him kept by the agency, rendered if necessary into 'plain English', provided the consumer has a) requested it in writing, b) given sufficient particulars to enable the agency to identify the file, and c) paid a fee of £1.[5] The agency must also send the consumer a statement[6] of his rights to have mistakes corrected under section 159. This latter section contains a statement of the consumer's right to have wrong and prejudicial information removed or amended from the file by giving notice to the agency that he requires this to be done. If the agency complies it must give to the consumer a notice stating that it has done so and sending him a copy of any amended entry. Section 159 also lays down the procedure to be followed if agreement cannot be reached. Either the consumer or the agency may apply to the Director, who may make such order as he thinks fit. If the consumer is a business consumer (i.e. a sole trader or a firm), his rights to receive information may be restricted in the interests of the effective operation of the credit reference agency, by revealing confidential sources of information. Here the Director may call for a copy of the file and disclose to the consumer such information as he thinks fit (section 160).

Breach of any of the above duties involves the commission of a

---

5 Increased from 15p by the Consumer Credit (Increase of Monetary Amounts) Order 1983, S.I. 1983/1571.

6 As prescribed in the Consumer Credit (Credit Reference Agency) Regulations 1977, S.I. 1977/329. See also OFT materials: 'Credit References You and Your Customer' (CCP 11), 'Guidance for Credit Reference Agencies' (CCP 6) and 'No Credit?'.

criminal offence, triable summarily with maximum penalty of level 4 on the standard scale (Schedule 1).[7]

In addition to controls under the Consumer Credit Act 1974, it should also be noted that the Data Protection Act 1984 has had an impact on the activities of credit reference agencies. The 1984 Act is concerned with personal data stored on computer and, in specified situations, allows access, correction and erasure.[8] Potential conflict with the Consumer Credit Act 1974, section 158, is prevented.[9] The Data Protection Registrar has been active in connection with credit reference agencies, requiring changes in the information passed on to creditors concerning other occupants of the debtor's premises.[10] However the Data Protection Tribunal has recently[11] permitted the inclusion of financial information about other household members in credit decisions.

11. PROBLEMS OF TITLE

It is an important general rule in commercial law that one person cannot pass a good title in goods 'sold' to another person unless the seller at the time of the sale owns those goods – *nemo dat quod non habet*. To this rule there are a number of exceptions which are explained in full in books on commercial law. A material exception in the case of transactions involving a buyer who pays for the goods by instalments, and to whom by agreement the property in the goods has not passed,[12] is contained in the Sale of Goods Act 1979, section 25.[13] This states, in short, that where a person having bought or agreed to buy goods obtains possession of them, the delivery or

---

7   As amended by the Criminal Justice Act 1982, s. 38. The Consumer Credit (Conduct of Business) (Credit References) Regulations 1977, S.I. 1977/330, also lay down a general duty by credit traders and hire traders to disclose to the credit-broker the particulars of any agency consulted, whether or not any request is made, if (inter alia) the introduction is made through a credit-broker and the prospective creditor or owner decides not to proceed with the agreement, informing only the credit-broker of this. Failure of duty is controlled through the licensing system in this case.

8   1984 Act, ss. 21 and 24.

9   1984 Act, s. 34(3), which requires such requests made under s. 21 to be treated as requests under the Consumer Credit Act 1974, s. 158.

10 Enforcement notices issued to Westcot Data; CCN Systems; Infolink and Credit and Data Marketing Services.

11 The Times, 14 March 1992.

12 Under the Sale of Goods Act 1979, s. 18, r. 1, where there is an unconditional contract for the sale of specific goods in a deliverable state, the property in the goods passes to the buyer when the contract is made, whether or not the time of payment and/or delivery is postponed. This is subject to a contrary intention.

13 See also Factors Act 1889, s. 9 in similar terms.

transfer of them to any person receiving them in good faith is as good as if he were validly authorised by the owner of the goods to sell them.

In early litigation it was held that where a customer was obliged to pay two instalments of 'rent' for furniture delivered under what purported to be a hiring agreement, and on payment of the second instalment but not before, the property should pass to the customer (who enjoyed no right to terminate the agreement) the transaction was a contract of sale and the customer had agreed to buy. So when the customer sold the goods to the defendant before having paid the full instalments, the defendant having taken in good faith, the defendant obtained a good title to the goods.[14] The blossoming piano and furniture industries needed a safer system to protect their interests where goods which had been delivered were to be paid for by instalments, and the concept of hire-purchase was first successfully tested in *Helby v Matthews*.[15] Here the subject matter of the hiring agreement was a piano, and the customer was obliged to pay a monthly rental over three years unless he terminated the agreement and redelivered to the owner possession of the piano. The agreement included two clauses the effect of which was to state that the property was to remain in the owner until all instalments had been paid, but if and when all instalments had been paid the piano should 'become the sole and absolute property of the hirer'. On a premature transfer by way of pledge by the hirer it was held, perhaps rather beneficently, that this was a hiring agreement with a mere option either to return the piano or to purchase it at the end. The hirer had not therefore agreed to buy and could not transfer title to the pawnbroker to whom he had pledged it. The piano accordingly had to be redelivered to the owner. Thereafter the hire-purchase agreement, defined as we have seen as essentially a hiring agreement containing an option in favour of the customer to purchase the subject matter after payment of the last instalment (and often for a further nominal consideration) became an established and well understood commercial agreement. It remains true that the hirer under a hire-purchase agreement cannot validly transfer title to a purchaser from him under this part of the sale of goods legislation.[16]

Credit sale agreements, under which the goods normally become the purchaser's as soon as the agreement is made, and conditional sale agreements, under which the property was expressed to pass on payment of the last instalment, were both vulnerable to premature

14   *Lee v Butler* [1893] 2 QB 318, CA.
15   [1895] AC 471, HL.
16   Conceivably title could be transferred under one of the other exceptions to the *nemo dat* rule, particularly by sale in market overt discussed above, p. 80.

sales by the purchaser. In the first case the purchaser was in fact the owner and in the second case he had 'agreed to buy' and could therefore pass a good title as described above. In the latter case, conditional sales, the 1974 Act made a significant change in the form of common law provision. It was stated formerly in Schedule 4 of the Act, and is now restated in the Sale of Goods Act 1979, section 25(2) that for the purposes of the Sale of Goods Act 1979, section 25(l) considered above, the buyer under a conditional sale agreement which is a consumer credit agreement shall be deemed not to be a person who has bought or agreed to buy goods.[17] It now makes no difference to questions of title whether a purported sale has taken place under such a conditional sale agreement or a hire-purchase agreement. In either case the original owner remains the true owner and can normally recover the goods from an innocent third party, subject to the exception next considered.

As a matter of policy the Hire-Purchase Act 1964 reversed the above position in the case of a purported sale of a motor car by a hirer under an undischarged hire-purchase agreement. The relevant provisions of the 1964 Act are reproduced in slightly amended form in the Consumer Credit Act 1974, Schedule 4. This states that where under a hire-purchase or conditional sale agreement a motor vehicle is disposed of to a private purchaser, and he takes in good faith and without notice of the relevant undischarged agreement, 'that disposition shall have effect as if the creditor's title to the vehicle has been vested in the debtor immediately before that disposition' (section 27(2)). The same result occurs when the debtor sells the vehicle to a trade or finance purchaser, who in turn passes the vehicle on to a private purchaser. The latter obtains a good title. The original debtor retains full criminal and civil liability for his actions.

The ascertainment of whether a buyer is a 'private purchaser' is often obvious but can cause difficulties. In *Stevenson v Beverley Bentinck Ltd*[18] a purchaser bought a car which was subject to an undischarged hire-purchase agreement, but the purchaser took in good faith and without notice. In the spare time after his full-time employment in a manufacturing company he carried on a part-time business of purchasing motor vehicles for resale. He bought this particular car for his private use. The finance company under the original hire-purchase agreement repossessed the car and resold it. The plaintiff purchaser claimed that he was the true owner by reason of the provisions discussed above in the Hire-Purchase Act 1964, but the defendant finance company denied that he was a private

---

17 See also Sch. 4 of the 1974 Act amending the Factors Act 1889, s. 9 to similar effect. Estoppel by conduct under s. 21(1) can also arise.

18 [1976] 2 All ER 606, [1976] 1 WLR 483, CA.

purchaser. This expression is elucidated in section 29 of the 1964 Act which defines a trade or finance purchaser as 'a purchaser who . . . carries on a business which consists, wholly or partly, (a) of purchasing motor vehicles for the purpose of offering or exposing them for sale.. .' and a 'private purchaser' as one who, at the time of the disposition to him, does not do so. It was held that the plaintiff was not a private purchaser because when he bought the car he was carrying on, in part, the business of a motor dealer. It was the status of the purchaser which mattered, not whether he happened to buy a car for his private use or for resale.

Trade purchasers are treated more severely than private purchasers because it is easier for them to check that cars are unencumbered. It was revealed in *Moorgate Mercantile Co Ltd v Twitchings*[19] that all the major finance companies were members of HP Information Ltd ('HPI') and about 8,000 motor dealers were affiliated to it. About 98 per cent of hire-purchase agreements relating to cars are registered with HPI by reference to the cars' registration numbers. Affiliated dealers can enquire by telephone whether a particular vehicle is registered with HPI. In this case a car was subject to a hire-purchase agreement with the plaintiffs, a finance company, who for some inexplicable reason failed to follow their usual practice of registering the hire-purchase agreement with HPI. The car was 'sold' by the hirer to the defendant motor dealers who enquired from HPI whether there was any hire-purchase agreement registered or recorded against the car and received a negative answer. The House of Lords held by a majority that HPI were not agents, in a general sense, of the finance companies who were members of it, nor did the answers given by HPI amount to a representation that none of the finance house members of the HPI had any interests in the car in question. Furthermore, the plaintiffs, in not registering the hire-purchase agreement with HPI, were not in breach of any duty of care to persons such as the defendants who might in future buy it, notwithstanding that both were members of HPI.[20]

---

19   [1977] AC 890, [1976] 2 All ER 641, HL.
20   Citizens' Advice Bureaux are equipped to make enquiries from HPI with regard to the status of second-hand cars on behalf of private purchasers. This is an extremely useful service and enquiries are usually answered within two or three days. It was reported in The Times, 27 January 1992, that 6,900 cars checked by HPI in the last quarter of 1990 were registered on the police computer as stolen. One in every 103 enquiries during that period traced a stolen car.

11 Fair trading

INTRODUCTION

The Fair Trading Act 1973 has been called 'potentially the most comprehensive measure ever passed' to protect the economic interests of the consumer.[1] Its importance and scope is indicated by this brief summary of its twelve Parts:

PART I provides for appointment of Director General of Fair Trading and establishment of Consumer Protection Advisory Committee; it reconstitutes the Monopolies and Mergers Commission.

PART II deals with references to Consumer Protection Advisory Committee and power of Secretary of State to make orders by statutory instrument imposing criminal sanctions in respect of conduct adversely affecting the economic interests of consumers.

PART III empowers the Director General to obtain undertakings from businessmen persisting in conduct detrimental to the interests of consumers and to take proceedings before the Restrictive Practices Court or other appropriate court if necessary.

PART IV deals with the functions of the Director General and the Monopolies and Mergers Commission in relation to monopoly situations, re-enacting with modification much of the previous law.

PART V deals in a similar way with mergers.

PART VI deals with other references to the Monopolies and Mergers Commission, such as restrictive labour practices relating to the employment of workers in commercial activities in the United Kingdom.

PART VII deals with procedural matters relating to references to the Consumer Protection Advisory Committee and the Monopolies and Mergers Commission.

1 Fair Trading and Consumer Protection in Britain, HMSO, p. 6.

PART VIII contains supplemental and procedural matters relating to monopoly references, including the criteria for determining the public interest.

PART IX transferred the functions of the former Registrar of Restrictive Trading Agreements to the Director General and contained other matters relating to restrictive trade practices now re-enacted in the Restrictive Trade Practices Act 1976.

PART X extended the ambit of the restrictive trade practices legislation to services (now comprised in Restrictive Trade Practices Act 1976).

PART XI deals with 'pyramid selling' whereunder, typically, an escalating number of participants not operating from business premises are enrolled by the promoter of a business in the expectation of receiving benefits; this Part gives the Secretary of State power to prescribe regulations for the purpose of preventing participants in such schemes from being unfairly treated and spelling out their rights and obligations. The current provisions are the Pyramid Selling Schemes Regulations 1989,[2] contravention of which involves a criminal offence (section 120(2)).[3]

PART XII deals with miscellaneous and supplemental matters including the duty of the Director General to make an annual report of his, the Advisory Committee's and the Monopolies and Mergers Commission's activities for each calendar year.

The Act contains 140 sections and 13 Schedules.

This chapter is concerned with the office of Director General and the organisation of and functions of the Office of Fair Trading, combined with a discussion of unfair trading practices and voluntary codes of conduct. The control of monopolies and mergers and the competition aspects of the work of the Director General have already been mentioned in ch. 1.

1. THE FUNCTIONS OF THE DIRECTOR GENERAL AND THE OFFICE OF FAIR TRADING

a) Genesis

On 24 November 1970 the new Conservative Government announced the abolition of the Consumer Council on the grounds of 'opposition to the use of public money for objectives which can be

---

2 S.I. 1989/2195 as amended by S.I. 1990/150.
3 . Two convictions under the earlier Regulations (S.I. 1973/1740) were noted in (1988) 11 Consumer Law Today, Pt 5, p.6.

achieved by private enterprise concerns using private money'[4] and because of the 'emergence and development of voluntary consumer organisations'.[5] As a valediction, the Chairman of the Consumer Council wrote in his final Annual Report, 'I am convinced that the axing of the Consumer Council cannot mean the axing of what we have done or what we have started. Some day someone will have to invent a new, publicly financed body to promote and protect the consumer's interests'.

Since the Fair Trading Bill, introduced into the Commons in November 1972, was not preceded by any sort of published enquiry, Green or White Paper,[6] it is difficult to trace the precise processes which led up to it. It seems probable that a draft Bill had been put in hand by the Civil Service, primarily within the Department of Trade and Industry, to improve the legislation on monopolies and mergers. This coincided with the appointment with Cabinet rank of a new and energetic Minister for Trade and Consumer Affairs, Sir Geoffrey Howe, within the giant Department of Trade and Industry. (A unique film was, however, made of some of the negotiations and deliberations which occurred at the committee stage, particularly on what is now section 2 – general functions of the Director – and section 13 – definition of 'consumer trade practice' (Granada Television – 'A Law in the Making').)

Speaking of the Bill on its second reading, and explaining its objects, Sir Geoffrey Howe remarked that the Bill had two complementary purposes; firstly the promotion of increased economic efficiency and secondly protection of the consumer against unfair trading practices. He continued,

> Just as fair trading is good business, so consumer protection is in itself an integral part of the market economy. That is why competition policy needs to be considered, as it is in the Bill, as a whole. It is this integrated view of competition policy that leads to the first institutional innovation proposed in the Bill – the appointment of a Director General of Fair Trading . . . The Government have concluded that given the specialist and detailed nature of the work and the need for continuity in its performance, it would best be done by an independent official body.[7]

The Bill with a number of amendments (about 125 of approximately 4,000 proposed) became law on 25 July 1973.

4 807 HC Official Report (5th series) col. 229 (24 November 1970).
5 807 HC Official Report (5th series) col. 895 (30 November 1970).
6 This feature attracted critical comment in debate – see 848 HC Official Report (5th series) col. 469 (13 December 1972).
7 848 HC Official Report (5th series) col. 454 (13 December 1972).

b) The Director General of Fair Trading

Section 1 provides for the appointment of an officer known as the Director General of Fair Trading (and referred to in the Act itself and here as 'the Director') by the Secretary of State for a renewable term of five years. The Director has power to appoint such staff as he thinks fit subject to the approval of the Minister for the Civil Service as regards numbers and conditions. The Director may not be an MP.[8] The first Director was appointed on 1 November 1973 (M. J. Methven). He was succeeded on 14 June 1976 by Gordon Borrie who served three five-year and one one-year terms as Director. The third Director, appointed from June 1992, is Sir Bryan Carsberg, who moves from being Director General of Telecommunications.

The Director's functions[9] are specified in section 2 and in various other sections of the Act. Additional functions have been added by subsequent legislation, for example, the Consumer Credit Act 1974. They may be summarised as follows:

1) He has various functions in relation to monopolies, mergers, restrictive practices and uncompetitive practices which have been considered in ch. 1.

2) He must keep under review the carrying on of commercial activities in the UK relating to the supply to consumers in the UK of goods and services, and collect information with a view to the ascertainment of practices which may adversely affect the economic interests of such consumers.

3) He must receive and collate evidence becoming available to him with respect to the activities in 2) above which appear to be evidence of practices which may adversely affect the interests (whether economic, or relating to health, safety or other matters) of UK consumers. He may refer such practices to the Consumer Protection Advisory Committee ('the Advisory Committee'), which may lead to the Secretary of State making an Order prohibiting or regulating the practice under Part II of the Act. Since there is some overlap here with the primary responsibilities of other Ministries (particularly the Ministry of Agriculture, Fisheries and Food) the duty is phrased as being 'to receive and collate evidence' which would then be passed on.

4) He may take action against persons carrying on business who

---

8   House of Commons Disqualification Act 1975, s. 1(1)(f) and Sch. 1, Pt III.
9   For a discussion of the powers and position of the Director see Sir Gordon Borrie *The Development of Consumer Law and Policy – Bold Spirits and Timorous Souls (The Hamlyn Lectures)* 1984 Stevens & Sons.

persist in conduct detrimental to the consumer, under Part III of the Act.

5) He may publish information and advice for UK consumers and encourage relevant associations to prepare and disseminate to their members codes of practice for guidance in safeguarding and promoting the interests of UK consumers, and to submit to the Secretary of State Annual Reports (Part XII).

6) The Consumer Credit Act 1974 imposed on the Director the duties relating to consumer credit originally envisaged as being those of an independent 'Commissioner for Consumer Credit'. These duties involve supervision of consumer credit activity generally, supervision of the enforcement of the Act and administration of the licensing system. Consumer credit is discussed in ch. 10.

7) The Estate Agents Act 1979, section 25, imposes a general duty upon the Director to superintend the working and enforcement of the Act.

8) The Control of Misleading Advertisements Regulations 1988[10] enable the Director to seek an injunction prohibiting misleading advertising.

The Office of Fair Trading

The Director performs his functions from and through the Office of Fair Trading ('OFT') at Field House, Breams Buildings, London EC4A 1PR. There is some academic controversy as to whether the OFT can more properly be classified as a 'Government Agency',[11] or as a Department of Government (which is apparently how it regards itself) the difficulty with the latter being that in conventional terminology a Department must be headed by a political Secretary of State or Minister. Nor is there any statutory recognition of the existence of the OFT in the 1973 Act.

The office is staffed by over 300 people headed by the Director General, a Deputy Director General and 'Directors' of Divisions dealing with Consumer Affairs, Competition Policy (Monopolies, Mergers and Anti-Competitive Restrictive Practices), and Legal Matters. It also has an Economics Branch, an Administration Branch and an Information Branch. It is important to note that the OFT does not formally deal with complaints received direct from the public other than as mentioned in section 34 (conduct by a person

---

10   S.I. 1988/915, as amended by the Broadcasting Act 1990, s. 203(1) and Sch. 20, para 51. See further ch. 2 at p. 41.

11   It is so described in the HMSO publication 'Fair Trading and Consumer Protection in Britain' p. 4.

detrimental to consumers) and regarding misleading advertising. Its information comes primarily from its own investigations and information supplied by trading standards departments of local authorities, the courts, who are authorised to inform the Director of material convictions, and the news media. Individual complaints should not normally, therefore, be sent to the OFT, since as can be seen, in most respects the Director is a 'watch dog' not a 'bloodhound'.

The OFT is financed by the Department of Trade and Industry.

References to the Consumer Protection Advisory Committee

Part II of the Act deals with references to the Advisory Committee. Its membership must consist of not less than ten and not more than fifteen members appointed by the Secretary of State for Trade and Industry, having regard to their experience in consumer protection work. Membership of the Advisory Committee is currently suspended as in 1982 the then Minister of Consumer Affairs, Dr. Gerard Vaughan, announced[12] that he would not be reappointing existing members nor appointing any new members to the Committee as there were no current or proposed references. The Advisory Committee will be reestablished should a reference be made.

References may be made by the Secretary of State, any other minister or the Director on the question of whether a consumer trade practice adversely affects the economic interests of UK consumers (section 14).[13] 'Consumer trade practice' is defined by section 13. The term means any practice carried on in connection with the supply of goods or services to consumers and which relates a) to the terms and conditions (whether as to price or otherwise) on which goods and services are to be supplied, or b) to the manner in which those terms and conditions are communicated to persons to whom goods or services are supplied (e.g. misleading 'small print' in documents), c) to all forms of promotion of the supply of goods or services, or d) to methods of salesmanship employed in dealing with consumers, or e) to the way in which goods are packed or otherwise got up for the purpose of being supplied, or f) to methods of demanding or securing payment for goods or services supplied. Section 15 excludes practices relating to services as specified in Schedule 4 which are subject to investigation by the Monopolies and Mergers Commission, and section 16 restricts references relating to specified

---

12 Department of Trade Press Notice, 24 September 1982; *Annual Report of the Director General of Fair Trading 1982* (HC Papers (1983–84) No. 20) at p. 45.
13 See M & H pp. 415–418.

supplies of goods and services mainly by publicly owned industries by requiring the consent of the appropriate minister.

References may be 'general' or purely investigative under section 14, but by section 17, where it appears to the Director that a consumer trade practice does or may –

a) mislead customers as to, or withhold from them adequate information as to, their rights and obligations, or

b) otherwise mislead or confuse with respect to any matter in connection with relevant consumer transactions, or

c) subject consumers to undue pressure to enter into relevant consumer transactions, or

d) cause the relevant terms or conditions to be so adverse as to be inequitable to them,

the Director's reference may then include proposals that the Secretary of State should exercise his order making powers to prohibit or modify the practice. A 'relevant consumer transaction' is any transaction to which a person is, or may be invited to become, a party in his capacity as consumer (section 17(5)). The word 'consumer' is also defined and its meaning may be summarised as a person to whom goods or services are supplied by a commercial supplier who does not receive the goods or services in the course of his business (section 137(2)).

Any such reference must specify which particular effect the Director considers the trade practice has and the reference is published in the London, Edinburgh and Belfast Gazettes (section 17).

The Advisory Committee must then report to the Secretary of State, normally within three months of the reference, stating whether or not it agrees with the Director's proposals (assuming it finds that there is an adverse consumer trade practice), or whether it would agree to modified proposals. The Advisory Committee itself, which consists partly of members experienced in consumer affairs and has a maximum of fifteen members, in the case of section 17 references must take into consideration representations by interested bodies who are normally also permitted to give to them oral evidence (section 81). Their report must, as far as practicable, exclude the private affairs of individuals or the affairs of a body of persons in so far as any such matter might, if published, seriously prejudice their interests (section 82). The report is then laid before Parliament in the manner specified by section 83.

Orders in pursuance of the report

In cases where the Advisory Committee agrees with the Director's proposals or agrees with specified modifications, then, the Secretary of State may, 'if he thinks fit', make an order under the powers in section 22. A draft of any such order must be laid before Parliament and approved by resolution of each House of Parliament (section 22(4)). Contravention of a prohibition in any such order confers no civil right of action (section 26), but constitutes a criminal offence punishable on summary conviction by a maximum fine of £5,000[14] and on conviction on indictment to a fine or imprisonment for a maximum of two years, or both (section 23). There are the defences familiar in trade descriptions law (inter alia) of mistake, act or default of another, accident, or cause beyond the defendant's control, provided in each case reasonable precautions were taken and due diligence shown (section 25).

The enforcement of any orders made is the responsibility of local weights and measures authorities. They are given power to make test purchases (section 28) and to enter premises and seize goods and documents, subject to some limitations (section 29). It is also an offence to obstruct an officer exercising his powers (section 30). In order to promote liaison with the Director, authorities are required to notify him of intended prosecutions under section 23 of the Act and for offences under the Trade Descriptions Act 1968, Part III of the Consumer Protection Act 1987 and the Property Misdescriptions Act 1991 (section 130, as amended).

References and orders made

Two references were made to the Advisory Committee in 1974. The first reference[15] covered the practice of some shops of informing the customer that no money would be refunded or otherwise misleading the customer, by a notice displayed or otherwise, as to his rights under the sale of goods legislation. This in due course resulted in the Consumer Transactions (Restrictions on Statements) Order 1976[16] which implements the proposed banning of these practices and has already been discussed in ch. 5. The second reference[17] covered practices connected with seeking to induce consumers to enter into mail order transactions with payment in advance without undertaking to return the money if the goods are not sent within a specified period, or without giving the seller's name and address. It was also the Director's view that any trader who took a prepayment of £10 or

14   Increased from £2,000 in October 1992 by the Criminal Justice Act 1991, s. 17(2).
15   OFT Dossier 17/1 'The Purported Exclusion of Inalienable Rights and Failure to Explain their Existence'; CPAC Report: 'Rights of Consumers' HC Papers (1974/75) No. 6.
16   S.I. 1976/1813 as amended by S.I. 1978/27.
17   OFT Dossier 17/2 'Prepayment in Mail Order Transactions and in Shops'; CPAC Report: 'Prepayment for Goods' HC Papers (1975/76) No. 285.

more should give the consumer a written commitment that if the goods are not supplied within a specified period, the money will be refunded within seven days of a request for it and the transaction annulled. These recommendations were partially adopted in the Mail Order Transactions (Information) Order 1976[18] which applies to written advertisements, circulars etc. in which persons in the course of business invite orders from consumers by post for goods for which payment in advance is required. Such advertisements must contain a legible description of the name and business address of the person inviting orders (and not, for example, purely a box number).

A reference[19] was made to the Advisory Committee in 1975 relating to the practice of seeking to sell goods to consumers without revealing (whether deliberately or not) that the goods are being sold in the course of a business – 'disguised business sales'. Advertisements in the classified columns of newspapers are the usual vehicles of communication used. The danger is that the consumer may not realise that he has the many rights given to him only when he buys from someone selling in the course of a business. This resulted in the promulgation of the Business Advertisements (Disclosure) Order 1977[20] under which a person seeking to sell goods in the course of a business[1] must make this fact clear in any advertisement.

In January 1977 a reference was made[2] to the Advisory Committee affecting the display of prices and quotations without a clear statement that VAT is included. The recommendation was that failure to show the VAT-inclusive price should be a criminal offence. The Advisory Committee agreed[3] with the Director's view that advertising, displaying or otherwise quoting to consumers VAT-exclusive prices or charges was economically detrimental to consumers and agreed the Director's proposals for control subject to two general modifications. For some four years no action followed this

---

18 S.I. 1976/1812.
19 OFT Dossier 17/3 'Seeking To Sell Goods Without Revealing That They Are Being Sold In The Course Of A Business'; CPAC Report: 'Disguised Business Sales' HC Papers (1975/76) No. 355. For extracts of the Dossier and the CPAC Report see M & H pp. 418–421.
20 S.I. 1977/1918, see M & H p. 421. For some information and statistics on the use of this Order in penalising disguised business sales of used cars, electrical goods, carpets and bicycles being goods commonly sold in classified columns of newspapers by businesses masquerading as private sellers, see (1981) 89 ITSA Monthly Review 147. There are between 50 to 100 convictions per annum under this Order.
 1 The meaning of 'in the course of a business' in this Order has been discussed in *Blakemore v Bellamy* (1982) 147 JP 89, [1983] RTR 303, QBD; see M & H pp. 421–424.
 2 OFT Dossier 17:4 'VAT-Exclusive Prices'.
 3 See CPAC Report 'VAT-Exclusive Prices' HC Paper (1977) No. 416.

recommendation, but on 23 July 1981 the Minister of State for Consumer Affairs announced in a written reply in the House of Commons that she proposed to make an order under the Prices Act 1974 on the price marking of VAT and ancillary charges. Consultations followed but no Order was made and on 29 July 1982 the new Minister for Consumer Affairs, Dr. Gerard Vaughan, announced, in reply to a Parliamentary question,[4] that the proposed Order had been dropped and that a comprehensive review of the controls over price comparisons, bargain offers, etc. would be undertaken.[5]

The rather slow reaction to the recommendations of the Director and comments of the Advisory Committee by the government caused disappointment in some circles. In his Second Report the Director commented, however, that whilst being disappointed, the references had had the beneficial effect of publicising and causing widespread discussion of the suspect trading practices in question. This itself tends to lead to a voluntary reduction in the operation of the practice.[6] It may also be supposed that the government showed understandable caution in implementing proposals which, however efficiently handled by the criminal courts, converted what were primarily breaches of the letter or spirit of the civil law into criminal offences.

If one looks at the operation of Part II, it is not the CPAC consultation process which causes difficulties or delays. The CPAC worked quickly and effectively, and generally supported the Director's proposals. There are, however, three major hurdles with the process. The first hurdle is that the practice in question must fall within the definition of a 'consumer trade practice' (section 13) and must affect the 'economic interests of consumers' (section 14). Sir Gordon Borrie cites the example of misdescriptions of house property as falling outside these provisions.[7]

The second hurdle is that the Director has to initiate the procedure. If he chooses not to do so then no further steps may be taken under Part II. From time to time the OFT issues consultation papers with a view to a possible CPAC reference, for example prepayments in non-mail order transactions[8] but these are not

4   Department of Trade Press Notice 29 July 1982, 28 HC Official Report (6th Series) col. 628–9 (29 July 1982).
5   See further ch. 12.
6   *The Second Report of the Director General 1975* at p. 9 (HC Papers (1975-1976) No. 288).
7   *The Development of Consumer Law and Policy* p. 127.
8   See *Annual Reports of the Director General for 1978 and 1979* (HC Papers (1978–1979) No. 79 at p. 21; HC Papers (1979–1980) No. 624 at p. 21).

always pursued as a section 17 reference. It is not always appropriate to seek new criminal offences as successive Directors have indicated.[9]

The third, and perhaps most important hurdle, is that the decision to act ultimately rests with the Minister. There is need for the Minister to support the proposals of the CPAC and no mechanism exists to prevent delays or to ensure that a draft statutory instrument is in fact laid before Parliament. Sir Gordon Borrie sums up Part II as:

> an example of a bold idea smothered by an excess of nervous caution so that the resulting provisions have inevitably heen a disappointment.[10]

Abolition of the Advisory Committee has been discussed[11] but this would need primary legislation, since Part II powers can only be fully exercised by and with the involvement of the Advisory Committee.

Undertakings from and action against traders

Part III of the Act gives the Director a 'bloodhound' as well as 'watchdog' function with regard to persons carrying on a business who persist in a course of conduct which a) is detrimental to the interests of UK consumers, whether economic or relating to health, safety or otherwise, and b) is to be regarded on the criteria stated as unfair to consumers (section 34). These criteria involve either contraventions of duties, prohibitions or restrictions imposed by the criminal law, whether or not the conduct has resulted in a conviction, and also breaches of contract or other breaches of duty enforceable by civil proceedings, whether or not proceedings have actually been brought (section 34(2) and (3)). The Director may take into account complaints received by him, whether from consumers or from other persons, as well as any other information collected by or furnished to him, to judge whether detrimental conduct has been persisted in. The

---

9   Borrie, *The Development of Consumer Law and Policy* p. 126; *1975 Director General's Report* (HC Papers 1975–1976) No. 288) at p. 9; *1977 Report of the Director General* (HC Papers (1977–1978) No. 228) at p. 7.
   Voluntary changes in practice, linked with licensing powers under the Consumer Credit Act 1974 (see ch. 10) have been used in connection with unfair contract terms and notices, see *1983 Director General's Report* (HC Papers (1983–1984) No. 495) at p. 14; *1980 and 1981 Director General's Reports* (HC Papers (1980–1981) No. 354 at p. 33 and HC Papers (1981–1982) No. 434 at p. 24 and *Bee Line* Nos. 30 and 34.
10   *The Development of Consumer Law and Policy* p. 127.
11   *Report on Non-Departmental Public Bodies* (Cmnd. 7797, January 1980); see also M & H p. 418.

following guidance has been issued by the OFT[12] itself to Trading Standards Officers and others as to whether complaints about problem traders are sufficiently serious for the Director to pursue:

> Most cases are sparked off by Trading Standards Officers, consumer advisers and others sending to the Office material about a specific trader for consideration. In submitting a case based on *complaints*, the answers to the following questions should be 'yes' before it is sent to the Office:
>   i) Do the complaints made against the trader show breaches of the existing civil or criminal law (whether or not any legal action is actually contemplated)?
>   ii) Are there sufficient complaints to show persistence by the trader in a course of 'unfair' conduct? (Persistence involves an element of deliberation by the trader.)
>   iii) Are the complaint forms sufficiently complete to establish clearly the facts of each case? (Any correspondence or additional documentation would always be valuable additional evidence.)
>   iv) Would the complainants allow their names to be quoted in the Office's approach to the trader?
> Although the final assessment of whether a case can be made is for the Office, in the light of the evidence from all sources and legal and policy consideration, these questions are a good guide to whether a case is likely to be a starter. The most difficult problem is judging 'persistent' behaviour. Although the number of complaints about a trader, considered in isolation, is not itself a sufficient trigger for Part III action, it is the only measure available in the first instance to assess persistence. In addition, however, account must be taken of the seriousness of individual complaints within the total, and the period which the complaints cover. A judgment also has to be made as to the overall picture shown by the total complaints when compared with the total size of business of the trader. 'Persistence' may also be shown if a trader has been warned by the Trading Standards Officer, but still continues the same course of conduct. And a case based on complaints might, of course, be reinforced by additional evidence such as convictions or county court judgments, details of which the Office or a Trading Standards Department can obtain.

The Director's first line of attack is to obtain a satisfactory written assurance that the trader will refrain from continuing that course of conduct and from carrying on any similar course of conduct in the course of that business. A number of these assurances are obtained each year from traders individually or from traders who consent to or connive at the course of conduct of a company. Of the 720 assurances, undertakings or orders obtained by the OFT to

---

12 *Bee Line* No. 23 at p. 3. See also *Assurances by Traders – an Introduction to the Operation of Part III of the Act* and *Assurances by Traders – Guidance on the Operation of Part III of the Act*, OFT, October 1985.

December 1990, 173 related to cars and motoring, 99 to house improvements, 84 to mail order transactions, 116 to electrical goods, 63 to carpets and furniture, 47 to food and catering, 26 to one-day and door-step sales, 14 to animals and 98 to other businesses. The texts of the undertakings are publicised and appear in the Annual Report. In many cases the traders in question have been convicted of criminal offences, particularly offences under the Trade Descriptions Act 1968, or have been unsuccessful defendants in more than one civil action arising out of their business conduct.

A case involving repeated offences and subsequent undertakings which were given publicity was *R v Director General of Fair Trading, ex p F H Taylor & Co Ltd*.[13] T. Ltd were the importers of toys and electrical equipment and had been convicted on thirteen occasions under the Consumer Protection Act 1961. They gave a written assurance to the Director that they would 'refrain from continuing a course of conduct and from carrying on a similar course of conduct in the course of a business'. The Director issued a press release which recorded, inter alia, that T. Ltd had only given the assurances after being warned that proceedings would be begun, and the number and nature of the convictions including the fines and costs ordered to be paid. T. Ltd complained that when asked to give the assurances they were not warned that the Director would make their compliance the subject of a press release, and the press release involved an abuse of the Director General's powers under section 124 (publication of information and advice) and a breach of section 133 (general restrictions on disclosure of information). It was held that the complaint must be dismissed, for if a press release was justifiable there was no reason why the Director should have warned T. Ltd, and in order to make good the complaint T. Ltd should have alleged that they were in some way misled into giving assurances. T. Ltd had been given an opportunity to make amendments to the draft press release, but had not done so, nor did they suggest limiting its circulation. The court did, however, raise some questions which the Director might wish to consider in framing press releases on assurances. There followed a period when little publicity was given to assurances but then, in January 1989, press announcements, usually in local newspapers and relevant trade journals, were introduced. The effectiveness of this policy was reviewed in 1991.

Should the Director be unsuccessful in receiving a satisfactory assurance, or if such an assurance is broken, the Director may either bring proceedings in the Restrictive Practices Court under section 35, or in smaller cases, in the county court for the district in which the

13   [1981] ICR 292, QBD; M & H p. 427.

practice is carried on (or sheriff's court in Scotland) (section 41). The first case was in fact brought in the Cardiff County Court, in respect of a broken undertaking, in February 1977. The trader in question, a gas central heating supplier, had not observed his undertaking to refrain from installing central heating equipment not in accordance with the contract with his customer and to refrain from committing offences under the Gas Safety Regulations 1972 by installing gas pipes which leaked gas.[14]

The powers of the courts specified include a) the obtaining of an undertaking to refrain from the specified course of conduct or b) to make an order in similar terms. The court also has power to obtain undertakings from or make orders against accessories, directors or officers of companies and other members of a group of interconnected bodies corporate. Legal aid is generally available to defend these proceedings, and appeals lie to the Court of Appeal, or Court of Session in Scotland (sections 35–42). Breach of any undertaking given or order made would put the defendant in contempt of court, punishable by imprisonment in the case of individuals, or a fine. Examples of contempt proceedings can be seen in the cases of Mr. Gilliam,[15] where imprisonment of fourteen days was ordered, and Saray Electronics (London) Ltd, where a fine of £1,950 was imposed for the initial contempt, followed by a further fine of £50,000 for the company and £10,000 for each director, with three months' imprisonment, suspended for two years, for a second contempt.[16]

In recent years approximately 40–65 assurances have been given each year, although only 15 were given in 1990, with 3–4 per annum necessitating court action under sections 35 and 38. A few actions for contempt of court are also taken. It is, however, difficult to evaluate the effectiveness of the assurance process. Despite the large number of people engaged in business activities and the large number of recorded complaints by consumers, comparatively few assurances have been given. The small number of court cases for breaches of assurances or court orders may be because, having given an assurance, traders modify their behaviour to comply with the law or even decide to cease trading altogether. In some cases, however, subsequent breaches have not been detected, especially where the

---

14   *Director General's Annual Report for 1977* (HC Papers (1977–78) No. 228) at p. 51. For a case taken before the Restrictive Practices Court in respect of traders with a large number of convictions under the Food and Drugs Act 1955, see *Director General of Fair Trading v Smiths Bakeries (Westfield) Ltd* (1978) Times, 12 May, Restrictive Practices Court. See generally M & H pp. 424–427.

15   See *Director General's Report for 1983* (HC Papers (1983–1984) No. 493) at p. 57; M & H p. 427; (1982) 90 ITSA MR 190; (1983) 91 ITSA MR 202.

16   See *Bee Line* No. 39 p. 17; OFT Press Release No 26/89 and *Director General's Annual Report for 1989* (HC Papers (1989–90) No. 502) at p. 65.

trader has set up a new company, possibly involving different goods or services, often in another part of the country. It is particularly difficult to keep track of such traders.[17]

The Director has put forward proposals for 'a complete overhaul of Part III'[18] as a result of reviewing the operation of assurances and also the effectiveness of voluntary codes of practice. These proposals will be examined after looking at the codes as they presently operate.

2. VOLUNTARY CODES OF PRACTICE

In his Second Report the then Director wrote:

> I believe that proposals to change the law should be made only when absolutely necessary because I have increasingly realised that extension of the law is no automatic panacea for consumer problems. It is all too easy to suggest measures for consumer protection which are either impractical or prohibitively costly. . . . I have always considered that one of my most important functions is the duty to encourage voluntary codes of practice. . . . Codes, to be effective, must be carefully constructed and precise. General expressions of goodwill towards the customer, or declarations of good intent, are not nearly enough. Once a code has been negotiated and publicised it cannot stop there. It must be kept up to date in the light of changing expectations and events, and it must be monitored to see if it is working effectively.[19]

The duty to which the Director was referring is contained in section 124(3), which states that it shall be the duty of the Director to encourage relevant associations to prepare, and to disseminate to their members, codes of practice for guidance in safeguarding and promoting the interests of UK consumers. This subsection, which as events have turned out, is the foundation of much of the OFT's work in the Consumer Affairs Division, was something of an afterthought, being inserted into the Bill during its passage through Parliament.

Creation of a new code or modification of an existing one should be quicker than legislation. No parliamentary time is needed, only the endorsement of the Director. In some cases, for example changes to the Association of British Travel Agents' (ABTA) Codes, this may occur regularly and quickly, whereas in other areas, for example car

17 For a discussion and analysis of assurances given up to 1980 see Hope (1981) 89 ITSA MR 96 and 180. See also Crossley, (1986) 94 ITSA MR 139 for a critical review of assurances and *Trading Malpractices,* OFT Report, 1990, paras. 4.8–4.18 for the Director's assessment.
18 *Trading Malpractices,* OFT Report, 1990, para. 1.8. See below pp. 336–337.
19 HC Papers (1975–1976) No. 288 at pp. 9–10.

auctions, negotiations have been conducted over several years without an OFT approved code materialising.

The advantage of the voluntary or self-regulating code is that it is tailor-made for the problems commonly met in a particular industry, and can thus be more detailed and specific than is practicable in legislation. On the other hand a code, being voluntary, lacks any direct way of enforcing it. A trade association may reprimand erring members, fine them[20] or ultimately expel them. Expelled members can, of course, still trade freely as there is no legal requirement of membership and unless there is publicity for expulsions, members of the public will not know of misdeeds. Some trade organisations are reluctant to publicise miscreants lest their industry is tainted. Others wish to draw attention to their 'strict' control of members.[1] Expulsion from a trade association or adverse notice from the OFT can be powerful indirect sanctions. This is particularly so if breaches are not widespread among members, if valuable benefits accrue from membership and if public awareness of the trade association and the benefits derived from the code is high, for example with the ABTA codes. A further disadvantage is that a voluntary code drawn up with an association can only be 'binding' on members of that association. Rogue operators are much less likely to join trade associations than honest and experienced traders.

In 1976 a survey was carried out for the OFT by Audits of Great Britain Limited on the working of the first code of practice, negotiated in 1974. This was with the Association of Manufacturers of Domestic Electrical Appliances ('AMDEA'). This survey showed a sharp decline in the number of complaints received by AMDEA's Conciliation Service – from 251 in the third quarter of 1974 to 49 in the second quarter of 1976 – and that in the main the code was being observed in such matters as the making and keeping of appointments, the customers involved describing themselves as 'satisfied' or 'very satisfied'. Nevertheless, these codes have not been without their critics. Some criticisms centre on the modest nature of the 'guarantees' given to the customer,[2] others with more general criticisms of the ineffectiveness of the codes.[3] The Director replied to the latter type of criticism in 1977 by asking for the codes to be given more

---

20   For details of disciplinary proceedings taken by ABTA in 1983 see M & H pp. 396–397.

1   See, for example, The Times, 11 February 1981, for the expulsion of a garage firm from the Motor Agents' Association.

2   See Susan E. Marsh 'Voluntary Codes of Practice' (1977) 127 NLJ 419, Gordon Borrie 'Laws and Codes for Consumers' [1980] JBL 315; also R. G. Lawson (1977) 121 Sol Jo 4; A. G. Page [1980] JBL 24; *A general duty to trade fairly, A discussion paper*, OFT, 1986, ch. 3.

3   See *Motoring Which?* January 1977 as to the Motor Trade Codes.

chance to prove themselves and deprecating premature criticism. He stated that he intended to place more emphasis on monitoring the performance of the codes. 'If performance is below par, I shall say so, loudly and publicly and, if necessary, will withdraw my blessing from a code which appears to be failing because traders are not observing it.'[4]

By 1982 the Director conceded that

> some measures of self-regulation may prove to be less effective than was hoped. . . self-regulatory codes have two principal weaknesses. First, they cannot be enforced against non-members – this may be felt to put member-firms, who are likely to be the more responsible traders, at a competitive disadvantage. Secondly, codes are difficult to enforce, even against members.[5]

He gave as an example difficulties encountered with the Motor Agents' Association Code and the requirement of displaying a pre-sales information report on used cars.

In 1991 the Director and the OFT announced[6] the adoption of a new approach regarding codes. Instead of becoming involved in detailed negotiations over the wording of codes, endorsement is now given for those codes which meet a series of criteria, setting out what the OFT regards as 'best practice'. The guidelines provided require the trade association to have a significant influence on the sector concerned, with compliance with the code as mandatory on members. Consultation with, inter alia, consumer oganisations and enforcement bodies is needed in preparing the code and the OFT must be consulted on competition aspects. The code must give genuine benefits to consumers beyond legal requirements, setting high standards and seeking to remove undesirable practices. There are requirements concerning provision of information to customers, publicity for the code and those complying with it, and availability of copies of the code. Adequate complaints handling machinery is needed, with a conciliation service and a low-cost independent scheme of redress as an alternative to court action. Monitoring of the code by the trade association is required, with annual reports

---

4 OFT Press Release, 3 March 1977. Since then successive annual reports have described monitoring exercises on a number of specific codes.

5 *Director's Report for 1982* (H of C Papers (1982–1983) No. 20) p. 11. See also *The Motor Code – A Report on a Monitoring Survey*, OFT, September 1986, paras. 7.8 and 7.19.

  For the pros and cons of codes see also *A general duty to trade fairly, A discussion paper*, OFT, August 1986, ch. 3, paras. 3.8–3.18; Borrie *The Development of Consumer Law and Policy* pp. 74–75; J. F. Pickering and D. C. Cousins 'The Benefits and Costs of Voluntary Codes of Practice' European Journal of Marketing (1982) (No. 6) p. 31 and M & H pp. 386–387 and 392–395.

6 See *Bee Line* No 91/1, pp. 3 and 24–25.

provided. Penalties for non-compliance must be instituted and, where appropriate, mechanisms established to ensure that judgments against members are met, in the event of members defaulting.

The main features of the OFT supported codes, which vary in some details, can be gathered from a short summary of those at present in existence. The conciliation and arbitration provisions require further explanation. Initially under some of the trade association arbitration schemes attended hearings before an arbitrator were offered, instead of the case being heard on a 'documents only' basis. This led to difficulties.[7] An arbitration in 1977 under the scheme established in its code by the Association of British Travel Agents ('ABTA') lasted for five days, cost six complaining holidaymakers £1,800 in legal costs and yielded only £25 damages. The costs included the arbitrator's own charge of £30 per hour. (This would not have occurred had a 'documents only' arbitration, where the maximum costs are limited, been chosen.) The adverse publicity given to this prompted the Director to write to the eight Associations who operated codes offering personal hearings before an arbitrator asking the Associations to warn their complaining customers that this type of hearing could be more expensive than taking action in the courts. In September 1980 a consultation document entitled *Redress Procedures under Codes of Practice* was issued by the OFT and this was followed, in December 1981, by a report of the same name. These both proposed a documents only arbitration scheme. A new model arbitration scheme, based on the OFT proposals, was introduced by the Chartered Institute of Arbitrators in 1983. Most of the schemes are administered by the Chartered Institute, although some use independent panels of arbitrators.[8]

The use of the trade association arbitration schemes is at the option of the customer with the complaint. There may, however, be a contractual agreement to submit a dispute to arbitration. If a customer signs a contract with an individual supplier of goods or services, and this contract contains a '*Scott v Avery* clause' stipulating that no right of action shall accrue until the amount of damages has been ascertained by arbitration, this could bar a court action, since it is a defence to court proceedings that arbitration has not taken place as agreed.[9] The Consumer Arbitration Agreements Act 1988, section 1 prevents compulsory arbitrations where a person is

---

7   For an assessment of consumer satisfaction with the trade association arbitration schemes see *Simple Justice*, NCC, 1979, ch. 10; *Out of Court*, NCC, 1991; *Consumer Redress Mechanisms*, OFT, 1991, paras. 4.47–4.57.

8   For details of all conciliation and arbitration schemes see *Consumer Redress Mechanisms*, OFT, 1991, pp. 79–86 and *Out of Court*, NCC, 1991, pp. 75–84.

9   *Scott v Avery* (1856) 5 HL Cas 811. See above p. 204.

'contracting as consumer' (section 3) if the dispute is within the county court jurisdiction limits. An option to go to arbitration under a voluntary code obviously involves no contract to do so, but once arbitration is in fact agreed to in writing then this can be enforced.[10]

Two reports, published in 1991, have examined the operation of consumer arbitration schemes and made proposals for improvements. First the National Consumer Council, in *Out of Court*, examined three low-cost arbitration schemes: those of the Association of British Travel Agents,[11] the Glass and Glazing Federation[12] and British Telecom.[13] The report, which involved surveys and questionnaires, produced a number of recommendations for improvements.[14] These include greater publicity for and commitment to arbitration, annual reports for each scheme, the option of personal hearings, some improvements in the information provided about the schemes, a speeding up of the process and specific recommendations for each of the three schemes studied. It is also felt that more research into the operation of conciliations is needed. Second, the OFT, in *Consumer Redress Mechanisms*,[15] also advocates greater publicity for the schemes and the production of annual reports. Consideration should be given to the idea of trade organisations providing independent conciliation services and the possibility of a common redress scheme is mooted. The suggestion of personal hearings being reintroduced is not supported.

INFORMATION ABOUT CODES

Included below are brief details[16] of the OFT-approved codes of practice currently in operation. The OFT publishes explanatory leaflets on some of the codes; these are indicated where relevant.

Cars

There are two Codes concerning the sale and repair of cars: the Code of Practice for the Motor Industry and the Vehicle Builders and Repairers Association's Code of Practice. Some information about

---

10 Consumer Arbitration Agreements Act 1988, s. 1. See also the discussion of arbitration in ch. 8.
11 See below p. 333.
12 See below p. 330.
13 See below p. 335 and ch. 4.
14 See *Out of Court*, NCC, 1991, pp. 72–73.
15 See paras 4.36–4.57 and ch. 6.
16 For the detailed texts of a number of these codes see Miller *Product Liability and Safety Encyclopaedia* Div. VI and O'Keefe *The Law Relating to Trade Descriptions*, Div. 5.

these Codes can be found in the OFT leaflet 'Used Cars – a guide for people who know little about them'.

Joint Code of the Society of Motor Manufacturers and Traders, the Retail Motor Industry Federation Ltd and the Scottish Motor Trade Association

This Joint Code (as revised in 1981) covers the advertising, sale, repair and servicing of new and used cars. Advertising controls include prohibition of misleading comparisons of models and pricing must make clear what is included and excluded. New car sales are governed by testing schedules and pre-delivery inspection checklists should be given to the customer, order forms and warranties must be clear, unexpired warranties must be transferable, and rectification work on a warranty must be capable of being done by any franchised dealer, not just the vendor dealer. Used cars are also subject to pre-sales inspections, mileage *must* be verified (or the customer told that the mileage is not verified) and where possible a signed statement from the previous owner as to mileage should be obtained and all relevant information such as service records, repair invoices, handbooks and warranties handed to the purchaser. Members must reveal any defects on an approved checklist which must be prominently displayed in the car and given to the customer before any sale. Repairs and servicing are governed by stipulations including the requirements of specifying minimum periods for the availability of spare parts by manufacturers, of giving where possible firm quotations for the cost of major repairs (with estimates also for major servicing) and of guarantees of workmanship for a specified mileage or period. With regard to complaints, if conciliation fails, 'low-cost' arbitration can be provided as an alternative to court proceedings. The arbitrator's award is binding not only as between manufacturer or dealer and customer, but also, where appropriate, between manufacturer and dealer.

This Code had been the subject of monitoring exercises by the OFT and three reports (in 1978, 1980 and 1986) have been produced.[17]

Vehicle Builders and Repairers Association (VBRA)

This Code, which was revised in 1989, governs the conduct of VBRA members carrying out vehicle body repairs and includes a comprehensive complaints and arbitration procedure. Written estimates

---

17　See *Bee Line* Special Edition Research Papers Nos. 4 and 7 and *The Motor Code: A Report on a Monitoring Survey*, September 1986.

must be offered, detailed invoices supplied, a minimum of twelve months or 12,000 miles guarantee of materials and workmanship provided, and reasonable care of vehicles in the charge of members exercised.

The earlier version of this Code was monitored by the OFT in 1986.[18]

Credit

To date six codes relating to the credit industry have been negotiated.

Consumer Credit Association of the United Kingdom

The Consumer Credit Association (CCA(UK)) was the first organisation in the consumer credit market to launch a Code in 1984. The updated version of 1989 achieved OFT approval. The CCA has over 900 members in six main areas of the unsecured credit market namely personal loans, credit sales, hire purchase, checks/vouchers, running account and hire/rental. The Code covers such matters as credit brokerage, checking the credit-worthiness of consumers, debt collection and default procedures and complaint handling. An arbitration scheme is included.

Consumer Credit Trade Association (CCTA)

This Code was launched in 1988 and is derived from the Finance Houses Association Code of Practice (see below) with modifications to suit CCTA members, involving hire purchase, store credit cards and personal loans. The CCTA has approximately 900 members, including finance houses, retailers and building societies. To avoid conflict with the work of the Building Societies Ombudsman, the Code does not apply to building societies who are members of CCTA. Conciliation and arbitration schemes operate.

Credit Services Association (CSA)

This Code was agreed in January 1991. The CSA represents debt-collecting agencies and the Code sets out guidelines of good business conduct in the collection of debts. In consumer transactions the Code requires the use of plain English, headed notepaper and clear identification of staff, with no collection charges levied on consumers in addition to those legally recoverable. There is a complaints procedure and a conciliation scheme.

18 See *The Code of Practice for Vehicle Body Repair: A Report on a Monitoring Survey*, OFT, November 1986.

Finance Houses Association (FSA)

The FSA, which represents 46 leading providers of instalment credit, launched its Code in 1987. The Code encourages responsible attitudes in granting credit, covers the refusal of credit, the use of credit-brokers and credit scoring techniques and requires monitoring of credit-granting practices and debt-collecting procedures. Conciliation and arbitration schemes operate.

London Personal Finance Association Ltd (LPFA)

Introduced in 1989, this Code is based on the FSA Code (see above). The LPFA has approximately 120 members representing both individuals and companies. Both conciliation and arbitration schemes operate.

National Consumer Credit Federation

In 1989 the Federation adopted the FSA Code (see above) on behalf of its members who are concerned with short-term shopping check business and companies who collect repayments of loans from customers' homes. Conciliation and arbitration schemes operate.

Direct selling

This Code of Practice, commenced in February 1980 and revised in 1987, is aimed particularly at the practice of selling goods at parties and by door-to-door salesmen.

The main points of the Code are: a) invitation cards to parties will make the purpose of a party clear to customers; b) party hostesses will be informed of their rights and responsibilities and will be fully insured by the company; c) provision for cancellation of orders within a minimum of fourteen days, and the consequential refund of deposits; d) when placing orders, customers will be given a copy of the order which must indicate where queries or complaints should be referred; e) the Trade Association (namely the Direct Selling Association Ltd) will provide prompt and informal conciliation on disputes referred to it, and customers will be told about this service; f) copies of the Code of Practice will be made available to customers. The Code Administrator can adjudicate in cases of dispute.

The DSA have published a consumer information leaflet called 'Shopping at Home' which contains the main points of this Code. In addition there is an OFT leaflet 'How to Cope with Doorstep Salesmen'.

Electrical goods and servicing

There are four Codes concerned with the sale and servicing of electrical goods. These are: the Association of Manufacturers of Domestic Electrical Appliances (AMDEA) Code, the two Codes produced by the former Electricity Councils and the Radio, Electrical and Television Retailers' Association (RETRA) Code.

The electrical Codes have been the subject of OFT monitoring in 1979.[19] As a result of this changes were made to the AMDEA and Electricity Councils' Codes.

Association of Manufacturers of Domestic Electrical Appliances

The AMDEA Code has been mentioned above. It was launched in 1975 and revised in 1984.[20] It requires members to answer requests for servicing equipment within three days and complete at least 80 per cent of all service jobs on the first visit, and the remaining 20 per cent within 15 days. Service appointments when made should be kept. Repair work and parts are provided with guarantees and detailed invoices have to be provided. On the important matter of spare parts, the Code requires manufacturers to stock sufficient parts to service current models and to maintain them for a minimum period after production ceases (e.g. 10 years for washing machines). An AMDEA Consumer Relations Department provides expert help and advice to CABx, Consumer Advice Centres and Trading Standards Departments, and assists with conciliation. An independent system of arbitration is also established, operated by the Institute of Arbitrators.

Electricity Council

This Code is unusual in being operated originally by a nationalised industry. Since privatisation the electricity companies have continued to operate the Code on an individual basis, there being no supervisory body now. The Code has somewhat similar terms to the AMDEA code considered above. There is a similar Code formerly operated by the Scottish Electricity Boards.

Radio Electrical and Television Retailers' Association (RETRA)

This Association represents more than 2,000 firms including the majority of companies with multiple outlets. The Code was launched in 1976. All members are required to give a comprehensive 12-

---

19 *Bee Line* Special Edition Research Paper No. 8 (1980).
20 See M & H p. 388 for the Code.

months guarantee, covering parts and labour, when selling new electrical appliances, radios and television sets. This is in addition to any manufacturer's guarantee. Members unable to repair appliances under guarantee within 15 days must supply a replacement, or if impractical, extend the period of the guarantee by the number of days over which the customer is deprived of his use of the appliance. Repairs are to be guaranteed for three months and completed within 15 days of any visit made. Deposits must be refunded for goods not available on time and receipts, detailed invoices and other information given to customers. Disputes may be referred by customer or member to the Secretary of RETRA and from there if still unresolved to the RETRA Customer Conciliation Panel.

Footwear

There are two Codes concerned with the sale and repair of footwear. The OFT has published an explanatory leaflet 'Shoes' referring to the Codes.

National Association of Multiple Shoe Repairers and Society of Master Shoe Repairers

Members of the above two Associations are responsible for about 85 per cent of shoe repairs in the UK. The Code includes a prohibition on members' limiting their liability for repairs carried out, a stipulation that prices for repairs inclusive of VAT will be displayed and customers should be issued with a ticket showing the cost and estimated date for collection. 'Worth', 'value' and 'price elsewhere' claims will not be made (and will in any event usually be contrary to pricing provisions), and where disputes cannot be resolved a test report will be obtained and honoured.

Footwear Distributors' Federation

In 1975 some 22,000 complaints were recorded for footwear. This Code was introduced in 1976 and is designed to improve customer relations and to ensure that more information is provided about shoes. Adherence to the Code is not obligatory on members of the FDF – only those members displaying the Code symbol must comply with it. This aspect has been criticised by the OFT. A Footwear Testing Centre has been set up, and customers may send shoes which are the subject matter of a dispute between them and the retailer to the Centre for testing and a report. If this is favourable, the customer's contribution to the test fee will be refunded. The Code also provides that all retailers of children's footwear will provide facilities for measuring children's feet, all prices shown will include

VAT, footwear will be labelled to show the material from which uppers and soles are made (leather or some other material), though this does not apply to wellington boots, plimsoles and most slippers. The Code has been monitored three times, in 1978, 1980 and 1985.[1]

Funeral directors

The Director was asked by the government to negotiate a Code of Practice with the National Association of Funeral Directors following the findings in the Price Commission's Report No. 22 (March 1977). This found, inter alia, that the pricing practices of funeral directors could be made fairer, for example by written estimates (often not asked for at a time of bereavement) and prominently displayed set prices for a simple, decent funeral. A Code was accordingly launched in 1979 and, following the publication of *Funerals: A Report* by the OFT in 1989, a revised version of the Code was issued in 1990. The Code details the specification for a basic funeral and covers the following additional matters: a) clients to be provided with full and fair information about services; b) price lists be made available and given to clients during a consultation; c) guidance to be provided on certification and registration of death, on the availability of Social Security benefits and on the application of insurance policies; d) a written estimate to be given of all funeral charges and an itemised account; e) advertising must be clear, honest and in good taste and in accordance with the British Code of Advertising Practice; f) complaints must be handled speedily and sympathetically, and backed up at national level with a clients' advisory service and conciliation and arbitration arrangements.

Furniture

A Code of Practice for the furniture industry came into operation in August 1978. The representative trade organisations are concerned with the manufacture and retailing of furniture (including carpets) and beds. The Code provides for the provision of point of sale literature or the attachment of labels to furniture giving information on construction, cleaning, dimensions and price, realistic delivery dates by retailers, the refund of deposits if delivery is delayed and a revised date is not acceptable to the customer, and the display of Code symbols by retail traders belonging to the Trade Associations to show the public their adherence to the Code. There is a conciliation scheme with an independent inspection service, the

1 *Bee Line* Special Edition Research Papers Nos. 5 (1978) and 9 (1980).

inspection fee being refundable if the customer's complaint is upheld. In addition an arbitration scheme is available.

In 1990 *Furniture and Carpets*, a report by the Director, was published. This highlighted a number of problems in the area, including with regard to the operation of the Code and proposed many changes and improvements for both retailers and manufacturers. An all-industry Action Group was formed to respond to the Report, which it did during 1991. A new consumer protection regime is anticipated in 1992 entitled Qualitas.[2]

Glass and glazing

The Glass and Glazing Federation's (GGF) Code of Ethical Practice was introduced in November 1981. Following the publication of *The Glass and Glazing Code: A Report on Monitoring Surveys* by the OFT in 1987, a revised Code was issued in 1988. Under the Code both the products and the installations are required to comply with the relevant BSI Codes of Practice and GGF Standards. Delivery periods and completion dates have to be provided and if the customer has made time of the essence, work uncompleted after six weeks may be cancelled without penalty. The Code also provides a right of cancellation for both cash and credit contracts which have been negotiated away from business premises. A Deposit Indemnity Fund is available to ensure the return of deposits or the completion of work in the event of a member going out of business. A conciliation and arbitration scheme is provided.[3]

Details of the Code may be found in the OFT leaflet entitled 'Double Glazing' and also in their booklet 'Home Improvements'.

Holiday caravans

Following a Monopolies and Mergers Commission Report on holiday caravans in Northern Ireland (in July 1983) the Director began negotiations with the National Caravan Council and the British Holiday and Home Parks Association Ltd. with a view to introducing a national Code. Two such Codes were finally introduced in January 1987, both of which offer conciliation and arbitration services.

Code of Practice for Letting Holiday Caravans

The Code requires caravan park owners to ensure that park facilities

---

2   See *Bee Line* 91/3, p. 10 and *Bee Line* 91/4 p. 8.
3   For a detailed examination of the operation of the arbitration scheme see *Out of Court*, NCC, 1991.

function correctly, site licence conditions are satisfied and staff are available during all reasonable hours. The condition of the caravans to be let is specified under the letting obligations and detailed information concerning the sites and the caravans must be sent to enquirers.

Code of Practice for Selling and Siting Holiday Caravans

This Code is concerned with the sale and siting of permanently sited caravans. It lays down terms as to tenure of pitches, the length of notice required to remove a caravan and to increase pitch fees. Details of the information to be included in written agreements for pitches are stipulated and rights regarding the resale of caravans and the substantial alteration of park arrangements are also included.

Laundry

The Textile Services Association Ltd (formerly ABLC)

This Code prohibits members from excluding liability for negligence by 'small print clauses',[4] and requiring them to pay fair compensation for loss or damage to property for which they are responsible. Members are also required to display current prices and to give customers a receipt showing the charge and the date for collection. Complaints about the quality of the work should be met by reprocessing the article free of charge. Disputes may be settled through the Association's Customer Advisory Service which will provide a free technical report if the TSA considers it necessary. The OFT explanatory leaflet is entitled 'Launderers and Dry Cleaners'.

Mail order trading

There are three Codes involved with mail order trading: first that of the Association of Mail Order Publishers, covering mainly book and record clubs, second the BDMA Direct Marketing Code of Practice, covering direct marketing activities and third the Mail Order Traders' Association Code, covering catalogue sales. An OFT leaflet entitled 'Buying by Post' covers the Codes.

---

4 For examples of written exemption clauses rendered ineffective by verbal misrepresentation see *Curtis v Chemical Cleaning and Dyeing Co* [1951] 1 KB 805, [1951] 1 All ER 631 (dry cleaning) and *J Evans & Son (Portsmouth) Ltd v Andrea Merzario Ltd* [1976] 2 All ER 930, [1976] 1 WLR 1078, CA (carriage of goods).

Association of Mail Order Publishers

This Code was originally drawn up in 1970, revised in 1977 and the third edition, published in conjunction with the British Direct Marketing Association (see below), was issued in 1989. The Code requires members' advertisements to include clear details of the essential points of an offer, including the cost of postage and packing, gifts given to every entrant in a competition must not be styled 'prizes', and book, record and other clubs must make clear the terms of their contracts and allow a customer time to reject the item. Special provisions cover telephone marketing, direct selling, prize draws, competitions and collectibles. The Mail Order Publishers' Authority has been established to investigate complaints. Customers should be supplied with the information that MOPA deals with complaints and its address. There is no low-cost arbitration scheme offered, only joint agreement for a standard arbitration. An earlier version of this Code was monitored by the OFT in 1977–78.[5]

The BDMA Direct Marketing Code of Practice

This Code was issued, as a first edition, in conjunction with the Association of Mail Order Publishers in 1989 (see above). Its terms are very similar, with the BDMA Council dealing with complaints against members and a conciliation service is offered. Ordinary arbitration is available by agreement between member and customer, no low-cost scheme is available.

Mail Order Traders' Association (MOTA)

This Code was launched in 1978 by MOTA which represents the leading firms selling goods through catalogues with part-time agents as intermediaries between the companies and their customers. The Code requires that the catalogues must contain the trading name of the advertiser and an address for enquiries and complaints, full information about the size, colour, materials, price including VAT and non-optional extras and restrictions on use for goods advertised. The goods must be dispatched 'on approval' without prior payment unless otherwise stated and customers have a minimum of 14 days in which to change their minds. A conciliation scheme is provided and if this does not satisfactorily resolve the dispute then there is also an arbitration scheme.

5   *Bee Line* Special Edition Research Paper No. 6 (1979).

Mechanical Breakdown Insurance Schemes

Operated by the Society of Motor Manufacturers and Traders (SMMT), a Code of Practice was adopted in 1989 covering what are often referred to as extended warranties. The Code provides that such schemes must be underwritten either by an insurance company or by a Lloyd's syndicate. It requires documentation in the form of booklets or certificates, written as a direct contract between the motorist and the insurer. If a dispute arises this can be referred to the Personal Insurance Arbitration Scheme or the Insurance Ombudsman, depending upon membership. There are also conciliation procedures with SMMT, Lloyd's Consumer Enquiries Department and the Association of British Insurers.

Motorcycles

A Code of Practice for the motorcycle industry was drawn up in 1984 by four organisations representing motorcycle manufacturers (the Motor Cycle Association) and retailers (the Motor Agents' Association, now the Retail Motor Industry Federation Ltd, the Scottish Motor Trade Association and the Motorcycle Retailers' Association, now the Motorcycle Association of Great Britain). The Code covers the supply of new and used motorcycles, parts and accessories, servicing and repairs. It requires the transfer of manufacturers' warranties on new motorcycles to subsequent owners and the inspection of used motorcycles, with a checklist to be made available to purchasers. In connection with repairs and servicing, quotations or estimates are to be provided, with repairs guaranteed for a specific time period or mileage. The Code provides a conciliation and arbitration service.

Package holidays

Association of British Travel Agents

ABTA operates two Codes of Conduct, one for Travel Agents and one for Tour Operators. These are regularly updated to take into account new situations and problems. Under the Tour Operators Code there are prohibitions on disclaiming responsibility for misrepresentations and for failing to exercise care and skill in making arrangements for package holidays. Also prohibited are clauses barring claims if not made within a fixed period unless that period is at least 28 days from completion of the holiday. The Code deals with unjustifiable cancellations, particularly as a result of overbooking, and where cancellations are unavoidable the client is to be offered a comparable alternative or a full refund of all money paid. Compensation must, in addition, be offered in some situations. Tour operators have to accept liability for the acts and/or omissions of their employees, agents, sub-contractors and suppliers for foreign inclusive holidays and tours. Where negligence is involved, claims for death and personal injury are included (except those involving air and sea carriers). Brochures must comply with ABTA Standards on Brochures and surcharges have to be in compliance with ABTA Standards on Surcharges. The Code also covers relations between tour operators and travel agents. Travel agents under their Code are required to give impartial and accurate information and keep clients fully informed. There are provisions relating to booking conditions, insurance, passport, visa and health requirements and relations between travel agents and tour operators are also covered.

ABTA ceased operating its conciliation service in 1991[6] as it was suggested this delayed dispute resolution. Instead it is has replaced it with a Consumer Affairs Department to monitor complaints against members, determine whether or not breaches have occurred and advise complainants on pursuing a remedy. In the case of disputes with a tour operator, the holidaymaker may either choose to go to arbitration under a scheme administered by the Institute of Arbitrators[7] or to court. This choice may be made after the extent of the loss has been calculated. The arbitration scheme does not apply to claims for more than £1,500 per person or £7,500 per booking form, nor does it apply to claims which are solely or mainly in respect of physical injury or illness. Alleged breaches of the Code are considered by the ABTA's Tour Operators' Council or Travel Agents' Council.

The ABTA Code has been monitored by the OFT in 1978 and 1988.[8] Further information about the Code is in the OFT leaflet 'Package Holidays'.

Photographic industry

A Code of Practice for the photographic industry came into operation in May 1979 and was revised in 1986. It is supported by eight Trade Associations representing all sectors of the industry. The main provisions for retailers are: a) retailers must provide informed information about the products which they sell; b) the manufacturer's guarantee will be available for inspection before purchase; c) delivery dates must be quoted in writing when a deposit is taken and

6 See *Bee Line* 91/2, p. 6.
7 For a detailed examination of the operation of the arbitration scheme see *Out of Court*, NCC, 1991.
8 *Bee Line* Special Edition Research Paper No. 3 (1978) and *The Package Holiday Codes: A Report on Monitoring Surveys*, OFT, July 1988.

refunds offered when those dates cannot be met; d) price lists for developing films will be displayed and customers given a receipt stating the estimated collection date; e) repairs are normally to be carried out within twenty-one days and customers to be warned if there is unforeseen delay or substantially more cost involved than was originally estimated; f) retailers will carry out detailed inspection of all second-hand equipment before sale and will guarantee second-hand items whenever possible.

Manufacturers have complementary duties to the above and must maintain stocks of spare parts for at least five years following the last sale to the trade. There are also provisions relating to professional photographers concerning information about fee structures and the quality of work produced. A conciliation and arbitration scheme is provided.

Postal and telecommunications services

Codes relating to the above were introduced in June 1979 and drawn up by the Post Office in consultation with the OFT and the Post Office Users National Council (see ch. 4). The drawing up of the Codes followed the exclusion of the Post Office from the scope of the Unfair Contract Terms Act 1977. The separation of British Telecom from the Post Office and its subsequent privatisation has led to the Code of Practice for Telecommunications now coming under the auspices of the Office of Telecommunications (Oftel) and the Director General of Telecommunications (discussed in ch. 4).[9]

Code of Practice for Postal Services

The Post Office Code has continued, with OFT approval, and was revised in 1982. It provides a complaints handling procedure and two arbitration schemes. One, which is legally binding, is for those areas where the Post Office is legally liable, i.e. most inland postal services; the other, which is voluntary and not legally binding, is for overseas mail and postal order complaints. Under the Code there are provisions for payment of compensation for loss or damage to inland and overseas letters and parcels; also for the refund of reasonable costs incurred by customers enquiring about lost or damaged postal packets, the refund of postage fees where, through the Post Office's negligence, a service has not been provided and delivery targets for first and second class mail.

9 For a detailed discussion of the arbitration scheme operated by British Telecom see *Out of Court*, NCC, 1991.

Criminal enforcement of voluntary Codes of Practice

It is, of course, a weakness of voluntary or self-enforcing codes of practice that they, by definition, bind only those traders who are members of an appropriate association. But, as regards trade association members, are the sanctions sufficient? Disciplinary action by the trade association may be taken but this does not always result in justice being seen to be done. It has been argued that a representation that a trader is adhering to a particular code of practice is akin to a statement that certain known services or facilities are provided. The provisions of the Codes contain statements of fact, and therefore if the requisite 'statement' as to adherence to the facilities which go with the Code is made falsely or recklessly, an offence under the Trade Descriptions Act 1968, section 14 has been committed.[10] In one case adjudicated upon by a magistrates' court the defendant car traders had misdescribed the car mileage on a used model and were charged that they 'in the course of trade or business recklessly made a statement which was false as to the provision of a service in the course of trade or business by a notice which read' that they subscribed to the Motor Agents' Association Code of Practice. The court convicted.[11]

3. TRADING MALPRACTICES

It has been accepted for some years that Codes of Practice in their present form do not always provide consumers with adequate protection from rogue traders. The Director, therefore, on a number of occasions[12] mooted the idea of introducing a general duty to trade fairly linked to the codes of practice. Following consultations, in August 1986, the Office of Fair Trading published *A general duty to trade fairly – A discussion paper*. The document made provisional recommendations on the establishment of a general duty and sought further comments. It proposed that the existing civil and criminal laws could be supplemented by the introduction of a broad statutory duty to trade fairly, supported by Codes of Practice, both vertical (by trading practice) and horizontal (by sector), which set out the trading practices regarded as acceptable or unacceptable. Resulting from the

---

10   See A. J. Street (1979) 87 ITSA Monthly Review 63.
11   See *Re V G Vehicles (Telford) Ltd* (1981) 89 ITSA Monthly Review 91.
12   See, for example, G. Borrie 'Laws and Codes for Consumers' [1980] JBL 315; *Home Improvements – A Discussion Paper*, OFT, March 1982, ch. 6; *Home Improvements: A Report by the Director General of Fair Trading*, June 1983, ch. 12; M & H pp. 428–431; G. Borrie *The Development of Consumer Law and Policy*, pp. 75–78.

comments received and further consideration of the proposals the Director published *Trading Malpractices* in July 1990. The arguments for and against a general duty to trade fairly were presented[13] and on balance the Director decided against pursuing the idea of a general duty.

The Director recognised that it is not possible within one measure both to raise trading standards generally and to assist in providing redress for consumers. The report, therefore, favours concentrating 'directly on tackling unlawful, deceptive or objectionable trading practices which have not been, or cannot be, controlled effectively by existing legislation.' (para. 1.6). To achieve this a radical overhaul of Part III of the Fair Trading Act 1973 is proposed. The definition of 'unfair' conduct, required before an assurance may be sought,[14] would be expanded to encompass 'deceptive or misleading' business practices (with a non-exhaustive list of illustrative acts or practices) and 'unconscionable' practices.[15] New enforcement procedures are also proposed, involving both local trading standards authorities and the Office of Fair Trading. Initially a caution would be served on the trader, indicating the unfair conduct concerned and requiring this to cease. The caution could be challenged by the trader in court. If the caution is then ignored, enforcement proceedings could be brought. The court would have powers to revoke cautions, accept undertakings and order the cessation of the conduct or similar conduct. Breach of court orders would amount to contempt of court.[16]

Since publishing its proposals the Office of Fair Trading has continued to consult on the area and to hold conferences to consider reactions to them. It can be seen that, having initially centred on Codes of Practice as a starting point for improving trading standards, these no longer form the core of proposals for future development – indeed they play very little part. There will be no foreseeable enhancement of the position of Codes of Practice. Instead assurances are seen as the way forward to remove trading malpractices.

4. BRIEF ASSESSMENT

This chapter has, it is hoped, given an impression which does not purport to be comprehensive, of the functions, powers and activities

13 *Trading Malpractices*, OFT, 1990, pp. 20–22.
14 See above pp. 315–316.
15 See op. cit. paras. 5.18–5.28.
16 See op. cit. paras. 4.19–4.38.

of the Director and the Office of Fair Trading outside the duties relating to competition policy, consumer credit and advertising. It has concentrated on his activities under Parts II and III of the Fair Trading Act 1973 and with Codes of Practice. This does not, however, fully reflect the Director's activities in the field of consumer protection. The Director and the OFT have been very active both in informing consumers and traders of their rights and obligations via leaflets, posters, booklets, etc. and also in proposing, introducing and supporting moves to improve the protection afforded to consumers. This has been done often by examining the practices of reputable traders and encouraging wider adoption of such practices, to the benefit of both traders and consumers. A glance at any Annual Report of the Director and *Bee Line* illustrates the range of his activities. Areas covered include insurance, marriage bureaux, prepayments for goods and services, guarantees and extended warranties, cars (selling and repairing), one-day sales, home improvements, mail order protection schemes, telephone selling, resale of electricity, micro-electronics and retailing and timeshare. The Director and the OFT have been and no doubt will be criticised by both consumer and trade interests for too little or too much activity but on balance it must be said that there has been a beneficial impact on the field on consumer protection. In the words of Sir Gordon Borrie:

> As one man's keen business practice is another man's unfair trading, it is never easy to be the referee.[17]

---

17   *Annual Report for 1985* (HC Papers (1985–1986) No. 403) at p. 13.

12 Trade descriptions and price indications

1. INTRODUCTION

Earlier chapters in this book have dealt with various examples of legislation aimed at the prohibition of false trade descriptions, hallmarking being an important and long standing example. Before the Trade Descriptions Act 1968 repealed them, the Merchandise Marks Acts 1887–1953 were the main body of legislation dealing specifically with the false or deceptive description of goods and the wrongful application of trade marks.

The Molony Committee received a considerable volume of evidence critical of the protection provided both to traders and consumers by the Merchandise Marks Acts. In particular, the definition of a 'trade description' in section 3 of the 1887 Act relating to 'the standard of quality of any goods, according to a classification commonly used or recognised in the trade' came under serious attack. It was apparent that in many trades no classifications were established, or where they were they could still be used in a way misleading to the public.[1] Evidence was also given, inter alia, of misleading price claims, especially at times of seasonal or 'special' sales and, as to government surplus implying a special rugged quality, a number of members of the public 'clearly doubted whether the needs of Her Majesty's Forces could be so consistently and seriously miscalculated as to throw up the large volume of goods regularly offered by traders to the general public' under such descriptions as 'ex-naval' or 'RAF surplus'. It was doubtful if the Acts applied to these practices and, if they did, the penalties were by modern standards absurdly low.[2] The Committee also noted the widespread view that the Acts were laxly enforced, particularly by the Board of Trade.

---

1 See Final Report, (1962) Cmnd. 1781, para 586, and see generally Part V of the Report.
2 Ibid, paras. 588, 589.

The Report recommended reform under five heads:
a) removal of defects in the Acts making the meaning of the Acts obscure, their application unfair or their administration difficult;
b) extension and amendment of the definition of trade description;
c) incorporation in the Acts of a power to define imprecise or corrupt terms used in trade descriptions;
d) extension and amendment of the definition of applying a trade description;
e) improvement in the enforcement of the Acts.[3]

Reform was implemented by the Trade Descriptions Act 1968. It applies to Scotland, and with the modification necessary for a different legal and administrative system, to Northern Ireland (section 40). Since the Crown is not 'named' in the Act, it does not bind the Crown, HM Forces or Visiting Forces. Nationalised industries and public corporations are controlled and 'owned' by *ad hoc* bodies which do not act for the Crown and they consequently cannot claim immunity.[4] The 1968 Act was extended in 1972 to require an indication of origin on certain imported goods but the 1972 Act was repealed in 1987 since its policy was regarded as in conflict with the Treaty of Rome.

A few general points can usefully be noted about the 1968 Act before its more important provisions are examined. Firstly, it is necessary to appreciate that though its primary purpose is to protect the public, it extends to transactions between traders. Secondly, the 1968 Act widens the law which it replaced. The provisions relating to misdescription of goods are a modern adaptation of the law contained in the Merchandise Marks Acts, but section 11 which concerned false price indications and section 14 covering false statements as to services, accommodation and facilities were both new provisions. Thirdly, under section 1, false trade descriptions of goods, there is no need to prove an intention to deceive.[5] The Act does, however, lay down a number of defences in sections 24 and 25 which mitigate the rigour of what is otherwise strict liability. Section 14, on the other hand, applies only to statements as to services etc.

---

3   Ibid, para. 575.
4   See generally O'Keefe *The Law Relating to Trade Descriptions* (Butterworths Looseleaf Encyclopaedia).
5   This was confirmed by the Divisional Court in *Alec Norman Garages Ltd v Phillips* (1984) 148 JP 741, [1985] RTR 164. But the defendant must know that there *is* a trade description attached to the goods – see *Cottee v Douglas Seaton (Used Cars) Ltd* [1972] 3 All ER 750, [1972] 1 WLR 1408, QBD, M & H p. 476.

known to be false or made *recklessly*. Here *mens rea* is required, the reason perhaps being that, unlike section 1 offences, there was no precedent for this particular provision and caution in introducing it was desirable. In view of the difficulties surrounding this provision it is perhaps, not without significance that it has been omitted from the otherwise very similar Hong Kong Trade Descriptions Ordinance (1980). Fourthly, the right to prosecute for an offence is not limited to local authorities.[6] Accordingly, as the common law right for any person, whether aggrieved or not, to prosecute in respect of an offence is not abrogated, private prosecutions may be brought. Fifthly, section 23 contains a provision familiar in criminal law to the effect that if a person commits an offence due to the act or default of some other party, that other person is guilty of the offence whether or not the first mentioned is proceeded against.

2. PENALTY FOR OFFENCES AND TIME LIMITS

Offences under the Act generally attract a penalty on summary conviction of a fine not exceeding £5,000[7] and on conviction on indictment of a fine without specific limit or imprisonment for up to two years or both. No prosecution may be commenced after the expiration of three years from the commission of the offence or one year from its discovery[8] by the prosecutor, whichever is the earlier. A magistrates' court may try an information laid at any time within twelve months from the commission of the offence notwithstanding section 127 of the Magistrates' Courts Act 1980, which requires informations normally to be laid within six months from the time when the offence was committed (section 19), unless the offence is triable 'either way', when the longer time limits specified above apply.

6 See *Snodgrass v Topping* (1952) 116 JP 312.
7 Section 18 as amended by the Criminal Law Act 1977, the Criminal Justice Act 1982, s. 37 and the Criminal Justice Act 1991, s. 17. The only purely summary offence in the 1968 Act is obstructing an authorised officer, which under s. 29 attracts a maximum fine of £1,000 (being level 3 on the standard scale).
8 What 'discovery' involves was elucidated in *R v Beaconsfield Justices, ex p Johnston & Sons Ltd* (1985) 149 JP 535, DC where it was held, in effect, that 'discovery' occurs where the prosecuting authority becomes aware of the relevant facts even though admissible evidence to support those facts still needs to be obtained. The time limit in s. 19(1) also applies to conspiracy to contravene s. 1 of the 1968 Act (*R v Pain* [1986] BTLC 142, CA).

3. ENFORCEMENT

It is the duty of every weights and measures authority to enforce within its area the Act and orders made under it. An authority may be required to report to the Secretary of State who also has power to investigate complaints of non-enforcement by ordering a local enquiry. Authorities and their duly authorised officers have wide powers to make test purchases, enter premises and seize goods and documents (sections 27, 28). Obstruction of an officer in pursuance of the Act is an offence (section 29).

Under sections 222 and 223 of the Local Government Act 1972 a local authority may prosecute, defend or appear in any legal proceedings where it is expedient for the promotion or protection of the interests of the inhabitants of their area, and may authorise any member or officer to prosecute, defend or appear on its behalf in proceedings before a magistrates' court whether or not the member or officer is a solicitor with a current practising certificate.

In practice proceedings are normally conducted by a solicitor employed by a local authority[9] or a senior member of staff of the Council's Trading Standards Department. Local authorities are required to inform the Office of Fair Trading of the results of prosecutions brought under the Trade Descriptions Act 1968, and results of convictions reported in 1989–90 were as follows:

False descriptions of goods	1,129
False price claims	26
False or reckless statements as to services etc.	129
TOTAL	1,284
Total fines	£823,633
Total compensation	£85,253

Various terms of imprisonment were also imposed. (*Source*: Annual Report of Director of Fair Trading 1990).

It may be noted that the Office of Fair Trading's Review of the Trade Descriptions Act 1968 (1976, Cmnd. 6628) referred to throughout this chapter, recommends that the Director General of Fair Trading be given a national role as enforcer of the Act (para. 224).

---

9 Normally the county council or metropolitan district council for the relevant area, or a London Borough Council – see redefinition of local weights and measures authorities in Weights and Measures Act 1985, s. 69.

4. PROHIBITION OF FALSE TRADE DESCRIPTIONS

Section 1(1) states that:
Any person who, in the course of a trade or business –
   a) applies a false trade description to any goods; or
   b) supplies or offers to supply any goods to which a false trade
      description is applied;
shall, subject to the provisions of this Act, be guilty of an offence.
This subsection, which is the core of the Act, must be read in
conjunction with sections 2 to 6 of the Act, which sections interpret
and expand the expressions used in section 1(1) (section 1(2)).

To understand subsection (1) it is necessary to analyse a number of
points in order, making reference to the first six sections where
appropriate.

'Any person'

This includes a limited company.[10] Section 20 contains special
provisions dealing with offences by corporations, making any
director, manager, secretary or other similar officer jointly liable if
the offence is proved to have been committed with their consent or
connivance. Although 'any person' will normally be the seller of
goods, it is also possible for a buyer to apply a false description. In
Fletcher v Budgen[11] a car dealer told a private customer that his car
was irreparable and fit only for scrap. The dealer then bought it for
£2, carried out repairs costing £56, obtained a test certificate and
advertised it for sale at £135. The Divisional Court held that an
offence could be committed by a buyer who applied a false trade
description to the goods (e.g. 'fit only for scrap') where buying them
in the course of his trade or business.

'In the course of a trade or business'

The Act is intended to penalise the dishonest businessman rather
than imposing strict criminal liability on private sellers who may or
may not be strictly honest, though it appears that there may be an
exception where section 23, considered below, can be used. (However, a dishonest private seller who, for instance, sells his car having
tampered with the odometer, a factor affecting the price obtained,
may well have obtained property by deception contrary to section 15
of the Theft Act 1968.) This expression is familiar in other areas of

10 Interpretation Act 1978, Sch. 1.
11 [1974] 2 All ER 1243, [1974] 1 WLR 1056; M & H p. 466. See also *Fletcher v
    Sledmore* [1973] RTR 371 (the false statement may be made by someone not privy
    to the contract of supply).

law such as income tax[12] and value added tax, and there have been a number of decisions on its meaning in the present context, there being no definition in the Act. In *John v Matthews*[13] it was held by the Divisional Court that it was not possible to commit an offence under section 11 (now repealed, but formerly catching misleading indications of price of goods) where the supply of goods was by a working men's club to a member, since the Act was designed to protect the public, not a husband from his wife or a club and its members. Its primary charging provisions relate only to transactions of a commercial nature, notwithstanding that under this particular section the requirement of the supply being in the course of a trade or business was not expressed. In *Havering London Borough v Stevenson*[14] a car sold by a car hire firm had a false trade description as to mileage. Though not car dealers, the firm regularly sold its cars after a period of use. It was held by the Divisional Court that the sale was in the course of its trade or business as a car hire firm. And in *Fletcher v Sledmore*[15] the defendant was a panel beater who bought, repaired and sold old cars. A dealer and his prospective customer visited him and he falsely stated that the car had a 'good little engine'. The panel beater sold the repaired car to the dealer and he resold to the customer who was influenced by the panel beater's remark. Despite the lack of any contractual relationship between the eventual buyer and the panel beater, the latter was directed to be convicted of applying a false trade description in the course of his trade or business contrary to section 1(1)(a).

In *Davies v Sumner*[16] the activities of a self-employed courier, whose car's odometer had gone right round the clock, thus presenting a false reading, were reviewed on his sale of that car. Here, he owned the car but in the past he had hired his vehicles. The House of Lords held that a normal business practice of buying and disposing of cars had not been established and the relevant sale was therefore not caught by section 1(1)(a).

In the civil context, the Court of Appeal held in *R & B Customs Brokers Co Ltd United Dominions Trust Ltd*[17] that a corporate purchaser had not bought a car 'in the course of a business' for the purposes of the Unfair Contract Terms Act 1977, section 12(1)(a).

---

12 See as to income tax, Sch. D. Cases 1 and 2, Income and Corporation Taxes Act 1988, and the many tax cases on the meaning of 'trade'. The expression is also relevant (inter alia) in bankruptcy and landlord and tenant law.
13 [1970] 2 QB 443, [1970] 2 All ER 643.
14 [1970] 3 All ER 609, [1970] 1 WLR 1375.
15 (1973) 117 Sol Jo 164.
16 [1984] 3 All ER 831, [1984] WLR 1301, H L; M & H p. 470. See also *Devlin v Hall* (1990) 155 JP 20.
17 [1988] 1 All ER 847.

This decision has been criticised for introducing a potential loophole in the ambit of protection of the criminal law in over-emphasising the need for regularity and trying vainly to equate the tests for buying in the course of a business and selling in the course of a business.[18]

'Applies'

The word 'applies' is amplified in section 4. A person applies a trade description to goods if he–

   a) affixes or annexes it to or in any manner marks it on or incorporates it with–

     i) the goods themselves, or

     ii) anything in, on or with which the goods are supplied; or

   b) places the goods in, on or with anything which the trade description has been affixed or annexed to, marked on or incorporated with, or places any such thing with the goods; or

   c) uses the trade description in any manner likely to be taken as referring to the goods.

This subsection is similar to section 5 of the Merchandise Marks Act 1887 as amended and there is a quantity of case law on the interpretation of the former provision which the draftsman no doubt had in mind in drafting section 4. An interesting illustrative case in which that part of section 4 referring to where a person 'affixes or annexes or in any manner marks it', with 'anything in, on or with which the goods are supplied' was relevant was *Donnelly v Rowlands*.[19] There a milk retailer sold milk in bottles the foil caps of which read 'Untreated milk Produced from TT Cows', followed by his name and address. The bottles themselves were marked with the name of various well known suppliers, such as CWS, to whom the actual bottles belonged. The prosecutor's appeal from the magistrate's dismissal of the informations alleging that he had sold bottles of milk to which false trade descriptions had been applied was also dismissed by the Divisional Court. It was held that the words on the cap were an accurate trade description and the words on the milk bottles, which could have been a false trade description had the public been misled into thinking that the names thereon had something to do with the production of milk, could only reasonably apply to the ownership of the bottles. The defendant was therefore

---

18 D Parry 'Business or Consumer A Trap for the Unwary' (1988) 6 Trading Law 270; D. Oughton *Consumer Law* p. 5.

19 [1971] 1 All ER 9, [1970] 1 WLR 1600. See also *Roberts v Severn Petroleum and Trading Co Ltd* [1981] RTR 312, DC, M & H p. 475, where the respondents were held to have infringed s. 1(1)(a) where they had falsely displayed Esso signs in the vicinity of petrol tanks not containing Esso petrol.

saved by the wording on the cap which was required by the Milk (Special Designation) Regulations 1963.[20]

Section 4(2) states that an oral statement may amount to the use of a trade description. Although there are similar provisions in food and drugs and weights and measures law,[1] this was a controversial innovation in trade descriptions law. The Molony Committee recognised that oral mis-statements were a widespread problem, but considered that to make oral misdescription an offence would 'put a very powerful weapon into the hands of a disappointed shopper'.[2] However, the government took the view that this provision was essential if a comprehensive system of protection was to be provided. No doubt because of the increasing fallibility of a witness's memory of alleged oral misdescriptions, section 19(4) expressly stipulates that prosecutions must be brought within the normal time of six months laid down by section 127(1) of the Magistrates' Courts Act 1980 (though since 1977 this is an either way offence not subject to time limits). The point was important where a prosecution was brought more than six months after the alleged offence was committed. In *Rees v Munday*[3] it was unsuccessfully argued that where a vehicle was falsely described ('first class condition, 12 yard capacity') in a trade journal, the operative misdescription occurred when the vendor stated to the purchaser orally that the vehicle he was buying was the one advertised. Some importance was attached by Lord Widgery CJ to the fact that there was only one lorry in the vendor's possession answering the relevant description. The description was therefore 'applied' when the advertisement was published. Section 4(3) also makes it clear that when goods are supplied in pursuance of a request in which a trade description is used, the supplier is deemed to have applied that trade description to the goods where the circumstances make it reasonable for that to be inferred.

Even though a trade description can be deemed to have been applied to goods in accordance with the Act, it is a necessary

20   S.I. 1963/1571; see now the Milk (Special Designation) Regulations 1989, S.I. 1989/2383.
1   See Food Safety Act 1990, s. 14 (misrepresentations as to nature, substance or quality of food) and Weights and Measures Act 1985, s. 28 (short quantity).
2   Cmnd. 1791, para. 659.
3   [1974] 3 All ER 506, [1974] 1 WLR 1284, M & H p. 571. In *Louis C Edwards & Sons (Manchester) Ltd v Miller* (19 January 1981, unreported), QBD (but see (1981) Monthly Rev 240), the Divisional Court convicted suppliers of meat to a local education authority under s. 1(1)(b) for failing to supply meat which complied with the specification in the tender. Since there was a standing contract which only required goods to be supplied when there was a request, s. 1(1)(b) applied by virtue of s. 4(3) considered below. But the court took care to stress that it was not every breach of contract for sale of goods which also contravened the Trade Descriptions Act.

ingredient of the offence that the offender should have knowledge at the time of the supply or offer to supply goods that a trade description is applied to them.[4]

'A false trade description to any goods'

The definition of 'false trade description' is contained in sections 2 and 3 in particular. Section 3 states that a *false* trade description is a trade description which is false to a material degree, and also includes within the expression 'false' descriptions which, though not false, are misleading. Anything likely to be taken for an indication of the matters specified in section 2 (discussed below), though not a 'trade description', will, if false, be deemed a false trade description (section 3(3)), and a similar provision applies to false indications of specified or recognised standards.

Again, this section is somewhat similar to section 3 of the Merchandise Marks Act 1887, as amended, on which repealed section there are a number of still relevant reported cases. For instance in *Sandeman v Gold*[5] it was held to be a false trade description to describe as 'port' what was in fact Tarragona wine, and in *Kat v Diment*[6] the term 'non-brewed vinegar' was held to be false when applied to a solution of acetic acid and caramel. A number of other examples are mentioned in the discussion of 'trade description' under section 2 below.

The term 'trade description' is defined comprehensively in section 2 (as amended). The section is a greatly extended version of the previous law. Subsection (1) states that a trade description is an indication, direct or indirect, and by whatever means given of any of the matters specified thereby with respect to any goods. Included in the list, lettered in paragraphs (a) to (j), are (a) quantity, size or gauge, (b) method of manufacture or production, (c) composition, (d) fitness for purpose, strength, performance, behaviour or accuracy, (e) any other physical characteristics, (f) testing by any person and the results thereof, (g) approval by any person or conformity with an approved type, (h) place or date of manufacture, production etc., (i) person by whom manufactured or processed, and (j) other history, including previous ownership or use.

In relation to '(a) quantity, size or gauge', quantity includes length, width, height, area, volume, capacity, weight and number (section 2(3)). There is some overlap here between this provision and the

4 See *Cottee v Douglas Seaton (Used Cars) Ltd* [1972] 3 All ER 750, [1972] 1 WLR 1408 (M & H p. 476).
5 [1924] 1 KB 107.
6 [1951] 1 KB 34, [1950] 2 All ER 657.

'short weight' etc. offences contained in the Weights and Measures Act 1985 and discussed in ch. 13 but technically it would be an offence under the Trade Descriptions Act to supply greater quantities than indicated.

In relation to '(c) composition', examples under the old law include misdescriptions such as 'natural mineral water', a mixture of cotton and linen described as 'linen' and artificial silk stockings described as 'silk'.[7] A modern case illustrates that 'composition' includes component parts. In *British Gas Corpn v Lubbock*[8] a Gas Board brochure stated, with regard to gas cookers for sale, 'Ignition is by hand-held battery torch supplied with the cooker'. This was held to be (inter alia) a trade description relating to composition of goods and an offence was committed when a cooker in a modified North Sea gas version was sold without a torch, despite a notice that specifications might be changed without notice. The description could also be regarded as coming within '(e) any physical characteristics not included in the preceding paragraphs'.

Linked with '(d) fitness for purpose' are 'strength, performance, behaviour or accuracy'. Thus for example, a 'diver's watch' described as 'waterproof' is not one which fills with water after being immersed in a bowl of water for an hour.[9] Second-hand car sales have not infrequently fallen foul of this paragraph. The courts have been willing to hold that such expressions as 'beautiful car' and 'immaculate condition' are either actually false descriptions within this paragraph where the car though good externally was internally in poor condition, or at least capable of being false, depending on the impact of the description on the ordinary man.[10]

The paragraph dealing with 'approval by any person' etc. lettered (g), was introduced to catch false claims such as that certain encyclopaedias were 'approved' by a well-known educational institution. Falsely stating that an article complies with a British Standard will also be caught here.

7   See *Allard v Selfridge & Co Ltd* [1925] 1 KB 129.
8   [1974] 1 All ER 188, [1974] 1 WLR 37. See also *Denard v Smith* [1991] Crim LR 63, DC, where a placard advertised a computer with a software package including a number of games. The package sold was known to be incomplete. This was held to be a supply of goods to which a false trade description as to composition had been applied.
9   *Sherratt v Geralds The American Jewellers Ltd* (1970) 114 Sol Jo 147; M & H p. 560.
10 Compare *Robertson v Dicicco* [1972] RTR 431, and *Kensington and Chelsea (Royal) London Borough Council v Riley* [1973] RTR 122, both decisions of the Divisional Court. See also *Hawkins v Smith* [1978] Crim LR 578 when it was held at the Portsmouth Crown Court that a dealer's advertisement that a car was in 'showroom condition throughout' contravened s. 1(1)(b), and (obiter) that 'showroom condition' referred to exterior, interior and mechanical condition.

Paragraph (i) deals with statements as to 'by whom manufactured, produced, processed or reconditioned'. It is debatable whether a name on 'own brand' goods necessarily denotes that the named person is the manufacturer. The practice of putting a trader's name on goods which he has imported, packed, bought wholesale or designed is so widespread that it could probably be argued that the description was not false so as to mislead the public.[11] Prosecutions founded on this paragraph could also be brought by or on behalf of manufacturers in respect of the 'passing off' of their goods by rival manufacturers. Examples might be marketing preserved milk labelled 'Nissley-brand', thus infringing Nestlé's trade mark[12] or marketing cough sweets in Singapore so packaged as to lead non-English speaking buyers to confuse them with 'Hacks' cough sweets.[13]

Paragraph (j) deals with 'other history, including previous ownership or use'. This covers such descriptions as 'Railway Lost Property', 'Army Surplus', 'one lady owner' and the like. An indication of a vehicle's age by reference to its date of registration or its suffix letter on a number plate is caught[14] as is the common case of a car's odometer registering a lower mileage than the true one, this being capable of being a trade description applied by the seller at the time of the offer for sale – a point discussed later in this chapter.

Section 2 goes on to state that the above matters in relation to animals include sex, breed or cross, fertility and soundness, and in relation to semen, the identity and characteristics of the animal from which it was taken and measure of dilution (section 2(2)). Descriptions and marks applied in pursuance of a number of statutes dealing with horticulture and agriculture are deemed not to be trade descriptions (section 2(4)), nor are descriptions applied pursuant to the food and drugs legislation (section 2(5)).

References in the Act to 'goods' include ships and aircraft, things attached to land and growing crops (section 39(1)).

Falsely indicating that goods or services are as supplied to the Royal Family or simulating the Queen's Award to Industry device

---

11   See *O'Keefe* op cit.
12   *Niblett Ltd v Confectioners Materials Co Ltd* [1921] 3 KB 387 (seller held to have broken condition as to right to sell the tins, under Sale of Goods Act 1893, s. 12).
13   *White Hudson & Co Ltd v Asian Organisation Ltd* [1965] 1 All ER 1040, [1964] 1 WLR 1466, PC. See also *J Bollinger v Costa Brava Wine Co Ltd* [1960] Ch 262, [1959] 3 All ER 800 (calling wine made in Spain 'Spanish Champagne', infringed the exclusive right of the wine producers of the Champagne district of France to that description).
14   See *R v Haesler* [1973] RTR 486. See also *Routledge v Ansa Motors (Chester-le-Street) Ltd* [1980] Crim LR 65 (car manufactured in 1972 but first registered in 1975 capable of being falsely described as 'one used 1975 Ford Escort').

are separate offences under section 12. Similar false indications of supply to 'any person' are caught by section 13.

'supplies or offers to supply any goods to which a false trade description is applied'

Section 6 elucidates the first part of the above by stating that a person exposing goods for supply or having goods in his possession for supply shall be deemed to offer to supply them. The section is deliberately widely drafted. It avoids the type of difficulty found in such cases as *Fisher v Bell*[15] where flick knives were displayed in a shop window, this being an invitation to treat rather than an 'offer for sale' contrary to section 1(1) of the Restriction of Offensive Weapons Act 1959. Such goods would have been 'exposed' for sale. Even if the goods to which a false trade description is applied belong to someone else so that it could not be said that the seller has them 'in his possession for supply', he still 'exposes them for supply'. The Trade Descriptions Act thus catches a variety of operations provided 'possession for supply' is proved, whether or not the supplier is e.g. a warehouseman selling to traders or a mail order firm selling to the public. The word 'supply' is wider than 'sale', and would seem to cover free gifts if the supply is made in the course of trade or business, as well as hire and hire-purchase transactions, goods for gift tokens and the like.[16]

It is clear from the expression 'is applied' that a sale etc. of goods already bearing a false description put on by a third party is caught.

Trade descriptions used in advertisements

Advertisements tend to generalise, so it is necessary to provide a fair test to enable the courts to identify whether a particular advertisement applicable to a class of goods has applied a trade description to particular goods. Section 5(2) states that the trade description shall be taken as referring to all goods of the class, whether or not in existence at the time the advertisement is published, for the purpose of determining whether an offence under section 1(1)(a) (applying a false trade description to goods) has been committed. The same applies to offences under section 1(1)(b) where goods of the class are supplied or offered to be supplied by a person publishing or displaying the advertisement – thus catching mail order sales for example.

15   [1961] 1 QB 394, [1960] 3 All ER 731.
16   For a decision illustrating the breadth of this concept see *Stainthorpe v Bailey* [1980] RTR 7, DC; M & H p. 481, considered post.

Section 5(3) states that when determining whether goods are of a class to which an advertised trade description relates regard shall be had not only to the form and content of the advertisement but also to the time, place, manner and frequency of its publication and all other matters making it likely or unlikely that a person to whom the goods are supplied would think of the goods belonging to the class in question. This is an attempt to ensure that the advertised trade description can fairly be regarded as current and applicable to the goods in question.

'Advertisement' is widely defined to include a catalogue, a circular and a price list (section 39(1)); but a printed, filmed, or broadcast trade description is not deemed to be made in the course of a trade or business unless it forms part of an advertisement (section 39(2)). This provision is designed to prevent prosecutions founded on descriptions contained in genuine news items.

Disclaimers

Offences arising out of the sale of cars with false odometer readings are the most prevalent offence dealt with by enforcement authorities. The question of disclaimers frequently arises in this context since an offence under section 1(1)(b) is committed if the odometer reading is false and undisclaimed, whether or not the seller is aware that the trade description is false. In *Norman v Bennett*[17] a purchaser looked at a second-hand car not yet prepared for sale in a saleroom. The exposed odometer reading was some 23,000 miles though the true mileage was about 68,000 miles. The purchaser questioned the low mileage and was told by a salesman that they had been told it was a director's car (apparently regarded as a sufficient explanation for low mileages). The purchaser agreed to buy it, knowing from previous dealings that he would have to sign an agreement. A little later he read and signed an agreement containing the words 'speedometer reading not guaranteed'. He had read and signed similar agreements before.

On appeal to the Divisional Court against dismissal of the information by the magistrates' court the Lord Chief Justice stated that, to be effective, a disclaimer 'must be as bold, precise and compelling as the trade description itself and must be as effectively brought to the notice of any person to whom the goods may be supplied. In other words, the disclaimer must equal the trade description in the extent to which it is likely to get home to anyone

17 [1974] 3 All ER 351.

interested in receiving the goods.'[18] This was not the case here, though on the particular facts since the buyer and seller were both experienced dealers in cars, a trade description had not been effectively applied.

It is now the practice of some car dealers thoroughly to cover odometer readings on dashboards with adhesive tape to prevent this being a trade description, it being established beyond doubt that a reading on the car's odometer is an indication of the use that it has had within section 2(1)(j). Another practice has been to 'zero' the odometer, which seemed to meet with the approval of the Divisional Court in *K Lill (Holdings) v White*.[19] In that case Lord Widgery said that he could see a great deal of merit in this practice because it seemed that, for the time being at all events, it put the problem of a false odometer out of the reckoning because no-one would be misled by such a record. However the Court of Appeal in *R v Southwood*[20] firmly stated that a person who zeroed the odometer was applying a false trade description just as much as a person who reduced it to, say, 15,000 miles. The Court of Appeal went on to confirm the proposition, discussed below in the context of 'clocking' cars, that it was not open to a person who had actively applied a false trade description in this way to purport to disclaim it by stickers or notices. If a disclaimer were to be effective at all it could only be appropriate to a charge laid under section 1(1)(b) where the false trade description had already been applied by somebody other than the supplier in question of the vehicle. Once the trade description has been made, a casual remark or 'small print' in a document are not enough to disclaim it. The true effect of an operative disclaimer is to negative the making of a trade description; it is not a defence once one has been made.[1]

The same point was reiterated in a case of importance to auctioneers, amongst some of whom there was thought to be a myth that the Act did not apply to those operating in the 'Art World'![2] An auction catalogue described a painting as being by JMW Turner

---

18   Ibid. at 354. The Lord Chief Justice also thought that 'applied' in s. 1(1)(b) meant applied at the time of supply or have been so applied in the course of negotiations leading to such supply. This decision was followed in *Zawadski v Sleigh* [1975] RTR 113.

19   [1979] JP 534, [1979] RTR 120, M & H p. 495.

20   (1987) 131 Sol Jo 1038.

1   See further on these points *R v Hammertons Cars Ltd* [1976] 3 All ER 758, [1976] 1 WLR 1243, CA (Criminal Division). The defence under Trade Descriptions Act 1968, s. 24 that the seller, by making enquiries of his own seller etc. has exercised all due diligence, is apparently not normally enough unless accompanied by a disclaimer; see *Simmons v Potter* [1975] RTR 347.

2   *May v Vincent* (1990) 154 JP 997, [1991] 1 EGLR 27, DC.

when the auctioneer knew that it was not. The catalogue contained a clear and comprehensive disclaimer. The Divisional Court allowed an appeal against the justices' acquittal on a charge of applying a false trade description to a painting. The disclaimer could not give a defence to applying a false trade description. (The point also arises in the context of clocking cars considered below.)

The concept of the disclaimer has been criticised as not clearly being permitted by section 1. The consultative document published by the Office of Fair Trading entitled 'Review of the Trade Descriptions Act 1968'[3] discussed the problem and recommends (inter alia) that disclaimers should be allowed to continue except in respect to descriptions applied by the trader to goods in his possession at the time. One reason given is that traders might otherwise cease to check second-hand goods and simply seek to repudiate all responsibilities for the accuracy of descriptions.[4] This conclusion by the Review Committee has also been strongly criticised on the grounds that the supposed difficulties of disallowing disclaimers are not 'insuperable' and that the decision in *Norman v Bennett* may encourage 'blanket' disclaimers as a substitute for checking descriptions already applied to goods properly before sale.[5] The most recent consultative document issued by the government (April 1990) suggests only that a new order-making power might be introduced controlling the use of disclaimers in specific areas of difficulty, such as descriptions of land and houses. 'Judicial decisions. . . have now more fully settled the scope for their legitimate and effective use'.[6]

Specific areas of difficulty

a) 'Clocking' cars

Reducing the mileage shown on the odometer of a used car is probably the most persistent offence under the Trade Descriptions Act and reference has already been made to it under 'Disclaimers' above. In October 1978 the Director General of Fair Trading stated that in the course of making 1,614 routine checks, over 50 per cent of vehicles were found to have been 'clocked', costing purchasers an estimated £50 million a year. The Director has threatened to use his powers to withhold, suspend or revoke a dealer's consumer credit licence or to demand assurances under Part 3 of the Fair Trading Act

---

3 Cmnd. 6628 (1976), discussed further below.
4 See R. G. Lawson (1974) 124 NLJ 622–623.
5 Gordon Borrie [1975] Crim LR 662, 667–669.
6 The text of the DTI's published consultative letter appears in (1990) 7 Trading Law 115–124. See also P Cartwright (1991) 141 NLJ 888. The proposals are further considered at p. 371.

1973 where dealers are found to be indulging in this practice. By March 1980 some fifty-three motor traders had had their licences revoked or renewals refused and almost three times that number had received warnings. In November 1980 a report was made by the Office of Fair Trading to the Secretary of State for Trade and the Minister of Transport recommending legislation a) for the compulsory provision by dealers of a pre-sales report about the condition of used cars under ten years old, b) for the introduction of tamper-proof mileometers, c) for the provision of a standard notice to be used by all dealers unable to verify a mileage reading, d) for the provision of an expanded vehicle registration document giving details of previous owners. The Director General explained that the background to these recommendations was a steep rise in the number of complaints about used cars (50,000 in 1979) and trade description convictions (used car dealers accounting for 65 per cent of all trade description offences). In March 1981 a revised Motor Code of Practice was promulgated making it compulsory for members to verify odometer readings or to warn the customer that this has not been done – as mentioned in chapter 11.

In the context of 'clocking', the strict attitude of the courts to the sale of cars bearing false odometer readings is illustrated by the following cases. In *Holloway v Cross*[7] a motor trader had been convicted by Chatham Justices on charges of applying a false trade description contrary to section 1(1)(a) and (b) of the Act. The dealer had bought a Triumph car, first registered in 1973, of which the mileage was in fact in excess of 70,000. However, when he bought it, the odometer read only 716 miles. When a buyer saw the car and asked the defendant about the mileage it was made clear that the defendant did not know the true mileage but promised to make enquiries. He subsequently gave an opinion that the mileage was probably about 45,000 and the defendant wrote on the used-car invoice 'recorded mileage 716, estimated mileage 45,000 miles'. The justices had concluded that such an estimate was an opinion, and it therefore did not fall within section 2(1)(j) which provides that a trade description is an indication, whether direct or indirect and by whatever means, of any matter with respect to goods, including their history, previous ownership and use. However, they held that it was within the extension to the concept of a false trade description provided by section 3(3) and the disparity between the estimate and the actual mileage was sufficiently large to render the estimate false to a material degree. Donaldson LJ considered that it was debatable whether or not section 2 applied to the situation bearing in mind that

---

7   [1981] 1 All ER 1012, DC; M & H p. 489. S. 3(3) is discussed above.

section 2(1) relates to an indication 'direct or indirect'. In any event it was clear that the defendant's estimate was likely to be taken by the buyer as an indication of the history of the vehicle and, if that was so, it was one which was false to a material degree. The defendant's opinion was only relevant in so far as the buyer wished for an indication as to what the mileage was. The words complained of therefore amounted to a false description within section 3(3). The appeal was dismissed.

Another 'clocking' case of particular interest to Trading Standards Officers is *Stainthorpe v Bailey*.[8] In this case the defendant motor dealer advertised a van for sale knowing that the odometer incorrectly recorded a mileage of 36,000 miles, the true mileage being more than 97,000 miles. An officer from the Trading Standards Department visited the firm's premises and was re-directed to the home of the defendant. The van was parked outside the house. The officer asked 'Is that van for sale?'; the defendant said 'Yes, the keys are in it if you want to have a look round', and dealt with a telephone call at his house. When the defendant went outside the officer had gone. The Divisional Court directed the magistrates to convict on the basis (inter alia) that the defendant had exposed goods for supply and having them in his possession for supply, he was deemed to offer to supply them by virtue of section 6 of the Act. Nor had the defendant taken reasonable precautions and exercised all due diligence to avoid the commission of the offence, such as making a disclaimer as to the accuracy of the recorded mileage.

Corfield v Starr[9] involved a purported disclaimer which the Divisional Court considered emphasised the point that some disclaimers could themselves give rise to a false trade description.[10] Here the disclaimer placed on a dashboard reading of 35,000 miles known by the defendant to be incorrect read: 'With deep regret due to Customer's Protection Act we can no longer verify that the mileage shown on this vehicle is correct.' As Bingham J pointed out, 'the notice here referred to an Act of Parliament which does not exist and gives to it an effect which no Act of Parliament in fact has . . . In my judgment, to counteract the statement (of mileage) on this odometer some statement would be needed clearly conveying to a customer or prospective customer that no reliance could be placed on the mileage

8   [1980] RTR 7, M & H p. 481.
9   [1981] RTR 380, DC, M & H p. 497.
10 This point is emphasised by the decision of the Divisional Court in *Newman v Hackney London Borough Council* [1982] RTR 296, M & H p. 498 where a car with an odometer reading of 46,000 miles had had the reading reduced deliberately by the defendants to 21,000 miles, which lower reading could still be seen despite a disclaimer stuck over it. The court held that it is not possible to disclaim the effect of one's own deliberate fraud.

reading for any purpose whatever, or that the reading was meaningless.' It was held that the justices should accordingly have convicted.

The Court of Appeal has now emphasised that the deliberate turning back of an odometer was in direct conflict with Parliament's intention that goods should be honestly described and convicted defendants should expect a term of imprisonment.[11]

b) Goods described as 'new'

The Molony Committee recommended that there should be added to the definition of 'trade description' formerly contained in the Merchandise Marks Acts, descriptions 'as to any goods being new in the sense of being unused' (para. 636), but this does not appear explicitly in the Act. The problem has arisen particularly in the context of sales of cars and components.

In *R v Ford Motor Co Ltd*[12] a dealer ordered from Ford a Cortina car and later sold it to a customer describing it in the invoice as 'one new Ford Cortina'. Unknown to dealer and customer the car had been damaged in process of delivery and repaired under insurance for about £50. Ford appealed against its conviction in the Crown Court for applying the false trade description 'new' contrary to section 1(1)(b) and causing the dealer to do the same, contrary to section 23. The Court of Appeal quashed the convictions because 1) the repairs were not intended to conceal defects but to restore the car to sound condition, and could not therefore themselves amount to a false description, and 2) although it could be deemed to have applied a trade description under section 4(3), a car was not necessarily falsely described as 'new' if such damage as occurs is 'perfectly repaired so that it can in truth be said after repairs have been effected that the car is as good as new'. The court added that there must nevertheless come a point when damage is so serious that a car could not be repaired so as to qualify it as 'new'. There are obvious difficulties if this decision is taken too far. Buyers can surely assume in the normal way that 'new' goods travel from production line to retail outlet in pristine condition. Any repair, however skilful, can affect the durability of goods.[13] However, it will be noted that even had the Molony Committee's suggestion been implemented the car in this case would still presumably have been 'unused'.

A similar problem can arise where a car manufactured in one year,

---

11   *R v Hewitt* (1991) Times, 21 June.
12   [1974] 3 All ER 489, [1974] 1 WLR 1220, M & H p. 484.
13   See discussion *obiter* in *Cottee v Douglas Seaton (Used Cars) Ltd* [1972] 3 All ER 750, [1972] 1 WLR 1408 as to whether a car which has been cleverly repaired so as to conceal corrosion 'tells a lie about itself' so as to apply a false trade description within Trade Descriptions Act 1968, s. 2 (indication of strength).

say 1972, is first registered in a later one, say 1975, and then advertised as a 'used 1975 Ford' – see *Routledge v Ansa Motors (Chester-le-Street) Ltd*.[14] The Divisional Court held that this could lead customers to think 1975 the year of manufacture and, in that event, the statement was false to a material degree. The practice of calling 'new' a car which is bought new from the manufacturer and then registered in the retail garage's name before a retail sale takes place (so that the purchaser is actually the second registered owner) was disapproved of in *R v Anderson*.[15] Although the cars here were undeniably mint, the description 'new' implied that there had been no previous registered owners.

5. FALSE OR MISLEADING STATEMENTS AS TO SERVICES, ETC.

Section 14 of the 1968 Act goes beyond the recommendations of the Molony Committee in laying down novel provisions to control statements about services, accommodation or facilities. As has already been noted, this is not an absolute offence, as can be seen from its wording:

1) It shall be an offence for any person in the course of any trade or business–
   a) to make a statement which he knows to be false; or
   b) recklessly to make a statement which is false;

as to any of the following matters in the course of any trade or business, and there then follow five provisions as to (i) the provision of, (ii) the nature of, (iii) the time at which, manner in which, or persons by whom services, accommodation or facilities are provided, or (iv) their examination, approval or evaluation by any person, or (v) the location or amenities of accommodation.

As to 'recklessly', a statement is deemed to be made recklessly if it is made regardless of whether it is true or false, whether or not the person making it had reasons for believing that it might be false (section 14(2)(b)). It was held in *MFI Warehouses Ltd v Nattrass*[16] that 'recklessly' does not imply dishonestly. The prosecution need only show that the defendant did not have regard to the truth or falsity of his statement, even though it cannot be proved he

---

14 [1980] RTR 1, and for used goods marked 'Display Stock Clearance' see (1985) 4 Trading Law 32.
15 (1987) 152 JP 373, CA.
16 [1973] 1 All ER 762, [1973] 1 WLR 307, M & H p. 513 (misleading advertisement for 'folding door gear (carriage free)' not intended by advertisers to mislead).

deliberately closed his eyes to the truth. This rather diminishes the force of the *mens rea* requirement.[17]

Section 14 was further and exhaustively analysed by the House of Lords in *Wings Ltd v Ellis*[18] where, as stated by Lord Scarman, 'the basic issue between the parties is whether on its proper construction s. 14(1)(a) of the 1968 Act creates an offence of strict, or more accurately semi-strict, liability or is one requiring the existence of full mens rea'. The actual point certified by the Divisional Court as being of general public importance was whether a defendant may properly be convicted of an offence under section 14(1)(a) of the Trade Descriptions Act 1968 where he had no knowledge of the falsity of the statement at the time of its publication but knew of the falsity at the time when the statement was read by the complainant. The facts, briefly, were that for the 1981/82 winter season the appellant tour operator had distributed to travel agents a brochure giving details of accommodation provided for customers. Shortly after the brochure was distributed the tour operator discovered that the brochure contained a statement which was false to a material degree, namely that the accommodation provided at a hotel in Sri Lanka was furnished with air conditioning. In May 1981 the mistake was discovered and steps were taken to mitigate its effects but W. had booked a holiday in January 1982 depending on an unamended brochure. At the time W. read the unamended brochure the tour operators were aware that the statement was false. The House of Lords unanimously upheld the prosecutor's appeal against the Divisional Court which had quashed the original conviction of the tour operators. 'The brochure was inaccurate, the respondent knew that it was inaccurate and W. was misled. The ingredients for an offence under s. 14 were compounded. To hold otherwise would be to emasculate s. 14 and to place a premium on carelessness by the respondents' (per Lord Templeman). It was pointed out that although the tour operators never intended to make a false statement to W. an offence had been committed under section 14 and the respondent tour operators had not attempted to put forward a defence under section 24, which might otherwise have been available, that the commission of the offence was due to a mistake etc. and all

17   See generally D. L. Rudkin 'Misdescriptions of Goods, Services and Property' (1978) 122 Sol Jo 119 et seq. In *Westminster City Council v Ray Alan (Manshops) Ltd* [1982] 1 All ER 771, [1982] 1 WLR 383 it was held that a suspect 'closing down sale' was not offering a 'facility' within the meaning of this section. The section applied to facilities *ejusdem generis* with services or accommodation, not, for instance, to shopping facilities.

18   [1985] AC 272, [1984] 3 All ER 577, M & H p. 516. See also *Yugotours v Wadsley* [1988] BTLC 300. (Failure to correct a statement known to be false can be reckless within s. 14(1) (b).)

reasonable precautions and all due diligence had been exercised to prevent the commission of the offence. Lord Brandon of Oakfield, in a concurring speech, added that he would have regarded the false statement about air conditioning contained in the respondent's brochures as having been a continuing false statement, that is to say a false statement which continued to be made so long as such brochures remained in circulation without effective correction. An advertisement exhibited on a street hoarding would be regarded in the same way.

Making a false statement about 'services' includes a person stating falsely, in the course of trade or business, that he has certain professional qualifications since this affects the likely quality of the services,[19] though employees with a tendency to overstatement are outside the ambit of the Act as regards their employers, since 'services' does not include anything done under a contract of service (section 14(4)). It was also made clear by the Divisional Court in *Newell v Hicks*[20] that where an advertisement offered 'a video cassette recorder absolutely free with every X registration Renault . . .' this was not a false statement as to the provision of services, accommodation or facilities within the meaning of section 14. This was because the word 'provision' could only be read as being concerned with the fact of providing services, accommodation or facilities and not as relating to the terms upon which they are provided. In other words section 14 does not comprehend statements as to price in relation to services, accommodation or facilities. Similarly, it was held in *Dixons Ltd v Roberts*[21] that the statement, 'refund the difference if you buy Dixon's Deal products cheaper locally at time of purchase and call within seven days' was not capable of giving rise to liability under section 14. 'It is impossible to accept that the offer of a refund on part of the price of goods could be taken as an offer to provide services' (per Forbes J).

A major problem under this section is as to where the line should

---

19 *R v Breeze* [1973] 2 All ER 1141, [1973] 1 WLR 994, M & H pp. 500 and 509, (person who had passed only the intermediate stage of an architect's qualification falsely described himself as an architect. The argument that s.14 applied to 'businesses' not 'professions' was also not approved.) In *R v Bow Street Magistrates Court, ex p Joseph* (1986) 150 JP 650, DC it was held that The Law Society did not carry on any trade or business and so could not commit any offence under this section.

20 (1983) 148 JP 308, (1983) 128 Sol Jo 63, M & H p. 509. Facts of this sort should be assessed instead in the light of the pricing provisions of Part III of the Consumer Protection Act 1987, below.

21 (1984) 148 JP 513, DC, M & H p. 512. Para 1.5.2. of the Code of Practice on Pricing (see below) states 'Do not make statements like "if you can buy this product elsewhere for less we will refund the difference" about your "own brand" products which other traders do not stock, unless your offer will also apply to other traders' equivalent goods.'

be drawn in distinguishing what is merely a breach of contract not within the mischief of the Act, and statements which are false or misleading within section 14 as well, in many cases, as being breaches of warranty. This point is illustrated by *R v Sunair Holidays Ltd.*[1] Travel agents had published a brochure in 1969 for the 1970 season relating to a Spanish hotel in the course of which they made a number of glowing references to hotel facilities, including a swimming pool, push chairs for hire at the hotel and special dishes for children. When the customer got there the swimming pool was empty and could not be filled, push chairs were not available at the hotel and there were no special dishes for children. The travel agents were convicted and the Court of Appeal allowed the appeal on the grounds that section 14 dealt with statements of which it could be said that they were false at the time they were made – i.e. statements of fact, past or present, but not promises or forecasts about the future, as such. Although in some cases a promise might imply a statement about the present, in this case the statements referred to the future.[2] Similarly in *Beckett v Cohen*[3] where a builder agreed to build for a customer a garage like his neighbour's 'within 10 days', and did not do so, the Divisional Court upheld the magistrates' court's dismissal of the information. This was a statement made in regard to the future. The Act could not be used to make a breach of contract into a criminal offence.

As the law now stands careful analysis is, therefore, required of the relevant statements to ascertain whether they are promises in the nature of a fallible forecast or whether the statement, although relating to services to be performed in the future, also contains a statement of existing fact. The point is again illustrated by the House of Lords decision in *British Airways Board v Taylor*.[4] There a prospective passenger was booked by BOAC on a flight to Bermuda and a letter 'confirming the following reservation London/Bermuda BA 679 Economy Class – 28 August' had been received. BOAC in common with many other airlines operated an 'overbooking' policy

1   [1973] 2 All ER 1233, [1973] 1 WLR 1105.
2   Cf. *R v Clarksons Holidays Ltd* (1972) 116 Sol Jo 728 where a number of statements about a hotel not yet built and illustrated by an 'artist's impression' were construed by the jury as being a representation of existing facts, and the ensuing conviction was upheld as being proper by the Court of Appeal.
3   [1973] 1 All ER 120, [1972] 1 WLR 1593.
4   [1975] 3 All ER 307, [1975] 1 WLR 1197. However, a pre- or post-contractual statement relating to services (as opposed to goods) may be caught by Trade Descriptions Act 1968, s. 14 as in *Breed v Cluett* [1970] 2 QB 459, [1970] 2 All ER 662, M & H p. 501 – statement after exchange of contracts that bungalow covered by National Housebuilders' Registration Council scheme made by builder-owner was false and builder convicted under s.14. See also *Cowburn v Focus Television Rentals Ltd* (1983) 2 Tr L 89, DC.

on the usually correct assumption that some passengers would fail to arrive at the airport. At the time of the letter the flight was not overbooked, but it subsequently became so and no seat was available for the passenger. The House of Lords held that the justices had been entitled to find as a fact that the statement in the letter was false within section 14, Lord Edmund Davies in particular stating that the facts illustrated that an assertion of existing fact and a promise of future conduct may both be found in one and the same statement. The factual statement here was that a booking could be confirmed when the overbooking policy made it impossible to do this. The appeal was in fact allowed in the Airline's favour on the technical ground that British Airways were not criminally liable for the acts of the former BOAC.

Property misdescriptions

Although section 14 of the Trade Descriptions Act 1968 applies to false or misleading statements as to any 'services, accommodation or facilities', it has been clear for many years that neither this section nor the Act generally applies to sales of interests in land (as opposed to the provision of short-term holiday accommodation). Thus paragraph 70 of the Review of the Trade Descriptions Act 1968 (1976) states:

> Although section 39 defines goods as including things attached to land, it is generally agreed that houses for sale do not come within this definition and are therefore outside the scope of section 1. In addition, although section 14 applies to statements about accommodation, this section is considered unlikely to cover statements relating to such matters as the disposal of a long lease.

The Review then goes on to state that though this omission is understandable there was a need to deal with false statements about house property 'which constitutes the ordinary person's most expensive purchase' (see para.71). In March 1990 the Director General of Fair Trading in his Report on Estate Agency, recommended new legislation to give more protection to consumers.

In 1990 a Private Member's Bill was introduced, sponsored by the Consumers' Association, to deal with property misdescriptions. The ambit of the Bill was widened considerably during its course to take account of statements made by builders, property developers and solicitors (when engaged in estate agency work), though the main target of the legislation is clearly a estate agency businesses. Its short title indicates its ambit – the Property Misdescriptions Act 1991.[5]

5   See Richard Bragg 'Regulation of Estate Agents' (1992) 55 MLR 368.

The Act makes it an offence to make a false or misleading statement about a prescribed matter in the course of an estate agency business or a property development business, otherwise than in providing conveyancing services (section 1). The Act makes it clear that where the making of a statement is attributable to the fault of an employee, the employee is guilty of an offence whether or not proceedings are also taken against the employer. The offence carries, on summary conviction, a fine of the statutory maximum and on conviction on indictment, an unlimited fine. The making of such a false statement does not affect the validity of the underlying contract, and no right of action in civil proceedings in respect of any loss arises by reason only of the commission of such an offence.

The terms 'false' and 'misleading' are defined in a similar way to that applicable to false trade descriptions generally and a 'prescribed matter' is any matter relating to land specified in an Order made by the Secretary of State under section 1 (5)(d). No Order has at present been made and, though the Act is in force, it follows that no prosecution could be brought under it pending the making of such an Order.

The statements in question must be made in the course of an estate agency business or a property development business. The latter means that the statement must be made 1) in the course of a business concerned wholly or substantially with the development of land, and 2) for the purpose of, or with a view to, disposing of an interest in land consisting of or including a building, or a part of a building, constructed or renovated in the course of the business. The ambit of section 1 is therefore wide since it covers not only the activities of 'an estate agency business' but also property development business concerned with the disposal of buildings or parts of buildings. An estate agency business involves 'estate agency work' as defined by section 1 of the Estate Agents Act 1979 – broadly, disposing of or acquiring an interest in land on the instructions of a client with a view to the introduction of a third party who wishes to acquire or dispose of the relevant interest in land.

There is a 'due diligence defence' whereby the defendant must show 'that he took all reasonable steps and exercised all due diligence to avoid committing the offence'. Where this involves reliance on information given by another it must be shown to have been reasonable to have relied on the information in the light of steps which had been taken to verify it and consideration of whether he had any reason to disbelieve the information (section 2). There is a requirement, common in trading law statutes, that if third parties are to be joined in, seven clear days' notice must be given to the prosecutor to identify the person who committed the act or default.

6. DEFENCES

The 1968 Act includes defences which are similar to defences provided by other penal consumer law statutes, e.g. weights and measures and food and drugs laws,[6] and mitigate the rigour of the strict liability imposed by sections 1 and (the former) 11.[7] The defences are primarily in section 24, but section 25 provides a defence that an advertisement committing an offence under the Act was published in the course of such a business and that the publisher 'did not know and had no reason to suspect that its publication would amount to an offence'. Section 23, dealing with offences due to the fault of some other person is not strictly a defence provision, but it is convenient to examine section 23 along with section 24.

Section 24(1) states that, subject to the procedure laid down in section 24(2), it shall be a defence for the accused to prove (on the balance of probabilities) that he comes within *both* the following paragraphs:

a) that the commission of the offence was due to a mistake or to reliance on information supplied to him or to the act or default of another person, an accident or some other cause beyond his control; and

b) that he took all reasonable precautions and exercised all due diligence to avoid the commission of such an offence by himself or any person under his control.

Subsection (2) provides, in effect, that an accused relying on the act or default of or on information supplied by another person must give, at least seven days before the hearing, written notice to the prosecution giving such information to identify the other person as was then in his possession.

Subsection (3) provides a further defence to charges of supplying or offering to supply goods to which a false trade description is applied. The accused must prove 'that he did not know, and could not with reasonable diligence have ascertained, that the goods did not conform to the description or that the description had been applied to the goods'. In *Barker v Hargreaves*[8] a second-hand car dealer advertised a car as being 'in good condition throughout' and sold it on that basis. The dealer had submitted it successfully for an MOT test and obtained the usual certificate containing printed warnings that the certificate should not be accepted as evidence of

---

6 See generally M & H ch. 14 – general statutory defences in consumer protection legislation.

7 They can less often be appropriate to s. 14 which has a built-in requirement of knowledge or recklessness.

8 (1980) 125 Sol Jo 165, M & H p. 554.

the car's condition. The car was in fact badly corroded on the underside, though this was partially hidden by undersealing and other factors. On a charge under section 1(1)(b) of applying a false trade description by advertisement the defendant relied on section 24(3) above – i.e. that he had relied on the information in the test certificate. The Divisional Court upheld the justices' conviction of the defendant. With reasonable diligence some of the corrosion could have been discovered. Nor could the defence under section 24(1) be prayed in aid. The defendant had relied solely on the certificate, which contained warnings and he had no system of his own for ascertaining the car's condition.

These defences have been the subject of considerable litigation and the main points of interpretation must be separately discussed.

Act or default of another person (section 24(1)(a)) and reasonable precautions etc. (section 24(1)(b))

Where the defendant is an individual, the expression 'another person' means any person other than himself. But if, for example, the individual blames his supplier, the individual must show that, in addition, he took all reasonable precautions under section 24(1)(b). So in *Naish v Gore*[9] a car originally sold with a recorded mileage of 83,060 ended up after several further sales with a recorded mileage of 35,000. On a charge brought against the last car dealer involved in respect of applying a false trade description as to the history of the car by means of an incorrect odometer reading the defendant was able to establish a defence under section 24(1)(a) and (b) when he showed that an independent opinion from an Automobile Association expert had been obtained that the car's appearance and performance were consistent with the lower mileage.[10] In the context of the meaning of reasonable precautions, O'Keefe states that the expression involves 'setting up a system to ensure that things will not go wrong: "due diligence" means seeing that the system works properly'.[11]

The words 'another person' cause more difficulty where the defendant is a company and the offence arises out of the act or default of one of its servants. The crucial issue is whether the person alleged for the purposes of the defence to be another person is really the 'ego' or 'alter ego' of the company. The point arose in *Beckett v*

---

9   [1971] 3 All ER 737.
10 This may no longer be enough. In *Simmons v Potter* [1975] RTR 347 the Divisional Court held on somewhat similar facts that the reasonable precaution of publishing an equally prominent disclaimer should have been adopted.
11 O'Keefe, *Law of Weights and Measures*, 2nd Edn. 1 (281). See also the discussion of 'due diligence' below.

Kingston Bros (Butchers) Ltd[12] where a turkey labelled 'Norfolk King Turkey' in fact came from Denmark. The mistake had been identified in the case of the consignment of which this was one, and all area managers had been warned by the managing director to alter the labels. One shop manager failed to comply with these instructions in respect of this turkey. The defendant company successfully established that the manager was 'another person', the Divisional Court stating that it would stultify the defence under section 24 if it were the law that because the person truly responsible for the offence was an employee the employer, provided he had taken reasonable precautions and shown due diligence, was still debarred from using the defence. The same question arose in the House of Lords' decision in *Tesco Supermarkets Ltd v Nattrass*.[13] One of the chain of supermarkets whose staff had been efficiently trained displayed a 'flash' offer on a poster relating to money off the usual price of washing powder. The shop had run out of the packets to which they intended to apply the reduced price, being packets bearing a special indication of reduced price, and a shopper failed to get the price of an ordinary packet reduced. This had occurred because the shop manager had failed to supervise the actions of his assistant who had put out on display only the remaining full price packets. The company was summonsed under the provisions of section 11(2) (giving an indication that goods are being offered at a price less than that at which they are in fact being offered). It was held that the shop manager was 'another person' from his employing company. He could not be identified with the company itself or its *alter ego*. Lord Reid said that managers to whom functions are delegated by the company's board of directors are capable of being part of the embodiment of the company (and see section 20), but here the board

> had set up a chain of command through regional and district supervisors, but they remained in control. The shop managers had to obey their general directions and also take orders from their superiors. The acts or omissions of shop managers were not acts of the company itself.[14]

The company's duty as to 'reasonable precautions' and 'due diligence' was to set up an efficient system of training and show due diligence in subsequent inspections to see that the law was complied with, which it had done. But, as regards the identification of the other

---

12 [1970] 1 QB 606, [1970] 1 All ER 715.
13 [1972] AC 153, M & H p. 555. See also *Lewin v Rothersthorpe Road Garage Ltd* (1984) 148 JP 87, to the same effect.
14 Ibid. at 175. See the criticism of this decision by Sir Gordon Borrie in *The Development of Consumer Law and Policy* pp. 52–53, M & H p. 559.

person, it has since been held that to avoid the administration of the Act becoming slipshod, the company must show that it has done all that could reasonably be expected in inquiring and investigating into the matter of who was responsible for the act or default, and identify him or them as far as possible.[15]

The concept of showing 'due diligence' is to be found in parallel defence sections of many other trading law statutes – and is mentioned again in this book in the context (for instance) of food offences. A full survey of the cases, some unreported, will be found in the standard trading law encyclopaedias. Suffice it to say here that the defendant will normally have to prove that 1) any staff responsible for the mischief in question were sensibly selected and properly trained, 2) a proper system exists for checking potentially offending stock, and if this is by sample, a reasonably comprehensive sample should be taken, and 3) any defect e.g. in a misdescribed car is truly latent. In summary, a positive and effective screening system must be shown to exist.

Mistake, accident, cause beyond accused's control

It was held in *Birkenhead and District Co-operative Society Ltd v Roberts*[16] that where the alleged offence arose out of the mis-labelling by the defendant's servant of a joint of beef, a 'mistake' by any person other than the one charged did not come within paragraph (a). If 'act or default of another person' had been pleaded the procedure as to seven days' notice would have had to be followed.

There are a number of reported decisions on the similar weights and measures legislation as to the meaning of these words. For instance, a manufacturer successfully established that a bag of crisps bore a wrong indication of its weight owing to an unforeseen fault in a well maintained and normally accurate machine, and this was a cause beyond the manufacturer's control.[17]

Section 24(3)

This involves what might be called a defence of 'innocent supply of goods' to a charge under section 1(1)(b) and is therefore more limited in its scope than the defence under section 24(1), which applies to any offence under the Act. It would be appropriate, for example, to the trader supplied with offending goods where he did not know and had

---

15   *McGuire v Sittingbourne Co-operative Society Ltd* [1976] Crim LR 268.
16   [1970] 3 All ER 391, [1970] 1 WLR 1497.
17   *Bibby-Cheshire v Golden Wonder Ltd* [1972] 3 All ER 738, [1972] 1 WLR 1487.

no cause to suspect that the goods did not conform to the description, or that a description had ever been applied to them.[18]

Section 23

This section allows the prosecution of a person other than the person actually committing the offence where 'the commission by any person of an offence' is due to the act or default of that other person. That other person may be charged and convicted whether or not the person actually committing the offence is prosecuted. Concurrent proceedings are, therefore, permitted and the position is similar to that under section 40 of the Consumer Protection Act 1987.

There is some difficulty with the meaning of 'commission by any person of an offence'. Strictly it might be argued that the first person would not have 'committed an offence' if he could show that he could bring himself within section 24(1)(a) and (b) by proving that it was due to the act or default of another and due diligence etc. However, Lord Widgery CJ explained in *Coupe v Guyett*[19] that where the first person referred to in section 23 had a defence on the merits and without reference to section 24, it is not possible to operate section 23 so as to render guilty the person whose act or default gave rise to the matter in complaint. Conversely, if the first person would have been convicted of an offence but for section 24, he or she can be properly regarded as having 'committed an offence' for the purposes of prosecuting the other person under section 23. (Section 24 would be clearer on the same point if section 24(1)(a) were to refer to 'the commission of the *alleged* offence'.)

It is essential to show a direct causal connection between the offence by the first person and the act or default to which it is due of the other person. Section 23 cannot be used where there are two separate offences or possible offences not causally connected. This point is particularly relevant in the case of the sale of a car with a false odometer reading where the seller thus prima facie commits an offence under section 1(1)(b) in offering to supply goods to which a false trade description is applied. What is the position where a

18 The overlap between ss. 24(1)(a) and 24(3) was discussed in *Naish v Gore*, above where it was suggested that s. 24(3) was more apt where the goods were defective than where there was a representation about them. See also for an unsuccessful attempt to use s. 24(3) where a car's false odometer reading could have been discovered with reasonable diligence, *Lewis v Moloney* [1977] Crim LR 436, DC.

19 [1973] 2 All ER 1058, [1973] 1 WLR 669, M & H p. 564 following dicta of Lord Diplock in *Tesco Supermarkets Ltd v Nattrass*, above. In this case a lady 'sleeping' proprietor of a garage was entirely unaware of a false statement made by her repair workshop manager and was acquitted of an offence under s. 14(1)(b) on this general ground. Accordingly, the 'other person', namely the manager, also had to be acquitted.

previous owner of the car has, for instance, sold it by auction at which the accused bought it some time before? It was held on similar facts found by the magistrates' court in *Tarleton Engineering Co Ltd v Nattrass*[20] that there was no causal connection between the events, the two sales being separated by a period of about three weeks, and even if the 'other person', i.e. the previous owner, had been separately charged under section 1, the 'other person' might have had a defence (e.g. a disclaimer, or act of a further third party under section 24). If a third party were actually found not guilty if separately charged under section 1(1)(b) it would indeed be strange if he were convicted by using section 23 in respect of a later event.

A further controversial point is whether a third party due to whose act or default an offence has been committed may be prosecuted by virtue of section 23 when he is a private individual. It is no objection, of course, to the section 24(1)(a) defence that the third party in question was a private individual (who, for example, turned back an odometer), but may he also be prosecuted if he was not acting in the course of trade or business? Section 23 refers to 'an offence under this Act' being due to another person's default. The offences in sections 1, 9, 12, 13 and 14 all expressly state that the accused must act in the course of a trade or business, and the courts have implied this into the actus reus of the former prices offence under section 11.[1] On the face of it this procedure is improper since the section, in stating that the 'other person shall be guilty of *the* offence' clearly refers back to the commission by any person of 'an offence *under this Act*'. The section also refers to the third party's being charged with 'the offence', similarly interpreted.[2] However the Divisional Court in *Olgeirsson v Kitching*[3] seemed to find little difficulty in extending criminal liability under section 23 to a private person who had falsely represented to a garage salesman that his vehicle had a true mileage of some 36,000 miles less than the reality. Stating that the words of section 23 must be given 'their plain and ordinary meaning', the court went on to decide that criminality was not confined to someone who is engaged in the same trade as the principal offender. The court did, however, query whether that was so only if his act or default was done with full knowledge that what he was doing was false or whether the result may be otherwise if the act or default is neither reckless nor careless. Although some comfort was found by the court

---

20 [1973] 3 All ER 699, [1973] 1 WLR 1261, DC, followed in *Taylor v Smith* [1974] RTR 190.

1 *John v Matthews* [1970] 2 QB 443, [1970] 2 All ER 643.

2 The private person may have committed an offence under some other statute, e.g. obtaining property by deception under Theft Act 1968, s. 15.

3 [1986] BTLC 72.

in the previous decision in *Meah v Roberts*[4] the decision results in the illogical situation that section 23 can apparently be used to prosecute a private individual misdescribing goods which happen to reach the hands of a trader, whereas no prosecution would lie where the goods remain subject to private sales.[5]

It is interesting to note that the government appears to share the concern about this extension in scope of section 23 by judicial decision. The 1990 consultative letter (referred to in more detail below) states (in Annexe A) that judicial decisions have confirmed 'that a private individual, i.e. a person not acting in the course of a trade or business, can be convicted by this means. There is a particular case for requiring knowledge or intention to be shown in such cases as an appropriate safeguard to protect persons who are otherwise generally outside the scope of the Act'. Pointing out that the Consumer Protection Act 1987 explicitly requires the relevant third party's acts or defaults to be done 'in the course of a business of his' thus exempting employees (as opposed to proprietors), a similar approach to that in the 1987 Act (above) could be adopted as an alternative to requiring *mens rea*.

On the question of defences generally, the point which seems to have given rise to the most disquiet is the refusal of the courts to hold companies in effect vicariously liable for the acts of their employees in such circumstances as arose in the *Tesco Supermarkets Ltd v Nattrass* case[6] The OFT's Review suggests that this decision is distorting the operation of the Act and encourages some companies to shoulder all the blame for offences within their organisation, whatever the circumstances, and others to establish due diligence and blame the staff responsible. In the latter case enforcement officers are reluctant to prosecute more lowly employees. The Committee points out (a) that in civil law corporations are vicariously responsible for the negligence of their servants and (b) that the Law Commission (see Working Paper No. 44 (1972)) considers that corporations should be subject to criminal liability in the regulatory field, including under the Trade Descriptions Act. But against this there is the 'potent argument' of Lord Reid in the *Tesco* case to the effect that since, to escape, the employer must show that he has done all that he could do to prevent an offence, 'how can he do more?' The

---

4 [1978] 1 All ER 97, [1977] 1 WLR 1187, discussed in the Food and Drugs context post p. 365.

5 See further the discussion in O'Keete *Law Relating to Trade Descriptions*, para 3 [234].

6 See p. 365, above. See also Gordon Borrie [1975] Crim LR 663–5, who is critical of the Committee's reluctance to impose vicarious responsibility which he considers would promote better trading standards. See also Borrie, *The Development of Consumer Law and Policy*, pp. 52–53.

Committee therefore reaches no decision as to recommendations on this point. The 1990 consultation document referred to below, suggests that a more modern version of the 'due diligence' defence might avoid these problems.

7. SENTENCING AND COMPENSATION ORDERS

As was noticed above, trials of Trade Descriptions Act offences may either be summary or on indictment and alternative penalties are laid down.[7] Whilst the maximum penalty on summary trial is £5,000 under section 18 (as amended), the same section provides for the penalties on conviction on indictment to be a fine (unlimited) or imprisonment for a term not exceeding two years or both. The Divisional Court in *R v Haesler*[8] said that offences under the Trade Descriptions Act, unless accompanied by dishonesty, would not normally be regarded as prison offences. But fines where the defendant has the ability to pay can be substantial. For instance in *R v Hammertons Cars Ltd* [9] the defendants were convicted in the Crown Court on two counts of supplying a motor car with false odometer readings under section 1(1) and fined £1,000 and £500 on each count respectively and ordered to pay cost. The application to the Court of Appeal for leave to appeal against sentence was also dismissed. And where dishonesty *is* involved, such as where a car has been deliberately clocked, the Court of Appeal has stated that a custodial sentence should be expected – see e.g. *R v Nash*.[10]

Since a false trade description can be proliferated by advertisements or holiday brochures, for example, the possibility of multiple prosecutions in different parts of the country, and correspondingly varying penalties, exists. In *R v Thomson Holidays Ltd*[11] the Court of Appeal in a reserved judgment held that false statements in a travel brochure contrary to section 14 are made when communicated to someone, so that each time a false statement was communicated to a reader a fresh offence was committed. It followed that a plea of *autrefois convict* in respect of a similar previous conviction was invalid, nor would the court stay the proceedings as being oppressive. Nevertheless, it was agreed by the OFT Review Committee that

---

7 Above, ch. 8. The offences are thus 'either way' and the procedure under the Magistrates' Courts Act 1980, s. 18 applies. The great majority of offences under the Act are tried summarily.

8 [1973] Crim LR 586 CA.

9 [1976] 3 All ER 758, [1976] 1 WLR 1243, above.

10 [1990] RTR 343 – written-off car cosmetically and inadequately repaired and described as 'in excellent condition'. In fact it was a potential death trap; and *R v Hewitt* (1991) Times, 21 June – turning back odometer.

11 [1974] QB 592, [1974] 1 All ER 823.

multiple prosecutions (though thought to be very rare) could be unduly burdensome both to the courts and the trader.

One complication is the problem of compensation orders. Under the Powers of Criminal Courts Act 1973 (section 35) the court has a discretionary power to impose a compensation order on persons convicted of an offence, or any other offence which is taken into consideration by the court in determining sentence. This provision applies generally, but is used notably in trade descriptions cases. The limit of such an order in the magistrates' courts is £5,000 for each offence of which the offender is convicted (Magistrates' Courts Act 1980, section 40 as amended). It is therefore natural for consumers to wish to encourage the bringing of what are collectively multiple prosecutions in the circumstances outlined above in order to obtain the benefit of a compensation order without incurring the trouble and expense of a separate civil action. The Review Committee state that 'there is clearly a conflict between the public interest in avoiding multiple prosecutions and the private interest in not losing the benefits of compensation which a successful prosecution might bring' (para. 231). They tentatively suggest that the best solution would be to make it a defence for a trader to prove a) that he has been convicted (or presumably acquitted) of an 'identical' offence (i.e. arising out of the same chain of events) before the offence charged and has since taken all reasonable steps to avoid the further commission of an offence, and b) that he has given ex gratia compensation to all aggrieved persons notifying him in writing that they have been injured by this or any 'identical' offence. The Committee draws a parallel with procedures under the Defamation Act 1952, but nevertheless realise that there are many unsolved difficulties in applying the proposed solution.

Compensation orders are discussed in more detail in chapter 8.

8. FUTURE OF THE 1968 ACT

As mentioned in the course of this chapter, the DTI put out a consultative letter in 1990[12] on the basis that although specific areas such as estate agency, timeshare and false environmental claims were already under consideration by either the DGFT or Ministers, 'in the light of these developments, and the fact that there has long been pressure for a more general review, we have decided that it is now appropriate to consider the Act as a whole'. The letter makes it

12 Reproduced in (1990) 7 Trading Law, 115–124. See also the NCC's Review, November 1990.

clear that changes are dependent on spaces in the legislative timetable.

The document suggests that areas where reform might be considered were i) scope of the Act and section 23 (considered above); ii) possibly introducing strict liability for misstatements as to services etc; iii) defences generally, which could be reformed by adopting a 'modern defence' regime involving all reasonable steps and exercising all due diligence to avoid committing the offence – which would encompass the need to show that sufficient had been done to guard against the inefficiency, incompetence etc. of employees; iv) extension of the Act to catch certain activities associated with services such as timeshare promotions, newspaper bingo and homework schemes; v) a minor clarification of disclaimers (considered above); vi) the removal of possible conflicts with EC law on certificates of origin; and vii) a possible reformulation of the existing order-making powers.

9. PRICE INDICATIONS

Legislation to curb abuses in the statement of prices was a novelty when introduced by the Act. The Molony Committee was unfashionably unsympathetic to complaints about deceptive pricing methods:

> Our reaction . . . is that consumers must be expected to go shopping with their eyes open and their wits reasonably alert. If it should happen to their cost that they fail to notice that the price on the bacon is quoted per ½lb and not per lb . . . they will have had a valuable lesson which might help them more than anything we could recommend (para. 813).

But in fact the Committee had included in its revised form of definition of a 'trade description' statements as to the 'former or usual price of any goods' (para. 636). This simple formula avoids the tortuousness of the language actually used in the relevant legislation, though if it had been adopted there would have been scope for much argument on the meaning of 'former' and 'usual'.

The main abuses identified and discussed in parliamentary debate before the Act was passed included a) disguising goods in fact bought by what is now advertised as 'special purchase' as goods reduced from their normal price, particularly during sales, b) goods displaying indications, perhaps marked on a shelf, of a lower price than the actual one, and c) other false claims as to 'bargains' or 'slashed prices'. The wording eventually adopted to attempt to deal with these abuses was contained in section 11. The two subsections creating the offences, the marginal note to which refers to 'false or misleading indications as to price of goods', were as follows:

1) If any person offering to supply goods of any description gives, by whatever means, any false indication to the effect that the price at which the goods are offered is equal to or less than
   a)   a recommended price; or
   b)   the price at which the goods or goods of the same description were previously offered by him;
   or is less than such a price by a specified amount, he shall, subject to the provisions of this Act, be guilty of an offence.

2) If any person offering to supply any goods gives, by whatever means, any indication likely to be taken as an indication that the goods are being offered at a price less than that at which they are in fact being offered he shall, subject to the provisions of this Act, be guilty of an offence.

In construing the above subsections various explanatory rules were contained in subsection (3).[13]

Section 11 received some critical comment in the Review of the Trade Descriptions Act 1968 by the OFT's inter-departmental committee.[14] They rejected the idea of a general prohibition, along the lines of the Canadian Combines Investigation Act 1960, of 'any materially misleading representation to the public. . .concerning the price at which such or like articles have been, are or will be ordinarily sold' (section 33c), on the grounds of the too vague boundaries to the offence and the consequential difficulties that would be caused to enforcement officers and the courts. The prevalence of reported litigation in the higher courts on the generally carefully drafted provisions of the Act, perhaps partly due to the resources of many of the defendants who can afford the best legal advice, does indeed indicate caution. But the Committee recommended that the ambit of the section should be widened beyond 'goods' to include hire and hire-purchase transactions, 'property' (by which is presumably meant private dwellinghouses) to prevent false claims of reductions in price by builders, and 'services, accommodation and facilities'. They also recommended some detailed amendments of section 11(3), including one to reduce the time limit relating to the period over which goods were previously offered at a higher price from six months to three months, and the period of 28 days during which they were continuously so offered should be immediately before the current selling price was adopted (instead of, under section 11, any 28 days within the preceding six months). Price comparisons should,

---

13   This provision, the cases on it, and the Bargain Offers Orders are discussed in M & H ch. 13. As will be seen, some of the older cases are still useful.

14   Review of the Trade Descriptions Act 1968, Cmnd. 6628 (1976), ch. viii. See also R. G. Lawson (1977) 141 JP 66.

also, be restricted to previous offers at the same premises and 'recommended prices' should, unless the contrary is indicated, be those of an independent manufacturer or producer, not the person offering the supply or his associates.

Bargain offers

'Bargain Offers' have proved singularly intractable to legislate against. The mischief involves the misleading advertisement of price comparisons – that is misleading in the sense that the comparison is meaningless, or not capable of substantiation or simply false. The main Order, hastily followed by two amending Orders,[15] followed a consultative document issued by the Office of Fair Trading in 1975 and recommendations subsequently made to the Secretary of State. There were extensive preliminary consultations with industry, trade and consumer groups. Despite this, and a helpful explanatory publication by the Department of Trade,[16] the Order was widely condemned as obscure, difficult to apply and to enforce, and arguably ambiguous in intent in some respects.[17] The Minister for Consumer Affairs announced in February 1981 that she had asked the Office of Fair Trading to review the Bargain Offers Order, (as to which, see below) and that she had asked the Director General of Fair Trading to pay particular attention to the increasing use of meaningless price comparisons technically complying with the Order and advocating slogans making generous claims as to value which might be interpreted as contrary to the Order. An example of 'meaningless price comparisons' might be comparisons with the 'after sales price' quoted during 'sales' by certain furniture outlets, or discounts off 'special order prices' where almost all goods on sale are available other than by 'special orders'.[18] The same applies to comparisons with 'RAP' – ready assembled price, when furniture is in practice normally sold unassembled.

In late October 1981 the Director reported to the Minister for Consumer Affairs as had been requested. The gist of his report was that although the criticism of the Bargain Offers Orders had been in some respects exaggerated, it was conceded that the wording contained substantial ambiguities which caused difficulties in both

15　Price Marking (Bargain Offers) Order 1979, S.I. 1979/364; S.I. 1979/633; S.I. 1979/1124, M & H ch. 13.
16　Notes for Guidance (5 December 1979).
17　See 'Practical Problems arising from the Price Marking (Bargain Offers) Order 1979', M Carlisle (1979) 129 NLJ 815; and 'Consumer Anger over Bargain Offer Muddle', The Times 14 April 1980.
18　See T. R. French 'More than was bargained for' (1981) 89 Monthly Rev 80.

interpretation and enforcement. There was therefore a case for amendment.

These proposals for review culminated in a Report of an Inter-Departmental Working Party on the review of legislation on false and misleading price information (1984).[19] This comprehensive review laid out a blueprint for what was to become the legislation now contained in the Consumer Protection Act 1987. Amongst the recommendations were that there should be a general legislative prohibition on traders providing consumers with false or misleading information about prices. However, it was pointed out that such a general legislative prohibition on its own would lead to severe practical difficulties. In the absence of detailed supplementary provisions the trade and the enforcement authorities would be unsure as to which practices the courts would hold to be misleading. Given the wide variety and ingenuity of marketing methods it would be many years and a large number of prosecutions before a satisfactory body of case law could be built up. It was therefore also recommended that a statutory Code of Practice containing practical guidance would be the best means of providing much of the necessary detailed support for a general prohibition on false or misleading price information. The report pointed out that during the previous 10 years a number of Acts had contained provisions for such a statutory code which is not legally binding – so that failure to observe any provision of the code does not itself render a person liable to any proceedings – but which is given a status which enables it to be admissible in evidence. It was also recommended that the primary legislation should contain provision for the Secretary of State to have power to make subordinate legislation. Enforcement should continue to be the responsibility of Trading Standards authorities.

Both these recommendations were adopted in the 1987 Act. In particular a Code of Practice explains with admirable clarity what is and what is not regarded as permitted by way of the sort of Bargain Offer mentioned above.

Consumer Protection Act 1987

Part III of this Act now deals with misleading price indications. It replaces section 11 of the Trade Descriptions Act 1968 and the Price Marking (Bargain Offers) Orders 1979. The new provisions create a general offence of giving a misleading price indication and empower the Secretary of State to approve a Code of Practice. Unlike section 11 of the 1968 Act, which it replaces, the new provisions apply not

19 See M & H p. 548.

only to goods but also to services, accommodation or facilities (as is the case for section 14 of the 1968 Act). The offence created by section 20(1) is that a person is guilty of an offence if, in the course of any business of his, he gives (by any means whatever) to any consumers an indication which is misleading as to the price at which any goods, services, accommodation or facilities are available (whether generally or from particular persons). Section 20(2) then goes on to add to subsection (1) above by stating that a person is also guilty of an offence if:

a) in the course of any business of his, he has given an indication to any consumers which, after it was given, has become misleading as mentioned in subsection (1); and

b) consumers might reasonably be expected to rely on the indication at a time after it has become misleading; and

c) he fails to take all such steps as are reasonable to prevent those consumers from relying on the indication. (Examples of price indications which become misleading are given in the extracts from the Statutory Code of Practice in Appendix II.)

The section also explains that it is immaterial:

a) whether the person who gives or gave the indication is or was acting on his own behalf or on behalf of another;

b) whether or not that person is the person from whom the goods, services, accommodation or facilities are available; and

c) whether the indication is or has become misleading in relation to all the consumers to whom it is or was given or only in relation to some of them (s. 20(3)).

Section 20(6) defines both the terms 'consumer' and 'price'. As far as 'consumer' is concerned this term is defined as follows:

a) in relation to any goods, it means any person who might wish to be supplied with the goods for his own private use or consumption;

b) in relation to any services or facilities, it means any person who might wish to be provided with the services or facilities otherwise than for the purposes of any business of his; and

c) in relation to any accommodation, it means any person who might wish to occupy the accommodation otherwise than for the purposes of any business of his.

It will be noted that, unlike under the Trade Descriptions Act 1968, this offence does not apply in a business-to-business situation; it applies *only* to a business-to-consumer one.

So far as 'price' is concerned, in relation to any goods, services, accommodation or facilities, 'price' is defined as follows:

a) the aggregate of the sums required to be paid by a consumer for or otherwise in respect of the supply of the goods or the provision of the services, accommodation or facilities; or

b) except in section 21 (regarding the meaning of 'misleading') any method which will be or has been applied for the purpose of determining that aggregate.

The meaning of 'misleading' is of crucial importance in defining the scope of the general offence discussed above. Section 21 is devoted to the meaning of 'misleading'. It can be summarised by saying that the price is misleading if a consumer might reasonably be expected to infer any of the following from the price indication:

a) The price is less than in fact it is. This covers the all too common situation in some supermarkets where goods purportedly reduced are charged for at full price at the cash till. (Section 11(2) of the Trade Descriptions Act 1968, reproduced above, was to similar effect.)

b) In effect, the price purports to be unconditional whereas in fact it is conditional – e.g. the advertised price of furniture is in fact applicable to that in one colour, anything else being more.[20]

c) The price covers matters in respect of which an extra charge is in fact made. An example would be a charge for VAT at the retail till when a customer assumed that the displayed price is net. Where the price differs when different methods of payment are made, for example by a credit card, the Price Indications (Method of Payment) Regulations 1991 prescribes that the differential pricing policy must be made clear, either by displaying the two prices or by expressing the one as a percentage of the indicated price of the other. Specifically as regards VAT, the Price Marking Order 1991 requires that in *retail* sales indicated prices are inclusive of VAT (art. 9) – see chapter 9.

d) The price is to be increased or reduced or maintained (whether or not at a particular time or by a particular amount) when the person giving the indication has no such expectation. For example, 'Prices now reduced by 10%. Hurry and buy now before prices return to normal' – or 'Buy before the price of this article rises', when neither event is expected to occur, infringe this subsection.

e) The price is linked to factual information by reference to which consumers might reasonably be expected to judge the validity of relevant comparison with the price indication, and these facts or circumstances are not in fact what they are. This is a very wide, catch-all, provision designed to prohibit all other false or misleading price comparisons. *Genuine* comparisons are to be encouraged, but if comparisons such as 'Our price £9,

---

20   See *Clive Sweeting v Northern Upholstery Ltd* (1983) 2 Tr L 5, DC.

£12 in X's supermarket', or 'Now reduced to £9, formerly £10', or 'Our price £9, mrp (manufacturer's recommended price) £10', are *falsely* made, an offence is committed. (Note that section 21(3) defines more closely what a 'relevant comparison' is (and includes by inference the above examples) and section 21(2) explains what is misleading as to a *method* of determining a price, so as to catch price comparisons expressed less directly.)

In summary it will be seen that the test is whether the information as to a price conveyed to a consumer includes any of the five misleading factors listed. With regard to section 21(1)(a) – an indication 'that the price is less than in fact it is' – this is a similar test to that formerly contained in section 11(2) of the 1968 Act. The implication continues to be that the well-known contractual principle that the indication of a price displayed with goods in, for example, a shop window has no contractual effect because it is merely an invitation to treat[1] is nevertheless likely to be a criminal offence under section 20. Section 21(1)(a) and (c) above will probably both apply to the facts of certain cases previously decided under the old section 11 of the 1968 Act.[2] Section 21(1)(e) is a general 'catch-all' provision which seeks to embrace many varieties of misleading comparisons of prices.

The former '28-day rule' for price comparisons with those previously charged in the same business is recast in the Code of Practice made under the Act's provisions and reproduced in Appendix II – see paragraph 1.2. The crucial rule is that the previous price with which comparison is made should be the *last* price at which the product was available in the previous six months for at least 28 consecutive days and in the same shop. Because this type of control over prices previously charged and followed by apparent reductions is difficult to enforce, the government has suggested new Regulations to require retailers to justify discount claims by producing written records. Trading Standards Officers have indi-

---

1   See e.g. *Pharmaceutical Society of Gt. Britain v Boots Cash Chemists (Southern) Ltd* [1952] 2 QB 795, [1952] 2 All ER 456; *Fisher v Bell* [1961] 1 QB 394, [1960] 3 All ER 731.

2   See in particular *Richards v Westminster Motors Ltd* (1975) 119 Sol Jo 626 – the price quoted for a vehicle did not indicate that VAT must be added and this was misleading to the ordinary consumer; *North Western Gas Board v Aspden* [1970] Crim LR 301 – Gas Board's displayed notice indicating that there was a ' £3 allowance when you buy any two gas fires at the same time', which was intended to apply only to 'fixed' hearth gas fires, not all gas fires, was an indication that the goods were being offered at a price £3 less than they were actually being offered, contrary to s. 11(2). See also *Sweeting v Northern Upholstery Ltd* (1983) 2 Tr L 5 and M & H pp. 532 et seq.

cated (through LACOTS) that they would prefer to have the same powers as the Advertising Standards Authority and enforce a duty on retailers not to make claims which cannot be substantiated.

Special provision is made to apply the general offence of giving a misleading price indication as to the provision of services and facilities. It had previously been held by the Divisional Court in *Newell v Hicks*[3] that section 14 of the 1968 Act did not catch a false statement as to the terms, including the price, at which services, accommodation or facilities were being offered. Equally the old section 11 clearly only applied to the supply of *goods*. There was therefore a lacuna which these new provisions now fill. Section 22 of the Act explains the application of the general offence to the provision of services and facilities in the following way:

22(1) Subject to the following provisions of this section, references in this Part to services or facilities are references to any services or facilities whatever including, in particular –

a) the provision of credit or of banking or insurance services and the provision of facilities incidental to the provision of such services;
b) the purchase or sale of foreign currency;
c) the supply of electricity;
d) the provision of a place, other than on a highway, for the parking of a motor vehicle;
e) the making of arrangements for a person to put or keep a caravan on any land other than arrangements by virtue of which that person may occupy the caravan as his only or main residence.

The section goes on in subsection (2) specifically to exclude from the ambit of the Act services provided to an employer under a contract of employment, and by subsection (3), the services of an investment business (which is separately dealt with in the Financial Services Act 1986).

The application of the general offence to the provision of 'accommodation or facilities' is severely circumscribed by section 23. The section in effect limits the ambit of the offence to *business* creations or disposals of major interests (fees simple or leaseholds of more than 21 years) in new dwellings – i.e. residences not previously occupied as such. Ordinary disposals of privately owned residences are therefore not within the ambit of this legislation.

Section 24 contains a self contained collection of defences. When charges are laid under section 20(1) or (2) these specific defences are as follows:

1) That the defendant's acts or omissions were authorised for the

purposes of section 24(1) by a regulation made under section 26 of the 1987 Act;

2) If the price indication is published in a book, newspaper, magazine, film or radio or television broadcast or on a programme included in a cable programme service, that the indication was not contained in an advertisement;

3) If the price indication is published in an advertisement there is the familiar defence of innocent publication available to the person who carries on a business of publishing such advertisements;

4) Section 24(4) attempts to deal with the situation where e.g. a manufacturer's published 'recommended' price is not adhered to by suppliers to consumers. It states that it is a defence for the accused to show that –

   a) the indication did not relate to the availability from him of any goods, services, accommodation or facilities;

   b) a price had been recommended to every person from whom the goods, services, accommodation or facilities were indicated as being available;

   c) the indication related to that price and was misleading as to that price only by reason of a failure by any person to follow the recommendation; and

   d) it was reasonable for the person who gave the indication to assume that the recommendation was for the most part being followed.

In addition to these specific defences there is the general defence contained in section 39 that in proceedings against any person for an offence to which the section applies it is a defence for that person to show that he took all reasonable steps and exercised all due diligence to avoid committing the offence (section 39(1)). If the due diligence defence involves implicating a third party whose act or default is allegedly to blame, it is necessary to serve the prosecution with a notice to enable that third party to be identified, normally not less than seven clear days before the proceedings (s 39(2) and (3)).

The defence of due diligence described above and contained in section 39(1) includes a refinement supplied by section 39(4). This states as follows:

4) It is hereby declared that a person shall not be entitled to rely on the defence provided by subsection (1) above by reason of his reliance on information supplied by another, unless he shows that it was reasonable in all the circumstances for him to have relied on the information, having regard in particular –

   a) to the steps which he took, and those which might reasonably have been taken, for the purpose of verifying the information; and

   b) to whether he had any reason to disbelieve the information.

These defences apply to section 20(1) of the 1987 Act and also to those sections of the Act dealing with the general safety requirement, offences against safety regulations and other matters dealing with consumer safety in the Act dealt with elsewhere in this book.

In the light of the recommendations of the Inter-Departmental Committee mentioned above, the legislative text of the 1987 Act has been supplemented by a Code of Practice approved by order of the Secretary of State. Its purpose is declared to be a) to give practical guidance and b) to promote desirable practices as to price indications of goods, services, accommodation or facilities (s 25(1)).

Section 25 further clarifies the status of the Code by stating that a contravention of a Code of Practice approved under this section does not of itself give rise to any criminal or civil liability, but in any proceedings against any person for an offence under section 20(1) or (2) above –

a) any contravention by that person of such a code may be relied on in relation to any matter for the purpose of establishing that that person committed the offence or of negativing any defence; and

b) compliance by that person with such a Code may be relied on in relation to any matter for the purpose of showing that the commission of the offence by that person has not been established or that that person has a defence.

Where the Secretary of State approves a Code of Practice under this section he may prescribe consultation, at any time by order –

a) approve any modification of the code; or

b) withdraw his approval; and references in subsection (2) above to a Code of Practice approved under this section are to be construed accordingly. The power to make an order under this section is exercisable by statutory instrument subject to annulment in pursuance of a resolution of either House of Parliament (s 25(2), (3) and (4)).

There was much debate in the consultation over the precise terms of a possible Code of Practice and as eventually promulgated it contains detailed guidance as to legitimate and illegitimate price comparisons and guidance as to statements of the actual price of goods and services to the customer. It should be particularly noted that contravention of the Code of Practice does not itself give rise to any criminal or civil liability, but contravention of the Code may be relied upon by the prosecutor for the purpose of establishing that the defendant has committed the offence or, for the purpose of negativing any defence. Similarly, compliance by the defendant with the Code may be relied on by him for the purpose of showing that the commission of the offence by that person has not been established, or that the person has a defence. The purpose of containing such provisions in a Code is that the Secretary of State is given power to alter the detailed provisions of the Code or withdraw approval to it. Consequently it should provide greater flexibility to deal with a constantly changing market situation.

Details of the Code

In practice the Code is widely relied on by retailers and gives important examples of some of the legitimate or illegitimate practices most often encountered. It is reproduced in Appendix II to this book.

Regulations

As noted above, the Secretary of State after consulting the Director General of Fair Trading and other appropriate persons, may make regulations for the purpose of regulating the circumstances and manner in which any person 1) gives any indication as to the price at which any goods, services, accommodation or facilities will or are available or have been supplied or provided; or 2) indicates any other matter in respect of which any such indication may be misleading. Regulations may also be made for the purpose of facilitating the enforcement of the provisions of section 20 or of relevant subsidiary legislation (section 26). Two Regulations have been made under these provisions: the Price Indications (Method of Payment) Regulations 1991[4] and the Price Indications (Bureaux de Change) (No. 2) Regulations 1992.

Punishments

Persons contravening section 20(1) or (2) are liable on conviction on indictment to a fine or on summary conviction to a fine not exceeding the statutory maximum (section 20(4)). Enforcement duties are imposed on every weights and measures authority in Great Britain. Enforcement authorities are given the usual power to make test purchases (section 28) and powers of search etc. (section 29). It is a separate offence to obstruct an authorised officer (section 32). Prosecutions under section 20(1) or (2) must be brought either by the end of the period of three years from the day that the offence was committed or within one year of its discovery by the prosecutor, whichever is the earlier (section 20(5)).

Section 40 contains a provision, familiar in trading law, enabling a third party whose act or default led to the offence being committed

---

4 Covering situations where different prices are charged depending upon the method of payment used by the customer.

to be prosecuted instead of, or along with, the principal offender – though here the misleading price offence must have been committed by the third party *in the course of any business of his*. This contrasts with the position under section 23 of the 1968 Act and may make it impossible to prosecute an erring employee of the employer-principal.[5]

Future of misleading prices regime

In a speech made to the Centre for Consumer Law, University of Brunel in February 1992 the relevant Minister was quoted as saying:

> When the present regime governing misleading prices under the Consumer Protection Act 1987 came into effect in March 1989 we established a Monitoring Committee to keep the regime under review and to report on its operation. The Monitoring Committee which consisted of representatives from a wide range of interests including retailers, enforcement officer, consumers and advertising, has now reported and has made a number of recommendations for action.
>
> Having considered those recommendations, whilst the Government appreciates that there are in some cases difficulties in enforcing the present regime, it is not convinced that making detailed regulations, particularly in the area of price comparisons, would necessarily solve the problem. The present regime replaced one which was governed by detailed regulation and which was widely felt to be ineffective. We, therefore, believe that the present regime which is based on a general offence backed up by a Code of Practice is, on balance, the better way to go.
>
> However, we have decided that it is right that consumers should, when buying tickets for theatre performances and other entertainment and sporting events, have proper information about the nature of the seat or place for which they are buying a ticket. We, therefore, propose to consult on proposed regulations which would require those who re-sell tickets for entertainment and sporting events to give sufficient information to the purchaser for him to know what sort of seat he is getting for his money.
>
> The Committee is also looking at the question of service charges in restaurants in the light of the widely differing practices operated by various establishments. I look forward to receiving the Committee's report on this matter in due course.

---

5 See discussion in O'Keefe *The Law Relating to Trade Descriptions* para. 2[3081].

13   Food; weights and measures

INTRODUCTION

The legislation relating to food contained in the Food Safety Act 1990 is massive and complex. The same is true of weights and measures. In both cases EEC requirements have complicated the law still further. These areas differ from most of the others discussed in this book because they depend for their effective enforcement on the high degree of technical training given to the local government officers responsible for enforcing them. The United Kingdom's unusual (by EEC standards) system of local authority, rather than central government, enforcement, will be noted.

Food Authorities charged with enforcement are County Councils, District Councils and London Borough Councils (and there are special arrangements for the City of London, the Inner and Middle Temple and the Scilly Isles, and Scotland).

The effect of this is that in the Metropolitan Districts District Councils remain the Food Authorities, but in non-Metropolitan counties both the County Councils and the District Councils are Food Authorities. Under powers given in the Act, the Food Safety Enforcement Authority (England and Wales) Order 1990 specifies that non-Metropolitan District Councils shall be responsible for the issue of emergency prohibition notices (where there is a health risk) under section 12 and County Councils deal with offences involving the false description or presentation of food under section 15, this dovetailing in with the latter's powers under the Trade Descriptions Act 1968. All other duties of local food authorities are exercisable concurrently but in order to prevent consumers having to go from one district to another to get their complaints dealt with, a Code of Practice has been issued setting out a sensible division of labour. So, cases involving contamination by micro-organisms should be dealt with by District Councils whereas County Councils deal with cases of chemical contamination which pose no immediate risk to health. Cases of foreign bodies and mould affecting food should be dealt with by District Councils under section 8 (the food safety requirement) or section 14 (food not of the nature or substance or quality demanded) – the appropriate officers in practice normally being environmental health officers and trading standards officers for Districts and Counties respectively. The Code goes on to recommend liaison arrangements to avoid duplication of effort or omission.[1] In the case of food offences private prosecutions are possible.[2] But in the case of weights and measures offences the prosecution must be brought by a weights and measures authority or a chief officer of police.[3] In most cases the private consumer will be concerned only with the recognition of the offences created by these Acts, and then usually only a small number of the possible ones, and the reporting of the matter to the local Environmental Health Department of the District Council or to the local Trading Standards (Weights and Measures) Department of the County Council. It should be noted that enforcement of food laws in the UK is primarily at retail level.

In order to fulfil their duties the officers responsible for the enforcement of the law in these two areas must have knowledge of, or at least access to, a forbidding mass of subsidiary legislation as well as the main Acts. Encyclopaedias exist for this purpose[4] and it would be both impractical and undesirable in a book of this nature to attempt to cover the whole ground. But it is important for the consumer and his adviser to be able to recognise the main offences under these Acts, which as collated statistically by the Director General in the OFT Annual Report of 1990 were as follows:

Food and Drugs Acts	*Number of convictions*
Not nature, substance or quality demanded	1,211
Unfit food	163
Labelling Regulations and others	592
TOTAL	1,966

Weights and Measures Acts	
False or unjust equipment	27
Short weight or measure	123
Average weight and quantity offences	12

1 Statutory Code of Practice No. 1: Responsibility for Enforcement of the Food Safety Act 1990.

2 *Snodgrass v Topping* (1952) 116 JP 312 (the decision suggests that the private prosecutor should be a purchaser prejudiced by the food).

3 Weights and Measures Act 1985, s. 83. In Scotland the Procurator Fiscal will prosecute.

4 See *Butterworth's Law of Food and Drugs* and O'Keefe *Law of Weights and Measures* (2nd Edn.) which are essential tools for those working in the field.

Packaged goods	51
Other offences	25
TOTAL	238

This chapter accordingly outlines the structure of the main Acts in the areas in question and examines in more detail the law relating to the more common offences.

Part 1. Food

1. FOOD SAFETY ACT 1990 – BACKGROUND

There has been legislation against impure food since Henry III's Assize of Bread and Ale in 1266, though legislative policy was directed at particular commodities, such as tea, coffee and bread. The first law against adulterated food generally was the Adulteration of Food or Drink Act 1860, and adulterated drugs were dealt with by the Pharmacy Act 1868. The parentage of the 1990 Act can be traced from the Sale of Food and Drugs Act 1875. There then appeared a number of consolidations of this and several *ad hoc* laws dealing with composition, labelling, the addition of preservatives and the like. By virtue of the Medicines Act 1968 (Commencement No. 7) Order 1977, references to 'drugs' in the former consolidating statute, the Food and Drugs Act 1955, were largely removed. Drugs are now dealt with by the Medicines Act 1968. The Food Act 1984 is largely replaced by the Food Safety Act 1990 which, despite its short title, deals not only with food safety but composition, labelling, advertising and other matters. This important Act, to which references in this Part relate unless the contrary is stated, was preceded by a White Paper '*Food Safety – Protecting the Consumer*' in July 1989. It should also be noted that Regulations made under the 1984 Act continue in force as if made by the 1990 Act (section 59(3)).

Food law can be very controversial, particularly in respect of additives which may be profitable to the manufacturer but are suspected to be less than healthy to the consumer. Furthermore there are considerations as to whether a food article such as a sausage can truly be described as such if there is very little meat in its actual composition. The government clearly requires expert advice on these topics and a Food Standards Committee was set up in 1947 to advise the appropriate Ministers and was normally required to be consulted before regulations relating to composition of food and Codes of Practice were issued. This Committee, together with the Food Additives and Contaminants Committee, issued a number of valuable reports which led to legislative changes of importance such as the Labelling of Food Regulations 1970. Compositional standards exist for many foods. In the case of sausages for example, beef sausages must contain at least 50 per cent meat and pork sausages at least 65 per cent. There is still debate as to whether existing compositional standards are extensive enough. Attention has been drawn to the use by unscrupulous producers of excessive water as a make-weight in food, and to machines called 'yield improvers' at one time advertised with the revealing adage – 'why sell meat when you could sell water?'[5]

On 1 November 1983 these two Committees were merged and became the Food Advisory Committee. The terms of reference of this Committee are to advise the Minister of Agriculture, Fisheries and Food and other relevant Secretaries of State on matters referred to it by the Ministers relating to the composition, labelling and advertising of food; and additives, contaminants and other substances which are, or may be, present in food or used in preparation. The enabling power to make regulations as to composition of food appears in section 16 of the Act and section 17 empowers Ministers to make regulations with respect to food as called for by any Community obligation – typically an EC Directive (see chapter 2). There are, for instance, detailed regulations concerning preservatives and colouring matter in food.

The sheer volume and complexity of the subsidiary legislation made under the Food Acts, much of it prompted by the EEC Directives, can be gauged by the fact that *Butterworth's Law of Food and Drugs* devotes some one and a half of the six looseleaf volumes to setting out their accumulated texts. Some, if by no means all, yield readily appreciated benefits to consumers. Thus, for instance, the Jam and Similar Products Regulations 1981 lay down that jam labelled 'extra jam' must have an (improved) fruit content of at least 45 per cent.

5 See now the Meat Products and Spreadable Fish Products Regulations 1984 (S.I. 1984/1566 as amended) which besides laying down detailed compositional standards requires a declaration of added water content – see Reg. 9. See also Reg. 17 of the Food Labelling Regulations 1984, discussed below.

2. THE MAIN OFFENCES

a) Rendering food injurious to health

Adulterating food is one of the most ancient of the offences encompassed by food legislation and this particular section can be traced to legislation of 1872. Adulteration of food by e.g. the addition of water to milk (as those who play 'Happy Families' may remember) used to be widespread. Nowadays there are detailed controls over the use of additives or treatments and the presence of contaminants and so there is little use in practice of this section, section 7, which makes it an offence to render food injurious to health by the addition or abstraction of articles or constituents with the intent that the food shall be sold for human consumption. The court is directed to have regard to the probable cumulative effect of food of substantially the same composition on the health of a person consuming it in ordinary quantities. The section forms a useful bench-mark for food control.

b) Selling food not complying with food safety requirements

Section 8 introduces an important new concept to food law – the food safety requirement – which is not dissimilar to the 'general safety requirement' in Part II of the Consumer Protection Act 1987 affecting products and discussed elsewhere in this book. Food is deemed to have failed to comply with the safety requirement if it has been rendered injurious to health by means of the operations mentioned in section 7 (above) or if it is unfit for human consumption or unreasonably contaminated. Authorised officers of the Food Authority may at all reasonable times inspect food intended for human consumption and if necessary seize and remove it (section 9). The ambit of the offence in section 8 is, typically, very widely drafted and affects any person who sells for human consumption, or offers, exposes, or advertises for sale for such consumption, or has in his possession for the purpose of such sale or of preparation for such sale, or has consigned it to any other person for the purpose of such sale, any food which fails to comply with the food safety requirements.

c) Selling food not of the nature etc. demanded

It is possible to trace the genesis of this offence back to the Sale of Food and Drugs Act of 1875. The offence (under section 14) involves any person selling to the purchaser's prejudice any food which is not of the nature or substance or quality demanded by the purchaser. The sale must be for human consumption.

The following summarises the main points on the interpretation of the section (in a similar form to which it appeared in former legislation).

'A person . . .'

The defendant may be an individual or limited company. This is well established by case law and Schedule 1 of the Interpretation Act 1978 which states that unless the contrary intention appears, the expression 'person' includes a body of persons corporate or unincorporate.

It was held in *Pearks, Gunston and Tee Ltd v Ward*[6] that there was no 'contrary intention' in this provision. In many cases the sale will be actually conducted by an employee of the proprietor of the business. In *Goodfellow v Johnson*[7] the Divisional Court considered the legal position arising out of a sale of watered gin in a public house by a barmaid to a duly authorised sampling officer. As Lord Parker CJ explained, this:

> constitutes an absolute offence . . . The forbidden act is the selling to the prejudice of the purchaser, and it has long been held that a person who has done the forbidden thing through somebody else like a servant or agent is himself liable . . . The forbidden act in a provision such as this is not the parting with the title by the owner but is the physical handling and handing over of the goods by way of sale: in other words the shop assistant, or in this case the barmaid, is liable, and accordingly, in view of the general principle to which I have referred, any person on whose behalf that act of handling and handing over is done is also liable.[8]

'Sells to the purchaser's prejudice'

It is specifically provided by subsection (2) that it shall not be a defence that the purchaser was not prejudiced because he bought for analysis or examination. Even where a servant buys on behalf of his employer, with the employer's money, it is open to the court to hold that the employer has been prejudiced.[9]

In most cases a purchaser of adulterated food or drugs is clearly 'prejudiced'. It has been long established, in addition, that he is prejudiced if he 'gets an article inferior to that which he demands and pays for', an unusual example of attaching criminal liability to a transaction which, in the absence of danger to health, would otherwise give rise only to civil liability in respect of breach of

---

6 [1902] 2 KB 1.
7 [1966] 1 QB 83, [1965] 1 All ER 941.
8 Ibid., at 88,89, and 944 respectively.
9 See *Garforth v Esam* (1892) 56 JP 521 (inspector bought through his servant).

warranty. Difficulties can be caused by notices disclaiming that the food is pure. In a number of cases it has been held that a notice, e.g. stating that spirits have been diluted, is capable of taking effect so that a purchaser therefore cannot be said to be prejudiced. In the Scottish case of *Brander v Kinnear*[10] it was held that such a notice must be clear and unambiguous and acquaint the purchaser with the prejudice that he is asked to accept. The courts tend to construe such notices strictly in the interests of purchasers.[11] In *Thomas Robinson, Sons & Co Ltd v Allardice*[12] the Divisional Court held that the standard of quality which a purchaser can expect is that applicable to an ordinary purchaser. The opinion of a public analyst that, for instance, a cordial must contain sugar to answer that description, is not necessarily by itself conclusive.[13]

'Not of the nature or substance or quality demanded by the purchaser'

It was emphasised in *Bastin v Davies*[14] that there are three distinct offences here relating to a) nature, b) substance and c) quality, of food demanded. An information alleging that a certain sale of food was 'not of the nature or not of the substance or not of the quality . . .' was held bad for uncertainty, the Divisional Court being influenced by a long-standing statement to this effect in the then leading textbook, *Bell's Sale of Food and Drugs*.[15]

As to 'nature' it was held in *Knight v Bowers*,[16] where a purchaser had asked for the drug 'Saffron' and had been supplied with pure 'Savin', an abortifacient, that it was no defence to show that the article supplied was pure in itself if it was not also the one demanded.

This decision was followed in the instructive case of *Meah v*

---

10 1923 JC 42.
11 See *Rodbourn v Hudson* [1925] 1 KB 225.
12 (1944) 170 LT 297.
13 Contrast *Collins Arden Products Ltd v Barking Corpn* [1943] KB 419, [1943] 2 All ER 249 and *Broughton v Whittaker* [1944] KB 269, [1944] 2 All ER 544; see also (1944) 108 JP 303, 'To the prejudice of the purchaser'.
14 [1950] 2 KB 579, [1950] 1 All ER 1095. The redrafted version appearing in the 1984 Act made this point clearer still. The 1990 Act has unfortunately telescoped the wording again.
15 Such an information would not now comply with Magistrates' Courts Rules 1981, S.I. 1981/552, r. 12. Earlier cases must be treated with caution because in s. 6 of the 1875 Act the phrase was drafted conjunctively. This was changed to its present disjunctive meaning in 1928.
16 (1885) 14 QBD 845. Section 14 on its previous form also applied to drugs. 'Nature' would also cover such matters as cod being sold after a demand for haddock.

Roberts[17] where a brewery employee visited a restaurant and cleaned a beer dispensing machine with caustic soda. He placed the residue of this fluid in an empty lemonade bottle, marking it 'cleaner', and left it for use by the restaurant. A customer's children were by mistake supplied with caustic soda from this bottle, having ordered lemonade. One of the children became seriously ill as a result. The restaurant proprietors and the brewery employee, joined in under the former Act's section 100 (see below), were convicted by the justices under the former Act's sections 2 (in that the food was not of the 'nature demanded') and 8 (in that the food was unfit for human consumption). The defendants appealed on the basis that there had been no food supplied and no sale. It was held by the Divisional Court that there had been a sale of lemonade although caustic soda had been supplied. The expression 'sells any food' means 'sells something as a food'. Furthermore, the third party employee's acts or omissions had caused the breaches of the sections and he was guilty of the offence whether he personally sold the food or not. The magistrates' decision was upheld in every respect.

As to 'substance', it has been held that milk is of the substance demanded if it is as it came from the cow, even if the milk supplied has a lesser fat content than specified by contract.[18] But if a significant foreign substance is found in the milk (e.g. penicillin) and this ought not to have been in the milk at the time of milking, an offence is committed.[19] Designated products may by usage develop a wider, generic, significance. Thus 'Demerara sugar', though originally referring to a certain type of brown sugar coming from the West Indies, is apt to describe the same type of sugar coming from Mauritius.[20] A prescribed standard for a food or drug, such as those of the British Pharmacopoeia, is prima facie the standard below which the article must not fall, unless there is evidence of a lower acceptable commercial standard.[1] In other cases the courts must apply such standards as are reasonable.[2] But this concept can cause apparent difficulties. Thus in both *T W Lawrence & Sons Ltd v Burleigh*[3] and *Goldup v John Manson Ltd*,[4] butchers were charged with

---

17 [1978] 1 All ER 97.
18 *Few v Robinson* [1921] 3 KB 504.
19 *Hall v Owen-Jones and Jones* [1967] 3 All ER 209.
20 *Anderson v Britcher* (1913) 78 JP 65.
1 *Boots Cash Chemists (Southern) Ltd v Cowling* (1903) 88 LT 539 (liniment of soap); *Dickins v Randerson* [1901] 1 KB 437 (mercury ointment).
2 See *Tonkin v Victor Value Ltd* [1962] 1 All ER 821, [1962] 1 WLR 339 – 'mock salmon cutlette' containing only 33 per cent fish held to be below any reasonable standard.
3 (1981) 146 JP 134.
4 [1982] QB 161, [1981] 3 All ER 257.

contravening section 2 of the 1984 Act in respect of excess fat in minced meat. In the *Lawrence* case the selling company's conviction was upheld in respect of selling mince with 30.8 per cent of fat when it had been ordered by telephone. The purchaser gave impressive evidence that she was 'prejudiced' and the analyst gave evidence to show that the fat content of the sample was at the top of the range of samples analysed in a survey of the fat content of mince. But in the *Goldup* case, where the meat contained 33 per cent fat, the magistrates' dismissal of the information was also upheld, partly, it seems, because minced meat was available both at a cheaper and more expensive price and partly because a notice in the shop stated that minced beef sold in the shop contained up to 30 per cent fat – the difference being dismissed as de minimis. It should be borne in mind, in this connection that similar facts could give rise to an offence against section 1 of the Trade Descriptions Act 1968 (applying a false trade description to any goods in the course of a business, including orally).

As to 'quality', it was held in *Anness* v *Grivell*,[5] a case concerning what was alleged to be an unduly insubstantial butter fat content in a butter and margarine mixture, that 'quality' meant commercial quality of the article sold and not merely its description. Extraneous matter, such as a dead fly found floating in an unopened bottle of milk,[6] or a nail in sweets[7] can make the food not of the quality demanded. In *Barber* v *Co-operative Wholesale Society Ltd*[8] a bottle of milk containing a green straw was delivered to a school and it was alleged that the food was not of the quality demanded by the purchaser. It was agreed by both parties that the presence of extraneous matter in the food could be evidence that it was not of the quality demanded and it was held, in addition, that it was unnecessary for the prosecution to prove that the matter was deleterious. The test was whether the purchaser could, in the context of the particular transaction, reasonably object to the presence of the matter.

The cases cited above as to the meaning of 'nature', 'substance' and 'quality' involve a degree of overlap. This was recognised in *Preston* v *Greenclose Ltd*[9] where the respondents were charged with selling to the prejudice of the purchaser a food, namely scampi, which was not of the substance demanded, being in part white fish and not scampi. The magistrates accepted the defence that the offence related to 'nature' and not 'substance of the food'. The

5   [1915] 3 KB 685.
6   *Newton* v *West Vale Creamery Co Ltd* (1956) 120 JP 318.
7   *Lindley* v *George W Horner & Co Ltd* [1950] 1 All ER 234.
8   (1983) 147 JP 296, 127 Sol Jo 424.
9   (1975) 139 JP Jo 245. See also *Shearer* v *Rowe* (1985) 149 JP 698.

Divisional Court allowed the prosecutor's appeal, holding that there was an area of common ground between the three words 'nature', 'substance' and 'quality'. They were not normally exclusive, and always to be precise in the selection of one or another could present difficult problems. In the present case it was impossible on a matter of law to pronounce as between the relevant appositeness of 'substance' or 'nature'. The overwhelming probability was that the case fell within both terms, in which event it was right for the prosecutor to choose one of the two terms he thought the more appropriate.

The significance of the 'demand' by the 'purchaser' is that it identifies the food in question, and it must then be shown that the particular article fails one of the tests for nature, substance or quality as charged.[10]

Subject to the general defence below, the section imposes absolute liability. It is not a defence to show absence of any negligence.[11]

It will be apparent from the above litigation that many prosecutions were brought under the predecessors of section 14. The scene was further enlivened by specific defences to those so prosecuted. For instance, if food contained some extraneous matter it was a defence to show that the presence of that matter was an unavoidable consequence of the process of collection or preparation. So, when (for instance) a hawk moth caterpillar was found in a tin of Smedleys' peas, and the appellants were charged with supplying food 'not of the substance demanded by the purchaser', the appellant argued that since the chances of this happening were 874,999 to 1 against and there was a highly sophisticated mechanical screening process plus visual inspection, the incident was an 'unavoidable consequence'. This gave the then members of the House of Lords some innocent amusement in commenting on whether by the time 'the immolated insect had at length plodded its way to the highest court in the land', and whose protein content might, perhaps, be beneficial, any good was served by bringing such a prosecution. In the event, the court convicted.[12] Under the 1990 Act the defendant must rely on the general defence of due diligence set out in section 21 (below).

It should also be borne in mind that there may be some overlap between section 14 and section 8 – selling food not complying with food safety requirements. Section 8, as has been mentioned above, covers 'contaminated' food and would certainly seem more

---

10   See *Collins Arden Products Ltd v Barking Corpn* [1943] KB 419, [1943] 2 All ER 249. See also *McDonald's Hamburger Ltd v Windle* (1986) 151 JP 333, DC – sale of liquid in response for demand for 'diet cola' not of quality demanded.
11   *Lindley v George W Horner & Co Ltd*, above.
12   *Smedleys Ltd v Breed* [1974] AC 839, [1974] 2 All ER 21, HL, M & H p. 567.

appropriate to cover food affected by mould, or which is rancid or stale – these offences formerly being prosecuted under the predecessor of section 14.

d) Falsely describing or presenting food

The offence here was formerly to be found in section 6 of the Food Act 1984 and has now been re-enacted with some important changes. Section 15 creates an offence of giving with any food sold or displaying with any food offered or exposed for sale or in possession for the purpose of sale, a label, whether or not attached to or printed on the wrapper or container which a) falsely describes the food; or b) is likely to mislead as to the nature or substance or quality of the food.

With regard to whether the label is misleading, this is a matter not for an expert witness, but for the court, which must decide whether the ordinary man is misled by it.[13]

The section also makes it an offence to publish or be a party to the publication of an advertisement which is false or calculated to mislead as above.

Section 15 is supplemented in particular by the Labelling of Food Regulations 1984[14] (as amended) made under the power conferred on Ministers to make regulations as to the labelling and description of food formerly under section 7 of the 1955 Act and sections 4, 7 and 118 of the 1984 Act and now under sections 16 and 17 of the 1990 Act.[15] The main features of these regulations (which replace earlier regulations) are as follows:

  a) they require all food, subject to certain exceptions, to be marked or labelled with the name of the food, a list of ingredients, an indication of minimum durability, any special storage conditions or conditions of use and the name and address of the manufacturer or packer or of the seller. In addition, by amending regulations of 1990 certain foods are required to be marked by a 'use by' date. This is appropriate to foods which are microbiologically highly perishable, and it is an offence to sell food after the 'use by' date shown (reg. 40(f));

  b) they specify additional labelling requirements for food sold from vending machines and for alcoholic drinks ('% vol.' or '% mas');

13　*Concentrated Foods Ltd v Champ* [1944] KB 342 at 350 per Wrottesley J.
14　S.I. 1984/1305 as amended.
15　The regulations continue to implement Council Directive No. 79/112/EEC. They supersede the Labelling of Food Regulations 1980.

c) they specify requirements as to the manner of marking or labelling of food;
d) they prohibit claims in the labelling or advertising of the food which has tonic properties or is equivalent or superior to mother's milk, and impose conditions for the making of a number of claims such as diabetic claims, slimming claims, medical claims, protein claims, vitamin claims, energy claims and cholesterol claims;
e) they prohibit the misleading presentation of food, including its shape, appearance or packing and the way it is arranged or displayed for sale;
f) they require, where the labelling of a food places special emphasis on the presence or low content of an ingredient in the food, an indication of the minimum or maximum percentage of that ingredient.
g) they make special provisions for the labelling of food which is not pre-packed and certain similar foods, pre-packed in small packages and food for immediate consumption.

With regard to the important question of minimum durability, regulation 21 indicates in some detail the form in which this must be expressed to consumers. For instance, in the case of food which, with proper storage, will lose its specific properties, minimum durability must be indicated by the words, 'best before' a specific date, this being the date up to which the food is reasonably expected to retain its specific properties if properly stored, plus any storage conditions. Regulation 21 does not prohibit the sale of food bearing an expired date, but such food may contravene sections 8 or 14 of the Act if not fit for human consumption or not of the nature or substance or quality demanded. On the other hand, a sale of expired 'use by' food is an offence. (The former 'sell by' indication is no longer legal.)

The regulations are enforced by local Food Authorities. The labelling of medicines is also tightly controlled under the Medicines (Labelling) Regulations 1976, as amended, made under section 85 of the Medicines Act 1968. Labels must show, inter alia, the name of the product, the quantity in the container, directions for use and the expiry date if within three years of manufacture.

Defences

The 1990 Act completely redesigns defences available for those charged with food offences under its provisions. This replaces the former system where there are a number of miscellaneous defences, including the 'warranty' defence (where retailers relied on their suppliers who gave them a 'warranty' involving a contractual description). Now the defences are as follows.

1. Third parties

There is the common form 'offence due to the fault of another person' provision to be found in section 20. This differs substantially from the old section 100 of the Food Act 1984 which enabled a person charged directly to bring in a third party. The current provision simply states that where the commission by any person of the relevant offence is due to an act or default of some other person, that other person shall be guilty of the offence. The third party may be charged with and convicted of the offence whether or not proceedings are taken against the original person. Although this section comes within the general heading of 'Defences' in the Act, it will be seen that it is not really a defence at all. Much will depend upon the discretion of the prosecutor. This may be exercised in the light of the availability of the section 21 'due diligence' defence discussed immediately below.

2. Defence of due diligence

The defence of due diligence is familiar in trading law statutes. Section 21 establishes a single-limbed defence of 'all reasonable precautions and all due diligence'. It is, in this form, in what is now its preferred version in trading law. In addition a person charged with an offence under section 8 (selling food not complying with the food safety requirements), section 14 (selling food not of the nature or substance or quality demanded) or section 15 (falsely describing or presenting food) has a specific defence. This is that if he has neither a) prepared the food in respect of which the offence is alleged to have been committed; nor b) imported it into Great Britain, the defendant is taken to have established the 'due diligence' defence provided certain other requirements are satisfied (section 21(2)). These are, in brief, that the defendant is able to prove that the commission of the offence was due to an act or default of another person not under his control, or to reliance on information supplied by such a person, and that he carried out all such checks of the food in question as were reasonable in all the circumstances (or reasonably relied on the checks carried out by a supplier); and that the defendant did not know and had no reason to suspect at the time of the commission of the alleged offence that his act or omission would amount to an offence under the relevant provision (section 21(3)). Section 21(4) contains a somewhat similar defence where the offence is due to the act or default of a third party not under the defendant's control and the sale is not under his name or mark – e.g. in typical non-own brand retailing situations.

  It will be seen that the primary defence in section 21(1) is simply of due diligence – there is no need to prove the fault of a third party under that subsection. A 'due diligence' system for the proper checking of food standards must be shown by the defendant. Section 21(2) then goes on to state that the due diligence shall be taken to have been established if the offence falls under sections 8, 14 or 15 *and* the other requirements outlined above (involving the act or default of the third party) are present.[16] Section 21(5) requires a defendant bringing in a third party to give the prosecution at least seven clear days' warning before the hearing. Otherwise that defence may not, without leave, be relied on.

3. Defence of innocent publication

Since there are offences involving the publication of advertisements for food, section 22 states that it is a defence for the person charged to prove that the advertisement was published in the course of a business of publishing or arranging for publication of advertisements and that the publisher had no reason to suspect that its publication would amount to an offence under the Act.

Enforcement powers

Food Authorities and authorised officers are given a range of enforcement powers in the new Act. Some of these have already been mentioned. In particular powers are given of inspection and seizure (section 9), of giving an 'improvement notice' requiring that a proprietor comply with food hygiene conditions and practices (section 10), and of issuing prohibition orders prohibiting the use of processes, treatments or equipment or persons from being the proprietor of a food business, if convicted of a relevant food offence (section 11).

Registration of food premises

The 1990 Act contains a section, section 19, which empowers regulations to be made requiring food premises to be registered. The object of this is to give local authorities responsible for enforcing food law a complete picture of all the food businesses in their area, so that they can target their enforcement resources effectively. Inspections of premises which represent a high risk to health can therefore be expected. Accordingly, the Food Premises

---

16   For a comprehensive analysis of 'due diligence' and the many illustrative cases on it, see *A Guide to the Food Safety Act 1990* (ed. Painter) (Butterworths) and *Butterworths Law of Food and Drugs.* See also *Food Safety Act 1990 – Guidelines on the Statutory Defence of Due Diligence* prepared by a consortium including LACOTS, the NCC and the Institute of Environmental Health Officers.

(Registration) Regulations 1991 (S.I. 1991/2825) have been made covering England, Wales and Scotland and are in force from 1 May 1992 since when it has been an offence to operate a food business from unregistered premises. Registration is with local Environmental Health Departments which have no discretion to refuse registration.

It will be noted that the registration will not make premises subject to the Food Safety Act 1990, since the Act *already* applies to all such premises and authorised officers have powers of entry to all premises whether registered or not. There are exceptions from the requirement to register, including premises used on less than five days in five consecutive weeks, domestic premises providing bed and breakfast in not more than three bedrooms, and premises, not storing food, used by voluntary organisations.

Code of Practice No. 11, issued under the Food Safety Act 1990, section 40, gives guidance on the enforcement of these regulations.

Part II. Weights and Measures

1. WEIGHTS AND MEASURES ACT 1985

The history of this complex subject has been outlined in chapter 1 (and see also the Introduction to this chapter for further background). Part II of this chapter concentrates on the structure of the 1985 Act (which consolidated previous legislation) the main offences of direct concern to the consumer created by it, and, to start with, an outline of the work of the weights and measures service.

2. THE WEIGHTS AND MEASURES SERVICE – CENTRAL AND LOCAL GOVERNMENT FUNCTIONS

Weights and measures functions are shared between central and local government. Section 2 of the Weights and Measures Act 1985 ('the Act') now states that it is the duty of the Secretary of State (currently for Trade and Industry by virtue of the Secretary of State for Trade Order 1979, and formerly the Board of Trade) to maintain standards of the yard, pound, metre and kilogramme. These standards are known as 'United Kingdom primary standards'. All other standards of those units and of any other unit of measurement derived wholly or partly from any of those units are maintained by reference to these primary standards. A 'unit of measurement' is not defined, but means (to adopt the definition used by the Hodgson Committee on Weights and Measures (1951), Cmd. 8219), 'a precisely defined and ideally invariable quantity of some particular kind, in terms of which the magnitudes of all other quantities of the same kind can be stated.' The scientifically minded might be interested to know that the true primary standards are the International Metre and International Kilogramme in the custody of the International Bureau of Weights and Measures at Sèvres. The International Metre is defined as 'the length of the path travelled by light in vacuum during a time interval of 1/299 792 458 of a second' (see Schedule I, Part I of the Act). The yard is defined as 0.9144 of a metre. For United Kingdom purposes the primary standards are defined by reference to the imperial standard bar of Baily's bronze metal for the yard, the imperial standard platinum cylinder for the pound, and British copies of the prototype metre and kilogramme (see Schedule 2). The Department of Trade and Industry is responsible for secondary and tertiary standards of weights and measures, these being the measures of length and capacity set out in Parts I and IV of Schedule 3, and the weights set out in Part V of that Schedule. The Department is also responsible for the standards of weight of each coin of the realm for the time being authorised by the Coinage Act 1971. This duty is fulfilled annually by 'the trial of the Pyx' at which the Chancellor of the Exchequer is notionally on trial before a jury in order to establish that the quality of the country's coinage is maintained. By sample weighing and testing it is ascertained whether the minted coins are of the prescribed quality in terms of weight, size and material content.

The central government function is, then, to maintain the primary and other standards mentioned above, though the actual enforcement of the legislation is left to local weights and measures authorities. The premise behind the hugely complex technology which goes into the testing of these standards is simply that since the consumer is normally unable to test the petrol pump with which he fills his car's fuel tank, the pint pot in which the landlord measures his beer, the price-computing and weighing machine with which the grocer and butcher weigh and price the food that he is buying, the baggage weighing equipment at the airport, the factory machines which measure the quantity of sugar or crisps in their packets, and so on, he is entitled to assume that these weights and measures are tolerably accurate. When the central government has established the standards and exhaustively tested any new pattern of equipment used in the trade for weighing and measuring and given to the machine 'pattern approval', the details are published. The local inspector, now usually known as the Trading Standards Officer, who is responsible for passing items of weighing and measuring equipment in his area, then knows that the design has been given the DTI's approval and can confidently proceed with the necessary testing and stamping of the equipment. The local standards used by local authorities are also periodically tested by the central government service by reference to the tertiary standards kept by the Department.

At the local level, section 69 of the Act states that the local weights and measures authority shall be in England and Wales the relevant non-metropolitan county, metropolitan district or London Borough Council,[17] the Common Council for the City and the Temples, and the Council of the Isles of Scilly.

Section 4 of the Act requires local authorities to keep local standards. These are kept at a particular place and there must be a certificate of fitness for the purpose in respect of them issued by the DTI. 'Working standards', i.e. those actually used by inspectors in testing traders' weighing and measuring equipment, must also be provided by the local authorities. These standards must be tested periodically by reference to the local standards (section 5). It can be seen, therefore, that there is a chain of uniformity from national standards, through local and working standards to the traders' equipment.

Local authorities are also required to appoint and reasonably remunerate a chief inspector of weights and measures and sufficient inspectors for the efficient discharge of the functions imposed on them by law (section 72). Inspectors are required to be properly qualified by examination (sections 72, 73). The present examination is the Diploma in Trading Standards conducted by the Local Government Training Board. The examination is designed to test not only a detailed knowledge of consumer protection law, but also ability in economics, materials technology and technical drawing, and statistics. The object is to ensure that inspectors have both the breadth and depth of knowledge to discharge their increasingly complex duties efficiently.

It is a feature of the office of inspector that he is himself criminally liable for falsely stamping equipment, deriving profit in connection with the marketing of weighing or measuring equipment, knowingly committing a breach of duty or otherwise misconducting himself in the execution of his office (section 75). Inspectors also have wide powers under section 79 of inspection and entry of premises within the inspector's area, subject to the production of credentials if

---

17   In England this means the 20 non-metropolitan counties and those metropolitan district councils which took over functions from the former metropolitan county councils pursuant to the Local Government Act 1985. In Wales this means the 8 counties.

requested. The inspector must have reasonable cause to believe that the equipment that he is to test is used for trade, and the premises must not be exclusively a private house.[18] He also has the power to seize and detain equipment liable to be forfeited under the Act. Forcible entry is only permitted under a written warrant by a justice on a sworn information that there is reasonable ground to believe that there are relevant equipment, goods, articles, or documents on any premises or that an offence under the Act is being or is about to be committed on the premises, and that entry has been refused, or (inter alia) that an application for entry would defeat the object of the entry. When an entry has been made, it is a criminal offence for the inspector or anyone accompanying him to disclose the proprietor's trade secrets otherwise than in the performance of his duty (section 79(7)). It is an offence wilfully to obstruct an inspector acting in the course of his duties (section 80). An offence is prima facie committed in any case where an inspector is refused entry after showing his credentials if required.

In the context of the functions of the trading standards inspectorate, its enforcement function under the Act must be differentiated from any consumer advisory services offered by councils to consumers in their area. The enforcement function must operate entirely impartially in the interests of both consumer and trader. It must be non-partisan and identified neither with buyer nor seller assessment of fault must regard the trade and the public equally. Trade secrets officially gained cannot be used for purposes other than enforcement.[19] Other bodies giving advice to aggrieved consumers may be free to be partisan.

3. THE MAIN OFFENCES

Weighing and measuring for trade

Part I having prescribed the various units of measurements and the various national and local standards described above, Part II goes on to deal with weighing and measuring for trade. In particular section 7 defines the expression 'use for trade' in the context of which only those weights and measures prescribed by the Act may be used. The core of the definition of 'use for trade' is 'the transferring or

---

18 See *Brunner v Williams* [1975] Crim LR 250, where the defendant coal merchants were acquitted of obstructing an inspector who unsuccessfully tried to stop them emptying coal bags, before weighing them, in the curtilage of a private dwellinghouse.

19 See the comprehensive review in *O'Keefe's Law of Weights and Measures*, (2nd Edn. by A. A. Painter), particularly Vol.(1)0. (132) et seq.

rendering of money or money's worth in consideration of money or money's worth', provided the transaction is by reference to quantity and the use is for the purpose of the determination or statement of that quantity (section 7(1)). An exchange of value by reference to quantity is therefore the essence of the test.

With the object of standardising weights and measures used for trade and so as not to confuse the consumer with weird and wonderful measurements which are difficult to understand and compare, the units of measurement now lawful for use for trade are those specified in section 8. Permissible units of measurement in which quantities may be expressed are set out in Schedule 1 (which may be amended by order of the Secretary of State). These are the measures of length, area, volume, capacity and mass or weight specified there in both imperial units and in metric units. The prescribed imperial units are now confined to the mile, yard, foot and inch; the acre, square yard and square foot; the gallon, quart, pint, gill and fluid ounce; and the pound, ounce, and troy ounce (as to length, area, volume, capacity and mass respectively). This list should be compared with the thirty-two permitted metric units. Familiar measurements such as the square mile are no longer lawful for use in trade. It is an offence to use for trade any unit of measurement not in the Schedule, except that only precious metals and stones may be measured in troy ounces and carats (metric).

Schedule 3 (which may also be amended by order – see section 8(6)) specifies the actual physical weights and measures which are lawful for use in trade when weighing or measuring quantities, the list being limited because it is necessary to keep these uniform as used in trade. These are the linear measures, the square measures, the cubic measure, the capacity measures, and the weights of both the imperial and metric system as specified. Thus, the specified linear measures of the imperial system range from measures of 100 feet to 1 inch, and those of the metric system range from measures of 50 metres to 1 centimetre. A linear measure may be marked in subdivisions. Whilst this Schedule lists the *physical* measures and weights lawful for use in trade, trade may lawfully be conducted by multiplying permitted *units* of measure and weight – see Schedule 1 and section 8(1)).

It is an offence to contravene section 8 and any unlawful measure or weight used is liable to forfeiture. The Secretary of State has power to add to, remove or vary the items listed in these Schedules.

In order to simplify the process of metrication, the Secretary of State is empowered to make regulations to require or authorise persons using metric units to afford information (by conversion charts, etc.) of the imperial equivalent (section 9).

Section 11 in Part II lays down the vital scheme for ensuring that the weights and measures used in everyday trade are accurate. It is an offence for any person to use for trade any such equipment as may be prescribed by regulation unless the equipment has been passed by an inspector as fit for such use, and bears a stamp that it has been so passed which remains undefaced except by reason of fair wear and tear. The trader must submit the equipment for testing by the inspector by means of such local or working standards as he considers appropriate. A weight or measure must be marked with its purported value before stamping. There are in force numerous regulations prescribing classes or descriptions of equipment and regulating their material, principles of construction, how they should be tested, and permissible margins of error. Some adaptation of UK law was made by the Measuring Instruments (EEC Requirements) Regulations 1988, implementing EEC Council Directive No. 71/316 as amended. One of the consequences of these Regulations is that measuring instruments bearing the sign of EEC pattern approval and exemption from EEC initial verification or the mark of EEC initial verification are exempted from the prohibition against use for trade in section 11.

Sections 16 and 17 create two further offences, one of which is commonly met. Section 16 relates to forging, counterfeiting, altering or defacing stamps and altering equipment so as to make it unjust after it has been stamped. Section 17 makes it an offence for a person to use for trade, or to have in his possession for use for trade, any weighing or measuring equipment which is false or unjust, and such equipment is liable to be forfeited (section 17(1)). In *Makinson v J K Dewhurst Ltd* [20] the Divisional Court dismissed the prosecutor's appeal against dismissal of a summons against the defendant butchers for having in their possession for use for trade unjust weighing equipment. They had a self-indicating and price-computing machine which had a built in tendency to give short weight unless a simple zeroing adjustment was made after a period of about two hours. Their employee failed to zero this when test purchases were made. The question was whether the machine was 'unjust'. The Divisional Court dismissed the prosecution appeal on the basis that as constructed the machine was a just one, even if as used without the recommended adjustment it was giving short

---

20 (1981) unreported, QBD, but see transcript in (1981) 89 Monthly Rev 87. See also the helpful discussion in *O'Keefe's Law of Weights and Measures* (2nd Edn., by A. A. Painter) para 1 (160). For a decision on the meaning here of 'in possession', see *Bellerby v Carle* [1983] 2 AC 101, [1983] 1 All ER 1031, HL, where it was held that two licensees were not in possession of unjust beer measuring equipment owned, supplied and maintained by Watney's Brewery pursuant to a contract with the licensees' company.

weight. The result might have been different if the prosecution had been brought under section 28 in respect of short weight.

Statistics collated by the Office of Fair Trading indicate that using false or unjust equipment is one of the more common weights and measures offences. This provision is construed strictly. The equipment must be just, both loaded and unloaded, neither showing too much or too little. Absence of fraud or acquiescence by the purchaser is irrelevant.

It is a defence under section 17 for the person charged to prove that he used the equipment in the course of employment by some other person and that he neither knew, nor might reasonably have been expected to know, nor had any reason to suspect, the equipment to be false or unjust.

Section 17(3) makes it an offence to commit fraud in the use of any weighing or measuring equipment or to be a party to such fraud. This offence is concerned with tricks such as tilting the scales or other manipulation of the equipment. It was held in *Harris v Allwood*[1] that no offence is committed here where goods such as tea, sugar or raisins are weighed in their wrapping paper in the customer's presence, or where it is customary in the trade to include wrappings.[2]

There is a presumption that where equipment is found in a person's possession who carries on trade, or on premises used for trade, that person or the occupier of the premises is presumed to have the equipment in his possession for use for trade until the contrary is proved (section 7(5)).

Public weighing or measuring equipment

This equipment is regulated by Part III. Keepers of public weighing or measuring equipment for the use of which a fee is charged must hold a certificate issued by the Chief Inspector of Weights and Measures. Local authorities are empowered to provide and maintain such equipment, and there are various offences connected with misuse of it.

Regulation of certain transactions in goods

Part IV of the Act contains a number of provisions of considerable importance to the consumer. In particular, Schedules 4 to 7 prescribe that certain commodities may be sold by quantity only whether

---

1 (1892) 57 JP 7; but in many cases now net weight or wrapper allowances are prescribed.
2 *King v Spencer* (1904) 68 JP 530.

expressed in net or gross weight, capacity measurement, or volume – rather than by 'tins' or 'packets'.[3] This Part also contains the offence of giving short weight, now further considered.

Short weight

The offence contained in section 28, giving short weight, measure or number applies to any goods whether or not they are listed in the Schedules mentioned under the previous heading. It also applies to sales at any point, not merely to retail sales.

The section states that any person who, in selling or purporting to sell any goods by weight or other measurement or by number, delivers or causes to be delivered to the buyer a lesser quantity than that purported to be sold or than corresponds with the price charged shall be guilty of an offence (section 28(1)). Under section 28(2)(a) the indicated quantity on a pre-package within that Act is to be taken as the 'nominal' quantity, a concept explained later.

Sections 29 and 30 create a number of other offences. In summarised form they are:

a) Misrepresenting by word of mouth or otherwise the quantity of the goods, or otherwise doing anything calculated to mislead another person as to the quantity, in connection with the sale *or purchase* of any goods (section 29(1));

b) Overstating the quantity of goods pre-packed in or on a container by means of a written statement of quantity (section 30(1));

c) Overstating the quantity of non pre-packed goods which are made up for sale or for delivery after sale in a container marked with a statement in writing of the quantity of the goods (section 30(2)). Subsections 30(3) and (4) modify the offences in section 30(1) and (2) by stating that an offence is committed notwithstanding that the quantity stated is expressed to be the quantity of the goods at a specified time falling before the time in question, except in specified circumstances. One of these is where the quantity is so expressed in pursuance of an express requirement of the Act;

d) Making false statements in documents associated with goods (e.g. coal) (section 31(1)).

It should be noted that the facts giving rise to a prosecution for short measure contrary to section 28 may also involve using false or

---

3 The detail is too complex to be dealt with in this book. Students involved in working in this area should refer to *O'Keefe's Law of Weights and Measures* (2nd edn. by A. A. Painter), where text and commentary will be found.

unjust equipment contrary to section 17 and may also amount to applying a false trade description to goods contrary to section 1(1) of the Trade Descriptions Act 1968.[4]

Although it is usually obvious when short weight has been delivered contrary to section 28(1), it is occasionally debatable what is meant by 'lesser quantity' in a particular context. Thus in *Marshall v Searles*[5] an inspector went to the defendant's public house and bought two pints of draught Guinness. Each pint glass that he was given included a head of froth. The total liquid content of each glass was about 6 per cent below a standard pint. The prosecution appealed against the justices' finding that no offence of selling less than a pint had been committed. The Divisional Court dismissed the appeal and held that reference to Guiness advertisements suggested that a general member of the public would expect to be served with a pint consisting of a composite mixture of liquid and gas. That was what was being sold and purported to be sold. In fact, section 43(1) states that gas comprised in any foam on beer or cider shall be disregarded in ascertaining quantity, but the section needed a commencement order. In 1992 the Secretary of State announced his intention of implementing the section. This was in response to public complaints of short measure and checks by trading standards officers tending to support these complaints. Accordingly, a commencement order[6] for section 43 has been made bringing the section into force on 1 April 1994. From this date, the gas in any foam is to be disregarded when measuring the volume of beer or cider. Brim measure glasses are not to be prohibited but licensees must see that they serve a full liquid pint of beer or cider.

The offence of misrepresenting quantities must be read in the light of section 28(2)(b), which states that any statement, whether oral or in writing, as to the weight of any goods shall be deemed, unless otherwise expressed, to be a statement of the net weight of the goods. A misrepresentation may also give rise to an offence under the Trade Descriptions Act 1968 (section 1), and give rise to civil remedies in tort and contract as discussed in previous chapters. But here the operative misrepresentation is not confined to one made by one party to a contract to the other. It is within the subsection if the

---

4   See, for example, *Kinchin v Haines* [1979] Crim LR 329, DC, mentioned below.
5   [1964] Crim LR 667. In late 1977 the Scottish High Court of Justiciary came to a similar conclusion with regard to ordinary beer, see *Dean v Scottish and Newcastle Breweries Ltd* 1978 SLT 24. These cases were followed in *Bennett v Markham King* [1982] 3 All ER 641, [1982] 1 WLR 1230
6   Weights and Measures (Commencement) Order 1992, S.I. 1992/770.

statement is made by an interested third party to the buyer or seller and is likely to mislead him.[7]

Offences under section 28 (short weight) are of strict liability.[8] For instance, when considering misrepresentations, a representation is false if at the material time it was a false statement of fact, irrespective of the knowledge or belief of the person making the statement. In addition, the words 'calculated to mislead' which might be thought to imply *mens rea*, are construed as meaning 'likely to mislead' rather than 'intended to mislead'.[9]

General defence

i) Warranty (section 33)

As was formerly the case with food it is a defence to an offence relating to the quantity or prepacking of goods that they were bought from some other person as being of a quantity represented by that person and with a *written* warranty that they were of the relevant quantity. The defendant must also show that he had no reason to believe the warranty inaccurate, that he did in fact believe it accurate, and if the warranty was given by a seller outside Great Britain that the defendant had taken reasonable steps to check its accuracy. Where the alleged offence relates to the quantity of goods, he must also show a) that he took all reasonable steps to ensure that the quantity remained unchanged while in his possession, and b) apart from any change in their quantity the goods remained in the same state as when he bought them. As with food and drugs, this latter provision is aimed against subtractions from the article, or breaking bulk.

The person by whom the warranty is alleged to be given is entitled to appear and give evidence (section 33(4)).

7 *Collett v Co-operative Wholesale Society Ltd* [1970] 1 All ER 274, DC (farmers sold milk to Milk Marketing Board but consigned it direct to respondent dairies, although no contract with them existed. The respondents were convicted of misrepresenting alleged deficiencies in quantity of milk received from the farmers, as a consequence of which they would feel obliged to accept less money for the milk).

8 *Winter v Hinckley and District Industrial Co-operative Society Ltd* [1959] 1 All ER 403 (servant in charge of vehicle delivering Society's coal had caused short weight of 112 lbs coal sacks by stealing some of their contents after leaving Society's premises. Held: no defence by Society that they did not know coal sacks were light, since no *mens rea* needed).

9 See *McDowell v Standard Oil Co (New Jersey)* [1927] AC 632 at 637, a case on similar wording in the Trade Marks Act 1905 and O'Keefe, op. cit. 1 (244).

ii) Additional defences and safeguards (section 34)

Section 34, which originates from the former 1979 Act (amending section 26 of the 1963 Act), lists a number of other defences, some of which are similar to those in trade descriptions or food and drug cases.

    a) It is a defence for the person charged to prove that he took all reasonable precautions and exercised all due diligence to avoid the commission of such an offence (section 34).

Before the amendments made to this defence by the Weights and Measures Act 1979 a 'mistake' or 'accident' also had to be proved, and the duty was for the defendant to have used all due diligence to avoid the commission of an offence by himself or any person under his control. The radically shortened version of the defence now substituted makes the other cases on the former section 26 not entirely reliable. The new version also makes it more likely that a defence will involve an employer 'passing the buck' to an employee. The employee may then often be prosecuted under section 34(2) (act or default of another person).[10]

    Although less onerous than formerly, it may not be easy to convince a court that all reasonable precautions have been taken and all due diligence exercised. These two duties have been described as 'first, the setting up of an efficient system for the avoidance of offences under the Act, and second, the proper operation of that system'.[11] It was held in *Kinchin v Haines*[12] that a self-employed coal-merchant charged under section 1(1)(a) of the Trade Descriptions Act 1968 with falsely describing sacks of fuel marked as '1 cwt' but which were lighter than this because of foreseeable evaporation of moisture caused by heavy rain, had not exercised reasonable precautions when weighing the wet coal and not allowing for the effects of evaporation.

    The defence has in its previous, more onerous, form been held to be applicable where an underweight packet of crisps was produced by an efficient and well maintained machine with an anticipated error of 6 underweight bags in every 10,000 of the weekly output or 0.0006 per cent of weekly production of 20 million bags.[13] The

---

10   See particularly *Tesco Supermarket Ltd v Nattrass* [1972] AC 153, [1971] 2 All ER 127, HL, discussed further in this book in the context of trade descriptions.
11   Per Fisher J in *Tesco Supermarkets v Nattrass* [1971] 1 QB 133, [1970] 3 All ER 357.
12   [1979] Crim LR 329, DC.
13   *Bibby-Cheshire v Golden Wonder Ltd* [1972] 3 All ER 738, DC, M & H p. 562.

reasoning seems to be that if a normally reliable machine causes the error for no anticipated reason, the defence is available.[14]

The requirements of reasonable precautions and due diligence have been extensively considered in trade description cases and the similar defence in section 24 of the Trade Descriptions Act 1968 is discussed above.[15] It is important to note, too, that this defence cannot be relied on unless notice to the prosecutor is given in accordance with section 34(2), discussed below.

b) It is a defence in proceedings involving goods in containers marked with wrong quantities, or goods having associated with them documents stating wrong quantities, that the deficiency arose after the marking of the container or completion of the document, *and* was attributable to factors for which reasonable allowance was made in stating the quantity of the goods in the marking or document (section 35(2)). A similar defence applies to retail sales of non-prepacked food where the deficiency is due wholly to unavoidable evaporation or drainage.[16] The defence under section 35(2) is available to the retailer as well as the person responsible for the marking, usually the manufacturer.[17]

c) Where the quantity of the goods is inaccurate because there is an excess, it is a defence to prove that the excess was attributable to the taking of measures reasonably necessary in order to avoid committing an offence in respect of a deficiency in those or other goods (section 36).[18]

d) There is a *de minimis* defence, the effect of which is that where one of a number of articles is tested and found deficient, the defendant shall not be convicted unless 'a reasonable number of those other articles was also tested'. Where the proceedings concern one or more of a number of articles tested on the same occasion, the court must have regard to the average quantity in all the articles tested; and if the proceedings are in respect of a single article, the court 'shall disregard any inconsiderable deficiency or excess'; and the court must 'have regard generally

14 Contrast the decision of the House of Lords in the food and drugs case of *Smedleys Ltd v Breed* [1974] AC 839, [1974] 2 All ER 21, above.

15 See above, p. 364. There is also a comprehensive discussion of how manufacturers can set up 'due diligence' systems in *O'Keefe,* op. cit. 1(281).

16 See s. 35(3).

17 *F W Woolworth & Co Ltd v Gray* [1970] 1 All ER 953. Here the retailer could not rely on the manufacturer's warranty because they had not taken steps to ensure that the quantity of the goods remained unchanged as required by Weights and Measures Act 1963, s. 25(1) (but the appeal succeeded under s. 26(2)).

18 See the facts of *Bibby-Cheshire v Golden Wonder Ltd,* above, where the machine was set to deliver bags of 17.5 drams instead of the 15 drams marked.

to all the circumstances of the case' (section 37). The effect of this important section is to emphasise that an inspector should check a reasonable quantity of similar articles in these circumstances. But it was held in *Sears v Smiths Food Group Ltd* [19] where a private purchaser had two bags of crisps tested by an inspector, one of the bags being in fact underweight, that the inspector was under no obligation to test other packets available at the 'time and place' in question – i.e. when and where the bag or bags were brought to the inspector for testing.

iii) Average quantities – EEC developments

A development of great importance bearing on the question of how far it is permissible for manufactured pre-packed goods to conform *on average* to a stated weight was contained in two Directives of the EEC Council (75/106/EEC and 76/211/EEC). These Directives refer, inter alia, to an earlier Directive (71/316/EEC) on the approximation of the laws of the member states relating to common provisions for both measuring instruments and methods of metrological control, and providing that there should be harmonisation of the requirements for marketing certain products and in particular as regards the measuring and marking of pre-packed quantities. The Directives relate to pre-packaged goods (called 'pre-packages'), which are intended for sale in constant unit nominal quantities equal to values predetermined by the packer, expressed in units of weight or volume, and not less than 5g or 5ml and not more than 10kg or 10l.

The Directive requires that all pre-packages must bear an indication of the weight or volume of the product which they are required to contain, known as 'nominal weight' or 'nominal volume'. They must also bear the EEC sign ('e') which guarantees that the requirements have been met by the packer or importer. Annex I of the Directives amplify these provisions. The 'nominal quantity' of a pre-package refers to the quantity of product which the package is *deemed to contain.* The 'actual contents' are the quantity of product which it in fact contains. The 'negative error' of a pre-package is the quantity by which the actual contents of the pre-package are less than the nominal quantity. The core of the Directive is the statement that completed pre-packages must satisfy the following requirements:

1) the actual contents shall not be less, on average, than the nominal quantity;
2) the proportion of pre-packages having a negative error greater

19   [1968] 2 QB 288, [1968] 2 All ER 721.

than the tolerable negative error laid down shall be sufficiently small to comply with the tests specified in Annex II of the Directive. Thus the tolerable negative error is first ascertained, and this factor is ignored for the purposes of the statistical checking of batches of pre-packages. The checking of the pre-packages is then done by sampling in two parts – a check covering the actual contents of each pre-package in the sample – and another check on the average of the actual contents of the pre-packages in the sample. A batch of pre-packages shall be considered acceptable if the results of both these checks satisfy the criteria laid down. Plans in Annex II indicate how samples should be tested (destructive or non-destructive testing) and the number in the sample according to the size of the batch. Criteria for acceptance or rejection according to the number of defective units found in the sample are then laid down. Thus, in the case of the single sampling non-destructive testing plan, if the batch contains between 501 and 1,200 pre-packages, 80 must be sampled. The whole batch of pre-packages is acceptable if the number of defective units in the sample does not exceed 5; otherwise it is rejected.

These Directives were implemented by the Weights and Measures Act 1979, an Act whose policy attracted opposition from consumer organisations in that for the first time in many centuries the consumer had no guarantee that a purchased pre-package had at least the quantities indicated. However, at the date of entry of the UK to the Community (1 January 1973) a system of average weights and measures was well established in most other member states. The UK was unusual in having a 'minimum system' enforced at the local, rather than central level. Since by sophisticated quality control techniques it is possible to fill pre-packages with lesser quantities than under the minimum system, a factor significant in large-scale production, to maintain the UK's competitiveness in overseas markets it was thought necessary to accept this change. It is still perfectly legal, however, for packers to pack to the minimum system (since the tests for average compliance will inevitably be satisfied) but a packer must still keep the records required by the legislation.

The 1979 Act, now consolidated in Part V of the 1985 Act, had introduced the following innovative features:

i) A Metrological Co-ordinating Unit was established to ensure uniform enforcement of the Act in every local authority's jurisdiction. Its existence reflected the unusual character of the UK's weights and measures enforcement machinery, based on weights and measures authorities in the UK but normally enforced centrally on the Continent. The body was set up experimentally and the Act confers power on the Secretary of

State to abolish it (sections 55 to 62). It was duly abolished (by the National Metrological Co-ordinating Unit (Transfer of Functions and Abolition) Order 1987) from 1 January 1988 and its functions transferred to the Secretary of State.

ii) The main thrust of enforcement moves from the traditional retail level to the packaging plant or point of importation. The 'reference test' referred to below can usually only be carried out if statistically acceptable samples are available, which will not be the case on retail premises. Tests on non-prepacked goods or exempted and catch-weight goods continue to be made at retail level.

iii) Persons other than the packer or importer, who have in their possession for sale, or agree to sell or sell a relevant package which is inadequate (i.e. has a negative error larger than twice the tolerable negative error) only incur criminal liability if they know that the package is inadequate – i.e. *mens rea* is necessary (section 50(5)).

iv) The Act makes provision for 'e' marked packages. Those bearing the EEC's 'e' mark are guaranteed to meet the requirements of the Directives and can circulate freely within the Community without further checks. There is therefore a special responsibility on packers and inspectors as regards goods so marked (section 54).

v) Special powers are given to inspectors to issue written instructions that suspect packages shall be kept at the disposal of the inspector with a view to their subsequent testing. No court order is necessary (section 63).

vi) The Act must be read in conjunction with the Weights and Measures (Packaged Goods) Regulations 1986, which in turn incorporates the Code of Practical Guidance for Packers and Importers and the Manual of Practical Guidance for Inspectors.

The Act establishes the 'three rules for packers and importers'. These are:

1) The actual contents of the packages shall not be less, on average, than the nominal quantity (i.e. the statement of quantity marked on the container).

2) Not more than $2\frac{1}{2}$ per cent of the packages may be non-standard, i.e. have negative errors larger than the tolerable negative error (TNE) specified for the nominal quantity.

3) No package may be 'inadequate', i.e. have a negative error larger than twice the specified TNE (section 47).

Details of the statistical test, known as the 'reference test' to be carried out by inspectors are contained in the 1986 Regulations referred to above. The packer's duty is to ensure that his tested goods pass the reference test. It is then statistically probable, but not inevitable, that he has complied with the three rules above.

The Act creates a number of offences, the main ones being failure by a packer or importer to fulfil his statutory duties or failure to keep proper records (or falsification thereof). The primary duties are specified in section 47 and relate to the three rules already discussed.

The only comprehensive, annotated, source of all relevant primary and secondary legislation, some of which is of great technical complexity to the layman, is *O'Keefe's Law of Weights and Measures* (2nd Edn.), ed. A.A. Painter. The Packers' Code contains a glossary of technical terms.

iv) Offences due to Third Party (section 32)

It is a condition of relying on the defence under section 34(1) of the Act (reasonable precautions taken and all due diligence exercised – see above) that the defendant give appropriate notice of this to the prosecutor at least seven days before the date of the hearing (section 34(2)). The person whose act or default caused the commission of the offence may then be convicted of the offence, under section 32, whether or not the original person is proceeded against. This procedure can be used against employees, suppliers and by and against a whole chain of distributors and sellers.

4. METRICATION

The UK response to EEC metrication policy has already been mentioned in Chapter 1.[20] The Metrication Board had been established before the UK's accession to the EEC in 1969 in order to simplify overseas trade processes. The Board was purely advisory, and responsible to the Secretary of State for Prices and Consumer Protection. Its main function was, obviously, to help acquaint the consumer with the significance of metric quantities and to ease the transition from imperial to metric units. The price control system under the Prices Acts is the mandatory element in this process, and can be used as a safeguard against unwarranted price increases. The Metrication Board itself was dissolved shortly after the return of the Conservative Government in 1979. In the light of the government's policy of slowing down the metrication process its continued existence as a 'quango' was thought to be unjustified.

---

20 For the recent history of this in the UK, see Norman Stone 'Metrication and the Consumer' in Morris (ed.) *Economics and Consumer Protection*. See also *O'Keefe*, op.cit. 0(23).

The Weights and Measures, &c. Act 1976 (now repealed and replaced by the 1985 Act) empowered the Secretary of State to:

   a) set dates not before 21 April 1978 from which only metric packs of prescribed quantities will be permitted;

   b) set dates ending the use of imperial units for other pre-packed goods or goods weighed or measured in front of customers. In the case of weighed-out meat, fish, fruit and vegetables sold retail, such dates not being before 1 January 1980;

   c) generally prohibit the use in trade of all imperial units except the mile, foot, inch, gallon and pint;

   d) restrict the use in trade of any imperial unit, sector by sector.

The Secretary of State may, under section 9 of the 1985 Act, require that where metric units are used for trade they are to be accompanied, for explanatory purposes, with information as to the equivalent imperial units. Conversion tables may also be required to be displayed. These powers are exercisable by statutory instrument subject to annulment in pursuance of a resolution of either House of Parliament. At the time of writing, compulsory metrication remains controversial. But by the end of 1981 the majority of goods, particularly those pre-packed, could be sold in S.I. units. The major exceptions are draught beer, cider, packaged milk and non-prepackaged goods at retail level. Concern about confusion has proved largely unfounded and little use has been made of section 9 above.

In the light of the fact that metrication is the norm in almost all the developed countries within and without the EEC with which the UK trades (the USA being the main exception) continued progress towards full metrication is inevitable. Countries such as New Zealand which have pursued a full metrication policy more vigorously do not appear to have found the oft-quoted 'confusion of the elderly' argument to have been a major obstacle, particularly if the policy is accompanied for a time by a dual marking system in metric units with imperial equivalents. Accordingly, it was not surprising in July 1991 that the Secretary of State made a statement that the government would take maximum advantage of the transitional arrangements in the Units of Measurement Directives (80/181/EEC and 71/617/EEC) and accordingly will:

   a) cease to authorise, after 31 December 1994, imperial units used for economic, public health, public safety and administrative purposes except for the units used for the purposes set out in b) and c) below;

   b) cease to authorise after 31 December 1999:

     I   the pound and ounce for goods sold loose from bulk;

     II the pint and fluid ounce for beer, cider, waters lemonades and fruit juices in returnable containers;

III the fathom for marine navigation;
IV the therm for gas supply;
c) authorise the continued use without limit of:
   I the mile, yard, foot and inch for road traffic signs and related distance and speed measurements;
   II the pint for dispensing draft beer and cider and for milk in returnable containers;
   III the troy ounce for transactions in precious metals;
   IV the acre for land registration purposes.

Metric units will continue to be authorised for use in the U.K. for economic, public health, public safety and administrative purposes. Changes to other legislation which refers to imperial units of measurement will be a matter for the government department and other bodies responsible for that legislation.

Appendix I

Safety regulations

a) Regulations made under the Consumer Protection Act 1987

As discussed in chapter 9 (pp. 233–234) safety regulations can be made under the Consumer Protection Act 1987, section 11. Listed below are all such current Regulations.

The Approval of Safety Standards Regulations 1987, S.I. 1987/1911. These regulations enable the Secretary of State to approve standards for the purposes of section 10(3). Approvals may also be cancelled. Details of how approvals and cancellations are to be effected are included and provision is made for a register of approvals to be kept.

The Benzene in Toys (Safety) Regulations 1987, S.I. 1987/2116. These regulations prohibit the supply etc. of toys, including balloon making kits, which contain benzene exceeding the specified concentration.

The Furniture and Furnishings (Fire)(Safety) Regulations 1988, S.I. 1988/1324 (amended by S.I. 1989/2358). These regulations replace earlier provisions and are concerned with new and, in some cases, second-hand domestic furniture including garden furniture for use indoors and caravan furniture. There is a requirement for upholstery to pass a cigarette test (reg. 5), for filling materials to pass ignitability tests (regs. 6 and 7), for permanent and loose covers to pass match tests (regs. 8 and 9) and for display and permanent labels to be attached to furniture (regs. 10 and 11). The regulations will be fully in force by 1 March 1993.

The Ceramic Ware (Safety) Regulations 1988, S.I. 1988/1647. These regulations replace earlier regulations and require ceramic ware to satisfy the requirements of BS 6748:1986 concerning the permissible release of lead and cadmium from ceramic ware for use with food.

The Gas Cooking Appliances (Safety) Regulations 1989, S.I. 1989/149. These regulations prohibit the supply etc of gas cookers which do not comply with either the requirements specified in the regulations or European Standard EN 30 or BSS 5386: Part 3: 1980 or Part 4: 1983. The requirements relate to such matters as the safety of burners, surface temperatures of the appliances, the heat emitted from them, the thickness of glass doors, lids etc., and the stability of appliances. There are also provisions covering instructions and warnings to be issued. The Secretary of State may approve amendments or revisions of the standards specified.

The Low Voltage Electrical Equipment (Safety) Regulations 1989, S.I. 1989/ 728. These regulations, made in conjunction with the European Communities Act 1972, section 2(2), apply to any electrical equipment designed or adapted for use with voltages of 50–1,000 (A.C.) and 75–1,500 (D.C.), unless excluded by Schedule 1 or for export outside the EEC. Electrical equipment is required to be safe and to be made in accordance with engineering practice generally accepted as good within the EEC (reg. 5). Compliance with certain harmonised standards, specified international safety provisions or, in the absence of these, with national safety provisions of a member state or with standards approved under the Approval of Safety Standards Regulations 1987[1] will suffice (reg. 7). There is provision for the marking and certification of goods (reg. 10). Enforcement duties and time limits for prosecution are also included.

The Toys (Safety) Regulations 1989, S.I. 1989/1275.[2] These regulations, made in conjunction with the European Communities Act 1972, section 2(2), replace the Toys (Safety) Regulations 1974[3] and are designed to provide for the safety of toys by applying European safety standards. The regulations apply to toys other than those supplied for the first time in the Community before 1 January 1990 and not bearing an EC mark (reg. 2). Toys are defined in reg. 3 as being products or materials designed or clearly intended for use in play by children under 14, providing they are not excluded by Sch. 3 which covers, for example, fashion jewellery for children and toy steam engines. Toys are required to satisfy the essential safety requirements as specified in Sch. 2. This may be achieved by either compliance with relevant national standards of any member state and carrying the EC mark (the symbol CE) (reg. 5) or compliance with EC type-examination certificates together with the EC mark (reg. 6). Provisions are included for approving bodies to test toys (reg. 7), application procedures for EC-type examinations certificates (reg. 8), for requiring EC marks to be applied (reg. 9), for information to be made available by manufacturers and Community importers (reg. 10), for prohibiting the supply of toys not conforming with the regulations (reg. 12) and for enforcement and prosecutions (regs. 13 and 14).

The Food Imitations (Safety) Regulations 1989, S.I. 1989/1291. These regulations replace earlier provisions and prohibit the supply etc. of

---

1 S.I. 1987/1911, see above.
2 See further 'Toy safety – too important to play around with?' D W Jenkins, (1987) 1 Fair Trader, Pt 12, p. 16; 'Toy safety in the EC' S Weatherill, (1989) 86 L S Gaz No 43, p. 30; *The Single Market, Standards: Toy Safety*, D.T.I., 1989.
3 S.I. 1974/1367, see below p. 420.

man·ifactured goods ordinarily intended for private use and which, although not food, have a form, odour, colour, appearance, packaging, labelling volume or size which makes them likely to be mistaken for food especially by children, and thereby being put into mouths or sucked or swallowed with a risk of death or injury. Excluded are all items excluded from section 11 of the Consumer Protection Act 1987 by section 11(7), marbles, products representing food for dolls houses, model scenes etc. and items entirely made from food ingredients.

The Cosmetic Products (Safety) Regulations 1989, S.I. 1989/2233 (amended by S.I. 1990/1812 and S.I. 1991/447). These regulations will replace the Cosmetic Products (Safety) Regulations 1984[4] by 1 January 1993. They were made in conjunction with the European Communities Act 1972, section 2(2) and are designed to implement a number of European Directives. Regulation 3 seeks to ensure that cosmetic products do not cause damage to human health when used under normal conditions. Products are prohibited from containing some 712 specified substances or may only contain other specified substances in specified circumstances (reg. 4). Substances may be authorised for use by the Secretary of State (reg. 5) and there are requirements of marking products with specified information (regs. 6 and 6A). Enforcement matters are also included.

The All-Terrain Motor Vehicles (Safety) Regulations 1989, S.I. 1989/2288. Introduced to supersede earlier regulations which had been made under the emergency procedure in section 11(5) of the Consumer Protection Act 1987,[5] these regulations prohibit the supply of regulated vehicles with three wheels (reg. 3). This encompasses vehicles propelled by internal combustion engines for leisure activities on all types of land but not those for disabled people nor two-wheeled motor-cycles with side cars. Four-wheeled vehicles designed or intended for use by children under 12 and for those aged between 12 and 16 are also prohibited unless they have maximum speeds within the specified limits and regulators to reduce the speed at which they can travel (regs. 4 and 5). Warnings are also required on the vehicles for use by the older children (reg. 5).

The Oral Snuff (Safety) Regulations 1989, S.I. 1989/2347. These regulations prohibit the supply etc. of oral snuff. They have been the subject of litigation[6]

---

4   S.I. 1984/1260, as amended, see below p. 422.
5   The Three-Wheeled All-Terrain Motor Vehicles (Safety) Regulations 1988, S.I. 1988/2122.
6   *R v Secretary of State for Social Security, ex p United States Tobacco International Inc* (21 July 1988, unreported) CA, re disclosure of representations by other interested parties; *United States Tobacco International Inc v Secretary of State for Health* (1990) 155 JP 144, QBD, re territorial extent of the regulations and *R v Secretary of State for Health, ex p United States Tobacco International Inc* [1992] 1 QB 353, [1992] 1 All ER 212, QBD, judicial review of regulations.

and, following a successful application for judicial review, have been quashed.[7]

Tobacco Products Labelling (Safety) Regulations 1991, S.I. 1991/1530. These regulations have been made in conjunction with the European Communities Act 1972 to implement a Council Directive. The regulations require producers of tobacco products to ensure that packets carry the specified general warning (reg. 3). Cigarettes are required to carry one of six additional health warnings as specified in Schedule 1 (reg. 4). There are also requirements to display tar and nicotine yields of cigarettes (reg. 6) with a testing system instituted (regs. 9 and 10). Compliance with equivalent measures from another Community state will suffice (reg. 8).

Heating Appliances (Fireguards) (Safety) Regulations 1991, S.I. 1991/2693. These regulations revoke earlier regulations and impose requirements relating to gas fires and oil heaters. Fireguards may either comply with BS 1945:1971 or with standards published in EC member states of an equivalent level of safety.

b) Summary of current regulations made under the Consumer Protection Act 1961

As mentioned in chapter 9, regulations made under the Consumer Protection Act 1961 which were still in force on 1 October 1987 continued to apply as if made under section 11 of the 1987 Act. Those still remaining are as follows.

Stands for Carry-Cots (Safety) Regulations 1966, S.I. 1966/1610. Carry-cot stands must have a durable label attached showing maximum length and width of the carry-cot to be accommodated. The regulations then specify that the stand should conform to various specifications (e.g. that the base shall be wider than the width of the carry-cot and at least as long as 3/4 of the length of the carry-cot as specified on the label, and the underside must be not more than 17" above floor-level, and withstand 60 lb pressure for 12 hours without distortion).

Electrical Appliances (Colour Code) Regulations 1969, S.I. 1969/310 (amended by S.I. 1970/811 and S.I. 1977/931). The main provision of these regulations is that in the case of domestic electrical appliances containing a mains lead with three wires, these wires must be coloured green and yellow (earth), brown (live wire) and blue (neutral). A label must be attached explaining the code. This requirement continues indefinitely.

---

7   *R v Secretary of State for Health, ex p United States Tobacco International Inc* [1992] 1 QB 353, [1992] 1 All ER 212, QBD.

Cooking Utensils (Safety) Regulations 1972, S.I. 1972/1957. Cooking utensils designed to come into contact with food must not have a metallic coating containing more than 20 parts in 10,000 of lead content.

Pencils and Graphic Instruments (Safety) Regulations 1974, S.I. 1974/226. These regulations control the proportion of poisonous metals in any part of pencils, pens and small paint brushes and other writing or drawing instruments.

Toys (Safety) Regulations 1974, S.I. 1974/1367.[8] The main features of these regulations are 1) that toys (other than table tennis balls) must not be made of flammable cellulose nitrate, 2) that the paint must not contain more than a minute specified limit of lead, arsenic, soluble antimony, barium, mercury, cadmium or chromium, 3) electrical toys must operate at not more than 24 volts from a separate transformer, 4) pile fabric must not be inflammable, 5) metal edges and points must generally be protected, 6) facial feature of dolls etc. must be safely fastened or embedded, and 7) plastic bags must be either too thick to cling to a child's face or have a narrow opening of less than 190 mm dimensions. Although these regulations are repealed by the Toys (Safety) Regulations 1989,[9] they still apply to toys supplied for the first time in the European Community before 1 January 1990 and which do not bear the EC Mark.

Children's Clothing (Hood Cords) Regulations 1976, S.I. 1976/2. These regulations prohibit the hood of a child's outer garment, defined to include raincoats, overcoats and anoraks, being designed to be secured by means of a cord drawn through the material.

Oil Heaters (Safety) Regulations 1977, S.I. 1977/167. These regulations impose controls (based on a re-draft of British Standard 3300) on domestic oil heaters as regards the amount of carbon monoxide emitted, the amount of fuel escaping from overturned heaters, the control of the flame, draught resistance, the performance of the heater when tilted and other matters relating to design, construction and performance. A warning must be affixed to the heater in respect of possible misuses. Tests must be carried out by organisations authorised by the Secretary of State.

Perambulators and Pushchairs (Safety) Regulations 1978, S.I. 1978/1372. These regulations lay down safety features with respect to parking devices, stability, harness attachment points and locking devices for perambulators

8   See *Which?*, December 1989, p. 627; also *Taylor v Lawrence Fraser (Bristol) Ltd* (1977) 121 Sol Jo 757, QBD (seller of dangerous toys cannot rely on manufacturer's assurances); *P & M Supplies (Essex) Ltd v Devon County Council* (1991) 156 JP 328, QBD (standard of sampling required for reasonable precautions defence); 'Are toys too dangerous to play around with?', A. Pugh (1985) 93 ITSA MR 214; 'Toy safety – too important to play around with?' D W Jenkins, (1987) 1 Fair Trader, Pt 12, p. 16.
9   S.I. 1989/1275, see above at p. 417.

and pushchairs. Since 1 June 1986 those aspects of the regulations relating to pushchairs have ceased to have effect and have been replaced by the Pushchair (Safety) Regulations 1985.[10]

Oil Lamps (Safety) Regulations 1979, S.I. 1979/1125. These regulations deal with the safe construction and use of domestic paraffin burning oil lamps. Certain warnings and instructions are to be given e.g. 'Warning: Use only Paraffin', and detailed tests and specifications are laid down to ensure a lamp's strength and safety in use.

c) Regulations made under the Consumer Safety Act 1978

The regulations below were made under the 1978 Act and continue in force, with prosecutions being brought under section 12 of the 1987 Act.

The Dangerous Substances and Preparations (Safety) Regulations 1980, S.I. 1980/136 (amended by S.I. 1985/127). These regulations prohibit the supply of aerosols which use chloroethylene as an aerosol propellant and the supply of ornamental lamps and other objects which contain certain dangerous substances. In addition the supply of children's nightwear and dressing-gowns containing Tris phosphate and certain other chemicals is banned. This replaced the Nightwear (Safety) Order 1978.[11]

Upholstered Furniture (Safety) Regulations 1980, S.I. 1980/725 (amended by S.I. 1983/519). These regulations apply to upholstered seating furniture designed or suitable for domestic use. They are being replaced by the Furniture and Furnishings (Fire) (Safety) Regulations 1988[12] which now apply except in the case of second-hand furniture. The new provisions come fully into force on 1 March 1993 which will complete the revocation of these regulations.

Novelties (Safety) Regulations 1980, S.I. 1980/958 (amended by S.I. 1985/128 and S.I. 1987/2116). These regulations apply to dangerous toys. They prohibit the supply etc. of any injurious tear-gas capsule and the supply etc. of any article containing more than 1.5 ml of sulphides of ammonia 'designed or intended to afford amusement to any person by causing discomfort to any other person by means of the use or exploitation of the obnoxious properties of such sulphides'; presumably 'stink-bombs' are the primary target here. The amendment of 1985 also prohibits the supply etc. of sneezing powder and similar substances designed to be used as jokes. These regulations include provisions originally contained in the Tear-Gas Capsules (Safety) Order 1979.[13]

---

10   S.I. 1985/2047, see below at p. 423.
11   S.I. 1978/1728.
12   S.I. 1988/1324 as amended by S.I. 1989/2358, see above p. 416.
13   S.I. 1979/887.

The Filament Lamps for Vehicles (Safety) Regulations 1982, S.I. 1982/444.
These regulations prohibit the supply etc., of filament lamps to which certain
EEC regulations apply without being marked in accordance with the Motor
Vehicles (Designation of Approval Marks) Regulations 1979.[14]

**The Pedal Bicycles (Safety) Regulations 1984, S.I. 1984/145 (amended by S.I.
1984/1057).** These regulations prohibit the supply etc. of two-wheeled pedal
cycles which are not constructed or adapted for mechanical propulsion
unless they comply with BS 6102 Parts 1 and 2 or are of an equivalent
standard. Parts for use in two-wheeled pedal cycles must also comply with
the British Standard or be of an equivalent standard.

The Motor Vehicles Tyres (Safety) Regulations 1984, S.I. 1984/1233. Subject
to certain exceptions these regulations prohibit the supply etc. of tyres (other
than remoulds) for passenger or dual purpose vehicles which do not comply
with the Geneva Agreement[15] on motor vehicle equipment and parts.
Remould tyres must comply with British Standard Automobile Series
144b:1977.

**The Cosmetic Products (Safety) Regulations 1984, S.I. 1984/1260 (amended
by S.I. 1985/2045, S.I. 1987/1920, S.I. 1988/802 and S.I. 1988/2121).** These
regulations are being replaced by the Cosmetic Products (Safety) Regulations 1989 (as amended)[16] over a number of years. This process will be
completed by 1 January 1993.

**Gas Catalytic Heaters (Safety) Regulations 1984, S.I. 1984/1802 (amended by
S.I. 1987/1979).** These regulations prohibit the supply etc. of any liquid
petroleum gas heater or catalytic unit or insulation device for gas catalytic
heaters containing any asbestos.

**The Asbestos Products (Safety) Regulations 1985, S.I. 1985/2042 (amended by
S.I. 1987/1979).** These regulations prohibit the supply etc. of crocidolite
asbestos minerals (blue asbestos) or amosite minerals (brown asbestos) or
products containing such minerals other than for research and development
or analysis (reg. 2). Certain exceptions are made for torque convertors and
brake bands for cars containing crocidolite providing warning labels are
attached. By reg. 3 the supply of further specified asbestos minerals is
prohibited unless labelled in accordance with the Schedule to the regulations
and, in the case of products specified in reg. 4 (e.g. toys, paints and
varnishes), any supply of those specified minerals is prohibited.

---

14 S.I. 1979/1088.
15 Cmnd. 2535 as amended by Cmnd. 3562.
16 S.I. 1989/2233 as amended by S.I. 1990/1812 and S.I. 1991/447, see above p. 418.

Nightwear (Safety) Regulations 1985, S.I. 1985/2043 (amended by S.I. 1987/ 286). These regulations revoked and replaced the Nightwear (Safety) Regulations 1967.[17] They prohibit the supply of children's nightwear (except pyjamas, babies' garments and cotton terry towelling bath robes) made out of fabrics which do not satisfy the flammability performance requirements of BS 5722 (regs. 4 and 5). Babies' garments, children's pyjamas, bath robes and adults' nightwear must be labelled in compliance with Sch. 2 and indicate 'KEEP AWAY FROM FIRE' and/or 'LOW FLAMMABILITY TO BS 5722' (regs. 4 and 6).

There are further labelling requirements for nightwear which has been treated with flame retardant chemicals (reg. 7 and Sch. 3) and certain advertisements must contain warning notices (reg. 9 and Sch. 4).

Pushchair (Safety) Regulations 1985, S.I. 1985/2047. These regulations replace those parts of the Perambulators and Pushchairs (Safety) Regulations 1978[18] which relate to pushchairs. They require that all pushchairs supplied etc. comply with BS 4792:1984 which covers, inter alia, the construction, materials, parking devices, stability, performance and instructions for use and maintenance of pushchairs. The new regulations cover some new dangers but others, for example finger traps in the folding frames, are not dealt with.[19]

Child Resistant Packaging (Safety) Regulations 1986, S.I. 1986/758 (amended by S.I. 1990/1736). These regulations prohibit the supply etc. of products listed in the Schedule, in quantities of 2 litres or less, unless the packaging complies with BS 6652:1989 (or BS 6652:1985 for certain products approved before 6 November 1990). The standard relates to packagings which are resistant to opening by children. The type of products contained in the Schedule include turpentine, white spirit, methanol, and products classified as 'very toxic', 'toxic', and 'corrosive'.[20] Exceptions include products to be used exclusively for business use and sprays.

Fireworks (Safety) Regulations 1986, S.I. 1986/1323. These regulations prohibit the supply etc. of fireworks to any person apparently under the age of 16.

Plugs and Sockets etc. (Safety) Regulations 1987, S.I. 1987/603. These regulations prohibit the supply etc. of specified electrical devices such as plugs, sockets, adaptors and fuse links which do not comply with the regulations. The main requirements are conformity with appropriate British Standards or approval by specified persons e.g. B.E.A.B. and B.S.I. Certain

---

17 S.I. 1967/839.
18 S.I. 1978/1372, see p. 420.
19 See *Which?* June 1982, October 1985 and May 1986.
20 See (1987) 1 Fair Trader Pt. 1 p. 14 for a discussion on the omission of bleach from the regulations and 'Child Poisoning – A Difficult Problem to Swallow', K Simpson, (1991) 99 Trading Standards Review, Pt 4 p. 8.

devices specified in reg. 3 and Sch. 1 are exempted and there are provisions for the granting, refusal, alteration and cancellation of approvals (regs. 7 and 8). In addition there are information requirements specified in reg. 9.

Bunk Beds (Entrapment Hazards) (Safety) Regulations 1987, S.I. 1987/1337. These regulations prohibit the supply etc. of bunk beds where there is a risk of a child under 6 becoming trapped in any part of it, thereby risking strangulation or injury. The regulations specify permissible gaps between sleeping surfaces and parts of the structure, the Schedule detailing how such gaps are to be measured.

d) Further regulations

Further regulations relating to safety have been made under other legislation. The table below indicates those which have been made under the European Communities Act 1972, s. 2(2) without involving either the Consumer Protection Act 1987 or earlier safety statutes.

Title	Number
Aerosol Dispensers (EEC Requirements)	S.I. 1977/1140
Regulations 1977 (as amended)	S.I. 1980/136
	S.I. 1981/1549
	S.I. 1985/1279
Notification of New Substances Regulations 1982	S.I. 1982/1496
(as amended)	S.I. 1984/1244
	S.I. 1985/1333
	S.I. 1986/890
	S.I. 1991/1914
Classification, Packaging and Labelling of	S.I. 1984/1244
Dangerous Substances Regulations 1984 (as	S.I. 1986/1922
amended)	S.I. 1986/1951
	S.I. 1988/766
	S.I. 1989/2208
	S.I. 1990/1255
Gas Cylinders (Pattern Approval) Regulations	S.I. 1987/116
1987	
Materials and Articles in Contact with Food	S.I. 1987/1523
Regulations 1987 (as amended)	S.I. 1990/2487
Pressure Vessels (Verification) Regulations 1988	S.I. 1988/896
Construction Products Regulations 1991	S.I. 1991/1620

The annotated text of all safety regulations is conveniently set out in Miller *Product Liability and Consumer Safety Encyclopaedia.*

Appendix II

The Consumer Protection (Code of Practice for Traders on Price Indications) Approval Order 1988 (S.I. 1988/2078)

1. This Order may be cited as the Consumer Protection (Code of Practice for Traders on Price Indications) Approval Order 1988 and shall come into force on 1 March 1989.

2. The code of practice, as set out in the Schedule to this Order, issued by the Secretary of State for the purpose of–

(a) giving practical guidance with respect to the requirements of section 20 of the Consumer Protection Act 1987; and

(b) promoting what appear to the Secretary of State to be desirable practices as to the circumstances and manner in which a person gives an indication as to the price at which goods, services, accommodation or facilities are available or indicates any other matter in respect of which any such indication may be misleading;

is hereby approved.

Arrangement of sections

Introduction
Definitions
Part 1 Price comparisons

Part 2 Actual Price to the Consumer

2.1 Indicating two different prices

2.2 Incomplete information and non-optional extras
Products available in limited numbers or range
Prices relating to differing forms of products
Postage, packing and delivery charges
Value added tax
Service, cover and minimum charges in hotels, restaurants and similar
establishments
Holiday and travel prices
Ticket prices
Call-out charges
Credit facilities
Insurance

Part 3   Price indications which become misleading after they have been given

3.1 General

3.2 Newspaper and magazine advertisements

3.3 Mail order advertisements, catalogues and leaflets

3.4 Selling through agents

3.5 Changes in the rate of value added tax

Part 4   Sale of new homes

Introduction

1 The Consumer Protection Act The Consumer Protection Act 1987 makes it
a criminal offence to give consumers a misleading price indication about
goods, services, accommodation (including the sale of new homes) or
facilities. It applies however you give the price indication – whether in a TV
or press advertisement, in a catalogue or leaflet, on notices, price tickets or
shelf-edge marking in stores, or if you give it orally, for example on the
telephone. The term 'price indication' includes price comparisons as well as
indications of a single price.

2 This code of practice is approved under section 25 of the Act which gives
the Secretary of State power to approve codes of practice to give practical
guidance to traders. It is addressed to traders and sets out what is good
practice to follow in giving price indications in a wide range of different
circumstances, so as to avoid giving misleading price indications. But the Act
does not require you to do as this code tells you. You may still give price
indications which do not accord with this code, provided they are not
misleading. 'Misleading' is defined in section 21 of the Act. The definition
covers indications about any conditions attached to a price, about what you
expect to happen to a price in future and what you say in price comparisons,
as well as indications about the actual price the consumer will have to pay.
It also applies in the same way to any indications you give about the way in
which a price will be calculated.

3 Price comparisons If you want to make price comparisons, you should do so only if you can show that they are accurate and valid. Indications which give only the price of the product are unlikely to be misleading if they are accurate and cover the total charge you will make. Comparisons with prices which you can show have been or are being charged for the same or similar goods, services, accommodation or facilities and have applied for a reasonable period are also unlikely to be misleading. Guidance on these matters is contained in this code.

4 Enforcement Enforcement of the Consumer Protection Act 1987 is the responsibility of officers of the local weights and measures authority (in Northern Ireland, the Department of Economic Development) – usually called Trading Standards Officers. If a Trading Standards Officer has reasonable grounds to suspect that you have given a misleading price indication, the Act gives the Officer power to require you to produce any records relating to your business and to seize and detain goods or records which the Officer has reasonable grounds for believing may be required as evidence in court proceedings.

5 It may only be practicable for Trading Standards Officers to obtain from you the information necessary to carry out their duties under the Act. In these circumstances the Officer may seek information and assistance about both the claim and the supporting evidence from you. Be prepared to cooperate with Trading Standards Officers and respond to reasonable requests for information and assistance. The Act makes it an offence to obstruct a Trading Standards Officer intentionally or to fail (without good cause) to give any assistance or information the Officer may reasonably require to carry out duties under the Act.

6 Court proceedings If you are taken to court for giving a misleading price indication, the court can take into account whether or not you have followed the code. If you have done as the code advises, that will not be an absolute defence but it will tend to show that you have not committed an offence. Similarly if you have done something the code advises against doing it may tend to show that the price indication was misleading. If you do something which is not covered by the code, your price indication will need to be judged only against the terms of the general offence. The Act provides for a defence of due diligence, that is, that you have taken all reasonable steps to avoid committing the offence of giving a misleading price indication, but failure to follow the code of practice may make it difficult to show this.

7 Regulations The Act also provides power to make regulations about price indications and you should ensure that your price indications comply with any such regulations. There are none at present.

8 Other legislation This code deals only with the requirements of Part III of the Consumer Protection Act 1987. In some sectors there will be other relevant legislation. For example, price indications about credit terms must comply with the Consumer Credit Act 1974 and the regulations made under it as well as with the Consumer Protection Act 1987.

Definitions

In this code:

Accommodation	includes hotel and other holiday accommodation and new homes for sale freehold or on a lease of over 21 years but does not include rented homes.
Consumer	means anyone who might want the goods, services, accommodation or facilities, other than for business use.
Price	means both the total amount the consumer will have to pay to get the goods, services, accommodation or facilities and any method which has been or will be used to calculate that amount.
Price comparison	means any indication given to consumers that the price at which something is offered to consumers is less than or equal to some other price.
Product	means goods, services, accommodation and facilities (but not credit facilities, except where otherwise specified).
Services and facilities	means any services or facilities whatever (including credit, banking and insurance services, purchase or sale of foreign currency, supply of electricity, off-street car parking and caravan sites) *except* those provided by a person who is an authorised person or appointed representative under the Financial Services Act 1986 in the course of an investment business, services provided by an employee to his employer and facilities for a caravan which is the occupier's main or only home.
Shop	means any shop, store, stall or other place (including a vehicle or the consumer's home) at which goods, services, accommodation or facilities are offered to consumers.
Trader	means anyone (retailers, manufacturers, agents, service providers and others) who is acting in the course of a business.

Part 1: Price comparisons

1.1 Price comparisons generally

1.1.1 Always make the meaning of price indications clear. Do not leave consumers to guess whether or not a price comparison is being made. If no price comparison is intended, do not use words or phrases which, in their normal, everyday use and in the context in which they are used, are likely to give your customers the impression that a price comparison is being made.

1.1.2 Price comparisons should always state the higher price as well as the price you intend to charge for the product (goods, services, accommodation or facilities). Do not make statements like 'sales price £5' or 'reduced to £39' without quoting the higher price to which they refer.

1.1.3 It should be clear what sort of price the higher price is. For example, comparisons with something described by words like 'regular price', 'usual price' or 'normal price' should say whose regular, usual or normal price it is (eg. 'our normal price'). Descriptions like 'reduced from' and crossed out higher prices should be used only if they refer to your own previous price. Words should not be used in price indications other than with their normal everyday meanings.

1.1.4 Do not use initials or abbreviations to describe the higher price in a comparison, except for the initials 'RRP' to describe a recommended retail price or the abbreviation 'man. rec. price' to describe a manufacturer's recommended price (see paragraph 1.6.2 below).

1.1.5 Follow the part of the code (sections 1.2 to 1.6 as appropriate) which applies to the type of comparison you intend to make.

1.2 Comparisons with the trader's own previous price

1.2.1 General In any comparison between your present selling price and another price at which you have in the past offered the product, you should state the previous price as well as the new lower price.

1.2.2 In any comparison with your own previous price:
(a) the previous price should be the *last* price at which the product was available to consumers in the previous 6 months;
(b) the product should have been available to consumers at that price for at least 28 consecutive days in the previous 6 months; and
(c) the previous price should have applied (as above) for that period at the *same* shop where the reduced price is now being offered.

The 28 days at (b) above may include bank holidays, Sundays or other days of religious observance when the shop was closed; and up to 4 days when, for reasons beyond your control, the product was not available for supply. The product must not have been offered at a different price between that 28 day period and the day when the reduced price is first offered.

1.2.3 If the previous price in a comparison does not meet one or more of the conditions set out in paragraph 1.2.2 above:
(i) the comparison should be fair and meaningful; and
(ii) give a clear and positive explanation of the period for which and the circumstances in which that higher price applied.

For example 'these goods were on sale here at the higher price from 1 February to 26 February' or 'these goods were on sale at the higher price in 10 of our 95 stores only'. Display the explanation clearly, and as prominently as the price indication. You should *not* use general disclaimers saying for example that the higher prices used in comparisons have not necessarily applied for 28 consecutive days.

1.2.4 Food, drink and perishable goods For any food and drink, you need not give a positive explanation if the previous price in a comparison has not applied for 28 consecutive days, *provided* it was the last price at which the goods were on sale in the previous 6 months and applied in the same shop where the reduced price is now being offered. This also applies to non-food perishables, if they have a shelf-life of less than 6 weeks.

1.2.5 Catalogue and mail order traders Where products are sold only through a catalogue, advertisement or leaflet, any comparison with a previous price should be with the price in your own last catalogue, advertisement or leaflet. If you sell the same products both in shops and through catalogues etc, the previous price should be the last price at which you offered the product. You should also follow the guidance in paragraphs **1.2.2** (a) and (b). If your price comparison does not meet these conditions, you should follow the guidance in paragraph **1.2.3**.

1.2.6 Making a series of reductions If you advertise a price reduction and then want to reduce the price further during the same sale or special offer period, the intervening price (or prices) need not have applied for 28 days. In these circumstances unless you use a positive explanation (paragraph **1.2.3**):

the highest price in the series must have applied for 28 consecutive days in the last 6 months at the same shop: and

you must show the highest price, the intervening price(s) and the current selling price (eg '£40, £20, £10, £5').

1.3 Introductory offers, after-sale or after-promotion prices

1.3.1 Introductory offers Do not call a promotion an introductory offer unless you intend to continue to offer the product for sale after the offer period is over and to do so at a higher price.

1.3.2 Do not allow an offer to run on so long that it becomes misleading to describe it as an introductory or other special offer. What is a reasonable period will depend on the circumstances (but, depending on the shelf-life of the product, it is likely to be a matter of weeks, not months). An offer is unlikely to be misleading if you state the date the offer will end and keep to it. If you then extend the offer period, make it clear that you have done so.

1.3.3 Quoting a future price If you indicate an after-sale or after-promotion price, do so only if you are certain that, subject only to circumstances beyond your control, you will continue to offer identical products at that price for at least 28 days in the 3 months after the end of the offer period or after the offer stocks run out.

1.3.4 If you decide to quote a future price, write what you mean in full. Do not use initials to describe it (eg "ASP', 'APP'). The description should be clearly and prominently displayed, with the price indication.

1.4 Comparisons with price related to different circumstances

1.4.1 This section covers comparisons with prices:
(a) for different quantities (eg '15p each, 4 for 50p');
(b) for goods in a different condition (eg 'seconds £20, when perfect £30');
(c) for a different availability (eg 'price £50, price when ordered specially £60');
(d) for goods in a totally different state (eg 'price in kit form £50, price ready-assembled £70'); or
(e) for special groups of people (eg 'senior citizens' price £2.50, others £5').

1.4.2 General Do not make such comparisons unless the product is available in the different quantity, conditions etc at the price you quote. Make clear to consumers the different circumstances which apply and show them prominently with the price indication. Do not use initials (eg 'RAP' for 'ready-assembled price') to describe the different circumstances, but write what you mean in full.

1.4.3 'When perfect' comparisons If you do not have the perfect goods on sale in the same shop:

(a) follow section **1.2** if the 'when perfect' price is your own previous price for the goods;

(b) follow section **1.5** if the 'when perfect' price is another trader's price; or

(c) follow section **1.6** if the 'when perfect' price is one recommended by the manufacturer or supplier.

1.4.4 Goods in a different state Only make comparisons with goods in a totally different state if:

(a) a reasonable proportion (say a third (by quantity)) of your stock of those goods is readily available for sale to consumers in that different state) (for example, ready assembled) at the quoted price and from the shop where the price comparison is made; *or*

(b) another trader is offering those goods in that state at the quoted price and you follow section **1.5** below.

1.4.5 Prices for special groups of people If you want to compare different prices which you charge to different groups of people (eg. one price for existing customers and another for new customers, or one price for people who are members of a named organisation (other than the trader) and another for those who are not), do not use words like "our normal" or "our regular" to describe the higher price, unless it applies to at least half your customers.

1.5 Comparisons with another trader's prices

1.5.1 Only compare your prices with another trader's price if:

(a) you know that his price which you quote is accurate and up-to-date;

(b) you give the name of the other trader clearly and prominently, with the price comparison;

(c) you identify the shop where the other trader's price applies, if that other trader is a retailer; and

(d) the other trader's price which you quote applies to the same products – or to substantially similar products and you state any differences clearly.

1.5.2 Do not make statements like 'if you can buy this product elsewhere for less, we will refund the difference' about your 'own brand' products which other traders do not stock, unless your offer will also apply to other traders' equivalent goods. If there are any conditions attached to the offer (eg. it only applies to goods on sale in the same town) you should show them clearly and prominently, with the statement.

1.6 Comparisons with 'Recommended Retail Price' or similar

1.6.1 General This Section covers comparisons with recommended retail prices, manufacturers' recommended prices, suggested retail prices, suppliers' suggested retail prices and similar descriptions. It also covers prices given to co-operative and voluntary group organisations by their wholesalers or headquarters organisations.

1.6.2 Do not use initials or abbreviations to describe the higher price in a comparison *unless*:

(a) you use the initials 'RRP' to describe a recommended retail price; or

(b) you use the abbreviation 'man. rec. price' to describe a manufacturer's recommended price.

Write all other descriptions out in full and show them clearly and prominently with the price indication.

1.6.3 Do not use a recommended price in a comparison unless:

(a) it has been recommended to you by the manufacturer or supplier as a price at which the product might be sold to consumers;

(b) you deal with that manufacturer or supplier on normal commercial terms. (This will generally be the case for members of co-operative or voluntary group organisations in relation to their wholesalers or headquarters organisations); and

(c) the price is not significantly higher than prices at which the product is generally sold at the time you first make that comparison.

1.7 Pre-printed prices

1.7.1 Make sure you pass on to consumers any reduction stated on the manufacturer's packaging (eg 'flash packs' such as '10p off RRP').

1.7.2 You are making a price comparison if goods have a clearly visible price already printed on the packaging which is higher than the price you will charge for them. Such pre-printed prices are, in effect, recommended prices (except for retailers' own label goods) and you should follow paragraphs **1.6.1** to **1.6.4**. You need not state that the price is a recommended price.

1.8 References to value or worth

1.8.1 Do not compare your prices with an amount described only as 'worth' or 'value'.

1.8.2 Do not present general advertising slogans which refer to 'value' or 'worth' in a way which is likely to be seen by consumers as a price comparison.

1.9 Sales or special events

1.9.1 If you have bought in items specially for a sale, and you make this clear, you should not quote a higher price when indicating that they are special purchases. Otherwise, your price indications for individual items in the sale which are reduced should comply with section **1.1** of the code and whichever of sections **1.2** to **1.6** applies to the type of comparison you are making.

1.9.2 If you just have a general notice saying, for example, that all products are at 'half marked price', the marked price on the individual items should be your own previous price and you should follow section **1.2** of the code.

1.9.3 Do not use general notices saying, eg 'up to 50% off' unless the maximum reduction quoted applies to at least 10% (by quantity) of the range of products on offer.

1.10 Free offers

1.10.1 Make clear to consumers, at the time of the offer for sale, exactly what they will have to buy to get the 'free offer'.

1.10.2 If you give any indication of the monetary value of the 'free offer', and that sum is not your own present price for the product, follow whichever of sections **1.2** to **1.6** covers the type of price it is.

1.10.3 If there are any conditions attached to the 'free offer', give at least the main points of those conditions with the price indication and make clear to consumers where, before they are committed to buy, they can get full details of the conditions.

1.10.4 Do not claim that an offer is free if:
(a) you have imposed additional charges that you would not normally make;
(b) you have inflated the price of any product the consumer must buy or the incidental charges (for example, postage) the consumer must pay to get the 'free offer'; or
(c) you will reduce the price to consumers who do not take it up.

Part 2: Actual price to consumer

2.1 Indicating two different prices

2.1.1 The Consumer Protection Act makes it an offence to indicate a price for goods or services which is lower than the one that actually applies, for example, showing one price in an advertisement, window display, shelf marking or on the item itself, and then charging a higher price at the point of sale or checkout.

2.2 Incomplete information and non-optional extras

2.2.1 Make clear in your price indications the full price consumers will have to pay for the product. Some examples of how to do so in particular circumstances are set out below.

2.2.2 Limited availability of product Where the price you are quoting for products only applies to a limited number of, say, orders, sizes or colours, you should make this clear in your price indication (eg 'available in other colours or sizes at additional cost').

2.2.3 Prices relating to differing forms of products If the price you are quoting for particular products does not apply to the products in the form they are displayed or advertised, say so clearly in your price indication. For example, advertisements for self-assembly furniture and the like should make it clear that the price refers to a kit of parts.

2.2.4 Postage, packing and delivery charges If you sell by mail order, make clear any additional charges for postage, packing or delivery on the order form or similar document, so that consumers are fully aware of them before being committed to buying. Where you cannot determine these charges in advance, show clearly on the order form how they will be calculated (eg 'Post Office rates apply'), or the place in the catalogue etc. where the information is given.

2.2.5 If you sell goods from a shop and offer a delivery service for certain items, make it clear whether there are any separate delivery charges (eg for delivery outside a particular area) and what those charges are, before the consumer is committed to buying.

Value added tax

2.2.6 (i) Price indications to consumers All price indications you give to private consumers, by whatever means, should include VAT.

2.2.7 (ii) Price indications to business customers Prices may be indicated exclusive of VAT in shops where or advertisements from which most of your business is with business customers. If you also carry out business with private consumers at those shops or from those advertisements you should make clear that the prices exclude VAT and:
(i)   display of VAT-inclusive prices with equal prominence, or
(ii) display prominent statements that on top of the quoted price customers will also have to pay VAT at 15% (or the current rate).

2.2.8 (iii) Professional fees Where you indicate a price (including estimates) for a professional fee, make clear what it covers. The price should generally include VAT. In cases where the fee is based on an as-yet-unknown sum of money (for example, the sale price of a house), either:
(i)   quote a fee which includes VAT: or
(ii) make it clear that in addition to your fee the consumer would have to pay VAT at the current rate (eg "fee of 1-% of purchase price, plus VAT at 15%).
Make sure that whichever method you choose is used for both estimates and final bills.

2.2.9 (iv) Building work In estimates for building work, either include VAT in the price indication or indicate with equal prominence the amount or rate of VAT payable in addition to your basic figure. If you give a separate amount for VAT, make it clear that if any provisional sums in estimates vary then the amount of VAT payable would also vary.

2.2.10 Service, cover and minimum charge in hotels, restaurants and similar establishments If your customers in hotels, restaurants or similar places must pay a non-optional extra charge, eg a 'service charge':
(i)   incorporate the charge within fully inclusive prices wherever practicable; and
(ii) display the fact clearly on any price list or priced menu, whether displayed inside or outside (eg by using statements like 'all prices include service').
Do not include suggested optional sums, whether for service or any other item, in the bill presented to the customer.

2.2.11 It will not be practical to include some non-optional extra charges in a quoted price; for instance, if you make a flat charge per person or per table in a restaurant (often referred to as a 'cover charge') or a minimum charge. In such cases the charge should be shown as prominently as other prices on any list or menu, whether displayed inside or outside.

2.2.12 Holiday and travel prices If you offer a variety of prices to give consumers a choice, (for example, paying more or less for a holiday depending on the time of year or the standard of accommodation), make clear in your brochure – or any other price indication – what the basic price is and what it covers. Give details of any optional additional charges and what those charges cover, or of the place where this information can be found, clearly and close to the basic price.

2.2.13 Any non-optional extra charges which are for fixed amounts should be included in the basic price and not shown as additions, unless they are only payable by some consumers. In that case you should specify, near to the details of the basic price, either what the amounts are and the circumstances in which they are payable, or where in the brochure etc. the information is given.

2.2.14 Details of non-optional extra charges which may vary, (such as holiday insurance) or of where in the brochure etc. the information is given should be made clear to consumers near to the basic price.

2.2.15 If you reserve the right to increase prices after consumers have made their booking, state this clearly with all indications of prices, and include prominently in your brochure full information on the circumstances in which a surcharge is payable.

2.2.16 Ticket prices If you sell tickets, whether for sporting events, cinema, theatre etc. and your prices are higher than the regular price that would be charged to the public at the box office, ie higher than the 'face value', you should make clear in any price indication what the 'face value' of the ticket is.

2.2.17 Call-out charges If you make a minimum call-out charge or other flat-rate charge (for example, for plumbing, gas or electrical applicance repairs etc. carried out in consumers' homes), ensure that the consumer is made aware of the charge and whether the actual price may be higher (eg. if work takes longer than a specific time) before being committed to using your services.

2.2.18 Credit facilities Price indications about consumer credit should comply with the relevant requirements of regulations under the Consumer Credit Act 1974 governing the form and content of advertisements.

2.2.12 Insurance Where actual premium rates for a particular consumer or the availability of insurance cover depend on an individual assessment, this should be made clear when any indication of the premium or the method of determining it is given to consumers.

Part 3: Price indications which become misleading after they have been given

3.1 General

3.1.1 The Consumer Protection Act makes it an offence to give a price indication which, although correct at the time, becomes misleading after you have given it, if:

(i) consumers could reasonably be expected still to be relying on it; and

(ii) you do not take reasonable steps to prevent them doing so.

Clearly it will not be necessary or even possible in many instances to inform all those who may have been given the misleading price indication. However, you should always make sure consumers are given the correct information before they are committed to buying a product and be prepared to cancel any transaction which a consumer has entered into on the basis of a price indication which has become misleading.

3.1.2 Do not give price indications which you know or intend will only apply for a limited period, without making this fact clear in the advertisement or price indication.

3.1.3 The following paragraphs set out what you should do in some particular circumstances.

3.2 Newspaper and magazine advertisements

3.2.1 If the advertisement does not say otherwise, the price indication should apply for a reasonable period (as a general guide, at least 7 days or until the next issue of the newspaper or magazine in which the advertisement was published, whichever is longer). If the price indication becomes misleading within this period make sure consumers are given the correct information before they are committed to buying the product.

3.3 Mail order advertisements, catalogues and leaflets

3.3.1 Paragraph **3.2.1** above also applies to the time for which price indications in mail order advertisements and in regularly published catalogues or brochures should apply. If a price indication becomes misleading within this period, make the correct price indication clear to anyone who orders the product to which it relates. Do so before the consumer is committed to buying the product and, wheverever practicable, before the goods are sent to the consumer.

3.4 Selling through agents

3.4.1 Holiday brochures and travel agents Surcharges are covered in paragraph **2.2.15**. If a price indication becomes misleading for any other reason, tour operators who sell direct to consumers should follow paragraph **3.3.1** above; and tour operators who sell through travel agents should follow paragraphs **3.4.2** and **3.4.3** below.

3.4.2 If a price indication becomes misleading while your brochure is still current, make this clear to the travel agents to whom you distributed the brochure. Be prepared to cancel any holiday bookings consumers have made on the basis of a misleading price indication.

3.4.3 In the circumstances set out in paragraph **3.4.2**, travel agents should ensure that the correct price indication is made clear to consumers before they make a booking.

3.4.4 Insurance and independent intermediaries Insurers who sell their products through agents or independent intermediaries should take all reasonable steps to ensure that all such agents who are known to hold information on the insurer's premium rates and terms of the cover provided are told clearly of any changes in those rates or terms.

3.4.5 Agents, independent intermediaries and providers of quotation systems should ensure that they act on changes notified to them by an insurer.

3.5 Changes in the rate of value added tax

3.5.1 If your price indications become misleading because of a change in the general rate of VAT, or other taxes paid at point of sale, make the correct price indication clear to any consumers who order products. Do so before the consumer is committed to buying the product and, wherever practicable, before the goods are sent to the consumer.

Part 4: Sale of new homes

4.1 A 'new home' is any building, or part of a building to be used only as private dwelling which is either:
(i) a newly-built house or flat, or
(ii) a newly-converted existing building which has not previously been used in that form as a private home.

4.2 The Consumer Protection Act and this code apply to new homes which are either for sale freehold or covered by a long lease, ie with more than 21 years to run. In this context the term 'trader' covers not only a business vendor, such as a developer, but also an estate agent acting on behalf of such a vendor.

4.3 You should follow the relevant provision of Part I of the code if:
(i) you want to make a comparison between the price at which you offer new homes for sale and any other price;
(ii) you offer an inclusive price for new homes which also covers such items as furnishings, domestic appliances and insurance and you compare their value with, for example, High Street prices for similar items.

4.4 Part 2 of the code gives details of the provisions you should follow if:
(i) the new houses you are selling, or any goods or services which apply to them, are only available in limited numbers or range;
(ii) the sale price you give does not apply to the houses as displayed; or
(iii) there are additional non-optional charges payable.

Appendix III

Varieties of consumer credit transactions in tabular form

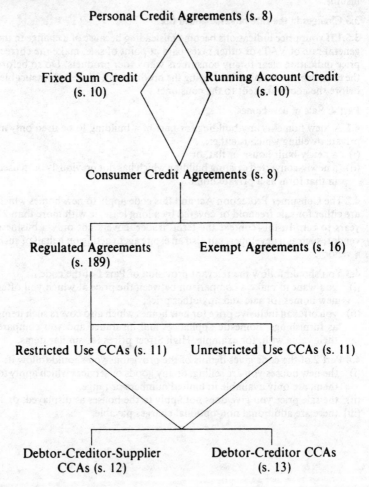

Personal Credit Agreements (s. 8)

Fixed Sum Credit (s. 10)　　　Running Account Credit (s. 10)

Consumer Credit Agreements (s. 8)

Regulated Agreements (s. 189)　　　Exempt Agreements (s. 16)

Restricted Use CCAs (s. 11)　　　Unrestricted Use CCAs (s. 11)

Debtor-Creditor-Supplier CCAs (s. 12)　　　Debtor-Creditor CCAs (s. 13)

N.B. A number of other 'sub-species' also exist – Credit Token Agreements (s. 14), Small Agreements (s. 17), Non-Commercial Agreements (s. 189), Multiple Agreements (s. 18), Linked Transactions (s. 19), Credit Agreements and Bargains (s. 137), Hire-purchase and Conditional Sale Agreements (s. 189).

Index